STUDENT SOLUTIONS MANUAL

Virginia Parks

INTERMEDIATE ALGEBRA WITH APPLICATIONS

Linda L. Exley
Vincent K Smith

DeKalb College
Clarkston, Georgia

Prentice Hall, Englewood Cliffs, New Jersey 07632

© 1990 by Prentice-Hall, Inc.
A Division of Simon & Schuster
Englewood Cliffs, New Jersey 07632

Printed in the United States of America

10 9 8 7 6 5 4 3 2 1

0-13-470428-2

Prentice-Hall International (UK) Limited, *London*
Prentice-Hall of Australia Pty. Limited, *Sydney*
Prentice-Hall Canada Inc., *Toronto*
Prentice-Hall Hispanoamericana, S.A., *Mexico*
Prentice-Hall of India Private Limited, *New Delhi*
Prentice-Hall of Japan, Inc., *Tokyo*
Simon & Schuster Asia Pte. Ltd., *Singapore*
Editora Prentice-Hall do Brasil, Ltda., *Rio de Janeiro*

TABLE OF CONTENTS

PRFFACE

This manual contains solutions to every odd-numbered problem in <u>INTERMEDIATE ALGEBRA WITH APPLICATIONS</u> by Linda Exley and Vincent Smith. It also includes solutions to all problems in the Chapter Tests. Every effort has been made to pattern the solutions after the examples in the text so that this manual is truly a supplement to the text.

I would like to thank Linda Exley and Vincent Smith for giving me the opportunity to participate in their project and also thank Susan White for checking my work.

Virginia Parks

CHAPTER 0

Problem Set 0.1.

1. True

3. True

5. False

7. False

9. False

11. $-2,0,2,4,6,8$

13. $\{-2,0,2\},\{-2,0\},\{-2,2\},$
$\{0,2\},\{-2\},\{0\},\{2\},\emptyset$

15. red, white, blue

17. a,b,c,d,e,f,g,h,i,j

19. $\{x|x$ is an even integer between
0 and 14$\}$

21. $\{x|x$ is a day of the week$\}$

23. $\frac{3}{4} = 0.75\overline{0}$

25. $\frac{5}{8} = 0.625\overline{0}$

27. rational

29. irrational

31. rational

33. False

35. True

37. True

39. True

41. True

43. $\frac{1}{2}, 2, \frac{9}{4}, 5$

45. $\{\frac{9}{4}, 5\}, \{\frac{9}{4}\}, \{5\}, \emptyset$

47. Friday

49. q,r,s,t,u,v,w,x,y,z

51. $\{x|x$ is an integer between -3
and 3$\}$

53. $\{x|x$ is a suit in a deck of
cards$\}$

55. rational

57. irrational

59. rational

61. $\frac{3}{5} = 0.6\overline{0}$

63. $\frac{7}{8} = 0.875\overline{0}$

65. $0.3 = \frac{3}{10}$

67. $0.655 = \frac{655}{1000}$

Problem Set 0.2.

1. $-\sqrt{3}$

3. $\frac{1}{3}$

5. 0

7. $-q$

9. $\frac{1}{7}$

11. $\frac{3}{2}$

13. $\frac{5}{8}$

15. Reflexive

17. Associative

19. Additive Identity

21. Multiplicative Identity

23. Multiplicative Inverse

25. Distributive

27. Substitution

29. 1) Commutative Property

    2) Distributive Property

    3) Addition

    4) Commutative Property

31. Commutative

33. Symmetric

35. Commutative

37. Commutative

39. Additive Inverse

41. Multiplication by zero

43. Transitive

45. Associative

47. 2

49. $-\dfrac{2}{3}$

51. p

53. 1

55. 4

57. $\dfrac{7}{3}$

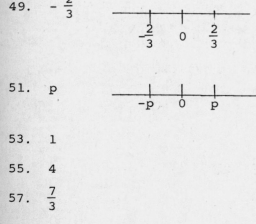

59. 1) Associative Property

    2) Addition

61.

$$\underline{\qquad\;\;|\qquad\;\;|\qquad}$$
$$0\quad\;\;p\text{-}q$$

Problem Set 0.3.

1. $|46| = 46$

3. $|7-11| = |-4|$

    $= 4$

5. $|0| = 0$

7. $|54| - |16| = 54 - 16$

    $= 38$

9. $-|13| = -13$

11. $-|32| - |-28| = -32 - 28$

    $= -60$

13. $|a| = a$

15. $|c|$ will not simplify

17. $|-a| = a$

19. $|-c| = |c|$

21. $|5y| = |5||y|$

    $= 5|y|$

23. $-|-53K| = -|-53||K|$

    $= -53|K|$

25. $\left|\dfrac{6}{z}\right| = \dfrac{|6|}{|z|}$

    $= \dfrac{6}{|z|}$

27.

$$\underline{\qquad\;\;|\qquad\;\;|\qquad}$$
$$2\qquad10$$

$|10-2| = |8|$

2

= 8

The distance is 8 units.

29.

$$\underline{\quad\vert\quad\vert\quad\quad}$$
$\sqrt{7}\quad\pi$

The distance is $\pi-\sqrt{7}$ units.

31. x and y can be anywhere on a

number line.

The distance is $|x-y|$ units.

33. $|-16| = 16$

35. $|19-22| = |-3|$

$\qquad = 3$

37. $|22| - |9| = 22 - 9$

$\qquad\qquad = 13$

39. $-|-47| = -47$

41. $|19| - |-22| = 19 - 22$

$\qquad\qquad = -3$

43. $-|-27| - |-81| = -27 - 81$

$\qquad\qquad\qquad = -108$

45. $|-21x| = |-21||x|$

$\qquad\quad = 21|x|$

47. $-|81g| = -|81||g|$

$\qquad\quad = -81|g|$

49. $\left|\dfrac{u}{9}\right| = \dfrac{|u|}{|9|}$

$\qquad = \dfrac{|u|}{9}$

51. $|p|$ will not simplify

53. $|r| = r$

55. $|s| = -s$

57. $|-r| = r$

59. $-|r| = -r$

61. $-|-r| = -r$

63. False

$|-(-3)| = -3$

65. True

$|-(-3)| = -(-3)$

67. True

$|7| = 7$

69.

$$\underline{\quad\vert\quad\vert\quad\quad}$$
$-1\quad 7$

$|7-(-1)| = |8|$

$\qquad\qquad = 8$

The distance is 8 units.

71.

$$\underline{\quad\vert\quad\vert\quad\quad}$$
$-9\quad -5$

$|-5-(-9)| = |-5+9|$

$\qquad\qquad = |4|$

$\qquad\qquad = 4$

The distance is 4 units.

73.

$$\underline{\quad\vert\quad\vert\quad\quad}$$
$-\sqrt{7}\quad -\sqrt{5}$

$|(-\sqrt{5})-(-\sqrt{7})| = \sqrt{7} - \sqrt{5}$

The distance is $|\sqrt{7} - \sqrt{5}|$

units.

75. $|-8+-5| = |-13|$

$\qquad\qquad = |13|$

$\qquad\qquad = 13$

77. $\dfrac{-8}{|-4|} = \dfrac{-8}{4}$

$\qquad\quad = -2$

79. $|-\sqrt{2}| + |\pi| = \sqrt{2} + \pi$

81. $|3-\pi| = |\pi-3|$

$\qquad = \pi - 3$

83. $|-\pi-3| = |-(\pi+3)|$

$\qquad = \pi + 3$

Problem Set 0.4.

1. $6 - (-3) = 6 + 3$

$\qquad = 9$

3. $\dfrac{-16}{4} = -4$

5. $\dfrac{16}{0}$ is undefined.

7. $|-12+4| \div 4 = |-8| \div 4$

$\qquad = 8 \div 4$

$\qquad = 2$

9. $\dfrac{1}{6} \div (-\dfrac{1}{3})^2 = \dfrac{1}{6} \div \dfrac{1}{9}$

$\qquad = \dfrac{1}{6} \cdot 9$

$\qquad = \dfrac{3}{2}$

11. $(2-3)^2 \cdot 5 = (-1)^2 \cdot 5$

$\qquad = 1 \cdot 5$

$\qquad = 5$

13. $15 \div (-3) \cdot \dfrac{-1}{5} = -5 \cdot -\dfrac{1}{5}$

$\qquad = 1$

15. $\dfrac{2-7+4}{3(2)-(-1)} = \dfrac{-5+4}{6+1}$

$\qquad = -\dfrac{1}{7}$

17. $5[6+2(-5+1)] = 5[6+2(-4)]$

$\qquad = 5[6+(-8)]$

$\qquad = 5(-2)$

$\qquad = -10$

19. $(-6)^2(-\dfrac{2}{3}) - (-7) = (36)(-\dfrac{2}{3}) + 7$

$\qquad = -24 + 7$

$\qquad = -17$

21. $(-13+4)^2 = (-9)^2$

$\qquad = 81$

23. $(-2)^2 - (-2)^3 = 4 - (-8)$

$\qquad = 4 + 8$

$\qquad = 12$

25. $7^2 - 8^2 = 49 - 64$

$\qquad = -15$

27. $-7 + (-7)^2 = -7 + 49$

$\qquad = 42$

29. $|-15-(-3)| \div (-3)$

$\qquad = |-15+3| \div (-3)$

$\qquad = |-12| \div (-3)$

$\qquad = 12 \div (-3)$

$\qquad = -4$

31. $(\dfrac{1}{8})/(-\dfrac{1}{4})^3 = \dfrac{1}{8}/(-\dfrac{1}{64})$

$\qquad = \dfrac{1}{8} \cdot -64$

$\qquad = -8$

33. $2^2 - 3 \cdot 5 = 4 - 15$

$\qquad = -11$

35. $\dfrac{3^2-4^2}{(-2)(-1)-1} = \dfrac{9-16}{2-1}$

$\qquad = \dfrac{-7}{1}$

$\qquad = -7$

37. $-2[6-3^2(\sqrt{5+4})] = -2[6-9(\sqrt{9})]$

$\qquad = -2[6-9(3)]$

$$= -2(6-27)$$

$$= -2(-21)$$

$$= 42$$

39. $-12 \div (-3)^3 \cdot -\frac{1}{3} = -12 \div (-27) \cdot -\frac{1}{3}$

$$= \frac{12}{27} \cdot -\frac{1}{3}$$

$$= -\frac{4}{27}$$

41. $(2-7)^2 - 7^2 = (-5)^2 - 7^2$

$$= 5^2 - 7^2$$

$$= 25 - 49$$

$$= -24$$

43. $\frac{3}{2} - (-\frac{1}{4} \div 4) = \frac{3}{2} - (-\frac{1}{4} \cdot \frac{1}{4})$

$$= \frac{3}{2} - (-\frac{1}{16})$$

$$= \frac{3}{2} + \frac{1}{16}$$

$$= \frac{24}{16} + \frac{1}{16}$$

$$= \frac{25}{16}$$

45. $6(-\frac{2}{3}-1) \div 3 = 6(-\frac{5}{3}) \div 3$

$$= -10 \div 3$$

$$= -\frac{10}{3}$$

47. $\dfrac{2(\frac{-1-(-7)}{4 \cdot 2-10})-8 \cdot 3}{-(-5)-7} = \dfrac{2(\frac{-1+7}{8-10})-24}{5-7}$

$$= \dfrac{2(\frac{6}{-2})-24}{-2}$$

$$= \dfrac{2(-3)-24}{-2}$$

$$= \dfrac{-6-24}{-2}$$

$$= \dfrac{-30}{-2}$$

$$= 15$$

49. $\dfrac{-4|-9-2|+8 \cdot 5}{2(\frac{-5-9}{5+2})-\frac{6-2 \cdot 3}{0-2}} = \dfrac{-4|-11|+40}{2(\frac{-14}{7})-\frac{6-6}{-2}}$

$$= \dfrac{-4(11)+40}{2(-2)-\frac{0}{-2}}$$

$$= \dfrac{-44+40}{-4-0}$$

$$= \dfrac{-4}{-4}$$

$$= 1$$

51. $\frac{3}{4}(-24+16) = \frac{3}{4}(-8)$

$$= -6$$

53. $\dfrac{\sqrt{-12+16}}{-2} = \dfrac{\sqrt{4}}{-2} = \dfrac{2}{-2} = -1$

55. $|-11| - (5+-7) = 11 - (-2)$

$$= 11 + 2 = 13$$

57. $\dfrac{\frac{2}{3}-\frac{3}{7}}{\frac{1}{7}+\frac{1}{3}}$ LCD = 21

$$\dfrac{21[\frac{2}{3}-\frac{3}{7}]}{21[\frac{1}{7}+\frac{1}{3}]} = \dfrac{14-9}{3+7} - \dfrac{5}{10} = \dfrac{1}{2}$$

Problem Set 0.5.

1. $\angle a = 45°$ $\angle f = 45°$ $\angle k = 90°$ $\angle p = 135°$

   $\angle b = 135°$ $\angle g = 45°$ $\angle l = 90°$ $\angle q = 45°$

   $\angle c = 135°$ $\angle h = 135°$ $\angle m = 135°$ $\angle r = 135°$

   $\angle d = 45°$ $\angle i = 90°$ $\angle n = 45°$ $\angle s = 135°$

   $\angle e = 135°$ $\angle j = 90°$ $\angle o = 45°$ $\angle t = 45°$

3. $180 - (30+30) = 180 - 60$

   $$= 120$$

   $\angle A$ is $120°$

5. $180 - 120 = 60$

    $A = 180 - (90+60)$

    $= 180 - 150$

    $= 30$

    $\angle A$ is $30°$

7. a) Two angles of one triangle
        are equal to two angles of
        the other triangle.

    b) Two angles of one triangle
        are equal to two angles of
        the other triangle.

9. False

11. False

13. True

15. False

17. False

19. True

21. $A = 180 - (85+45)$

    $= 180 - (130)$

    $= 50$

    $\angle A$ is $50°$

23. $A = 180 - 40$

    $= 140$

    $\angle A$ is $140°$

25. $180 - 115 = 65$

    $180 - 133 = 47$

    $A = 180 - (65+47)$

    $= 180 - 112$

    $= 68$

$\angle A$ is $68°$

27. $6^2 + 8^2 = 36 + 64$

    $= 100$

    $10^2 = 100$

29. $\frac{3}{4} = \frac{6}{8}$

    Corresponding sides are
    proportional.

31. True

33. True

35. False

37. True

39. True

41. $(n-2)180°$

Problem Set 0.6

1. $3 + 4 + 5 = 12$

    The perimeter is 12 in.

3. $2(13) + 2(4) = 26 + 8$

    $= 34$

    The perimeter is 34 cm.

5. $2(20) + 2(17) = 40 + 34$

    $= 74$

    The perimeter is 74 yd.

7. $4(90) = 360$

    He must run 360 ft.

9. $(4)(7) = 28$

    The area is 28 sq. m. (m^2).

11. $\frac{1}{2}(12)(10) = 60$

    The area is 60 cm^2.

13. $(5)^3 = 125$

The volume is 125 units^3.

15. $(35)(25)(6) = 5250$

It will take 5250 ft^3 of water.

17. $\frac{1}{3}\pi(1.1)^2(3.6) = \frac{1}{3}\pi(1.21)(3.6)$

$$= 1.452\pi$$

The volume is 1.452π in^3.

19. $4(3.14)(4000)^2 = 200{,}960{,}000$

The surface area is 200,960,000

mi^2.

21. $2(6\frac{1}{2})(3\frac{1}{2}) + 2(3\frac{1}{2})(14) + 2(6\frac{1}{2})(14)$

$$= 2(\frac{13}{2})(\frac{7}{2}) + 2(\frac{7}{2})(14)$$

$$+ 2(\frac{13}{2})(14)$$

$$= \frac{91}{2} + 98 + 182$$

$$= 45\frac{1}{2} + 98 + 182 = 325\frac{1}{2}$$

The surface area is $325\frac{1}{2}$ in^2.

23. $3(2.5) = 7.5$

The perimeter is 7.5 in.

25. $2(23) + 2(8) = 46 + 16$

$$= 62$$

The perimeter is 62 ft.

27. $2(20.3) + 2(17.23)$

$$= 40.6 + 34.4$$

$$= 75.06$$

The perimeter is 75.06 yds.

29. $\pi(4000) = 4000\pi$

He would walk 4000π miles.

31. Radius is $\frac{1}{2}(3)$ or $\frac{3}{2}$.

Area $= \frac{1}{2}\pi(\frac{3}{2})^2$

$$= \frac{1}{2}\pi(\frac{9}{4})$$

$$= \frac{9\pi}{8}$$

The area is $\frac{9\pi}{8}$ in^2.

33. $(2\frac{1}{3})^3 = (\frac{7}{3})^3$

$$= \frac{343}{27}$$

The volume is $\frac{343}{27}$ in^3.

35. $(5\frac{1}{2})(3\frac{1}{4})(1\frac{1}{2}) = (\frac{11}{2})(\frac{13}{4})(\frac{3}{2})$

$$= \frac{429}{16}$$

$$= 26\frac{13}{16}$$

It would take $26\frac{13}{16}$ in^3.

37. $\frac{1}{3}\pi(12)^2(5) = \frac{1}{3}\pi(144)(5)$

$$= 240\pi$$

The volume is 240π yd^3.

39. $\frac{4}{3}\pi(4000)^3 = \frac{4}{3}\pi(64{,}000{,}000{,}000)$

$$= \frac{256{,}000{,}000{,}000}{3}\pi$$

The volume is $\frac{256{,}000{,}000{,}000}{3}\pi$

mi^3.

41.

$\frac{1}{2}(1\frac{1}{2})(2) = \frac{1}{2}(\frac{3}{2})(2) = \frac{3}{2}$

It will hold $\frac{3}{2}$ ft^3.

7

43. Radius is $\frac{1}{2}(\frac{5}{2}) = \frac{5}{4}$

$10,000[2\pi(\frac{5}{4})^2 + 2\pi(\frac{5}{4})(4)]$

$= 10.000[2\pi(\frac{25}{16})+10\pi]$

$= 10,000(\frac{50\pi}{16}+10\pi)$

$= 10,000(\frac{50\pi}{16}+\frac{160\pi}{16})$

$= 10,000(\frac{210\pi}{16})$

$= 131,250\pi$

The amount of material needed is

$131,250\pi$ in^2.

45.

$\frac{1}{2}(2)(2) = 2$

It will hold 2 ft^3.

47. Ends: $2[\frac{1}{2}(6)(4)] = 24$

Sides: $3^2 + 4^2 = 9 + 16$

$= 25$

So the height of a side is 5 ft.

Area: $2(15)(5) = 150$

Ends + sides $= 24 + 150 = 174$

The surface area is 174 ft^2.

Review Problems.

1. $-(-7)[2-(5-8)] = 7[2-(-3)]$

$= 7(2+3)$

$= 7(5)$

$= 35$

3. $\dfrac{-6(-7)}{(-2-19)-\sqrt{30-5}} = \dfrac{42}{(-21)-\sqrt{25}}$

$= \dfrac{42}{-21-5}$

$= \dfrac{42}{-26}$

$= \dfrac{-21}{13}$

5. $\dfrac{(-3)(-4)-(-4)(-5)}{-5-2+(-1)} = \dfrac{12-20}{-8}$

$= \dfrac{-8}{-8}$

$= 1$

7. $-|6+(-11)| - 6^2 = -|-5| - 36$

$= -5 - 36$

$= -41$

9. $|(-4)(5)|-6-19| = |-20| - |-13|$

$= 20 - 13$

$= 7$

11. $(6-8)^2 + 9/3 = (-2)^2 + 3$

$= 4 + 3$

$= 7$

13. $(-9)^2 - [17-(4-12)]$

$= 81 - [17-(-8)]$

$= 81 - (17+8)$

$= 81 - 25$

$= 56$

15. Commutative

17. Distributive

19. Multiplicative Identity

21. Irrational

23. Rational

25. Rational

27. c

29. 1, 3, 5

31. $|-5| - |25| = 5 - 25$

$\qquad = -20$

33. $-|-25| = -25$

35. $-|-4| - |-17| = -4 - 17$

$\qquad = -21$

37. $|b| = -b$

39. $|-a| = a$

41. Perimeter

$3(8) + 6 + 10 = 24 + 16$

$\qquad = 40$

Perimeter is 40 in.

Area

$(10)(8) + \frac{1}{2}(8)(16) = 80 + 24$

$\qquad = 104$

Area is 104 in^2.

43. Diameter is 5 m.

Circumference $= \pi(5)$

The circumference is 5π m.

Area $= \pi(2.5)^2$

$\qquad = \pi(6.25)$

The area is 6.25π m^2.

45. Volume

$\frac{1}{3}\pi(3)^2(4) = \frac{1}{3}\pi(9)(4)$

$\qquad = 12\pi$

The volume is 12π units^3.

Surface Area

$\pi(3)^2 + \pi(3)5 = 9\pi + 15\pi$

$\qquad = 24\pi$

The surface area is 24π units^2.

47. Volume

$\frac{4}{3}\pi(5)^3 = \frac{4}{3}\pi(125)$

$\qquad = \frac{500}{3}\pi$

The volume is $\frac{500}{3}\pi$ units^3.

Surface area

$4\pi(5)^2 = 4\pi(25)$

$\qquad = 100\pi$

The surface area is 100π units^2.

49. Corresponding sides are pro-

portional.

Chapter Test

1. B

2. D

3. $6\overline{\smash{)}1.000}$ .166...

$\qquad \underline{6}$

$\qquad 40$

$\qquad \underline{36}$

$\qquad 40$

$\qquad \underline{36}$

$\qquad 4$

B

4. C

5. C

6. $|p-(-5)| = |p+5|$

D

7. $-(2-x) = -2 + x$

$\qquad = x - 2$

C

8. C

9. B

10. $(-7)^2 - (-13) = 49 + 13$

$\qquad = 62$

11. $\dfrac{-5}{9} \div (-15) = \dfrac{-5}{9} \cdot -\dfrac{1}{15}$

$\qquad = \dfrac{1}{27}$

12. $-5^2 + 4.6 = -25 + 24$

$\qquad = -1$

13. $3\{2-3[5+2(8-9)]\}$

$\qquad = 3\{2-3[5+2(-1)]\}$

$\qquad = 3\{2-3[5+(-2)]\}$

$\qquad = 3[2-3(3)]$

$\qquad = 3(2-9)$

$\qquad = 3(-7)$

$\qquad = -21$

14. $\dfrac{16-4^2}{8} = \dfrac{16-16}{8}$

$\qquad = \dfrac{0}{8}$

$\qquad = 0$

15. $-\dfrac{2}{3}(3-\dfrac{9}{2}) = \dfrac{-2}{3}(\dfrac{6}{2}-\dfrac{9}{2})$

$\qquad = \dfrac{-2}{3}(\dfrac{-3}{2})$

$\qquad = 1$

16. $3|11-17| = 3|-6|$

$\qquad = 3(6)$

$\qquad = 18$

17. $6 + (-7) = -7 + 6$

18. $x(6+y) = x(6) + x(y)$

19. $-5 + 5 = 0$

20. $2(x+t) = (x+t)2$

21. $\angle a = 130^\circ \qquad \angle d = 30^\circ$

$\angle b = 50^\circ \qquad \angle e = 150^\circ$

$\angle c = 100^\circ \qquad \angle f = 50^\circ$

$\qquad\qquad\qquad \angle g = 130^\circ$

22. $\pi(4)^2 12 = \pi(16)(12)$

$\qquad = 192\pi$

The volume is 192π ft^3.

23. $2(28) + 2(22) = 56 + 44$

$\qquad = 100$

The **amount** needed is 100 m.

24. $4\pi(3\frac{1}{2})^2 = 4\pi(\frac{7}{2})^2$

$\qquad = 4\pi(\frac{49}{4})$

$\qquad = 49\pi$

The surface area is 49π cm^2.

25. $(28)(11) = 308$

The area is 308 yd^2.

CHAPTER 1

Problem Set 1.1

1. $2^4 = 2 \cdot 2 \cdot 2 \cdot 2$
    $= 16$

3. $-4^2 = -4 \cdot 4$
    $= -16$

5. $-4^3 = -4 \cdot 4 \cdot 4$
    $= -64$

7. $(-3)(-2)^2 = (-3)(4)$
    $= -12$

9. $(-x)^8 = x^8$

11. $(-s)^{11} = -s^{11}$

13. $2^2 \cdot 2^3 = 2^{2+3}$
    $= 2^5$

15. $-x^2 \cdot x^3 = -x^{2+3}$
    $= -x^5$

17. $(2^3)^2 = 2^{3 \cdot 2}$
    $= 2^6$

19. $(-x^2)^5 = -x$
    $= -x^{10}$

21. $(\dfrac{-3}{2})^2 = \dfrac{-3}{2} \cdot \dfrac{-3}{2}$
    $= \dfrac{9}{4}$

23. $\dfrac{x^{12}}{x^4} = x^{12-4}$
    $= x^8$

25. $[(-x)^2]^3 = (-x)^{3 \cdot 2}$
    $= (-x)^6$
    $= x^6$

27. $(2xy^2)^3 = 2^3 x^3 (y^2)^3$
    $= 8x^3 y^6$

29. $[(x+y)^4]^5 = (x+y)^{20}$

31. $(\dfrac{2x}{y^2})^3 = \dfrac{(2x)^3}{(y^2)^3}$
    $= \dfrac{2^3 x^3}{y^6}$
    $= \dfrac{8x^3}{y^6}$

33. $(\dfrac{x^2}{-y^4})^2 = \dfrac{(x^2)^2}{(-y^4)^2}$
    $= \dfrac{x^4}{y^8}$

35. $\left[\dfrac{(x-1)^3}{(x-1)^2}\right]^5 = [(x-1)^{3-2}]^5$
    $= [(x-1)^1]^5$
    $= (x-1)^5$

37. $(\dfrac{-x^4 y z^3}{2s^2})^5 = \dfrac{(-x^4)^5 y^5 (z^3)^5}{2^5 (s^2)^5}$
    $= \dfrac{-x^{20} y^5 z^{15}}{2^5 s^{10}}$

39. $\dfrac{(25x^5 z)^2}{(5x^3 z^3)^3} = \dfrac{25^2 (x^5)^2 z^2}{5^3 (x^3)^3 (z^3)^3}$
    $= \dfrac{625 x^{10} z^2}{125 x^9 z^9}$
    $= \dfrac{5x}{z^7}$

41. $\dfrac{(-xyz)^3}{(-x^2 y z^4)^2} = \dfrac{(-x)^3 y^3 z^3}{(-x^2)^2 y^2 (z^4)^2}$
    $= \dfrac{-x^3 y^3 z^3}{x^4 y^2 z^8}$
    $= \dfrac{-y}{xz^5}$

43. $-2^0 (-\dfrac{1}{2})^4 = -1 \cdot \dfrac{1}{16}$
    $= -\dfrac{1}{16}$

45. $2^3 = 8$

47. $-3^3 = -27$

49. $-3^2 = -9$

51. $3^0(\frac{1}{2})^2 = 1 \cdot \frac{1}{4}$

$= \frac{1}{4}$

53. $(-2)(-3)^3 = (-2)(-27)$

$= 54$

55. $(3^2)^2(3^2)^3 = 3^4 \cdot 3^6$

$= 3^{10}$

57. $-3^0(-\frac{1}{2})^2 = -1 \cdot \frac{1}{4}$

$= -\frac{1}{4}$

59. $(-2)^3 \cdot 3^2 = -8 \cdot 9$

$= -72$

61. $2^2(-3^2) = 4 \cdot -9$

$= -36$

63. $(-2)^2(-3^2) = 4 \cdot -27$

$= -108$

65. $-2^3 \cdot (2^3)^2 = -2^3 \cdot 2^6$

$= -2^9$

67. $2^2(-2)^2 = 4 \cdot 4$

$= 16$

69. $(2 \cdot 3)^3 = 6^3$

$= 216$

71. $(-2 \cdot 3)^2 = (-6)^2$

$= 36$

73. $(-\frac{3}{2})^3 = \frac{-27}{8}$

75. $(\frac{2 \cdot 3}{5})^2 = (\frac{6}{5})^2$

$= \frac{36}{25}$

77. $\frac{2^3}{2^2} = 2$

79. $\frac{-2}{(-2)^9} = \frac{1}{(-2)^8}$

$= \frac{1}{2^8}$

81. $\frac{-3^4}{3^7} = -\frac{1}{3^3}$

$= -\frac{1}{27}$

83. $\frac{(-7)^9}{-7^8} = \frac{-7^9}{-7^8}$

$= 7^1$

85. $-8^0 = -1$

87. $x^3 \cdot x^4 = x^7$

89. $(-x^3)(x^2) = -x^5$

91. $(-x)^3 \cdot x^2 = -x^3 \cdot x^2$

$= -x^5$

93. $x - (-x)^2 = x \cdot x^2$

$= x^3$

95. $(-x^2)^3 = -x^6$

97. $(x^5y)^7 = (x^5)^7 y^7$

$= x^{35} y^7$

99. $(-4x)^3 = (-4)^3 x^3$

$= -4^3 x^3$

101. $[(x+7)^4]^4 = (x+7)^{16}$

103. $(\frac{-2x}{y^2})^5 = \frac{(-2x)^5}{(y^2)^5}$

$= \frac{(-2)^5 x^5}{y^{10}}$

$= \frac{-2^5 x^5}{y^{10}}$

105. $[\frac{(x+4)^4}{(x+4)^3}]^5 = [(x+4)^1]^5$

$= (x+4)^5$

107. $\dfrac{(-3x^3y)^4}{(2^3x^3y^4)^3} = \dfrac{(-3)^4(x^3)^4y^4}{(2^3)^3(x^3)^3(y^4)^3}$

$\qquad = \dfrac{3^4x^{12}y^4}{2^9x^9y^{12}}$

$\qquad = \dfrac{3^4x^3}{2^9y^8}$

109. $\dfrac{(14xz)^2}{(7x^2z)^3} = \dfrac{14^2x^2z^2}{7^3(x^2)^2z^3}$

$\qquad = \dfrac{196x^2z^2}{343x^6z^3}$

$\qquad = \dfrac{4}{7x^4z}$

111. $\dfrac{(-xyz)^2}{(-x^2yz^3)^3} = \dfrac{(-x)^2y^2z^2}{(-x^2)^3y^3(z^3)^3}$

$\qquad = \dfrac{x^2y^2z^2}{-x^6y^3z^9}$

$\qquad = -\dfrac{1}{x^4yz^7}$

113. $\left[\dfrac{-30x^5yz^8}{45x^5yz^3}\right]^2 = \left[\dfrac{-2z^5}{3}\right]^2$

$\qquad = \dfrac{(-2z^5)^2}{3^2}$

$\qquad = \dfrac{(-2)^2(z^5)^2}{9}$

$\qquad = \dfrac{4z^{10}}{9}$

115. $(3x^2y^3)^2 = 3^2(x^2)^2(y^3)^2$

$\qquad = 9x^4y^6$

117. $\left(\dfrac{11x^5z}{7y^3}\right)^2 = \dfrac{11^2(x^5)^2z^2}{7^2(y^3)^2}$

$\qquad = \dfrac{121x^{10}z^2}{49y^6}$

119. $(3x)^2 = 3^2(x)^2$

$\qquad = 9x^2$

The area is $9x^2$ ft.^{2}.

121. $(4t)^3 = 4^3t^3$

$\qquad = 64t^3$

The volume is $64t^3$ in.^{3}.

123. $6^n \cdot 6^2 = 6^{n+2}$

125. $(8^n)^2 = 8^{2n}$

127. $2 \cdot 2^n = 2^{1+n}$

129. $x^n \cdot x^{2n} = x^{3n}$

Problem Set 1.2.

1. $x + 6$; degree: 1

3. $x^2 - 3x + 4$; degree: 2

5. $-3x^3 + 4x^2 + \dfrac{1}{2}x - 7$; degree: 3

7. $3(-2) + 7 = -6 + 7$

$\qquad = 1$

9. $2(-2)^3 - (-2) + 2 = 2(-8) + 2 - 2$

$\qquad = -16 + 0$

$\qquad = -16$

11. $(1)(-1) + 6 = -1 + 6$

$\qquad = 5$

13. $2(1)^3(-1) - 5(1)^2(-1)^2$

$\qquad + (1)(-1) + (-1)^2$

$\qquad = 2(-1) - 5(1) + (-1) + 1$

$\qquad = -2 + (-5)$

$\qquad = -7$

15. $5x^3 - 7x^2 + 3x^3 - x^2$

$\qquad = 5x^3 + 3x^3 - 7x^2 - x^2$

$\qquad = 8x^3 - 8x^2$

13

17. $3z^2 - 4z - z^2 + 6z$

$\quad = 3z^2 - z^2 - 4z + 6z$

$\quad = 2z^2 + 2z$

19. $17xyz - 11xy - 13z$ no like terms

21. $w^5 - w + 6 - w^5 + w$

$\quad = w^5 - w^5 - w + w + 6$

$\quad = 6$

23. $z - 4$; degree: 1; binomial

25. $x^2 - x + 1$; degree: 2; trinomial

27. $-2x^5 + 7x^4 + \frac{2}{5}x - 9$; degree: 5

29. $x^5 + y^5$; degree: 5: binomial

31. $x^7y^2 - x^4y^3 + y^7$; degree: 9;

trinomial

33. $3(-3) + 7 = -9 + 7$

$\quad\quad\quad\quad = -2$

35. $8 - (-3) = 8 + 3$

$\quad\quad\quad\quad = 11$

37. $1 - (-3)^2 = 1 - 9$

$\quad\quad\quad\quad = -8$

39. $(-2)(3) + 6 = -6 + 6$

$\quad\quad\quad\quad\quad = 0$

41. $(-2)^2 + 2(-2)(3) + (3)^2$

$\quad = 4 + -12 + 9$

$\quad = 1$

43. $(-2)^2 - (3)^2 = 4 - 9$

$\quad\quad\quad\quad\quad = -5$

45. $6x - 7 - 5x + 3 = 6x - 5x - 7 + 3$

$\quad\quad\quad\quad\quad\quad = x - 4$

47. $7y - 2z - 3y - 2z$

$\quad = 7y - 3y - 2z - 2z$

$\quad = 4y - 4z$

49. $4x^3 - x^2 + 2 - x^3 + 2x^2$

$\quad = 4x^3 - x^3 - x^2 + 2x^2 + 2$

$\quad = 3x^3 + x^2 + 2$

51. $-x^3 - w^3 + x^3 + w^3$

$\quad = -x^3 + x^3 - w^3 + w^3$

$\quad = 0$

53. $t = 3, \ 64(3) - 16(3)^2$

$\quad\quad = 192 - 16 \cdot 9$

$\quad\quad = 192 - 144$

$\quad\quad = 48$

After 3 seconds, 48 ft.

$t = 4, \ 64(4) - 16(4)^2$

$\quad\quad = 256 - 16 \cdot 16$

$\quad\quad = 256 - 256$

$\quad\quad = 0$

After 4 seconds, 0 ft.

55. $n = 5, \ \frac{1}{3}(5)^3 + \frac{1}{2}(5)^2 + \frac{1}{6}(5)$

$\quad = \frac{125}{3} + \frac{25}{2} + \frac{5}{6}$

$\quad = \frac{250+75+5}{6}$

$\quad = \frac{330}{6}$

$\quad = 55$

The sum of the squares of the first five natural numbers is 55.

$n = 6, \ \frac{1}{3}(6)^3 + \frac{1}{2}(6)^3 + \frac{1}{6}(6)$

$\quad = \frac{216}{3} + \frac{36}{2} + 1$

$\quad = 72 + 18 + 1$

$\quad = 91$

The sum of the squares of the first six natural numbers is 91.

57. $(-1)^{2n} + 1 = 1 + 1$

$\quad\quad\quad\quad = 2$

59. $(-1)^{2n-1} - 1 = -1 - 1$

$\qquad\qquad\qquad = -2$

Problem Set 1.3.

1. $(4x-5) + (3x-9) = 7x - 14$

3. $(x^2+4xy+y^2) + (4x^2-7xy-4y^2)$

$\qquad = 5x^2 - 3xy - 3y^2$

5. $-(5x^6-3x^4+3) = -5x^6 + 3x^4 - 3$

7. $-(15x^4y-12x^3y^2+7x^2y^2-12)$

$\qquad = -15x^4y + 12x^3y^2 - 7x^2y^2 + 12$

9. $(5x-8) - (7x+4) = (5x-8)$

$\qquad\qquad\qquad + (-7x-4)$

$\qquad\qquad\qquad\qquad = -2x - 12$

11. $(2x^2-5xy+3y^2) - (6x^2+3xy-8y^2)$

$\qquad = (2x^2-5xy+3y^2) + (-6x^2-3xy+8y^2)$

$\qquad = -4x^2 - 8xy + 11y^2$

13. $[(x^2+2x+5)+(4x^2-8)] - (5x^2-x)$

$\qquad = [(x^2+2x+5)+(4x^2-8)] + (-5x^2+x)$

$\qquad = (5x^2+2x-3) + (-5x^2+x)$

$\qquad = 3x - 3$

15. $[(5x^3y-x^2y^2+7xy+5)$

$\qquad - (3x^3y+2x^2y^2-4xy)]$

$\qquad + (2x^3y+7)$

$\qquad = [(5x^3y-x^2y^2+7xy+5)$

$\qquad + (-3x^3y-2x^2y^2+4xy)]$

$\qquad + (2x^3y+7)$

$\qquad = (2x^3y-3x^2y^2+11xy+5) + (2x^3y+7)$

$\qquad = 4x^3y - 3x^2y^2 + 11xy + 12$

17. $(x-5) + (23x+9) = 24x + 4$

19. $(3y^2+4y-8) + (3y^2-9)$

$\qquad = 6y^2 + 4y - 17$

21. $(x^2-4xy-y^2) - (3x^2+7xy-5y^2)$

$\qquad = (x^2-4xy-y^2) + (-3x^2-7xy+5y^2)$

$\qquad = -2x^2 - 11xy + 4y^2$

23. $(3x^3-4x^2+3x-9) + (12x^3+6x^2+x+1)$

$\qquad = 15x^3 + 2x^2 + 4x - 8$

25. $(8x^5-4x^3+7x) - (3x^4-17x^3+x^2-12)$

$\qquad = (8x^5-4x^3+7x)$

$\qquad + (-3x^4+17x^3-x^2+12)$

$\qquad = 8x^5 - 3x^4 + 13x^3 - x^2 + 7x$

$\qquad + 12$

27. $(4x^3y-2x^2y^2+8xy-12)$

$\qquad \div (2x^3y-7x^2y^2+7xy-1)$

$\qquad = 6x^3y - 9x^2y^2 + 15xy - 13$

29. $(13x^5-4x^3-7x) + (11x^5+14x^4-3x)$

$\qquad =24x^5 + 14x^4 - 4x^3 - 10x$

31. $(x^2-7x-5) - (x^2+6x-4) + (x^2-2x+11)$

$\qquad = (x^2-7x-5) + (-x^2-6x+4)$

$\qquad + (x^2-2x+11)$

$\qquad = x^2 - 15x + 10$

33. $(z^2-3) - (z^2+3) + (z^2-2z-1)$

$\qquad = (z^2-3) + (-2^2-3) + (2^2-2z-1)$

$\qquad = z^2 - 2z - 7$

35. $[(3x^2-4x+7) + (2x^2+10)] - (7x^2-x)$

$\qquad = [(3x^2-4x+7)+(2x^2+10)]$

$\qquad + (-7x^2+x)$

$\qquad = (5x^2-4x+17) + (-7x^2+x)$

$\qquad = -2x^2 - 3x + 17$

37. $(4v^4-v^2+4)$

    $- [(2v^4-v+8)+(2v^3+3v^2-5v+8)]$

    $= (4v^4-v^2+4)$

      $- (2v^4+2v^3+3v^2-6v+16)$

    $= (4v^4-v^2+4)$

      $+ (2v^4-2v^3-3v^2+6v-16)$

    $= 2v^4 - 2v^3 - 4v^2 + 6v - 12$

39. $[(z^2-2z)-(2z^2+8)] - (6z^2-2z-7)$

    $= [(z^2-2z)+(-2z^2-8)]$

      $+ (-6z^2+2z+7)$

    $= (-z^2-2z-8) + (-6z^2+2z+7)$

    $= -7z^2 - 1$

41. $(s^2+7s-6) - (3s+2)$

    $= (s^2+7s-6) + (-3s-2)$

    $= s^2 + 4s - 8$

43. $[(x^2+1)+(x^2+2x+1)] - (x^2+x+1)$

    $= (2x^2+2x+2) + (-x^2-x-1)$

    $= x^2 + x + 1$

45. $[(6x-5y)+(3x-13y)]$

    $- [(3x+y)+(4x-8y)]$

    $= (9x-18y) - (7x-7y)$

    $= (9x-18y) + (-7x+7y)$

    $= 2x - 11y$

47. $(2x^2+2x+2) + (-x^2-4x-4)$

    $+ (6x^2+7x-3)$

    $= 7x^2 + 5x - 5$

49. Perimeter: $2w + 2(2w-3)$

    $= 2w + 4w - 6$

    $= 6w - 6$

$w = 7, \ 6(7) - 6 = 42 - 6$

          $= 36$

When the width is 7 ft., the perimeter is 36 ft.

51. $65x + (54x+27) = 119x + 27$

They are $119x + 27$ miles apart.

53. $42 - x$ are Penn.

55. $(10x+4) - (6x-22)$

    $= (10x+4) + (-6x+22)$

    $= 4x + 26$

Kitty has saved $4x + 26$ dollars.

57. $180 - (x^2-2x+30)$

    $= 180 + (-x^2+2x-30)$

    $= -x^2 + 2x + 150$

The supplement is $-x^2 + 2x + 150$ degrees.

59. $(2x^{2n}-x^n+1) + (5x^{2n}+2x^n+3)$

    $= 7x^{2n} + x^n + 4$

61. $(x^m-5x^m y^n+y^n) + (2x^m+x^m y^n-5y^n)$

    $= 3x^m - 4x^m y^n - 4y^n$

Problem Set 1.4.

1. $(x+2)(x+1) = x^2 + x + 2x + 2$

                $= x^2 + 3x + 2$

3. $(\frac{1}{2}x+2)(\frac{1}{2}x+1) = \frac{1}{4}x^2 + \frac{1}{2}x + x + 2$

                    $= \frac{1}{4}x^2 + \frac{3}{2}x + 2$

5. $(x-6)(x-7) = x^2 - 7x - 6x + 42$

                $= x^2 - 13x + 42$

7. $(x+7)(x-5) = x^2 - 5x + 7x - 35$

                $= x^2 + 2x - 35$

9. $(4ab)(-3a^2b) = -12a^3b^2$

11. $(rs)s^3 = rs^4$

13. $-3x^2(1-x) = -3x^2 + 3x^3$

15. $(5x-7)(3x-8) = 15x^2 - 40x - 21x$

$\qquad + 56$

$\qquad = 15x^2 - 61x + 56$

17. $(x-y)(x^2-2xy^2+y^3)$

$\qquad = x(x^2) - x(2xy^2) + x(y^3)$

$\qquad - y(x^2) + y(2xy^2) - y(y^3)$

$\qquad = x^3 - 2x^2y^2 + xy^3 - x^2y$

$\qquad + 2x^y3 - y^4$

$\qquad = x^3 - 2x^2y^2 - x^2y + 3xy^3 - 4^4$

19. $(x+5)^2 = x^2 + 2(5x) + 25$

$\qquad = x^2 + 10x + 25$

21. $(3x-4y)^2 = 9x^2 - 2(12xy) + 16y^2$

$\qquad = 9x^2 - 24xy + 16y^2$

23. $(x-2)(x+2) = x^2 - 2^2$

$\qquad = x^2 - 4$

25. $(5x+7)(5x-7) = (5x)^2 - 7^2$

$\qquad = 25x^2 - 49$

27. $(x-2)(x^2+2x+4) = x^3 - 2^3$

$\qquad = x^3 - 8$

29. $(x+5)(x^2-5x+25) = x^3 + 5^3$

$\qquad = x^3 + 125$

31. $(x+2)^3 = x^3 + 3x^2(2) + 3(x)(2)^2$

$\qquad + 2^3$

$\qquad = x^3 + 6x^2 + 12x + 8$

33. $(3a-b)^3 = (3a)^3 - 3(3a)^2(b)$

$\qquad + 3(3a)(b)^2 - b^3$

$\qquad = 27a^3 - 27a^2b + 9ab^2 - b^3$

35. $(x+3)(x-1) + 2x(x-7)$

$\qquad = x^2 - 2x - 3 + 2x^2 - 14x$

$\qquad = 3x^2 - 12x - 3$

37. $5 - 2[3(x^2-x)+(x+1)(x+3)]$

$\qquad = 5 - 2(3x^2-3x+x^2+4x+3)$

$\qquad = 5 - 2(4x^2+x+3)$

$\qquad = 5 - 8x^2 - 2x - 6$

$\qquad = -8x^2 - 2x - 1$

39. $(2ab)(-4a^3b) = -8a^4b^2$

41. $(2rs)s^4 = 2rs^5$

43. $-2^3xy^3(x^4y) = -2^3x^5y^4$

45. $3b^5(-3^2abc)^3 = 3b^5(-3^6a^3b^3c^3)$

$\qquad = -3^7a^3b^8c^3$

47. $(-r^4t)^5 = -r^{20}t^5$

49. $(rst^5)^3(-3r^7)^2 = (r^3s^3t^{15})(9r^{14})$

$\qquad = 9r^{17}s^3t^{15}$

51. $(abc^5)(a^3bc)^7(-ab^2c)^4$

$\qquad = (abc^5)(a^{21}b^7c^7)(a^4b^8c^4)$

$\qquad = a^{26}b^{16}c^{16}$

53. $a^3bc(3a+5ab^3c^6-4b)$

$\qquad = 3a^4bc + 5a^4b^4c^7 - 4a^3b^2c$

55. $-\frac{3}{5}x^5yz(5xz-3y^5z^7-1)$

$\qquad = -3x^6yz^2 + \frac{9}{5}x^5y^6z^8 + \frac{3}{5}x^5yz$

57. $\frac{1}{3}x^4(3x^7-9x^6+x^3-3)$

$\qquad = x^{11} - 3x^{10} + \frac{1}{3}x^7 - x^4$

59. $(x+1)(x+9) = x^2 + 9x + x + 9$

$\qquad = x^2 + 10x + 9$

61. $(x-3)(x+7) = x^2 + 7x - 3x - 21$

$\qquad\qquad\quad = x^2 + 4x - 21$

63. $(5+x)(7+x) = 35 + 5x + 7x + x^2$

$\qquad\qquad\qquad = 35 + 12x + x^2$

65. $(x-4)(x-6) = x^2 - 6x - 4x + 2x$

$\qquad\qquad\qquad = x^2 - 10x + 24$

67. $(x-\frac{1}{3})(x+\frac{2}{3}) = x^2 + \frac{2}{3}x - \frac{1}{3}x - \frac{2}{9}$

$\qquad\qquad\qquad\quad = x^2 + \frac{1}{3}x - \frac{2}{9}$

69. $(3-x)(2-x) = 6 - 3x - 2x + x^2$

$\qquad\qquad\qquad = 6 - 5x + x^2$

71. $(7-x^2)(4+x^2) = 28 + 7x^2 - 4x^2$

$\qquad\qquad\qquad\qquad\quad - x^4$

$\qquad\qquad\qquad\quad = 28 + 3x^2 - x^4$

73. $(4x+5)(2x+5) = 8x^2 + 20x + 10x$

$\qquad\qquad\qquad\qquad + 25$

$\qquad\qquad\qquad = 8x^2 + 30x + 25$

75. $(11x+5)(3x+1) = 33x^2 + 11x + 15x$

$\qquad\qquad\qquad\qquad + 5$

$\qquad\qquad\qquad = 33x^2 + 26x + 5$

77. $(4-x)(5-4x) = 20 - 16x - 5x + 4x^2$

$\qquad\qquad\qquad = 20 - 21x + 4x^2$

79. $(5x^2-6)(x^2-7) = 5x^4 - 35x^2 - 6x^2$

$\qquad\qquad\qquad\qquad + 42$

$\qquad\qquad\qquad = 5x^4 - 41x^2 + 42$

81. $(10x-7)(3x-5) = 30x^2 - 50x - 21x$

$\qquad\qquad\qquad\qquad + 35$

$\qquad\qquad\qquad = 30x^2 - 71x + 35$

83. $[(u-z)-5][(u-z)+3]$

$\qquad = (u-z)^2 + 3(u-z) - 5(u-z) - 15$

$\qquad = (u-z)^2 - 2(u-z) - 15$

85. $(2x-3y)(x^2-2xy+3y^2)$

$\qquad = 2x(x^2) - 2x(2xy) + 2x(3y^2)$

$\qquad\quad - 3y(x^2) + 3y(2xy)$

$\qquad\quad - 3y(3y^2)$

$\qquad = 2x^3 - 4x^2y + 6xy^2 - 3x^2y$

$\qquad\quad + 6xy^2 - 9y^3$

$\qquad = 2x^3 - 7x^2y + 12xy^2 - 9y^3$

87. $(2x+7)(x-7)(3x+1)$

$\qquad = (2x^2-14x+7x-49)(3x+1)$

$\qquad = (2x^2-7x-49)(3x+1)$

$\qquad = 2x^2(3x) + 2x^2(1) - 7x(3x)$

$\qquad\quad - 7x(1) - 49(3x) - 49(1)$

$\qquad = 6x^3 + 2x^2 - 21x^2 - 7x - 147x$

$\qquad\quad - 49$

$\qquad = 6x^3 - 19x^2 - 154x - 49$

89. $(x-4)^2 = x^2 - 2(4x) + 4^2$

$\qquad\qquad = x^2 - 8x + 16$

91. $(11x+12)^2 = (11x)^2 + 2(11x)(12)$

$\qquad\qquad\qquad\quad + 12^2$

$\qquad\qquad = 121x^2 + 264x + 144$

93. $(5x-4)^2 = (5x)^2 - 2(5x)(4) + 4^2$

$\qquad\qquad = 25x^2 - 40x + 16$

95. $(x-5y)(x+5y) = x^2 - (5y)^2$

$\qquad\qquad\qquad = x^2 - 25y^2$

97. $(7x+6)^2 = (7x)^2 + 2(7x)(6) + 6^2$

$\qquad\qquad = 49x^2 + 84x + 36$

99. $(ax-2by)^2 = (ax)^2 - 2(ax)(2by)$

$\qquad\qquad\qquad\quad + (2by)^2$

$\qquad\qquad = a^2x^2 - 4abxy + 4b^2y^2$

101. $(7a+3b)(4a^2-21ab+9b^2) = (7a)^3$

$\qquad + (3b)^3$

$\qquad = 343a^3 + 2b^3$

103. $(t+4r)(t^2-4rt+16r^2) = t^3 + (4r)^3$

$\qquad\qquad = t^3 + 64r^3$

105. $(x-6)(x^2+6x+36) = x^3 - 6^3$

$\qquad\qquad = x^3 - 216$

107. $(x-5)^3 = x^3 - 3(x)^2(5)$

$\qquad\qquad + 3(x)(5)^2 - 5^3$

$\qquad = x^3 - 15x^2 + 75x - 125$

109. $(x+2y)^3 = x^3 + 3(x)^2(2y)$

$\qquad\qquad + 3(x)(2y)^2 + (2y)^3$

$\qquad = x^3 + 6x^2y + 12xy^2 + 8y^3$

111. $(4s-3t)^3 = (4s)^3 - 3(4s)^2(3t)$

$\qquad\qquad + 3(4s)(3t)^2 - (3t)^3$

$\qquad = 64s^3 - 9t(16s^2)$

$\qquad\qquad + 12s(9t^2) - 27t^3$

$\qquad = 64s^3 - 144s^2t + 108st^2$

$\qquad\qquad - 27t^3$

113. $[(x-y)+7][(x-y)-7] = (x-y)^2 - 7^2$

$\qquad\qquad = (x-y)^2 - 49$

115. $[(s+t)+3]^2 = (s+t)^2 + 2(s+t)(3)$

$\qquad\qquad + 3^2$

$\qquad = (s+t)^2 + 6(s+t) + 9$

117. $(x+6)(x-3) - 3x(x-5)$

$\qquad = x^2 + 3x - 18 - 3x^2 + 15x$

$\qquad = -2x^2 + 18x - 18$

119. $7 - 3[3(x^2+x)-(x-1)(x+3)]$

$\qquad = 7 - 3[3x^2+3x-(x^2+2x-3)]$

$\qquad = 7 - 3[3x^2+3x-x^2-2x+3]$

$\qquad = 7 - 3[2x^2+x+3]$

$\qquad = 7 - 6x^2 - 3x - 9$

$\qquad = -6x^2 - 3x - 2$

121. $(n+2)(n+4) = n^2 + 6n + 8$

123. $(n+1)(n+2) = n^2 + 3n + 2$

125. $\frac{4}{3}\pi(x-5)^3$

$\qquad = \frac{4}{3}(x^3-3(x)^2(5)+3(x)(5)^2-5^3)$

$\qquad = \frac{4}{3}(x^3-15x^2+75x-125)$

$\qquad = \frac{4}{3}\pi x^3 - 20\pi x^2 + 100\pi x - \frac{500}{3}\pi$

The volume is $\frac{4}{3}\pi x^3 - 20\pi x^2$

$\qquad + 100\pi x - \frac{500}{3}\pi$ m^3.

127. $(w)(3w^2)(\frac{1}{2}) = \frac{3}{2}w^3$

The volume is $\frac{3}{2}w^3$ in^3.

129. $2x^2(x^{2n}+3x^n+1)$

$\qquad = 2x^{2+2n} + 6x^{2+n} + 2x^2$

131. $(x^n+2)(x^n-2) = (x^n)^2 - 2^2$

$\qquad\qquad = x^{2n} - 4$

133. $(x^n+1)^3 = (x^n)^3 + 3(x^n)^2(1)$

$\qquad\qquad + 3(x^n)(1)^2 + 1^3$

$\qquad = x^{3n} + 3x^{2n} + 3x^n + 1$

Problem Set 1.5.

1. $(x+1)^3 = x^3 + 3(x)^2(1)$

$\qquad + 3(x)(1)^2 + (1)^3$

$\qquad = x^3 + 3x^2 + 3x + 1$

3. $(x+2)^4 = x^4 + 4(x)^2(2) + 6(x)^2(2)^2$

$\qquad + 4(x)(2)^3 + (2)^4$

$\qquad = x^4 + 8x^3 + 24x^2 + 32x+16$

5. $(2x+3y)^6 = (2x)^6 + 6(2x)^5(3y)$

   $+ 15(2x)^4(3y)^2$

   $+ 20(2x)^3(3y)^3$

   $+ 15(2x)^2(3y)^4$

   $+ 6(2x)(3y)^5 + (3y)$

   $= 64x^6 + 18y(32x^5)$

   $+ 135y^2(16x^4)$

   $+ 540y^3(8x^3)$

   $+ 1215y^4(4x^2)$

   $+ 12x(243y^5) + 729y^6$

   $= 64x^6 + 576x^5y$

   $+ 2160x^4y^2 + 4320x^3y^3$

   $+ 4860x^2y^4 + 2916xy^5$

   $+ 729y^6$

7. $(u-2w)^6 = u^6 - 6(u)^5(2w)$

   $+ 15(u)^4(2w)^2$

   $- 20(u)^3(2w)^3$

   $+ 15(u)^2(2w)^4$

   $- 6(u)(2w)^5 + (2w)^6$

   $= u^6 - 12u^5w + 60u^4w^2$

   $- 160u^3w^3 + 240u^2w^4$

   $- 192uw^5 + 64w^6$

9. $(x-2)^{10} = x^{10} - 10x^9(2)$

   $+ 45x^8(2)^2 - 120x^7(2)^3$

   $+ 210x^6(2)^4 - 252x^3(2)^5$

   $+ 210x^4(2)^6 - 120x^3(2)^7$

   $+ 45x^2(2)^8 - 10x(2)^9$

   $+ (2)^{10}$

$= x^{10} - 20x^9 + 180x^8 - 960x^7$

$+ 3360x^6 - 8064x^5$

$+ 13,440x^4 - 15,360x^3$

$+ 11,520x^2 - 5120x + 1024$

11. $(x-1)^3 = x^3 - 3(x)^2(1)$

   $+ 3(x)(1)^2 - 1^3$

   $= x^3 - 3x^2 + 3x - 1$

13. $(y-2)^4 = y^4 - 4(y)^3(2)$

   $+ 6(y)^2(2)^2 - 4(y)(2)^3$

   $+ (2)^4$

   $= y^4 - 8y^3 + 24y^2 - 32y$

   $+ 16$

15. $(b-3)^5 = b^5 - 5(b)^4(3)$

   $+ 10(b)^3(3)^2 - 10(b)^2(3)^3$

   $+ 5b(3)^4 - 3^5$

   $= b^5 - 15b^4 + 90b^3 - 270b^2$

   $+ 405b - 243$

17. $(2x-1)^4 = (2x)^4 - 4(2x)^3(1)$

   $+ 6(2x)^2(1)^2 - 4(2x)(1)^3$

   $+ 1^4$

   $= 16x^4 - 32x^3 + 24x^2$

   $- 8x + 1$

19. $(a+1)^5 = a^5 + 5a^4(1) + 10a^3(1)^2$

   $+ 10a^2(1)^3 + 5a(1)^4 + 1^5$

   $= a^5 + 5a^4 + 10a^3 + 10a^2 + 5a + 1$

21. $(2x+3)^4 = (2x)^4 + 4(2x)^3(3)$

   $+ 6(2x)^2(3)^2 + 4(2x)(3)^3$

   $+ 3^4$

   $= 16x^4 + 46x^3 + 216x^2$

   $+ 216x + 81$

23. $(3x-2)^3 = (3x)^3 - 3(3x)^2(2)$

$+ 3(3x)(2)^2 - 2^3$

$= 27x^3 - 54x^2 + 36x - 8$

25. $(3x+2)^5 = (3x)^5 + 5(3x)^4(2)$

$+ 10(3x)^3(2)^2$

$+ 10(3x)^2(2)^3$

$+ 5(3x)(2)^4 + 2^5$

$= 243x^5 + 810x^4 + 1080x^3$

$+ 720x^2 + 240x + 32$

27. $(x-y)^6 = x^6 - 6x^5y + 15x^4y^2$

$- 20x^3y^3 + 15x^2y^4 - 6xy^5$

$+ y^6$

29. $(x-2)^8 = x^8 - 8x^7(2) + 28x^6(2)^2$

$- 56x^5(2)^3 + 70x^4(2)^4$

$- 56x^3(2)^5 + 28x^2(2)^6$

$- 8x(2)^7 + (2)^8$

$= x^8 - 16x^7 + 112x^6 - 448x^5$

$+ 1120x^4 - 1792x^3 + 1792x^2$

$- 1024x + 256$

31. 4th term: $-165(3x)^8(y)^3$

$= -165(6561x^8)(y^3)$

$= -1,082,565x^8y^3$

33. 5th term: $70(5z)^4(2)^4$

$= 70(625z^4)(16)$

$= 700,000z^4$

Problem Set 1.6.

1. $\dfrac{a^4b^2}{b} = a^4b$

3. $\dfrac{(x-y)^4z^2}{(x-y)^2z} = (x-y)^2z$

5. $\dfrac{6x^2+12y}{6x} = \dfrac{6x^2}{6x} + \dfrac{12y}{6x}$

$= x + \dfrac{2y}{x}$

7.
$$
\begin{array}{r}
z-6 \\
z+2\,\overline{\smash{)}\,z^2-4z-12} \\
\underline{-z^2+2z} \\
-6z-12 \\
\underline{-6z-12} \\
0
\end{array}
$$

$\dfrac{z^2-4z-12}{z+2} = z-6$

9.
$$
\begin{array}{r}
x-3 \\
2x+1\,\overline{\smash{)}\,2x^2-5x-3} \\
\underline{-2x^2+\ x} \\
-6x-3 \\
\underline{-6x-3} \\
0
\end{array}
$$

$\dfrac{2x^2-5x-3}{2x+1} = x - 3$

11.
$$
\begin{array}{r}
x-1 \\
x+3\,\overline{\smash{)}\,x^2+2x-4} \\
\underline{-x\ +3x} \\
-\ x-4 \\
\underline{-\ x-3} \\
-1
\end{array}
$$

$\dfrac{x^2+2x-4}{x+3} = x - 1 + \dfrac{-1}{x+3}$

13.
$$
\begin{array}{r}
x^3-x^2-4x-7 \\
x^2-2x+3\,\overline{\smash{)}\,x^5-3x^4+\ x^3-2x^2+\ 5x+4} \\
\underline{-x^5-2x^4+3x^3} \\
-\ x^4-2x^3-2x^2 \\
\underline{-\ x^4+2x^3-3x^2} \\
-4x^3+\ x^2+\ 5x \\
\underline{-4x^3+8x^2-12x} \\
-7x^2+17x+4 \\
\underline{7x^2+14x-2} \\
3x+25
\end{array}
$$

$\dfrac{x^5-3x^4+x^3-2x^2+5x+4}{x^2-2x+3}$

21

$$= x^3 - x^2 - 4x - 7$$

$$+ \frac{3x+25}{x^2-2x+3}$$

15.
$$
\begin{array}{r}
x^2-xy+y^2 \\
x+2y\overline{\smash{\big)}\,x^3 + x^2y - xy^2+2y^3} \\
\underline{-x^3+2x^2y} \\
- x^2y - xy^2 \\
\underline{- x^2y-2xy^2} \\
xy^2+2y^3 \\
\underline{- xy^2+2y^3} \\
0
\end{array}
$$

$$\frac{x^3+x^2y-xy^2+2y^3}{x+2y} = x^2 - xy + y^2$$

17.
$$
\begin{array}{r}
x^2-x+2 \\
x^2+0x-1\overline{\smash{\big)}\,x^4 - x^3 + x^2+0x+1} \\
\underline{-x^4+0x^3 - x^2} \\
- x^3+2x^2+0x \\
\underline{- x^3+0x^2+ x} \\
2x^2 - x+1 \\
\underline{- 2x^2+0x-2} \\
- x+3
\end{array}
$$

$$\frac{(x^4+x^2-x^3+1)}{(x^2-1)} = x^2 - x + 2 + \frac{-x+3}{x^2-1}$$

19. $\dfrac{27ab}{18b^2} = \dfrac{3a}{2b}$

21. $\dfrac{5x^2+10x-15}{10y} = \dfrac{5x^2}{10y} + \dfrac{10x}{10y} - \dfrac{15}{10y}$

$$= \frac{x^2}{2y} + \frac{x}{y} - \frac{3}{2y}$$

23. $\dfrac{x^2-xy+y^2}{xy} = \dfrac{x^2}{xy} - \dfrac{xy}{xy} + \dfrac{y^2}{xy}$

$$= \frac{x}{y} - 1 + \frac{y}{x}$$

25.
$$
\begin{array}{r}
3x-1 \\
3x+3\overline{\smash{\big)}\,6x^2+7x-3} \\
\underline{-6x^2+9x} \\
-2x-3 \\
\underline{-2x-3} \\
0
\end{array}
$$

$$\frac{6x^2+7x-3}{3x+3} = 3x-1$$

27.
$$
\begin{array}{r}
y+3 \\
y-1\overline{\smash{\big)}\,y^2+2y-3} \\
\underline{-y^2- y} \\
3y-3 \\
\underline{3y-3} \\
0
\end{array}
$$

$$\frac{y^2+2y-3}{y-1} = y+3$$

29.
$$
\begin{array}{r}
x^2-x-1 \\
2x+1\overline{\smash{\big)}\,2x^3 - x^2-3x+3} \\
\underline{-2x^3+ x^2} \\
-2x^2-3x \\
\underline{- -2x^2- x} \\
-2x+3 \\
\underline{-2x-1} \\
4
\end{array}
$$

$$(2x^3-x^2-3x+3) \div (2x+1)$$

$$= x^2 - x - 1 + \frac{4}{2x+1}$$

31.
$$
\begin{array}{r}
2x^2-x+1 \\
3x+2\overline{\smash{\big)}\,6x^3 + x^2+ x-5} \\
\underline{-6x^3+4x^2} \\
-3x^2+ x \\
\underline{- -3x^2-2x} \\
3x-5 \\
\underline{3x+2} \\
-7
\end{array}
$$

$$\frac{x^2+6x^3+x-5}{3x+2} = 2x^2-x+1 + \frac{-7}{3x+2}$$

33.
```
           2x+1
x-3 ) 2x²-5x-3
     -2x²-6x
     ────────
          x-3
          x-3
          ───
           0
```

$$\frac{2x^2-5x-3}{x-3} = 2x + 1$$

35.
```
          3x+y
2x+y ) 6x²+5xy+y²
      -6x²+3xy
      ─────────
           2xy+y²
          -2xy+y²
          ───────
             0
```

$$\frac{(6x^2+5xy+y^2)}{(2x+y)} = 3x + y$$

37.
```
            x²-x+1
3x²+x-1 ) 3x⁴-2x³+ x²-2x+4
        -3x⁴+ x³- x²
         ─────────────
           -3x³+2x²-2x
         -  -3x³- x²+ x
            ──────────
              3x²-3x+4
              3x²+ x-1
              ────────
               -4x+5
```

$$\frac{(3x^4-2x^3-2x+x^2+4)}{(x+3x^2-1)}$$

$$= x^2 - x + 1 + \frac{-4x+5}{3x^2+x-1}$$

39.
```
           3x²-x+1
7x+4 ) 21x³+ 5x²+3x+8
      -21x³+12x²
      ───────────
         -7x²+3x
      -  -7x²- x
         ────────
             7x+8
             7x+4
             ────
              4
```

$$\frac{21x^3+5x^2+3x+8}{7x+4} = 3x^2 - x + 1$$

41.
```
           x³-3x²+9x-28
x+3 ) x⁴+0x³+0x²- x+ 2
     -x⁴+3x³
     ───────────
       -3x³+0x²
     -  -3x³-9x²
        ─────────
          9x²-  x
          9x²+27x
          ───────
          -28x+ 2
          -28x-84
          ───────
           86
```

$$\frac{x^4-x+2}{3+x} = x^3 - 3x^2 + 9x - 28$$

$$+ \frac{86}{3+x}$$

43.
```
                   x³+2
x³+0x²+0x-1 ) x⁶+0x⁵+0x⁴+x³+0x²+0x-3
             -x⁶+0x⁵+0x⁴-x³
             ─────────────────
                       2x³+0x²+0x-3
                     -2x³+0x²+0x-2
                     ─────────────
                       -1
```

$$\frac{x^3+x^6-3}{x^3-1} = x^3 + 2 + \frac{-1}{x^3-1}$$

45.
```
                    2x³-4x+1
2x²+0x+1 ) 4x⁵+0x⁴-6x³+2x²+0x+1
          -4x⁵+0x⁴+2x³
          ──────────────
            -8x³+2x²+0x
          -  -8x³+0x²-4x
             ────────────
               2x²+4x+1
               2x²+0x+1
               ────────
                4x
```

$$\frac{4x^5-6x^3+2x^2+1}{2x^2+1} = 2x^3 - 4x + 1$$

$$+ \frac{4x}{2x^2+1}$$

47.
$$\begin{array}{r} x^2+3x-4 \\ \hline x-2 \overline{\smash{\big)}\ x^3+\ x^2-10x+8} \\ -\underline{x^3-2x^2} \\ 3x^2-10x \\ -\underline{3x^2-\ 6x} \\ -\ 4x+8 \\ -\underline{\ 4x+8} \\ 0 \end{array}$$

$(x^3+x^2-10x+8) \div (x-2) = x^2$
$\qquad\qquad\qquad\qquad\quad + 3x - 4$

49.
$$\begin{array}{r} 2t^2-3t+5 \\ \hline 3t-2 \overline{\smash{\big)}\ 6t^3-13t^2+21t+17} \\ -\underline{6t^3-\ 4t^2} \\ -9t^2+21t \\ -\underline{-9t^2+\ 6t} \\ 15t+17 \\ -\underline{15t-10} \\ 27 \end{array}$$

The remainder is 27.

51.
$$\begin{array}{r} x^n-3 \\ \hline x^n+1 \overline{\smash{\big)}\ x^{2n}-2x^n+4} \\ -\underline{x^{2n}+\ x^n} \\ -3x^n+4 \\ -\underline{-3x^2-3} \\ 7 \end{array}$$

$\dfrac{x^{2n}-2x^n+4}{x^n+1} = x^n - 3 + \dfrac{7}{x^n+1}$

53.
$$\begin{array}{r} x^2-x+4 \\ \hline x+3 \overline{\smash{\big)}\ x^3+2x^2+\ x+K} \\ -\underline{x^3+3x^2} \\ -x^2+\ x \\ -\underline{-x^2+3x} \\ -4x+\ K \\ \underline{4x+12} \\ 0 \end{array}$$

K - 12 = 0, so K = 12.

1.
$$\begin{array}{r|rrr} 3 & 2 & -5 & -3 \\ & & 6 & 3 \\ \hline & 2 & 1 & 0 \end{array}$$

$\dfrac{2x^2-5x-3}{x-3} = 2x + 1$

3.
$$\begin{array}{r|rrrr} -1 & 1 & 3 & 3 & 1 \\ & & -1 & -2 & -1 \\ \hline & 1 & 2 & 1 & 0 \end{array}$$

$\dfrac{x^3+3x^2+3x+1}{x+1} = x^2 + 2x + 1$

5.
$$\begin{array}{r|rrrr} 4 & 1 & 0 & 0 & -64 \\ & & 4 & 16 & 64 \\ \hline & 1 & 4 & 16 & 0 \end{array}$$

The remainder is 0.

7.
$$\begin{array}{r|rrrrr} 1 & 1 & 0 & -2 & 0 & 1 \\ & & 1 & 1 & -1 & -1 \\ \hline & 1 & 1 & -1 & -1 & 0 \end{array}$$

$\dfrac{x^4-2x^2+1}{x-1} = x^3 + x^2 - x - 1$

9.
$$\begin{array}{r|rrrr} -2 & 4 & 7 & 1 & 5 \\ & & -8 & 2 & -6 \\ \hline & 4 & -1 & 3 & -1 \end{array}$$

$\dfrac{7x^2+4x^3+x+5}{x+2} = 4x^2 - x + 3 + \dfrac{-1}{x+2}$

11.
$$\begin{array}{r|rrr} 3 & 2 & -9 & 9 \\ & & 6 & -9 \\ \hline & 2 & -3 & 0 \end{array}$$

$(2x^2-9x+9) \div (x-3) = 2x - 3$

13.
$$\begin{array}{r|rrrrr} 2 & 1 & 0 & -2 & -5 & 3 \\ & & 2 & 4 & 4 & -2 \\ \hline & 1 & 2 & 2 & -1 & 1 \end{array}$$

$$\frac{x^4-2x^2-5x+3}{x-2} = x^3 + 2x^2 + 2x - 1$$
$$+ \frac{1}{x-2}$$

15.
```
2 |  2 -1 -3 -4
        4  6  6
     2  3  3  2
```

$$\frac{(2x^3-x^2-3x-4)}{(x-2)} = 2x^2 + 3x + 3$$
$$+ \frac{2}{x-2}$$

17.
```
-1 |  1  0  0  0  1
        -1  1 -1  1
      1 -1  1 -1  2
```

$$\frac{(y^4+1)}{(y+1)} = y^3 - y^2 + y - 1 + \frac{2}{y+1}$$

19.
```
1 |  1  0  1  0 -2
        1  1  2  2
     1  1  2  2  0
```

$$(x^4+x^2-2) \div (x-1) = x^3 + x^2 + 2x$$
$$+ 2$$

21.
```
1 |  1  1  1  1  1
        1  2  3  4
     1  2  3  4  5
```

$$\frac{x^4+x^3+x^2+x+1}{x-1} = x^3 + 2x^2 + 3x + 4$$
$$+ \frac{5}{x-1}$$

23.
```
2 |  2 -4  1 -1 -2
        4  0  2  2
     2  0  1  1  0
```

The remainder is 0.

Review problems.

1. $1^3 - (1)(-3)^2 + (-3)^3$

$= 1 - 9 - 27$

$= -35$

3. $(-5)^2 = 25$

5. $(-2)^2(-3)^3 = 4(-27)$

$= -108$

7. $(xy^3)^4 = x^4(y^3)^4$

$= x^4 y^{12}$

9. $(a+b)^4(a+b) = (a+b)^5$

11. $\left(\frac{-2x}{y}\right)^2 = \frac{(-2x)^2}{y^2}$

$= \frac{(-2)^2 x^2}{y^2}$

$= \frac{4x^2}{y^2}$

13. $\frac{-10^0}{10} = -\frac{1}{10}$

15. $\frac{(-6)^4}{(-6)^5} = \frac{1}{-6}$ or $-\frac{1}{6}$

17. $\frac{-5^3}{-2^4} = \frac{125}{16}$

19. $abc(a^2b^3c-ac^4) = a^3b^4c^2 - a^2bc^5$

21. $(7p^3-4p^2-7) - (p^3+6p-5)$

$= 7p^3 - 4p^2 - 7 - p^3 - 6p + 5$

$= 6p^3 - 4p^2 - 6p - 2$

23. $\frac{xy^3z^2}{x^2yz} = \frac{y^2z}{x}$

25. $(r^3s^2t)(r^3st^4) = r^6s^3t^5$

27. $(x^4-x^3y+3x^2y^2-5xy+y^5)$

$-(2x^4+2x^3y-x^2y^2+7xy)$

$= x^4 - x^3y + 3x^2y^2 - 5xy + y^5$

$$-2x^4 - 2x^3y + x^2y^2 - 7xy$$

$$= -x^4 - 3x^3y + 4x^2y^2 - 12xy + y^5$$

29.
$$\begin{array}{r} x^2-2x+1 \\ x+7\overline{\smash{\big)}\,x^3+5x^2-10x+20} \\ \underline{-x^3+7x^2} \\ -2x^2-10x \\ \underline{--2x^2-14x} \\ 4x+20 \\ \underline{-4x+28} \\ -8 \end{array}$$

$$\frac{x^3+5x^2-10x+20}{x+7} = x^2 - 2x + 4$$
$$+ \frac{-8}{x+7}$$

31. $(t-5)^3 = t^3 - 3(t)^2(5)$
$$+ 3(t)(5)^2 - 5^3$$
$$= t^3 - 15t^2 + 75t - 125$$

33. $(7r-2)(2r-1) = 14r^2 - 7r - 4r + 2$
$$= 14r^2 - 11r + 2$$

35. $(c+3d)(-3d) = c^2 - (3d)^2$
$$= c^2 - 9d^2$$

37. $(x-y) - (x+y) = x - y - x - y$
$$= -2y$$

39. $xy^2(xy-1) = x^2y^3 - xy^2$

41.
$$\begin{array}{r} 4s^2-6s+9 \\ 2s+3\overline{\smash{\big)}\,8s^3+0s^2+0s+27} \\ \underline{-8s^3+12s^2} \\ -12s^2+0s \\ \underline{-12s-18s} \\ 18s+27 \\ \underline{18s+27} \\ 0 \end{array}$$

$$\frac{8s^3+27}{2s+3} = 4s^2 - 6s + 9$$

43. $(x+3)^2 - (x-2)^2$

$$= x^2 + 6x + 9 - (x^2-4x+4)$$

$$= x^2 + 6x + 9 - x^2 + 4x - 4$$

$$= 10x + 5$$

45.
$$\begin{array}{r} x^2+3x \\ x^2-x+2\overline{\smash{\big)}\,x^4+2x^3-x^2+0+6} \\ \underline{-x^4-x^3+2x^2} \\ 3x^3-3x^2+0 \\ \underline{3x^3-3x^2+6x} \\ -6x+6 \end{array}$$

$$\frac{x^4+2x^3-x^2+6}{x^2-x+2} = x^2 + 3x$$
$$+ \frac{-6x+6}{x^2-x+2}$$

47. $r(r-t) + (2r-t)(2r+t)$
$$= r^2 - rt + 4r^2 - t^2$$
$$= 5r^2 - rt - t^2$$

49. $6 - [x(x-1)-2(x+3)]$
$$= 6 - (x^2-x-2x-6)$$
$$= 6 - (x^2-3x-6)$$
$$= 6 - x^2 + 3x + 6$$
$$= -x^2 + 3x + 12$$

51. height: x ft.

base: 2x ft.

area $= \frac{1}{2}(2x)(x) = x^2$

The area is x^2 ft.^{2}.

53. 3 terms

55. $(2x)^2 = 2^2x^2$
$$= 4x^2$$

57. $(x-2)(x+2) = x^2 - 2^2$
$$= x^2 - 4$$

26

59. $(x+1)^3 = x^3 + 3x^2(1) + 3x(1)^2$
$$+ 1^3$$
$$= x^3 + 3x^2 + 3x + 1$$

61. $(-3)^3 = -27$

63. $(-b)^2 = b^2$

Test.

1. $2x^3[(3x)^2-x^5] = 2x^3(9x^2-x^5)$
$$= 18x^5 - 2x^8$$

A.

2. $3(-1)^3 - 2(-1)^2(3)^2$
$$= 3(-1) - 2(1)(9)$$
$$= -3 - 18$$
$$= -21$$

D.

3. $(\dfrac{-2a^5 b}{b^4})^2 = \dfrac{(-2)^2(a^5)^2 b^2}{(b^4)^2}$
$$= \dfrac{4a^{10}b^2}{b^8}$$
$$= \dfrac{4a^{10}}{b^6}$$

A.

4. $\dfrac{(-3)^4}{(-3)^6} = \dfrac{1}{(-3)^2}$
$$= \dfrac{1}{9}$$

B.

5. $-3^2 ab^4(2ab)(-a^4) = 18a^6 b^5$

B.

6. $\dfrac{6x^2-4x^3}{x^2} = \dfrac{6x^2}{x^2} - \dfrac{4x^3}{x^2}$
$$= 6 - 4x.$$

7. $(2x-3)(5x+7) = 10x^2 + 14x - 15x-21$
$$= 10x^2 - x - 21$$

8. $(5x^3 y^2-4x^2 y+3xy) + (-3x^3 y^2+x^2 y-7xy)$
$$= 2x^3 y^2 - 3x^2 y - 4xy$$

9. $(4x-7)^2 = (4x)^2 - 2(4x)(7) + (-7)^2$
$$= 16x^2 - 56x + 49$$

10. $(2x+3)(4x^2-6x+9) = (2x)^3 + 3^3$
$$= 8x^3 + 27$$

11. $(x^4-2x^3+3x-2) + (x^2-1)$
$$- (2x^4-x^3+2x^2+3x)$$
$$= x^4 - 2x^3 + 3x - 2 + x^2 - 1$$
$$- 2x^4 + x^3 - 2x^2 - 3x$$
$$= -x^4 - x^3 - x^2 - 3$$

12. $(x+3)^3 = x^3 + 3(x)^2(3) + 3(x)(3)^2$
$$+ 3^3$$
$$= x^3 + 9x^2 + 27x + 27$$

13.
$$\begin{array}{r} 6x^2-8x+9 \\ x+1\overline{\smash{\big)}\,6x^3-2x^2+ x- 2} \\ \underline{-6x^3+6x^2} \\ -8x^2+ x \\ \underline{-8x^2-8x} \\ 9x- 2 \\ \underline{9x+ 9} \\ -11 \end{array}$$

$(6x^3-2x^2+x-2) \div (x+1)$
$$= 6x^2 - 8x + 9 + \dfrac{-11}{x+1}$$

14. $(5x^3-x^2+4) - (x^3-2x-7)$
$$= 5x^3 - x^2 + 4 - x^3 + 2x + 7$$
$$4x^3 - x^2 + 2x + 11$$

27

15. $7 - [2(x+4)-(x+2)(x-2)]$

   $= 7 - [2x+8-(x^2-4)]$

   $= 7 - (2x+8-x^2+4)$

   $= 7 - (2x-x^2+12)$

   $= 7 - 2x + x^2 - 12$

   $= x^2 - 2x - 5$

CHAPTER 2

Problem Set 2.1.

1. $64 = 2 \cdot 32$

   $= 2 \cdot 2 \cdot 16$

   $= 2 \cdot 2 \cdot 2 \cdot 8$

   $= 2 \cdot 2 \cdot 2 \cdot 2 \cdot 4$

   $= 2 \cdot 2 \cdot 2 \cdot 2 \cdot 2$

   $= 2^6$

3. $45 = 3 \cdot 15$

   $= 3 \cdot 3 \cdot 5$

   $= 3^2 \cdot 5$

5. $162 = 2 \cdot 81$

   $= 2 \cdot 3 \cdot 27$

   $= 2 \cdot 3 \cdot 3 \cdot 9$

   $= 2 \cdot 3 \cdot 3 \cdot 3 \cdot 3$

   $= 2 \cdot 3^4$

7. $243 = 3 \cdot 81$

   $= 3 \cdot 3^4$

   $= 3^5$

9. $216 = 2 \cdot 108$

   $= 2 \cdot 2 \cdot 54$

   $= 2 \cdot 2 \cdot 2 \cdot 27$

   $= 2 \cdot 2 \cdot 2 \cdot 3^3$

   $= 2^3 \cdot 3^3$

11. $24 = 2 \cdot 12$ $48 = 2 \cdot 24$

   $= 2 \cdot 2 \cdot 6$ $= 2 \cdot 2^3 \cdot 3$

   $= 2 \cdot 2 \cdot 2 \cdot 3$ $= 2^4 \cdot 3$

   $= 2^3 \cdot 3$

   The GCF is $2^3 \cdot 3$ or 24.

28

13. $36 = 2 \cdot 18$ $54 = 2 \cdot 27$

    $= 2 \cdot 2 \cdot 9$ $= 2 \cdot 3^3$

    $= 2 \cdot 2 \cdot 3 \cdot 3$

    $= 2^2 \cdot 3^2$

The GCF is $2 \cdot 3^2$ or 18.

15. $x^3 y^2$

17. st^2

19. $96 = 2 \cdot 48$ $80 = 2 \cdot 40$

    $= 2 \cdot 2^4 \cdot 3$ $= 2 \cdot 2 \cdot 20$

    $= 2^5 \cdot 3$ $= 2 \cdot 2 \cdot 2 \cdot 10$

                       $= 2 \cdot 2 \cdot 2 \cdot 2 \cdot 5$

                       $= 2^4 \cdot 5$

GCF for 96 and 80 is 2^4 or 16.

GCF for $96x^2 y$ and $80x$ is $16x$.

21. $192 = 2 \cdot 96$ $48 = 2^4 \cdot 3$

    $= 2 \cdot 2 \cdot 48$

    $= 2 \cdot 2 \cdot 2^4 \cdot 3$

    $= 2^6 \cdot 3$

    $72 = 2 \cdot 36$

    $= 2 \cdot 2^2 \cdot 3$

    $= 2^3 \cdot 3^2$

The GCF for 192, 48, 72 is $2^3 \cdot 3$
or 24.

The GCF for $192x^2 y^3$, $48x^2 y^4$,
$72x^2 y^3$ is $24 x^2 y^3$.

23. $48a^2 b^3 c + 64a^3 b^2 c$

    $= 16a^2 b^2 c(3b+4a)$

25. $20p^2 q^7 - 28p^5 q^5 + 36p^8 q^3$

$= 4p^2 q^3 (5q^4 - 7p^3 q^2 + 9p^6)$

27. $15t^3 - 15t^2 = 15t^2 (t-1)$

29. $120 = 2 \cdot 60$ $72 = 2 \cdot 36$

    $= 2 \cdot 2 \cdot 30$ $= 2 \cdot 2^2 \cdot 3^2$

    $= 2 \cdot 2 \cdot 2 \cdot 15$ $= 2^3 \cdot 3^2$

    $= 2 \cdot 2 \cdot 2 \cdot 5 \cdot 3$

    $= 2^2 \cdot 5 \cdot 3$

    $48 = 2^4 \cdot 3$

GCF for 120, 72, 48 is $2^3 \cdot 3 = 24$

$120m^2 n^3 - 72m^4 n^4 + 48m^3 n^5$

    $= 24m^2 n^3 (5-3m^2 n+2mn^2)$

31. $-6x^2 + 3x = -3x(2x-1)$

33. $-6uv + 3v = -3v(2u-1)$

35. $m(p-q) + n(p-q) = (p-q)(m+n)$

37. $(x+y)^2 + 3(x+y) = (x+y)(x+y+3)$

39. $5(1-r)^4 + 3(1-r)^3 - (1-r)^2$

    $= (1-r)^2 [5(1-r)^2 + 3(1-r)-1]$

41. $r(s-t) - u(t-s)$

    $= r(s-t) - u[-(s-t)]$

    $= r(s-t) + u(s-t)$

    $= (s-t)(r+u)$

43. $w(3u-v)^3 - 3u(3u-v)^2 + v(v-3u)$

    $= w(3u-v)^3 - 3u(3u-v)^2$

        $+ v[-(3u-v)]$

    $= w(3u-v)^3 - 3u(3u-v)^2 - v(3u-v)$

    $= (3u-v)[w(3u-v)^2 - 3u(3u-v)-v]$

45. $7x + 7y + ax + ay$

    $= 7(x+y) + a(x+y)$

    $= (x+y)(7+a)$

47. $a^2 = ab + 2a - 2b$

   $= a(a-b) + 2(a-b)$

   $= (a-b)(a+2)$

49. $a2 + ab + a + b$

   $= a(a+b) + (a+b)$

   $= (a+b)(a+1)$

51. $5r + s^2 - 5s - rs$

   $= 5r - 5s + s^2 - rs$

   $= 5(r-s) + s(s-r)$

   $= 5(r-s) + s[-(r-s)]$

   $= 5(r-s) - s(r-s)$

   $= (r-s)(5-s)$

53. $uv + wv - u - w = v(u+w) - (u+w)$

   $= (u+w)(v-1)$

55. $a^3 - a^2c + a^2b - abc$

   $= a(a^2 -ac+ab-bc)$

   $= a[a(a-c)+b(a-c)]$

   $= a(a-c)(a+b)$

57. $xz^2 - z^2 + xz - z = z(xz-z+x-1)$

   $= z[z(x-1)+(x-1)]$

   $= z(x-1)(z+1)$

59. $15abx - 15aby - 25acx + 25acy$

   $= 5a(3bx-3by-5cx+5cy)$

   $= 5a[3b(x-y)-5c(x-y)]$

   $= 5a(x-y)(3b-5c)$

61. $42a^4b^2c + 54a^2b^5c$

   $= 6a^2b^2c(7a^2+9b^3)$

63. $24r^4s^4 - 48r^3s^3 = 24r^3s^3(rs-2)$

65. $27a^4b - 18ab^5 + 9ab$

   $= 9ab(3a^3-2b^4+1)$

67. $-16x^3 - 24x^6 = -8x^3(2+3x^3)$

69. $12t^4 - 12t^3 = 12t^3(t-1)$

71. $a^3x - 2a^3y + a^3w = a^3(x-2y+w)$

73. $36m^3n^3 - 48m^5n^3 + 60m^4n^6$

   $= 12m^3n^3(3-4m^2+5mn^3)$

75. $c(d-2) + b(-2) = (d-2)(c+b)$

77. $a(s-t) + u(t-s)$

   $= a(s-t) + u[-(s-t)]$

   $= a(s-t) - u(s-t)$

   $= (s-t)(a-u)$

79. $(x+y)^3 - 5(x+y)^2 = (x+y)^2(x+y-5)$

81. $3(1-r)^3 - 3(1-r)^4 - 4(1-r)^2$

   $= (1-r)^2[3(1-r)-3(1-r)^2-4]$

83. $2t(a-x) - t(x-a)$

   $= 2t(a-x) - t[-(a-x)]$

   $= 2t(a-x) + t(a-x)$

   $= (a-x)(2t+t)$

   $= (a-x)3t$

85. $c^2(5+b)^4 - d^2(5+b)^5 - 2(b+5)^2$

   $= (5+b)^2[c^2(5+b)^2-d^2(5+b)^3-2]$

87. $15(a-b)^4 + 45(a-b)^2 - 35(b-a)$

   $= 15(a-b)^4 + 45(a-b)^2$

   $-35[-(a-b)]$

   $= 15(a-b)^4 + 45(a-b)^2 + 35(a-b)$

   $= 5(a-b)[3(a-b)^3+9(a-b)+7]$

89. $xy + 6y + x + 6 = y(x+6) + (x+6)$

   $= (x+6)(y+1)$

30

91. $ar - br - as + bs$

    $= r(a-b) - s(a-b)$

    $= (a-b)(r-s)$

93. $a + b^2 - b - ab = a - b + b^2 - ab$

                  $= (a-b) + b(b-a)$

                  $= (a-b) + b[-(a-b)]$

                  $= (a-b) - b(a-b)$

                  $= (a-b)(1-b)$

95. $4s + 12 - 3b - bs$

    $= 4(s+3) - b(3+s)$

    $= (s+3)(4-b)$

97. $t^5 + t^4 + s^4 t + s^4$

    $= t^4(t+1) + s^4(t+1)$

    $= (t+1)(t^4+s^4)$

99. $q^4 - q^2 t + q^2 - t$

    $= q^2(q^2-t) + (q^2-t)$

    $= (q^2-t)(q^2+1)$

101. $ax^2 + b^2 x^2 - ax - b^2 x$

    $= x(ax+b^2x-a-b^2)$

    $= x[x(a+b^2)-(a+b^2)]$

    $= x(a+b^2)(x-1)$

103. $16c^2 r + 32c^2 s - 8cr - 16cs$

    $= 8c(2cr+4cs-r-2s)$

    $= 8c[2c(r+2s)-(r+2s)]$

    $= 8c(r+2s)(2c-1)$

105. $w^3 - w^2 t + w^3 t - w^4$

    $= w^2(w-t+wt-w)$

    $= w^2[(w-t)+w(t-w)]$

    $= w^2\{(w-t)+w[-(w-t)]\}$

    $= w^2[(w-t)-w(w-t)]$

    $= w^2(w-t)(1-w)$

107. $x^{n+2} - x^{n+3} = x^{n+2}(1-x)$

109. $x^{2mn} + x^{4mn} = x^{2mn}(1+x^{2mn})$

Problem Set 2.2.

1. $x^2 - 9 = (x-3)(x+3)$

3. $x^4 - 25 = (x^2-5)(x^2+5)$

5. $9x^8 - 4y^4 = (3x^4-2y^2)(3x^4+2y^2)$

7. $x^3 + 1 = (x+1)(x^2-x+1)$

9. $64 - x^3 = (4-x)(16+4x+x^2)$

11. $1 - 8x^3 = (1-2x)(1+2x+4x^2)$

13. $r^3 - s^3 = (r-s)(r^2+rs+s^2)$

15. $x^6 + y^3 = (x^2+y)(x^4-x^2y+y^2)$

17. $27a^3 - 8b^3$

    $= (3a-2b)(9a^2+6ab+4b^2)$

19. $(x+y)^2 - 4 = (x+y+2)(x+y-2)$

21. $81 - (r+t)^2 = [9-(r+t)][9+(r+t)]$

               $= (9-r-t)(9+r+t)$

23. $64 - (a-b)^3$

    $= [4-(a-b)][16+4(a-b)+(a-b)^2]$

    $= (4-a+b)[16+4(a-b)+(a-b)^2]$

25. $(a+b)^2 - (x+y)^2$

    $= [(a+b)-(x+y)][(a+b)+(x+y)]$

    $= (a+b-x-y)(a+b+x+y)$

27. $(s+t)^3 - (u+v)^3$

    $= [(s+t)-(u+v)][(s+t)^2$

           $+ (s+t)(u+v)+(u+v)^2]$

    $= (s+t-u-v)[(s+t)^2+(s+t)(u+v)$
                  $+ (u+v)^2]$

29. $a^9 - b^9 = (a^3-b^3)(a^6+a^3b^3+b^6)$

$= (a-b)(a^2+ab+b^2)$

$(a^6+a^3b^3+b^6)$

31. $25(x+1) - r^2(x+1) = (x+1)(25-r^2)$

$= (x+1)(5-r)(5+r)$

33. $5(x+y)^2 - 20$

$= 5[(x+y)^2-4]$

$= 5[(x+y)-2][(x+y)+2]$

$= 5(x+y-2)(x+y)+2)$

35. $4x^2 - 64 = 4(x^2-16)$

$= 4(x-4)(x+4)$

37. $x^2 - 81 = (x-9)(x+9)$

39. $x^4 - 36 = (x^2-6)(x^2+6)$

41. $4x^2 - 25y^4 = (2x^3-5y^2)(2x^3+5y^2)$

43. $x^3 + 27 = (x+3)(x^2-3x+9)$

45. $27 - x^3 = (3-x)(9+3x+x^2)$

47. $1 - 27x^3 = (1-3x)(1+3x+9x^2)$

49. $r^3 - 8s^3 = (r-2s)(r^2+2rs+4s^2)$

51. $x^6 + 8y^3 = (x^2+2y)(x^4-2x^2y+4y^2)$

53. $125a^2 - 64b^3$

$= (5a-4b)(25a^2+20ab+16b^2)$

55. $(x-y)^2 - 16 = [(x-y)-4][(x-y)+4]$

$= (x-y-4)(x-y+4)$

57. $8 - (r-t)^3$

$= [2-(r-t)][4+2(r-t)+(r-t)^2]$

$= (2-r+t)[4+2(r-t)+(r-t)^2]$

59. $125 - (a-b)^3$

$= [5-(a-b)][25+5(a-b)+(a-b)^2]$

$= [5-a+b][25+5(a-b)+(a-b)^2]$

61. $(a-b)^2 - (x-y)^2$

$= [(a-b)-(x-y)][(a-b)+(x-y)]$

$= (a-b-x+y)(a-b+x-y)$

63. $8(a+b) + y^3(a+b) = (a+b)(8+y^3)$

$= (a+b)(2+y)(4-2y+y^2)$

65. $3x^4 - 1875 = 3(x^4-625)$

$= 3(x^2-25)(x^2+25)$

$= 3(x+5)(x-5)(x^2+25)$

67. $1 - x^9 = (1-x^3)(1+x^3+x^6)$

$= (1-x)(1+x+x^2)(1+x^3+x^6)$

69. $5(t^3-125s^3)$

$= 5(t-5s)(t^2+5st+25s^2)$

71. $16 + 2(s-t)^3 = 2[8+(s-t)^3]$

$= 2[2+(s-t)][4-2(s-t)+(s-t)^2]$

$= 2(2+s-t)[4-2(s-t)+(s-t)^2]$

73. $64 + s^2$ is prime

75. 16

77. Shaded volume is $\pi x^2 h - \pi y^2 h$

$= \pi h(x^2-y^2)$

$= \pi h(x-y)(x+y)$

79. Shaded area is $\pi y^2 - \pi x^2$

$= \pi(y^2-x^2)$

$= \pi(y-x)(y+x)$

81. $x^{2p} - 1 = (x^p-1)(x^p+1)$

83. $x^{3p} + 1 = (x^p+1)(x^{2p}-x^p+1)$

85. $x^6 - 1 = (x^3-1)(x^3+1)$

$(x-1)(x^2+x+1)(x+1)(x^2-x+1)$

$$x^6 - 1 = (x^2-1)(x^4+x^2+1)$$
$$= 4(y^3-2)(y+1)(y^2-y+1)$$

Problem Set 2.3.

1. $x^2 + 3x + 2 = (x+2)(x+1)$

3. $x^2 - 14x + 49 = (x-7)^2$

5. $r^2 - 2rs - 15s^2 = (r-5s)(r+3s)$

7. $x^2 - x + 2$ is prime.

9. $z^2 - 3z - 10 = (z-5)(z+2)$

11. $y^2 - 7y - 60 = (y-12)(y+5)$

13. $2z^2 + 32 + 1 = (2z+1)(z+1)$

15. $20y^2 + 27yz + 9z^2 = (5y+3z)(4y+3z)$

17. $8x^2 - 22x + 15 = (4x-5)(2x-3)$

19. $2 - 13x + 21x^2 = (2-7x)(1-3x)$

21. $12z^2 + 4z - 1 = (6z-1)(2z+1)$

23. $4a^2 - 4a - 8 = 4(a^2-a-2)$
$$= 4(a-2)(a+1)$$

25. $-6b^2 + 6bc + 12c^2 = -6(b^2-bc-2c^2)$
$$= -6(b-2c)(b+c)$$

27. $z^3 + 2z^2 + z = z(z^2+2z+1)$
$$= z(z+1)^2$$

29. $x^4 + 6x^2 + 5 = (x^2+5)(x^2+1)$

31. $x^6 + 5x^3 - 14 = (x^3+7)(x^3-2)$

33. $6y^4 - y^2 - 2 = (3y^2-2)(2y^2+1)$

35. $x^4 - 2x^2 + 1 = (x^2-1)^2$
$$= (x^2-1)(x^2-1)$$
$$= (x-1)(x+1)(x-1)(x+1)$$
$$= (x-1)^2(x+1)^2$$

37. $x^4 + x^2 - 2 = (x^2+2)(x^2-1)$
$$= (x^2+2)(x-1)(x+1)$$

39. $x^2 + 9x + 8 = (x+8)(x+1)$

41. $x^2 + 4x + 4 = (x+2)^2$

43. $x^2 - 6x + 8 = (x-4)(x-2)$

45. $x^2 - 2x - 1$ is prime

47. $r^2 - 5rs - 14s^2 = (r-7s)(r+2s)$

49. $x^2 - x - 12 = (x-4)(x+3)$

51. $z^2 - 3z - 54 = (z-9)(z+6)$

53. $y^2 - y - 56 = (y-8)(y+7)$

55. $2z^2 + 5z + 3 = (2z+3)(z+1)$

57. $6y^2 + 25yz + 4z^2 = (6y+z)(y+4z)$

59. $6x^2 - 17x + 12 = (3x-4)(2x-3)$

61. $35 - 31x + 6x^2 = (7-2x)(5-3x)$

63. $3z^2 - z - 10 = (3z+5)(z-2)$

65. $3t^2 - 2t - 1 = (3t+1)(t-1)$

67. $14s^2 - 11s - 15 = (7s+5)(2s-3)$

69. $28r^2 + r - 15 = (7r-5)(4r+3)$

71. $5a^2 - 5a - 30 = 5(a^2-a-6)$
$$= 5(a-3)(a+2)$$

73. $-6b^2 - 3bc + 3c^2 = -3(2b^2+bc-c^2)$
$$= -3(2b-c)(b+c)$$

75. $z^4 - 2z^3 - 8z^2 = z^2(z^2-2z-8)$
$$= z^2(z-4)(z+2)$$

77. $x^4 - 7x^3 - 60x^2 = x^2(x^2-7x-60)$
$$= x^2(x-12)(x+5)$$

79. $x^4 + x^3 - 12x^2 = x^2(x^2+x-12)$
$$= x^2(x+4)(x-3)$$

81. $x^6 - 8x^3 + 15 = (x^3-5)(x^3-3)$

83. $4y^6 - 4y^3 - 8 = 4(y^6-y^3-2)$

$$= 4(y^3-2)(y^3+1)$$
$$= 4(y^3-2)(y+1)(y^2-y+1)$$

85. $x^6 - 7x^3 - 8 = (x^3+8)(x^3-1)$

$$= (x+2)(x^2-2x+4)(x-1)(x^2+x+1)$$

87. $x^4 - 2x^2 - 8 = (x^2-4)(x^2+2)$

$$= (x-2)(x+2)(x^2+2)$$

89. $t^2 + kt - 7$ factors as $(t-7)(t+1)$

or $(t+7)(t-1)$. When $t^2 + kt - 7$

$= (t-7)(t+1)$, $k = -6$. When

$t^2 + kt - 7 = (t+7)(t-1)$, $k = 6$.

91. $x^2 + kx - 3$ factors as $(x-3)(x+1)$

or $(x+3)(x-1)$. When

$x^2 + kx - 3 = (x-3)(x+1)$,

$k = -2$. When $x^2 + kx - s$

$= (x+3)(x-1)$, $k = 2$.

93. $x^{2n} + 2x^n - 8 = (x^n+4)(x^n-2)$

95. $x^{2n} + 2x^n y^m + y^{2m} = (x^n+y^m)^2$

Problem Set 2.4.

1. $16x^2 - 16 = 16(x^2-1)$

$$= 16(x-1)(x+1)$$

3. $x^2 - x = x(x-1)$

5. $x(x^2y-1)$ is factored.

7. $225a^5b^2c - 90a^2b^2c$

$$= 45a^2b^2c(5a^3-2)$$

9. $4x^2 - 1 = (2x-1)(2x+1)$

11. $16 - 25x^2 = (4-5x)(4+5x)$

13. $(z+t)^3 + 1$

$$= [(z+t)+1][(z+t)^2-(z+t)+1]$$

$$= (z+t+1)[(z+t)^2-z-t+1]$$

15. $8w^3 - 27 = (2w-3)(4w^2+6w+9)$

17. $x^{10} - 16 = (x^5-4)(x^5+4)$

19. $a^2b + c$ is prime.

21. $2ab + 2ax - by - xy$

$$= 2a(b+x) - y(b+x)$$

$$= (b+x)(2a-y)$$

23. $16 + 15y^2 - y^4$

$$= (1+y^2)(16-y^2)$$

$$= (1+y^2)(4-y)(4+y)$$

25. $2x^2 - 5x - 7 = (2x-7)(x+1)$

27. $x^6 + x^3 - 2 = (x^3+2)(x^3-1)$

$$= (x^3+2)(x-1)(x^3+x+1)$$

29. $x^6 + x^5 + x^4 + x^3$

$$= x^3(x^3+x^2+x+1)$$

$$= x^3[x^2(x+1)+(x+1)]$$

$$= x^3(x+1)(x^2+1)$$

31. $x^2(x+y)$ is factored.

33. $9r^2 - 23r - 8$ is prime.

35. $2x^2 + x + 1$ is prime.

37. $x^2 + 6x + 9 - z^2$

$$= (x^2+6x+9) - z^2$$

$$= (x+3)^2 - z^2$$

$$= [(x+3)-z][(x+3)+z]$$

$$= (x+3-z)(x+3+z)$$

39. $x^2 + 9x + 14 = (x+7)(x+2)$

41. $135r^3t^5 + 225r^2t^4$

$$= 45r^2t^4(3rt+5)$$

43. $1 - 27a^3b^3 = (1-3ab)(1+3ab+9a^2b^2)$

45. $x^2 - y^2 + x + y = (x^2-y^2) + x + y$

$= (x-y)(x+y) + (x+y)$

$= (x+y)[(x-y)+1]$

$= (x+y)(x-y+1)$

47. $s^3 t(2st+u)$ is factored.

49. $32 - 2x^2 = 2(16-x^2)$

$\qquad = 2(4-x)(4+x)$

51. $r^3(x-t) + (t-x)$

$= r^3(x-t) - (x-t)$

$= (x-t)(r^3-1)$

$= (x-t)(r-1)(r^2+r+1)$

53. $(z+4)^2 - x^2 y^2$

$= [(z+4)-xy][(z+4)+xy]$

$= (z+4-xy)(z+4+xy)$

55. $a^2 b + ab^2 + a + b = ab(a+b) + (a+b)$

$\qquad\qquad\qquad\qquad = (a+b)(ab+1)$

57. $x^4 + 3x^2 + 2 = (x^2+2)(x^2+1)$

59. $8x^9 + y^3 = (2x^3+y)(4x^6-2x^3 y+y^2)$

61. $x^2 + 12x + 36 = (x+6)^2$

63. $3x^2 + x + 1$ is prime.

65. $(t+8)^3 + z^3$

$= [(t+8)+z][(t+8)^2-z(t+8)+z^2]$

$= (t+8+z)[(t+8)^2-z(t+8)+z^2]$

67. $x^4 + x^2 - 20 = (x^2+5)(x^2-4)$

$\qquad\qquad\qquad = (x^2+5)(x-2)(x+2)$

69. $81 - 18x + x^2 = (9-x)^2$

71. $a^9 + 8 = (a^3+2)(a^6-2a^3+4)$

73. $a^7 b^5 c^4 - a^6 b^6 c^6 + a^5 b^6 c^3$

$= a^5 b^5 c^3(a^2 c-abc^3+b)$

75. $16 - x^2 - 2xy - y^2$

$= 16 - (x^2+2xy+y^2)$

$= 16 - (x+y)^2$

$= [4-(x+y)][4+(x+y)]$

$= (4-x-y)(4+x+y)$

77. $x^{4n} - 2x^{2n} + 1 = (x^{2n}-1)^2$

$= [(x^{2n}-1)(x^{2n}-1)]$

$= [(x^n-1)(x^n+1)(x^n-1)(x^n+1)]$

$= (x^n-1)^2(x^n+1)^2$

79. $x^{4n} - x^{2n} = x^{2n}(x^{2n}-1)$

$= x^{2n}(x^n-1)(x^n+1)$

81. a) $x^4 + 3x^2 + 4$

$= x^4 + 3x^2 + 4 + x^2 - x^2$

$= (x^4+4x^2+4) - x^2$

$= (x^2+2)^2 - x^2$

$= [(x^2+2)-x][x^2+2+x]$

$= (x^2-x+2)(x^2+x+2)$

b) $x^4 + 2x^2 + 9$

$= x^4 + 2x^2 + 9 + 4x^2 - 4x^2$

$= (x^4+6x^2+9) - 4x^2$

$= (x^2+3)^2 - 4x^2$

$= [(x^2+3)-2x][(x^2+3)+2x]$

$= (x^2-2x+3)(x^2+2x+3)$

c) $x^4 + 7x^2 + 16$

$= x^4 + 7x^2 + 16 + x^2 - x^2$

$= (x^4+8x^2+16) - x^2$

$= (x^2+4)^2 - x^2$

$= [(x^2+4)-x][(x^2+4)+x]$

$= (x^2-x+4)(x^2+x+4)$

d) $x^4 - 8x^2 + 4$

$$= x^4 - x^2 + 4 - 4x^2$$

$$= (x^2-2)^2 - 4x^2$$

$$= [(x^2-2)-2x][(x^2-2)+2x]$$

$$= (x^2-2x-2)(x^2+2x-2)$$

e) $x^4 - 11x^2 + 25$

$$= x^4 - 10x^2 + 25 - x^2$$

$$= (x^2-5)^2 - x^2$$

$$= [(x^2-5)-x][(x^2-5)+x]$$

$$= (x^2-x-5)(x^2+x-5)$$

Review Problems.

1. $2x^2 - 162 = 2(x^2-81)$

$$= 2(x-9)(x+9)$$

3. $at - 4z^2 - 2az + 2zt$

$$= at + 2zt - 4z^2 - 2az$$

$$= t(a+2z) - 2z(2z+a)$$

$$= (a+2z)(t-2z)$$

5. $(x+4z)^2 - 4$

$$= [(x+4z)+2][(x+4z)-2]$$

$$= (x+4z+2)(x+4z-2)$$

7. $12x^2 - 38x - 14$

$$= 2(6x^2-19x-7)$$

$$= 2(3x+1)(2x-7)$$

9. $12a^2b^2c - 96a^2b^3c + 54abc$

$$= 6abc(2ab-16ab^2+9)$$

11. $x^4 - 15x^2 - 16 = (x^2-16)(x^2+1)$

$$= (x-4)(x+4)(x^2+1)$$

13. $x^6 + 28x^3 + 27 = (x^3+27)(x^3+1)$

$$= (x+3)(x^2-3x+9)(x+1)(x^2-x+1)$$

15. $2a^2b + 4a^2y - 3abz - 6ayz$

$$= a(2ab+4ay-3bz-6yz)$$

$$= a[2a(b+2y)-3z(b+2y)]$$

$$= a(b+2y)(2a-3z)$$

17. $2ax + 4x + 2a + 4$

$$= 2(ax+2x+a+2)$$

$$= 2[x(a+2)+(a+2)]$$

$$= 2(a+2)(x+1)$$

19. $x^2 + 18x + 81 = (x+9)^2$

21. $w^2 - x^2 - 4x - 4$

$$= w^2 - (x^2+4x+4)$$

$$= w^2 - (x+2)^2$$

$$= [w-(x+2)][w+(x+2)]$$

$$= (w-x-2)(w+x+2)$$

23. $x^8 - 81 = (x^4-9)(x^4+9)$

$$= (x^2-3)(x^2+3)(x^4+9)$$

25. $3x^2 + 4x + 5$ is prime.

27. $27a^3 - 1 = (3a-1)(9a^2+3a+1)$

29. $x^2 + 4x + 4 - z^2$

$$= (x^2+4x+4) - z^2$$

$$= (x+2)^2 - z^2$$

$$= [(x+2)-z][(x+2)+z]$$

$$= (x+2-z)(x+2+z)$$

31. $(2x+5)^3$ is factored.

33. $(s+t)^3 - a(s+t)^2$

$$= (s+t)^2[(s+t)-a]$$

$$= (s+t)^2(s+t-a)$$

35. $12ab^2$ is factored.

37. $y^2 - 49 = (y-7)(y+7)$
two terms; $y + 7$ is a factor.

39. $y^2 + 6y - 7 = (y+7)(y-1)$

three terms; $y + 7$ is a factor.

41. $4(y+7) - (7+y) = (y+7)(4-1)$
$$= 3(y+7)$$

two term; $y + 7$ is a factor.

43. $(3x-2)^2 = 9x^2 - 12x + 4$

45. $-5^2 = -25$

47. $(-5)^2 = 25$

49. $(-x)^3 = -x^3$

Chapter Test.

1. $48 = 2^4 \cdot 3$ $80 = 2^4 \, 5$

   GCF of $48x^2y$ and $80xy$ is 2^4xy

   B.

2. $x^3 - 64 = (x-4)(x^2+4x+16)$

   C.

3. $x(a-1) + y(1-a)$
$$= x(a-1) + y[-(a-1)]$$
$$= x(a-1) - y(a-1)$$
$$= (a-1)(x-y)$$

   B.

4. $x^2 - 12x + 36 = (x-6)^2$

   D.

5. $x^4 - 16 = (x^2-4)(x^2+4)$
$$= (x-2)(x+2)(x^2+4)$$

   D.

6. $(x+2)^3$ is factored

   D.

7. $8a^3 - 27 = (2a-3)(4a^2+6a+9)$

8. $4x^2 + 18x - 10 = 2(2x^2+9x-5)$
$$= 2(2x-1)(x+5)$$

9. $ax - bx + 2a - 2b$
$$= x(a-b) + 2(a-b)$$
$$= (a-b)(x+2)$$

10. $x(p-q) - y(p-q)$
$$= x(p-q) - y[-(p-q)]$$
$$= x(p-q) + y(p-q)$$
$$= (p-q)(x+y)$$

11. $a^4 - 2a^2 - 8 = (a^2-4)(a^2+2)$
$$= (a-2)(a+2)(a^2+2)$$

12. $x^2 + 14x + 49 = (x+7)^2$

13. $(x+y)^2 - 9 = [(x+y)-3][(x+y)+3]$
$$= (x+y-3)(x+y+3)$$

14. $4y^2 - 25 = (2y+5)(2y-5)$

15. $27a^2b^3 - 36a^3b^2 + 45a^4b^4$
$$= 9a^2b^2(3b-4a+5a^2b^2)$$

CHAPTER 3

Problem Set 3.1.

1. 3

3. 5

5. None

7. None

9. 2

11. $-3, 1$

13. $0, 2$

15. $\dfrac{x^2 - 2x - 3}{x^2 - 4} = \dfrac{x^2 - 2x - 3}{(x-2)(x+2)}$

    undefined when $x = 2$ or -2

17. $\dfrac{-3}{x} = \dfrac{3}{-x} = -\dfrac{3}{x}$

19. $-\dfrac{7}{x} = \dfrac{-7}{x} = \dfrac{7}{-x}$

21. $\dfrac{2x}{-(x+3)} = \dfrac{-2x}{x+5} = -\dfrac{2x}{x+5}$

23. $\dfrac{x-1}{-x^2} = \dfrac{-(x-1)}{x^2} = -\dfrac{x-1}{x^2}$

25. $-\dfrac{x-7}{x+4} = \dfrac{-(x-7)}{x+4} = \dfrac{x-7}{-(x+4)}$

27. -6

29. 0

31. 0

33. 7

35. -9

37. $5, 2$

39. $\dfrac{x-4}{x^2 - x - 2} = \dfrac{x-4}{(x-2)(x+1)}$

    undefined when $x = 2$ or -1

41. $\dfrac{x}{x^2 - 6x + 9} = \dfrac{x}{(x-3)^2}$

    undefined when $x = 3$

43. $\dfrac{x^2}{-2} = \dfrac{-x^2}{2} = -\dfrac{x^2}{2}$

45. $\dfrac{-(x+1)}{x} = \dfrac{x+1}{-x} = -\dfrac{x+1}{x}$

47. $-\dfrac{x}{x-3} = \dfrac{-x}{x-3} = \dfrac{x}{-(x-3)}$

49. $\dfrac{-x-5}{x+1} = \dfrac{-(x+5)}{x+1}$

    $= \dfrac{x+5}{-(x+1)}$

    $= -\dfrac{x+5}{x+1}$

51. $\dfrac{160x}{x+12}$ hours

53. distance is $2N$

    time $= \dfrac{2N}{8-N}$ hours

55. $\dfrac{x+1}{x^2 + 4x + 3} = \dfrac{x+1}{(x+1)(x+3)}$

    undefined when $x = -1$ or -3

57. $\dfrac{x+2}{x^4 - 16} = \dfrac{x+2}{(x^2-4)(x^2+4)}$

    $= \dfrac{x+2}{(x-2)(x+2)(x^2+4)}$

    undefined when $x = 2$ or -2

Problem Set 3.2.

1. $\dfrac{x^7}{x^2} = \dfrac{x^5 \cdot x^2}{x^2}$

    $= x^5$

3. $\dfrac{28t^2}{21t} = \dfrac{4(7)t \cdot t}{3(7)t}$

    $= \dfrac{4t}{3}$

5. $\dfrac{(-3)^2 a^2}{3a} = \dfrac{9a^2}{3a}$

$$= \frac{3(3)a \cdot a}{3a}$$

$$= 3a$$

$$= \frac{(c+d)(a+b)}{(c-d)(a+b)}$$

$$= \frac{c+d}{c-d}$$

7. $\dfrac{5x^2(x+y)^2}{10x(x+y)^3} = \dfrac{5x \cdot x(x+y)^2}{2 \cdot 5x(x+y)^2(x+y)}$

$$= \frac{x}{2(x+y)}$$

9. $\dfrac{(x+y)^5}{(x+y)^2} = \dfrac{(x+y)^2(x+y)^3}{(x+y)^2}$

$$= (x+y)^3$$

11. $\dfrac{12x^2-12x}{18x1^2} = \dfrac{12x(x-1)}{18x^2}$

$$= \frac{2(6)x(x-1)}{3(6)x \cdot x}$$

$$= \frac{2(x-1)}{3x}$$

13. $\dfrac{x^2-16}{x-4} = \dfrac{(x-4)(x+4)}{(x-4)}$

$$= x + 4$$

15. $\dfrac{x^2-3x-10}{x^2-2x-15} = \dfrac{(x-5)(x+2)}{(x-5)(x+3)}$

$$= \frac{x+2}{x+3}$$

17. $\dfrac{s^2-1}{1+s^3} = \dfrac{(s-1)(s+1)}{(1+s)(1-s+s^2)}$

$$= \frac{s-1}{1-s+s^2}$$

19. $\dfrac{6x^2+x-2}{3x^2-4x-4} = \dfrac{(3x+2)(2x-1)}{(3x+2)(x-2)}$

$$= \frac{2x-1}{x-2}$$

21. $\dfrac{ac+ad+bc+bd}{ac-ad+bc-bd} = \dfrac{a(c+d)+b(c+d)}{a(c-d)}$

23. $\dfrac{s-1}{1-s} = \dfrac{s-1}{-(s-1)}$

$$= -1$$

25. $\dfrac{(2x-1)^2}{(1-2x)(x+2)} = \dfrac{(2x-1)^2}{-(2x-1)(x+2)}$

$$= \frac{2x-1}{-(x+2)} \text{ or } \frac{-(2x-1)}{x+2}$$

$$\text{or } \frac{1-2x}{x+2}$$

27. $\dfrac{x^2-3x+2}{3-2x-x^2} = \dfrac{(x-1)(x-2)}{(3+x)(1-x)}$

$$= \frac{(x-1)(x-2)}{(3+x)[-(1-x)]}$$

$$= \frac{x-2}{-(3+x)} \text{ or } \frac{-(x-2)}{x+3}$$

$$\text{or } \frac{2-x}{x+3}$$

29. $\dfrac{5}{x} \cdot \dfrac{10}{10} = \dfrac{50}{10x}$

31. $\dfrac{r^2}{6} \cdot \dfrac{(m+n)}{(m+n)} = \dfrac{r^2(m+n)}{6m+6n}$

33. $\dfrac{3}{a} \cdot \dfrac{4}{4} = \dfrac{12}{4a}$

35. $\dfrac{-3x}{(x+1)} \cdot \dfrac{(x-1)}{(x-1)} = \dfrac{-3x(x-1)}{x^2-1}$

37. $x - x^2 = x(1-x)$

$$= x[-(x-1)]$$

$$= -x(x-1)$$

$$\frac{x+1}{x-1} \cdot \frac{-x}{-x} = \frac{-x(x+1)}{x-x^2}$$

39. $x^2 - 9 = (x-3)(x+3)$

$$= [-(3-x)](x+3)$$

$$= -(3-x)(x+3)$$

$$\frac{x}{3-x} \cdot \frac{-(x+3)}{-(x+3)} = \frac{-x(x+3)}{x^2-9}$$

41. $\dfrac{x^8}{x^3} = \dfrac{x^3 \cdot x^5}{x^3}$

$$= x^5$$

43. $\dfrac{48t^3}{16t} = \dfrac{3(16)t \cdot t^2}{16t}$

$$= 3t^2$$

45. $\dfrac{-2x^2 y}{-8xy} = \dfrac{-2x \cdot x \cdot y}{4(-2)xy}$

$$= \frac{x}{4}$$

47. $\dfrac{-3^3 xy}{3^2 x^3 y^3} = \dfrac{-3^2 \cdot 3xy}{3^2 \cdot x \cdot x^2 \cdot y \cdot y^2}$

$$= \frac{-3}{x^2 y^2}$$

49. $\dfrac{7^2 5^3 x^2 y}{7^3 5^2 xy^3} = \dfrac{7^2 \cdot 5^2 \cdot 5 \cdot x \cdot xy}{7^2 \cdot 7 \cdot 5^2 \cdot x \cdot y \cdot y^2}$

$$= \frac{5x}{7y^2}$$

51. $\dfrac{-n^5(n-m)}{n^4(n-m)^4} = \dfrac{n^4 \cdot n(n-m)}{n^4(n-m)(n-m)^3}$

$$= \frac{-n}{(n-m)^3}$$

53. $\dfrac{(x+2)(5+x)}{(x-1)(x+5)^2} = \dfrac{(x+2)(5+x)}{(x-1)(x+5)(x+5)}$

$$= \frac{x+2}{(x-1)(x+5)}$$

55. $\dfrac{(a-3)(a+3)}{(3-a)(1+a)} = \dfrac{(a-3)(a+3)}{-(a-3)(1+a)}$

$$= \frac{a+3}{-(1+a)} \text{ or } -\frac{a+3}{1+a}$$

57. $\dfrac{4a^2-8a}{8-4a} = \dfrac{4a(a-2)}{4(2-a)}$

$$= 4a[-(2-a)]$$

$$= \frac{-4a(2-a)}{4(2-a)}$$

$$= -a$$

59. $\dfrac{5x}{25x-15x^2} = \dfrac{5x}{5x(5-3x)}$

$$= \frac{1}{5-3x}$$

61. $\dfrac{3y + 12y^4}{15y^3-25y} = \dfrac{3y(1+4y^3)}{5y(3y^2-5)}$

$$= \frac{3(1+4y^3)}{5(3y^2-5)}$$

63. $\dfrac{ab^2}{ab+b} = \dfrac{ab^2}{b(a+1)}$

$$= \frac{b \cdot b}{b(a+1)}$$

$$= \frac{ab}{a+1}$$

65. $\dfrac{3y^4+15y^2}{3y^3+9y^5} = \dfrac{3y^2(y^2+5)}{3y^3(1+3y^2)}$

$$= \frac{3y^2(y^2+5)}{3y^2 \cdot y(1+3y^2)}$$

$$= \frac{y^2+5}{y(1+3y^2)}$$

67. $\dfrac{4x^3-24x}{x^3-6x} = \dfrac{4x(x^2-6)}{x(x^2-6)}$

$$= 4$$

69. $\dfrac{x^2-25}{x+5} = \dfrac{(x-5)(x+5)}{(x+5)}$

$$= x - 5$$

71. $\dfrac{x^2+8x+16}{x+4} = \dfrac{(x+4)^2}{x+4}$

$$= \frac{(x+4)(x+4)}{x+4}$$

$$= x + 4$$

73. $\dfrac{p^3-8}{p^2-5p+6} = \dfrac{(p-2)(p^2+2p+4)}{(p-2)(p-3)}$

$= \dfrac{p^2+2p+4}{p-3}$

75. $\dfrac{b^2-1}{b^2+b-2} = \dfrac{(b-1)(b+1)}{(b+2)(b-1)}$

$= \dfrac{b+1}{b+2}$

77. $\dfrac{x^2-x-12}{x^2-3x-4} = \dfrac{(x-4)(x+3)}{(x-4)(x+1)}$

$= \dfrac{x+3}{x+1}$

79. $\dfrac{x^2+3x-10}{8-2x-x^2} = \dfrac{(x+5)(x-2)}{(4+x)(2-x)}$

$= \dfrac{(x+5)[-(2-x)]}{(4+x)(2-x)}$

$= \dfrac{-(x+5)}{(4+x)} \quad \text{or} \quad -\dfrac{x+5}{x+4}$

81. $\dfrac{3x^4-3x}{6x^3-6x} = \dfrac{3x(x^3-1)}{6x(x^2-1)}$

$= \dfrac{3x(x-1)(x^2+x+1)}{2(3)x(x-1)(x+1)}$

$= \dfrac{x^2+x+1}{2(x+1)}$

83. $\dfrac{x^4-x^2-2}{x^4+x^2-6} = \dfrac{(x^2-2)(x^2+1)}{(x^2-2)(x^2+3)}$

$= \dfrac{x^2+1}{x^2+3}$

85. $\dfrac{9-4x^2}{2x^2-x-3} = \dfrac{(3-2x)(3+2x)}{(2x-3)(x+1)}$

$= \dfrac{[-(2x-3)](3+2x)}{(2x-3)(x+1)}$

$= \dfrac{-(3+2x)}{x+1} \quad \text{or} \quad -\dfrac{3+2x}{x+1}$

87. $\dfrac{x^4-25}{x^2-5} = \dfrac{(x^2-5)(x^2+5)}{x^2-5}$

$= x^2 + 5$

89. $\dfrac{m^2-n^2}{n^3-m^3} = \dfrac{(m+n)(m-n)}{(n-m)(n^2+nm+m^2)}$

$= \dfrac{(m+n)[-(n-m)]}{(n-m)(n^2+nm+m^2)}$

$= \dfrac{-(m+n)}{n^2+nm+m^2} \quad \text{or} \quad -\dfrac{m+n}{n^2+mn+m^2}$

91. $\dfrac{am+3m-2a-6}{cm-2c+6m-12} = \dfrac{m(a+3)-2(a+3)}{c(m-2)+6(m-2)}$

$= \dfrac{(a+3)(m-2)}{(m-2)(c+6)}$

$= \dfrac{a+3}{c+6}$

93. $\dfrac{ps-pt-qs+qt}{pt+qt-ps-qs} = \dfrac{p(s-t)-q(s-t)}{t(p+q)-s(p+q)}$

$= \dfrac{(s-t)(p-q)}{(p+q)(t-s)}$

$= \dfrac{[-(t-s)](p-q)}{(p+q)(t-s)}$

$= \dfrac{-(p-q)}{p+q} \quad \text{or} \quad \dfrac{p-q}{p+q}$

95. $\dfrac{x^3-xy+x^2y-y^2}{x^3-x^2y-xy+y^2} = \dfrac{x(x^2-y)+y(x^2-y)}{x^2(x-y)-y(x-y)}$

$= \dfrac{(x^2-y)(x+y)}{(x-y)(x^2-y)}$

$= \dfrac{x+y}{x-y}$

97. $\dfrac{5}{x} \cdot \dfrac{12x}{12x} = \dfrac{60x}{12x^2}$

99. $\dfrac{r^2}{3} \cdot \dfrac{2(x+y)}{2(x+y)} = \dfrac{2r^2(x+y)}{6(x+y)}$

$= \dfrac{2r^2(x+y)}{6x+6y}$

101. $\dfrac{3}{a} \cdot \dfrac{4a}{4a} = \dfrac{12a}{4a^2}$

103. $\dfrac{-10a}{3xy} \cdot \dfrac{10xy^2}{10xy} = \dfrac{-100axy^2}{30x^2y^3}$

105. $\dfrac{a^2}{a+b} \cdot \dfrac{4}{4} = \dfrac{4a^2}{4(a+b)}$

$\qquad\qquad = \dfrac{4a^2}{4a+4b}$

107. $\dfrac{p}{p-4} \cdot \dfrac{2}{2} = \dfrac{2p}{2(p-4)}$

$\qquad\qquad = \dfrac{2p}{2p-8}$

109. $\dfrac{-3x}{x-1} \cdot \dfrac{(x+1)}{(x+1)} = \dfrac{-3x(x+1)}{(x-1)(x+1)}$

$\qquad\qquad\qquad = \dfrac{-3x(x+1)}{x^2-1}$

111. $\dfrac{2z}{z+3} \cdot \dfrac{z+3}{z+3} = \dfrac{2z(z+3)}{(z+3)^2}$

$\qquad\qquad\qquad = \dfrac{2z(z+3)}{z^2+6z+9}$

113. $\dfrac{x-2}{x} \cdot \dfrac{x-3}{x-3} = \dfrac{(x-2)(x-3)}{x(x-3)}$

$\qquad\qquad\qquad = \dfrac{(x-2)(x-3)}{x^2-3x}$

115. $x^2-4 = (x+2)(x-2) = (x+2)[-(2-x)]$

$\qquad \dfrac{x}{2-x} \cdot \dfrac{-(x+2)}{-(x+2)} = \dfrac{-x(x+2)}{x^2-4}$

117. $\dfrac{2x}{x+y} \cdot \dfrac{(x^2-xy+y^2)}{(x^2-xy+y^2)} = \dfrac{2x(x^2-xy+y^2)}{x^3+y^3}$

119. $\dfrac{2x}{x-y} \cdot \dfrac{(x^2+xy+y^2)}{(x^2+xy+y^2)} = \dfrac{2x(x^2+xy+y^2)}{x^3-y^3}$

121. $\dfrac{w^2+3w+9}{w+3} \cdot \dfrac{(w-3)}{(w-3)} = \dfrac{w^3-27}{w^2-9}$

123. $\dfrac{x^3}{1} \cdot \dfrac{2z}{2z} = \dfrac{2x^3z}{2z}$

125. $\dfrac{(x+2)^{n+1}}{(x+2)^n} = \dfrac{(x+2)^n(x+2)}{(x+2)^n}$

$\qquad\qquad = x + 2$

Problem Set 3.3.

1. $\dfrac{xy^2}{z} \cdot \dfrac{z^2}{x^4y} = \dfrac{xy^2z^2}{x^4yz}$

$\qquad\qquad = \dfrac{yz}{x^3}$

3. $\dfrac{-2^3m}{n} \cdot \dfrac{n}{(-2)^2m^3} = \dfrac{-2mn}{2^2nm^3}$

$\qquad\qquad\qquad = \dfrac{-2}{m^2}$

5. $\dfrac{z}{x^2y} \cdot \left(\dfrac{-xy}{z}\right)^3 = \dfrac{z}{x^2y} \cdot \dfrac{-x^3y^3}{z^3}$

$\qquad\qquad\qquad = \dfrac{-x^3y^3z}{x^2yz^3}$

$\qquad\qquad\qquad = \dfrac{-xy^2}{z^2}$

7. $\dfrac{17a+17b}{3} \cdot \dfrac{-39}{51a+51b}$

$\qquad = \dfrac{17(a+b)}{3} \cdot \dfrac{-39}{51(a+b)}$

$\qquad = \dfrac{-39(17)(a+b)}{3(51)(a+b)}$

9. $\dfrac{-4}{a^4-5a^2+6} \cdot a^4 - 4$

$\qquad = \dfrac{-4}{(a^2-3)(a^2-2)} \cdot (a^2-2)(a^2+2)$

$\qquad = \dfrac{-4(a^2-2)(a^2+2)}{(a^2-3)(a^2-2)} = \dfrac{-4(a^2+2)}{a^3-3}$

11. $\dfrac{2x^2+2x-12}{x^2-x-12} \cdot \dfrac{x^2-3x-4}{4x^2-4x-8}$

$$\frac{2(x+3)(x-2)}{(x-4)(x+3)} \cdot \frac{(x-4)(x+1)}{4(x-2)(x+1)}$$

$$= \frac{2}{4} = \frac{1}{2}$$

13. $\dfrac{6a^2-6b^2}{a^2+2ab+b^2} \cdot \dfrac{a^2-ab-2b^2}{3a^2+3ab-6b^2}$

$$= \frac{6(a^2-b^2)}{(a+b)^2} \cdot \frac{(a-2b)(a+b)}{3(a^2+ab-2b^2)}$$

$$= \frac{6(a+b)(a-b)}{(a+b)^2} \cdot \frac{(a-2b)(a+b)}{3(a+2b)(a-b)}$$

$$= \frac{6(a+b)(a-b)(a-2b)(a+b)}{3(a+b)^2(a+2b)(a-b)}$$

$$= \frac{2(a-2b)}{a+2b}$$

15. $\dfrac{6x^2+7x-3}{10x^2-x-2} \cdot \dfrac{5x^2-3x-2}{4x^2+4x-3} \cdot \dfrac{6x^2-5x+1}{3x^2-4x+1}$

$$= \frac{(3x-1)(2x+3)}{(5x+2)(2x-1)} \cdot \frac{(5x+2)(x-1)}{(2x+3)(2x-1)}$$

$$\cdot \frac{(3x-1)(2x-1)}{(3x-1)(x-1)}$$

$$= \frac{(3x-1)(2x+3)(5x+2)(x-1)(3x-1)(2x-1)}{(5x+2)(2x-1)(2x+3)(2x-1)(3x-1)(x-1)}$$

$$= \frac{3x-1}{2x-1}$$

17. $\dfrac{s-t}{t^2} \cdot \dfrac{t}{t-s} = \dfrac{-(t-s)}{t^2} \cdot \dfrac{t}{t-s}$

$$= \frac{-t(t-s)}{t^2(t-s)}$$

$$= -\frac{1}{t}$$

19. $\dfrac{16-x^2}{x^2+3x+2} \cdot \dfrac{x^2+x-2}{x^2-5x+4}$

$$= \frac{(4-x)(4+x)}{(x+1)(x+2)} \cdot \frac{(x+2)(x-1)}{(x-1)(x-4)}$$

$$= \frac{-(x-4)(4+x)(x+2)(x-1)}{(x+1)(x+2)(x-1)(x-4)}$$

$$= \frac{-(4+x)}{x+1} \text{ or } -\frac{4+x}{x+1}$$

21. $\dfrac{(2x)^2 y}{15} \div \dfrac{(2x)^3}{75} = \dfrac{(2x)^2 y}{15} \cdot \dfrac{75}{(2x)^3}$

$$= \frac{75(2x)^2 y}{15(2x)^3}$$

$$= \frac{5y}{2x}$$

23. $\dfrac{(-2a)^3}{x^5} \div \dfrac{(-2a)^2}{x^2} = \dfrac{(-2a)^3}{x^5} \cdot \dfrac{x^2}{(-2a)^2}$

$$= \frac{(-2a)^3 x^2}{(-2a)^2 x^5}$$

$$= \frac{-2a}{x^3}$$

25. $\dfrac{(-3)^2 r}{(2st)^2} \div \dfrac{3r^2}{8t} = \dfrac{9r}{4s^2 t^2} \cdot \dfrac{8t}{3r^2}$

$$= \frac{9(8)rt}{3(4)r^2 s^2 t^2}$$

$$= \frac{6}{rs^2 t}$$

27. $\dfrac{50-2x^2}{x^2+2x} \div \dfrac{4x+20}{4-x^2} = \dfrac{2(25-x^2)}{x(x+2)} \cdot \dfrac{4-x^2}{4(x+5)}$

$$= \frac{2(5-x)(5+x)(2-x)(2+x)}{4x(x+2)(x+5)}$$

$$= \frac{(5-x)(2-x)}{2x}$$

29. $\dfrac{2x^2+5x-3}{2x^2+5x+3} \div \dfrac{2x^3-x^2}{2x^2+x-3}$

$= \dfrac{(2x-1)(x+3)}{(2x+3)(x+1)} \cdot \dfrac{2x^2+x-3}{2x^3-x^2}$

$= \dfrac{(2x-1)(x+3)}{(2x+3)(x+1)} \cdot \dfrac{(2x+3)(x-1)}{x^2(2x-1)}$

$= \dfrac{(2x-1)(x+3)(2x+3)(x-1)}{x^2(2x+3)(x+1)(2x-1)}$

$= \dfrac{(x+3)(x-1)}{x^2(x+1)}$

31. $\dfrac{2x^2-8x-42}{x^2+2x+1} \div \dfrac{4x^2+8x-12}{x+x^2}$

$= \dfrac{2(x^2-4x-21)}{(x+1)^2} \cdot \dfrac{x+x^2}{4(x^2+2x-3)}$

$= \dfrac{2(x-7)(x+3)}{(x+1)^2} \cdot \dfrac{x(x+1)}{4(x+3)(x-1)}$

$= \dfrac{2x(x-7)(x+3)(x+1)}{4(x+1)^2(x+3)(x-1)}$

$= \dfrac{x(x-7)}{2(x+1)(x-1)}$

33. $\dfrac{p^2-q^2}{r^2-2rs+s^2} \div \dfrac{pr+ps+rq+qs}{pr-ps-rq+qs}$

$= \dfrac{(p+q)(p-q)}{(r-s)^2} \cdot \dfrac{p(r-s)-q(r-s)}{p(r+s)+q(r+s)}$

$= \dfrac{(p+q)(p-q)}{(r-s)^2} \cdot \dfrac{(r-s)(p-q)}{(r+s)(p+q)}$

$= \dfrac{(p+q)(p-q)^2(r-s)}{(r-s)^2(r+s)(p+q)}$

$= \dfrac{(p-q)^2}{(r-s)(r+s)}$

35. $(x-y) \div \dfrac{y-x}{y} = x - y \cdot \dfrac{y}{y-x}$

$= -(y-x) \cdot \dfrac{y}{y-x}$

$= \dfrac{-y(y-x)}{(y-x)}$

$= -y$

37. $\dfrac{x^3+3x^2+4x+12}{x^2+x-2} \div \dfrac{x^4-16}{1-x^2}$

$= \dfrac{x^2(x+3)+4(x+3)}{(x+2)(x-1)} \cdot \dfrac{(1-x)(1+x)}{(x^2-4)(x^2+4)}$

$= \dfrac{(x+3)(x^2+4)(1-X)(1+x)}{(x+2)(x-1)(x+2)(x-2)(x^2+4)}$

$= \dfrac{(x+3)(x^2+4)[-(x-1)](1+x)}{(x+2)^2(x-1)(x-2)(x^2+4)}$

$= \dfrac{-(x+3)(1+x)}{(x+2)^2(x-2)}$ or $- \dfrac{(x+3)(x+1)}{(x+2)^2(x-2)}$

39. $\dfrac{xy^3}{z} \cdot \dfrac{z^4}{x^2y} = \dfrac{xy^3z^4}{x^2yz}$

$= \dfrac{y^2z^3}{x}$

41. $\dfrac{-3^3m}{n} \cdot \dfrac{n}{(-3)^2m^4} = \dfrac{-3^3mn}{3^2m^4n}$

$= \dfrac{-3}{m^3}$

43. $\dfrac{z}{x^4y} \cdot \left[\dfrac{-xy}{z^2}\right]^3 = \dfrac{-zx^3y^3}{x^4yz^6}$

$= \dfrac{-y^2}{xz^5}$

45. $\dfrac{(ab^4)^3}{c(dx)^2} \cdot \dfrac{(c^3d)^2}{(-a)^3b^3}$

44

$$= \frac{a^3b^{12}}{cd^2x^2} \cdot \frac{c^6d^2}{-a^3b^3}$$

$$= \frac{a^3b^{12}c^6d^2}{-a^3b^3cd^2x^2}$$

$$= -\frac{b^9c^5}{x^2}$$

47. $\dfrac{(abc)^3}{xy} \cdot \dfrac{(xy)^2}{(abc)^2} = \dfrac{(abc)^3(xy)^2}{(abc)^2(xy)}$

$$= (abc)(xy)$$

$$= abcxy$$

49. $\dfrac{a-b}{t^3} \cdot \dfrac{t}{b-a} = \dfrac{-(b-a)}{t^3} \cdot \dfrac{t}{(b-a)}$

$$= \frac{-t(b-a)}{t^3(b-a)}$$

$$= \frac{-1}{t^2}$$

51. $\dfrac{pq+pq^2}{p-p^2} \cdot \dfrac{q-qp}{p^2q^2+p^2q}$

$$= \frac{pq(1+q)}{p(1-p)} \cdot \frac{q(1-p)}{p^2q(q+1)}$$

$$= \frac{pq^2(1+q)(1-p)}{p^3q(1-p)(q+1)}$$

$$= \frac{q}{p^2}$$

53. $\dfrac{r^4s^5-r^3s^3}{t^2u^2+t^4u^4} \cdot \dfrac{t^3u^2}{r^2s^5}$

$$= \frac{r^3s^3(rs^2-1)}{t^2u^2(1+t^2u^2)} \cdot \frac{t^3u^2}{r^2s^5}$$

$$= \frac{r^3s^3t^3u^2(rs^2-1)}{r^2s^5t^2u^2(1+t^2u^2)}$$

$$= \frac{rt(rs^2-1)}{s^2(1+t^2u^2)}$$

55. $\dfrac{s+t}{s-t} \cdot \dfrac{t^2-s^2}{t+s} = \dfrac{s+t}{s-t} \cdot \dfrac{(t-s)(t+s)}{t+s}$

$$= \frac{(s+t)[-(s-t)](t+s)}{(s-t)(t+s)}$$

$$= -(s+t)$$

57. $(x^3-125) \cdot \dfrac{x^3}{5-x}$

$$= (x-5)(x^2+5x+25) \cdot \frac{x^3}{-(x-5)}$$

$$= \frac{-x^3(x-5)(x^2+5x+25)}{(x-5)}$$

$$= -x^3(x^2+5x+25)$$

59. $\dfrac{r^3+s^3}{r^2-s^2} \cdot \dfrac{r+s}{r^2-rs+s^2}$

$$= \frac{(r+s)(r^2-rs+s^2)}{(r+s)(r-s)} \cdot \frac{(r+s)}{r^2-rs+s^2}$$

$$= \frac{(r+s)^2(r^2-rs+s^2)}{(r+s)(r-s)(r^2-rs+s^2)}$$

$$= \frac{r+s}{r-s}$$

61. $\dfrac{3m^2-3n^2}{m^2+2mn+n^2} \cdot \dfrac{m^2+3mn+2n^2}{6m^2-6mn-12n^2}$

$$= \frac{3(m^2-n^2)}{(m+n)^2} \cdot \frac{(m+n)(m+2n)}{6(m^2-mn-2n^2)}$$

$$= \frac{3(m-n)(m+n)^2(m+2n)}{6(m+n)^2(m-2n)(m+n)}$$

$$= \frac{(m-n)(m+2n)}{2(m-2n)(m+n)}$$

63. $\dfrac{as+st+a+t}{ax^2-bx^2+2a-2b} \cdot \dfrac{bx^2-ax^2+2b-2a}{as-2a+st-2t}$

$= \dfrac{s(a+t)+(a+t)}{x^2(a-b)+2(a-b)} \cdot \dfrac{x^2(b-a)+2(b-a)}{s(a+t)-2(a+t)}$

$= \dfrac{(a+t)(s+1)}{(a-b)(x^2+2)} \cdot \dfrac{(b-a)(x^2+2)}{(a+t)(s-2)}$

$= \dfrac{(a+t)(s+1)[-(a-b)](x^2+2)}{(a-b)(x^2+2)(a+t)(s-2)}$

$= \dfrac{-(s+1)}{(s-2)} \quad \text{or} \quad -\dfrac{s+1}{s-2}$

65. $\dfrac{abc^3}{xyz^4} \div \dfrac{ab^2c}{xy} = \dfrac{abc^3}{xyz^4} \cdot \dfrac{xy^3}{ab^2c}$

$\qquad = \dfrac{abc^3xy}{ab^2cxyz^4}$

$\qquad = \dfrac{c^2y^2}{bz^4}$

67. $\dfrac{m^5(n^3p)^2}{rst^3} \div \dfrac{(mnp)^3}{r^3s^2t^2}$

$\qquad = \dfrac{m^5r^6p^2}{rst^3} \cdot \dfrac{r^3s^2t^2}{m^3n^3p^3}$

$\qquad = \dfrac{m^5n^6p^2r^3s^2t^2}{m^3n^3p^3rst^3}$

$\qquad = \dfrac{m^2n^3r^2s}{pt}$

69. $\dfrac{-5^2x}{ab} \div \dfrac{5^3x^2y}{a^3} = \dfrac{-5^2x}{ab} \cdot \dfrac{a^3}{5^3x^2y}$

$\qquad = \dfrac{-5^2xa^3}{5^3x^2aby}$

$\qquad = \dfrac{a^2}{5xby}$

71. $\dfrac{(-ab)^3}{r^3s} \div \dfrac{a^5b}{(rs^3)^4}$

$\qquad = \dfrac{-a^3b^3}{r^3s} \cdot \dfrac{r^4s^{12}}{a^5b}$

$\qquad = \dfrac{-a^3b^3r^4s^{12}}{a^5br^3s}$

$\qquad = -\dfrac{b^2rs^{11}}{a^2}$

73. $\dfrac{p}{p-q} \div \dfrac{q}{q-p} = \dfrac{p}{p-q} \cdot \dfrac{q-p}{q}$

$\qquad = \dfrac{p[-(p-q)]}{(p-q)(q)}$

$\qquad = \dfrac{-p}{q}$

75. $\dfrac{ax-bx}{ay+by} \div \dfrac{a^2-ab}{2a+2b} = \dfrac{x(a-b)}{y(a+b)} \cdot \dfrac{2(a+b)}{a(a-b)}$

$\qquad = \dfrac{2x(a-b)(a+b)}{ay(a+b)(a-b)}$

$\qquad = \dfrac{2x}{ay}$

77. $\dfrac{p^2+p^t}{p-p^2} \div \dfrac{pq+qt}{pq-q} = \dfrac{p(p+t)}{p(1-p)} \cdot \dfrac{q(p-1)}{q(p+t)}$

$\qquad = \dfrac{pq(p+t)(p-1)}{pq[-(p-1)](p+t)}$

$\qquad = -1$

79. $\dfrac{16x^2-1}{x^2+8x+16} \div \dfrac{64x^3-1}{x+4}$

$= \dfrac{(4x-1)(4x+1)}{(x+4)^2} \cdot \dfrac{x+4}{(4x-1)(16x^2+4x+1)}$

$= \dfrac{(4x-1)(4x+1)(x+4)}{(x+4)^2(4x-1)(16x^2+4x+1)}$

$$= \frac{4x+1}{(x+4)(16x^2+4x+1)}$$

81. $\dfrac{x^2-4x-12}{x^2-4x-5} \div \dfrac{x^2-3x-18}{x^2-7x+10}$

$$= \frac{(x-6)(x+2)}{(x-5)(x+1)} \cdot \frac{(x-2)(x-5)}{(x-6)(x+3)}$$

$$= \frac{(x-6)(x+2)(x-2)(x-5)}{(x-5)(x+1)(x-6)(x+3)}$$

$$= \frac{(x+2)(x-2)}{(x+1)(x+3)}$$

83. $\dfrac{x^2-3x-10}{2x^2+5x+3} \div \dfrac{5+4x-x^2}{2x^2+7x+6}$

$$= \frac{(x-5)(x+2)}{(2x+3)(x+1)} \cdot \frac{(2x+3)(x+2)}{(5-x)(1+x)}$$

$$= \frac{[-(5-x)](x+2)(2x+3)(x+2)}{(2x+3)(x+1)(5-x)(1+x)}$$

$$= -\frac{(x+2)^2}{(x+1)^2}$$

85. $\dfrac{x^2+10x+21}{x^2-4x+3} \div \dfrac{x^3+7x^2}{x^2-2x+1}$

$$= \frac{(x+3)(x+7)}{(x-1)(x-3)} \cdot \frac{(x-1)^2}{x^2(x+7)}$$

$$= \frac{(x+3)(x+7)(x-1)^2}{x^2(x-1)(x-3)(x+7)}$$

$$= \frac{(x+3)(x-1)}{x^2(x-3)}$$

87. $\dfrac{b^3-2b^2+3b-6}{b^2-b-6} \div \dfrac{b^4-9}{b^2-9}$

$$= \frac{b^2(b-2)+3(b-2)}{(b-3)(b+2)} \cdot \frac{(b-3)(b+3)}{(b^2-3)(b^2+3)}$$

$$= \frac{(b-2)(b^2+3)(b-3)(b+3)}{(b-3)(b+2)(b^2-3)(b^2+3)}$$

$$= \frac{(b-2)(b+3)}{(b+2)(b^2-3)}$$

89. $\dfrac{ac+bc+2ad+2bd}{a^2-d^2} \div \dfrac{ac-bc+2ad-2bd}{a^2+2ab-ad-2bd}$

$$= \frac{c(a+b)+2d(a+b)}{(a-d)(a+d)}$$

$$\cdot \frac{a(a+2b)-d(a+2b)}{c(a-b)+2d(a-b)}$$

$$= \frac{(a+b)(c+2d)(a+2b)(a-d)}{(a-d)(a+d)(a-b)(c+2d)}$$

$$= \frac{(a+b)(a+2b)}{(a+d)(a-b)}$$

91. $\dfrac{2x^2+5x-3}{3x^2+2x-5} \cdot \dfrac{3x^2-x-10}{x^2+2x-3} \cdot \dfrac{x^2-2x+1}{2x^2+x-1}$

$$= \frac{(2x-1)(x+3)}{(3x+5)(x-1)} \cdot \frac{(3x+5)(x-2)}{(x+3)(x-1)}$$

$$\cdot \frac{(x-1)^2}{(2x-1)(x+1)}$$

$$= \frac{(2x-1)(x+3)(3x+5)(x-2)(x-1)^2}{(3x+5)(x-1)(x+3)(x-1)(2x-1)(x+1)}$$

$$= \frac{x-2}{x+1}$$

93. $\dfrac{p^2+pt-2t^2}{2p^2-5pt-3t^2} \cdot \dfrac{p^2-2pt-3t^2}{p^2-3pt+2t^2}$

$$\cdot \frac{4p^2+4pt+t^2}{2p^2+3pt-2t^2}$$

$$= \frac{(p+2t)(p-t)}{(2p+t)(p-3t)} \cdot \frac{(p-3t)(p+t)}{(p-t)(p-2t)}$$

$$\cdot \frac{(2p+t)^2}{(2p-t)(p+2t)}$$

$$= \frac{(p+2t)(p-t)(p-3t)(p+t)(2p+t)^2}{(2p+t)(p-3t)(p-t)(p-2t)(2p-5)(p+2t)}$$

$$= \frac{(p+t)(2p+t)}{(p-2t)(2p-t)}$$

95. $\dfrac{ac+bc-ad-bd}{2ac+4ad+bc+2bd} \cdot \dfrac{c^4+2c^3d}{ac-bc-ad+bd}$

$$\div \frac{ac+ad+bc+bd}{2a^2-ab-b^2}$$

$$= \frac{c(a+b)-d(a+b)}{2a(c+2d)+b(c+2d)} \cdot \frac{c^3(c+2d)}{c(a-b)-d(a-b)}$$

$$\cdot \frac{(2a+b)(a-b)}{a(c+d)+b(c+d)}$$

$$= \frac{(a+b)(c-d)c^3(c+2d)(2a+b)(a-b)}{(c+2d)(2a+b)(a-b)(c-d)(c+d)(a+b)}$$

$$= \frac{c^3}{c+d}$$

97. $\dfrac{x^{2n}-x^n-6}{x^{2p}+2x^p-3} \cdot \dfrac{x^{2p}-1}{x^{2n}+4x^n+4}$

$$= \frac{(x^n+2)(x^n-3)}{(x^p+3)(x^p-1)} \cdot \frac{(x^p-1)(x^p+1)}{(x^n+2)^2}$$

$$= \frac{(x^n+2)(x^n-3)(x^p-1)(x^p+1)}{(x^p+3)(x^p-1)(x^n+2)^2}$$

$$= \frac{(x^n-3)(x^p+1)}{(x^p+3)(x^n+2)}$$

Problem Set 3.4.

1. $\dfrac{7}{x^2} - \dfrac{x+2}{x^2} = \dfrac{7-(x+2)}{x^2}$

$$= \frac{7-x-2}{x^2}$$

$$= \frac{5-x}{x^2}$$

3. $\dfrac{x+y}{xy} + \dfrac{x-y}{xy} = \dfrac{x+y+x-y}{xy}$

$$= \frac{2x}{xy}$$

$$= \frac{2}{y}$$

5. $\dfrac{x}{x+y} + \dfrac{x+y}{x+y} = \dfrac{x+(x+y)}{x+y}$

$$= \frac{2x+y}{x+y}$$

7. $\dfrac{3}{m-2} - \dfrac{2-m}{m-2} = \dfrac{3-(2-m)}{m-2}$

$$= \frac{3-2+m}{m-2}$$

$$= \frac{1+m}{m-2}$$

9. $\dfrac{3y}{x-5} - \dfrac{2y}{5-x} = \dfrac{3y}{x-5} - \dfrac{2y}{-(x-5)}$

$$= \frac{3y}{x-5} + \frac{2y}{x-5}$$

$$= \frac{3y+2y}{x-5}$$

$$= \frac{5y}{x-5}$$

11. $\dfrac{p}{pq^2} + \dfrac{q}{p^2q} = \dfrac{p(q)}{pq^2(q)} + \dfrac{q(p)}{p^2q(q)}$

$$= \frac{p^2}{p^2q^2} + \frac{q^2}{p^2q^2}$$

$$= \frac{p^2+q^2}{p^2q^2}$$

13. $\dfrac{1}{r+2} + \dfrac{2}{r-3} = \dfrac{1(r-3)}{(r+2)(r-3)}$

$$+ \frac{2(r+2)}{(r-3)(r+3)}$$

$$= \frac{r-3+2(r+2)}{(r+2)(r-3)}$$

$$= \frac{r-3+2r+4}{(r+2)(r-3)}$$

$$= \frac{3r+1}{(r+2)(r-3)}$$

15. $\dfrac{2}{5a+10} + \dfrac{7}{3a+6} = \dfrac{2}{5(a+2)} + \dfrac{7}{3(a+2)}$

$$= \frac{2(3)}{5(a+2)(3)} + \frac{7(5)}{3(a+2)(5)}$$

$$= \frac{6}{15(a+2)} + \frac{35}{15(a+2)}$$

$$= \frac{6+35}{15(a+2)}$$

$$= \frac{41}{15(a+2)}$$

17. $\dfrac{x}{x^2-4x+4} + \dfrac{2}{x^2-4}$

$$= \frac{x}{(x-2)^2} + \frac{2}{(x-2)(x+2)}$$

$$= \frac{x(x+2)}{(x-2)^2(x+2)} \quad \frac{2(x-2)}{(x-2)(x+2)(x-2)}$$

$$= \frac{x(x+2)+2(x-2)}{(x-2)^2(x+2)}$$

$$= \frac{x^2+2x+2x-4}{(x-2)^2(x+2)}$$

$$= \frac{x^2+4x-4}{(x-2)^2(x+2)}$$

19. $\dfrac{x+5}{x^2-2x-15} - \dfrac{x}{x^2-6x+5}$

$$= \frac{x+5}{(x-5)(x+3)} - \frac{x}{(x-1)(x-5)}$$

$$= \frac{(x+5)(x-1)}{(x-5)(x+3)(x-1)}$$

$$- \frac{x(x+3)}{(x-1)(x-5)(x+3)}$$

$$= \frac{(x+5)(x-1)-x(x+3)}{(x-5)(x+3)(x-1)}$$

$$= \frac{x^2+4x-5-(x^2+3x)}{(x-5)(x+3)(x-1)}$$

$$= \frac{x^2+4x-5-x^2-3x}{(x-5)(x+3)(x-1)}$$

$$= \frac{(x-5)}{(x-5)(x+3)(x-1)}$$

$$= \frac{1}{(x+3)(x-1)}$$

21. $\dfrac{3y+6}{8-y^3} + \dfrac{4}{4-y^2}$

$$= \frac{3y+6}{(2-y)(4+2y+y^2)} + \frac{4}{(2-y)(2+y)}$$

$$= \frac{(3y+6)(2+y)}{(2-y)(4+2y+y^2)(2+y)}$$

$$+ \frac{4(4+2y+y^2)}{(2-y)(2+y)(4+2y+y^2)}$$

$$= \frac{3y^2+12y+12}{(2-y)(4+2y+y^2)(2+y)}$$

$$+ \frac{16+8y+4y^2}{(2-y)(2+y)(4+2y+y^2)}$$

$$= \frac{7y^2+20y+28}{(2-y)(4+2y+y^2)(2+y)}$$

23. $x + \dfrac{2}{x} = \dfrac{x(x)}{x} + \dfrac{2}{x}$

$$= \frac{x^2}{x} + \frac{2}{x}$$

$$= \frac{x^2+2}{x}$$

49

25. $a + \dfrac{3}{a+b} = \dfrac{a(a+b)}{(a+b)} + \dfrac{3}{a+b}$

$\qquad = \dfrac{a^2+ab+3}{a+b}$

27. $\dfrac{1}{a} - \dfrac{1}{a+1} + \dfrac{1}{a^2+a} = \dfrac{1}{a} - \dfrac{1}{a+1} + \dfrac{1}{a(a+1)}$

$\qquad = \dfrac{a+1}{a(a+1)} - \dfrac{a}{(a+1)a} + \dfrac{1}{a(a+1)}$

$\qquad = \dfrac{a+1-a+1}{a(a+1)}$

$\qquad = \dfrac{2}{a(a+1)}$

29. $\dfrac{p}{p+2} + \dfrac{p+1}{p+3} + \dfrac{2}{p^2+5p+6}$

$\qquad = \dfrac{p}{p+2} + \dfrac{p+1}{p+3} + \dfrac{2}{(p+2)(p+3)}$

$\qquad = \dfrac{p(p+3)}{(p+2)(p+3)} + \dfrac{(p+1)(p+2)}{(p+3)(p+2)}$

$\qquad\qquad + \dfrac{2}{(p+2)(p+3)}$

$\qquad = \dfrac{p^2+3p+p^2+3p+2+2}{(p+2)(p+3)}$

$\qquad = \dfrac{2p^2+6p+4}{(p+2)(p+3)}$

$\qquad = \dfrac{2(p^2+3p+2)}{(p+2)(p+3)}$

$\qquad = \dfrac{2(p+2)(p+1)}{(p+2)(p+3)}$

$\qquad = \dfrac{2(p+1)}{p+3}$

31. $\dfrac{3}{p^2-p} + \dfrac{7}{1-p} = \dfrac{3}{p(p-1)} + \dfrac{7}{1-p}$

$\qquad\qquad = \dfrac{3}{p(p-1)} + \dfrac{7}{-(p-1)}$

$\qquad\qquad = \dfrac{3}{p(p-1)} - \dfrac{7p}{p(p-1)}$

$\qquad\qquad = \dfrac{3-7p}{p(p-1)}$

33. $\dfrac{2}{x-2} + \dfrac{3}{x+2} - \dfrac{5}{4-x^2}$

$\qquad = \dfrac{2}{x-2} + \dfrac{3}{x+2} - \dfrac{5}{(2-x)(2+x)}$

$\qquad = \dfrac{2}{x-2} + \dfrac{3}{x+2} - \dfrac{5}{[-(x-2)](x+2)}$

$\qquad = \dfrac{2(x+2)}{(x-2)(x+2)} + \dfrac{3(x-2)}{(x+2)(x-2)}$

$\qquad\qquad + \dfrac{5}{(x-2)(x+2)}$

$\qquad = \dfrac{2x+4}{(x-2)(x+2)} + \dfrac{3x-6}{(x+2)(x-2)}$

$\qquad\qquad + \dfrac{5}{(x-2)(x+2)}$

$\qquad = \dfrac{2x+4+3x-6+5}{(x-2)(x+2)}$

$\qquad = \dfrac{5x+3}{(x-2)(x+2)}$

35. $\dfrac{x+2}{x+1} - \dfrac{x+4}{x+1} = \dfrac{x+2-(x+4)}{x+1}$

$\qquad\qquad = \dfrac{x+2-x-4}{x+1}$

$\qquad\qquad = \dfrac{-2}{x+1}$

37. $\dfrac{2}{r^2t} - \dfrac{1}{rt^4} = \dfrac{2(t^3)}{r^2t(t^3)} - \dfrac{1(r)}{rt^4(r)}$

$\qquad\qquad = \dfrac{2t^3}{r^2t^4} - \dfrac{r}{r^2t^4}$

$\qquad\qquad = \dfrac{2t^3-r}{r^2t^4}$

50

39. $\dfrac{1}{x} + \dfrac{1}{y} - \dfrac{1}{z} = \dfrac{1(y^2)}{x(y^2)} + \dfrac{1(xz)}{y(xz)} - \dfrac{1(xy)}{z(xy)}$

$\qquad\qquad = \dfrac{yz+xz-xy}{xyz}$

41. $\dfrac{r}{r+2} + \dfrac{1}{2} - \dfrac{3}{2r+4} = \dfrac{r}{r+2} + \dfrac{1}{2} - \dfrac{3}{2(r+2)}$

$\qquad\qquad = \dfrac{r(2)}{(r+2)(2)} + \dfrac{1(r+2)}{2(r+2)} \cdot \dfrac{3}{2(r+2)}$

$\qquad\qquad = \dfrac{2r+r+2-3}{2(r+2)}$

$\qquad\qquad = \dfrac{3r-1}{2(r+2)}$

43. $\dfrac{3}{s+1} - \dfrac{1}{s-1}$

$\qquad\qquad = \dfrac{3(s-1)}{(s+1)(s-1)} - \dfrac{1(s+1)}{(s-1)(s+1)}$

$\qquad\qquad = \dfrac{3s-3-(s+1)}{(s+1)(s-1)}$

$\qquad\qquad = \dfrac{3s-3-s-1}{(s+1)(s-1)}$

$\qquad\qquad = \dfrac{2s-4}{(s+1)(s-1)}$

45. $\dfrac{5}{p+5} - \dfrac{7}{p-7}$

$\qquad\qquad = \dfrac{5(p-7)}{(p+5)(p-7)} - \dfrac{7(p+5)}{(p+5)(p-7)}$

$\qquad\qquad = \dfrac{5p-35}{(p+5)(p-7)} - \dfrac{7p+35}{(p+5)(p-7)}$

$\qquad\qquad = \dfrac{5p-35-(7p+35)}{(p+5)(p-7)}$

$\qquad\qquad = \dfrac{5p-35-7p-35}{(p+5)(p-7)}$

$\qquad\qquad = \dfrac{-2p-70}{(p+5)(p-7)}$

47. $\dfrac{v}{v-3} - \dfrac{1}{v+7}$

$\qquad\qquad = \dfrac{v(v+7)}{(v-3)(v+7)} - \dfrac{1(v-3)}{(v+7)(v-3)}$

$\qquad\qquad = \dfrac{v^2+7v-(v-3)}{(v-3)(v+7)}$

$\qquad\qquad = \dfrac{v^2+7v-v+3}{(v-3)(v+7)}$

$\qquad\qquad = \dfrac{v^2+6v+3}{(v-3)(v+7)}$

49. $\dfrac{4}{x-y} - \dfrac{2}{y-x} = \dfrac{4}{x-y} - \dfrac{2}{-(x-y)}$

$\qquad\qquad = \dfrac{4}{x-y} + \dfrac{2}{x-y}$

$\qquad\qquad = \dfrac{6}{x-y}$

51. $\dfrac{x}{x^2-2x} + \dfrac{4}{2x^2-x^3} = \dfrac{x}{x(x-2)} + \dfrac{4}{x^2(2-x)}$

$\qquad\qquad = \dfrac{x}{x(x-2)} + \dfrac{4}{x^2[-(x-2)]}$

$\qquad\qquad = \dfrac{x}{x(x-2)} - \dfrac{4}{x^2(x-2)}$

$\qquad\qquad = \dfrac{x(x)}{x(x-2)(x)} - \dfrac{4}{x^2(x-2)}$

$\qquad\qquad = \dfrac{x^2}{x^2(x-2)} - \dfrac{4}{x^2(x-2)}$

$\qquad\qquad = \dfrac{x^2-4}{x^2(x-2)}$

$\qquad\qquad = \dfrac{(x-2)(x+2)}{x^2(x-2)}$

$\qquad\qquad = \dfrac{x+2}{x^2}$

53. $\dfrac{3r+1}{1-r^2} + \dfrac{2}{r-1} = \dfrac{3r+1}{(1-r)(1+r)} + \dfrac{2}{r-1}$

$$= \frac{3r+1}{(1-r)(1+r)} + \frac{2}{-(1-r)}$$

$$= \frac{3r+1}{(1-r)(1+r)} - \frac{2}{(1-r)}$$

$$= \frac{3r+1}{(1-r)(1+r)} - \frac{2(1+r)}{(1-r)(1+r)}$$

$$= \frac{3r+1-(2+2r)}{(1-r)(1+r)}$$

$$= \frac{3r+1-2-2r}{(1-r)(1+r)}$$

$$= \frac{r-1}{(1-r)(1+r)}$$

$$= \frac{-(1-r)}{(1-r)(1+r)}$$

$$= \frac{-1}{(1+r)}$$

55. $\dfrac{a}{b+a} - \dfrac{2b^2}{a^2-b^2}$

$$= \frac{a}{b+a} - \frac{2b^2}{(a+b)(a-b)}$$

$$= \frac{a(a-b)}{(a+b)(a-b)} - \frac{2b^2}{(a+b)(a-b)}$$

$$= \frac{a(a-b)-2b^2}{(a+b)(a-b)}$$

$$= \frac{a^2-ab-2b^2}{(a+b)(a-b)}$$

$$= \frac{(a-2b)(a+b)}{(a+b)(a-b)}$$

$$= \frac{a-2b}{a-b}$$

57. $\dfrac{2x}{x-5} - \dfrac{14x+20}{x^2-x-20}$

$$= \frac{2x}{x-5} - \frac{14x+20}{(x-5)(x+4)}$$

$$= \frac{2x(x+4)}{(x-5)(x+4)} - \frac{14x+20}{(x-5)(x+4)}$$

$$= \frac{2x^2+8x}{(x-5)(x+4)} - \frac{14x+20}{(x-5)(x+4)}$$

$$= \frac{2x^2+8x-(14x+20)}{(x-5)(x+4)}$$

$$= \frac{2x^2+8x-14x-20}{(x-5)(x+4)}$$

$$= \frac{2x^2-6x-20}{(x-5)(x+4)}$$

$$= \frac{2(x^2-3x-10)}{(x-5)(x+4)}$$

$$= \frac{2(x-5)(x+2)}{(x-5)(x+4)}$$

$$= \frac{2(x+2)}{x+4}$$

59. $\dfrac{y}{y-5} + \dfrac{y^2}{5+4y-y^2}$

$$= \frac{y}{y-5} + \frac{y^2}{(5-y)(1+y)}$$

$$= \frac{y}{y-5} + \frac{y^2}{-(y-5)(y+1)}$$

$$= \frac{y(y+1)}{(y-5)(y+1)} - \frac{y^2}{(y-5)(y+1)}$$

$$= \frac{y^2+y-y^2}{(y-5)(y+1)}$$

$$= \frac{y}{(y-5)(y+1)}$$

61. $\dfrac{2t}{t^2-2t-3} - \dfrac{t}{t^2-8t+15}$

$$= \frac{2t}{(t-3)(t+1)} - \frac{t}{(t-3)(t-5)}$$

$$= \frac{2t(t-5)}{(t-3)(t+1)(t-5)}$$

$$\qquad - \frac{t(t+1)}{(t-3)(t-5)(t+1)}$$

$$= \frac{2t^2-10t-(t^2+t)}{(t-3)(t+1)(t-5)}$$

$$= \frac{2t^2 - 10t - t^2 - t}{(t-3)(t+1)(t-5)}$$

$$= \frac{t^2 - 11t}{(t-3)(t+1)(t-5)}$$

63. $\dfrac{3b-23}{b^2 + 8b - 9} + \dfrac{35}{b^2 + 11b + 18}$

$$= \frac{3b-23}{(b-1)(b+9)} + \frac{35}{(b+9)(b+2)}$$

$$= \frac{(3b-23)(b+2)}{(b-1)(b+9)(b+2)}$$

$$\qquad + \frac{35(b-1)}{(b+9)(b+2)(b-1)}$$

$$= \frac{3b^2 - 17b - 46 + 35b - 35}{(b-1)(b+9)(b+2)}$$

$$= \frac{3b^2 + 18b - 81}{(b-1)(b+9)(b+2)}$$

$$= \frac{3(b^2 + 6b - 27)}{(b-1)(b+9)(b+2)}$$

$$= \frac{3(b+9)(b-3)}{(b-1)(b+9)(b+2)}$$

$$= \frac{3(b-3)}{(b-1)(b+2)} \quad \text{or} \quad \frac{3b-9}{(b-1)(b+2)}$$

65. $\dfrac{14x+63}{x^2 + 9x + 14} + \dfrac{8x}{7 - 6x - x^2}$

$$= \frac{14x+63}{(x+7)(x+2)} + \frac{8x}{(7+x)(1-x)}$$

$$= \frac{14x+63}{(x+7)(x+2)} + \frac{8x}{(x+7)[-(x-1)]}$$

$$= \frac{14x+63}{(x+7)(x+2)} - \frac{8x}{(x+7)(x-1)}$$

$$= \frac{(14x+63)(x-1)}{(x+7)(x+2)(x-1)}$$

$$\qquad - \frac{8x(x+2)}{(x+7)(x-1)(x+2)}$$

$$= \frac{14x^2 + 49x - 63}{(x+7)(x+2)(x-1)}$$

$$\qquad - \frac{8x^2 + 16x}{(x+7)(x-1)(x+2)}$$

$$= \frac{14x^2 + 49x - 63 - (8x^2 + 16x)}{(x+7)(x+2)(x-1)}$$

$$= \frac{14x^2 + 49x - 63 - 8x^2 - 16x}{(x+7)(x+2)(x-1)}$$

$$= \frac{6x^2 + 33x - 63}{(x+7)(x+2)(x-1)}$$

$$= \frac{3(2x^2 + 11x - 21)}{(x+7)(x+2)(x-1)}$$

$$= \frac{3(2x-3)(x+7)}{(x+7)(x+2)(x-1)}$$

$$= \frac{3(2x-3)}{(x+2)(x-1)} \quad \text{or} \quad \frac{6x-9}{(x+2)(x-1)}$$

67. $\dfrac{3t+19}{t^2 + t - 2} + \dfrac{3t-46}{t^2 + 4t - 5}$

$$= \frac{3t+19}{(t+2)(t-1)} + \frac{3t-46}{(t+5)(t-1)}$$

$$= \frac{(3t+19)(t+5)}{(t+2)(t-1)(t+5)}$$

$$\qquad + \frac{(3t-46)(t+2)}{(t+5)(t-1)(t+2)}$$

$$= \frac{3t^2 + 34t + 95 + 3t^2 - 40t - 92}{(t+2)(t-1)(t+5)}$$

$$= \frac{6t^2 - 6t + 3}{(t+2)(t-1)(t+5)} \quad \text{or}$$

$$\frac{3(2t^2 - 2t + 1)}{(t+2)(t-1)(t+5)}$$

69. $\dfrac{5}{p+1} + p = \dfrac{5}{(p+1)} + \dfrac{p(p+1)}{(p+1)}$

$$= \frac{5 + p^2 + p}{p+1}$$

$$= \frac{p^2 + 5p + 5}{p+1}$$

53

71. $r + \dfrac{rt}{r+t} = \dfrac{r(r+t)}{r+t} + \dfrac{rt}{r+t}$

$= \dfrac{r^2+rt+rt}{r+t}$

$= \dfrac{r^2+2rt}{r+t}$

73. $\dfrac{2}{x} - \dfrac{3}{x+2} + \dfrac{4}{x^2+2x}$

$= \dfrac{2}{x} - \dfrac{3}{x+2} + \dfrac{4}{x(x+2)}$

$= \dfrac{2(x+2)}{x(x+2)} - \dfrac{3x}{x(x+2)} + \dfrac{4}{x(x+2)}$

$= \dfrac{2x+4-3x+4}{x(x+2)}$

$= \dfrac{-x+8}{x(x+2)}$

75. $\dfrac{1}{x+4} - \dfrac{1}{x+3} - \dfrac{1}{x+2}$

$= \dfrac{(x+3)(x+2)}{(x+4)(x+3)(x+2)}$

$\qquad - \dfrac{(x+4)(x+2)}{(x+4)(x+3)(x+2)}$

$\qquad - \dfrac{(x+4)(x+3)}{(x+4)(x+3)(x+2)}$

$= \dfrac{x^2+5x+6}{(x+4)(x+3)(x+2)}$

$\qquad - \dfrac{x^2+6x+8}{(x+4)(x+3)(x+2)}$

$\qquad - \dfrac{x^2+7x+12}{(x+4)(x+3)(x+2)}$

$= \dfrac{x^2+5x+6-(x^2+6x+8)-(x^2+7x+12)}{(x+4)(x+3)(x+2)}$

$= \dfrac{x^2+5x+6-x^2-6x-8-x^2-7x-12}{(x+4)(x+3)(x+2)}$

$= \dfrac{-x^2-8x-14}{(x+4)(x+3)(x+2)}$

$\text{or} \quad - \dfrac{x^2+8x+14}{(x+4)(x+3)(x+2)}$

77. $\dfrac{4x}{x^2+2x-3} + \dfrac{1}{1-x} - \dfrac{2}{x+3}$

$= \dfrac{4x}{(x-1)(x+3)} + \dfrac{1}{-(x-1)} - \dfrac{2}{x+3}$

$= \dfrac{4x}{(x-1)(x+3)} - \dfrac{x+3}{(x-1)(x+3)}$

$\qquad - \dfrac{2(x-1)}{(x-1)(x+3)}$

$= \dfrac{4x-x-3-2x+2}{(x-1)(x+3)}$

$= \dfrac{x-1}{(x-1)(x+3)}$

$= \dfrac{1}{x+3}$

79. $\dfrac{n^3}{m^3+m^2n} + \dfrac{n}{m} - 1$

$= \dfrac{n^3}{m^2(m+n)} + \dfrac{n}{m} - 1$

$= \dfrac{n^3}{m^2(m+n)} + \dfrac{n[m(m+n)]}{m[m(m+n)]}$

$\qquad - \dfrac{m^2(m+n)}{m^2(m+n)}$

$= \dfrac{n^2+mn(m+n)-m^2(m+n)}{m^2(m+n)}$

$= \dfrac{n^2+m^2n+mn^2-m^3-m^2n}{m^2(m+n)}$

$= \dfrac{n^3+mn^2-m^3}{m^2(m+n)}$

81. $\dfrac{3(r+1)}{r^2-9} - \dfrac{40}{r^2-4r-21} + \dfrac{16}{r^2-10r+21}$

$= \dfrac{3(r+1)}{(r+3)(r-3)} - \dfrac{40}{(r-7)(r+3)}$

$\qquad\qquad + \dfrac{16}{(r-3)(r-7)}$

$= \dfrac{3(r+1)(r-7)}{(r+3)(r-3)(r-7)}$

$\qquad - \dfrac{40(r-3)}{(r+3)(r-3)(r-7)}$

$\qquad + \dfrac{16(r+3)}{(r+3)(r-3)(r-7)}$

$= \dfrac{3(r^2-6r-7)-40r+120+16r+48}{(r+3)(r-3)(r-7)}$

$= \dfrac{3r^2-18r-21-40r+120+16r+48}{(r+3)(r-3)(r-7)}$

$= \dfrac{3r^2-42r+147}{(r+3)(r-3)(r-7)}$

$= \dfrac{3(r^2-14r+49)}{(r+3)(r-3)(r-7)}$

$= \dfrac{3(r-7)^2}{(r+3)(r-3)(r-7)}$

$= \dfrac{3(r-7)}{(r+3)(r-3)}$ or $\dfrac{3r-21}{(r+3)(r-3)}$

83. $\dfrac{1}{f} = \dfrac{1}{x} + \dfrac{1}{x+5}$

$= \dfrac{x+5}{x(x+5)} + \dfrac{x}{x+5}$

$= \dfrac{2x+5}{x(x+5)}$

85. $\dfrac{1}{R_t} = \dfrac{1}{x+1} + \dfrac{1}{2x-3}$

$= \dfrac{2x-3}{(x+1)(2x-3)} + \dfrac{x+1}{(x+1)(2x-3)}$

$= \dfrac{2x-3+x+1}{(x+1)(2x-3)}$

$= \dfrac{3x-2}{(x+1)(2x-3)}$

87. $(x+2)(\dfrac{3}{x+2} + \dfrac{1}{x-1})$

$= (x+2)(\dfrac{3(x-1)}{(x+2)(x-1)} + \dfrac{x+2}{(x+2)(x-1)})$

$= (x+2)(\dfrac{3x-3+x+2}{(x+2)(x-1)})$

$= (x+2)(\dfrac{4x-1}{(x+2)(x-1)})$

$= \dfrac{4x-1}{x-1}$

89. $(\dfrac{3}{x-3} - \dfrac{x}{x+3})(\dfrac{3}{x+3} + \dfrac{x}{x-3})$

$= (\dfrac{3(x+3)}{(x-3)(x+3)} - \dfrac{x(x-3)}{(x-3)(x+3)})$

$\quad (\dfrac{3(x-3)}{(x+3)(x-3)} + \dfrac{x(x+3)}{(x+3)(x-3)})$

$= (\dfrac{3x+9-x^2+3x}{(x-3)(x+3)})(\dfrac{3x-9+x^2+3x}{(x+3)(x-3)})$

$= \dfrac{(9+6x-x^2)(x^2+6x-9)}{(x-3)^2(x+3)^2}$

Problem Set 3.5.

1. $\dfrac{\dfrac{2}{a}}{\dfrac{4}{a^2}} \cdot \dfrac{a^2}{a^2} = \dfrac{2a}{4}$

$\qquad\qquad = \dfrac{a}{2}$

3. $\dfrac{\dfrac{-3r^3}{54}}{\dfrac{18r^4}{56}} \cdot \dfrac{s^6}{s^6} = \dfrac{-3r^3s^2}{18r^4}$

$\qquad\qquad = -\dfrac{s^2}{6r}$

55

5.
$$\frac{\frac{xy}{x+1} \cdot (x+1)}{\frac{x}{x+1} \cdot (x+1)} = \frac{xy}{x}$$
$$= y$$

7.
$$\frac{\frac{4}{s-1}}{\frac{8}{1-s}} = \frac{\frac{4}{s-1}}{\frac{8}{-(s-1)}}$$

$$= \frac{\frac{4}{s-1} \cdot (s-1)}{\frac{-8}{s-1} \cdot (s-1)}$$

$$= \frac{4}{-8}$$

$$= -\frac{1}{2}$$

9.
$$\frac{\frac{-12}{5r+5s}}{\frac{18}{r+s}} = \frac{\frac{-12}{5(r+s)}}{\frac{18}{r+s}}$$

$$= \frac{\frac{-12}{5(r+s)} \cdot 5(r+s)}{\frac{18}{r+s} \cdot 5(r+s)}$$

$$= \frac{-12}{90}$$

$$= -\frac{2}{15}$$

11.
$$\frac{1+\frac{1}{r+1}}{1-\frac{1}{r+1}} = \frac{(1+\frac{1}{r+1}) \cdot (r+1)}{(1-\frac{1}{r+1}) \cdot (r+1)}$$

$$= \frac{(r+1)+1}{(r+1)-1}$$

$$= \frac{r+2}{r}$$

13.
$$\frac{\frac{1}{m}+\frac{1}{n}}{\frac{1}{m}-\frac{1}{n}} = \frac{(\frac{1}{m}+\frac{1}{n}) \cdot mn}{(\frac{1}{m}-\frac{1}{n}) \cdot mn}$$

$$= \frac{n+m}{n-m}$$

15.
$$\frac{\frac{2t^2-st-s^2}{st}}{\frac{2}{s}+\frac{1}{t}} = \frac{[\frac{(2t+s)(t-s)}{st}] \cdot st}{[\frac{2}{s}+\frac{1}{t}] \cdot st}$$

$$= \frac{(2t+s)(t-s)}{(2t+s)}$$

$$= t-s$$

17.
$$\frac{\frac{2}{m+n}+\frac{1}{m-n}}{\frac{1}{m+n}-\frac{2}{m-n}} = \frac{(\frac{2}{m+n}-\frac{1}{m-n}) \cdot (m+n)(m-n)}{(\frac{1}{m+n}-\frac{2}{m-n}) \cdot (m+n)(m-n)}$$

$$= \frac{2(m-n)-(m+n)}{(m-n)-2(m+n)}$$

$$= \frac{2m-2n-m-n}{m-n-2m-2n}$$

$$= \frac{m-3n}{-m-3n} \text{ or } -\frac{m-3n}{m+3n}$$

19.
$$\frac{\frac{w+18}{4-w^2}+\frac{w}{w+2}}{\frac{2}{w+2}-\frac{1}{w-2}} = \frac{\frac{w+18}{(2-w)(2+w)}+\frac{w}{w+2}}{\frac{2}{w+2}-\frac{1}{w-2}}$$

$$= \frac{[\frac{w+18}{-(w-2)(w+2)}+\frac{w}{w+2}] \cdot (w-2)(w+2)}{[\frac{2}{w+2}-\frac{1}{w-2}] \cdot (w-2)(w+2)}$$

$$= \frac{-(w+18)+w(w-2)}{2(w-2)-(w+2)}$$

$$= \frac{-w-18+w^2-2w}{2w-4-w-2}$$

$$= \frac{w^2-3w-18}{w-6}$$

$$= \frac{(w-6)(w+3)}{w-6}$$

$$= w+3$$

21.
$$\frac{\frac{a-b}{a+b}-\frac{a+b}{a-b}}{\frac{a-b}{a+b}+\frac{a+b}{a-b}} = \frac{[\frac{a-b}{a+b}-\frac{a+b}{a-b}] \cdot (a+b)(a-b)}{[\frac{a-b}{a+b}+\frac{a+b}{a-b}] \cdot (a+b)(a-b)}$$

$$= \frac{(a-b)^2 - (a+b)^2}{(a-b)^2 + (a+b)^2}$$

$$= \frac{a^2 - 2ab + b^2 - (a^2 + 2ab)}{a^2 - 2ab + b^2 + a^2 + 2ab + b^2}$$

$$= \frac{a^2 - 2ab + b^2 - a^2 - 2ab - b^2}{2a^2 + 2b^2}$$

$$= \frac{-4ab}{2(a^2 + b^2)}$$

$$= \frac{-2ab}{a^2 + b^2}$$

23. $$\frac{\dfrac{xyz^3}{t^5}}{\dfrac{x^2 y}{t^7}} = \frac{\dfrac{xyz^3}{t^5} \cdot t^7}{\dfrac{x^2 y}{t^7} \cdot t^7}$$

$$= \frac{t^2 xyz^3}{x^2 y}$$

$$= \frac{t^2 z^3}{x}$$

25. $$\frac{\dfrac{64a^4 b}{m^3 n}}{\dfrac{-48ab^5}{mn^2}} = \frac{\dfrac{64a^4 b}{m^3 n} \cdot m^3 n^2}{\dfrac{-48ab^5}{mn^2} \cdot m^3 n^2}$$

$$= \frac{64a^4 bn}{-48ab^5 m^2}$$

$$= \frac{4a^3 n}{-3b^4 m^2} \text{ or } -\frac{4a^3 n}{3b^4 m^2}$$

27. $$\frac{\dfrac{7s^3}{p-3}}{\dfrac{28s}{p-3}} = \frac{\dfrac{7s^3}{p-3} \cdot (p-3)}{\dfrac{28s}{p-3} \cdot (p-3)}$$

$$= \frac{7s^3}{28s}$$

$$= \frac{s^2}{4}$$

29. $$\frac{\dfrac{15}{t-1}}{\dfrac{35}{1-t}} = \frac{\dfrac{15}{t-1}}{\dfrac{35}{-(t-1)}}$$

$$= \frac{\dfrac{15}{t-1} \cdot (t-1)}{\dfrac{-35}{t-1} \cdot (t-1)}$$

$$= \frac{15}{-35}$$

$$= -\frac{3}{7}$$

31. $$\frac{\dfrac{x}{bc+bd}}{\dfrac{4x}{ab}} = \frac{\dfrac{x}{b(c+d)} \cdot ab(c+d)}{\dfrac{4x}{ab} \cdot ab(c+d)}$$

$$= \frac{xa}{4x(c+d)}$$

$$= \frac{a}{4(c+d)}$$

33. $$\frac{\dfrac{16}{u-v}}{\dfrac{8}{u+v}} = \frac{\dfrac{16}{u-v} \cdot (u-v)(u+v)}{\dfrac{8}{u+v} \cdot (u-v)(u+v)}$$

$$= \frac{16(u+v)}{8(u-v)}$$

$$= \frac{2(u+v)}{(u-v)}$$

35. $$\frac{\dfrac{m+1}{m^2-1}}{\dfrac{3}{m-1}} = \frac{\dfrac{m+1}{(m-1)(m+1)} \cdot (m-1)(m+1)}{\dfrac{3}{(m-1)} \cdot (m-1)(m+1)}$$

$$= \frac{(m+1)}{3(m+1)}$$

$$= \frac{1}{3}$$

37. $$\frac{\dfrac{x}{x^2-x-6}}{\dfrac{x}{x-3}} = \frac{\dfrac{x}{(x-3)(x+2)} \cdot (x-3)(x+2)}{\dfrac{x}{(x-3)} \cdot (x-3)(x+2)}$$

$$= \frac{x}{x(x+2)} = \frac{1}{(x+2)}$$

39. $\dfrac{\dfrac{3}{y}-2}{\dfrac{1}{y}+4} = \dfrac{\left(\dfrac{3}{y}-2\right)\cdot y}{\left(\dfrac{1}{y}+4\right)\cdot y}$

$\quad = \dfrac{3-2y}{1+4y}$

41. $\dfrac{\dfrac{1}{a-2}+1}{\dfrac{1}{a-2}-1} = \dfrac{\left(\dfrac{1}{a-2}+1\right)\cdot(a-2)}{\left(\dfrac{1}{a-2}-1\right)\cdot(a-2)}$

$\quad = \dfrac{1+(a-2)}{1-(a-2)}$

$\quad = \dfrac{1+a-2}{1-a+2}$

$\quad = \dfrac{a-1}{3-a} \quad \text{or} \quad -\dfrac{a-1}{a-3}$

43. $\dfrac{\dfrac{2}{a}+\dfrac{2}{b}}{\dfrac{a^3+b^3}{ab}} = \dfrac{\left(\dfrac{2}{a}+\dfrac{2}{b}\right)\cdot ab}{\left(\dfrac{a^3+b^3}{ab}\right)\cdot ab}$

$\quad = \dfrac{2b+2a}{a^3+b^3}$

$\quad = \dfrac{2(b+a)}{(a+b)(a^2-ab+b^2)}$

$\quad = \dfrac{2}{a^2-ab+b^2}$

45. $\dfrac{\dfrac{1}{2-b}+1}{1-\dfrac{1}{b-2}} = \dfrac{\dfrac{1}{-(b-2)}+1}{1-\dfrac{1}{b-2}}$

$\quad = \dfrac{\left(\dfrac{-1}{b-2}+1\right)\cdot b-2}{\left(1-\dfrac{1}{b-2}\right)\cdot b-2}$

$\quad = \dfrac{-1+b-2}{b-2-1}$

$\quad = \dfrac{b-3}{b-3}$

$\quad = 1$

47. $\dfrac{\dfrac{t+5}{t^2-16}}{1+\dfrac{1}{t+4}} = \dfrac{\dfrac{t+5}{(t-4)(t+4)}}{1+\dfrac{1}{t+4}}$

$\quad = \dfrac{\left(\dfrac{t+5}{(t-4)(t+4)}\right)\cdot(t-4)(t+4)}{\left(1+\dfrac{1}{t+4}\right)\cdot(t-4)(t+4)}$

$\quad = \dfrac{t+5}{(t-4)(t+4)\div(t-4)}$

$\quad = \dfrac{t+5}{t^2-16+t-4}$

$\quad = \dfrac{t+5}{t^2+t-20}$

$\quad = \dfrac{t+5}{(t+5)(t-4)}$

$\quad = \dfrac{1}{t-4}$

49. $\dfrac{\dfrac{x}{x^2-x-12}}{\dfrac{x}{x-4}} = \dfrac{\dfrac{x}{(x-4)(x+3)}\cdot(x-4)(x+3)}{\dfrac{x}{x-4}\cdot(x-4)(x+3)}$

$\quad = \dfrac{x}{x(x+3)}$

$\quad = \dfrac{1}{x+3}$

51. $\dfrac{\dfrac{2x+1}{x^2+x}}{\dfrac{2x}{x+1}-\dfrac{1}{x}} = \dfrac{\dfrac{2x+1}{x(x+1)}\cdot x(x+1)}{\left(\dfrac{2x}{x+1}-\dfrac{1}{x}\right)\cdot x(x+1)}$

$\quad = \dfrac{2x+1}{2x^2-(x+1)}$

$\quad = \dfrac{2x+1}{2x^2-x-1}$

$$= \frac{2x+1}{(2x+1)(x-1)}$$

$$= \frac{1}{x-1}$$

53. $\dfrac{\dfrac{m+3}{m-3}-\dfrac{m+3}{m-3}}{\dfrac{m+3}{m-3}+\dfrac{m+3}{m-3}} = \dfrac{0}{\dfrac{2(m+3)}{m-3}}$

$$= 0$$

55. $\dfrac{1+\dfrac{1}{x}-\dfrac{1}{x+1}}{\dfrac{x^2+1}{x+1}-\dfrac{1}{x}} = \dfrac{(1+\dfrac{1}{x}-\dfrac{1}{x+1}) \cdot x(x+1)}{(\dfrac{x^2+1}{x+1}-\dfrac{1}{x}) \cdot x(x+1)}$

$$= \frac{x(x+1)+(x+1)-x}{x(x^2+1)-(x+1)}$$

$$= \frac{x^2+x+x+1-x}{x^3+x-x-1}$$

$$= \frac{x^2+x+1}{x^3-1}$$

$$= \frac{(x^2+x+1)}{(x-1)(x^2+x+1)}$$

$$= \frac{1}{x-1}$$

57. $\dfrac{\dfrac{3}{x}-\dfrac{2}{y}-\dfrac{4}{z}}{\dfrac{1}{x}-\dfrac{1}{y}-\dfrac{1}{z}} = \dfrac{(\dfrac{3}{x}-\dfrac{2}{y}-\dfrac{4}{2}) \cdot xyz}{(\dfrac{1}{x}-\dfrac{1}{y}-\dfrac{1}{2}) \cdot xyz}$

$$= \frac{3yz-2xz-4xy}{yz-xz-xy}$$

59. $1 + \dfrac{1}{1+\dfrac{1}{1+1}} = 1 + \dfrac{1}{1+\dfrac{1}{2}}$

$$= 1+ \frac{1 \cdot 2}{(1+\frac{1}{2}) \cdot 2}$$

$$= 1 + \frac{2}{2+1}$$

$$= 1 + \frac{2}{3}$$

$$= \frac{5}{3}$$

61. $\dfrac{1+\dfrac{1}{1-\dfrac{1}{x}}}{1-\dfrac{1}{1+\dfrac{1}{x}}} = \dfrac{1+\dfrac{1}{(1-\dfrac{1}{x}) \cdot x} \cdot x}{1-\dfrac{1}{(1+\dfrac{1}{x}) \cdot x} \cdot x}$

$$= \frac{1+\dfrac{x}{x-1}}{1-\dfrac{x}{x+1}}$$

$$= \frac{(1+\dfrac{x}{x-1})}{(1-\dfrac{x}{x+1}) \cdot (x-1)(x+1)}$$

$$= \frac{(x-1)(x+1)+x(x+1)}{(x-1)(x+1)-x(x-1)}$$

$$= \frac{x^2-1+x^2+x}{x^2-1-(x^2-x)}$$

$$= \frac{2x^2+x-1}{x^2-1-x^2+x}$$

$$= \frac{2x^2+x-1}{x-1}$$

Review Problems.

1. 0

3. None

5. $\dfrac{x-1}{x^2+4x+3} = \dfrac{x-1}{(x+1)(x+3)}$

Undefined when $x = -1$ or -3.

7. $\dfrac{4}{3p} = \dfrac{4[2p(p-2)]}{6p^2(p-2)}$

$$= \frac{8p(p-2)}{6p^2(p-2)} = \frac{8p^2-16p}{6p^2(p-2)}$$

$$= \frac{-3(x+2)(x+1)}{(x+3)(x-2)}$$

9. $\dfrac{x+3}{x-4} = \dfrac{(x+3)(x-4)}{(x-4)^2}$

$$= \frac{x^2-x-12}{(x-4)^2}$$

$$= \frac{x^2-x-12}{x^2-8x+16}$$

11. $\dfrac{m^5n}{m^7n^3} = \dfrac{m^5n}{m^5n(m^2n^2)}$

$$= \frac{1}{m^2n^2}$$

13. $\dfrac{x^2-4x-5}{x^3+1} = \dfrac{(x-5)(x+1)}{(x+1)(x^2-x+1)}$

$$= \frac{x-5}{x^2-x+1}$$

15. $\dfrac{s^3t-st}{s^2+s} = \dfrac{st(s^2-1)}{s(s+1)}$

$$= \frac{st(s-1)(s+1)}{s(s+1)}$$

$$= t(s-1)$$

17. $\dfrac{12-3x^2}{2x^2+x-15} \cdot \dfrac{2x^2-3x-5}{x^2-4x+4}$

$$= \frac{3(4-x^2)}{(2x-5)(x+3)} \cdot \frac{(2x-5)(x+1)}{(x-2)^2}$$

$$= \frac{3(2-x)(2+x)}{(2x-5)(x+3)} \cdot \frac{(2x-5)(x+1)}{(x-2)^2}$$

$$= \frac{3[-(x-2)(x+2)]}{(2x-5)(x+3)} \cdot \frac{(2x-5)(x+1)}{(x-2)^2}$$

$$= \frac{-3(x-2)(x+2)(2x-5)(x+1)}{(2x-5)(x+3)(x-2)^2}$$

19. $\dfrac{a^2-3a+9}{a^3-ab^2} \div \dfrac{a^3+27}{a^4+2a^3b+a^2b^2}$

$$= \frac{a^2-3a+9}{a(a^2-b^2)} \cdot \frac{a^4+2a^3b+a^2b^2}{a^3+27}$$

$$= \frac{a^2-3a+9}{a(a-b)(a+b)} \cdot \frac{a^2(a^2+2ab+b^2)}{(a+3)(a^2-3a+9)}$$

$$= \frac{a^2-3a+9}{a(a-b)(a+b)} \cdot \frac{a^2(a+b)^2}{(a+3)(a^2-3a+9)}$$

$$= \frac{a^2(a^2-3a+9)(a+b)^2}{a(a-b)(a+b)(a+3)(a^2-3a+9)}$$

$$= \frac{a(a+b)}{(a-b)(a+3)}$$

21. $\dfrac{r^2st^3}{u^4v} \cdot \dfrac{-t^5}{u} \cdot \dfrac{u^2v^3}{rst} = \dfrac{-r^2st^8u^2v^3}{rstu^5v}$

$$= -\frac{rt^7v^2}{u^3}$$

23. $\dfrac{u^2-uv+2uw-2vw}{u^3+8w^3} \div \dfrac{u^2+4uw+4w^2}{u^2-2uw+4w^2}$

$$= \frac{u(u-v)+2w(u-v)}{(u+2w)(u^2-2uw+4w^2)}$$

$$\cdot \frac{u^2-2uw+4w^2}{(u+2w)^2}$$

$$= \frac{(u-v)(u+2w)(u^2-2uw+4w^2)}{(u+2w)(u^2-2uw+4w^2)(u+2w)^2}$$

$$= \frac{u-v}{(u+2w)^2}$$

25. $\dfrac{1-2y+y^2}{6y^2-y-1} \cdot \dfrac{y^2+7y+12}{3y^2+y-4} \cdot \dfrac{6y^2+5y-4}{y^2+2y-3}$

$$= \frac{(y-1)^2}{(3y+1)(2y-1)} \cdot \frac{(y+3)(y+4)}{(3y+4)(y-1)}$$

$$\frac{(3y+4)(2y-1)}{(y+3)(y-1)}$$

$$= \frac{(y-1)^2(y+3)(y+4)(3y+4)(2y-1)}{(3y+1)(2y-1)(3y+4)(y-1)^2(y+3)}$$

$$= \frac{y+4}{3y+1}$$

27. $\frac{12x^2-5x-2}{x^2+2xy+y^2} \div \frac{12x^2+x-6}{x+y}$

$$= \frac{(4x+1)(3x-2)}{(x+y)^2} \cdot \frac{(x+y)}{(4x+3)(3x-2)}$$

$$= \frac{(4x+1)(3x-2)(x+y)}{(x+y)^2(4x+3)(3x-2)}$$

$$= \frac{4x+1}{(x+y)(4x+3)}$$

29. $\frac{12t^3-27t}{t^8-16} \cdot \frac{t^4+2t^2}{2t^2-3t-9}$

$$= \frac{3t(4t^2-9)}{(t^4-4)(t^4+4)} \cdot \frac{t^2(t^2+2)}{(2t+3)(t-3)}$$

$$= \frac{3t(2t+3)(2t-3)}{(t^2-2)(t^2+2)(t^4+4)}$$

$$\cdot \frac{t^2(t^2+2)}{(2t+3)(t-3)}$$

$$= \frac{3t^3(2t+3)(2t-3)(t^2+2)}{(t^2-2)(t^2+2)(t^4+4)(2t+3)(t-3)}$$

$$= \frac{3t^3(2t-3)}{(t^2-2)(t^4+4)(t-3)}$$

31. $\frac{96t^7}{375s^2} \div \frac{-72t^4}{125s^7}$

$$= \frac{96t^7}{375s^2} \cdot \frac{125s^7}{-72t^4}$$

$$= \frac{(96)(125)s^7t^7}{(-72)(375)s^2t^4}$$

$$= \frac{4t^3s^5}{-9} \quad \text{or} \quad -\frac{4t^3s^5}{9}$$

33. $\frac{a3+a^2b+ab^2+b^3}{32a^7b^3} \cdot \frac{-768a^2b}{a^4-b^4}$

$$= \frac{a^2(a+b)+b^2(a+b)}{32a^7b^3}$$

$$\cdot \frac{-768a^2b}{(a^2-b^2)(a^2+b^2)}$$

$$= \frac{(a+b)(a^2+b^2)(-768)a^2b}{32a^7b^3(a+b)(a-b)(a^2+b^2)}$$

$$= \frac{-24}{a^5b^2(a-b)} \quad \text{or} \quad -\frac{24}{a^5b^2(a-b)}$$

35. $\frac{m^2-16n^2}{6m^4+3m^2} \div \frac{64n^3-m^3}{12m^2}$

$$= \frac{(m-4n)(m+4n)}{3m^2(2m^2+1)}$$

$$\cdot \frac{12m^2}{(4n-m)(16n^2+4nm+m^2)}$$

$$= \frac{-(4n-m)(m+4n)(12m^2)}{3m^2(2m^2+1)(4n-m)(16n^2+4nm+m^2)}$$

$$= \frac{-4(m+4n)}{(2m^2+1)(16n^2+4nm+m^2)}$$

37. $\frac{\frac{x^2y}{x+1}}{\frac{x}{x+1}} = \frac{\frac{x^2y}{x+1} \cdot (x+1)}{\frac{x}{x+1} \cdot (x+1)}$

$$= \frac{x^2y}{x}$$

$$= xy$$

39. $\frac{\frac{1}{x}-\frac{2}{xy}}{\frac{2}{x}+\frac{1}{xy}} = \frac{(\frac{1}{x}-\frac{2}{xy}) \cdot xy}{(\frac{2}{x}+\frac{1}{xy}) \cdot xy} = \frac{y-2}{2y+1}$

61

$$41. \quad \frac{\dfrac{3t^2+5t}{t^2-25}}{\dfrac{2}{t5}+\dfrac{1}{t+5}} = \frac{\dfrac{t(3t+5)}{(t-5)(t+5)} \cdot (t-5)(t+5)}{\left(\dfrac{2}{t-5}+\dfrac{1}{t+5}\right) \cdot (t-5)(t+5)}$$

$$= \frac{t(3t+5)}{2(t+5)+(t-5)}$$

$$= \frac{t(3t+5)}{2t+10+t-5}$$

$$= \frac{t(3t+5)}{3t+5}$$

$$= t$$

$$43. \quad \frac{\dfrac{1}{x-5}-\dfrac{1}{x+3}}{\dfrac{16^2+16}{x^2-2x-15}} = \frac{\left(\dfrac{1}{x-5}-\dfrac{1}{x+3}\right) \cdot (x-5)(x+3)}{\dfrac{16(x^2+1)}{(x-5)(x+3)} \cdot (x-5)(x+3)}$$

$$= \frac{(x+3)-(x-5)}{16(x^2+1)}$$

$$= \frac{x+3-x+5}{16(x^2+1)} = \frac{8}{16(x^2+1)}$$

$$= \frac{1}{2(x^2+1)}$$

$$45. \quad \frac{\dfrac{1}{s-5}+\dfrac{s+5}{s^2+5s+25}}{\dfrac{2s+5}{s^3-125}}$$

$$= \frac{\left(\dfrac{1}{s-5}+\dfrac{s+5}{s^2+5s+25}\right) \cdot (s-5)(s^2+5s+25)}{\left(\dfrac{2s+5}{(s-5)(s^2+5s+25)}\right) \cdot (s-5)(s^2+5s+25)}$$

$$= \frac{(s^2+5s+25)+(s+5)(s-5)}{(2s+5)}$$

$$= s^2 + 5s + 25 + s^2 - 25$$

$$= \frac{2s^2+5s}{2s+5}$$

$$= \frac{s(2s+5)}{(2s+5)}$$

$$= s$$

47. $27x^3 - 1 = (3x-1)(9x^2+3x+1)$

49. $3s^2t(st+1)$ factored

51. $x^3 + 1$ has two terms.

 $x^3 + 1 = (x+1)(x^2-x+1)$

 $x - 1$ is not a factor.

53. $x^2 - x - 2$ has three terms.

 $x^2 - x - 2 = (x-2)(x+1)$

 $x - 1$ is not a factor.

55. $3(x-1) - (x-1)^2$ has two terms.

 $3(x-1) - (x-1)^2 = (x-1)[3-(x-1)]$

$$= (x-1)(3-x-1)$$

$$= (x-1)(2-x)$$

 $x - 1$ is a factor.

57. $(x+2y)^2 = x^2 + 4xy + 4y^2$

59. $-2^2 = -4$

61. $(-2)^3 = -8$

63. $(-a)^5 = -a^5$

$$65. \quad \frac{a(y+z)-b(y+z)}{(y+z)(y-z)} = \frac{(y+z)(a-b)}{(y+z)(y-z)}$$

$$= \frac{a-b}{y-z}$$

$$67. \quad \frac{\dfrac{4}{x-2}+1}{\dfrac{2x}{x+2}-1} = \frac{\left(\dfrac{4}{x-2}+1\right) \cdot (x-2)(x+2)}{\left(\dfrac{2x}{x+2}-1\right) \cdot (x-2)(x+2)}$$

$$= \frac{4(x+2)+(x-2)(x+2)}{2x(x-2)-(x-2)(x+2)}$$

$$= \frac{4x+8+x^2-4}{2x^2-4x-(x^2-4)}$$

$$= \frac{x^2+4x+4}{2x^2-4x-x^2+4}$$

$$= \frac{x^2+4x+4}{x^2-4x+4} \quad \text{or} \quad \frac{(x+2)^2}{(x-2)^2}$$

$$= \frac{3y+x}{9y^2-x^2}$$

$$= \frac{3y+x}{(3y-x)(3y+x)}$$

$$= \frac{1}{3y-x}$$

B.

Chapter Test.

1. $\frac{x-2}{x(x+3)}$ is undefined when $x = 0$ or

   $x + 3 = 0$

   C.

6. $\frac{a}{ab-b^2} \div \frac{b}{a^2-ab} = \frac{a}{b(a-b)} + \frac{b}{a(a-b)}$

$$= \frac{a \cdot a}{ab(a-b)} + \frac{b \cdot b}{ab(a-b)}$$

$$= \frac{a^2+b^2}{ab(a-b)}$$

2. $x^2 - 14x + 49 = (x-7)^2$

$$\frac{3x}{x-7} = \frac{3x(x-7)}{(x-7)(x-7)}$$

$$= \frac{3x^2-21x}{x^2-14x+49}$$

B.

3. $\frac{x^3-8y^3}{x^2-4y^2} = \frac{(x-2y)(x^2+2xy+4y^2)}{(x-2y)(x+2y)}$

$$= \frac{x^2+2xy+4y^2}{x+2y}$$

7. $\frac{(a+2)^2}{a^2+6a+8} \cdot \frac{a^2-2a-8}{(a+2)^3}$

$$= \frac{(a+2)^2}{(a+4)(a+2)} \cdot \frac{(a-4)(a+2)}{(a+2)^3}$$

$$= \frac{(a+2)^2(a-4)(a+2)}{(a+4)(a+2)(a+2)^3}$$

$$= \frac{(a-4)}{(a+4)(a+2)}$$

A.

4. $\frac{x}{x+4} - \frac{x-3}{x-2}$

$$= \frac{x(x-2)}{(x+4)(x-2)} - \frac{(x-3)(x+4)}{(x+4)(x-2)}$$

$$= \frac{x^2-2x-(x^2+x-12)}{(x+4)(x-2)}$$

$$= \frac{x^2-2x-x^2-x+12}{(x+4)(x-2)}$$

$$= \frac{-3x+12}{(x+4)(x-2)}$$

$$= \frac{-3(x-4)}{(x+4)(x-2)}$$

C.

8. $\frac{x^3+3x^2}{x^3-6x^2+9x} \div \frac{x^2+2x-3}{x^2-9}$

$$= \frac{x^2(x+3)}{x(x^2-6x+9)} \cdot \frac{x^2-9}{x^2+2x-3}$$

$$= \frac{x^2(x+3)}{x(x-3)^2} \cdot \frac{(x-3)(x+3)}{(x+3)(x-1)}$$

$$= \frac{x^2(x+3)(x-3)(x+3)}{x(x-3)^2(x+3)(x-1)}$$

5. $\frac{\frac{3}{x}+\frac{1}{y}}{\frac{9y}{x}-\frac{x}{y}} = \frac{(\frac{3}{x}+\frac{1}{x}) \cdot xy}{(\frac{9y}{x}-\frac{x}{y}) \cdot xy}$

$$= \frac{x(x+3)}{(x-3)(x-1)}$$

63

9. $\dfrac{y+1}{y-2} - \dfrac{y^2+5y+1}{y^2+y-6}$

$= \dfrac{y+1}{y-2} - \dfrac{y^2+5y+1}{y^2+y-6}$

$= \dfrac{y+1}{y-2} - \dfrac{y^2+5y+1}{(y+3)(y-2)}$

$= \dfrac{(y+1)(y+3)}{(y+3)(y-2)} - \dfrac{y^2+5y+1}{(y+3)(y-2)}$

$= \dfrac{y^2+4y+3-(y^2+5y+1)}{(y+3)(y-2)}$

$= \dfrac{y^2+4y+3-y^2-5y-1}{(y+3)(y-2)}$

$= \dfrac{-y+2}{(y+3)(y-2)}$

$= \dfrac{-(y-2)}{(y+3)(y-2)}$

$= \dfrac{-1}{y+3}$

10. $\dfrac{6x^2+13x+6}{9x^2-4} \cdot \dfrac{9x^2-12x+4}{2x^2+x-3}$

$= \dfrac{(3x+2)(2x+3)}{(3x-2)(3x+2)} \cdot \dfrac{(3x-2)^2}{(2x+3)(x-1)}$

$= \dfrac{(3x+2)(2x+3)(3x-2)^2}{(3x-2)(3x+2)(2x+3)(x-1)}$

$= \dfrac{3x-2}{x-1}$

11. $\dfrac{ar+at+2br+2bt}{a^2-ab+b^2} \div \dfrac{r^2+rt}{a^3+b^3}$

$= \dfrac{a(r+t)+2b(r+t)}{a^2-ab+b^2} \cdot \dfrac{a^3+b^3}{r(r+t)}$

$= \dfrac{(r+t)(a+2b)}{a^2-ab+b^2} \cdot \dfrac{(a+b)(a^2-ab+b^2)}{r(r+t)}$

$= \dfrac{(r+t)(a+2b)(a+b)(a^2-ab+b^2)}{(a^2-ab+b^2)r(r+t)}$

$= \dfrac{(a+2b)(a+b)}{r}$

12. $\dfrac{\dfrac{2t}{s+t}+1}{\dfrac{4t}{s+t}-1} = \dfrac{\left(\dfrac{2t}{s+t}+1\right)\cdot(s+t)}{\left(\dfrac{4t}{s+t}-1\right)\cdot(s+t)}$

$= \dfrac{2t+(s+t)}{4t-(s+t)}$

$= \dfrac{3t+s}{3t-s}$

13. $\dfrac{x^2-4x+4}{16x^2-4x^4} = \dfrac{(x-2)^2}{4x^2(4-x)}$

$= \dfrac{(x-2)^2}{4x^2(2-x)(2+x)}$

$= \dfrac{(x-2)^2}{4x^2[-(x-2)](2+x)}$

$= \dfrac{x-2}{-4x^2(x+2)}$ or

$-\dfrac{x-2}{4x^2(x+2)}$

14. $\dfrac{w}{5} = \dfrac{w\cdot 3w^3}{5\cdot 3w^3}$

$= \dfrac{3w^4}{15w^3}$

15. (A) $\dfrac{5}{x^2-x-2} = \dfrac{5}{(x-2)(x+1)}$

undefined when $x = 2$ or -1

(B) $\dfrac{x-1}{8}$ - None.

64

CHAPTER 4

Problem Set 4.1.

1. $x - 4 = 2$

$x = 6$ $\{6\}$

3. $2x = 10$

$x = 5$ $\{5\}$

5. $3x - 5 = 4$

$3x = 4 + 5$

$3x = 9$

$x = 3$ $\{3\}$

7. $5 + 3x = 5x - 1$

$5 + 1 = 5x - 3x$

$6 = 2x$

$3 = x$ $\{3\}$

9. $5x - 3 = 3x + 7$

$5x - 3x = 7 + 3$

$2x = 10$

$x = 5$ $\{5\}$

11. $6 + 3x = 3x + 6$

$3x - 3x = 6 - 6$

$0 = 0$ $\mathbb{R}$

13. $2(x+1) = 3x - 4$

$2x + 2 = 3x - 4$

$2x - 3x = -4 - 2$

$-x = -6$

$x = 6$ $\{6\}$

15. $2(x-6) - 3(2x-2) = 0$

$2x - 12 - 6x + 6 = 0$

$-4x - 6 = 0$

$-4x = 6$

$x = \dfrac{-6}{4}$ or $-\dfrac{3}{2}$ $\{-\dfrac{3}{2}\}$

17. $-1(1-2x) = 3 + 5x$

$-1 + 2x = 3 + 5x$

$2x - 5x = 3 + 1$

$-3x = 4$

$x = -\dfrac{4}{3}$ $\{-\dfrac{4}{3}\}$

19. $1 + 3x = 3(2+x)$

$1 + 3x = 6 + 3x$

$3x - 3x = 6 - 1$

$0 = 5$ $\emptyset$

21. $2(x+3) - 3[2(x-3)+4] = 0$

$2x + 6 - 3(2x-6+4) = 0$

$2x + 6 - 3(2x-2) = 0$

$2x + 6 - 6x + 6 = 0$

$4x + 12 = 0$

$-4x = -12$

$x = 3$ $\{3\}$

23. $\dfrac{1}{2}x - 1 = \dfrac{1}{3}x$

$6(\dfrac{1}{2}x-1) = 6(\dfrac{1}{3}x)$

$3x - 6 = 2x$

$-6 = 2x - 3x$

$-6 = -x$

$6 = x$ $\{6\}$

25. $\dfrac{8}{9}x - \dfrac{1}{3} = \dfrac{2}{3} + 2$

$9(\dfrac{8}{9}x-\dfrac{1}{3}) = 9(\dfrac{2}{3}x+2)$

$8x - 3 = 6x + 18$

65

$$8x - 6x = 18 + 3$$

$$2x = 21$$

$$x = \frac{21}{2} \qquad \{\frac{21}{2}\}$$

27. $\quad \frac{x}{6} = \frac{5}{12}(x+2)$

$$12\left(\frac{x}{6}\right) = 12\left[\frac{5}{12}(x+2)\right]$$

$$2x = 5(x+2)$$

$$2x = 5x + 10$$

$$2x - 5x = 10$$

$$-3x = 10$$

$$x = -\frac{10}{3} \qquad \{-\frac{10}{3}\}$$

29. $\quad \frac{x+1}{2} = 2$

$$2\left(\frac{x+1}{2}\right) = 2(2)$$

$$x + 1 = 4$$

$$x = 4 - 1$$

$$x = 3 \qquad \{3\}$$

31. $\quad \frac{1-3x}{2} - 3x = 5$

$$2\left(\frac{1-3x}{2}-3x\right) = 2(5)$$

$$1 - 3x - 6x = 10$$

$$1 - 9x = 10$$

$$-9x = 10 - 1$$

$$-9x = 9$$

$$x = -1 \qquad \{-1\}$$

33. $\quad \frac{7x-3}{7} - \frac{5x+7}{5} = 1$

$$35\left(\frac{7x-3}{7}-\frac{5x+7}{5}\right) = 35 \cdot 1$$

$$5(7x-3) - 7(5x+7) = 35$$

$$35x - 15 - 35x - 49 = 35$$

$$-54 = 35 \qquad \emptyset$$

35. $\quad x + 0.4 = 1.5$

$$x = 1.5 - 0.4$$

$$x = 1.1 \qquad \{1.1\}$$

37. $\quad 1.3x - 6.1 = 2x + 5.8$

$$1.3x - 2x = 5.8 + 6.1$$

$$-0.7x = 11.9$$

$$x = -17 \qquad \{-17\}$$

39. $\quad 1.1x = 2.3(x+2)$

$$1.1x = 2.3x + 4.6$$

$$1.1x - 2.3x = 4.6$$

$$-1.2x = 4.6$$

$$x = -3.8\overline{3}$$

41. width: w

length: w + 5

$$2w + 2(w+5) = 78$$

$$2w + 2w + 10 = 78$$

$$4w + 10 = 78$$

$$4w = 78 - 10$$

$$4w = 68$$

$$w = 17$$

$$w + 5 = 22$$

The strawberry patch is 17m. by 22m.

43. 1st number: x

2nd number: 5x

3rd number: x + 10

$$x + 5x + x + 10 = 24$$

$$7x + 10 = 24$$

66

$$7x = 24 - 10$$

$$7x = 14$$

$$x = 2, \quad 5x = 10, \quad x + 10 = 12$$

The numbers are 2, 10, and 12.

45. $x + 5 = 9$

   $x = 9 - 5$

   $x = 4 \qquad \{4\}$

47. $2x - 12 = 7$

   $2x = 7 + 12$

   $2x = 19$

   $x = \dfrac{19}{2} \qquad \{\dfrac{19}{2}\}$

49. $5 - 3x = 2$

   $-3x = 2 - 5$

   $-3x = -3$

   $x = 1 \qquad \{1\}$

51. $5x + 8 = 11x$

   $8 = 11x - 5x$

   $8 = 6x$

   $\dfrac{8}{6} = x \qquad \{\dfrac{4}{3}\}$

53. $x + 7 = x + 3$

   $x - x = 3 - 7$

   $0 = -4 \qquad\qquad \emptyset$

55. $2y + 3 = -y - 6$

   $2y + y = -6 - 3$

   $3y = -9$

   $y = -3 \qquad \{-3\}$

57. $5x - 22 = 17x - 16$

   $5x - 17x = -16 + 22$

   $-12x = 6$

$$x = -\dfrac{6}{12} \qquad \{-\dfrac{1}{2}\}$$

59. $7x + 15 = 5x + 31$

   $7x - 5x = 31 - 15$

   $2x = 16$

   $x = 8 \qquad \{8\}$

61. $2(3-x) = 5(x+4)$

   $6 - 2x = 5x + 20$

   $-2x - 5x = 20 - 6$

   $-7x = 1x$

   $x = -2 \qquad \{-2\}$

63. $(1+s)3 = 7(-1-s)$

   $3 + 3s = -7 - 7s$

   $10s = -10$

   $s = -1 \qquad \{-1\}$

65. $4(2x+1) - (4-x) = 18$

   $8x + 4 - 4 + x = 18$

   $9x = 18$

   $x = 2 \qquad \{2\}$

67. $3(x+1) - 3 = 2(x-1) + x + 2$

   $3x + 3 - 3 = 2x - 2 + x + 2$

   $3x = 3x$

   $0 = 0 \qquad \{\mathbb{R}\}$

69. $2[1-3(x+2)] = 0$

   $2(1-3x-6) = 0$

   $2(-3x-5) = 0$

   $-6x - 10 = 0$

   $-6x = 10$

   $x = -\dfrac{10}{6} \qquad \{-\dfrac{5}{3}\}$

71.　　$-6\{x+3[x+3(2x-5)]\} = 5 - 3(44x+8)$

　　　　$-6[x+3(x+6x-15)] = 5 - 132x - 24$

　　　　　$-6(x+3(7x-15)) = -19 - 132x$

　　　　　　$-6(x+21x-45) = -19 - 132x$

　　　　　　　$-6(22x-45) = -19 - 132x$

　　　　　　　$-132x + 270 = -19 - 132x$

　　　　　　$-132x + 132x = -19 - 270$

　　　　　　　　　　$0 = -289$　　$\emptyset$

73.　　　　$\frac{1}{2}x - \frac{1}{4} = \frac{1}{3}x$

　　　　$12\left(\frac{1}{2}x-\frac{1}{4}\right) = 12\left(\frac{1}{3}x\right)$

　　$12\cdot\frac{1}{2}x - 12\cdot\frac{1}{4} = 12\cdot\frac{1}{3}x$

　　　　　　$6x - 3 = 4x$

　　　　　　　$-3 = 4x - 6x$

　　　　　　　$-3 = -2x$

　　　　　　$\frac{3}{2} = x$　　　　$\left\{\frac{3}{2}\right\}$

75.　　　$\frac{1}{6} - \frac{1}{3}x = \frac{1}{9}(2x+1)$

　　　$18\left(\frac{1}{6}-\frac{1}{3}x\right) = 18\left[\frac{1}{9}(2x+1)\right]$

　$18\cdot\frac{1}{6} - 18\cdot\frac{1}{3}x = 18\cdot\frac{1}{9}(2x+1)$

　　　　　$3 - 6x = 2(2x+1)$

　　　　　$3 - 6x = 4x + 2$

　　　　$-6x - 4x = 2 - 3$

　　　　　$-10x = -1$

　　　　　　$x = \frac{1}{10}$　　$\left\{\frac{1}{10}\right\}$

77.　　　$\frac{2x}{7} + \frac{x}{2} = 11$

　　　$14\left(\frac{2x}{7}+\frac{x}{2}\right) = 14\cdot 11$

　$14\cdot\frac{2x}{7} + 14\cdot\frac{x}{2} = 156$

　　　　$4x + 7x = 156$

　　　　　$11x = 156$

　　　　　　$x = 14$　　　$\{14\}$

79.　　$\frac{3}{4}(x-3) = \frac{5}{8}x$

　　$8\left[\frac{3}{4}(x-3)\right] = 8\left(\frac{5}{8}x\right)$

　　$8\cdot\frac{3}{4}(x-3) = 8\cdot\frac{5}{8}x$

　　　　$6(x-3) = 5x$

　　　　$6x - 18 = 5x$

　　　　　$-18 = 5x - 6x$

　　　　　$-18 = -x$

　　　　　$18 = x$　　　　$\{18\}$

81.　　$\frac{x-2}{3} = 4$

　　$3\left(\frac{x-2}{3}\right) = 3\cdot4$

　　$x - 2 = 12$

　　　$x = 14$　　　$\{14\}$

83.　　$\frac{x+3}{5} - \frac{2-x}{10} = 7$

　　$10\left(\frac{x+3}{5}-\frac{2-x}{10}\right) = 10\cdot7$

　$10\cdot\frac{x+3}{5} - 10\cdot\frac{2-x}{10} = 70$

　$2(x+3) - (2-x) = 70$

　$2x + 6 - 2 + x = 70$

　　　$3x + 4 = 70$

　　　　$3x = 70 - 4$

　　　　$3x = 66$

　　　　$x = 22$　　$\{22\}$

85.　　$\frac{3t-7}{7} = \frac{t+1}{2}$

　　$14\left(\frac{3t-7}{7}\right) = 14\left(\frac{t+1}{2}\right)$

$2(3t-7) = 7(t+1)$

$6t - 14 = 7t + 7$

$6t - 7t = 7 + 14$

$-t = 21$

$t = -21 \qquad \{-21\}$

87. $\dfrac{5x-10}{3} + \dfrac{x-8}{2} = -3$

$6\left(\dfrac{5x-10}{3} + \dfrac{x-8}{2}\right) = 6 \cdot -3$

$6 \cdot \dfrac{5x-10}{3} + 6 \cdot \dfrac{x-8}{2} = -18$

$2(5x-10) + 3(x-8) = -18$

$10x - 20 + 3x - 2x = -18$

$13x - 44 = -18$

$13x = -18 + 4$

$13x = 26$

$x = 2 \qquad \{2\}$

89. $\dfrac{2x-3}{6} = \dfrac{3x}{2} + \dfrac{6-x}{3}$

$6\left(\dfrac{2x-3}{6}\right) = 6\left(\dfrac{3x}{2} + \dfrac{6-x}{3}\right)$

$6 \cdot \dfrac{2x-3}{6} = 6 \cdot \dfrac{3x}{2} + 6 \cdot \dfrac{6-x}{3}$

$2x - 3 = 3(3x) + 2(6-x)$

$2x - 3 = 9x + 12 - 2x$

$2x - 3 = 7x + 12$

$2x - 7x = 12 + 3$

$-5x = 15$

$x = -3 \qquad \{-3\}$

91. $3x + 6.03 = 3.42$

$3x = 3.42 - 6.03$

$3x = -2.61$

$x = -0.87 \qquad \{-0.87\}$

93. $1.4x + 0.5 = 1.1x + 1.5$

$1.4x - 1.1x = 1.5 - 0.5$

$0.3x = 1.0$

$x = \dfrac{1.0}{0.3} = 3.\overline{3} \qquad \{3.\overline{3}\}$

95. $1.5(x+2) = 2.8 + x$

$1.5x + 3 = 2.8 + x$

$1.5x - x = 2.8 - 3$

$0.5x = -0.2$

$x = \dfrac{-0.2}{0.5} = -0.4 \qquad \{-0.4\}$

97. width: w

length: w + 8

$2w + 2(w+8) = 104$

$2w + 2w + 16 = 104$

$4w + 16 = 104$

$4w = 104 - 16$

$4w = 88$

$w = 22$

$w + 8 = 30$

The dimensions are 22 ft. by 30 ft.

99. 1st number: x

2nd number: 5 + x

3rd number: 2x

$x + 5 + x + 2x = 29$

$4x + 5 = 29$

$4x = 29 - 5$

$4x = 24$

$x = 6, \; 5 + x = 11,$

$$2x = 12$$

The numbers are 6, 11, 12.

101. 1st angle: x

    2nd angle: 2x

$$x + 2x = 90$$

$$3x = 90$$

$$x = 30 \quad 2x = 60$$

The measures of the angle are 30° and 60°.

103. $x - a = b$

$$x = b + a \qquad \{a + b\}$$

105. $\dfrac{x-a}{2} = \dfrac{4-x}{3}$

$$6\left(\dfrac{x-a}{2}\right) = 6\left(\dfrac{4-x}{3}\right)$$

$$3(x-a) = 2(4-x)$$

$$3x - 3a = 8 - 2x$$

$$3x + 2x = 8 + 3a$$

$$5x = 8 + 3a$$

$$x = \dfrac{8+3a}{5} \qquad \left\{\dfrac{8+3a}{5}\right\}$$

Problem Set 4.2.

1. $C = 2\pi r \quad$ for r

$$\dfrac{C}{2\pi} = r$$

3. $F = \dfrac{9}{5}c + 32 \quad$ for c

$$5 \cdot F = 5\left(\dfrac{9}{5}c + 32\right)$$

$$5F = 5 \cdot \dfrac{9}{5}c + 5 \cdot 32$$

$$5F = 9c + 160$$

$$5F - 160 = 9c$$

$$\dfrac{5F-160}{9} = c$$

5. $A = P\left(1 + \dfrac{i}{m}\right) \quad$ for i

$$A = P + \dfrac{pi}{m}$$

$$m \cdot A = m\left(P + \dfrac{pi}{m}\right)$$

$$mA = mP + m \cdot \dfrac{pi}{m}$$

$$mA = mP + Pi$$

$$mA - mP = Pi$$

$$\dfrac{mA - mP}{P} = i$$

7. $s = 2(\ell h + hw + \ell w) \quad$ for w

$$s = 2\ell h + 2hw + 2\ell w$$

$$s - 2\ell h = 2hw + 2\ell w$$

$$s - 2\ell h = w(2h + 2\ell)$$

$$\dfrac{s - 2\ell h}{2h + 2\ell} = w$$

9. $2x - 7 = a$

$$2x = a + 7$$

$$x = \dfrac{a+7}{2}$$

11. $\dfrac{2}{3}x - a = \dfrac{1}{3}$

$$3\left(\dfrac{2}{3}x - a\right) = 3 \cdot \dfrac{1}{3}$$

$$3 \cdot \dfrac{2}{3}x - 3a = 1$$

$$2x - 3a = 1$$

$$2x = 1 + 3a$$

$$x = \dfrac{1+3a}{2}$$

13. $b - ax = 4b$

$$-ax = 4b - b$$

$$-ax = 3b$$

$$x = \dfrac{3b}{-a} \quad \text{or} \quad \dfrac{3b}{a}$$

15. $\dfrac{x-b}{3} = \dfrac{2}{5}$

$15\left(\dfrac{x-b}{3}\right) = 15\left(\dfrac{2}{5}\right)$

$5(x-b) = 3 \cdot 2$

$5x - 5b = 6$

$5x = 6 + 5b$

$x = \dfrac{6+5b}{5}$

17. $0.1x + b = 1.0$

$0.1x = 1.0 - b$

$x = \dfrac{1.0-b}{0.1}$

$x = 10.0 - 10b$

19. $ax + b = bx$

$ax - bx = -b$

$x(a-b) = -b$

$x = \dfrac{-b}{a-b}$ or $\dfrac{-b}{-(b-a)} = \dfrac{b}{b-a}$

21. $a(x-b) = b(x+b)$

$ax - ab = bx + b^2$

$ax - bx = b^2 + ab$

$x(a-b) = b^2 + ab$

$x = \dfrac{b^2+ab}{a-b}$

23. $\dfrac{3bx}{4} - a - b = \dfrac{x}{3}$

$12\left(\dfrac{3bx}{4}-a-b\right) = 12\left(\dfrac{x}{3}\right)$

$3 \cdot 3bx - 12a - 12b = 4 \cdot x$

$9bx - 12a - 12b = 4x$

$9bx - 4x = 12a + 12b$

$x(9b-4) = 12a + 12b$

$x = \dfrac{12a+12b}{9b-4}$

25. $\dfrac{7}{x} - \dfrac{a}{3} = \dfrac{b}{2}$

$6x\left(\dfrac{7}{x}-\dfrac{a}{3}\right) = 6x\left(\dfrac{b}{2}\right)$

$6x \cdot \dfrac{7}{x} - 6x \cdot \dfrac{a}{3} = 6x \cdot \dfrac{b}{2}$

$42 - 2ax = 3bx$

$42 = 3bx + 2ax$

$42 = x(3b+2a)$

$\dfrac{42}{3b+2a} = x$

27. $(x-b)^2 - (x+b)^2 = 2$

$x^2 - 2xb + b^2 - (x^2+2xb+b^2) = 2$

$x^2 - 2xb + b^2 - x^2 - 2xb - b^2 = 2$

$-4xb = 2$

$x = \dfrac{2}{-4b}$ or $-\dfrac{1}{2b}$

29. $\dfrac{3}{2}(bx+a) = \dfrac{3}{2}ax + a^2$

$2\left[\dfrac{3}{2}(bx+a)\right] = 2\left(\dfrac{3}{2}ax+a^2\right)$

$2 \cdot \dfrac{3}{2}(bx+a) = 2 \cdot \dfrac{3}{2}ax + 2a^2$

$3(bx+a) = 3ax + 2a^2$

$3bx + 3a = 3ax + 2a^2$

$3bx - 3ax = 2a^2 - 3a$

$\quad = 2a^2 - 3a$

$x = \dfrac{2a^2-3a}{3(b-a)}$ or $\dfrac{2a^2-3a}{3b-3a}$

31. $A = \ell w$ for ℓ

$\dfrac{A}{w} = \ell$

71

33. $v = \ell wh$ for w

$$\frac{v}{\ell h} = w$$

35. $I = prt$ for t

$$\frac{I}{Pr} = t$$

37. $\dfrac{1}{R} = \dfrac{1}{R_1} + \dfrac{1}{R_2}$ for R

$$RR_1R_2\left(\frac{1}{R}\right) = RR_1R_2\left(\frac{1}{R_1}+\frac{1}{R_2}\right)$$

$$\frac{RR_1R_2}{R} = RR_1R_2 \cdot \frac{1}{R_1} + RR_1R_2 \cdot \frac{1}{R_2}$$

$$R_1R_2 = RR_2 + RR_1$$

$$R_1R_2 = R(R_2+R_1)$$

$$\frac{R_1R_2}{R_2+R_1} = R$$

39. $A = P + Prt$ for t

$$A - P = Prt$$

$$\frac{A-P}{Pr} = t$$

41. $P = 2\ell + 2w$ for ℓ

$$P - 2w = 2\ell$$

$$\frac{P-2w}{2} = \ell$$

43. $s^2 = 1 - \dfrac{a}{r}$ for r

$$r(s^2) = r\left(1-\frac{a}{r}\right)$$

$$rs^2 = r - r \cdot \frac{a}{r}$$

$$rs^2 = r - a$$

$$rs^2 - r = -a$$

$$r(s^2-1) = -a$$

$$r = \frac{-a}{s^2-1} \quad \text{or} \quad \frac{-a}{-(1-s^2)} = \frac{a}{1-s^2}$$

45. $E = IR$ for R

$$\frac{E}{I} = R$$

47. $S = \dfrac{a}{1-r}$ for

$$(1-r)S = 1 - r\left(\frac{a}{1-r}\right)$$

$$(1-r)S = a$$

$$S - Sr = a$$

49. Area is 46.7 ft^2.

Width is 6.6 ft.

$$\ell = \frac{A}{w}$$

$$= \frac{46.7}{6.6}$$

$$= 7.0\overline{75}$$

The length is $7.0\overline{75}$ ft.

51. $d = 10$ Km.

$t = 55$ m.

$$r = \frac{d}{t}$$

$$= \frac{10}{55}$$

$$= \frac{2}{11}$$

His rate is $\dfrac{2}{11}$ Km/min.

53. $C = 100$

$$F = \frac{9C+160}{5}$$

$$= \frac{9(100)+160}{5}$$

$$= \frac{900+160}{5}$$

$$= \frac{1060}{5} \quad \text{or} \quad 212$$

$100^{\circ}C = 212^{\circ}F$

55. $x - b = 6$

$$x = b + 6$$

57. $4bx + a = 7$

$$4bx = 7 - a$$

$$x = \frac{7-a}{4b}$$

59. $ax + ab = b$

$$ax = b - ab$$

$$x = \frac{b-ab}{a}$$

61. $\frac{x+a}{3} = 1$

$$3\left(\frac{x+a}{3}\right) = 3 \cdot 1$$

$$x + a = 3$$

$$x = 3 - a$$

63. $b(2-x) = a$

$$2b - bx = a$$

$$-bx = a - 2b$$

$$x = \frac{a-2b}{-b} \quad \text{or}$$

$$\frac{-(a-2b)}{b} = \frac{2b-a}{b}$$

65. $3(5+ax) = 1$

$$15 + 3ax = 1$$

$$3ax = 1 - 15$$

$$3ax = -14$$

$$x = \frac{-14}{3a}$$

67. $ax - 2 = bx$

$$-2 = bx - ax$$

$$-2 = x(b-a)$$

$$\frac{-2}{b-a} = x$$

So, $x = \frac{-2}{b-a}$ or $\frac{-2}{-(a-b)} = \frac{2}{a-b}$

69. $2b - (x-a) = a(x-2)$

$2b - x + a = ax - 2a$

$$2b + a + 2a = ax + x$$

$$2b + 3a = x(a+1)$$

$$\frac{2b+3a}{a+1} = x$$

71. $bx + 4 - a^2 = ax$

$$4 - a^2 = ax - bx$$

$$4 - a^2 = x(a-b)$$

$$\frac{4-a^2}{a-b} = x$$

So $x = \frac{4-a^2}{a-b}$ or $\frac{-(a^2-4)}{-(b-a)} = \frac{a^2-4}{b-a}$

73. $(x-b)(x+ \ ) = x^2 + ab$

$x^2 + ax - bx \quad ab = x^2 + ab$

$x^2 + ax - bx - x^2 = ab + ab$

$$ax - bx = 2ab$$

$$x(a-b) = 2ab$$

$$x = \frac{2ab}{a-b}$$

75. $\frac{2}{3}bx + a + b = \frac{2}{5}x$

$$15\left(\frac{2}{3}bx+a+b\right) = 15\left(\frac{2}{5}x\right)$$

$$15 \cdot \frac{2}{3}bx + 15a + 15b = 6x$$

$$10bx + 15a + 15b = 6x$$

$$15a + 15b = 6x - 10bx$$

$$15a + 15b = x(6-10b)$$

$$\frac{15a+15b}{6-10b} = x$$

77. $\frac{5}{6}(bx+2a) = \frac{1}{6}ax + b^2$

$$6\left[\frac{5}{6}(bx+2a)\right] = 6\left(\frac{1}{6}ax+b^2\right)$$

$$6 \cdot \frac{5}{6}(bx+2a) = 6 \cdot \frac{1}{6}ax + 6b^2$$

$$5(bx+2a) = ax + 6b^2$$

$$5bx + 10a = ax + 6b^2$$

$$5bx - ax = 6b^2 - 10a$$

$$x(5b-a) = 6b^2 - 10a$$

$$x = \frac{6b^2 - 10a}{5b-a} \text{ or } \frac{-(10a-6b^2)}{-(a-5b)}$$

$$= \frac{10a-6b^2}{a-5b}$$

79. $a(x-2) = a + x$

$ax - 2a = a + x$

$ax - x = a + 2a$

$x(a-1) = 3a$

$x = \frac{3a}{a-1}$

81. a) $a(a-x) = x + 1$

$a^2 - ax = x + 1$

$a^2 - 1 = x + ax$

$a^2 - 1 = x(1+a)$

$\frac{a^2-1}{1+a} = x$

So, $x = \frac{a^2-1}{a+1}$

$x = \frac{(a-1)(a-1)}{a+1}$

$x = a - 1, \quad a \neq -1$

b) $2(x+2) = b(b+x)$

$2x + 4 = b^2 + bx$

$2x - bx = b^2 - 4$

$x(2-b) = b^2 - 4$

$x = \frac{b^2-4}{2-b}$

$x = \frac{(b-2)(b+2)}{2-b}$

$$x = \frac{(b-2)(b+2)}{-(b-2)}$$

$$x = \frac{b+2}{-1} \text{ or } -b - 2, \ b \neq 2$$

c) $(b+2)(x-b+3) = 0$

$b(x-b+3) + 2(x-b+3) = 0$

$bx - b^2 + 3b + 2x - 2b + 6 = 0$

$bx - b^2 + b + 2x + 6 = 0$

$bx + 2x = b^2 - b - 6$

$x(b+2) = b^2 - b - 6$

$x = \frac{b^2-b-6}{b+2}$

$x = \frac{(b-3)(b+2)}{b+2}$

$x = b - 3, \quad b \neq -2$

d) $a(x-a) = x - 1$

$ax - a^2 = x - 1$

$ax - x = a^2 - 1$

$x(a-1) = a^2 - 1$

$x = \frac{a^2-1}{a-1}$

$x = \frac{(a-1)(a+1)}{a-1}$

$x = a + 1, \ a \neq 1$

Problem Set 4.3.

1. x: number of gallons of 60%
    solution to be added

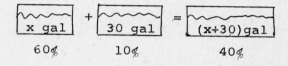

$$\frac{60}{100}x + \frac{10}{100}(30) = \frac{40}{100}(x+30)$$

74

$$100(\frac{60}{100}x+\frac{300}{100}) = 100[\frac{40}{100}(x+30)]$$

$$60x + 300 = 40(x+30)$$

$$60x + 300 = 40x + 1200$$

$$60x - 40x = 1200 - 300$$

$$20x = 900$$

$$x = 45$$

45 gallons of 60% solution should be added.

3. x: number of gallons of pure alcohol to be added.

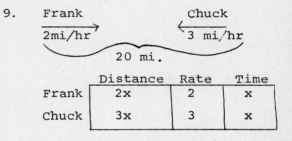

$$\frac{30}{100}(10) + \frac{100}{100}x = \frac{40}{100}(10+x)$$

$$100(\frac{300}{100}+\frac{100}{100}x) = 100[\frac{40}{100}(10+x)]$$

$$300 + 100x = 40(10+x)$$

$$300 + 100x = 400 + 40x$$

$$100x - 40x = 400 - 300$$

$$60x = 100$$

$$x = \frac{100}{60} \quad or \quad \frac{5}{3}$$

$\frac{5}{3}$ gallons of alcohol should be added.

5. x: number of hours it takes both pipes working together to fill the pool.

$$\frac{x}{2} + \frac{x}{4} = 1$$

$$4(\frac{x}{2}+\frac{x}{4}) = 4\cdot1$$

$$2x + x = 4$$

$$3x = 4$$

$$x = \frac{4}{3}$$

It takes $\frac{4}{3}$ hours for both pipes to fill the pool.

7. x: number of minutes it takes Rowland and Dan working together to mow the lawn

$$\frac{x}{21} + \frac{x}{28} = 1$$

$$84(\frac{x}{21}+\frac{x}{28}) = 84\cdot1$$

$$4x + 3x = 84$$

$$7x = 84$$

$$x = 12$$

It takes 12 minutes for both of them to mow the lawn if they work together.

9. Frank   Chuck
2mi/hr   3 mi/hr
        20 mi.

	Distance	Rate	Time
Frank	2x	2	x
Chuck	3x	3	x

x: number of hours until they meet

$$2x + 3x = 20$$

$$5x = 20$$

$$x = 4 \quad 2x = 8 \quad 3x = 12$$

They will meet in 4 hrs. Frank walked 8 mi. Chuck walked 12 mi.

11.

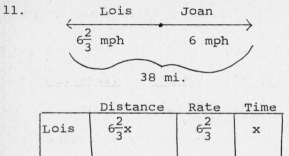

	Distance	Rate	Time
Lois	$6\frac{2}{3}x$	$6\frac{2}{3}$	x
Joan	6x	6	x

x: number of hours when they are 38 mi. apart

$$6\frac{2}{3}x + 6x = 38$$

$$\frac{20}{3}x + 6x = 38$$

$$3(\frac{20}{3}x+6x) = 3 \cdot 38$$

$$20x + 18x = 114$$

$$38x = 114$$

$$x = 3$$

In 3 hours they will be 38 miles apart.

13. x: amount to invest at 5%

100,000-x: amount to invest at 6%

$$560 = \frac{5}{100}x + \frac{6}{100}(10,000-x)$$

$$100 \cdot 560 = 100[\frac{5}{100}x+\frac{6}{100}(10,000-x)]$$

$$56,000 = 5x + 6(10,000-x)$$

$$56,000 = 5x + 60,000 - 6x$$

$$56,000-60,000 = 5x - 6x$$

$$-4,000 = -x$$

$$4,000 = x$$

$$10,000 - x = 10,000 - 4,000$$

$$= 6,000$$

Invest $4,000 at 5% and $6,000 at 6%.

15. x: rate at which 16,000 must be invested

$$\frac{8}{100} \cdot 14,000 + x(16,000)$$

$$= \frac{12}{100}(14,000+16,000)$$

$$\overline{100} + 16,000x = \frac{12}{100}(30,000)$$

$$100(\frac{112,000}{100} + 16,000x \quad \frac{360,000}{100}$$

$$112,000 + 1,600,000x = 360,000$$

$$1,600,000x = 248,000$$

$$x = \frac{248,000}{1,600,000}$$

$$= 0.155 \quad or \quad 15.5\%$$

She needs a yield of 15.5% on the $16,000.

17.

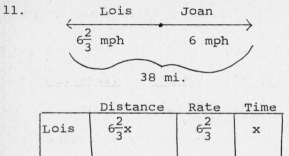

original △   New △
Area: $\frac{1}{2}(x)(2x)$ Area: $\frac{1}{2}(x+2)(2x+2)$

x: length of one leg of the original △.

2x: length of other leg in the original △.

$$\frac{1}{2}(x)(2x) + 17 = \frac{1}{2}(x+2)(2x+2)$$

$$x^2 + 17 = \frac{1}{2}(2x^2+6x+4)$$

$$x^2 + 17 = x^2 + 3x + 2$$

$$17 - 2 = x^2 - x^2 + 3x$$

$$15 = 3x$$

$$5 = x \qquad 2x = 10$$

76

The lengths of the legs of the
   original triangle are 5 m.
   and 10 m.

19. x: width of the original
     rectangle

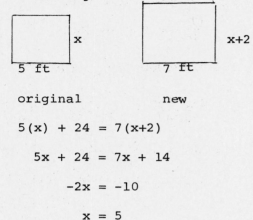

original   new

5(x) + 24 = 7(x+2)

5x + 24 = 7x + 14

-2x = -10

x = 5

Yes the original rectangle was
   5 ft. by 5 ft., a square.

21. x: number of oz. of 50% silver
     alloy to add

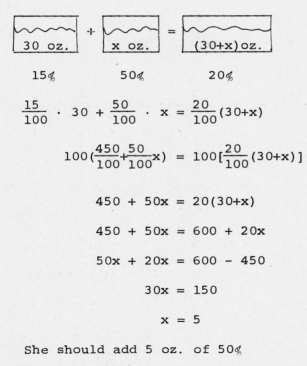

15%   50%   20%

$$\frac{15}{100} \cdot 30 + \frac{50}{100} \cdot x = \frac{20}{100}(30+x)$$

$$100(\frac{450}{100}+\frac{50}{100}x) = 100[\frac{20}{100}(30+x)]$$

450 + 50x = 20(30+x)

450 + 50x = 600 + 20x

50x + 20x = 600 - 450

30x = 150

x = 5

She should add 5 oz. of 50%
   silver alloy.

23. x: number of ml of water to add

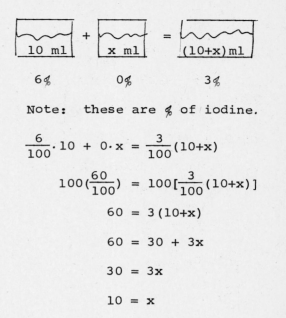

6%   0%   3%

Note: these are % of iodine.

$$\frac{6}{100} \cdot 10 + 0 \cdot x = \frac{3}{100}(10+x)$$

$$100(\frac{60}{100}) = 100[\frac{3}{100}(10+x)]$$

60 = 3(10+x)

60 = 30 + 3x

30 = 3x

10 = x

She should add 10 ml. of water.

25. x: number of kg. of pure lead
      to add

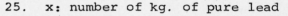

20%   100%   24%

$$\frac{20}{100} \cdot 532 + \frac{100}{100}x = \frac{24}{100}(532+x)$$

$$100(\frac{10,640}{100}+\frac{100}{100}x) = 100[\frac{24}{100}(532+x)]$$

10,640 + 100x = 24(532+x)

10,640 + 100x = 12,768 + 24x

100x - 24x = 12,768 - 10,640

76x = 2,128

x = 28

28 kg. of molten lead should
   be added.

27. x: number of hours it takes both pipes working together to fill the tank

$$\frac{x}{5} + \frac{x}{6} = 1$$

$$30\left(\frac{x}{5} + \frac{x}{6}\right) = 30 \cdot 1$$

$$6x + 5x = 30$$

$$11x = 30$$

$$x = \frac{30}{11}$$

It takes $\frac{30}{11}$ hrs. for both pipes to fill the tank.

29. x: number of minutes to fill the faulty tire

$$\frac{x}{3} - \frac{x}{5} = 1$$

$$15\left(\frac{x}{3} - \frac{x}{5}\right) = 15 \cdot 1$$

$$5x - 3x = 15$$

$$2x = 15$$

$$x = \frac{15}{2} \quad \text{or} \quad 7\frac{1}{2}$$

It will take Jose $7\frac{1}{2}$ min. to fill the tire.

31. x: number of minutes to fill the sink to overflow level

$$\frac{x}{3} + \frac{x}{4} = \frac{1}{2}$$

$$12\left(\frac{x}{3} + \frac{x}{4}\right) = 12 \cdot \frac{1}{2}$$

$$4x + 3x = 6$$

$$7x = 6$$

$$x = \frac{6}{7}$$

It will take $\frac{6}{7}$ min. to fill the sink to overflow level.

33. x: number of hours to empty the tank with both valves and the drain open

$$\frac{x}{\frac{5}{2}} - \frac{x}{5} - \frac{x}{10} = 1$$

$$10\left(\frac{2}{5}x - \frac{4}{5}\frac{x}{10}\right) = 10 \cdot 1$$

$$4x - 2x - x = 10$$

$$x = 10$$

It will take 10 hrs. to empty the tank.

35. x: number of minutes to chop the slaw with Jo and Jo Ann working together

	working alone	working together
Jo	30 min	60 min
Jo Ann	42 min	84 min

$$\frac{x}{60} + \frac{x}{84} = 1$$

$$420\left(\frac{x}{60} + \frac{x}{84}\right) = 420 \cdot 1$$

$$7x + 5x = 420$$

$$12x = 420$$

$$x = 35$$

[420 is LCD for 60, 84]

It will take them 35 minutes working together to chop the slaw.

37.

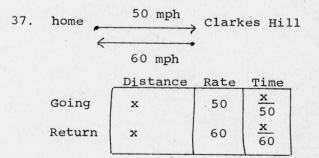

	Distance	Rate	Time
Going	x	50	$\frac{x}{50}$
Return	x	60	$\frac{x}{60}$

78

x: distance from home to Clarkes
   Hill

$$\frac{x}{50} + \frac{x}{60} = 5.5$$

$$300(\frac{x}{50} + \frac{x}{60}) = 300(5.5)$$

$$6x + 5x = 1650$$

$$11x = 1650$$

$$x = 150$$

It is 150 mi. from Henry's home
   to Clarkes Hill.

39.

	Distance	Rate	Time
Midnight Express	(2x)4	2x	4
Freight Train	x(2)	x	2

x: rate of travel of the freight
   train

$$8x = 2x + 210$$

$$6x = 210$$

$$x = 35 \qquad 2x = 70$$

The freight train has traveled
   70 mi. at 4 am.

41. $\frac{1}{8}$ mi/min

$\frac{1}{6}$ mi/min

	Distance	Rate	Time
John	$\frac{1}{6}(3)$	$\frac{1}{6}$	3
Jim	$\frac{1}{8}(x)$	$\frac{1}{8}$	x

x: Jim's time

$$\frac{1}{6}(3) = \frac{1}{8}x$$

$$\frac{1}{2} = \frac{1}{8}x$$

$$8(\frac{1}{2}) = 8(\frac{1}{8}x)$$

$$4 = x \qquad 4 - 3 = 1$$

John started 1 min. after
   Jim started.

43. x: amount invested at 5.5%

12,000-x: amount invested at
   6.5%

$$700 = \frac{5.5}{100} \cdot x + \frac{6.5}{100}(12,000-x)$$

$$100(700) = 100[\frac{5.5}{100}x + \frac{6.5}{100}(12,000-x)]$$

$$70,000 = 5.5x + 6.5(12,000-x)$$

$$70,000 = 5.5x + 78,000 - 6.5x$$

$$70,000 = 78,000 - 1.0x$$

$$70,000 - 78,000 = -x$$

$$-8,000 = -x$$

$$8,000 = x \quad 12,000 - x$$
$$= 4,000$$

He invested $8,000 at 5.5% and
   $4.000 at 6.5%.

45. x: amount invested at 18%

100,000 - x: amount invested at
   12%

$$16,200 = \frac{18}{100}x + \frac{12}{100}(100,000-x)$$

$$100(16,200)$$

$$= 100[\frac{18}{100}x + \frac{12}{100}(100.000-x)]$$

$$1,620,000 = 18x + 12(100,000-x)$$

$$1,620,000 = 18x + 1,200,000 - 12x$$

$1,620,000 - 1,200,000 = 6x$

$420,000 = 6x$

$70,000 = x$

$100,000 - x = 30,000$

He invested \$70,000 at 18% and
  \$30,000 at 12%.

47. x: amount to invest at 8.25%

100,000 - x: amount to invest at
  9.25%

$8,500 = \frac{8.25}{100}x + \frac{9.25}{100}(100,000-x)$

$100(8,500)$

$= 100[\frac{8.25}{100}x + \frac{9.25}{100}(100,000-x)]$

$850,000 = 8.25x + 9.25(100,000-x)$

$850,000 = 8.25x + 925,000 - 9.25x$

$850,000 = -1.0x + 925,000$

$850,000 - 925,000 = -x$

$-75,000 = -x$

$75,000 = x$

$100,000 - x = 25,000$

He should invest \$75,000 in AAAA
  bonds and \$25,000 in AA bonds.

49. x: amount invested at 20%

240,000 - x: amount invested at
  5%.

$\frac{13.75}{100}(240,000) = \frac{20}{100}x$

$- \frac{5}{100}(240,000-x)$

$100[\frac{13.75}{100}(240,000)]$

$= 100[\frac{20}{100}x-\frac{5}{100}(240,000-x)]$

$13.75(240,000)$

$= 20x - 5(240,000-x)$

$3,300,000 = 20x - 1,200,000 + 5x$

$3,300,000 = 25x - 1,200,000$

$3,300,000 + 1,200,000 = 25x$

$4,500,000 = 25x$

$180,000 = x$

$240,000 - x = 60,000$

He invested \$180,000 at 20%
  and \$60,000 at 5%.

51.

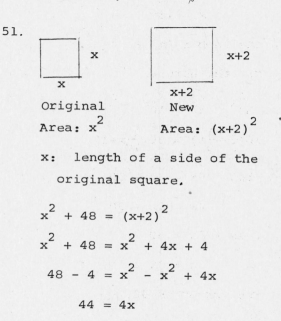

Original   New
Area: x^2 Area: $(x+2)^2$

x: length of a side of the
  original square.

$x^2 + 48 = (x+2)^2$

$x^2 + 48 = x^2 + 4x + 4$

$48 - 4 = x^2 - x^2 + 4x$

$44 = 4x$

$11 = x$

The length of a side of the square
  is 11 in.

53. x: number of tickets given away.

$\frac{1}{2}x = \frac{1}{5}x + 3$

$10(\frac{1}{2}x) = 10(\frac{1}{5}x+3)$

$5x = 2x + 30$

$5x - 2x = 30$

$$3x = 30$$

$$x = 10$$

He gave 10 tickets away.

55. x: the number

$$\frac{1}{2}x + \frac{2}{3}x = x + 3$$

$$6\left(\frac{1}{2}x + \frac{2}{3}x\right) = 6(x+3)$$

$$3x + 4x = 6x + 18$$

$$7x = 6x + 18$$

$$7x - 6x = 18$$

$$x = 18$$

The number is 18.

57. x: the number

$$\frac{1}{3}x - \frac{1}{5}x = \frac{1}{10}x + 1$$

$$30\left(\frac{1}{3}x - \frac{1}{5}x\right) = 30\left(\frac{1}{10}x + 1\right)$$

$$10x - 6x = 3x + 30$$

$$4x = 3x + 30$$

$$4x - 3x = 30$$

$$x = 30$$

The number is 30.

59. shack •⸻⟶ long
          ⟵⸻• bridge

	Distance	Rate	Time
Upstream	20	4-x	$\frac{20}{4-x}$
Downstream	20	4+x	$\frac{20}{4+x}$

x: speed of the current

$$\frac{20}{4-x} = 2\left(\frac{20}{4+x}\right) \quad \text{[Note: LCD is}$$
$$(4-x)(4+x)]$$

$$(4-x)(4+x)\left(\frac{20}{4-x}\right)$$

$$= (4-x)(4+x)2\left(\frac{20}{4+x}\right)$$

$$(4+x)20 = (4-x)40$$

$$80 + 20x = 160 - 40x$$

$$20x + 40x = 160 - 80$$

$$60x = 80$$

$$x = \frac{80}{60} \quad \text{or} \quad \frac{4}{3}$$

The speed of the current is $\frac{4}{3}$ km/hr.

Problem Set 4.4.

1. $$\frac{1}{x} + 2 = 3$$

$$x\left(\frac{1}{x} + 2\right) = x \cdot 3$$

$$x \cdot \frac{1}{x} + x \cdot 2 = 3x$$

$$1 + 2x = 3x$$

$$1 = 3x - 2x$$

$$1 = x \qquad \{1\}$$

3. $$\frac{3}{x} - 1 = \frac{1}{2}$$

$$2x\left(\frac{3}{x} - 1\right) = 2x \cdot \frac{1}{2}$$

$$2x\frac{3}{x} - 2x = x$$

$$6 - 2x = x$$

$$6 = x + 2x$$

$$6 = 3x$$

$$2 = x \qquad \{2\}$$

5. $$\frac{1}{2x} + \frac{1}{x} = \frac{1}{2}$$

$$2x\left(\frac{1}{2x} + \frac{1}{x}\right) = 2x\left(\frac{1}{2}\right)$$

$$2x \cdot \frac{1}{2x} + 2x \cdot \frac{1}{x} = \frac{2x}{2}$$

$$1 + 2 = x$$

$$3 = x \qquad \{3\}$$

7.
$$\frac{2}{3t} + \frac{1}{4} = \frac{3}{4t}$$

$$12t\left(\frac{2}{3t}+\frac{1}{4}\right) = 12t\left(\frac{3}{4t}\right)$$

$$12t\left(\frac{2}{3t}\right) + 12t\left(\frac{1}{4}\right) = 3 \cdot 3$$

$$4 \cdot 2 + 3t = 9$$

$$8 + 3t = 9$$

$$3t = 9 - 8$$

$$3t = 1$$

$$t = \frac{1}{3} \qquad \{\frac{1}{3}\}$$

9.
$$\frac{3}{x-1} + 2 = \frac{5}{x-1}$$

$$(x-1)\left(\frac{3}{x-1}+2\right) = (x-1)\left(\frac{5}{x-1}\right)$$

$$(x-1) \cdot \frac{3}{x-1} + 2(x-1) = (x-1) \cdot \frac{5}{x-1}$$

$$3 + 2(x-1) = 5$$

$$3 + 2x - 2 = 5$$

$$2x + 1 = 5$$

$$2x = 5 - 1$$

$$2x = 4$$

$$x = 2 \qquad \{2\}$$

11.
$$\frac{5}{2x+3} = \frac{1}{2x+3} + 1$$

$$(2x+3)\left(\frac{5}{2x+3}\right) = (2x+3)\left(\frac{1}{2x+3}+1\right)$$

$$(2x+3) \cdot \frac{5}{2x+3} = (2x+3) \cdot \frac{1}{2x+3}$$

$$+ 1(2x+3)$$

$$5 = 1 + 2x + 3$$

$$5 = 4 + 2x$$

$$5 - 4 = 2x$$

$$1 = 2x$$

$$\frac{1}{2} = x \qquad \{\frac{1}{2}\}$$

13.
$$\frac{1.4}{x} + \frac{3.2}{2x} = -1.2$$

$$2x\left(\frac{1.4}{x}+\frac{3.2}{2x}\right) = 2x(-1.2)$$

$$2x \cdot \frac{1.4}{x} + 2x \cdot \frac{3.2}{2x} = -2.4x$$

$$2.8 + 3.2 = -2.4x$$

$$6.0 = -2.4x$$

$$-2.5 = x \qquad \{-2.5\}$$

15.
$$\frac{1}{x+2} + \frac{1}{x} = \frac{12}{x^2+2x}$$

$$\frac{1}{x+2} + \frac{1}{x} = \frac{12}{x(x+2)}$$

$$x(x+2)\left(\frac{1}{x+2}+\frac{1}{x}\right) = x(x+2)\left(\frac{12}{x(x+2)}\right)$$

$$x(x+2) \cdot \frac{1}{x+2} + x(x+2) \cdot \frac{1}{x}$$

$$= x(x+2) \cdot \frac{12}{x(x+2)}$$

$$x(1) + (x+2)(1) = 12$$

$$x + x + 2 = 12$$

$$2x + 2 = 12$$

$$2x = 12 - 2$$

$$2x = 10$$

$$x = 5 \qquad \{5\}$$

17.
$$\frac{2}{x-3} = \frac{4}{x+4}$$

$$(x-3)(x+4) \cdot \frac{2}{x-3} = (x-3)(x+4) \cdot \frac{4}{x+4}$$

$$(x+4)2 = (x-3)4$$

$$2x + 8 = 4x - 12$$

$$2x - 4x = -12 - 8$$

$$-2x = -20$$

$$x = 10 \qquad \{10\}$$

19. $\dfrac{6}{x-3} - \dfrac{3}{x+2} = \dfrac{12}{x^2-x-6}$

$$\dfrac{6}{x-3} - \dfrac{3}{x+2} = \dfrac{12}{(x-3)(x+2)}$$

$$(x-3)(x+2)\left(\dfrac{6}{x-3} - \dfrac{3}{x+2}\right)$$

$$= (x-3)(x+2)\left(\dfrac{12}{(x+3)(x-2)}\right)$$

$$(x-3)(x+2)\cdot\dfrac{6}{x-3} - (x-3)(x+2)\dfrac{3}{x+2}$$

$$= (x-3)(x+2)\cdot\dfrac{12}{(x+3)(x-2)}$$

$$6(x+2) - 3(x-3) = 12$$

$$6x + 12 - 3x + 9 = 12$$

$$3x + 21 = 12$$

$$3x = 12 - 21$$

$$3x = -9$$

$$x = -3 \qquad \{3\}$$

21. $\dfrac{x-3}{x+4} = \dfrac{x-2}{x+3}$

$$(x+4)(x+3)\left(\dfrac{x-3}{x+4}\right) = (x+4)(x+3)\left(\dfrac{x-2}{x+3}\right)$$

$$(x+3)(x-3) = (x+4)(x-2)$$

$$x^2 - 9 = x^2 + 2x - 8$$

$$-9 + 8 = x^2 - x^2 + 2x$$

$$-1 = 2x$$

$$-\dfrac{1}{2} = x \qquad \left\{-\dfrac{1}{2}\right\}$$

23. $\dfrac{-4}{5(x+2)} = \dfrac{3}{x+2}$

$$5(x+2)\left(\dfrac{-4}{5(x+2)}\right) = 5(x+2)\left(\dfrac{3}{x+2}\right)$$

$$-4 = 5\cdot 3$$

$$-4 = 15 \qquad \varnothing$$

25. $\dfrac{4}{1-x} + \dfrac{1}{x} = \dfrac{5}{x^2-x}$

$$\dfrac{4}{1-x} = \dfrac{1}{x} = \dfrac{5}{x(x-1)}$$

$$\dfrac{4}{-(x-1)} + \dfrac{1}{x} = \dfrac{5}{x(x-1)}$$

$$x(x-1)\left(\dfrac{-4}{x-1}+\dfrac{1}{x}\right) = x(x-1)\left(\dfrac{5}{x(x-1)}\right)$$

$$x(x-1)\cdot\dfrac{-4}{x-1} + x(x-1)\cdot\dfrac{1}{x}$$

$$= x(x-1)\cdot\dfrac{5}{x(x-1)}$$

$$-4x + x - 1 = 5$$

$$-3x - 1 = 5$$

$$-3x = 6$$

$$x = -2 \qquad \{-2\}$$

27. $\dfrac{3}{2+x} + \dfrac{2}{2-x} = \dfrac{2x}{x^2-4}$

$$\dfrac{3}{2+x} + \dfrac{2}{2-x} = \dfrac{2x}{(x-2)(x+2)}$$

$$\dfrac{3}{x+2} + \dfrac{2}{-(x-2)} = \dfrac{2x}{(x-2)(x+2)}$$

$$\dfrac{3}{x+2} - \dfrac{2}{x-2} = \dfrac{2x}{(x-2)(x+2)}$$

$$(x-2)(x+2)\left(\dfrac{3}{x+2}-\dfrac{2}{x-2}\right)$$

$$= (x-2)(x+2)\left(\dfrac{2x}{(x-2)(x+2)}\right)$$

$$(x-2)(x+2)\cdot\dfrac{3}{x+2} - (x-2)(x+2)\cdot\dfrac{2}{x-2}$$

$$= (x-2)(x+2)\cdot\dfrac{2x}{(x-2)(x+2)}$$

$$3(x-2) - 2(x+2) = 2x$$

$$3x - 6 = 2x$$

$$x - 10 = 2x$$

$$-10 = 2x - x$$

$$-10 = x \qquad \{-10\}$$

29. JP

K

	D	R	T
John Phillips	56	x	$\frac{56}{x}$
Kenneth	49	x-2	$\frac{49}{x-2}$

x: John Phillip's average rate

$$\frac{56}{x} = \frac{49}{x-2}$$

$$x(x-2)\left(\frac{56}{x}\right) = x(x-2)\left(\frac{49}{x-2}\right)$$

$$(x-2)56 = x \cdot 49$$

$$56x - 112 = 49x$$

$$-112 = -7x$$

$$16 = x$$

His average rate is 16 mph.

31. x: one number

2x: other number

$$\frac{1}{x} + \frac{1}{2x} = \frac{1}{2}$$

$$2x\left(\frac{1}{x}+\frac{1}{2x}\right) = 2x \cdot \frac{1}{2}$$

$$2x \cdot \frac{1}{x} + 2x \cdot \frac{1}{2x} = \frac{2x}{2}$$

$$2 + 1 = x$$

$$3 = x \qquad 2x = 6$$

The numbers are 3 and 6.

33. x: number of girls in the class

$$\frac{32}{x} = \frac{4}{5}$$

$$5x\left(\frac{32}{x}\right) = 5x\left(\frac{4}{5}\right)$$

$$5 \cdot 32 = x \cdot 4$$

$$160 = 4x$$

$$40 = x$$

There are 40 girls in the class.

35. x: number of centimeters in foot

$$\frac{2.54}{1} = \frac{x}{12}$$

$$12(2.54) = 12 \cdot \frac{x}{12}$$

$$30.48 = x$$

There are 30.48 cm. in one foot.

37.
$$\frac{1}{x} + \frac{1}{3} = \frac{1}{4}$$

$$12x\left(\frac{1}{x}+\frac{1}{3}\right) = 12x \cdot \frac{1}{4}$$

$$12x \cdot \frac{1}{x} + 12x \cdot \frac{1}{3} = 12x \cdot \frac{1}{4}$$

$$12 + 4x = 3x$$

$$12 = 3x - 4x$$

$$12 = -x$$

$$-12 = x \qquad \{-12\}$$

39.
$$\frac{2}{y} - \frac{1}{5} = -\frac{1}{4}$$

$$20y\left(\frac{2}{y}-\frac{1}{5}\right) = 20y\left(-\frac{1}{4}\right)$$

$$20y \cdot \frac{2}{4} - 20y \cdot \frac{1}{5} = 20y \cdot \frac{-1}{4}$$

$$40 - 4y = -5y$$

$$40 = -5y + 4y$$

$$40 = -y$$

$$-40 = y \qquad \{-40\}$$

41.
$$\frac{2}{x} - \frac{3}{4} = \frac{1}{x}$$

$$4x\left(\frac{2}{x}-\frac{3}{4}\right) = 4x\left(\frac{1}{x}\right)$$

$$4x \cdot \frac{2}{x} - 4x \cdot \frac{3}{4} = 4x \cdot \frac{1}{x}$$

$$8 - 3x = 4$$

$$-3x = 4 - 8$$

$$-3x = -4$$

$$x = \frac{4}{3} \qquad \left\{\frac{4}{3}\right\}$$

43.
$$\frac{1}{x+1} - \frac{2}{x} = 0$$

$$x(x+1)\left(\frac{1}{x+1} - \frac{2}{x}\right) = x(x+1)(0)$$

$$x(x+1) \cdot \frac{1}{x+1} - x(x+1) \cdot \frac{2}{x} = 0$$

$$x - (x+1)2 = 0$$

$$x - 2x - 2 = 0$$

$$-x - 2 = 0$$

$$-x = 2$$

$$x = -2 \quad \{-2\}$$

45.
$$\frac{4}{2-x} - 1 = \frac{3}{2-x}$$

$$(2-x)\left(\frac{4}{2-x} - 1\right) = (2-x)\left(\frac{3}{2-x}\right)$$

$$(2-x) \cdot \frac{4}{2-x} - (2-x) = (2-x) \cdot \frac{3}{2-x}$$

$$4 - 2 + x = 3$$

$$2 + x = 3$$

$$x = 3 - 2$$

$$x = 1 \qquad \{1\}$$

47.
$$\frac{3}{x} = \frac{5}{x+4}$$

$$x(x+4)\left(\frac{3}{x}\right) = x(x+4)\left(\frac{5}{x+4}\right)$$

$$(x+4)3 = x \cdot 5$$

$$3x + 12 = 5x$$

$$12 = 5x - 3x$$

$$12 = 2x$$

$$6 = x \qquad \{6\}$$

49.
$$\frac{14.3}{w} - \frac{3.1}{2w} = 1.1$$

$$2w\left(\frac{14.3}{w} - \frac{3.1}{2w}\right) = 2w(1.1)$$

$$2w \cdot \frac{14.3}{w} - 2w \cdot \frac{3.1}{2w} = (2w)(1.1)$$

$$2(14.3) - 3.1 = 2.2w$$

$$28.6 - 3.1 = 2.2w$$

$$25.5 = 2.2w$$

$$11.59\overline{0} = w \qquad \{11.5\overline{90}\}$$

51.
$$\frac{16.4}{x} + 12.2 = 1.4$$

$$x\left(\frac{16.4}{x} + 12.2\right) = x(1.4)$$

$$x \cdot \frac{16.4}{x} + x(12.2) = 1.4x$$

$$16.4 + 12.2x = 1.4x$$

$$16.4 = 1.4x - 12.2x$$

$$16.4 = -10.8X$$

$$-1.\overline{518} = x \qquad \{-1.\overline{518}\}$$

53.
$$\frac{4}{x} + \frac{3}{5-x} = \frac{-20}{x^2-5x}$$

$$\frac{4}{x} + \frac{3}{5-x} = \frac{-20}{x(x-5)}$$

$$\frac{4}{x} + \frac{3}{-(x-5)} = \frac{-20}{x(x-5)}$$

$$x(x-5)\left(\frac{4}{x} - \frac{3}{x-5}\right) = x(x-5)\left[\frac{-20}{x(x-5)}\right]$$

$$x(x-5) \cdot \frac{4}{x} - x(x-5) \cdot \frac{3}{x-5}$$

$$= x(x-5) \cdot \frac{-20}{x(x-5)}$$

$$(x-5)4 - x \cdot 3 = -20$$

$$4x - 20 - 3x = -20$$

$$x - 20 = -20$$

$$x = 0$$

$\emptyset$ since $\frac{4}{x}$ is undefined for $x = 0$.

55.
$$\frac{3}{2(x+2)} + \frac{3}{(x+2)^2} = 0$$

$$2(x+2)^2\left[\frac{3}{2(x+2)} + \frac{3}{(x+2)^2}\right] = 2(x+2)^2 \cdot 0$$

$$2(x+2)^2 \cdot \frac{3}{2(x+2)} + 2(x+2)^2 \cdot \frac{3}{(x+2)^2}$$

$$= 0$$

85

$(x+2)3 + 2 \cdot 3 = 0$

$3x + 6 + 2 \cdot 3 = 0$

$3x + 12 = 0$

$3x = -12$

$x = -4 \qquad \{-4\}$

57. $\dfrac{2}{x+1} + \dfrac{3}{x+2} = \dfrac{-3}{x^2+3x+2}$

$\dfrac{2}{x+1} + \dfrac{3}{x+2} = \dfrac{-3}{(x+2)(x+1)}$

$(x+1)(x+2)\left(\dfrac{2}{x+1}+\dfrac{3}{x+2}\right)$

$= (x+1)(x+2) \cdot \left[\dfrac{-3}{(x+2)(x+1)}\right]$

$(x+1)(x+2)\cdot\dfrac{2}{x+1} + (x+1)(x+2)\cdot\dfrac{3}{x+2}$

$= (x+1)(x+2)$

$(x+2)2 + (x+1)3 = -3$

$2x + 4 + 3x + 3 = -3$

$5x + 7 = -3$

$5x = -3 + -7$

$5x = -10$

$x = -2$

$\emptyset$ since $\dfrac{3}{x+2}$ and $\dfrac{-3}{(x+2)(x+1)}$ are

undefined for $x = -2$.

59. $\dfrac{u-2}{u+3} = \dfrac{u-1}{u+2}$

$(u+3)(u+2)\left(\dfrac{u-3}{u+3}\right) = (u+3)(u+2)\left(\dfrac{u-1}{u+2}\right)$

$(u+2)(u-2) = (u+3)(u-1)$

$u^2 - 4 = u^2 + 2u - 3$

$-4 + 3 = u^2 - u^2 + 2u$

$-1 = 2u$

$-\dfrac{1}{2} = u \qquad \{-\dfrac{1}{2}\}$

61. $\dfrac{3}{x-1} + x = \dfrac{x^2}{x-1}$

$(x-1)\left(\dfrac{3}{x-1}+x\right) = \left(x-1(\dfrac{x^2}{x-1}\right)$

$(x-1)\cdot\dfrac{3}{x-1} + (x-1)x = (x-1)\cdot\dfrac{x^2}{x-1}$

$3 + x^2 - x = x^2$

$3 = x^2 - x^2 + x$

$3 = x \qquad \{3\}$

63. $\dfrac{1}{x-5} + \dfrac{x}{25-x^2} = 0$

$\dfrac{1}{x-5} + \dfrac{x}{(5-x)(x+x)} = 0$

$\dfrac{1}{-(5-x)} + \dfrac{x}{(5-x)(5+x)} = 0$

$\dfrac{-1}{5-x} + \dfrac{x}{(5-x)(5+x)} = 0$

$(5-x)(5+x)\left[\dfrac{-1}{5-x}+\dfrac{x}{(5-x)(5+x)}\right]$

$= (5-x)(5+x)\cdot 0$

$-1(5+x) + x = 0$

$-5 - x + x = 0$

$-5 = 0 \qquad\qquad \emptyset$

65. $\dfrac{3}{x-1} - \dfrac{1}{x+2} = \dfrac{9}{x^2+x-2}$

$\dfrac{3}{x-1} - \dfrac{1}{x+2} = \dfrac{9}{(x+2)(x-1)}$

$(x+2)(x-1)\left(\dfrac{3}{x-1}-\dfrac{1}{x+2}\right)$

$= (x+2)(x-1)\left[\dfrac{9}{(x+2)(x-1)}\right]$

$3(x+2) - 1(x-1) = 9$

$3x + 6 - x + 1 = 9$

$2x + 7 = 9$

$2x = 9 - 7$

$2x = 2$

$$x = 1$$

$\emptyset$ since $\frac{3}{x-1}$ and $\frac{9}{(x+2)(x-1)}$ are undefined for $x = 1$.

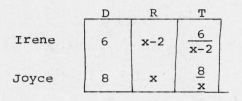

	D	R	T
Irene	6	x-2	$\frac{6}{x-2}$
Joyce	8	x	$\frac{8}{x}$

x: Joyce's rate

$$\frac{6}{x-2} = \frac{8}{x}$$

$$x(x-2)(\frac{6}{x-2}) = x(x-2)\frac{8}{x}$$

$$6x = (x-2)8$$

$$6x = 8x - 16$$

$$6x - 8x = -16$$

$$-2x = -16$$

$$x = 8$$

Her rate is 8mph.

69.

$$\xrightarrow{\quad x \quad} \text{Work}$$

Home $\xleftarrow{\quad x+20 \quad}$

	D	R	T
Going	15	x	$\frac{15}{x}$
Return	25	x+20	$\frac{25}{x+20}$

x: speed going to work

$$x(x+20)(\frac{15}{x}) = x(x+20)(\frac{25}{x+20})$$

$$(x+20)15 = x\cdot 25$$

$$15x + 300 = 25x$$

$$300 = 25x - 15x$$

$$300 = 10x$$

$$30 = x$$

His speed going to work is 30 mph.

71. x: the number

$$\frac{1}{x-1} = 2(\frac{1}{x})$$

$$\frac{1}{x-1} = \frac{2}{x}$$

$$x(x-1)(\frac{1}{x-1}) = x(x-1)\frac{2}{x}$$

$$x = (x-1)2$$

$$x = 2x - 2$$

$$x - 2x = -2$$

$$-x = -2$$

$$x = 2$$

The number is 2.

73. x: number of republicans

$$\frac{3}{8} = \frac{45}{x}$$

$$8x(\frac{3}{8}) = 8x(\frac{45}{x})$$

$$3x = 8\cdot 45$$

$$3x = 360$$

$$x = 120$$

There are 120 republicans.

75. x: number of liters in 5 gallons.

$$\frac{3.8}{1} = \frac{x}{5}$$

$$5(3.8) = 5(\frac{x}{5})$$

$$19 = x$$

There are 19 ℓ. in 5 gallons.

77.

$$\frac{x}{x+4} - 1 = \frac{x}{x+4}$$

$$(x+4)(\frac{x}{x+4}-1) = (x+4)(\frac{x}{x+4})$$

$$(x+4)\cdot\frac{x}{x+4} - (x+4)1$$
$$= (x+4)\cdot\frac{x}{x+4}$$

$$x - (x+4) = x$$

$$x - x - 4 = x$$

$$-4 = x$$

$\emptyset$ since $\frac{x}{x+4}$ is undefined when

$x = -4$.

Problem Set 4.5.

1. $|x| = 3$

   $x = 3$ or $x = -3$ $\{3,-3\}$

3. $|2x| = 5$

   $2x = 5$ or $2x = -5$

   $x = \frac{5}{2}$ or $x = -\frac{5}{2}$ $\{\frac{5}{2},-\frac{5}{2}\}$

5. $|1-2x| = 4$

   $1 - 2x = 4$ or $1 - 2x = -4$

   $-2x = 4 - 1$ $-2x = -4 - 1$

   $-2x = 3$ $- 2x = -5$

   $x = \frac{-3}{2}$ or $x = \frac{5}{2}$ $\{-\frac{3}{2},\frac{5}{2}\}$

7. $|\frac{1}{4}x| = 1$

   $\frac{1}{4}x = 1$ or $\frac{1}{4}x = -1$

   $4(\frac{1}{4}x) = 4 \cdot 1$ $4(\frac{1}{4}x) = 4 \cdot (-1)$

   $x = 4$ or $x = -4$ $\{4,-4\}$

9. $|\frac{3x}{2} - \frac{1}{2}| = \frac{1}{4}$

   $\frac{3x}{2} - \frac{1}{2} = \frac{1}{4}$ or $\frac{3x}{2} - \frac{1}{2} = -\frac{1}{4}$

   $4(\frac{3x}{2}-\frac{1}{2}) = 4 \cdot \frac{1}{4}$ $4(\frac{3x}{2}-\frac{1}{2}) = 4(-\frac{1}{4})$

   $4 \cdot \frac{3x}{2} - 4 \cdot \frac{1}{2} = 4 \cdot \frac{1}{4}$

   $4 \cdot \frac{3x}{2} - 4 \cdot \frac{1}{2} = 4(-\frac{1}{4})$

   $6x - 2 = 1$ $6x - 2 = -1$

$6x = 1 + 2$ $6x = -1 + 2$

$6x = 3$ $6x = 1$

$x = \frac{3}{6} = \frac{1}{2}$ or $x = \frac{1}{6}$ $\{\frac{1}{2},\frac{1}{6}\}$

11. $|x| = -2$ $\emptyset$

13. $|x| = 0$

   $x = 0$ $\{0\}$

15. $|2x-5| = 0$

   $2x - 5 = 0$

   $2x = 5$

   $x = \frac{5}{2}$ $\{\frac{5}{2}\}$

17. $|2x-3| - 5 = 0$

   $|2x-3| = 5$

   $2x - 3 = 5$ or $2x - 3 = -5$

   $2x = 5 + 3$ $2x = -5 + 3$

   $2x = 8$ $2x = -2$

   $x = 4$ or $x = -1$ $\{4,-1\}$

19. $|5-2x| + 2 = 5$

   $|5-2x| = 5 - 2$

   $|5-2x| = 3$

   $5 - 2x = 3$ or $5 - 2x = -3$

   $-2x = 3 - 5$ $-2x = -3 - 5$

   $-2x = -2$ $-2x = -8$

   $x = 1$ or $x = 4$ $\{1,4\}$

21. $7 + |2x+3| =$

   $|2x+3| = -2$ $\emptyset$

23. $|x+2| = |x|$

   $x + 2 = x$ or $x + 2 = -x$

   $2 = x - x$ $2 = -x - x$

   $2 = 0$ $2 = -2x$

       $\emptyset$ $-1 = x$ $\{-1\}$

88

25. $|x+1| - |x-3| = 0$

$|x+1| = |x-3|$

$x + 1 = x - 3$ or $x + 1 = -(x-3)$

$x - x = -3 - 1$ $\qquad$ $x + 1 = -x + 3$

$\qquad 0 = -4$ $\qquad\qquad$ $x + x = 3 - 1$

$\qquad \emptyset$ $\qquad\qquad\qquad$ $2x = 2$

$\qquad\qquad\qquad\qquad$ $x = 1$ $\{1\}$

27. $|2x-1| = |x+3|$

$2x - 1 = x + 3$ or $2x - 1 = -(x+3)$

$2x - x = 3 + 1$ $\qquad$ $2x - 1 = -x - 3$

$\qquad x = 4$ $\qquad\qquad$ $2x + x = -3 + 1$

$\qquad\qquad\qquad\qquad$ $3x = -2$

$\qquad\qquad\qquad\qquad$ $x = -\dfrac{2}{3}$

$\qquad\qquad\qquad\qquad$ $\{-\dfrac{2}{3}, 4\}$

29. $\left|\dfrac{x+1}{3}\right| - |x| = 0$

$\left|\dfrac{x+1}{3}\right| = |x|$

$\dfrac{x+1}{3} = x$ or $\dfrac{x+1}{3} = -x$

$3\left(\dfrac{(x+1)}{3}\right) = 3 \cdot x$ $\qquad$ $3\left(\dfrac{x+1}{3}\right) = 3(-x)$

$x + 1 = 3x$ $\qquad\qquad$ $x + 1 = -3x$

$1 = 3x - x$ $\qquad\qquad$ $1 = -3x - x$

$1 = 2x$ $\qquad\qquad\qquad$ $1 = -4x$

$\dfrac{1}{2} = x$ or $\qquad$ $-\dfrac{1}{4} = x$ $\quad \{-\dfrac{1}{4}, \dfrac{1}{2}\}$

31. $|x| = 6$

$x = 6$ or $x = -6$ $\qquad$ $\{6, -6\}$

33. $|2x| = 0$

$2x = 0$

$x = 0$ $\qquad\qquad$ $\{0\}$

35. $|x-4| = 2$

$x - 4 = 2$ $\qquad$ or $\qquad$ $x - 4 = -2$

$x = 2 + 4$ $\qquad\qquad$ $x = -2 + 4$

$x = 6$ $\qquad$ or $\qquad$ $x = 2$

$\qquad\qquad\qquad\qquad$ $\{2, 6\}$

37. $|x-6| = -7$ $\qquad\qquad$ $\emptyset$

39. $|x+13| = 7$

$x + 13 = 7$ $\qquad$ or $\qquad$ $x + 13 = -7$

$x = 7 - 13$ $\qquad\qquad$ $x = -7 - 13$

$x = -6$ $\qquad$ or $\qquad$ $x = -20$

$\qquad\qquad\qquad\qquad$ $\{-20, -6\}$

41. $|4x+5| - 4 = 4$

$|4x+5| = 4 + 4$

$|4x+5| = 8$

$4x + 5 = 8$ $\qquad$ or $\qquad$ $4x + 5 = -8$

$4x = 8 - 5$ $\qquad\qquad$ $4x = -8 - 5$

$4x = 3$ $\qquad\qquad\qquad$ $4x = -13$

$x = \dfrac{3}{4}$ $\qquad\qquad\qquad$ $x = \dfrac{-13}{4}$

$\qquad\qquad\qquad\qquad$ $(\dfrac{-13}{4}, \dfrac{3}{4}\}$

43. $|10x-3| = 0$

$10x - 3 = 0$

$10x = 3$

$x = \dfrac{3}{10}$ $\qquad\qquad$ $\{\dfrac{3}{10}\}$

45. $|5x+11| = 9$

$5x + 11 = 9$ $\qquad$ or $\qquad$ $5x + 11 = -9$

$5x = 9 - 11$ $\qquad\qquad$ $5x = -9 - 11$

$5x = -2$ $\qquad\qquad\qquad$ $5x = -20$

$x = \dfrac{-2}{5}$ $\qquad$ or $\qquad$ $x = -4$

$\qquad\qquad\qquad\qquad$ $\{-4, -\dfrac{2}{5}\}$

47. $6 - |2.5x-4| = 0$

$\quad 6 = |2.5x-4|$

$\quad 6 = 2.5x - 4 \quad$ or $\quad -6 = 2.5x - 4$

$\quad 4+6 = 2.5x \qquad\quad -6+4 = 2.5x$

$\quad 10 = 2.5x \qquad\qquad -2 = 2.5x$

$\quad 4 = x \qquad\qquad\quad -0.8 = x \quad \{-0.8, 4\}$

49. $|2.3-x| = 4.5$

$\quad 2.3 - x = 4.5 \qquad 2.3 - x = -4.5$

$\quad -x = 4.5 - 2.3 \qquad -x = -4.5 - 2.3$

$\quad -x = 2.2 \qquad\qquad -x = -6.8$

$\quad x = -2.2 \quad$ or $\quad x = 6.8$

$\qquad\qquad\qquad\qquad \{-2.2, 6.8\}$

51. $|2s| = |s+3|$

$\quad 2s = s + 3 \quad$ or $\quad 2s = -(s+3)$

$\quad 2s - s = 3 \qquad\qquad 2s = -s - 3$

$\qquad\quad s = 3 \qquad\qquad 2s + s = -3$

$\qquad\qquad\qquad\qquad\quad 3s = -3$

$\qquad\qquad\qquad\qquad\quad s = -1$

$\qquad\qquad\qquad\qquad\quad (-1, 3\}$

53. $|x+7| = |x-4|$

$\quad x + 7 = x - 4 \quad$ or $\quad x + 7 = -(x-4)$

$\quad x - x = -4 - 7 \qquad x + 7 = -x + 4$

$\qquad 0 = -11 \qquad\qquad x + x = 4 - 7$

$\qquad \emptyset \qquad\qquad\qquad 2x = -3$

$\qquad\qquad\qquad\qquad\qquad x = -\dfrac{3}{2}$

$\qquad\qquad\qquad\qquad\qquad \{-\dfrac{3}{2}\}$

55. $|3x+4| = |x-2|$

$3x + 4 = x - 2 \quad$ or $\quad 3x + 4 = -(x-2)$

$3x - x = -2 - 4 \qquad 3x + 4 = -x + 2$

$\quad 2x = -6 \qquad\qquad 3x + x = 2 - 4$

$\qquad x = -3 \qquad\qquad\quad 4x = -2$

$\qquad\qquad\qquad\qquad\qquad x = -\dfrac{2}{4}$

$\qquad\qquad\qquad\qquad\qquad\ = -\dfrac{1}{2}$

$\qquad\qquad\qquad\qquad \{-3, -\dfrac{1}{2}\}$

57. $|x+1| = |2x+1|$

$\quad x + 1 = 2x + 1 \quad$ or $\quad x + 1 = -(2x+1)$

$\quad x - 2x = 1 - 1 \qquad\quad x + 1 = -2x - 1$

$\qquad -x = 0 \qquad\qquad x + 2x = -1 - 1$

$\qquad x = 0 \qquad\qquad\quad 3x = -2$

$\qquad\qquad\qquad\qquad\qquad x = -\dfrac{2}{3}$

$\qquad\qquad\qquad\qquad \{-\dfrac{2}{3}, 0\}$

59. $|2x-5| = |4x+3|$

$\quad 2x - 5 = 4x + 3 \quad$ or $\quad 2x - 5 = -(4x+3)$

$\quad 2x - 4x = 3 + 5 \qquad\quad 2x - 5 = -4x - 3$

$\qquad -2x = 8 \qquad\qquad 2x + 4x = -3 + 5$

$\qquad x = -4 \qquad\qquad\quad 6x = 2$

$\qquad\qquad\qquad\qquad\qquad x = \dfrac{2}{6}$

$\qquad\qquad\qquad\qquad\qquad\ = \dfrac{1}{3}$

$\qquad\qquad\qquad\qquad \{-4, \dfrac{1}{3}\}$

61. $|2x+9| = |7-x|$

$\quad 2x + 9 = 7 - x \quad$ or $\quad 2x + 9 = -(7-x)$

$\quad 2x + x = 7 - 9 \qquad\quad 2x + 9 = -7 + x$

$\qquad 3x = -2 \qquad\qquad 2x - x = -7 - 9$

$\qquad x = -\dfrac{2}{3} \qquad\qquad\quad x = -16$

$\qquad\qquad\qquad\qquad \{-16, -\dfrac{2}{3}\}$

63. $|9x-5| = |x+3|$

$9x - 5 = x + 3$ or $9x - 5 = -(x+3)$

$9x - x = 3 + 5$ $\qquad 9x - 5 = -x - 3$

$8x = 8$ $\qquad 9x + x = -3 + 5$

$x = 1$ $\qquad 10x = 2$

$$x = \frac{2}{10}$$

$$= \frac{1}{5}$$

$$\{1, \tfrac{1}{5}\}$$

65. $|x+1| = |\tfrac{1}{2}x|$

$x + 1 = \tfrac{1}{2}x$ $\qquad$ or $x + 1 = -\tfrac{1}{2}x$

$2(x+1) = 2(\tfrac{1}{2}x)$ $\qquad 2(x+1) = 2(-\tfrac{1}{2}x)$

$2x + 2 = x$ $\qquad 2x + 2 = -x$

$2 = x - 2x$ $\qquad 2 = -x - 2x$

$2 = -x$ $\qquad 2 = -3x$

$-2 = x$ $\qquad$ or $-\tfrac{2}{3} = x$

$$\{-2, -\tfrac{2}{3}\}$$

67. x: the number

$|x| = 3$

$x = 3$ $\quad$ or $\quad x = -3$

The numbers are 3 and -3.

69. x: the number

$|4x-3| = 1$

$4x - 3 = 1$ $\quad$ or $\quad 4x - 3 = -1$

$4x = 1 + 3$ $\qquad 4x = -1 + 3$

$4x = 4$ $\qquad 4x = 2$

$x = 1$ $\quad$ or $\quad x = \tfrac{2}{4} = \tfrac{1}{2}$

The numbers are $\tfrac{1}{2}$ and 1.

71. $|x-5| = a.$ $\quad a > 0$

$x - 5 = a$ $\qquad$ or $\qquad x - 5 = -a$

$x = a + 5$ $\qquad\qquad x = -a + 5$

$\qquad\qquad\qquad\qquad = 5 - a$

$$\{a+5 \ \ 5-a\}$$

73. $|x-a| = b,$ $b > 0$

$x - a = b$ $\quad$ or $\quad x - a = -b$

$x = a + b$ $\qquad\qquad x = a - b$

$$\{a+b, a-b\}$$

75. $|2x-a| = |x|$

$2x - a = x$ $\quad$ or $\quad 2x - a = -x$

$-a = x - 2x$ $\qquad\qquad -a = -x - 2x$

$-a = -x$ $\qquad\qquad -a = -3x$

$a = x$ $\qquad\qquad\qquad \dfrac{a}{3} = x$

$$\{a, \tfrac{a}{3}\}$$

77. $|2x-3| = x + 1$

$2x - 3 = x + 1$ or $2x - 3 = -(x+1)$

$2x - x = 1 + 3$ $\qquad 2x - 3 = -x - 1$

$x = 4$ $\qquad\qquad 2x + x = -1 + 3$

$$3x = 2$$

$$x = \frac{2}{3}$$

Checking,

LS: $|2(4)-3| = |8-3| = |5| = 5$

RS: $4 + 1 = 5$ $\qquad$ Yes

Checking,

LS: $|2(\tfrac{2}{3})-3| = |\tfrac{4}{3}-3| = |\tfrac{-5}{3}| = \tfrac{5}{3}$

RS: $\tfrac{2}{3} + 1 = \tfrac{5}{3}$

$$\{4\}$$

79. $|x+5| = x + 2$

79. $x + 5 = x + 2$ or $x + 5 = -(x+2)$

　　$x - x = 2 - 5$ 　　 $x + 5 = -x - 2$

　　　$0 = -3$ 　　　 $x + x = -2 - 5$

　　　$\emptyset$ 　　　　 $2x = -7$

　　　　　　　　 $x = -\dfrac{7}{2}$ 　$\emptyset$

Checking,

LS: $\left| -\dfrac{7}{2}+5 \right| = \left| \dfrac{3}{2} \right| = \dfrac{3}{2}$

RS: $-\dfrac{7}{2} + 1 = -\dfrac{3}{2}$ 　No

Problem Set 4.6.

1. 　　$\sqrt{x+1} = 2$

　　$(\sqrt{x+1})^2 = (2)^2$

　　　$x + 1 = 4$

　　　　$x = 4 - 1$

　　　　$x = 3$

Checking,

LS: $\sqrt{3+1} = \sqrt{4} = 2$

RS: 2

$\{3\}$ is the solution set.

3. 　　$\sqrt{2t+3} = 5$

　　$(\sqrt{2t+3})^2 = (5)^2$

　　　$2t + 3 = 25$

　　　　$2t = 25 - 3$

　　　　$2t = 22$

　　　　$t = 11$

Checking,

LS: $\sqrt{2(11)+3} = \sqrt{22+3} = \sqrt{25} = 5$

RS: 5

$\{11\}$ is the solution set.

5. 　　$\sqrt{2-x} = 3$

　　$(\sqrt{2-x})^2 = 3^2$

　　　$2 - x = 9$

　　　$-x = 9 - 2$

　　　$-x = 7$

　　　$x = -7$

Checking,

LS: $\sqrt{2--7} = \sqrt{9} = 3$

RS: 3

$\{-7\}$ is the solution set

7. 　　$\sqrt{x} = 0$

　　$(\sqrt{x})^2 = 0^2$

　　　$x = 0$

Checking,

LS: $= \sqrt{0} = 0$

RS: $= 0$

$\{0\}$ is the solution set.

9. 　　$\sqrt{x-3} = -8$

　　$(\sqrt{x-3})^2 = (-8)^2$

　　　$x - 3 = 64$

　　　　$x = 64 + 3$

　　　　$x = 67$

Checking,

LS: $\sqrt{67-3} = \sqrt{64} = 8$

RS: -8

$\emptyset$ is the solution set.

11. 　　$\sqrt{w+1} = \sqrt{3w-1}$

　　$(\sqrt{w+1})^2 = (\sqrt{3w-1})^2$

　　　$w + 1 = 3w - 1$

$$1 + 1 = 3w - w$$

$$2 = 2w$$

$$1 = w$$

Checking,

LS: $\sqrt{1+1} = \sqrt{2}$

RS: $\sqrt{3(1)-1} = \sqrt{3-1} = \sqrt{2}$

$\{1\}$ is the solution set.

13.
$$\sqrt{3x+2} + \sqrt{2x+7} = 0$$

$$\sqrt{3x+2} = -\sqrt{2x+7}$$

$$(\sqrt{3x+2})^2 = (-\sqrt{2x+7})^2$$

$$3x + 2 = 2x + 7$$

$$3x - 2x = 7 - 2$$

$$x = 5$$

Checking,

LS: $\sqrt{3(5)+2} + \sqrt{2(5)+7}$

$$= \sqrt{15+2} + \sqrt{10+7}$$

$$= \sqrt{17} + \sqrt{17} = 2\sqrt{17}$$

RS: 0

$\emptyset$ is the solution set.

15.
$$\sqrt{x+1} = \sqrt{2x-2}$$

$$(\sqrt{x+1})^2 = (\sqrt{2x-2})^2$$

$$x + 1 = 2x - 2$$

$$x - 2x = -2 - 1$$

$$-x = -3$$

$$x = 3$$

Checking,

LS: $\sqrt{3+1} = \sqrt{4} = 2$

RS: $\sqrt{2(3)-2} = \sqrt{6-2} = \sqrt{4} = 2$

$\{3\}$ is the solution set.

17.
$$\sqrt{x-1} = \sqrt{x+1}$$

$$(\sqrt{x-1})^2 = (\sqrt{x+1})^2$$

$$x - 1 = x + 1$$

$$x - X = 1 + 1$$

$$0 = 2$$

$\emptyset$ is the solution set.

19.
$$12 = 3\sqrt{x-1}$$

$$(12)^2 = (3\sqrt{x-1})^2$$

$$144 = 9(x-1)$$

$$144 = 9x - 9$$

$$144 + 9 = 9x$$

$$153 = 9x$$

$$17 = x$$

Checking,

LS: 12

RS: $3\sqrt{17-1} = 3\sqrt{16} = 3 \cdot 4 = 12$

$\{17\}$ is the solution set.

21.
$$\sqrt{2x+3} - 3\sqrt{x-2} = 0$$

$$\sqrt{2x+3} = 3\sqrt{x-2}$$

$$(\sqrt{2x+3})^2 = (3\sqrt{x-2})^2$$

$$2x + 3 = 9(x-2)$$

$$2x + 3 = 9x - 18$$

$$3 + 18 = 9x - 2x$$

$$21 = 7x$$

$$3 = x$$

Checking,

LS: $\sqrt{2(3)+3} - 3\sqrt{3-2}$

$$= \sqrt{6+3} - 3\sqrt{1}$$

$$= \sqrt{9} - 3\sqrt{1}$$

$$3 - 3 = 0$$

RS: 0

{3} is the solution set.

23. $\sqrt{x^2+3} = x + 1$

$(\sqrt{x^2+3})^2 = (x+1)^2$

$x^2 + 3 = x^2 + 2x + 1$

$3 - 1 = x^2 - x^2 + 2x$

$2 = 2x$

$1 = x$

Checking,

LS: $\sqrt{1^2+3} = \sqrt{1+3} = \sqrt{4} = 2$

RS: $1 + 1 = 2$

{1} is the solution set.

25. $\sqrt{y^2-2y} = -y$

$(\sqrt{y^2-2y})^2 = (-y)^2$

$y^2 - 2y = y^2$

$y^2 - y^2 - 2y = 0$

$-2y = 0$

$y = 0$

Checking.

LS: $\sqrt{0^2-2\cdot0} = \sqrt{0} = 0$

RS: $-0 = 0$

{0} is the solution set.

27. $\sqrt{x^2+x} = x$

$(\sqrt{x^2+x})^2 = (x)^2$

$x^2 + x = x^2$

$x^2 - x^2 + x = 0$

$x = 0$

Checking:

LS: $\sqrt{0^2+0} = \sqrt{0} = 0$

RS: 0

{0} is the solution set.

29. $\sqrt{x^2-4} = x + 2$

$(\sqrt{x^2-4})^2 = (x+2)^2$

$x^2 - 4 = x^2 + 4x + 4$

$-4 - 4 = x^2 - x^2 + 4x$

$-8 = 4x$

$-2 = x$

Checking,

LS: $\sqrt{(-2)^2-4} = \sqrt{4-4} = \sqrt{0} = 0$

RS: $-2 + 2 = 0$

{-2} is the solution set.

31. $\sqrt{4x^2+9} + 1 = 2x$

$\sqrt{4x^2+9} = 2x - 1$

$(\sqrt{4x^2+9})^2 = (2x-1)^2$

$4x^2 + 9 = 4x^2 - 4x + 1$

$ = 4x^2 - 4x^2 - 4x$

$8 = -4x$

$-2 = x$

Checking,

LS: $\sqrt{4(-2)^2+9} + 1 = \sqrt{16+9} + 1$

$= \sqrt{25} + 1$

$= 5 + 1$

$= 6$

RS: $2(-2) = -4$

$\emptyset$ is the solution set.

33. $\sqrt{z-5} = -7$

$(\sqrt{z-5})^2 = (-7)^2$

94

$$z - 5 = 49$$
$$z = 49 + 5$$
$$z = 54$$

Checking

LS: $\sqrt{54-5} = \sqrt{49} = 7$

RS: -7

$\emptyset$ is the solution set.

35. $\sqrt{3x+4} = 4$

$$(\sqrt{3x+4})^2 = (4)^2$$
$$3x + 4 = 16$$
$$3x = 16 - 4$$
$$3x = 12$$
$$x = 4$$

Checking,

LS: $\sqrt{3(4)+4} = \sqrt{12+4} = \sqrt{16} = 4$

RS: 4

$\{4\}$ is the solution set.

37. $\sqrt{1-x} = 5$

$$(\sqrt{1-x})^2 = (5)^2$$
$$1 - x = 25$$
$$-x = 25 - 1$$
$$-x = 24$$
$$x = 24$$

Checking,

LS: $\sqrt{1-(-24)} = \sqrt{1+24} = \sqrt{25} = 5$

RS: 5

$\{-24\}$ is the solution set.

39. $\sqrt{3-5x} = -2$

$$(\sqrt{3-5x})^2 = (-2)^2$$

$$3 - 5x = 4$$
$$-5x = 4 - 3$$
$$-5x = 1$$
$$x = \frac{-1}{5}$$

Checking,

LS: $\sqrt{3-5(-\frac{1}{5})} = \sqrt{3+1} = \sqrt{4} = 2$

RS: -2

$\emptyset$ is the solution set.

41. $\sqrt{2-t} = 0$

$$(\sqrt{2-t})^2 = 0^2$$
$$2 - t = 0$$
$$-t = 0 - 2$$
$$-t = -2$$
$$t = 2$$

Checking,

LS: $\sqrt{2-t} = \sqrt{2-2} = \sqrt{0} = 0$

RS: 0

$\{2\}$ is the solution set.

43. $\sqrt{2x-1} = 3$

$$(\sqrt{2x-1})^2 = 3^2$$
$$2x - 1 = 9$$
$$2x = 9 + 1$$
$$2x = 10$$
$$x = 5$$

Checking,

LS: $\sqrt{2x-1} = \sqrt{2(5)-1} = \sqrt{10-1}$

$$= \sqrt{9} = 3$$

RS: 3

$\{5\}$ is the solution set.

45. $\sqrt{2-x} = \sqrt{x+3}$

   $(\sqrt{2-x})^2 = (\sqrt{x+3})^2$

   $2 - x = x + 3$

   $-x - x = 3 - 2$

   $-2x = 1$

   $x = -\dfrac{1}{2}$

Checking,

LS: $\sqrt{2-(-\dfrac{1}{2})} = \sqrt{2+\dfrac{1}{2}} = \sqrt{\dfrac{5}{2}}$

RS: $\sqrt{x+3} = \sqrt{-\dfrac{1}{2}+3} = \sqrt{\dfrac{5}{2}}$

$\{-\dfrac{1}{2}\}$ is the solution set.

47. $\sqrt{1-3s} + \sqrt{2s+11} = 0$

   $\sqrt{1-3s} = -\sqrt{2s+11}$

   $(\sqrt{1-3s})^2 = (-\sqrt{2s+11})^2$

   $1 - 3s = 2s + 11$

   $-3s - 2s = 11 - 1$

   $-5s = 10$

   $s = -2$

Checking,

LS: $\sqrt{1-3(-2)} + \sqrt{2(-2)+11}$

   $= \sqrt{1+6} + \sqrt{-4+11}$

   $= \sqrt{7} + \sqrt{7}$

RS: 0

$\emptyset$ is the solution set.

49. $\sqrt{1+3x} = \sqrt{3x}$

   $(\sqrt{1+3x})^2 = (\sqrt{3x})^2$

   $1 + 3x = 3x$

   $1 = 3x - 3x$

   $1 = 0$

$\emptyset$ is the solution set.

51. $3\sqrt{6-x} = 2\sqrt{x+46}$

   $(3\sqrt{6-x})^2 = (2\sqrt{x+46})^2$

   $9(6-x) = 4(x+46)$

   $54 - 9x = 4x + 184$

   $-9x - 4x = 184 - 54$

   $-13x = 130$

   $x = -10$

Checking,

LS: $3\sqrt{6-(-10)} = 3\sqrt{6+10} = 3\sqrt{16}$

   $= 3.4 = 12$

RS: $2\sqrt{-10+46} = 2\sqrt{36} = 2.6 = 12$

$\{-10\}$ is the solution set.

53. $2\sqrt{x} = \sqrt{3x+1}$

   $(2\sqrt{x})^2 = (\sqrt{3x+1})^2$

   $4x = 3x + 1$

   $4x - 3x = 1$

   $x = 1$

Checking,

LS: $2\sqrt{1} = 2 \cdot 1 = 2$

RS: $\sqrt{3(1)+1} = \sqrt{3+1} = \sqrt{4} = 2$

$\{1\}$ is the solution set.

55. $\sqrt{x^2-1} = 1 - x$

   $(\sqrt{x^2-1})^2 = (1-x)^2$

   $x^2 - 1 = 1 - 2x + x^2$

   $-1 - 1 = -2x + x^2 - x^2$

   $-2 = -2x$

   $1 = x$

96

Checking,

LS: $\sqrt{1^2-1} = \sqrt{1-1} = \sqrt{0} = 0$

RS: $1 - 1 = 0$

{1} is the solution set.

57. $\sqrt{x^2-3x} = x - 3$

$(\sqrt{x^2-3x})^2 = (x-3)^2$

$x^2 - 3x = x^2 - 6x + 9$

$x^2 - x^2 - 3x + 6x = 9$

$3x = 9$

$x = 3$

Checking,

LS: $\sqrt{3^2-3\cdot3} = \sqrt{9-9} = \sqrt{0} = 0$

RS: $3 - 3 = 0$

{3} is the solution set.

59. $\sqrt{x^2+11} = x + 1$

$(\sqrt{x^2+11})^2 = (x+1)^2$

$x^2 + 11 = x^2 + 2x + 1$

$11 - 1 = x^2 - x^2 + 2x$

$10 = 2x$

$5 = x$

Checking

LS: $\sqrt{5^2+11} = \sqrt{25+11} = \sqrt{36} = 6$

RS: $5 + 1 = 6$

{5} is the solution set.

61. $\sqrt{x^2-1} = x + 1$

$(\sqrt{x^2-1})^2 = (x+1)^2$

$x^2 - 1 = x^2 + 2x + 1$

$-1 - 1 = x^2 - x^2 + 2x$

$-2 = 2x$

$-1 = x$

Checking,

LS: $\sqrt{(-1)^2-1} = \sqrt{1-1} = \sqrt{0} = 0$

RS: $-1 + 1 = 0$

{-1} is the solution set.

63. $v = \sqrt{32h}$ and $v = 4$

$4 = \sqrt{32h}$

$(4)^2 = (\sqrt{32h})^2$

$16 = 32h$

$\frac{1}{2} = h$

Checking,

LS: 4

RS: $\sqrt{32\cdot\frac{1}{2}} = \sqrt{16} = 4$

The wave height is $\frac{1}{2}$ ft.

Review

1. $6(x-5) - (2-x) = 2x + 1$

$6x - 30 - 2 + x = 2x + 1$

$7x - 32 = 2x + 1$

$7x - 2x = 32 + 1$

$5x = 33$

$x = \frac{33}{5}$ $\{\frac{33}{5}\}$

3. $|2z-3| = 4$

$2z - 3 = 4$ or $2z - 3 = -4$

$2z = 7$ $2z = -1$

$z = \frac{7}{2}$ $z = -\frac{1}{2}$

$\{-\frac{1}{2},\frac{7}{2}\}$

5. $\frac{1}{x-3} + \frac{1}{x+3} = \frac{4}{x^2-9}$

$$\frac{1}{x-3} + \frac{1}{x+3} = \frac{4}{(x-3)(x+3)}$$

$$(x-3)(x+3)\left(\frac{1}{x-3}+\frac{1}{x+3}\right)$$

$$= (x-3)(x+3)\left[\frac{4}{(x-3)(x+3)}\right]$$

$$(x-3)(x+3)\cdot\frac{1}{x-3} + (x-3)(x+3)\cdot\frac{1}{x+3}$$

$$= (x-3)(x+3)\cdot\frac{4}{(x-3)(x+3)}$$

$$x + 3 + x - 3 = 4$$

$$2x = 4$$

$$x = 2 \qquad \{2\}$$

7. $$\sqrt{x} = -3$$

$$(\sqrt{x})^2 = (-3)^2$$

$$x = 9$$

Checking,

LS: $\sqrt{9} = 3$

RS: -3

$\emptyset$ is the solution set.

9. $$\frac{1}{x+1} + 1 = \frac{x-2}{x}$$

$$x(x+1)\left(\frac{1}{x+1}+1\right) = x(x+1)\left(\frac{x-2}{x}\right)$$

$$x(x+1)\cdot\frac{1}{x+1} + x(x+1)\cdot 1$$

$$= x(x+1)\cdot\frac{x-2}{x}$$

$$x + x(x+1) = (x+1)(x-2)$$

$$x + x^2 + x = x^2 - x - 2$$

$$x^2 + 2x = x^2 - x - 2$$

$$x^2 - x^2 + 2x + x = -2$$

$$3x = -2$$

$$x = \frac{-2}{3} \qquad \left\{\frac{-2}{3}\right\}$$

11. $$\left|\frac{3+y}{2}\right| = 5$$

$$\frac{3+y}{2} = 5 \quad \text{or} \quad \frac{3+y}{2} = -5$$

$$2\cdot\frac{3+y}{2} = 5\cdot 2 \qquad 2\cdot\frac{3+y}{2} = 2(-5)$$

$$3 + y = 10 \qquad 3 + y = -10$$

$$y = 10 - 3 \qquad y = -10 - 3$$

$$y = 7 \quad \text{or} \quad y = -13$$

$$\{-13,7\}$$

13. $$\frac{3}{2}(x+2) = \frac{1}{2}(x-2)$$

$$2\left[\frac{3}{2}(x+2)\right] = 2\left[\frac{1}{2}(x-2)\right]$$

$$3(x+2) = 1(x-2)$$

$$3x + 6 = x - 2$$

$$3x - x = -2 - 6$$

$$2x = -8$$

$$x = -4 \qquad \{-4\}$$

15. $$\sqrt{1+x^2} = x + 1$$

$$(\sqrt{1+x^2})^2 = (x+1)^2$$

$$1 + x^2 = x^2 + 2x + 1$$

$$1 - 1 = x^2 - x^2 + 2x$$

$$0 = 2x$$

$$0 = x$$

Checking,

LS: $\sqrt{1+0^2} = \sqrt{1+0} = \sqrt{1} = 1$

RS: $0 + 1 = 1$

$\{0\}$ is the solution set.

17. $$\frac{1}{x} - \frac{1}{3x} = \frac{1}{2}$$

$$6x\left(\frac{1}{x}-\frac{1}{3x}\right) = 6x\cdot\frac{1}{2}$$

$$6x\cdot\frac{1}{x} - 6x\cdot\frac{1}{3x} = 3x$$

$$6 - 2 = 3x$$

$$4 = 3x$$

$$\frac{4}{3} = x \qquad \left\{\frac{4}{3}\right\}$$

19.　　$\sqrt{3s+2} = 2$

　　　$(\sqrt{3s+2})^2 = (2)^2$

　　　　$3s + 2 = 4$

　　　　　$3s = 4 - 2$

　　　　　$3s = 2$

　　　　　$s = \dfrac{2}{3}$

Checking,

LS:　$\sqrt{3(\frac{2}{3})+2} = \sqrt{2+2} = \sqrt{4} = 2$

RS:　2

$\{\frac{2}{3}\}$ is the solution set.

21.　　$\dfrac{5}{2}(1-x) = \dfrac{1}{3}(2x+1)$

　$6[\dfrac{5}{2}(1-x)] = 6[\dfrac{1}{3}(2x+1)]$

　　　$15(1-x) = 2(2x+1)$

　　　$15 - 15x = 4x + 2$

　　　$15 - 2 = 4x + 15x$

　　　　　$13 = 19x$

　　　　$\dfrac{13}{19} = x$　　　　$\{\dfrac{13}{19}\}$

23.　　$\sqrt{3x+4} = \sqrt{x+2}$

　　$(\sqrt{3x+4})^2 = (\sqrt{x+2})^2$

　　　$3x + 4 = x + 2$

　　　$3x - x = -4 + 2$

　　　　$2x = -2$

　　　　$x = -1$　　　$\{-1\}$

25.　　$\dfrac{3}{x+1} - 2 = \dfrac{2x}{1-x}$

　　　$\dfrac{3}{x+1} - 2 = \dfrac{2x}{-(x-1)}$

$(x+1)(x-1)(\dfrac{3}{x+1}-2)$

　$= (x+1)(x-1)(\dfrac{-2x}{x-1})$

$(x+1)(x-1)\cdot\dfrac{3}{x+1} - 2(x+1)(x-1)$

　$= (x+1)(x-1)\cdot\dfrac{-2x}{x-1}$

$3(x-1) - 2(x^2-1) = (x+1)(-2x)$

$3x - 3 - 2x^2 + 2 = -2x^2 - 2x$

　　　　$-1 = -2x^2+2x^2-2x-3x$

　　　　$-1 = -5x$

　　　　$\dfrac{1}{5} = x$　　　$\{\dfrac{1}{5}\}$

27.　　$\sqrt{1-x} = \sqrt{2-x}$

　　$(\sqrt{1-x})^2 = (\sqrt{2-x})^2$

　　　$1 - x = 2 - x$

　　　$1 - 2 = -x + x$

　　　　$1 = 0$

$\emptyset$ is the solution set.

29.　　$6x + 5 = 2x - 3$

　　　$6x - 2x = -3 - 5$

　　　　$4x = -8$

　　　　$x = -2$　　　$\{-2\}$

31.　　$\dfrac{1}{4-x} + \dfrac{8}{16-x^2} = \dfrac{1}{4+x}$

　$\dfrac{1}{4-x} + \dfrac{8}{(4-x)(4+x)} = \dfrac{1}{4+x}$

　$(4-x)(4+x)[\dfrac{1}{4-x}+\dfrac{8}{(4-x)(4+x)}]$

　　$= (4-x)(4+x)\cdot\dfrac{1}{4+x}$

$(4-x)(4+x)\cdot\dfrac{1}{4-x}$

　　$+ (4-x)(4+x)\cdot\dfrac{8}{(4-x)(4+x)}$

　$= (4-x)(4+x)\dfrac{1}{4+x}$

$4 + x + 8 = 4 - x$

$12 + x = 4 - x$

$12 - x = -x - x$

$8 = -2x$

$-4 = x$

$\emptyset$ since $\dfrac{1}{4-x}$ and $\dfrac{8}{(4-x)(4+x)}$ are

undefined for $x = -4$.

33. $\sqrt{x^2+3} = x + 3$

$(\sqrt{x^2+3})^2 = (x+3)^2$

$x^2 + 3 = x^2 + 6x + 9$

$3 - 9 = x^2 - x^2 + 6x + 9 - 9$

$-6 = 6x$

$-1 = x$

Checking,

LS: $\sqrt{(-1)^2+3} = \sqrt{1+3} = \sqrt{4} = 2$

RS: $-1 + 3 = 2$

$\{-1\}$ is the solution set.

35. $3[4-(2x+7)] = 6(x+4)$

$3(4-2x-7) = 6x + 24$

$3(-2x-3) = 6x + 24$

$-6x - 9 = 6x + 24$

$-9 - 24 = 6x + 6x$

$-33 = 12x$

$\dfrac{-11}{4}$ or $-\dfrac{33}{12} = x$ $\{\dfrac{-11}{4}\}$

37. $\dfrac{2}{3(w+3)} - \dfrac{1}{3} = \dfrac{2}{w+3}$

$3(w+3)[\dfrac{3}{3(w+3)} - \dfrac{1}{3}] = 3(w+3)\cdot\dfrac{2}{w+3}$

$3(w+3)\cdot\dfrac{2}{3(w+3)} - 3(w+3)\cdot\dfrac{1}{3}$

$= 3(w+3)\cdot\dfrac{2}{w+3}$

$2 - (w+3) = 3\cdot 2$

$2 - w - 3 = 6$

$-1 - w = 6$

$-w = 6 + 1$

$-w = 7$

$w = -7$ $\{-7\}$

39. $\sqrt{1-x} = 4$

$(\sqrt{1-x})^2 = (4)^2$

$1 - x = 16$

$-x = 16 - 1$

$-x = 15$

$x = -15$

Checking,

LS: $\sqrt{1-(-15)} = \sqrt{16} = 4$

RS: 4

$\{-15\}$ is the solution set.

41. $\dfrac{3x}{x+2} = \dfrac{3}{2}$

$2(x+2)\cdot\dfrac{3x}{x+2}$

$2(3x) = 3(x+2)$

$6x = 3x + 6$

$6x - 3x = 6$

$3x = 6$

$x = 2$ $\{2\}$

43. $\sqrt{x+4} = \sqrt{2x}$

$(\sqrt{x+4})^2 = (\sqrt{2x})^2$

$x + 4 = 2x$

$4 = 2x - x$

$4 = x$

Checking,

LS: $\sqrt{4+4} = \sqrt{8}$

RS: $\sqrt{2(4)} = \sqrt{8}$

$\{4\}$ is the solution set.

45. $\dfrac{2}{1-x} = \dfrac{2x}{1-x^2}$

$\dfrac{2}{1-x} = \dfrac{2x}{(1-x)(1+x)}$

$(1-x)(1+x)\cdot\dfrac{2}{1-x}$

$= (1-x)(1+x)\dfrac{2x}{(1-x)(1+x)}$

$$(1+x)2 = 2x$$
$$2 + 2x = 2x$$
$$2 = 2x - 2x$$
$$2 = 0 \qquad \emptyset$$

47. $\sqrt{x^2-15} = x + 5$

$(\sqrt{x^2-15})^2 = (x+5)^2$

$x^2 - 15 = x^2 + 10x + 25$

$-15 - 25 = x^2 - x^2 + 10x$

$-40 = 10x$

$-4 = x$

Checking,

LS: $\sqrt{(-4)^2-15} = \sqrt{16-15} = \sqrt{1} = 1$

RS: $-4 + 5 = 1$

$\{-4\}$ is the solution set.

49. $|2x-7| = -3 \qquad \emptyset$

51. $\dfrac{1}{x+2} - 1 = \dfrac{x}{4-x^2}$

$\dfrac{1}{x+2} - 1 = \dfrac{x}{(2-x)(2+x)}$

$\dfrac{1}{x+2} - 1 = \dfrac{x^2}{(-x-2)(x+2)}$

$(x-2)(x+2)(\dfrac{1}{x+2}-1)$

$= (x-2)(x+2) \cdot \dfrac{-x^2}{(x-2)(x+2)}$

$(x-2)(x+2) \cdot \dfrac{1}{x+2} - (x-2)(x+2) \cdot 1$

$= -x^2$

$x - 2 - (x^2-4) = -x^2$

$x - 2 - x^2 + 4 = -x^2$

$2 = -x^2 + x^2 - x$

$2 = -x$

$-2 = x$

$\emptyset$, since $\dfrac{1}{x+2}$ and

$\dfrac{-x^2}{(x-2)(x+2)}$ are undefined for

$x = -2$.

53. $3[2-(6-x)+3(x+2)] = 3(x-2)$

$3(2-6+x+3x+6) = 3x - 6$

$3(4x+2) = 3x - 6$

$12x + 6 = 3x - 6$

$12x - 3x = -6 - 6$

$9x = -12$

$x = \dfrac{-12}{9}$ or $\dfrac{-4}{3}$

$\{-\dfrac{4}{3}\}$

55. $|t-17| = 14$

$t - 17 = 14$ or $t - 17 = -14$

$t = 14 + 17 \qquad t = -14 + 17$

$t = 31$ or $t = 3$

$\{3,31\}$

57. $\dfrac{1}{x} - \dfrac{2}{3} = \dfrac{1}{2}$

$6x(\dfrac{1}{x}-\dfrac{2}{3}) = 6x \cdot \dfrac{1}{2}$

$6x \cdot \dfrac{1}{x} - 6x \cdot \dfrac{2}{3} = 3x$

$6 - 4x = 3x$

$6 = 3x + 4x$

$6 = 7x$

$\dfrac{6}{7} = x \qquad \{\dfrac{6}{7}\}$

59. $\sqrt{1+x} = 3$

$(\sqrt{1+x})^2 = (3)^2$

$1 + x = 9$

$x = 9 - 1$

$$x = 8$$

Checking,

LS: $\sqrt{1+8} = \sqrt{9} = 3$

RS: 3

$\{8\}$ is the solution set.

61. $\left|\dfrac{1-x}{2}\right| = 2$

$\dfrac{1-x}{2} = 2$ or $\dfrac{1-x}{2} = -2$

$2\left(\dfrac{1-x}{2}\right) = 2 \cdot 2$ $2\left(\dfrac{1-x}{2}\right) = 2(-2)$

$1 - x = 4$ $1 - x = -4$

$-x = 4 - 1$ $-x = -4 - 1$

$-x = 3$ $-x = -5$

$x = -3$ or $x = 5$

$\{-3, 5\}$

63. $\dfrac{1}{x-2} = \dfrac{2}{x-2}$

$(x-2)\left(\dfrac{1}{x+2}\right) = (x-2)\left(\dfrac{2}{x-2}\right)$

$1 = 2$

$\emptyset$

65. $0.2s - 0.9 = 0.3$

$0.2s = 0.3 + 0.9$

$0.2s = 1.2$

$s = \dfrac{1.2}{0.2}$ or 6 $\{6\}$

67. $\sqrt{x+2} = \sqrt{x-5}$

$\left(\sqrt{x+2}\right)^2 = \left(\sqrt{x-5}\right)^2$

$x + 2 = x - 5$

$x - x = -5 - 2$

$0 = -7$

$\emptyset$

69. $\dfrac{3}{4}(x-2) + (x-1) = 1$

$4\left[\dfrac{3}{4}(x-2)+(x-1)\right] = 4 \cdot 1$

$4 \cdot \dfrac{3}{4}(x-2) + 4(x-1) = 4$

$3(x-2) + 4(x-1) = 4$

$3x - 6 + 4x - 4 = 4$

$7x - 10 = 4$

$7x = 4 + 10$

$7x = 14$

$x = 2$ $\{2\}$

71. $\dfrac{1}{2x-1} + \dfrac{1}{2x+1} = \dfrac{2}{1-4x^2}$

$\dfrac{1}{2x-1} + \dfrac{1}{2x+1} = \dfrac{2}{(1-2x)(1+2x)}$

$\dfrac{1}{2x-1} + \dfrac{1}{2x+1} = \dfrac{2}{-(2x-1)(2x+1)}$

$(2x-1)(2x+1)\left(\dfrac{1}{2x-1}+\dfrac{1}{2x+1}\right)$

$\qquad = (2x-1)(2x+1)\left[\dfrac{-2}{(2x-1)(2x+1)}\right]$

$(2x-1)(2x+1)\cdot\dfrac{1}{2x-1} +$

$\qquad\qquad (2x-1)(2x+1)\cdot\dfrac{1}{2x+1}$

$\qquad = (2x-1)(2x+1)\cdot\dfrac{-2}{(2x-1)(2x+1)}$

$2x + 1 + 2x - 1 = -2$

$4x = -2$

$x = \dfrac{-2}{4}$ or $-\dfrac{1}{2}$

$\emptyset$ since $\dfrac{1}{2x+1}$ and $\dfrac{2}{(1-2x)(1+2x)}$

are undefined when $x = -\dfrac{1}{2}$.

73. $6x - (1-x) = 6$

$6x - 1 + x = 6$

$7x - 1 = 6$

$7x = 6 + 1$

$7x = 7$

$x = 1$ $\{1\}$

102

75. $\left|\frac{1}{2}x+1\right| = 4$

$\frac{1}{2}x + 1 = 4$ or $\frac{1}{2}x + 1 = -4$

$2(\frac{1}{2}x+1) = 2\cdot 4$ $2(\frac{1}{2}x+1) = 2(-4)$

$2\cdot\frac{1}{2}x + 2\cdot 1 = 8$ $2\cdot\frac{1}{2}x + 2\cdot 1 = -8$

$x + 2 = 8$ $x + 2 = -8$

$x = 8 - 2$ $x = -8 - 2$

$x = 6$ $x = -10$

$\{-10, 6\}$

77. $\frac{5}{x+2} = \frac{6}{2x+3}$

$(x+2)(2x+3)\cdot\frac{5}{x+2}$

$\quad = (x+2)(2x+3)\cdot\frac{6}{2x+3}$

$(2x+3)5 = (x+2)6$

$10x + 15 = 6x + 12$

$10x - 6x = 12 - 15$

$4x = -3$

$x = -\frac{3}{4}$ $\{-\frac{3}{4}\}$

79. $|6x-7| = 0$

$6x - 7 = 0$

$6x = 7$

$x = \frac{7}{6}$ $\{\frac{7}{6}\}$

81. x: first   x+2: second

   x+4: third

$x + 2(x+2) + 3(x+4) = 94$

$x + 2x + 4 + 3x + 12 = 94$

$6x + 16 = 94$

$6x = 94 - 16$

$6x = 78$

$x = 13$

The consecutive odd integers are

13, 15, 17.

83. x: number of gallons of water

   to add.

$\frac{8}{100}\cdot 15 + 0\cdot x = \frac{5}{100}(15+x)$

$100(\frac{8}{100}\cdot 15) = 100[\frac{5}{100}(15+x)]$

$120 = 5(15+x)$

$120 = 75 + 5x$

$120 - 75 = 5x$

$45 = 5x$

$9 = x$

She should add 9 gal. of water.

85. width: x

   length: 2x - 2

$2x + 2(2x-2) = 86$

$2x + 4x - 4 = 86$

$6x - 4 = 86$

$6x = 86 + 4$

$6x = 90$

$x = 15$ $2x - 2 = 28$

The dimensions are 15m. by 28m.

87. Factored.

89. $(x+y) - 4(x+y)^2$

$\quad = (x+y)[1-4(x+y)]$

$\quad = (x+y)(1-4x-4y)$

91. Factored

93. $(x+2)^2$ has one term.

    $(x+2)$ is a factor.

95. $xy(x+2)$ has one term.

    $(x+2)$ is a factor.

97. $x^2 + 4x + 4 = (x+2)^2$

    $x^2 + 4x + 4$ has three terms.

    $(x+2)$ is a factor.

99. $(-8)^2 = (-8)(-8)$

    $= 64$

101. $(a+2b)^3 = a^3 + 3a^2(2b)$

$$+ 3a(2b)^2 + (2b)^3$$

$$= a^3 + 6a^2b + 3a \cdot 4b^2 + 8b^3$$

$$= a^3 + 6a^2b + 12ab^2 + 8b^3$$

103. $x^3(x^2y - xy) = x^5y - x^4y$

105. $\dfrac{2(x-3)-(3+x)}{x^2-9} = \dfrac{2(x-3)-(3+x)}{(x+3)(x-3)}$

        will not factor

$$= 2x - 6 - 3 - x$$

$$= \dfrac{x-9}{x^2-9}$$

107. $\dfrac{1}{2x} - \dfrac{1}{3} = \dfrac{1 \cdot 3}{6x} - \dfrac{1 \cdot 2x}{6x}$

$$= \dfrac{3-2x}{6x}$$

109. $\dfrac{1}{x+1} - \dfrac{x}{x+2}$ Expression

$$= \dfrac{1 \cdot (x+2)}{(x+1)(x+2)} - \dfrac{x \cdot (x+1)}{(x+1)(x+2)}$$

$$= \dfrac{x+2}{(x+1)(x+2)} - \dfrac{x^2+x}{(x+1)(x+2)}$$

$$= \dfrac{x+2-(x^2+x)}{(x+1)(x+2)}$$

$$= \dfrac{x+2-x^2-x}{(x+1)(x+2)}$$

$$= \dfrac{2-x^2}{(x+1)(x+2)}$$

111. $\dfrac{1}{x+3} - \dfrac{2}{x-2} = \dfrac{3}{x^2+x-6}$ Equation

$$\dfrac{1}{x+3} - \dfrac{2}{x-2} = \dfrac{3}{(x+3)(x-2)}$$

$$(x+3)(x-2)\left(\dfrac{1}{x+3} - \dfrac{2}{x-2}\right)$$

$$= (x+3)(x-2)\left[\dfrac{3}{(x+3)(x-2)}\right]$$

$$(x+3)(x-2) \cdot \dfrac{1}{x+3} - (x+3)(x-2)\dfrac{2}{(x-2)}$$

$$= (x+3)(x-2) \cdot \dfrac{3}{(x+3)(x-2)}$$

$$x - 2 - (x+3)2 = 3$$

$$x - 2 - 2x - 6 = 3$$

$$-x - 8 = 3$$

$$-x = 3 + 8$$

$$-x = 11$$

$$x = -11 \qquad \{-11\}$$

113. $|x+3| = 6$ Equation

$$x + 3 = 6 \quad \text{or} \quad x + 3 = -6$$

$$x = 6 - 3 \qquad x = -6 - 3$$

$$x = 3 \quad \text{or} \qquad x = -9$$

$$(-9, 3\}$$

115. $\dfrac{4}{x-y} - \dfrac{8}{y-x}$ Expression

$$= \dfrac{4}{x-y} - \dfrac{8}{-(x-y)}$$

$$= \dfrac{4}{x-y} + \dfrac{8}{x-y}$$

$$= \dfrac{12}{x-y}$$

Chapter Test.

1. $3(2x-1) - 4x = 3(5-x)$

$$6x - 3 - 4x = 15 - 3x$$

$$2x - 3 = 15 - 3x$$

$$2x + 3x = 15 + 3$$

$$5x = 18$$

$$x = \frac{18}{5} \qquad \{\frac{18}{5}\}$$

C.

2.
$$\frac{2x}{x-1} - \frac{1}{x+2} = 2$$

$$(x-1)(x+2)\left(\frac{2x}{x-1} - \frac{1}{x+2}\right) = 2(x-1)(x+2)$$

$$(x-1)(x+2)\cdot\frac{2x}{x-1} - (x-1)(x+2)\cdot\frac{1}{x+2}$$

$$= 2(x^2+x-2)$$

$$(x+2)2x - (x-1)\cdot 1 = 2x^2 + 2x - 4$$

$$2x^2 + 4x - x + 1 = 2x^2 + 2x - 4$$

$$2x^2 + 3x + 1 = 2x^2 + 2x - 4$$

$$2x^2 - 2x^2 + 3x - 2x = -4 - 1$$

$$x = -5 \qquad \{-5\}$$

A.

3.
$$b(1-6x) = 2ax$$

$$b - 6bx = 2ax$$

$$b = 2ax + 6bx$$

$$b = x(2a+6b)$$

$$\frac{b}{2a+6b} = x$$

B.

4.
$$\sqrt{x+1} = \sqrt{2x-2}$$

$$(\sqrt{x+1})^2 = (\sqrt{2x-2})^2$$

$$x + 1 = 2x - 2$$

$$x - 2x = -2 - 1$$

$$-x = -3$$

$$x = 3$$

Checking,

LS: $\sqrt{3+1} = \sqrt{4} = 2$

RS: $\sqrt{2(3)-2} = \sqrt{6-2} = \sqrt{4} = 2$

$\{3\}$ is the solution set.

D.

5. x: smallest   x+2: second

x+4: third

$$x+2(x+2) + 4(x+4)$$

C.

6. $|2x+3| = 7$

$$2x + 3 = 7 \quad \text{or} \quad 2x + 3 = -7$$

$$2x = 7 - 3 \qquad\qquad 2x = -7 - 3$$

$$2x = 4 \qquad\qquad\qquad 2x = -10$$

$$x = 2 \quad \text{or} \qquad\qquad x = -5$$

$$\{-5,2\}$$

7. $\sqrt{x+3} + \sqrt{2x-3} = 0$

$$\sqrt{x+3} = -\sqrt{2x-3}$$

$$(\sqrt{x+3})^2 = (-\sqrt{2x-3})^2$$

$$x + 3 = 2x - 3$$

$$x - 2x = -3 - 3$$

$$-x = -6$$

$$x = 6$$

Checking,

LS: $\sqrt{6+3} + \sqrt{2(6)-3} = \sqrt{9} + \sqrt{9}$

$$= 3 + 3 = 6$$

RS: 0

$\emptyset$ is the solution set.

8.
$$\frac{1}{3x} - \frac{3}{2x} = \frac{1}{3}$$

$$6x\left(\frac{1}{3x} - \frac{3}{2x}\right) = 6x\left(\frac{1}{3}\right)$$

$$6x\cdot\frac{1}{3x} - 6x\cdot\frac{3}{2x} = 2x$$

$$2 - 3 \cdot 3 = 2x$$

$$2 - 9 = 2x$$

$$-7 = 2x$$

$$\frac{-7}{2} = x \qquad \{-\frac{7}{2}\}$$

9. $\quad \frac{2}{3}(x-1) = \frac{1}{6} + x$

$$6[\frac{2}{3}(x-1)] = 6(\frac{1}{6}+x)$$

$$6 \cdot \frac{2}{3}(x-1) = 6 \cdot \frac{1}{6}+6 \cdot x$$

$$4(x-1) = 1 + 6x$$

$$4x - 4 = 1 + 6x$$

$$4x - 6x = 1 + 4$$

$$-2x = 5$$

$$x = -\frac{5}{2} \qquad \{-\frac{5}{2}\}$$

10. $\quad |1-2x| = -3 \qquad \emptyset$

11. $\quad \frac{a-x}{2} + y = ax$

$$2(\frac{a-x}{2}+y) = 2 \cdot ax$$

$$2 \cdot \frac{a-x}{2} + 2 \cdot y = 2ax$$

$$a - x + 2y = 2ax$$

$$a + 2y = 2ax + x$$

$$a + 2y = x(2a+1)$$

$$\frac{a+2y}{2a+1} = x$$

12. $\quad F^2 = \frac{1}{LC} - \frac{R}{4L^2}$

$$4CL^2(F^2) = 4CL^2(\frac{1}{LC}-\frac{R}{4L^2})$$

$$4CF^2L^2 = 4CL^2 \cdot \frac{1}{LC} - 4CL^2\frac{R}{4L^2}$$

$$4CF^2L^2 = 4L - CR$$

$$4CF^2L^2 + CR = 4L$$

$$C(4F^2L^2+R) = 4L$$

$$C = \frac{4L}{4F^2L^2+R}$$

13. $\quad$ x: rate of Honda

	D	R	T
Honda	5x	x	5
Bus	9(x+20)	x+20	9

$$5x + 9(x+20) = 600$$

$$5x + 9x + 180 = 600$$

$$14x = 600 - 180$$

$$14x = 420$$

$$x = 30$$

The Honda went 30 mph.

14. $\quad$ width: x

length: x + 5

$$2x + 2(x+5) = 134$$

$$2x + 2x + 10 = 134$$

$$4x + 10 = 134$$

$$4x = 134 - 10$$

$$4x = 124$$

$$x = 31$$

$$x + 5 = 36$$

The dimensions of the largest picture frame are 31 in. by 36 in.

15. $\quad$ x: number of quarts of 20% vinegar solution to add.

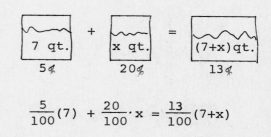

$$\frac{5}{100}(7) + \frac{20}{100} \cdot x = \frac{13}{100}(7+x)$$

$$100\left(\frac{5}{100}\cdot 7+\frac{20}{100}\cdot x\right) = 100\left[\frac{13}{100}(7+x)\right]$$

$$5\cdot 7 + 20\cdot x = 13(7+x)$$

$$35 + 20x = 91 + 13x$$

$$20x - 13x = 91 - 35$$

$$7x = 56$$

$$x = 8$$

She should add 8 qts. of 20%

vinegar solution.

CHAPTER 5

Problem Set 5.1.

1. $2^{-3} = \dfrac{1}{2^3}$

      $= \dfrac{1}{8}$

3. $6^{-1} = \dfrac{1}{6}$

5. $-2^{-4} = -\dfrac{1}{2^4}$

      $= -\dfrac{1}{16}$

7. $-2^{-3} = -\dfrac{1}{2^3}$

      $= -\dfrac{1}{8}$

9. $\left(\dfrac{1}{3}\right)^{-2} = \dfrac{1}{\left(\dfrac{1}{3}\right)^2}$

      $= \dfrac{1}{\dfrac{1}{9}}$

      $= 9$

11. $3^{-2}x = \dfrac{1}{3^2}x$

      $= \dfrac{1}{9}x$ or $\dfrac{x}{9}$

13. $2^3 \cdot 2^{-2} = 2^1$ or   2

15. $5^{-1} \cdot 5^4 = 5^3$

      $= 125$

17. $(3^2)^{-2} = 3^{-4}$

      $= \dfrac{1}{3^4}$

      $= \dfrac{1}{81}$

19. $(xy)^{-1} = \dfrac{1}{xy}$

21. $(-3x)^{-3} = \dfrac{1}{(-3x)^3}$

      $= \dfrac{1}{(-3)^3 x^3}$

      $= \dfrac{1}{-27x^3}$ or $-\dfrac{1}{27x^3}$

23. $\dfrac{2^3}{2^{-2}} = 2^{3-(-2)}$

      $= 2^5$

      $= 32$

25. $(-5^{-1})^{-2} = 5^{(-1)(-2)}$

      $= 5^2$

      $= 25$

27. $(-x^{-3})^{-2} = x^{(-3)(-2)}$

      $= x^6$

29. $\left(-\dfrac{x^{-1}}{2y}\right)^{-3} = -\dfrac{x^{(-1)(-3)}}{(2y)^{-3}}$

      $= -\dfrac{x^3}{2^{-3}y^{-3}}$

      $= -x^3 \cdot 2^3 \cdot y^3$

      $= -8x^3 y^3$

31. $\dfrac{2^{-3}}{3} = \dfrac{1}{2^3 \cdot 3}$

      $= \dfrac{1}{24}$

33. $-\dfrac{6^{-1}}{5^{-2}} = -\dfrac{5^2}{6}$

      $= -\dfrac{25}{6}$

35. $-\left(-\dfrac{3x^{-2}}{yz^{-1}}\right)^{-1} = \dfrac{3^{-1}x^{(-2)(-1)}}{y^{(-1)}z^{(-1)(-1)}}$

      $= \dfrac{x^2 y}{3z}$

37. $\dfrac{(2x^{-1}y^2)^{-2}}{(3xy^{-2})^{-1}} = \dfrac{2^{-2}x^{(-1)(-2)}y^{2(-2)}}{3^{-1}x^{-1}y^{(-2)(-1)}}$

$$= \frac{3x^2 y^{-4} x}{2^2 y^2}$$

$$= \frac{3x^3}{4y^2 y^4}$$

$$= \frac{3x^3}{4y^6}$$

39. $\dfrac{(2x)^{-3} yz^{-2}}{2x(y^2 z)^{-1}} = \dfrac{2^{-3} x^{-3} yz^{-2}}{2xy^{-2} z^{-1}}$

$$= \frac{y \cdot y^2 z}{2^3 x^3 z^2 \cdot 2x}$$

$$= \frac{y^3 z}{16x^4 z^2} = \frac{y^3}{16x^4 z}$$

41. $3^{-2} - 2^{-3} = \dfrac{1}{3^2} - \dfrac{1}{2^3}$

$$= \frac{1}{9} - \frac{1}{8}$$

$$= \frac{8}{72} - \frac{9}{72}$$

$$= -\frac{1}{72}$$

43. $\dfrac{2^{-1} + 2^{-2}}{2^{-1}} = \dfrac{\frac{1}{2} + \frac{1}{4}}{\frac{1}{2}}$

$$= \frac{4\left(\frac{1}{2} + \frac{1}{4}\right)}{4\left(\frac{1}{2}\right)}$$

$$= \frac{4 \cdot \frac{1}{2} + 4 \cdot \frac{1}{4}}{2}$$

$$= \frac{2+1}{2}$$

$$= \frac{3}{2}$$

45. $\dfrac{2^{-3} + x^{-1}}{x^{-2}} = \dfrac{\frac{1}{8} + \frac{1}{x}}{\frac{1}{x^2}}$

$$= \frac{8x^2\left(\frac{1}{8} + \frac{1}{x}\right)}{8x^2\left(\frac{1}{x^2}\right)}$$

$$= \frac{8x^2 \cdot \frac{1}{8} + 8x^2 \cdot \frac{1}{x}}{8x^2 \cdot \frac{1}{x^2}}$$

$$= \frac{x^2 + 8x}{8}$$

47. $-0.0000012345 = -1.2345 \times 10^{-6}$

49. $77,722,000,000,000$

$$= 7.7722 \times 10^{13}$$

51. $5.43 \times 10^{-5} = 0.0000543$

53. $-80 \times 10^{11} = -800,000,000,000$

55. $2^{-2} = \dfrac{1}{2^2}$

$$= \frac{1}{4}$$

57. $-3^{-4} = -\dfrac{1}{3^4}$ $-3 \cdot 3 \cdot 3 \cdot 3$

$$= \frac{1}{81}$$

59. $(-3)^{-3} = \dfrac{1}{(-3)^3}$

$$= \frac{1}{-27} \quad \text{or} \quad -\frac{1}{27}$$

61. $-10^{-2} = -\dfrac{1}{10^2}$ $10 \cdot 10$

$$= -\frac{1}{100}$$

63. $\left(\dfrac{2}{3}\right)^{-3} = \dfrac{1}{\left(\frac{2}{3}\right)^3}$

$$= \frac{1}{\frac{8}{27}}$$

$$= \frac{27}{8}$$

65. $-\left(\dfrac{3}{5}\right)^{-1} = -\dfrac{1}{\left(\frac{3}{5}\right)^1}$

$$= -\frac{5}{3}$$

67. $2^{-3}x = \frac{1}{x}$

$$= \frac{1}{8}x \quad \text{or} \quad \frac{x}{8}$$

69. $-6x^{-2}y^{-1} = \frac{-6}{x^2 y}$

71. $3t^{-21} = \frac{3}{t^{21}}$

73. $\frac{5}{4^{-2}} = 5 \cdot 4^2$

$$= 5 \cdot 16$$

$$= 80$$

75. $\frac{-2x^{-2}}{y^{-3}} = \frac{-2y^3}{x^2}$

77. $4^{-1} + 4^{-2} = \frac{1}{4} + \frac{1}{16}$

$$= \frac{4}{16} + \frac{1}{16}$$

$$= \frac{5}{16}$$

79. $3^{-2} + 2^{-3} = \frac{1}{3^2} + \frac{1}{2^3}$

$$= \frac{1}{9} + \frac{1}{8}$$

$$= \frac{8}{72} + \frac{9}{72}$$

$$= \frac{17}{72}$$

81. $\dfrac{3^{-1} + 3^{-2}}{3^{-1}} = \dfrac{\frac{1}{3} + \frac{1}{9}}{\frac{1}{3}}$

$$= \frac{9\left(\frac{1}{3} + \frac{1}{9}\right)}{9 \cdot \frac{1}{3}}$$

$$= \frac{9 \cdot \frac{1}{3} + 9 \cdot \frac{1}{9}}{9 \cdot \frac{1}{3}}$$

$$= \frac{3+1}{3}$$

$$= \frac{4}{3}$$

83. $\dfrac{3^{-2} - x^{-1}}{x^{-2}} = \dfrac{\frac{1}{3^2} - \frac{1}{x^1}}{\frac{1}{x^2}}$

$$= \frac{9x^2 \left(\frac{1}{9} - \frac{1}{x}\right)}{9x^2 \frac{1}{x^2}}$$

$$= \frac{9x^2 \cdot \frac{1}{9} - 9x^2 \cdot \frac{1}{x}}{9}$$

$$= \frac{x^2 - 9x}{9}$$

85. $\left(\frac{2}{x}\right)^{-3} + x^3 = \dfrac{1}{\left(\frac{2}{x}\right)^3} + x^3$

$$= \frac{1}{\frac{2^3}{x^3}} + x^3$$

$$= \frac{x^3}{2^3} + x^3$$

$$= \frac{x^3}{8} + \frac{8x^3}{8}$$

$$= \frac{9x^3}{8}$$

87. $3^2 \cdot 3^{-3} = 3^{2 + -3}$

$$= 3^{-1}$$

$$= \frac{1}{3}$$

89. $6^{-1} \cdot 6^4 = 6^{-1+4}$

$$= 6^3 \quad \text{or} \quad 216$$

91. $3^{-3} \cdot 3^{-1} = 3^{-3 + (-1)}$

$$= 3^{-4}$$

$$= \frac{1}{3^4}$$

$$= \frac{1}{81}$$

93. $(3^{-2})^3 = 3^{(-2)(3)}$

$$= 3^{-6}$$

$$= \frac{1}{3^6}$$

95. $(3^{-3})^{-2} = 3^6$

97. $(-4^{-1})^2 = 4^{(-1)(2)}$

$$= 4^{-2}$$

$$= \frac{1}{4^2}$$

$$= \frac{1}{16}$$

99. $(-4^{-1})^{-2} = 4^{(-1)(-2)}$

$$= 4^2$$

$$= 16$$

101. $(-x^{-3})^{-4} = x^{(-3)(-4)}$

$$= x^{12}$$

103. $(3x)^{-3} = 3^{-3}x^{-3}$

$$= \frac{1}{3^3 x^3}$$

$$= \frac{1}{27x^3}$$

105. $(x^{-2}y^4)^{-3} = (x^{-2})^{-3}(y^4)^{-3}$

$$= x^{(-2)(-3)}y^{4(-3)}$$

$$= x^6 y^{-12}$$

$$= \frac{x^6}{y^{12}}$$

107. $-(3x^{-2}y)^{-3} = -3^{-3}(x^{-2})^{-3}y^{-3}$

$$= -3^{-3}x^{(-2)(-3)}y^{-3}$$

$$= -3^{-3}x^6 y^{-3}$$

$$= \frac{-x^6}{3^3 y^3}$$

$$= \frac{-x^6}{27y^3}$$

109. $\left(\frac{x-1}{3y}\right)^{-2} = \frac{(x^{-1})^{-2}}{(3y)^{-2}}$

$$= \frac{x^{(-1)(-2)}}{3^{-2}y^{-2}}$$

$$= \frac{x^2}{3^{-2}y^{-2}}$$

$$= 3^2 x^2 y^2$$

$$= 9x^2 y^2$$

111. $\left(\frac{-2}{x^3}\right)^{-3} = \frac{(-2)^{-3}}{(x^3)^{-3}}$

$$= \frac{-2^{-3}}{x^{(3)(-3)}}$$

$$= \frac{-2^{-3}}{x^{-9}}$$

$$= \frac{-x^9}{2^3}$$

$$= \frac{-x^9}{8}$$

113. $-\left(-\frac{(-x^{-3})y^3}{(-2^{-3})^2}\right)^0 = -1$

115. $\frac{3^2}{3^{-3}} = 3^2 \cdot 3^3$

$$= 3^5 \quad \text{or} \quad 243$$

117. $\dfrac{(-y)^{-4}}{(-y)^{-2}} = \dfrac{y^2}{y^4}$

$\qquad = \dfrac{1}{y^{4-2}}$

$\qquad = \dfrac{1}{y^2}$

119. $\dfrac{3t^{-3}}{3t^{-6}} = \dfrac{3t^6}{3t^3}$

$\qquad = t^3$

121. $\dfrac{7(x+2)^{-2}}{(x+2)^3} = \dfrac{7}{(x+2)^2(x+2)^3}$

$\qquad = \dfrac{7}{(x+2)^5}$

123. $\dfrac{(3x^2y^2)^{-2}}{(2xy^2)^{-1}} = \dfrac{3^{-2}x^{(2)(-2)}y^{(2x-2)}}{2^{-1}x^{-1}y^{(2)(-1)}}$

$\qquad = \dfrac{3^{-2}x^{-4}y^{-4}}{2^{-1}x^{-1}y^{-2}}$

$\qquad = \dfrac{2xy^2}{3x^4y^4}$

$\qquad = \dfrac{2}{3x^{(4-1)}y^{(4-2)}}$

$\qquad = \dfrac{2}{9x^3y^2}$

125. $\dfrac{(2x)^{-2}y^2z^{-3}}{2x(y^{-2}z)^{-1}} = \dfrac{2^{-2}x^{-2}y^2z^{-3}}{2xy^{(-2)(-1)}z^{-1}}$

$\qquad = \dfrac{2^{-2}x^{-2}y^2z^{-3}}{2xy^2z^{-1}}$

$\qquad = \dfrac{z}{2 \cdot 2^2 x \cdot x^2 z^3}$

$\qquad = \dfrac{z}{2^3 x^3 z^3}$

$\qquad = \dfrac{z}{8x^3z^3}$

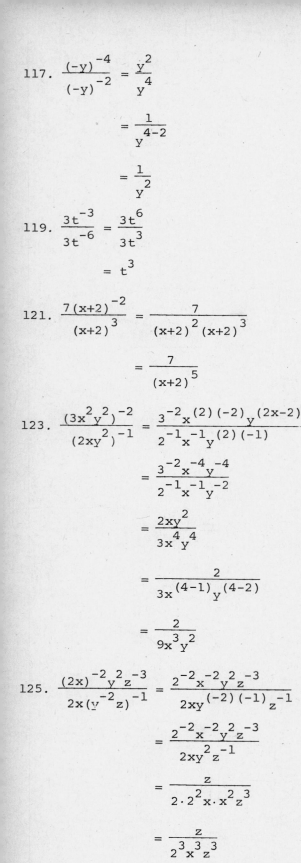

$\qquad = \dfrac{1}{8x^3z^{3-1}}$

$\qquad = \dfrac{1}{8x^3z^2}$

127. $0.05432 = 5.432 \times 10^{-2}$

129. $4402 = 4.402 \times 10^3$

131. $-0.901 = -9.01 \times 10^{-1}$

133. $1.43 \times 10^5 = 143{,}000$

135. $1.1 \times 10^{-11} = 0.000000000011$

137. $-1.0 \times 10^{-1} = -0.1$

139. $(4.3)(365)(24)(60)(60)(2.99)(10^{10})$

$\qquad = 4.05 \times 10^{18}$

141. $x^{-4} \cdot x^{-1} = \dfrac{1}{x^4} \cdot \dfrac{1}{x^1}$

$\qquad = \dfrac{1}{x^{4+1}}$

$\qquad = \dfrac{1}{x^5}$

$\qquad = x^{-5}$

143. $(x \cdot y)^{-5} = \dfrac{1}{(xy)^5}$

$\qquad = \dfrac{1}{x^5 y^5}$

$\qquad = x^{-5} \cdot y^{-5}$

145. $\dfrac{x^3}{x^{-2}} = x^3 \cdot x^2$

$\qquad = x^5$

$\qquad = x^{3-(-2)}$

147. $(x^j + x^k)(x^j - x^k) = x^{2j} - x^{2k}$

149. $(x^j - x^{-j})^2 = x^{2j} - 2x^j x^{-j} + x^{-2j}$

$$= x^{2j} - 2x^0 + \frac{1}{x^{2j}}$$

$$= x^{2j} - 2 + \frac{1}{x^{2j}}$$

151. $(x^j y^k)^2 = x^{2j} y^{2k}$

153. $(x^{-2} - x^{-1} - 6 = (x^{-1} - 3)(x^{-1} + 2)$

Problem Set 5.2.

1. $2\sqrt{49} = 2 \cdot 7$

   $= 14$

3. $\sqrt{121} = 11$

5. $3\sqrt[3]{-64} = 3(-4)$

   $= -12$

7. $\sqrt{\dfrac{25}{49}} = \dfrac{5}{7}$

9. $3\sqrt{\dfrac{27}{64}} = \dfrac{3}{4}$

11. $\sqrt[3]{-8x^6 y^3} = -2x^2 y$

13. $-\sqrt{144 j^6 k^3 \ell^4} = \sqrt{12^2 j^6 k^2 \ell^4 \cdot k}$

    $= -12 j^3 k \ell^2 \sqrt{k}$

15. $\sqrt{\dfrac{36x^{10}}{y^8}} = \dfrac{6x^5}{y^4}$

17. $-2\sqrt{45} = -2\sqrt{9 \cdot 5}$

    $= -2 \cdot 3\sqrt{5}$

    $= -6\sqrt{5}$

19. $\sqrt{240} = \sqrt{2^4 \cdot 5 \cdot 3}$

    $= 2^2 \sqrt{5 \cdot 3}$

    $= 4\sqrt{15}$

21. $-3\sqrt[3]{-108} = -3\sqrt[3]{-27 \cdot 4}$

$$= -3\sqrt[3]{(-3)^3 \cdot 4}$$

$$= -3 \cdot -3\sqrt[3]{4}$$

$$= 9\sqrt[3]{4}$$

23. $\sqrt[6]{320} = \sqrt[6]{2^6 \cdot 5}$

    $= 2\sqrt[6]{5}$

25. a) $\sqrt{4y^2} = 2y$

    b) $\sqrt{4 + y^2}$ won't simplify

    c) $\sqrt{(2+y)^2} = 2 + y$

27. $3\sqrt{36} = 3 \cdot 6$

    $= 18$

29. $-\sqrt{100} = -10$

31. $\sqrt[3]{216} = \sqrt[3]{6^3}$

    $= 6$

33. $-\sqrt{16x^4 y^2} = -4x^2 y$

35. $\sqrt{72} = \sqrt{9 \cdot 4 \cdot 2}$

    $= 3 \cdot 2\sqrt{2}$

    $= 6\sqrt{2}$

37. $\sqrt{288} = \sqrt{12^2 \cdot 2}$

    $= 12\sqrt{2}$

39. $3\sqrt{54} = 3\sqrt{3^3 \cdot 2}$

    $= 3\sqrt[3]{2}$

41. $\sqrt[5]{-486} = \sqrt[5]{(-3)^5 \cdot 2}$

    $= -3\sqrt[5]{2}$

43. $\sqrt{\dfrac{16}{81}} = \dfrac{4}{9}$

45. $\sqrt{\dfrac{27}{49}} = \sqrt{\dfrac{3^2 \cdot 3}{7^2}}$

        $= \dfrac{3\sqrt{3}}{7}$

47. $-3\sqrt{\dfrac{8}{9}} = -3\sqrt{\dfrac{2^2 \cdot 2}{3^2}}$

        $= \dfrac{-3 \cdot 2}{3}\sqrt{2}$

        $= -2\sqrt{2}$

49. $\sqrt{9x^3y^2} = \sqrt{3^2 x^2 y^2 \cdot x}$

        $= 3xy\sqrt{x}$

51. $3\sqrt{\dfrac{64}{27}} = 3\sqrt{\dfrac{4^3}{3^3}}$

        $= \dfrac{4}{3}$

53. $\sqrt{\dfrac{75}{49}} = \sqrt{\dfrac{5^2 \cdot 3}{7}}$

        $= \dfrac{5\sqrt{3}}{7}$

55. $3\sqrt{\dfrac{56}{27}} = 3\sqrt{\dfrac{2^3 \cdot 7}{3^3}}$

        $= \dfrac{2\sqrt[3]{7}}{3}$

57. $3\sqrt{7x^2y^3z} = 3\sqrt{x^2y^2 \cdot 7yz}$

        $= 3xy\sqrt{7yz}$

59. $-\sqrt{450x^3y^9} = -\sqrt{2 \cdot 3^2 \cdot 5^2 x^3 y^9}$

        $= -\sqrt{3^2 \cdot 5^2 x^2 y^8 \cdot 2xy}$

        $= -3 \cdot 5xy^4\sqrt{2xy}$

        $= -15xy^4\sqrt{2xy}$

61. $\sqrt{\dfrac{196}{p^4q^2}} = \sqrt{\dfrac{2^2 \cdot 7^2}{p^4q^2}}$

        $= \dfrac{2 \cdot 7}{p^2q}$

        $= \dfrac{14}{p^2q}$

63. $3\sqrt{16z^3} = 3\sqrt{2^3 \cdot 2z^3}$

        $= 3\sqrt{2^3 \cdot z^3 \cdot 2}$

        $= 2z\sqrt[3]{2}$

65. $3\sqrt{\dfrac{216a^6b^{12}c^4}{d^{27}}} = 3\sqrt{\dfrac{6^3 a^6 b^{12} c^3}{d^{27}}}$

        $= \dfrac{6a^2b^4c^3\sqrt{c}}{d^9}$

67. $5\sqrt{-96x^{15}z^{26}} = 5\sqrt{(-2)^5 3x^{15}z^{25} \cdot z}$

        $= -2x^3z^5 \sqrt[5]{3z}$

69. $\sqrt{(13+2x)^2} = 13 + 2x$

71. $\sqrt{36+9v^2} = \sqrt{9(4+v^2)}$

        $= 3\sqrt{4+v^2}$

73. $\sqrt{x^2} = -x$ when $x < 0$

75. $\sqrt{a^2} = a$

77. $\sqrt{c^2} = |c|$

79. $\sqrt{(b-1)^2} = -(b-1)$

        $= -b + 1$ or $1 - b$

Problem Set 5.3.

1. $\sqrt{11} - 3\sqrt{11} = -2\sqrt{11}$

3. $\sqrt{121} + 2\sqrt{36} = 11 + 2 \cdot 6$

        $= 11 + 12$

        $= 23$

5. $\sqrt[3]{54} - \sqrt[3]{-16} = \sqrt[3]{3^3 \cdot 2} - \sqrt[3]{(-2)^3 \cdot 2}$

$$= 3\sqrt[3]{2} - (-2)\sqrt[3]{2}$$

$$= 3\sqrt[3]{2} + 2\sqrt[3]{2}$$

$$= 5\sqrt[3]{2}$$

7. $\sqrt{72} - \sqrt{1250} + 11\sqrt{8}$

$$= \sqrt{36 \cdot 2} - \sqrt{25^2 \cdot 2} + 11\sqrt{4 \cdot 2}$$

$$= 6\sqrt{2} - 25\sqrt{2} + 11 \cdot 2\sqrt{2}$$

$$= 6\sqrt{2} - 25\sqrt{2} + 22\sqrt{2}$$

$$= 3\sqrt{2}$$

9. $5x\sqrt{27y^5} - xy\sqrt{3y^3} + 2y^2\sqrt{12x^2 y}$

$$= 5x\sqrt{3^2 \cdot 3y^4 \cdot y} - xy\sqrt{3 \cdot y^2 \cdot y}$$

$$+ 2y^2\sqrt{4 \cdot 3x^2 y}$$

$$= (5x)(3y^2)\sqrt{3y} - xy(y)\sqrt{3y}$$

$$+ 2y^2(2x)\sqrt{3y}$$

$$= 15xy^2\sqrt{3y} - xy^2\sqrt{3y} + 4xy^2\sqrt{3y}$$

$$= 18xy^2\sqrt{3y}$$

11. $\sqrt[3]{-432} - 2\sqrt[3]{-250}$

$$= \sqrt[3]{(-6)^3 \cdot 2} - 2\sqrt[3]{(-5)^3 \cdot 2}$$

$$= -6\sqrt[3]{2} - 2(-5)\sqrt[3]{2}$$

$$= -6\sqrt[3]{2} + 10\sqrt[3]{2}$$

$$= 4\sqrt[3]{2}$$

13. $\sqrt{xy} \cdot \sqrt{x^3 y^5} = \sqrt{x^4 y^6}$

$$= x^2 y^3$$

15. $\sqrt{5}(2\sqrt{3} + \sqrt{5}) = 2\sqrt{15} + \sqrt{25}$

$$= 2\sqrt{15} + 5$$

17. $(1 - \sqrt{2})(2\sqrt{2} + 3) = 2\sqrt{2} + 3 - 2\sqrt{4}$

$$- 3\sqrt{2}$$

$$= 2\sqrt{2} + 3 - 2 \cdot 2 - 3\sqrt{2}$$

$$= 2\sqrt{2} - 3\sqrt{2} + 3 - 4$$

$$= -\sqrt{2} - 1$$

19. $(2\sqrt{x} + \sqrt{y})^2 = (2\sqrt{x})^2 + 2 \cdot 2\sqrt{x} \cdot \sqrt{y}$

$$+ (\sqrt{y})^2$$

$$= 4x + 4\sqrt{xy} + y$$

21. $(1 - \sqrt{2})(1 + \sqrt{2}) = 1 - \sqrt{4}$

$$= 1 - 2$$

$$= -1$$

23. $\dfrac{\sqrt{48}}{\sqrt{6}} = \sqrt{\dfrac{48}{6}}$

$$= \sqrt{8}$$

$$= \sqrt{4 \cdot 2}$$

$$= 2\sqrt{2}$$

25. $\dfrac{\sqrt[3]{108}}{\sqrt[3]{4}} = \sqrt[3]{\dfrac{108}{4}}$

$$= \sqrt[3]{27}$$

$$= 3$$

27. $\dfrac{1}{\sqrt{5}} = \dfrac{1}{\sqrt{5}} \cdot \dfrac{\sqrt{5}}{\sqrt{5}}$

$$= \dfrac{\sqrt{5}}{\sqrt{25}}$$

$$= \dfrac{\sqrt{5}}{5}$$

29. $\dfrac{5}{2\sqrt{5}} = \dfrac{5\sqrt{5}}{2\sqrt{5}\sqrt{5}}$

$= \dfrac{5\sqrt{5}}{2\sqrt{25}}$

$= \dfrac{5\sqrt{5}}{2\cdot 5}$

$= \dfrac{\sqrt{5}}{2}$

31. $\dfrac{\sqrt{14}}{2\sqrt{2x}} = \dfrac{1}{2}\sqrt{\dfrac{14}{2x}}$

$= \dfrac{1}{2}\sqrt{\dfrac{7}{x}}$

$= \dfrac{1}{2}\sqrt{\dfrac{7\cdot x}{x\cdot x}}$

$= \dfrac{1}{2x}\sqrt{7x}$ or $\dfrac{\sqrt{7x}}{2x}$

33. $\dfrac{1}{\sqrt[3]{7}} = \dfrac{\sqrt[3]{7^2}}{\sqrt[3]{7\cdot 7^2}}$

$= \dfrac{\sqrt[3]{49}}{7}$

35. $\dfrac{5}{\sqrt[3]{5}} = \dfrac{5\sqrt[3]{5^2}}{\sqrt[3]{5\cdot 5^2}}$

$= \dfrac{5\sqrt[3]{5^2}}{5}$

$= \sqrt[3]{25}$

37. $\dfrac{1}{\sqrt[4]{4}} = \dfrac{1\sqrt[4]{2^2}}{\sqrt[4]{2^2\cdot 2^2}}$

$= \dfrac{\sqrt[4]{4}}{2}$

39. $\dfrac{\sqrt{2}}{1-\sqrt{2}} = \dfrac{\sqrt{2}}{(1-\sqrt{2})}\cdot\dfrac{(1+\sqrt{2})}{(1+\sqrt{2})} = \dfrac{\sqrt{2}+\sqrt{4}}{1-\sqrt{4}}$

$= \dfrac{\sqrt{2}+2}{1-2}$

$= \dfrac{\sqrt{2}+2}{-1}$

$= -\sqrt{2} - 2$

41. $\dfrac{2\sqrt{3}}{\sqrt{2}-\sqrt{3}} = \dfrac{2\sqrt{3}(\sqrt{2}+\sqrt{3})}{(\sqrt{2}-\sqrt{3})(\sqrt{2}+\sqrt{3})}$

$= \dfrac{2\sqrt{6}+2\sqrt{9}}{\sqrt{4}-\sqrt{9}}$

$= \dfrac{2\sqrt{6}+3\cdot 2}{2-3}$

$= \dfrac{2\sqrt{6}+6}{-1}$

$= -2\sqrt{6} - 6$

43. $\dfrac{\sqrt{k}-1}{\sqrt{k}+1} = \dfrac{(\sqrt{k}-1)(\sqrt{k}-1)}{(\sqrt{k}+1)(\sqrt{k}-1)}$

$= \dfrac{(\sqrt{k})^2-2\sqrt{k}+1}{(\sqrt{k})^2-1}$

$= \dfrac{k-2\sqrt{k}+1}{k-1}$

45. $\sqrt{13} + 3\sqrt{13} = 4\sqrt{13}$

47. $\sqrt{72} + 2\sqrt{98} = \sqrt{36\cdot 2} + 2\sqrt{49\cdot 2}$

$= 6\sqrt{2} + 2\cdot 7\sqrt{2}$

$= 6\sqrt{2} + 14\sqrt{2}$

$= 20\sqrt{2}$

49. $\sqrt[3]{108} + \sqrt[3]{32} = \sqrt[3]{3^3\cdot 2^2} + \sqrt[3]{2^3\cdot 2^2}$

$= 3\sqrt[3]{4} + 2\sqrt[3]{4}$

$= 5\sqrt[3]{4}$

51. $\sqrt{18} - 2\sqrt{32} = \sqrt{3^2\cdot 2} - 2\sqrt{2^4\cdot 2}$

$= 3\sqrt{2} - 2\cdot 2^2\sqrt{2}$

$= 3\sqrt{2} - 8\sqrt{2}$

$= -5\sqrt{2}$

$$= 4 + 2\sqrt{3}$$

53. $\sqrt{75} - \sqrt{1587} + 8\sqrt{12}$

$$= \sqrt{5^2 \cdot 3} - \sqrt{23^2 \cdot 3} + 8\sqrt{2^2 \cdot 3}$$

$$= 5\sqrt{3} - 23\sqrt{3} + 8 \cdot 2\sqrt{3}$$

$$= 5\sqrt{3} - 23\sqrt{3} + 16\sqrt{3}$$

$$= -2\sqrt{3}$$

55. $7x\sqrt{108y^7} + xy^2\sqrt{3y^3} - 12y^2\sqrt{27x^3y^3}$

$$= 7x\sqrt{3^2 \cdot 2^2 \cdot y^6 \cdot 3y} + xy^2\sqrt{y^2 \cdot 3y}$$
$$\qquad - 12y^2\sqrt{3^2 x^2 y^2 \cdot 3y}$$

$$= (7x)(3 \cdot 2 \cdot y^3)\sqrt{3y} + xy^2(y)\sqrt{3y}$$
$$\qquad - 12y^2(3xy)\sqrt{3y}$$

$$= 42xy^3\sqrt{3y} + xy^3\sqrt{3y} - 36xy^3\sqrt{3y}$$

$$= 7xy^3\sqrt{3y}$$

57. $\sqrt[3]{-192} - 2\sqrt[3]{-375}$

$$= \sqrt[3]{(-4)^3 \cdot 3} - 2\sqrt[3]{(-5)^3 3}$$

$$= -4\sqrt[3]{3} - 2(-5)\sqrt[3]{3}$$

$$= -4\sqrt[3]{3} + 10\sqrt[3]{3}$$

$$= 6\sqrt[3]{3}$$

59. $\sqrt[3]{-3a^4b} - \sqrt[3]{16ab^2} = \sqrt[3]{-3 \cdot 16a^5b^3}$

$$= \sqrt[3]{(-2)^3 a^3 b^3 \cdot 2 \cdot 3 \cdot a^2}$$

$$= -2ab\sqrt[3]{6a^2}$$

61. $\sqrt{2}(2\sqrt{2} + \sqrt{6}) = 2\sqrt{4} + \sqrt{12}$

$$= 2 \cdot 2 + \sqrt{2^2 \cdot 3}$$

63. $(1+\sqrt{x})(3\sqrt{x}-2)$

$$= 3\sqrt{x} + 3\sqrt{x^2} - 2 - 2\sqrt{x}$$

$$= 3\sqrt{x} - 2\sqrt{x} + 3x - 2$$

$$= \sqrt{x} + 3x - 2$$

65. $(2+\sqrt{5})(3\sqrt{2}+2\sqrt{3})$

$$= 6\sqrt{2} + 3\sqrt{10} + 4\sqrt{3} + 2\sqrt{15}$$

67. $(1-\sqrt{3})^2 = 1 - 2\sqrt{3} + (\sqrt{3})^2$

$$= 1 - 2\sqrt{3} + 3$$

$$= 4 - 2\sqrt{3}$$

69. $(2\sqrt{3}-\sqrt{2})^2$

$$= (2\sqrt{3})^2 - 2(2\sqrt{3})(\sqrt{2}) + (\sqrt{2})^2$$

$$= 4 \cdot 3 - 4\sqrt{6} + 2$$

$$= 12 + 2 - 4\sqrt{6}$$

$$= 14 - 4\sqrt{6}$$

71. $(1-\sqrt{k})(1+\sqrt{k}) = 1 - (\sqrt{k})^2$

$$= 1 - k$$

73. $(\sqrt{6}-\sqrt{5})(\sqrt{6}+\sqrt{5}) = (\sqrt{6})^2 - (\sqrt{5})^2$

$$= 6 - 5$$

$$= 1$$

75. $\dfrac{\sqrt{72}}{\sqrt{6}} = \sqrt{\dfrac{72}{6}}$

$$= \sqrt{12}$$

$$= \sqrt{2^2 3}$$

$$= 2\sqrt{3}$$

77. $\dfrac{\sqrt[3]{32}}{\sqrt[3]{2}} = \sqrt[3]{\dfrac{32}{2}}$

$\quad = \sqrt[3]{16}$

$\quad = \sqrt[3]{2^3 \cdot 2}$

$\quad = 2\sqrt[3]{2}$

79. $\dfrac{1}{\sqrt{7}} = \dfrac{1\sqrt{7}}{\sqrt{7} \cdot \sqrt{7}}$

$\quad = \dfrac{\sqrt{7}}{7}$

81. $\dfrac{3}{2\sqrt{x}} = \dfrac{3\sqrt{x}}{2\sqrt{x}\sqrt{x}}$

$\quad = \dfrac{3\sqrt{x}}{2x}$

83. $\dfrac{\sqrt{22}}{2\sqrt{2x}} = \dfrac{1}{2}\sqrt{\dfrac{22}{2x}}$ $= \dfrac{11}{2\cancel{2}x} \cdot \dfrac{x}{x} = \dfrac{\sqrt{11}x}{2x}$

$\quad = \dfrac{1}{2}\sqrt{\dfrac{11}{x}}$

$\quad = \dfrac{1}{2}\sqrt{\dfrac{11 \cdot x}{x \cdot x}}$

$\quad = \dfrac{1}{2}\dfrac{\sqrt{11x}}{x}$ or $\dfrac{\sqrt{11x}}{2x}$

85. $\dfrac{\sqrt{3}}{2+\sqrt{3}} = \dfrac{\sqrt{3}(2-\sqrt{3})}{(2+\sqrt{3})(2-\sqrt{3})}$

$\quad = \dfrac{2\sqrt{3}-3}{4-3}$

$\quad = \dfrac{2\sqrt{3}-3}{1}$

$\quad = 2\sqrt{3}-3$

87. $\dfrac{3\sqrt{2}}{\sqrt{3}-\sqrt{2}} = \dfrac{3\sqrt{2}\,(\sqrt{3}+\sqrt{2})}{(\sqrt{3}-\sqrt{2})(\sqrt{3}+\sqrt{2})}$

$\quad = \dfrac{3\sqrt{6}+3\cdot 2}{3-2}$

$\quad = \dfrac{3\sqrt{6}+6}{1}$

$\quad = 3\sqrt{6}+6$

89. $\dfrac{3\sqrt{2}-1}{\sqrt{2}+1} = \dfrac{(3\sqrt{2}-1)(\sqrt{2}-1)}{(\sqrt{2}+1)(\sqrt{2}-1)}$

$\quad = \dfrac{3\sqrt{4}-\sqrt{2}-3\sqrt{2}+1}{2-1}$

$\quad = \dfrac{6-4\sqrt{2}+1}{1}$

$\quad = 7 - 4\sqrt{2}$

91. $\dfrac{\sqrt{2k}-3}{\sqrt{2k}+3} = \dfrac{(\sqrt{2k}-3)(\sqrt{2k}-3)}{(\sqrt{2k}+3)(\sqrt{2k}-3)}$

$\quad = \dfrac{(\sqrt{2k})^2-2(3\sqrt{2k})+9}{(\sqrt{2k})^2-9}$

$\quad = \dfrac{2k-6\sqrt{2k}+9}{2k-9}$

93. $\dfrac{2\sqrt{k}+3\sqrt{m}}{\sqrt{k}+2\sqrt{m}} = \dfrac{(2\sqrt{k}+3\sqrt{m})(\sqrt{k}-2\sqrt{m})}{(\sqrt{k}+2\sqrt{m})(\sqrt{k}-2\sqrt{m})}$

$\quad = \dfrac{2\cdot k+3\sqrt{mk}-4\sqrt{mk}-6\cdot m}{k-4\cdot m}$

$\quad = \dfrac{2k-\sqrt{mk}-6m}{k-4m}$

95. $\dfrac{1}{\sqrt[3]{49}} = \dfrac{1}{\sqrt[3]{7^2}}$

$\quad = \dfrac{\sqrt[3]{7}}{\sqrt[3]{7^2}\,\sqrt[3]{7}}$

$\quad = \dfrac{\sqrt[3]{7}}{\sqrt[3]{7^3}}$

$\quad = \dfrac{\sqrt[3]{7}}{7}$

97. $\dfrac{1}{\sqrt[4]{9}} = \dfrac{1}{\sqrt[4]{3^2}}$

$\quad = \dfrac{\sqrt[4]{3^2}}{\sqrt[4]{3^2} \cdot \sqrt[4]{3^2}}$

118

$$= \frac{\sqrt[4]{3^2}}{\sqrt[4]{3^4}}$$

$$= \frac{\sqrt[4]{9}}{3}$$

99. $(\sqrt[3]{a}-\sqrt[3]{b})(\sqrt[3]{a^2}+\sqrt[3]{ab}+\sqrt[3]{b^2}) = a - b$

　　 Difference of cubes.

101. $\dfrac{1}{\sqrt[3]{3}-\sqrt[3]{2}} = \dfrac{(\sqrt[3]{9}+\sqrt[3]{6}+\sqrt[3]{4})}{(\sqrt[3]{3}-\sqrt[3]{2})(\sqrt[3]{9}+\sqrt[3]{6}+\sqrt[3]{4})}$

$$= \frac{\sqrt[3]{9}+\sqrt[3]{6}+\sqrt[3]{4}}{3-2}$$

$$= \frac{\sqrt[3]{9}+\sqrt[3]{6}+\sqrt[3]{4}}{1}$$

$$= \sqrt[3]{9} + \sqrt[3]{6} + \sqrt[3]{4}$$

103. $\dfrac{\sqrt[3]{2}}{\sqrt[3]{2}-1} = \dfrac{\sqrt[3]{2}(\sqrt[3]{4}+\sqrt[3]{2}+1)}{(\sqrt[3]{2}-1)(\sqrt[3]{4}+\sqrt[3]{2}+1)}$

$$= \frac{\sqrt[3]{8}+\sqrt[3]{4}+\sqrt[3]{2}}{2-1}$$

$$= \frac{\sqrt[3]{2^3} + \sqrt[3]{4}+\sqrt[3]{2}}{1}$$

$$= 2 + \sqrt[3]{4} + \sqrt[3]{2}$$

105. $x^2 - 8 = (x-\sqrt{8})(x+\sqrt{8})$

$$= (x\cdot\sqrt{2^2\cdot2})(x+\sqrt{2^2\cdot2})$$

$$= (x-2\sqrt{2})(x+2\sqrt{2})$$

Problem Set 5.4.

1. $49^{1/2} = \sqrt{49}$

$$= 7$$

3. $169^{1/2} = \sqrt{169}$

$$= 13$$

5. $(-100)^{1/2} = \sqrt{-100}$

　　 $\sqrt{-100}$ is not a real number.

7. $81^{1/4} = \sqrt[4]{81}$

$$= 3$$

9. $1024^{1/10} = \sqrt[10]{1024}$

$$= 2$$

11. $64^{5/6} = 64^{(1/6)5}$

$$= (64^{1/6})^5$$

$$= (\sqrt[6]{64})^5$$

$$= 2^5$$

$$= 32$$

13. $4^{7/2} = 4^{(1/2)7}$

$$= (4^{1/2})^7$$

$$= (\sqrt{4})^7$$

$$= 2^7$$

$$= 128$$

15. $27^{-2/3} = 27^{(1/3)(-2)}$

$$= (27^{1/3})^{-2}$$

$$= (\sqrt[3]{27})^{-2}$$

$$= 3^{-2}$$

$$= \frac{1}{3^2}$$

$$= \frac{1}{9}$$

17. $(-49)^{-3/2} = (-49)^{(t)(-3)}$

$$= (\sqrt{-49})$$

　　 $\sqrt{-49}$ is not a real number.

119

19. $(\frac{8}{125})^{2/3} = (\frac{8}{125})^{1/3(2)}$

$\qquad = (\sqrt[3]{\frac{8}{125}})^2$

$\qquad = (\frac{2}{5})^2$

$\qquad = \frac{4}{25}$

21. $(\frac{196}{169})^{3/2} = (\frac{196}{169})^{1/2(3)}$

$\qquad = (\sqrt{\frac{196}{169}})^3$

$\qquad = (\frac{14}{13})^3$

$\qquad = \frac{2744}{2197}$

23. $(\frac{100}{121})^{-3/2} = (\frac{100}{121})^{1/2(-3)}$

$\qquad = (\sqrt{\frac{100}{121}})^{-3}$

$\qquad = (\frac{10}{11})^{-3}$

$\qquad = \frac{10^{-3}}{11^{-3}}$

$\qquad = \frac{11^3}{10^3}$

$\qquad = \frac{1331}{1000}$

25. $2^{1/2} \cdot 2^{5/2} = 2^{1/2+5/2}$

$\qquad = 2^{6/2}$

$\qquad = 2^3$

$\qquad = 8$

27. $(25^{3/8})^{4/3} = 25^{3/8 \cdot 4/3}$

$\qquad = 25^{1/2}$ Note: $\frac{3}{8} \cdot \frac{4}{3}$

$\qquad\qquad\qquad = \frac{4}{8} = \frac{1}{2}$

$\qquad = \sqrt{25}$

$\qquad = 5$

29. $\frac{2^{7/3}}{2^{1/3}} = 2^{7/3-1/3} = 2^{6/3}$

$\qquad\qquad = 2^2$

$\qquad\qquad = 4$

31. $(36x^2)^{1/2} = 36^{1/2}(x^2)^{1/2}$

$\qquad = \sqrt{36}\ x^{2/2}$

$\qquad = 6x$

33. $(49x^2y^{-2}) = 49^{1/2}(x^2)^{1/2}(y^{-2})^{1/2}$

$\qquad = \sqrt{49}\ x^{2/2}y^{-2/2}$

$\qquad = 7xy^{-1}$

$\qquad = \frac{7x}{y}$

35. $(-64x^{-6}z)^{-1/3}$

$\qquad = (-64)^{-1/3}(x^{-6})^{-1/3}z^{-1/3}$

$\qquad = (\sqrt[3]{-64})^{-1}x^{6/3}z^{-1/3}$

$\qquad = (-4)^{-1}x^2z^{-1/3}$

$\qquad = \frac{x^2}{-4z^{1/3}}$ or $\frac{-x^2}{4z^{1/3}}$

37. $(8x^{-2}y)^{1/2} = 8^{1/2}(x^{-2})^{1/2}y^{1/2}$

$\qquad = \sqrt{8}\ x^{-2/2}y^{1/2}$

$\qquad = \sqrt{4 \cdot 2}\ x^{-1}y^{1/2}$

$\qquad = \frac{2\sqrt{2}\ y^{1/2}}{x}$

39. $(3a^{2/3}x^{-1/3})^3 = 3^3a^{2/3(3)}x^{-1/3(3)}$

$\qquad = 27a^2x^{-1}$

$$= \frac{27a^2}{x}$$

41. $2x^2(3x^{1/6} - 5x^{-5/6})$

$= 2x^2 \cdot 3x^{1/6} - 2x^2 \cdot 5x^{-5/6}$

$= 6x^{2+1/6} - 10x^{2-5/6}$

$= 6x^{13/6} - 10x^{7/6}$

43. $(x^{1/2} + x^{-1/2})$

$= (x^{1/2})^2 + 2 \cdot x^{1/2} \cdot x^{-1/2}$

$\qquad + (x^{-1/2})$

$= x^{2/2} + 2x^0 + x^{-2/2}$

$= x + 2 + x^{-1}$

$= x + 2 + \frac{1}{x}$

45. $36^{1/2} = \sqrt{36}$

$= 6$

47. $225^{1/2} = \sqrt{225}$

$= 15$

49. $-(100)^{1/2} = -\sqrt{100}$

$= -10$

51. $81^{1/2} = \sqrt{81}$

$= 9$

53. $-64^{1/6} = -\sqrt[6]{64}$

$= -2$

55. $216^{1/3} = \sqrt[3]{216}$

$= 6$

57. $(-81)^{1/4} = \sqrt[4]{-81}$

$\sqrt[4]{-81}$ is not a real number.

59. $1024^{3/10} = (1024^{1/10})^3$

$= (\sqrt[10]{1024})^3$

$= 2^3$

$= 8$

61. $32^{7/5} = (32^{1/5})^7$

$= (\sqrt[5]{32})^7$

$= 2^7$

$= 128$

63. $9^{5/2} = (9^{1/2})^5$

$= (\sqrt{9})^5$

$= 3^5$

$= 243$

65. $64^{-2/3} = (64^{1/3})^{-2}$

$= (\sqrt[3]{64})^{-2}$

$= (4)^{-2}$

$= \frac{1}{4^2}$

$= \frac{1}{16}$

67. $(-27)^{-2/3} = (-27^{1/3})^{-2}$

$= (\sqrt[3]{-27})^{-2}$

$= (-3)^{-2}$

$= \frac{1}{(-3)^2}$

$= \frac{1}{9}$

69. $(\frac{64}{343})^{2/3} = (\frac{64}{343})^{1/3(2)}$

$$= (\sqrt[3]{\frac{64}{343}})^2$$

$$= (\frac{4}{7})^2$$

$$= \frac{16}{49}$$

71. $(\frac{256}{225})^{3/2} = (\frac{256}{225})^{1/2(3)}$

$$= (\sqrt{\frac{256}{225}})^3$$

$$= (\frac{16}{15})^3$$

$$= \frac{4096}{3375}$$

73. $(\frac{169}{324})^{-3/2} = (\frac{169}{324})^{1/2(-3)}$

$$= (\sqrt{\frac{169}{324}})^{-3}$$

$$= (\frac{13}{18})^{-3}$$

$$= \frac{13^{-3}}{18^{-3}}$$

$$= \frac{18^3}{13^3}$$

$$= \frac{5832}{2197}$$

75. $(25y^2)^{1/2} = 25^{1/2}(y^2)^{1/2}$

$$= \sqrt{25}\ y^{2/2}$$

$$= 5y$$

77. $(16x^4y^{-6})^{1/2}$

$$= 16^{1/2}(x^4)^{1/2}(y^{-6})^{1/2}$$

$$= \sqrt{16}\ x^{4/2}y^{-6/2}$$

$$= 4x^2y^{-3}$$

$$= \frac{4x^2}{y^3}$$

79. $(64x^{-3}z)^{-1/3}$

$$= 64^{-1/3}(x^{-3})^{-1/3}z^{-1/3}$$

$$= (\sqrt[3]{64})^{-1}x^{3/3}z^{-1/3}$$

$$= 4^{-1}xz^{-1/3}$$

$$= \frac{x}{4z^{1/3}}$$

81. $(18x^2y^{-2})^{1/2}$

$$= 18^{1/2}(x^2)^{1/2}(y^{-2})^{1/2}$$

$$= \sqrt{18}\ x^{2/2}y^{-2/2}$$

$$= \sqrt{9 \cdot 2}\ xy^{-1}$$

$$= 3\sqrt{2}\ xy^{-1}$$

$$= \frac{3\sqrt{2}\ x}{y}$$

83. $-3(3a^{3/2}x^{-1/2})^2$

$$= -3 \cdot 3^2 \cdot a^{3/2(2)}x^{-1/2(2)}$$

$$= -27\ a^{6/2}x^{-2/2}$$

$$= -27\ a^3x^{-1}$$

$$= \frac{-27a^3}{x}$$

85. $\frac{5x^{-1/3}y^{1/3}}{y^{2/3}} = \frac{5}{x^{1/3}y^{2/3-1/3}}$

$$= \frac{5}{x^{1/3}y^{1/3}}$$

87. $(\frac{2x^{1/3}y}{3z^{2/3}})^{-3} = \frac{2^{-3}(x^{1/3})^{-3}y^{-3}}{3^{-3}(z^{2/3})^{-3}}$

$$= \frac{2^{-3}x^{-1}y^{-3}}{3^{-3}z^{-2}}$$

$$= \frac{3^3 z^2}{2^3 xy^3}$$

$$= \frac{27z^2}{8xy^3}$$

89. $\left(\frac{25x^{-2/3}}{y^{2/3}}\right)^{-3/2} = \frac{25^{-3/2} x^{-2/3(-3/2)}}{y^{2/3(-3/2)}}$

$$= \frac{25^{1/2(-3)} x^{6/6}}{y^{-6/6}}$$

$$= \frac{(\sqrt{25})^{-3} x}{y^{-1}}$$

$$= \frac{5^{-3} x}{y^{-1}}$$

$$= \frac{xy}{5^3} \quad \text{or} \quad \frac{xy}{125}$$

91. $3x^3 (2x^{1/3} - 5x^{-5/3})$

$$= 3x^3 \cdot 2x^{1/3} - 3x^3 \cdot 5x^{-5/3}$$

$$= 6x^{3+1/3} - 15x$$

$$= 6x^{10/3} - 15x^{9/3}$$

93. $2a^{-1/2} b^{3/2} (3a^{1/2} b^{-3/2} + 1)$

$$= 2a^{-1/2} b^{3/2} \cdot 3a^{1/2} b^{-3/2}$$

$$\quad + 2a^{-1/2} b^{3/2}$$

$$= 6a^{-1/2+1/2} b^{3/2-3/2}$$

$$\quad + 2a^{-1/2} b^{3/2}$$

$$= 6a^0 b^0 + 2a^{-1/2} b^{3/2}$$

$$= 6 + \frac{2b^{3/2}}{a^{1/2}}$$

95. $(x^{3/2} + x^{-3/2})(x^{3/2} - x^{-3/2})$

$$= (x^{3/2})^2 - (x^{-3/2})^2$$

$$= x^{3/2(2)} - x^{(-3/2)(2)}$$

$$= x^3 - x^{-3}$$

$$= x^3 - \frac{1}{x^3}$$

97. $(a^{1/3} + b^{1/3})^3$

$$= (a^{1/3})^3 + 3(a^{1/3})^2 b^{1/3}$$

$$\quad + 3a^{1/3} (b^{1/3})^2 + (b^{1/3})^3$$

$$= a^{1/3(3)} + 3a^{1/3(2)} b^{1/3}$$

$$\quad + 3a^{1/3} b^{1/3(2)} + b^{1/3(3)}$$

$$= a + 3a^{2/3} b^{1/3} + 3a^{1/3} b^{2/3} + b$$

99. $(x^{1/3} - x^{-1/3})^3$

$$= (x^{1/3})^3 - 3(x^{1/3})^2 (x^{-1/3})$$

$$\quad + 3x^{1/3} (x^{-1/3})^2 - (x^{-1/3})^3$$

$$= x^{1/3(3)} - 3x^{1/3(2)} x^{-1/3}$$

$$\quad + 3x^{1/3} x^{(-1/3)(2)} - x^{(-1/3)(3)}$$

$$= x - 3x^{2/3} x^{-1/3} + 3x^{1/3} x^{-2/3}$$

$$\quad - x^{-1}$$

$$= x - 3x^{1/3} + 3x^{-1/3} - \frac{1}{x}$$

$$= x - 3x^{1/3} + \frac{3}{x^{1/3}} - \frac{1}{x}$$

101. $x^{2/3} - x^{1/3} - 6$

$$= (x^{1/3} - 3)(x^{1/3} + 2)$$

103. $(-1)^{2/2} \neq \sqrt{(-1)^2}$ since $\sqrt{-1}$ is not a real number.

105. $\sqrt[8]{x^4 y^4} = x^{4/8} y^{4/8}$

$\qquad = x^{1/2} y^{1/2}$

$\qquad = (xy)^{1/2}$

$\qquad = \sqrt{xy}$

Problem Set 5.5.

1. $\sqrt{-9} = \sqrt{9}\, i$

$\qquad = 3i$

$\qquad = 0 + 3i$

3. $-\sqrt{-121} = -\sqrt{121}\, i$

$\qquad = -11i$

$\qquad = 0 + (-11)i$

5. $3-\sqrt{-4} = 3-\sqrt{4}\,i$

$\qquad = 3 - 2i$

$\qquad = 3 + (-2)i$

7. $\sqrt{50} = \sqrt{25 \cdot 2}$

$\qquad = 5\sqrt{2}$

$\qquad = 5\sqrt{2} + 0i$

9. $(\sqrt{-2})^2 = -2$

$\qquad = -2 + 0i$

11. $i^{11} = i^3$

$\qquad = -i$

13. $i^{48} = i^0$

$\qquad = 1$

15. $i^{-235} = \dfrac{1}{i^{235}}$

$\qquad = \dfrac{1}{i^3} \qquad\qquad 4\,\overline{)235}$

$\qquad = \dfrac{1}{-i} \cdot \dfrac{i}{i} \qquad\qquad \begin{array}{r} 58 \\ \underline{20} \\ 35 \\ \underline{32} \\ 3 \end{array}$

$\qquad = \dfrac{i}{-i^2}$

$\qquad = \dfrac{i}{-(-1)}$

$\qquad = \dfrac{i}{1}$

$\qquad = i$

17. $(3+5i) - (2+3i) = 3 - 2 + 5i - 3i$

$\qquad = 1 + 2i$

19. $(-4-i) + (1+5i) = -4 + 1 - i + 5i$

$\qquad = -3 + 4i$

21. $i(14i) = 14i^2$

$\qquad = 14(-1)$

$\qquad = -14$

23. $3i(-2-5i) = -6i - 15i^2$

$\qquad = -6i - 15(-1)$

$\qquad = -6i + 15$

$\qquad = 15 - 6i$

25. $(1-i)(5+2i) = 5 - 5i + 2i - 2i$

$\qquad = 5 - 3i - 2(-1)$

$\qquad = 5 - 3i + 2$

$\qquad = 7 - 3i$

27. $(2-3i)^2 = 4 - 2(2)(3i) + (3i)^2$

$\qquad = 4 - 12i + 9i^2$

$\qquad = 4 - 12i + 9(-1)$

$\qquad = 4 - 9 - 12i$

$\qquad = -5 - 12i$

124

29. $(\sqrt{8}-\sqrt{-12})^2 = (\sqrt{4\cdot2}-\sqrt{12}i)^2$

$\qquad = (2\sqrt{2}-2\sqrt{3}i)^2$

$\qquad = (2\sqrt{2})^2 - 2[2\sqrt{2}\cdot(2\sqrt{3}i)]$

$\qquad\qquad + (2\sqrt{3}i)^2$

$\qquad = 4\sqrt{4} - 8\sqrt{6}i + 4\sqrt{9}i^2$

$\qquad = 4\cdot2 - 8\sqrt{6}i + (-1)$

$\qquad = 8 - 12 - 8\sqrt{6}i$

$\qquad = -4 - 8\sqrt{6}i$

31. $(5+2i)(5-2i) = 5^2 - (2i)^2$

$\qquad = 25 - 4i^2$

$\qquad = 25 - 4(-1)$

$\qquad = 25 + 4$

$\qquad = 29$

33. $(\sqrt{7}+\sqrt{-5})(\sqrt{7}-\sqrt{-5})$

$\qquad = (\sqrt{7}+\sqrt{5}i)(\sqrt{7}-\sqrt{5}i)$

$\qquad = (\sqrt{7})^2 - (\sqrt{5}i)^2$

$\qquad = 7 - 5i^2$

$\qquad = 7 - 5(-1)$

$\qquad = 7 + 5$

$\qquad = 12$

35. $\dfrac{1}{2-i} = \dfrac{1}{(2-i)}\dfrac{(2+i)}{(2+i)} = \dfrac{2+i}{4-i^2}$

$\qquad\qquad = \dfrac{2+i}{4-(-1)}$

$\qquad\qquad = \dfrac{2+i}{5}$

$\qquad\qquad = \dfrac{2}{5} + \dfrac{1}{5}i$

37. $\dfrac{1+2i}{1+3i} = \dfrac{(1+2i)(1-3i)}{(1+3i)(1-3i)}$

$\qquad = \dfrac{1+2i-3i-6i^2}{1-9i^2}$

$\qquad = \dfrac{1-i-6(-1)}{1-9(-1)}$

$\qquad = \dfrac{1-i+6}{1+9}$

$\qquad = \dfrac{7-i}{10}$

$\qquad = \dfrac{7}{10} - \dfrac{1}{10}i$

39. $(2-i) \div (2+i) = \dfrac{2-i}{2+i}$

$\qquad = \dfrac{(2-i)(2-i)}{(2+i)(2-i)}$

$\qquad = \dfrac{4-2(2i)-i^2}{4-i^2}$

$\qquad = \dfrac{4-4i}{4-(-1)}$

$\qquad = \dfrac{3-4i}{5}$

$\qquad = \dfrac{3}{5} - \dfrac{4}{5}i$

41. $\sqrt{-25} = \sqrt{25}i$

$\qquad = 5$

$\qquad = 0 + 5i$

43. $2 - \sqrt{-5} = 2 - \sqrt{5}i$

45. $\sqrt{-7} = \sqrt{7}i$

$\qquad = 0 + \sqrt{7}i$

47. $2\sqrt{-2} = 2\sqrt{2}i$

$\qquad = 0 + 2\sqrt{2}i$

49. $i^7 = i^3$

$\qquad = -i$

51. $i^{30} = i^2$

$\qquad = -1$

53. $i^{-3} = \dfrac{1}{i^3}$

$= \dfrac{1}{i^3} \cdot \dfrac{i}{i}$

$= \dfrac{i}{i^4}$

$= \dfrac{i}{1}$

$= i$

55. $(1-i) + (2-3i) = 1 + 2 - i - 3i$

$= 3 - 4i$

57. $(5+2i) + (3+5i) = 5 + 3 + 2i + 5i$

$= 8 + 7i$

59. $(3+3i) - (5+5i) = 3 + 3i - 5 - 5i$

$= 3 - 5 + 3i - 5i$

$= -2 - 2i$

61. $i(9i) = 9i^2$

$= 9(-1)$

$= -9$

63. $i(2-3i) = 2i - 3i^2$

$= 2i - 3(-1)$

$= 2i + 3$

$= 3 + 2i$

65. $(1-i)(3+2i) = 3 - 3i + 2i - 2i^2$

$= 3 - i - 2(-1)$

$= 3 + 2 - i$

$= 5 - i$

67. $(1-3i)(2-3i) = 2 - 6i - 3i + 9i$

$= 2 - 9i + 9(-1)$

$= 2 - 9 - 9i$

$= -7 - 9i$

69. $(-2-3i)(1-2i) = -2 - 3i + 4i + 6i^2$

$= -2 + i + 6(-1)$

$= -2 - 6 + i$

$= -8 + i$

71. $(1-i)^2 = 1^2 - 2i + i^2$

$= 1 - 2i + (-1)$

$= -2i$

73. $(3+4i)^2 = 3^2 + 2(3 \cdot 4i) + (4i)^2$

$= 9 + 24i + 16i^2$

$= 9 + 24i + 16(-1)$

$= 9 - 16 + 24i$

$= -7 + 24i$

75. $(\sqrt{3}+3i)^2 = (\sqrt{3})^2 + 2\sqrt{3}(3i) + (3i)^2$

$= 3 + 6\sqrt{3}i + 9i^2$

$= 3 + 6\sqrt{3}i + 9(-1)$

$= 3 - 9 + 6\sqrt{3}i$

$= -6 + 6\sqrt{3}i$

77. $(\sqrt{3}+\sqrt{2}i)^2 = (\sqrt{3})^2 + 2\sqrt{3}\sqrt{2}i$

$+ (\sqrt{2}i)^2$

$= 3 + 2\sqrt{6}i + 2i^2$

$= 3 + 2\sqrt{6}i + 2(-1)$

$= 3 - 2 + 2\sqrt{6}i$

$= 1 + 2\sqrt{6}i$

79. $(3-i)(3+i) = 9 - i^2$

$= 9 - (-1)$

$= 10$

81. $(7-10i)(7+10i) = 49 - 100i^2$

$= 49 - 100(-1)$

$= 49 + 100$

$= 149$

83. $(\sqrt{3}-2i)(\sqrt{3}+2i) = (\sqrt{3})^2 - (2i)^2$

$$= 3 - 4i^2$$

$$= 3 - 4(-1)$$

$$= 3 + 4$$

$$= 7$$

85. $(\sqrt{2}-\sqrt{3}i)(\sqrt{2}+\sqrt{3}i) = (\sqrt{2})^2 - (\sqrt{3}i)^2$

$$= 2 - 3i^2$$

$$= 2 - 3(-1)$$

$$= 2 + 3$$

$$= 5$$

87. $\dfrac{1}{1-i} = \dfrac{1}{(1-i)} \dfrac{(1+i)}{(1+i)}$

$$= \dfrac{1+i}{1-i^2}$$

$$= \dfrac{1+i}{1-(-1)}$$

$$= \dfrac{1+i}{1+1}$$

$$= \dfrac{1+i}{2}$$

$$= \dfrac{1}{2} + \dfrac{1}{2}i$$

89. $\dfrac{3}{1-2i} = \dfrac{3(1+2i)}{(1-2i)(1+2i)}$

$$= \dfrac{3+6i}{1-4i^2}$$

$$= \dfrac{3+6i}{1-4(-1)}$$

$$= \dfrac{3+6i}{1+4}$$

$$= \dfrac{3+6i}{5}$$

$$= \dfrac{3}{5} + \dfrac{6}{5}i$$

91. $\dfrac{i}{4+4i} = \dfrac{i(4-4i)}{(4+4i)(4-4i)}$

$$= \dfrac{4i-4i^2}{16-16i^2}$$

$$= \dfrac{4i-4(-1)}{16-16(-1)}$$

$$= \dfrac{4i+4}{16+16}$$

$$= \dfrac{4i}{32}$$

$$= \dfrac{4}{32} + \dfrac{4}{32}i$$

$$= \dfrac{1}{8} + \dfrac{1}{8}i$$

93. $\dfrac{2+i}{1-3i} = \dfrac{(2+i)(1+3i)}{(1-3i)(1+3i)}$

$$= \dfrac{2+i+6i+3i^2}{1-9i^2}$$

$$= \dfrac{2+7i+3(-1)}{1-9(-1)}$$

$$= \dfrac{2-3+7i}{1+9}$$

$$= \dfrac{-1+7i}{10}$$

$$= \dfrac{-1}{10} + \dfrac{7}{10}i$$

95. $(5-i) \div (5+i) = \dfrac{5-i}{5+i}$

$$= \dfrac{(5-i)(5-i)}{(5+i)(5-i)}$$

$$= \dfrac{5^2-10i+i^2}{25-i^2}$$

$$= \dfrac{25-10i-1}{25-(-1)}$$

$$= \dfrac{25-1-10i}{26}$$

$$= \dfrac{24-10i}{26}$$

$$= \dfrac{24}{26} - \dfrac{10}{26}i$$

$$= \dfrac{12}{13} - \dfrac{5}{13}i$$

127

$(2+3i)^3$

$$= 2^3 + 3(2)^2(3i) + 3(2)(3i)^2$$
$$+ (3i)^3$$
$$= 8 + 3\cdot4\cdot3i + 6\cdot9i^2 + 27i^3$$
$$= 8 + 36i + 54i^2 + 27i^3$$
$$= 8 + 36i + 54(-1) + 27(-i)$$
$$= 8 + 36i - 54 - 27i$$
$$= 8 - 54 + 36i - 27i$$
$$= -46 + 9i$$

99. Consider $x^2 + 1 = 0$

Checking i,

LS: $(i)^2 + 1 = -1 + 1$
$$= 0$$

RS: $= 0$ i checks

Another solution: $-i$

Checking $-i$

LS: $(-i)^2 + 1 = i^{-2} + 1$
$$= -1 + 1$$
$$= 0$$

RS: $= 0$ $-i$ checks

101. $x^2 + 9 = x^2 - (-9)$
$$= x^2 - (9i^{-2})$$
$$= x^2 - (3i)^2$$
$$= (x-3i)(x+3i)$$

Review

1. $5^{-2} = \dfrac{1}{5^2}$
$$= \dfrac{1}{25}$$

3. $(-2)^{-6} = \dfrac{1}{(-2)^6}$
$$= \dfrac{1}{2^6}$$
$$= \dfrac{1}{64}$$

5. $7q^{-3} = \dfrac{7}{q^3}$

7. $6^{-4}\cdot6^6 = 6^2$
$$= 36$$

9. $\dfrac{4x^{-2}}{y^{-1}} = \dfrac{4y}{x^2}$

11. $\left(\dfrac{7^{-5}}{7^{-3}}\right)^{-1} = \dfrac{(7^{-5})^{-1}}{(7^{-3})^{-1}}$
$$= \dfrac{7^{(-5)(-1)}}{7^{(-3)(-1)}}$$
$$= \dfrac{7^5}{7^3}$$
$$= 7^{5-3}$$
$$= 7^2$$
$$= 49$$

13. $\left(\dfrac{3x^2y^{-3}}{z^{-1}}\right)^{-3} = \dfrac{3^{-3}x^{2(-3)}y^{(-3)(-3)}}{z^{(-1)(-3)}}$
$$= \dfrac{3^{-3}x^{-6}y^9}{z^3}$$
$$= \dfrac{y^9}{3^3x^6z^3} \quad \text{or} \quad \dfrac{y^9}{27x^6z^3}$$

15. $\dfrac{p}{q} - \left(\dfrac{p}{q}\right)^{-2} = \dfrac{p}{q} - \dfrac{p^{-2}}{q^{-2}}$
$$= \dfrac{p}{q} - \dfrac{q^2}{p^2}$$
$$= \dfrac{p\cdot p^2}{q\cdot p^2} - \dfrac{q^2\cdot2}{p^2\cdot q}$$
$$= \dfrac{p^3-q^3}{p^2q}$$

17. $\sqrt[3]{-128} = \sqrt[3]{-64 \cdot 2}$

$\qquad = \sqrt[3]{(-4)^3 \cdot 2}$

$\qquad = -4 \sqrt[3]{2}$

19. $\sqrt{\dfrac{24x^5}{54x}} = \sqrt{\dfrac{4x^4 \cdot 6x}{9 \cdot 6x}}$

$\qquad = \dfrac{2x^2}{3} \sqrt{1}$

$\qquad = \dfrac{2x^2}{3}$

21. $\sqrt{4+x^2}$ will not simplify.

23. $32^{4/5} = (32^{1/5})^4$

$\qquad = 2^4$

$\qquad = 16$

25. $\left(\dfrac{49}{121}\right)^{-3/2} = \left(\dfrac{49}{121}\right)^{1/2(-3)}$

$\qquad = \left(\sqrt{\dfrac{49}{121}}\right)^{-3}$

$\qquad = \left(\dfrac{7}{11}\right)^{-3}$

$\qquad = \dfrac{7^{-3}}{11^{-3}}$

$\qquad = \dfrac{11^3}{7^3}$

$\qquad = \dfrac{1331}{343}$

27. $\left(\dfrac{4x^6 y^{-4}}{9z^{-2}}\right)^{-1/2}$

$\qquad = \dfrac{4^{-1/2} x^{6(-1/2)} y^{-4(-1/2)}}{9^{-1/2} z^{-2(-1/2)}}$

$\qquad = \dfrac{9^{1/2} x^{-3} y^2}{4^{1/2} z^1}$

$= \dfrac{3y^2}{2x^3 z}$

29. $\left(\dfrac{-8x^{3/2} y^{-1/2}}{z^{-3}}\right)^{-2/3}$

$\qquad = \dfrac{-8^{-2/3} x^{3/2(-2/3)} y^{(-1/2)(-2/3)}}{z^{-3(-2/3)}}$

$\qquad = \dfrac{(-8)^{1/3 \cdot (-2)} x^{-1} y^{1/3}}{z^2}$

$\qquad = \dfrac{(3\sqrt{-8})^{-2} x^{-1} y^{1/3}}{z^2}$

$\qquad = \dfrac{(-2)^{-2} x^{-1} y^{1/3}}{z^2}$

$\qquad = \dfrac{y^{1/3}}{(-2)^2 xz^2}$

$\qquad = \dfrac{y^{1/3}}{4xz^2}$

31. $\sqrt{50} - 3\sqrt{8} = \sqrt{25 \cdot 2} - 3\sqrt{4 \cdot 2}$

$\qquad = 5\sqrt{2} - 3 \cdot 2\sqrt{2}$

$\qquad = 5\sqrt{2} - 6\sqrt{2}$

$\qquad = -\sqrt{2}$

33. $\sqrt[3]{16x^4} + x\sqrt[3]{2x} - \sqrt[3]{54x^4}$

$\qquad = \sqrt[3]{8x^3 \cdot 2x} + x\sqrt[3]{2x} - \sqrt[3]{27x^3 \cdot 2x}$

$\qquad = 2x\sqrt[3]{2x} + x\sqrt[3]{2x} - 3x\sqrt[3]{2x}$

$\qquad = 0\sqrt[3]{2x}$

$\qquad = 0$

35. $(\sqrt{3}-1)(2+\sqrt{2}) = 2\sqrt{3} - 2 + \sqrt{6} - \sqrt{2}$

37. $(2\sqrt{5}+\sqrt{7})(2\sqrt{5}-\sqrt{7}) = (2\sqrt{5})^2 - (\sqrt{7})^2$

$\qquad = 4\sqrt{25} - \sqrt{49}$

$\qquad = 4 \cdot 5 - 7$

$$= 20 - 7$$

$$= 13$$

39. $(x^{1/2} + y^{-1/2})^2$

$$= (x^{1/2})^2 + 2x^{1/2}y^{-1/2} + (y^{-1/2})^2$$

$$= x^{2/2} + 2x^{1/2}y^{-1/2} + y^{-2/2}$$

$$= x + \frac{2x^{1/2}}{y^{1/2}} + \frac{1}{y}$$

41. $\dfrac{2}{\sqrt{6}} = \dfrac{2\sqrt{6}}{\sqrt{6}\sqrt{6}}$

$$= \frac{2\sqrt{6}}{6}$$

$$= \frac{\sqrt{6}}{3}$$

43. $\dfrac{\sqrt{3}}{\sqrt{5}} = \dfrac{\sqrt{3}\cdot\sqrt{5}}{\sqrt{5}\,\sqrt{5}}$

$$= \frac{\sqrt{15}}{\sqrt{25}}$$

$$= \frac{\sqrt{15}}{5}$$

45. $\dfrac{4}{\sqrt[5]{16}} = \dfrac{4}{\sqrt[5]{2^4}}$

$$= \frac{4}{\sqrt[5]{2^4}} \cdot \frac{\sqrt[5]{2}}{\sqrt[5]{2}}$$

$$= \frac{4\sqrt[5]{2}}{\sqrt[5]{2^5}}$$

$$= \frac{4\sqrt[5]{2}}{2}$$

$$= 2\sqrt[5]{2}$$

47. $\dfrac{6}{\sqrt{5}-1} = \dfrac{6(\sqrt{5}+1)}{(\sqrt{5}-1)(\sqrt{5}+1)}$

$$= \frac{6\sqrt{5}+6}{\sqrt{25}-1}$$

$$= \frac{6\sqrt{5}+6}{5-1}$$

$$= \frac{6\sqrt{5}+6}{4}$$

$$= \frac{3\sqrt{5}+3}{2}$$

49. $\dfrac{\sqrt{3}-2}{\sqrt{3}+2} = \dfrac{(\sqrt{3}-2)(\sqrt{3}-2)}{(\sqrt{3}+2)(\sqrt{3}-2)}$

$$= \frac{(\sqrt{3})^2 - 2(2\sqrt{3}) + 2^2}{(\sqrt{3})^2 - 2^2}$$

$$= \frac{3 - 4\sqrt{3} + 4}{3 - 4}$$

$$= \frac{7 - 4\sqrt{3}}{-1}$$

$$= -7 + 4\sqrt{3}$$

51. $0.000007681 = 7.681 \times 10^{-6}$

53. $-0.00000000000988 = -9.88 \times 10^{-12}$

55. 9.006×10^{14}

$$= 900,600,000,000,000$$

57. -3.2×10^{-11}

$$= -0.000000000032$$

59. $\sqrt{18} + \sqrt{-18} = \sqrt{9\cdot 2} + \sqrt{9\cdot 2}i$

$$= 3\sqrt{2} + 3\sqrt{2}i$$

61. $(2-3i) + (7-11i)$

$$= 2 + 7 - 3i - 11i$$

$$= 9 - 14i$$

63. $4i(3-2i) = 12i - 8i^2$

$$= 12i - 8(-1)$$

$$= 12i + 8$$

$$= 8 + 12i$$

65. $(3-5i)^2 = 3^2 - 2(3\cdot5i) + (5i)^2$

$\quad = 9 - 30i + 25i^2$

$\quad = 9 - 30i + 25(-1)$

$\quad = 9 - 25 - 30i$

$\quad = -16 - 30i$

67. $\dfrac{3-7i}{5+5i} = \dfrac{(3-7i)(5-5i)}{(5+5i)(5-5i)}$

$\quad = \dfrac{15-35i-15i+35i^2}{25-25i^2}$

$\quad = \dfrac{15-50i+35(-1)}{25-25(-1)}$

$\quad = \dfrac{15-35-50i}{25+25}$

$\quad = \dfrac{-20-50i}{50}$

$\quad = \dfrac{-2}{5} - i$

69. $(x-3)^2$ is factored.

71. $(2x+3)(4x^2-6x+9)$ is factored.

73. $8x^3 - 27 = (2x-3)(4x^2+6x+9)$

75. $1 - x^2$ has two terms.

$\quad 1 - x^2 = (1-x)(1+x)$

$\quad 1 - x$ is a factor.

77. $2 - x - x^2$ has three terms.

$\quad 2 - x - x^2 = (2+x)(1-x)$

$\quad 1 - x$ is a factor.

79. $1 - x + x^2$ has three terms.

$\quad 1 - x + x^2$ is prime.

$\quad 1 - x$ is not a factor.

81. $\dfrac{-5x^{-1}}{y^2 z^{-3}} = \dfrac{-5z^3}{xy^2}$

83. $\left(\dfrac{27a^{-6}}{8b^{-9}}\right)^{-1/3} = \dfrac{27^{-1/3}a^{-6(-1/3)}}{8^{-1/3}b^{-9(-1/3)}}$

$\quad = \dfrac{8^{1/3}a^{6/3}}{27^{1/3}b^{9/3}}$

$\quad = \dfrac{\sqrt[3]{8}\,a^2}{\sqrt[3]{27}b^3}$

$\quad = \dfrac{2a^2}{3b^3}$

85. $\dfrac{\sqrt{12}-\sqrt{14}}{2} = \dfrac{\sqrt{4\cdot3}-\sqrt{4}i}{2}$

$\quad = \dfrac{2\sqrt{3}-2i}{2}$

$\quad = \dfrac{2\sqrt{3}}{2} - \dfrac{2i}{2}$

$\quad = \sqrt{3} - i$

87. $\sqrt{6}(\sqrt{2}+\sqrt{6}) = \sqrt{6}\cdot\sqrt{2} + \sqrt{6}\sqrt{6}$

$\quad = \sqrt{12} + \sqrt{36}$

$\quad = \sqrt{4\cdot3} + 6$

$\quad = 2\sqrt{3} + 6$

89. $(2-x)^3 = 2^3 - 3(2)^2x + 3(2)x^2 - x^3$

$\quad = 8 - 12x + 6x^2 - x^3$

91. $\dfrac{4+\sqrt{8}}{4} = \dfrac{4+\sqrt{4\cdot2}}{4}$

$\quad = \dfrac{4+2\sqrt{2}}{4}$

$\quad = \dfrac{4}{4} + \dfrac{2\sqrt{2}}{4}$

$\quad = 1 + \dfrac{\sqrt{2}}{2}$

93. $\dfrac{4}{x+1} - \dfrac{1}{x-2} = \dfrac{4(x-2)}{(x+1)(x-2)}$

$\quad - \dfrac{1(x+1)}{(x+1)(x-2)}$

$\quad = \dfrac{4x-8}{(x+1)(x-2)} - \dfrac{x+1}{(x+1)(x-2)}$

$$= \frac{4x-8-(x+1)}{(x+1)(x-2)}$$

$$= \frac{4x-8-x-1}{(x+1)(x-2)}$$

$$= \frac{3x-9}{(x+1)(x-2)}$$

95. $\left|\frac{2x-5}{3}\right| = 3$ equation

$$\frac{3x-5}{3} = 3 \quad \text{or} \quad \frac{2x-5}{3} = -3$$

$$3\left(\frac{2x-5}{3}\right) = 3\cdot 3 \qquad 3\left(\frac{2x-5}{3}\right) = 3(-3)$$

$$2x - 5 = 9 \qquad\qquad 2x - 5 = -9$$

$$2x = 9 + 5 \qquad\qquad 2x = -9 + 5$$

$$2x = 14 \qquad\qquad 2x = -4$$

$$x = 7 \quad \text{or} \qquad x = -2$$

$$\{-2, 7\}$$

97. $\dfrac{x}{x^2+x-6} - \dfrac{1}{x+3}$ expression

$$= \frac{x}{(x+3)(x-2)} - \frac{1}{(x+3)}$$

$$= \frac{x}{(x+3)(x-2)} - \frac{x-2}{(x+3)(x-2)}$$

$$= \frac{x-(x-2)}{(x+3)(x-2)}$$

$$= \frac{x-x+2}{(x+3)(x-2)}$$

$$= \frac{2}{(x+3)(x-2)}$$

99. $(4-3x)^2$ expression

$$= 16 - 24x + 9x^2$$

Chapter Test.

1. $(6^{-1/2})^{-2} = 6^{(-1/2)(-2)}$

$$= 6^{2/2}$$

$$= 6^1$$

$$= 6$$

A.

2. $\dfrac{(b^{1/2})^6}{(b^{-1})^2} = \dfrac{b^{1/2(6)}}{b^{-1(2)}}$

$$= \frac{b^3}{b^{-2}}$$

$$= b^3 \cdot b^2$$

$$= b^5$$

B.

3. $\sqrt[3]{-8x^4y^2} = \sqrt[3]{(-2)^3 x^3 \cdot xy^2}$

$$= -2x\sqrt[3]{xy^2}$$

C.

4. $\sqrt{32} + \sqrt{18} - \sqrt{50}$

$$= \sqrt{16\cdot 2} + \sqrt{9\cdot 2} - \sqrt{25\cdot 2}$$

$$= 4\sqrt{2} + 3\sqrt{2} - 5\sqrt{2}$$

$$= 2\sqrt{2}$$

B.

5. $i^{117} = i^1$

$$= i$$

B.

6. $(\sqrt{5}-2)^2 = (\sqrt{5})^2 - 2(2\sqrt{5}) + 2^2$

$$= 5 - 4\sqrt{5} + 4$$

$$= 9 - 4\sqrt{5}$$

D.

7. $\left(\dfrac{729}{64}\right)^{2/3} = \left(-\dfrac{729}{64}\right)^{1/3(2)}$

$$= \left(\sqrt[3]{-\frac{729}{64}}\right)^2$$

$$= \left(\frac{-9}{4}\right)^2$$

$$= \frac{81}{16}$$

$$= \frac{\sqrt{4}a^{-2}b^{6}}{\sqrt{36}\,c^{3}}$$

A.

8. $\sqrt{-3}\,(2+\sqrt{-3}) = \sqrt{3}i(2+\sqrt{3}i)$

$$= 2\sqrt{3}i + \sqrt{9}i^{2}$$

$$= \frac{2b^{6}}{6a^{2}c^{3}}$$

$$= 2\sqrt{3}i + 3(-1)$$

$$= \frac{b^{6}}{3a^{2}c^{3}}$$

$$= 2\sqrt{3}i - 3$$

$$= -3 + 2\sqrt{3}i$$

13. $\dfrac{i}{1+i} = \dfrac{i(1-i)}{(1+i)(1-i)}$

C.

9. $(5-2i)^{2} = 5^{2} - 2(5\cdot 2i) + (2i)^{2}$

$$= \frac{i-i^{2}}{1-i^{2}}$$

$$= 25 - 20i + 4i^{2}$$

$$= \frac{i-(-1)}{1-(-1)}$$

$$= 25 - 20i + 4(-1)$$

$$= \frac{i+1}{2}$$

$$= 25 - 4 - 20i$$

$$= \frac{1}{2} + \frac{1}{2}i$$

$$= 21 - 20i$$

14. $\dfrac{3}{2\sqrt{6}} = \dfrac{3\sqrt{6}}{2\sqrt{6}\sqrt{6}}$

D.

10. $\dfrac{-2x^{-1}}{y^{-2}} = \dfrac{-2y^{2}}{x}$

$$= \frac{3\sqrt{6}}{2\cdot 6}$$

11. $\dfrac{x^{-1}+y^{-1}}{(xy)^{-1}} = \dfrac{\frac{1}{x}+\frac{1}{y}}{\frac{1}{xy}}$

$$= \frac{3\sqrt{6}}{12}$$

$$= \frac{\sqrt{6}}{4}$$

$$= \frac{xy}{1}\left(\frac{1}{x}+\frac{1}{y}\right)$$

15. $\dfrac{7-\sqrt{2}}{1+\sqrt{2}} = \dfrac{(7-\sqrt{2})(1-\sqrt{2})}{(1+\sqrt{2})(1-\sqrt{2})}$

$$= xy\cdot\frac{1}{x} + xy\cdot\frac{1}{y}$$

$$= \frac{7-\sqrt{2}-7\sqrt{2}+\sqrt{4}}{1-\sqrt{4}}$$

$$= y + x$$

$$= \frac{7-8\sqrt{2}+2}{1-2}$$

12. $\left(\dfrac{36a^{4}b^{-12}}{4c^{-6}}\right)^{-1/2}$

$$= \frac{9-8\sqrt{2}}{-1}$$

$$= \frac{36^{-1/2}a^{4(-1/2)}b^{-12(-1/2)}}{4^{-1/2}c^{-6(-1/2)}}$$

$$= -9+8\sqrt{2}$$

$$= \frac{4^{1/2}a^{-4/2}b^{12/2}}{36^{1/2}c^{6/2}}$$

CHAPTER 6

Problem Set 6.1.

1. $(x+7)(x+3) = 0$

$x + 7 = 0$ or $x + 3 = 0$

$x = -7$ $\qquad x = -3$

$\{-7,-3\}$

3. $(x+5)(x-5) = 0$

$x + 5 = 0$ or $x - 5 = 0$

$x = -5$ $\qquad x = 5$

$\{-5,5\}$

5. $2x(x+5) = 0$

$2x = 0$ or $x + 5 = 0$

$x = 0$ $\qquad x = -5$

$\{-5,0\}$

7. $(x-7)(7x+1) = 0$

$x - 7 = 0$ or $7x + 1 = 0$

$x = 7$ $\qquad 7x = -1$

$x = -\dfrac{1}{7}$

$\{-\dfrac{1}{7},7\}$

9. $(5x-1)(5x+1) = 0$

$5x - 1 = 0$ or $5x + 1 = 0$

$5x = 1$ $\qquad 5x = -1$

$= \dfrac{1}{5}$ $\qquad x = -\dfrac{1}{5}$

$\{-\dfrac{1}{5},\dfrac{1}{5}\}$

11. $(3x+7)(2x-5) = 0$

$3x + 7 = 0$ or $2x - 5 = 0$

$3x = -7$ $\qquad 2x = 5$

$x = -\dfrac{7}{3}$ $\qquad x = \dfrac{5}{2}$

$\{-\dfrac{7}{3},\dfrac{5}{2}\}$

13. $x^2 = 0$

$x = 0$ $\qquad \{0\}$

15. $-2(t-3)(2t-9) = 0$

$t - 3 = 0$ or $2t - 9 = 0$

$t = 3$ $\qquad 2t = 9$

$t = \dfrac{9}{2}$

$\{3,\dfrac{9}{2}\}$

17. $(z-2i)(z+2i) = 0$

$z - 2i = 0$ or $z + 2i = 0$

$z = 2i$ $\qquad z = -2i$

$\{-2i,2i\}$

19. $x^2 - x - 2 = 0$

$(x-2)(x+1) = 0$

$x - 2 = 0$ or $x + 1 = 0$

$x = 2$ $\qquad x = -1$

$\{-1,2\}$

21. $x^2 + 6x = -5$

$x^2 + 6x + 5 = 0$

$(x+1)(x+5) = 0$

$x + 1 = 0$ or $x + 5 = 0$

$x = -1$ $\qquad x = -5$

$\{-5,-1\}$

23. $x^2 - 8x + 15 = 0$

$(x-2)(x-5) = 0$

$x - 3 = 0$ or $x - 5 = 0$

$x = 3$ $\qquad x = 5$

$\{3,5\}$

25. $4v^2 + 5v + 1 = 0$

    $(4v+1)(v+1) = 0$

    $4v + 1 = 0$ or $v + 1 = 0$

        $4v = -1$ $v = -1$

          $v = -\dfrac{1}{4}$ $\{-1,-\dfrac{1}{4}\}$

27. $x^2 - 2x = 0$

    $x(x-2) = 0$

    $x = 0$ or $x - 2 = 0$

               $x = 2$ $\{0,2\}$

29. $x^2 = -7x$

    $x^2 + 7x = 0$

    $x(x+7) = 0$

    $x = 0$ or $x + 7 = 0$

               $x = -7$ $\{-7,0\}$

31. $(x+6)(x-1) = -10$

      $x^2 + 5x - 6 = -10$

   $x^2 + 5x - 6 + 10 = 0$

       $x^2 + 5x + 4 = 0$

       $(x+1)(x+4) = 0$

   $x + 1 = 0$ or $x + 4 = 0$

      $x = -1$ $x = -4$

                  $\{-4,-1\}$

33. $(x+4)^2 = 9$

    $x^2 + 8x + 16 = 9$

  $x^2 + 8x + 16 - 9 = 0$

     $x^2 + 8x + 7 = 0$

     $(x+1)(x+7) = 0$

  $x + 1 = 0$ or $x + 7 = 0$

        $x = -1$ $x = -7$ $\{-7,-1\}$

35. $\dfrac{2}{5}x^2 - \dfrac{3}{5}x - 1 = 0$

    $5(\dfrac{2}{5}x^2 - \dfrac{3}{5}x - 1) = 5\cdot 0$

    $2x^2 - 3x - 5 = 0$

    $(2x-5)(x+1) = 0$

    $2x - 5 = 0$ or $x + 1 = 0$

        $2x = 5$ $x = -1$

         $x = \dfrac{5}{2}$ $\{-1,\dfrac{5}{2}\}$

37. $\dfrac{3}{2}t^2 + \dfrac{5}{2}t = 1$

   $\dfrac{3}{2}t^2 + \dfrac{5}{2}t - 1 = 0$

   $2(\dfrac{3}{2}t^2 + \dfrac{5}{2}t - 1) = 2\cdot 0$

   $3t^2 + 5t - 2 = 0$

    $(3t-1)(t+2) = 0$

    $3t - 1 = 0$ $t + 2 = 0$

      $3t = 1$ $t = -2$

       $t = \dfrac{1}{3}$ $\{-2,\dfrac{1}{3}\}$

39. $\dfrac{1}{2}x^2 + \dfrac{7}{6}x - 1 = 0$

    $6(\dfrac{1}{2}x^2 + \dfrac{7}{6}x - 1) = 6\cdot 0$

    $3x^2 + 7x - 6 = 0$

    $(3x-2)(x+3) = 0$

    $3x - 2 = 0$ or $x + 3 = 0$

        $3x = 2$ $x = -3$

         $x = \dfrac{2}{3}$ $\{-3,\dfrac{2}{3}\}$

41. $x^2 - 4 = 0$

    $(x-2)(x+2) = 0$

    $x - 2 = 0$ or $x + 2 = 0$

        $x = 2$ $x = -2$ $\{-2,2\}$

43. $\quad x^2 - 9 = 0$

$\quad (x-3)(x+3) = 0$

$\quad x - 3 = 0 \quad$ or $\quad x + 3 = 0$

$\quad x = 3 \qquad\qquad x = -3$

$\qquad\qquad\qquad\qquad \{3,-3\}$

45. $\quad 2x^2 - 6x = 0$

$\quad 2x(x-3) = 0$

$\quad 2x = 0 \quad$ or $\quad x - 3 = 0$

$\quad x = 0 \qquad\qquad x = 3 \quad \{0,3\}$

47. $\quad 2x^2 - 8x = 0$

$\quad 2x(x-4) = 0$

$\quad 2x = 0 \quad$ or $\quad x - 4 = 0$

$\quad x = 0 \qquad\qquad x = 4$

49. $\quad -6x^2 + 5x + 1 = 0$

$\quad -1(-6x^2+5x+1) = -1 \cdot 0$

$\quad 6x^2 - 5x - 1 = 0$

$\quad (6x+1)(x-1) = 0$

$\quad 6x + 1 = 0 \quad$ or $\quad x - 1 = 0$

$\quad 6x = -1 \qquad\qquad x = 1$

$\quad x = -\dfrac{1}{6} \qquad\qquad \{-\dfrac{1}{6},1\}$

51. $\quad x^2 - 16x + 64 = 0$

$\quad (x-8)(x-8) = 0$

$\quad x - 8 = 0$

$\quad x = 8 \qquad \{8\}$

53. $\quad x^2 - 6x - 6 = 0$

$\quad (x-6)(x+1) = 0$

$\quad x - 6 = 0 \quad$ or $\quad x + 1 = 0$

$\quad x = 6 \qquad\qquad x = -1$

$\qquad\qquad\qquad\qquad\qquad\qquad \{-1,6\}$

55. $\quad x^2 + 7x + 12 = 0$

$\quad (x+4)(x+3) = 0$

$\quad x + 4 = 0 \quad$ or $\quad x + 3 = 0$

$\quad x = -4 \qquad\qquad x = -3$

$\qquad\qquad\qquad\qquad \{-4,-3\}$

57. $\quad x^2 - 6x - 7 = 0$

$\quad (x-7)(x+1) = 0$

$\quad x - 7 = 0 \quad$ or $\quad x + 1 = 0$

$\quad x = 7 \qquad\qquad x = -1$

$\qquad\qquad\qquad\qquad \{-1,7\}$

59. $\quad x^2 - 6x - 16 = 0$

$\quad (x-8)(x+2) = 0$

$\quad x - 8 = 0 \quad$ or $\quad x + 2 = 0$

$\quad x = 8 \qquad\qquad x = -2$

$\qquad\qquad\qquad\qquad \{-2,8\}$

61. $\qquad (x-7)(x-8) = 6$

$\quad x^2 - 15x + 56 = 6$

$\quad x^2 - 15x + 56 - 6 = 0$

$\quad x^2 - 15x + 50 = 0$

$\quad (x-5)(x-10) = 0$

$\quad x - 5 = 0 \quad$ or $\quad x - 10 = 0$

$\quad x = 5 \qquad\qquad x = 10$

$\qquad\qquad\qquad\qquad \{5,10\}$

63. $\quad x^2 - 24x + 144 = 0$

$\quad (x-12)(x-12) = 0$

$\quad x - 12 = 0$

$\quad x = 12 \qquad \{12\}$

65. $\quad 5x^2 - 11x + 2 = 0$

$(5x-1)(x-2) = 0$

$5x - 1 = 0$ or $x - 2 = 0$

$5x = 1$ $x = 2$

$x = \dfrac{1}{5}$ $\{\dfrac{1}{5}, 2\}$

67. $3x^2 + 5x + 2 = 0$

$(3x+2)(x+1) = 0$

$3x + 2 = 0$ or $x + 1 = 0$

$3x = -2$ $x = -1$

$x = -\dfrac{2}{3}$ $\{-1, -\dfrac{2}{3}\}$

69. $2x^2 - 7x + 6 = 0$

$(2x-3)(x-2) = 0$

$2x - 3 = 0$ or $x - 2 = 0$

$2x = 3$ $x = 2$

$x = \dfrac{3}{2}$ $\{\dfrac{3}{2}, 2\}$

71. $5x^2 - 6x - 8 = 0$

$(5x+4)(x-2) = 0$

$5x + 4 = 0$ or $x - 2 = 0$

$4x = -4$ $x = 2$

$x = -\dfrac{4}{5}$ $\{-\dfrac{4}{5}, 2\}$

73. $3x^2 + x - 10 = 0$

$(3x-5)(x+2) = 0$

$3x - 5 = 0$ or $x + 2 = 0$

$3x = 5$ $x = -2$

$x = \dfrac{5}{3}$ $\{-2, \dfrac{5}{3}\}$

75. $5x^2 - 4x - 33 = 0$

$(5x+11)(x-3) = 0$

$5x + 11 = 0$ or $x - 3 = 0$

$5x = -11$ $x = 3$

$x = -\dfrac{11}{5}$ $\{-\dfrac{11}{5}, 3\}$

77. $6x^2 + x - 12 = 0$

$(3x-4)(2x+3) = 0$

$3x - 4 = 0$ or $2x + 3 = 0$

$3x = 4$ $2x = -3$

$x = \dfrac{4}{3}$ $x = \dfrac{-3}{2}$

79. $4x^2 + 4x - 3 = 0$

$(2x+3)(2x-1) = 0$

$2x + 3 = 0$ or $2x - 1 = 0$

$2x = -3$ $2x = 1$

$x = \dfrac{-3}{2}$ $x = \dfrac{1}{2}$

$\{-\dfrac{3}{2}, \dfrac{1}{2}\}$

81. $2s^2 - 2s - 4 = 0$

$\dfrac{1}{2}(2s^2-2s-4) = \dfrac{1}{2} \cdot 0$

$s^2 - s - 2 = 0$

$(s-2)(s+1) = 0$

$s - 2 = 0$ or $s + 1 = 0$

$s = 2$ $s = -1$

$\{-1, 2\}$

83. $-x^2 + x + 12 = 0$

$-1(-x^2+x+12) = -1 \cdot 0$

$x^2 - x - 12 = 0$

$(x-4)(x+3) = 0$

$x - 4 = 0$ or $x + 3 = 0$

$x = 4$ $x = -3$

$\{-3, 4\}$

85. $-2t^2 + 24t + 26 = 0$

$-\dfrac{1}{2}(-2t^2+24t+26) = -\dfrac{1}{2} \cdot 0$

137

$$t^2 - 12t - 13 = 0$$

$$(t-13)(t+1) = 0$$

$$t - 13 = 0 \quad \text{or} \quad t + 1 = 0$$

$$t = 13 \qquad\qquad t = -1$$

$$\{-1, 13\}$$

87. $\quad 5x^2 + \frac{1}{3}x = 2$

$$5x^2 + \frac{1}{3}x - 2 = 0$$

$$3(5x^2 + \frac{1}{3}x - 2) = 3 \cdot 0$$

$$15x^2 + x - 6 = 0$$

$$(3x+2)(5x-3) = 0$$

$$3x + 2 = 0 \quad \text{or} \quad 5x - 3 = 0$$

$$3x = -2 \qquad\qquad 5x = 3$$

$$x = -\frac{2}{3} \qquad\qquad x = \frac{3}{5}$$

$$\{-\frac{2}{3}, \frac{3}{5}\}$$

89. $\quad 5x^2 + \frac{7}{4}x - \frac{3}{2} = 0$

$$4(5x^2 + \frac{7}{4} - \frac{3}{2}) = 4 \cdot 0$$

$$20x^2 + 7x - 6 = 0$$

$$(4x+3)(5x-2) = 0$$

$$4x + 3 = 0 \quad \text{or} \quad 5x - 2 = 0$$

$$4x = -3 \qquad\qquad 5x = 2$$

$$x = \frac{-3}{4} \qquad\qquad x = \frac{2}{5}$$

$$\{-\frac{3}{4}, \frac{2}{5}\}$$

91. $\qquad x^2 - 5 = 0$

$$(x - \sqrt{5})(x + \sqrt{5}) = 0$$

$$x - \sqrt{5} = 0 \quad \text{or} \quad x + \sqrt{5} = 0$$

$$x = \sqrt{5} \qquad\qquad x = -\sqrt{5}$$

$$\{-\sqrt{5}, \sqrt{5}\}$$

93. $\qquad x^2 + 5 = 0$

$$(x - \sqrt{5}i)(x + \sqrt{5}i) = 0$$

$$x - \sqrt{5}i = 0 \quad \text{or} \quad x + \sqrt{5}i = 0$$

$$x = \sqrt{5}i \qquad\qquad x = -\sqrt{5}i$$

$$\{-\sqrt{5}i, \sqrt{5}i\}$$

95. $\qquad 4x^2 + 25 = 0$

$$(2x+5i)(2x-5i) = 0$$

$$2x + 5i = 0 \quad \text{or} \quad 2x - 5i = 0$$

$$2x = -5i \qquad\qquad 2x = 5i$$

$$x = -\frac{5}{2}i \qquad\qquad x = \frac{5}{2}i$$

$$\{-\frac{5}{2}i, \frac{5}{2}i\}$$

97. $\{1, 2\}$ is the solution set.

$$(x-1)(x-2) = 0$$

$$x^2 - 3x + 2 = 0$$

99. $\{\pm 2\}$ is the solution set.

$$(x-2)(x+2) = 0$$

$$x^2 - 4 + 0$$

101. $\{\pm 2i\}$ is the solution set.

$$(x-2i)(x+2i) = 0$$

$$x^2 - 4i^2 = 0$$

$$x^2 - 4(-1) = 0$$

$$x^2 + 4 = 0$$

Problem Set 6.2.

1. 1st girl's age: x

   2nd girl's age: x + 2

$$x(x+2) = 224$$

$$x^2 + 2x = 224$$

138

$x^2 + 2x - 224 = 0$

$(x+16)(x-14) = 0$

$x + 16 = 0$ or $x - 14 = 0$

$x = -16$ $x = 14$ $x + 2 = 16$

$x \neq -16$ since x must be
   positive.

The girls'ages are 14 and 16.

3.   length of first trail: x

length of second trail: $20 - x$

$x(20-x) = 143$

$20x - x^2 = 143$

$0 = x^2 - 20x + 143$

$0 = (x-7)(x-13)$

$x = 7$ $x = 13$ $20 - x = 7$

The length of the trails is
   7 mi. and 13 mi.

5.   1st: x 2nd: $x+1$ 3rd: $x+2$

$x^2 + (x+1)^2 + (x+2)^2 = 77$

$x^2 + x^2 + 2x + 1 + x^2 + 4x + 4$

$= 77$

$3x^2 + 6x + 5 = 77$

$3x^2 + 6x + 5 - 77 = 0$

$3x^2 + 6x - 72 = 0$

$\frac{1}{3}(3x^2+6x-72) = \frac{1}{3} \cdot 0$

$x^2 + 2x - 24 = 0$

$(x+6)(x-4) = 0$

$x = -6$ or $x = 4$ $x+1 = 5$, $x+2 = 6$

$x \neq -6$ since x is positive.

The numbers are 4, 5, and 6.

7. x: width

$2x - 4$: length

$x(2x-4) = 70$

$2x^2 - 4x = 70$

$2x^2 - 4x - 70 = 0$

$(2x+10)(x-7) = 0$

$2x + 10 = 0$ or $x - 7 = 0$

$2x = -10$ $x = 7$

$x = -5$ $2x - 4 = 10$

$x \neq -5$ since x must be
   positive

The dimensions are 7 in. by 10 in.

9. x: width

$\frac{120}{x}$: length

$2x + 2(\frac{120}{x}) = 44$

$2x + \frac{240}{x} = 44$

$x(2x+\frac{240}{x}) = x \cdot 44$

$2x^2 + 240 = 44x$

$2x^2 - 44x + 240 = 0$

$\frac{1}{2}(2x^2-44x+240) = \frac{1}{2} \cdot 0$

$x^2 - 22x + 120 = 0$

$(x-10)(x-12) = 0$

$x = 10$ $x = 12$

$\frac{120}{x} = 12$ $\frac{120}{x} = 10$

The dimensions are 10m. by 12m.

11. x: width of frame

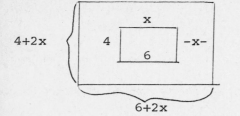

Outer dimensions: 4+2x and 6+2x

$$(4+2x)(6+2x) = 48$$
$$24 + 20x + 4x^2 = 48$$
$$4x^2 + 20x + 24 - 48 = 0$$
$$4x^2 + 20x - 24 = 0$$
$$\frac{1}{4}(4x^2+20x-24) = \frac{1}{4} \cdot 0$$
$$x^2 + 5x - 6 = 0$$
$$(x+6)(x-1) = 0$$

x = -6 or x = 1

x ≠ -6 since x must be positive.

The width of the frame should be 1 ft.

13. x: length of one side of the copper.

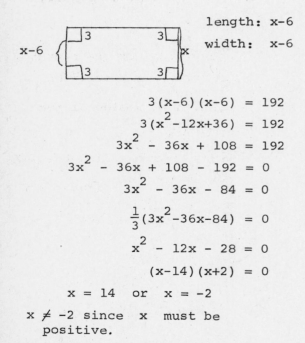

length: x-6

width: x-6

$$3(x-6)(x-6) = 192$$
$$3(x^2-12x+36) = 192$$
$$3x^2 - 36x + 108 = 192$$
$$3x^2 - 36x + 108 - 192 = 0$$
$$3x^2 - 36x - 84 = 0$$
$$\frac{1}{3}(3x^2-36x-84) = 0$$
$$x^2 - 12x - 28 = 0$$
$$(x-14)(x+2) = 0$$

x = 14 or x = -2

x ≠ -2 since x must be positive.

The copper sheet should be 14 in. by 14 in.

15. altitude: x

base: x + 9

$$\frac{1}{2}(x+9)(x) = 56$$
$$\frac{1}{2}x^2 + \frac{9}{2}x = 56$$
$$2(\frac{1}{2}x^2+\frac{9}{2}x) = 2 \cdot 56$$
$$x^2 + 9x = 112$$
$$x^2 + 9x - 112 = 0$$
$$(x+16)(x-7) = 0$$

x = -16 or x = 7, x + 9 = 16

x ≠ -16 since x is positive.

The base is 16 ft. and the altitude is 7 ft.

17. x: length along the wall

$$4^2 + x^2 = 8^2$$
$$x^2 + 16 = 64$$
$$x^2 + 16 - 64 = 0$$
$$x^2 - 48 = 0$$
$$(x-\sqrt{48})(x+\sqrt{48}) = 0$$

x = √48 or x = -√48

x = 4√3   x = -4√3

x ≠ -4√3 since x is positive.

The length along the wall is 4√3 m.

19. leg 1: x   leg 2: x+1

hypotenuse: x + 2

$$x^2 + (x+1)^2 = (x+2)^2$$
$$x^2 + x^2 + 2x + 1 = x^2 + 4x + 4$$
$$2x^2 + 2x + 1 = x^2 + 4x + 4$$
$$2x^2 - x^2 + 2x - 4x + 1 - 4 = 0$$
$$x^2 - 2x - 3 = 0$$
$$(x+1)(x-3) = 0$$

x = -1 or x = 3, x + 1 = 4, x + 2 = 5

x ≠ -1 since x is positive.

The lengths of the sides of the right triangle are 3, 4, and 5 units.

21. points Bob scored: x

points Jack scored: $x + 2$

$$x(x+2) = 168$$

$$x^2 + 2x = 168$$

$$x^2 + 2x - 168 = 0$$

$$(x+14)(x-12) = 0$$

$$x = -14 \text{ or } x = 12, \quad x + 2 = 14$$

$x \neq -14$ since x is positive.

Bob scored 12 points and
  Jack scored 14 points.

23. 1st: x   2nd: $\dfrac{51}{x}$

$$x + \frac{51}{x} = 20$$

$$x(x+\frac{51}{x}) = x \cdot 20$$

$$x^2 + 51 = 20x$$

$$x^2 - 20x + 51 = 0$$

$$(x-3)(x-17) = 0$$

$$x = 3, \frac{51}{x} = 17 \text{ or } x = 17,$$

$$\frac{51}{x} = 3$$

The numbers are 3 and 17.

25. 1st: x   2nd: x+2   3rd: x+4

$$x^2 + (x+2)^2 + (x+4)^2 = 200$$

$$x^2 + x^2 + 4x + 4 + x^2 + 8x + 16$$
$$= 200$$

$$3x^2 + 12x + 20 = 200$$

$$3x^2 + 12x + 20 - 200 = 0$$

$$3x^2 + 12x - 180 = 0$$

$$\frac{1}{3}(3x^2+12x-180) = \frac{1}{3} \cdot 0$$

$$x^2 + 4x - 60 = 0$$

$$(x+10)(x-6) = 0$$

$$x = -10 \text{ or } x = 6, x + 2 = 8,$$
$$x + 4 = 10$$

$x \neq -10$ since x is positive.

The integers are 6, 8, and 10.

27. x: width of the search zone

$\dfrac{165}{x}$: length of the search zone

$$2x + 2(\frac{165}{x}) = 52$$

$$2x + \frac{330}{x} = 52$$

$$x(2x+\frac{330}{x}) = x \cdot 52$$

$$2x^2 + 330 = 52x$$

$$2x^2 - 52x + 330 = 0$$

$$\frac{1}{2}(2x^2-52x+330) = \frac{1}{2} \cdot 0$$

$$x^2 - 26x + 165 = 0$$

$$(x-11)(x-15) = 0$$

$$x = 11, \frac{165}{x} = 15 \text{ or } x = 15,$$

$$\frac{165}{x} = 11$$

The dimensions of the search
  zone are 11 mi. by 15 mi.

29. x: length of a side of the
    cardboard

length: x-4

width: x-4

height: 2

$$2(x-4)(x-4) = 98$$

$$2(x-4)^2 = 98$$

$$2(x^2-8x+16) = 98$$

$$2x^2 - 16x + 32 = 98$$

$$2x^2 - 16x + 32 - 98 = 0$$

$$2x^2 - 16x - 66 = 0$$

$\frac{1}{2}(2x^2 - 16x - 6) = 0$

$x^2 - 8x - 33 = 0$

$(x+3)(x-11) = 0$

$x = -3$ or $x = 11$

$x \neq -3$ since x is positive.

The cardboard should be 11 in.
  by 11 in.

31. height: x   base: 4x

$\frac{1}{2}(4x)(x) = 8$

$2x^2 = 8$

$2x^2 - 8 = 0$

$\frac{1}{2}(2x^2 - 8) = 0$

$x^2 - 4 = 0$

$(x+2)(x-2) = 0$

$x = -2$ or $x = 2$, $4x = 8$

$x \neq -2$ since x must be positive.

The base is 8 ft. and the height
  is 2 ft.

33. $h = 48t - 16t^2$

Find t when h = 32

$32 = 48t - 16t^2$

$16t^2 - 48t + 32 = 0$

$\frac{1}{16}(16t^2 - 48t + 32) = 0$

$t^2 - 3t + 2 = 0$

$(t-1)(t-2) = 0$

$t = 1$ or $t = 2$

It will take 1 sec. to reach 32
  feet going up and 2 sec. to be
  at a height of 32 ft. coming
  down.

35. $V = t(3t-14)$

Find t when V = 160 cu. ft.

$160 = t(3t-14)$

$160 = 3t^2 - 14t$

$0 = 3t^2 - 14t - 160$

$0 = (3t+16)(t-10)$

$3t + 16 = 0$ or $t - 10 = 0$

$3t = -16$ $t = 10$

$t = \frac{-16}{3}$

$t \neq \frac{-16}{3}$ since t must be positive.

It takes 10 min. to fill the
  pool.

37. x: rate of eastbound train

x+70: rate of southbound train

	D	R	T
eastbound train	2x	x	2
southbound train	2(x+70)	x+70	2

GCS

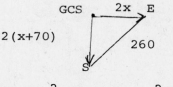

$(2x)^2 + [2(x+70)]^2 = (260)^2$

$4x^2 + (2x+140)^2 = 67,600$

$4x^2 + 4x^2 + 2(2x)(140) + (140)^2$
  $= 67,600$

$8x^2 + 560x + 19,600 = 67,000$

$8x^2 + 560x + 19,600 - 67,600 = 0$

$8x^2 + 560x - 48,000 = 0$

$\frac{1}{8}(8x^2+560x-48,000) = \frac{1}{8} \cdot 0$

$\quad x^2 + 70x - 6,000 = 0$

$\quad\quad (x+120)(x-50) = 0$

$x = -120 \quad \text{or} \quad x = 50, \; x + 70$

$\quad\quad\quad\quad\quad\quad\quad = 120$

$x \neq -120$ since x is positive.

The eastbound train is traveling
   50 mph and the southbound
   train is traveling 120 mph.

Problem Set 6.3.

1. $x^2 - 25 = 0$

$\quad x^2 = 25$

$\quad\quad x = \pm 5 \quad\quad\quad\quad \{\pm 5\}$

3. $x^2 + 9 = 0$

$\quad x^2 = -9$

$\quad\quad x = \pm\sqrt{-9}$

$\quad\quad x = \pm 3i \quad\quad\quad \{\pm 3i\}$

5. $x^2 - 5 = 0$

$\quad x^2 = 5$

$\quad\quad x = \pm\sqrt{5} \quad\quad\quad \{\pm\sqrt{5}\}$

7. $x^2 + 5 = 0$

$\quad x^2 = -5$

$\quad\quad x = \pm\sqrt{-5}$

$\quad\quad x = \pm\sqrt{5}i \quad\quad\quad \{\pm\sqrt{5}i\}$

9. $x^2 - 48 = 0$

$\quad x^2 = 48$

$\quad\quad x = \pm\sqrt{48}$

$\quad\quad x = \pm 4\sqrt{3} \quad\quad\quad \{\pm 4\sqrt{3}\}$

11. $x^2 + 18 = 0$

$\quad x^2 = -18$

$\quad\quad x = \pm\sqrt{-18}$

$\quad\quad x = \pm\sqrt{18}i$

$\quad\quad x = \pm 3\sqrt{2}i \quad\quad \{\pm 3\sqrt{2}i\}$

13. $2t^2 + 16 = 0$

$\quad 2t^2 = -16$

$\quad\quad t^2 = -8$

$\quad\quad t = \pm\sqrt{-8}$

$\quad\quad t = \pm\sqrt{8}i$

$\quad\quad t = \pm 2\sqrt{2}i \quad\quad \{\pm 2\sqrt{2}i\}$

15. $-6s^2 - 18 = 0$

$\quad s^2 + 3 = 0$

$\quad\quad s^2 = -3$

$\quad\quad s = \pm\sqrt{3} \quad\quad \{\pm\sqrt{3}i\}$

17. $(x+3)^2 = 4$

$\quad x + 3 = \pm 2$

$\quad\quad x = -3 \pm 2$

$x = -3 + 2 \quad \text{or} \quad x = -3 - 2$

$x = -1 \quad\quad\quad x = -5 \quad \{-5,-1\}$

19. $(x-7)^2 = 8$

$\quad x - 7 = \pm\sqrt{8}$

$\quad\quad x = 7 \pm\sqrt{8}$

$\quad\quad x = 7 \pm 2\sqrt{2} \quad\quad \{7\pm 2\sqrt{2}\}$

21. $(x-5)^2 = -7$

$\quad x - 5 = \pm\sqrt{-7}$

$\quad x - 5 = \pm\sqrt{7}i$

$\quad\quad x = 5 \pm \sqrt{7}i \quad\quad \{5\pm\sqrt{7}i\}$

23. $x^2 + 4x$ add: $(\frac{1}{2}4)^2 = 2^2$

                                $= 4$

25. $x^2 - 6x$ add: $[\frac{1}{2}(-6)]^2 = (-3)^2$

                                $= 9$

27. $x^2 + 7x$ add: $(\frac{1}{2}\cdot 7)^2 = (\frac{7}{2})^2$

                                $= \frac{49}{4}$

29. $x^2 + x$ add: $(\frac{1}{2}\cdot 1)^2 = (\frac{1}{2})^2$

                                $= \frac{1}{4}$

31. $u^2 + 11u$ add: $(\frac{1}{2}\cdot 11)^2 = (\frac{11}{2})^2$

                                $= \frac{121}{4}$

33. $x^2 - 4x - 5 = 0$

     $x^2 - 4x = 5$

$x^2 - 4x + 4 = 5 + 4$

    $(x-2)^2 = 9$

      $x - 2 = \pm\sqrt{9}$

      $x - 2 = \pm 3$

        $x = 2 \pm 3$

$x = 2 + 3$ or $x = 2 - 3$

$x = 5$ $x = -1$ $\{-1.5\}$

35. $x^2 - 4x + 5 = 0$

      $x^2 - 4x = -5$

$x^2 - 4x + 4 = -5 + 4$

     $(x-2)^2 = -1$

      $x - 2 = \pm\sqrt{-1}$

      $x - 2 = \pm i$

        $x = 2 \pm i$ $\{2\pm i\}$

37. $x^2 + x - 6 = 0$

      $x^2 + x = 6$

$x^2 + x + \frac{1}{4} = 6 + \frac{1}{4}$

    $(x+\frac{1}{2})^2 = \frac{25}{4}$

    $x + \frac{1}{2} = \pm\sqrt{\frac{25}{4}}$

    $x + \frac{1}{2} = \pm\frac{5}{2}$

       $x = -\frac{1}{2} \pm \frac{5}{2}$

$x = \frac{-1}{2} + \frac{5}{2}$ or $x = -\frac{1}{2} - \frac{5}{2}$

   $= \frac{4}{2}$ $= \frac{-6}{2}$

   $= 2$ $= -3$ $\{-3,2\}$

39. $x^2 + 2x = 4$

$x^2 + 2x + 1 = 4 + 1$

    $(x+1)^2 = 5$

     $x + 1 = \pm\sqrt{5}$

        $x = -1 \pm\sqrt{5}$ $\{-1\pm\sqrt{5}\}$

41. $t^2 - t + 3 = 0$

      $t^2 - t = -3$

$t^2 - t + \frac{1}{4} = -3 + \frac{1}{4}$

    $(t-\frac{1}{2})^2 = \frac{-12}{4} + \frac{1}{4}$

    $(t-\frac{1}{2})^2 = \frac{-11}{4}$

    $t - \frac{1}{2} = \pm\sqrt{\frac{-11}{4}}$

    $t - \frac{1}{2} = \pm\frac{\sqrt{11}\ i}{2}$

        $t = \frac{1}{2} \pm \frac{\sqrt{11}\ i}{2}$

               $\{\frac{1}{2}\pm\frac{\sqrt{11}\ i}{2}\}$

43. $2z^2 + 2z = 7$

      $z^2 + z = \frac{7}{2}$

$z^2 + z + \frac{1}{4} = \frac{7}{2} + \frac{1}{4}$

144

$$\left(z+\tfrac{1}{2}\right)^2 = \frac{14}{4} + \frac{1}{4}$$

$$\left(z+\tfrac{1}{2}\right)^2 = \frac{15}{4}$$

$$z + \frac{1}{2} = \pm\sqrt{\frac{15}{4}}$$

$$z = -\frac{1}{2} \pm \frac{\sqrt{15}}{2} \quad \{-\tfrac{1}{2}\pm\tfrac{\sqrt{15}}{2}\}$$

45. $2x^2 - 2x + 5 = 0$

$$x^2 - x + \frac{5}{2} = 0$$

$$x^2 - x = -\frac{5}{2}$$

$$x^2 - x + \frac{1}{4} = \frac{1}{4} - \frac{5}{2}$$

$$\left(x-\tfrac{1}{2}\right)^2 = \frac{1}{4} - \frac{10}{4}$$

$$\left(x-\tfrac{1}{2}\right)^2 = \frac{-9}{4}$$

$$x - \frac{1}{2} = \pm\sqrt{\frac{-9}{4}}$$

$$x - \frac{1}{2} = \pm\frac{3i}{2}$$

$$x = \frac{1}{2} \pm \frac{3i}{2} \quad \{\tfrac{1}{2}\pm\tfrac{3}{2}i\}$$

47. $2x^2 - 5x + 1 = 0$

$$x^2 - \frac{5}{2}x + \frac{1}{2} = 0$$

$$x^2 - \frac{5}{2}x = -\frac{1}{2}$$

$$x^2 - \frac{5}{2}x + \frac{25}{16} = -\frac{1}{2} + \frac{25}{16}$$

$$\left(x-\tfrac{5}{4}\right)^2 = \frac{-8}{16} + \frac{25}{16}$$

$$\left(x-\tfrac{5}{4}\right)^2 = \frac{17}{16}$$

$$x - \frac{5}{4} = \pm\sqrt{\frac{17}{16}}$$

$$x = \frac{5}{4} \pm \frac{\sqrt{17}}{4}$$

$$\{\tfrac{5}{4}\pm\tfrac{\sqrt{17}}{4}\}$$

49. $x^2 - 2x - 8 = 0$

$$x^2 - 2x = 8$$

$$x^2 - 2x + 1 = 8 + 1$$

$$(x-1)^2 = 9$$

$$x - 1 = \pm\sqrt{9}$$

$$x - 1 = \pm 3$$

$$x = 1 \pm 3$$

$$x = 1 + 3 \quad \text{or} \quad x = 1 - 3$$

$$x = 4 \qquad x = -2 \quad \{-2, 4\}$$

51. $x^2 - 2x + 1 = 0$

$$(x-1)^2 = 0$$

$$x - 1 = 0$$

$$x = 1 \qquad \{1\}$$

53. $3x^2 - 12x = -9$

$$x^2 - 4x = -3$$

$$x^2 - 4x + 4 = -3 + 4$$

$$(x-2)^2 = 1$$

$$x - 2 = \pm 1$$

$$x = 2 \pm 1$$

$$x = 2 + 1 \quad \text{or} \quad x = 2 - 1$$

$$x = 3 \qquad x = 1 \quad \{1, 3\}$$

55. $x^2 - 3x - 4 = 0$

$$x^2 - 3x = 4$$

$$x^2 - 3x + \frac{9}{4} = 4 + \frac{9}{4}$$

$$\left(x-\tfrac{3}{2}\right)^2 = \frac{16}{4} + \frac{9}{4}$$

$$\left(x-\tfrac{3}{2}\right)^2 = \frac{25}{4}$$

$$x - \frac{3}{2} = \pm\sqrt{\frac{25}{4}}$$

$$x - \frac{3}{2} = \pm\frac{5}{2}$$

$$x = \frac{3}{2} \pm \frac{5}{2}$$

$$x = \frac{3}{2} + \frac{5}{2} \quad \text{or} \quad x = \frac{3}{2} - \frac{5}{2}$$

$$= \frac{8}{2} \qquad\qquad = \frac{-2}{2}$$

$$= 4 \qquad\qquad = -1 \quad \{-1, 4\}$$

57. $4x^2 - 20x + 16 = 0$

$$x^2 - 5x + 4 = 0$$

$$x^2 - 5x = -4$$

$$x^2 - 5x + \frac{25}{4} = -4 + \frac{25}{4}$$

$$\left(x - \frac{5}{2}\right)^2 = \frac{-16}{4} + \frac{25}{4}$$

$$\left(x - \frac{5}{2}\right)^2 = \frac{9}{4}$$

$$x - \frac{5}{2} = \pm\frac{3}{2}$$

$$x = \frac{5}{2} \pm \frac{3}{2}$$

$$x = \frac{5}{2} + \frac{3}{2} \quad \text{or} \quad x = \frac{5}{2} - \frac{3}{2}$$

$$= \frac{8}{2} \qquad\qquad = \frac{2}{2}$$

$$= 4 \qquad\qquad = 1 \quad \{1, 4\}$$

59. $2u^2 - 2u = 2$

$$u^2 - u = 1$$

$$u^2 - u + \frac{1}{4} = 1 + \frac{1}{4}$$

$$\left(u - \frac{1}{2}\right)^2 = \frac{5}{4}$$

$$u - \frac{1}{2} = \pm\sqrt{\frac{5}{4}}$$

$$u - \frac{1}{2} = \pm\frac{\sqrt{5}}{2}$$

$$u = \frac{1}{2} \pm \frac{\sqrt{5}}{2} \qquad \left\{\frac{1}{2} \pm \frac{\sqrt{5}}{2}\right\}$$

61. $2x^2 + 5x - 4 = 0$

$$x^2 + \frac{5}{2}x - 2 = 0$$

$$x^2 + \frac{5}{2}x = 2$$

$$x^2 + \frac{5}{2}x + \frac{25}{16} = 2 + \frac{25}{16}$$

$$\left(x + \frac{5}{4}\right)^2 = \frac{32}{16} + \frac{25}{16}$$

$$\left(x + \frac{5}{4}\right)^2 = \frac{57}{16}$$

$$x + \frac{5}{4} = \pm\sqrt{\frac{57}{16}}$$

$$x + \frac{5}{4} = \pm\frac{\sqrt{57}}{4}$$

$$x = \frac{-5}{4} \pm \frac{\sqrt{57}}{4}$$

$$\left\{-\frac{5}{4} \pm \frac{\sqrt{57}}{4}\right\}$$

63. $3v^2 - 4v + 10 = 0$

$$v^2 - \frac{4}{3}v + \frac{10}{3} = 0$$

$$v^2 - \frac{4}{3}v = \frac{-10}{3}$$

$$v^2 - \frac{4}{3}v + \frac{4}{9} = \frac{-10}{3} + \frac{4}{9}$$

$$\left(v - \frac{2}{3}\right)^2 = \frac{-30}{9} + \frac{4}{9}$$

$$\left(v - \frac{2}{3}\right)^2 = \frac{-26}{9}$$

$$v - \frac{2}{3} = \pm\sqrt{\frac{-26}{9}}$$

$$v - \frac{2}{3} = \pm\frac{\sqrt{26}}{3}i$$

$$v = \frac{2}{3} \pm \frac{\sqrt{26}}{3}i$$

$$\left\{\frac{2}{3} \pm \frac{\sqrt{26}}{3}i\right\}$$

65. $2x^2 - 7x + 5 = 0$

$$x^2 - \frac{7}{2}x + \frac{5}{2} = 0$$

$$x^2 - \frac{7}{2}x = -\frac{5}{2}$$

$$x^2 - \frac{7}{2}x + \frac{49}{16} = -\frac{5}{2} + \frac{49}{16}$$

$$\left(x - \frac{7}{4}\right)^2 = \frac{-40}{16} + \frac{49}{16}$$

$$(x-\tfrac{7}{4})^2 = \tfrac{9}{16}$$

$$x - \tfrac{7}{4} = \pm\sqrt{\tfrac{9}{16}}$$

$$x - \tfrac{7}{4} = \pm\tfrac{3}{4}$$

$$x = \tfrac{7}{4} \pm \tfrac{3}{4}$$

$$x = \tfrac{7}{4} + \tfrac{3}{4} \quad \text{or} \quad x = \tfrac{7}{4} - \tfrac{3}{4}$$

$$= \tfrac{10}{4} \qquad\qquad = \tfrac{4}{4}$$

$$= \tfrac{5}{2} \qquad\qquad = 1 \quad \{1, \tfrac{5}{2}\}$$

67. $4x^2 - 6x + 10 = 0$

$$x^2 - \tfrac{6}{4}x + \tfrac{10}{4} = 0$$

$$x^2 - \tfrac{3}{2}x + \tfrac{5}{2} = 0$$

$$x^2 - \tfrac{3}{2}x = \tfrac{-5}{2}$$

$$x^2 - \tfrac{3}{2}x + \tfrac{9}{16} = -\tfrac{5}{2} + \tfrac{9}{16}$$

$$(x-\tfrac{3}{4})^2 = \tfrac{-40}{16} + \tfrac{9}{16}$$

$$(x-\tfrac{3}{4})^2 = \tfrac{-31}{16}$$

$$x - \tfrac{3}{4} = \pm\sqrt{\tfrac{-31}{16}}$$

$$x - \tfrac{3}{4} = \pm\tfrac{\sqrt{31}\,i}{4}$$

$$x = \tfrac{3}{4} \pm \tfrac{\sqrt{}i}{4}$$

$$\{\tfrac{3}{4} \pm \tfrac{\sqrt{31}\,i}{4}\}$$

69. x: length of the missing leg

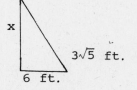

71. $x^2 = a + b$

$$x = \pm\sqrt{a+b} \qquad\qquad \{\pm\sqrt{a+b}\}$$

73. $(x+1)^2 = a$

$$x + 1 = \pm\sqrt{a}$$

$$x = -1 \pm\sqrt{a} \qquad \{-1\pm\sqrt{a}\}$$

75. $(x+b)^2 = 8$

$$x + b = \pm\sqrt{8}$$

$$x = -b \pm 2\sqrt{2} \qquad \{-b\pm 2\sqrt{2}\}$$

77. $4x^2 + 4ax - a = 0$

$$x^2 + ax - \tfrac{a}{4} = 0$$

$$x^2 + ax = \tfrac{a}{4}$$

$$x^2 + ax + \tfrac{a^2}{4} = \tfrac{a}{4} + \tfrac{a^2}{4}$$

$$(x+\tfrac{a}{2})^2 = \pm\sqrt{\tfrac{a+a^2}{4}}$$

$$x + \tfrac{a}{2} = \pm\tfrac{\sqrt{a+a^2}}{2}$$

$$x = -\tfrac{a}{2} \pm \tfrac{\sqrt{a+a^2}}{2}$$

$$\{-\tfrac{a}{2} \pm \tfrac{\sqrt{a+a^2}}{2}\}$$

79. $0.8x^2 - 0.48x + 0.01 = 0$

$$x^2 - 0.6x + 0.0125 = 0$$

Right column, problem 70:

$$x^2 + 6^2 = (3\sqrt{5})^2$$

$$x^2 + 36 = 9 \cdot 5$$

$$x^2 + 36 = 45$$

$$x^2 = 45 - 36$$

$$x^2 = 9$$

$$x = \pm 3$$

$x \neq -3$ since x is positive.

The length of the leg is 3 ft.

$$x^2 - 0.6x = -0.0125$$

$$x^2 - 0.6x + 0.09 = -0.0125 + 0.09$$

$$(x-0.3)^2 = 0.0775$$

$$x - 0.3 = \pm\sqrt{0.0775}$$

$$x = 0.3 \pm \sqrt{0.0775} \qquad \{0.3 \pm \sqrt{0.0775}\}$$

81. $ax^2 + bx + c = 0 \qquad a \neq 0$

$$x^2 + \frac{b}{a}x + \frac{c}{a} = 0$$

$$x^2 + \frac{b}{a}x = -\frac{c}{a}$$

$$x^2 + \frac{b}{a}x + \frac{b^2}{4a^2} = \frac{b^2}{4a^2} - \frac{c}{a}$$

$$(x+\frac{b}{2a})^2 = \frac{b^2}{4a^2} - \frac{4ac}{4a^2}$$

$$x + \frac{b}{2a} = \pm\sqrt{\frac{b^2-4ac}{4a^2}}$$

$$x + \frac{b}{2a} = \pm\frac{\sqrt{b^2-4ac}}{2a}$$

$$x = \frac{-b}{2a} \pm \frac{\sqrt{b^2-4ac}}{2a}$$

$$x = \frac{-b \pm \sqrt{b^2-4ac}}{2a}$$

$$\{\frac{-b \pm \sqrt{b^2-4ac}}{2a}, a \neq 0\}$$

Problem Set 6.4.

1. $x^2 + 2x - 8 = 0$

$a = 1 \quad b = 2 \quad c = -8$

$$x = \frac{-2 \pm \sqrt{4-4(1)(-8)}}{2(1)}$$

$$= \frac{-2 \pm \sqrt{4+32}}{2}$$

$$= \frac{-2 \pm \sqrt{36}}{2}$$

$$= \frac{-2 \pm 6}{2}$$

$$x = \frac{-2+6}{2} \quad \text{or} \quad x = \frac{-2-6}{2}$$

$$= \frac{4}{2} \qquad\qquad = \frac{-8}{2}$$

$$= 2 \qquad\qquad = -4 \quad \{-4,2\}$$

3. $x^2 + 2x = 0$

$a = 1 \quad b = 2 \quad c = 0$

$$x = \frac{-2 \pm \sqrt{4-4(1)0}}{2(1)}$$

$$= \frac{-2 \pm \sqrt{4}}{2}$$

$$= \frac{-2 \pm 2}{2}$$

$$x = \frac{-2+2}{2} \quad \text{or} \quad x = \frac{-2-2}{2}$$

$$= \frac{0}{2} \qquad\qquad = \frac{-4}{2}$$

$$= 0 \qquad\qquad = -2 \quad \{-2,0\}$$

5. $x^2 - x - 1 = 0$

$a = 1 \quad b = -1 \quad c = -1$

$$x = \frac{-(-1) \pm \sqrt{(-1)^2-4(1)(-1)}}{2(1)}$$

$$= \frac{1 \pm \sqrt{1+4}}{2}$$

$$= \frac{1 \pm \sqrt{5}}{2} \quad \text{or} \quad \frac{1}{2} \pm \frac{\sqrt{5}}{2} \quad \{\frac{1}{2} \pm \frac{\sqrt{5}}{2}\}$$

7. $x^2 + 4x + 4 = 0$

$a = 1 \quad b = 4 \quad c = 4$

$$x = \frac{-4 \pm \sqrt{16-4(1)(4)}}{2(1)}$$

$$= \frac{-4 \pm \sqrt{16-16}}{2}$$

$$= \frac{-4 \pm 0}{2}$$

$$= \frac{-4}{2}$$

$$= -2 \qquad\qquad \{-2\}$$

9. $x^2 - x + 1 = 0$

$a = 1 \quad b = -1 \quad c = 1$

$$x = \frac{-(-1)\pm\sqrt{(-1)^2-4(1)(1)}}{2(1)}$$

$$= \frac{1\pm\sqrt{1-4}}{2}$$

$$= \frac{1\pm\sqrt{-3}}{2}$$

$$= \frac{1\pm\sqrt{3}i}{2} \quad \text{or} \quad \frac{1}{2}\pm\frac{\sqrt{3}i}{2} \quad \left\{\frac{1}{2}\pm\frac{\sqrt{3}i}{2}\right\}$$

11. $x^2 + 1 = 0$

$a = 1 \quad b = 0 \quad c = 1$

$$x = \frac{-0\pm\sqrt{0^2-4(1)(1)}}{2(1)}$$

$$= \frac{0\pm\sqrt{-4}}{2}$$

$$= \frac{\pm\sqrt{4}i}{2}$$

$$= \pm\frac{2i}{2}$$

$$= \pm i \qquad\qquad \{\pm i\}$$

13. $x^2 + 5x + 9 = 0$

$a = 1 \quad b = 5 \quad c = 9$

$$x = \frac{-5\pm\sqrt{25-4(1)(9)}}{2(1)}$$

$$= \frac{-5\pm\sqrt{25-36}}{2}$$

$$= \frac{-5\pm\sqrt{-11}}{2}$$

$$= \frac{-5\pm\sqrt{11}i}{2} \quad \text{or} \quad \frac{-5}{2}\pm\frac{\sqrt{11}}{2}i$$

15. $x^2 - 2x = 1$

$x^2 - 2x - 1 = 0$

$a = 1 \quad b = -2 \quad c = -1$

$$x = \frac{-(-2)\pm\sqrt{(-2)^2-4(1)(-1)}}{2(1)}$$

$$= \frac{2\pm\sqrt{4+4}}{2}$$

$$= \frac{2\pm\sqrt{8}}{2}$$

$$= \frac{2+2\sqrt{2}}{2}$$

$$= 1 \pm \sqrt{2} \qquad \{1\pm\sqrt{2}\}$$

17. $x^2 + 2x - 1 = 0$

$a = 1 \quad b = 2 \quad c = -1$

$$x = \frac{-2\pm\sqrt{4-4(1)(-1)}}{2(1)}$$

$$= \frac{-2\pm\sqrt{4+4}}{2}$$

$$= \frac{-2\pm\sqrt{8}}{2}$$

$$= \frac{-2+2\sqrt{2}}{2}$$

$$= -1 \pm \sqrt{2} \qquad \{-1\pm\sqrt{2}\}$$

19. $x^2 - 6x - 2 = 0$

$a = 1 \quad b = -6 \quad c = -2$

$$x = \frac{-(-6)\pm\sqrt{(-6)^2-4(1)(-2)}}{2(1)}$$

$$= \frac{6\pm\sqrt{36+8}}{2}$$

$$= \frac{6\pm\sqrt{44}}{2}$$

$$= \frac{6^2 \pm 2\sqrt{11}}{2}$$

$$= 3 \pm \sqrt{11} \qquad \{3\pm\sqrt{11}\}$$

21. $x^2 + 2x + 2 = 0$

$a = 1 \quad b = 2 \quad c = 2$

$$x = \frac{-2\pm\sqrt{4-4(1)(2)}}{2(1)}$$

$$= \frac{-2\pm\sqrt{4-8}}{2}$$

$$= \frac{-2\pm\sqrt{-4}}{2}$$

$$= \frac{-2\pm\sqrt{4}\,i}{2}$$

$$= \frac{-2\pm2i}{2}$$

$$= -1 \pm i \qquad \{-1\pm i\}$$

23. $\qquad 4x^2 + 3 = 8x$

$4x^2 - 8x + 3 = 0$

$a = 4 \quad b = -8 \quad c = 3$

$$x = \frac{-(-8)\pm\sqrt{(-8)^2-4(4)(3)}}{2(4)}$$

$$= \frac{8\pm\sqrt{64-48}}{8}$$

$$= \frac{8\pm\sqrt{16}}{8}$$

$$= \frac{8+4}{8}$$

$$x = \frac{8+4}{8} \quad \text{or} \quad x = \frac{8-4}{8}$$

$$= \frac{12}{8} \qquad\qquad = \frac{4}{8}$$

$$= \frac{3}{2} \qquad\qquad = \frac{1}{2} \qquad \{\tfrac{1}{2},\tfrac{3}{2}\}$$

25. $6x^2 + 5x - 6 = 0$

$a = 6 \quad b = 5 \quad c = -6$

$$x = \frac{-5\pm\sqrt{25-4(6)(-6)}}{2(6)}$$

$$= \frac{-5\pm\sqrt{25+144}}{12}$$

$$= \frac{-5\pm\sqrt{169}}{12}$$

$$= \frac{-5\pm13}{12}$$

$$x = \frac{-5+13}{12} \quad \text{or} \quad x = \frac{-5-13}{12}$$

$$= \frac{8}{12} \qquad\qquad = \frac{-18}{12}$$

$$= \frac{2}{3} \qquad\qquad = \frac{-3}{2} \qquad \{-\tfrac{3}{2},\tfrac{2}{3}\}$$

27. $2s^2 - 2s - 1 = 0$

$a = 2 \quad b = -2 \quad c = -1$

$$s = \frac{-(-2)\pm\sqrt{(-2)^2-4(2)(-1)}}{2(2)}$$

$$= \frac{2\pm\sqrt{4+8}}{4}$$

$$= \frac{2\pm\sqrt{12}}{4}$$

$$= \frac{2\pm2\sqrt{3}}{4}$$

$$= \frac{1\pm\sqrt{3}}{2} \quad \text{or} \quad \frac{1}{2} \pm \frac{\sqrt{3}}{2} \qquad \{\tfrac{1}{2}\pm\tfrac{\sqrt{3}}{2}\}$$

29. $3x^2 - x + 2 = 0$

$a = 3 \quad b = -1 \quad c = 2$

$$x = \frac{-(-1)\pm\sqrt{(-1)^2-4(3)(2)}}{2(3)}$$

$$= \frac{1\pm\sqrt{1-24}}{6}$$

$$= \frac{1 \pm \sqrt{-23}}{6}$$

$$= \frac{1 \pm \sqrt{23}\, i}{6} \quad \text{or} \quad \frac{1}{6} \pm \frac{\sqrt{23}}{6} i$$

$$\left\{ \frac{1}{6} \pm \frac{\sqrt{23}}{6} i \right\}$$

$$= \frac{8 \pm \sqrt{64 \cdot 3}\ i}{8}$$

$$= \frac{8 \pm 8\sqrt{3}\, i}{8}$$

$$= 1 \pm \sqrt{3}\, i \qquad \{1 \pm \sqrt{3}\, i\}$$

31. $6t^2 - t = 5$

$6t^2 - t - 5 = 0$

$a = 6 \quad b = -1 \quad c = -5$

$$t = \frac{-(-1) \pm \sqrt{(-1)^2 - 4(6)(-5)}}{2(6)}$$

$$= \frac{1 \pm \sqrt{1 + 120}}{12}$$

$$= \frac{1 \pm \sqrt{121}}{12}$$

$$= \frac{1 \pm 11}{12}$$

$$t = \frac{1+11}{12} \quad \text{or} \quad t = \frac{1-11}{12}$$

$$= \frac{12}{12} \qquad\qquad = \frac{-10}{12}$$

$$= 1 \qquad\qquad\quad = -\frac{5}{6} \quad \left\{ -\frac{5}{6}, 1 \right\}$$

33. $8x - 16 = 4x^2$

$$0 = 4x^2 - 8x + 16$$

$a = 4 \quad b = -8 \quad c = 16$

$$x = \frac{-(-8) \pm \sqrt{(-8)^2 - 4(4)(16)}}{2(4)}$$

$$= \frac{8 \pm \sqrt{64 - 256}}{8}$$

$$= \frac{8 \pm \sqrt{-192}}{8}$$

$$= \frac{8 \pm \sqrt{192}\ i}{8}$$

35. $\frac{2}{3}x^2 + \frac{11}{3}x - 7 = 0$

$$3\left(\frac{2}{3}x^2 + \frac{11}{3}x - 7\right) = 3 \cdot 0$$

$$2x^2 + 11x - 21 = 0$$

$a = 2 \quad b = 11 \quad c = -21$

$$x = \frac{-(11) \pm \sqrt{11^2 - 4(2)(-21)}}{2(2)}$$

$$= \frac{-11 \pm \sqrt{121 + 168}}{4}$$

$$= \frac{-11 \pm \sqrt{289}}{4}$$

$$= \frac{-11 \pm 17}{4}$$

$$x = \frac{-11 + 17}{4} \quad \text{or} \quad x = \frac{-11 - 17}{4}$$

$$= \frac{6}{4} \qquad\qquad\qquad = \frac{-28}{4}$$

$$= \frac{3}{2} \qquad\qquad\qquad = -7$$

$$\left\{ -7, \frac{3}{2} \right\}$$

37. $r(r-6) - (2r-1) = 0$

$$r^2 - 6r - 2r + 1 = 0$$

$$r^2 - 8r + 1 = 0$$

$a = 1 \quad b = -8 \quad c =$

$$r = \frac{-(-8) \pm \sqrt{(-8)^2 - 4(1)(1)}}{2(1)}$$

$$= \frac{8 \pm \sqrt{64 - 4}}{2}$$

$$= \frac{8 \pm \sqrt{60}}{2}$$

$$= \frac{8 \pm 2\sqrt{15}}{2}$$

$$= 4 \pm \sqrt{15} \qquad \{4 \pm \sqrt{15}\}$$

39. $(2y+3)(y-1) = 3$

$2y^2 + y - 3 = 3$

$2y^2 + y - 6 = 0$

$a = 2 \quad b = 1 \quad c = -6$

$$y = \frac{-1 \pm \sqrt{1^2 - 4(2)(-6)}}{2(2)}$$

$$= \frac{-1 \pm \sqrt{1 + 48}}{4}$$

$$= \frac{-1 \pm \sqrt{49}}{4}$$

$$= \frac{-1 \pm 7}{4}$$

$y = \frac{-1+7}{4} \quad$ or $\quad y = \frac{-1-7}{4}$

$\quad = \frac{6}{4} \qquad\qquad = \frac{-8}{4}$

$\quad = \frac{3}{2} \qquad\qquad = -2 \quad \{-2, \frac{3}{2}\}$

41. $x^2 - x + 4 = 0$

$a = 1 \quad b = -1 \quad c = 4$

$d = (-1)^2 - 4(1)(4)$

$\quad = 1 - 16$

$\quad = -15 < 0 \quad$ so there are two

complex solutions.

43. $\qquad 2x^2 + 3x = 4$

$2x^2 + 3x - 4 = 0$

$a = 2 \quad b = 3 \quad c = -4$

$d = 3^2 - 4(2)(-4)$

$\quad = 9 + 32$

$\quad = 41 > 0$, so there are two

real solutions.

45. $x^2 + 6x + 9 = 0$

$(x+3)^2 = 0$

$x + 3 = 0$

$x = -3 \qquad \{-3\}$

47. $2x^2 - x - 1 = 0$

$(2x+1)(x-1) = 0$

$2x + 1 = 0 \quad$ or $\quad x - 1 = 0$

$2x = -1 \qquad\qquad x = 1$

$x = \frac{-1}{2} \qquad\qquad \{-\frac{1}{2}, 1\}$

49. $x^2 - 2(x+4) = 0$

$x^2 - 2x - 8 = 0$

$(x-4)(x+2) = 0$

$x - 4 = 0 \quad$ or $\quad x + 2 = 0$

$x = 4 \qquad\qquad x = -2 \quad \{-2, 4\}$

51. $\qquad\qquad 5x^2 = 13x + 6$

$5x^2 - 13x - 6 = 0$

$(5x+2)(x-3) = 0$

$5x + 2 = 0 \quad$ or $\quad x - 3 = 0$

$5x = -2 \qquad\qquad x = 3$

$x = -\frac{2}{5} \qquad\qquad \{-\frac{2}{5}, 3\}$

53. $6x^2 + x - 2 = 0$

$(3x+2)(2x-1) = 0$

$3x + 2 = 0 \qquad 2x - 1 = 0$

$3x = -2 \qquad\qquad 2x = 1$

$x = -\frac{2}{3} \qquad\qquad x = \frac{1}{2} \quad \{-\frac{2}{3}, \frac{1}{2}\}$

55. $x(x-1) = 0$

    $x = 0$ or $x - 1 = 0$

                          $x = 1$ $\{0,1\}$

57. $x^2 + 25 = 0$

    $(x-5i)(x+5i) = 0$

    $x - 5i = 0$ or $x + 5i = 0$

        $x = 5i$ $x = -5i$

                        $\{\pm 5i\}$

59. $x^2 + x - 4 = 0$

    $a = 1$ $b = 1$ $c = -4$

$$x = \frac{-1 \pm \sqrt{1-4(1)(-4)}}{2(1)}$$

$$= \frac{-1 \pm \sqrt{1+16}}{2}$$

$$= \frac{-1 \pm \sqrt{17}}{2} \text{ or } -\frac{1}{2} \pm \frac{\sqrt{17}}{2} \quad \{-\frac{1}{2} \pm \frac{\sqrt{17}}{2}\}$$

61. $(y-\frac{3}{2})^2 = -\frac{11}{4}$

$$y - \frac{3}{2} = \pm \sqrt{\frac{-11}{4}}$$

$$y = \frac{3}{2} \pm \frac{\sqrt{-11}}{2}$$

$$y = \frac{3}{2} \pm \frac{\sqrt{11}\,i}{2} \quad \{\frac{3}{2} \pm \frac{\sqrt{11}}{2}i\}$$

63. $x^2 - 2x + 2 = 0$

    $a = 1$ $b = -2$ $c = 2$

$$x = \frac{-(-2) \pm \sqrt{(-2)^2 - 4(1)(2)}}{2(1)}$$

$$= \frac{2 \pm \sqrt{4-8}}{2}$$

$$= \frac{2 \pm \sqrt{-4}}{2}$$

$$= \frac{2 \pm \sqrt{4}\,i}{2}$$

$$= \frac{2 \pm 2i}{2}$$

$$= 1 \pm i \quad\quad \{1 \pm i\}$$

65. $x^2 - 6x + 10 = 0$

    $a = 1$ $b = -6$ $c = 10$

$$x = \frac{-(-6) \pm \sqrt{(-6)^2 - 4(1)(10)}}{2(1)}$$

$$= \frac{6 \pm \sqrt{36-40}}{2}$$

$$= \frac{6 \pm \sqrt{-4}}{2}$$

$$= \frac{6 \pm \sqrt{4}\,i}{2}$$

$$= \frac{6 \pm 2i}{2}$$

$$= 3 \pm i \quad\quad \{3 \pm i\}$$

67. $(2x+1)(x+3) = 2$

        $2x^2 + 7x + 3 = 2$

  $2x^2 + 7x + 3 - 2 = 0$

        $2x^2 + 7x + 1 = 0$

    $a = 2$ $b = 7$ $c = 1$

$$x = \frac{-7 \pm \sqrt{7^2 - 4(2)(1)}}{2(2)}$$

$$= \frac{-7 \pm \sqrt{49-8}}{4}$$

$$= \frac{-7 \pm \sqrt{41}}{4} \text{ or } -\frac{7}{4} \pm \frac{\sqrt{41}}{4}$$

$$\{-\frac{7}{4} \pm \frac{\sqrt{41}}{4}\}$$

69. $y^2 + 0.1y - 0.06 = 0$

    $a = 1$ $b = 0.1$ $c = -0.06$

$$y = \frac{-0.1 \pm \sqrt{(0.1)^2 - 4(1)(-0.06)}}{2(1)}$$

$$= \frac{-0.1 \pm \sqrt{0.01 + .2}}{2}$$

$$= \frac{-0.1 \pm \sqrt{.25}}{2}$$

$$= \frac{-0.1 \pm 0.5}{2}$$

$$x = \frac{-0.1 + 0.5}{2} \quad \text{or} \quad x = \frac{-0.1 - 0.5}{2}$$

$$= \frac{0.4}{2} \qquad\qquad = \frac{-0.6}{2}$$

$$= 0.2 \qquad\qquad = -0.3$$

$$\{-0.3, 0.2\}$$

71. $x^2 + 8x + 7 = 0$

$(x+1)(x+7) = 0$

$x + 1 = 0 \quad \text{or} \quad x + 7 = 0$

$x = -1 \qquad\qquad x = -7$

$$\{-7, -1\}$$

73. $2x^2 - 6 = 0$

$\qquad 2x^2 = 6$

$\qquad x^2 = 3$

$\qquad x = \pm\sqrt{3} \qquad\qquad \{\pm\sqrt{3}\}$

75. $3x^2 - 2x - 1 = 0$

$(3x+1)(x-1) = 0$

$3x + 1 = 0 \quad \text{or} \quad x - 1 = 0$

$\qquad 2x = -1 \qquad\qquad x = 1$

$\qquad x = -\frac{1}{3} \qquad\qquad \{-\frac{1}{3}, 1\}$

77. $2x^2 - x = 0$

$x(2x-1) = 0$

$x = 0 \quad \text{or} \quad 2x - 1 = 0$

$2x = 1$

$x = \frac{1}{2} \qquad \{0, \frac{1}{2}\}$

79. $z^2 = 4$

$z = \pm 2 \qquad\qquad \{\pm 2\}$

81. $2x^2 - 2x + 1 = 0$

$a = 2 \quad b = -2 \quad c = 1$

$$x = \frac{-(-2) \pm \sqrt{(-2)^2 - 4(2)(1)}}{2(2)}$$

$$= \frac{2 \pm \sqrt{4-8}}{}$$

$$= \frac{2 \pm \sqrt{-4}}{4}$$

$$= \frac{2 \pm \sqrt{4}i}{4}$$

$$= \frac{2 \pm 2i}{4}$$

$$= \frac{1 \pm i}{2} \quad \text{or} \quad \frac{1}{2} \pm \frac{1}{2}i \qquad \{\frac{1}{2} \pm \frac{1}{2}i\}$$

83. $9x^2 + 12x + 4 = 0$

$(3x+2)^2 = 0$

$3x + 2 = 0$

$3x = -2$

$x = \frac{-2}{3} \qquad \{-\frac{2}{3}\}$

85. $5 = 2s^2 - s$

$0 = 2s^2 - s - 5$

$a = 2 \quad b = -1 \quad c = -5$

$$s = \frac{-(-1) \pm \sqrt{(-1)^2 - 4(2)(-5)}}{2(2)}$$

$$= \frac{1 \pm \sqrt{1 + 40}}{4}$$

$$= \frac{1 \pm \sqrt{41}}{4} \quad \text{or} \quad \frac{1}{4} \pm \frac{\sqrt{41}}{4}$$

$$\{\frac{1}{4} \pm \frac{\sqrt{41}}{4}\}$$

87. $5x^2 - x = 0$

   $a = 5 \quad b = -1 \quad c = 0$

   $d = (-1)^2 - 4(5)(0)$

   $d = 1 > 0$ so there are two
                real solutions.

89. $5 + x^2 = 0$

   $a = 1 \quad b = 0 \quad c = 5$

   $d = 0^2 - 4(1)(5)$

   $= -20 < 0$ so there are two
                complex solutions.

91. $ax^2 + 3x - 2 = 0$

   $a = a \quad b = 3 \quad c = -2$

   $x = \dfrac{-3 \pm \sqrt{9 - 4(a)(-2)}}{2(a)}$

   $= \dfrac{-3 \pm \sqrt{9 + 8a}}{2a}$

   So, $x = \dfrac{-3 \pm \sqrt{9 + 8a}}{2a}$

93. $x^2 + (n-m)x - mn = 0$, solve for x

   $a = 1 \quad b = n - m \quad c = -mn$

   $x = \dfrac{-(n-m) \pm \sqrt{(n-m)^2 - 4(1)(-mn)}}{2(1)}$

   $= \dfrac{-n+m \pm \sqrt{n^2 - 2mn + m^2 + 4mn}}{2}$

   $= \dfrac{-n+m \pm \sqrt{n^2 + 2mn + m^2}}{2}$

   $= \dfrac{-n+m \pm \sqrt{(n+m)^2}}{2}$

   $= \dfrac{-n+m \pm (n+m)}{2}$

$x = \dfrac{-n+m+(n+m)}{2} \qquad x = \dfrac{-n+m-(n+m)}{2}$

$= \dfrac{-n+n+2m}{2} \qquad\qquad = \dfrac{-n+m-n-m}{2}$

$= \dfrac{2m}{2} \qquad\qquad\qquad = -2$

$x = m \qquad$ or $\qquad x = -n$

So $x = m$ or $x = -n$.

95. $V = \dfrac{2}{3}pr^2h$, solve for r

   $0 = \left(\dfrac{2}{3}ph\right)r^2 - V$

   $a = \dfrac{2}{3}ph \quad b = 0 \quad c = -V$

   $r = \dfrac{-0 \pm \sqrt{0^2 - 4\left(\dfrac{2}{3}ph\right)(-V)}}{2\left(\dfrac{2}{3}ph\right)}$

   $= \dfrac{\pm\sqrt{4\left(\dfrac{2}{3}phV\right)}}{\dfrac{4}{3}ph}$

   $= \dfrac{\pm\dfrac{3}{4}\cdot 2\sqrt{\dfrac{2}{3}phV}}{ph}$

   $= \pm\dfrac{3}{2ph}\sqrt{\dfrac{2phV}{3}}$

   $= \pm\dfrac{3}{2ph}\sqrt{\dfrac{2phV}{3}} \cdot \dfrac{3}{3}$

   $= \pm\dfrac{3\sqrt{6phV}}{6ph}$

   $= \pm\dfrac{\sqrt{6phV}}{2ph}$

   So, $r = \pm\dfrac{\sqrt{6phV}}{2ph}$ or $\pm\sqrt{\dfrac{6phV}{4p^2h^2}}$

   $= \pm\sqrt{\dfrac{3V}{2ph}}$

97. $L = \dfrac{2}{R^2} - d^2$, $R > 0$ solve for d

   $d^2 + L - \dfrac{2}{R^2} = 0$

   $a = 1 \quad b = 0 \quad c = L - \dfrac{2}{R^2}$

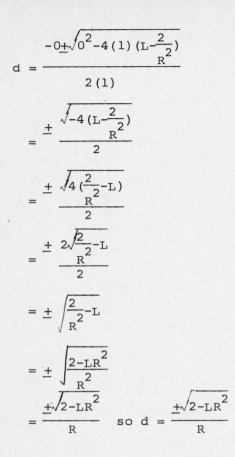

$$d = \frac{-0 \pm \sqrt{0^2 - 4(1)\left(L - \frac{2}{R^2}\right)}}{2(1)}$$

$$= \pm \frac{\sqrt{-4\left(L - \frac{2}{R^2}\right)}}{2}$$

$$= \pm \frac{\sqrt{4\left(\frac{2}{R^2} - L\right)}}{2}$$

$$= \pm \frac{2\sqrt{\frac{2}{R^2} - L}}{2}$$

$$= \pm \sqrt{\frac{2}{R^2} - L}$$

$$= \pm \sqrt{\frac{2 - LR^2}{R^2}}$$

$$= \frac{\pm\sqrt{2 - LR^2}}{R} \quad \text{so } d = \frac{\pm\sqrt{2 - LR^2}}{R}$$

99. $x^2 - 2x + K = 0$ has two complex solutions when the discriminant is negative.

$a = 1 \quad b = -2 \quad c = K$

$d = (-2)^2 - 4(1)(K)$

$d = 4 - 4K$

So, $4 - 4K < 0$.

$-4K < -4$

$K > 1$

$x^2 - 2x + K = 0$ has two complex solutions when $k > 1$.

101. $x^2 - Kx - 1 = 0$ has two distinct real solutions when the discriminant is positive.

$a = 1 \quad b = -K \quad e = -1$

$d = (-K)^2 - 4(1)(-1)$

$d = K^2 + 4$

$K^2 + 4$ is positive for all values of K so $x^2 - Kx - 1$ has two distinct real solutions when K is any real number.

103. $x^2 + K = 0$ has two complex solutions when the discriminant is negative.

$a = 1 \quad b = 0 \quad c = K$

$d = 0^2 - 4(1)(K)$

$d = -4K$

So, $-4K < 0$

$K > 0$

$x^2 + K$ has two complex solutions when $K > 0$.

105. If $b^2 - 4ac$ is a perfect square, there are rational solutions. If $b^2 - 4ac$ is not a perfect square, there are irrational solutions.

107. $ax^2 + c = 0$

$d = 0^2 - 4(a)(c)$

$\quad = -4ac$

The discriminant is $-4ac$.

When $ac < 0$ $(-4ac > 0)$ there are real solutions. When $ac > 0$ $(-4ac < 0)$ there are complex solutions.

109. $ax^2 + bx + c = 0$

$R_1 = \frac{-b + \sqrt{b^2 - 4ac}}{2a} \quad R_2 = \frac{-b - \sqrt{b^2 - 4ac}}{2a}$

$$R_1R_2 = \left(\frac{-b+\sqrt{b^2-4ac}}{2a}\right)\left(\frac{-b-\sqrt{b^2-4ac}}{2a}\right)$$

$$= \frac{b^2-(b^2-4ac)}{4a^2}$$

$$= \frac{b^2-b^2+4ac}{4a^2}$$

$$= \frac{4ac}{4a^2}$$

$$= \frac{c}{a}$$

111. $x^2 - 5x + 10 = 0$

$a = 1 \quad b = -5 \quad c = 10$

$$\text{sum} = \frac{-(-5)}{1}$$

$$= 5$$

$$\text{product} = \frac{10}{1}$$

$$= 10$$

113. $3x^2 - 11 = 0$

$a = 3 \quad b = 0 \quad c = -11$

$$\text{sum} = \frac{-0}{3}$$

$$= 0$$

$$\text{product} = \frac{-11}{3}$$

115. $Kx^2 + (Q-P)x + Q + P = 0$

$a = K \quad b = Q - P \quad c = Q + P$

$$\text{sum} = \frac{-(Q-P)}{K}$$

$$= \frac{P-Q}{K}$$

$$\text{product} = \frac{Q+P}{K}$$

Problem Set 6.5.

1. $(x-5)(x+4)(x+3) = 0$

$x - 5 = 0$ or $x + 4 = 0$ or

$x + 3 = 0$

$x = 5 \qquad x = -4 \qquad x = -3$

$\{-4, -3, 5\}$

3. $x(x+\frac{3}{2})(x+17) = 0$

$x = 0$ or $x + \frac{3}{2} = 0$ or $x + 17 = 0$

$2(x+\frac{3}{2}) = 2 \cdot 0 \qquad x = -17$

$2x + 3 = 0$

$2x = -3$

$x = \frac{-3}{2}$

$\{-17, -\frac{3}{2}, 0\}$

5. $x^4 - 10x^2 + 9 = 0$

$(x^2-1)(x^2-9) = 0$

$(x+1)(x-1)(x+3)(x-3) = 0$

$x+1=0$ or $x-1=0$ or $x+3=0$ or $x-3=0$

$x=-1 \qquad x=1 \qquad x=-3 \qquad x=3$

$\{\pm 1, \pm 3\}$

7. $x^4 - 2x^2 + 1 = 0$

$(x^2-1)^2 = 0$

$(x-1)(x+1)(x-1)(x+1) = 0$

$x-1=0$ or $x+1=0$ or $x-1=0$ or $x+1=0$

$x=1 \qquad x=-1 \qquad x=1 \qquad x=-1$

$\{\pm 1\}$

9. $x^4 - 3x^2 - 4 = 0$

$(x^2-4)(x^2+1) = 0$

$(x-2)(x+2)(x^2+1) = 0$

$x-2=0$ or $x+2=0$ or $x^2+1=0$

$x = 2 \qquad x = -2 \qquad x^2 = -1$

$x = \pm\sqrt{-1}$

157

$\{\pm 2, \pm i\}$

11. $x^4 + x^2 - 6 = 0$

$(x^2 + 3)(x^2 - 2) = 0$

$x^2 + 3 = 0$ or $x^2 - 2 = 0$

$x^2 = -3$ $\qquad x^2 = 2$

$x = \pm\sqrt{-3}$ $\qquad x = \pm\sqrt{2}$

$x = \pm\sqrt{3}i$

$\{\pm\sqrt{2}, \pm\sqrt{3}i\}$

13. $x^4 - 13x^2 + 12 = 0$

$(x^2 - 12)(x^2 - 1) = 0$

$(x^2 - 12)(x + 1)(x - 1) = 0$

$x^2 - 12 = 0$ or $x + 1 = 0$ or $x - 1 = 0$

$x^2 = 12$ $\quad x = -1 \quad x = 1$

$x = \pm\sqrt{12}$

$x = \pm 2\sqrt{3}$

$\{\pm 2\sqrt{3}, \pm 1\}$

15. $x^4 + 2x^2 = 0$

$x^2(x^2 + 2) = 0$

$x^2 = 0$ or $x^2 + 2 = 0$

$x = 0$ $\qquad x^2 = -2$

$\qquad\qquad x = \pm\sqrt{-2}$

$\qquad\qquad = \pm\sqrt{2}i$

$\{0, \pm\sqrt{2}i\}$

17. $x^4 - 4 = 0$

$(x^2 + 2)(x^2 - 2) = 0$

$x^2 + 2 = 0$ or $x^2 - 2 = 0$

$x^2 = -2$ $\qquad x^2 = 2$

$x = \pm\sqrt{-2}$ $\qquad x = \pm\sqrt{2}$

$x = \pm\sqrt{2}i$

$\{\pm\sqrt{2}, \pm\sqrt{2}i\}$

19. $4x^4 + 5x^2 - 6 = 0$

$(4x^2 - 3)(x^2 + 2) = 0$

$4x^2 - 3 = 0$ or $x^2 + 2 = 0$

$4x^2 = 3$ $\qquad x^2 = -2$

$x^2 = \dfrac{3}{4}$ $\qquad x = \pm\sqrt{-2}$

$x = \pm\dfrac{\sqrt{3}}{2}$ $\qquad x = \pm\sqrt{2}i$

$\{\pm\dfrac{\sqrt{3}}{2}, \pm\sqrt{2}i\}$

21. $16x^4 - 8x^2 + 15 = 0$

$(4x^2 + 3)(4x^2 - 5) = 0$

$4x^2 + 3 = 0$ or $4x^2 - 5 = 0$

$4x^2 = -3$ $\qquad 4x^2 = 5$

$x^2 = \dfrac{-3}{4}$ $\qquad x^2 = \dfrac{5}{4}$

$x = \pm\dfrac{\sqrt{-3}}{2}$ $\qquad x = \pm\dfrac{\sqrt{5}}{2}$

$x = \pm\dfrac{\sqrt{3}i}{2}$

$\{\pm\dfrac{\sqrt{5}}{2}, \pm\dfrac{\sqrt{3}\,i}{2}\}$

23. $\dfrac{1}{4}w^4 - 1 = 0$

$4(\dfrac{1}{4}w^4 - 1) = 4 \cdot 0$

$w^4 - 4 = 0$

$(w^2 + 2)(w^2 - 2) = 0$

$w^2 + 2 = 0$ or $w^2 - 2 = 0$

$w^2 = -2$ $\qquad w^2 = 2$

$w = \pm\sqrt{2}i$ $\qquad x = \pm\sqrt{2}$

$\{\pm\sqrt{2}, \pm\sqrt{2}i\}$

25. $x^3 + 1 = 0$

$(x + 1)(x^2 - x + 1) = 0$

$\{\pm\sqrt{2}, \pm\sqrt{2}i\}$

$$x = -1 \text{ or } x = \frac{1 \pm \sqrt{(-1)^2 - 4(1)(1)}}{2(1)}$$

$$= \frac{1 \pm \sqrt{-3}}{2}$$

$$= \frac{1 \pm \sqrt{3}i}{2}$$

$$= \frac{1}{2} \pm \frac{\sqrt{3}i}{2}$$

$$\left\{-1, \frac{1}{2} \pm \frac{\sqrt{3}i}{2}\right\}$$

27.
$$y^3 - 8 = 0$$

$$(y-2)(y^2+2y+4) = 0$$

$$y = 2 \quad \text{or} \quad y = \frac{-2 \pm \sqrt{2^2 - 4(1)(4)}}{2(1)}$$

$$= \frac{-2 \pm \sqrt{4-16}}{2}$$

$$= \frac{-2 \pm \sqrt{-12}}{2}$$

$$= \frac{-2 \pm 2\sqrt{3}i}{2}$$

$$= -1 \pm \sqrt{3}i$$

$$\{2, -1 \pm \sqrt{3}i\}$$

29.
$$x^3 - 125 = 0$$

$$(x-5)(x^2+5x+25) = 0$$

$$x = 5 \quad \text{or} \quad x = \frac{-5 \pm \sqrt{5^2 - 4(1)(25)}}{2(1)}$$

$$= \frac{-5 \pm \sqrt{25-100}}{2}$$

$$= \frac{-5 \pm \sqrt{-75}}{2}$$

$$= \frac{-5 \pm 5\sqrt{3}i}{2}$$

$$= -\frac{5}{2} \pm \frac{5}{2}\sqrt{3}i$$

$$\left\{5, \frac{-5}{2} \pm \frac{5\sqrt{3}}{2}i\right\}$$

31.
$$s^5 - s^2 = 0$$

$$s^2(s^3-1) = 0$$

$$s^2(s-1)(s^2+s+1) = 0$$

$$s^2 = 0 \quad \text{or} \quad s - 1 = 0$$
$$s = 0 \qquad\qquad s = 1$$

$$\text{or} \quad s = \frac{-1 \pm \sqrt{1^2 - 4(1)(1)}}{2(1)}$$

$$= \frac{-1 \pm \sqrt{1-4}}{2}$$

$$= \frac{-1 \pm \sqrt{-3}}{2}$$

$$= \frac{-1 \pm \sqrt{3}i}{2}$$

$$= -\frac{1}{2} \pm \frac{\sqrt{3}}{2}i$$

$$\left\{0, 1, -\frac{1}{2} \pm \frac{\sqrt{3}}{2}i\right\}$$

33.
$$125x^3 + 8 = 0$$

$$(5x+2)(25x^2-10x+4) = 0$$

$$5x + 2 = 0$$

$$5x = -2$$

$$x = -\frac{2}{5}$$

$$\text{or} \quad x = \frac{-(-10) \pm \sqrt{(-10)^2 - 4(25)(4)}}{2(25)}$$

$$= \frac{10 \pm \sqrt{100-400}}{50}$$

$$= \frac{10 \pm \sqrt{-300}}{50}$$

$$= \frac{10 \pm 10\sqrt{3}i}{50}$$

$$= \frac{1 \pm \sqrt{3}i}{5} \quad \text{or} \quad \frac{1}{5} \pm \frac{\sqrt{3}}{5}i$$

$$\left\{\frac{-2}{5}, \frac{1}{5} \pm \frac{\sqrt{3}}{5}i\right\}$$

35.
$$x^4 - 37x^2 + 36 = 0$$
$$(x^2 - 36)(x^2 - 1) = 0$$
$$(x+6)(x-6)(x+1)(x-1) = 0$$
$$x+6 = 0 \text{ or } x-6 = 0 \text{ or } x+1 = 0 \text{ or } x-1 = 0$$
$$x = -6 \qquad x = 6 \qquad x = -1 \qquad x = 1$$
$$\{\pm 1, \pm 6\}$$

37.
$$2x^4 - 6x^2 = 0$$
$$2x^2(x^2 - 3) = 0$$
$$2x^2 = 0 \text{ or } x^2 - 3 = 0$$
$$x^2 = 0 \qquad\qquad x^2 = 3$$
$$x = 0 \qquad\qquad x = \pm\sqrt{3}$$
$$\{0, \pm\sqrt{3}\}$$

39.
$$x^4 - x^2 - 42 = 0$$
$$(x^2 - 7)(x^2 + 6) = 0$$
$$x^2 - 7 = 0 \text{ or } x^2 + 6 = 0$$
$$x^2 = 7 \qquad\qquad x^2 = -6$$
$$x = \pm\sqrt{7} \qquad\qquad x = \pm\sqrt{-6}$$
$$\qquad\qquad\qquad\qquad x = \pm\sqrt{6}i$$
$$\{\pm\sqrt{7}, \pm\sqrt{6}i\}$$

41.
$$x^4 - x^2 - 12 = 0$$
$$(x^2 - 4)(x^2 + 3) = 0$$
$$(x-2)(x+2)(x^2 + 3) = 0$$
$$x-2 = 0 \text{ or } x+2 = 0 \text{ or } x^2 + 3 = 0$$
$$x = 2 \qquad x = -2 \qquad x^2 + -3$$
$$\qquad\qquad\qquad\qquad x = \pm\sqrt{-3}$$

$$x = \pm\sqrt{3}i$$
$$\{\pm 2, \pm\sqrt{3}i\}$$

43.
$$-x^4 + x^2 + 6 = 0$$
$$-1(-x^4 + x^2 + 6) = -1.0$$
$$x^4 - x^2 - 6 = 0$$
$$(x^2 - 3)(x^2 + 2) = 0$$
$$x^2 - 3 = 0 \text{ or } x^2 + 2 = 0$$
$$x^2 = 3 \qquad\qquad x^2 = -2$$
$$x = \pm\sqrt{3} \qquad\qquad x = \pm\sqrt{-2}$$
$$\qquad\qquad\qquad\qquad x = \pm\sqrt{2}i$$
$$\{\pm\sqrt{3}, \pm\sqrt{2}i\}$$

45.
$$4x^4 - x^2 - 3 = 0$$
$$(4x^2 + 3)(x^2 - 1) = 0$$
$$(4x^2 + 3)(x-1)(x+1) = 0$$
$$4x^2 + 3 = 0 \text{ or } x-1 = 0 \text{ or } x+1 = 0$$
$$4x^2 = -3 \qquad x = 1 \qquad x = -1$$
$$x^2 = \frac{-3}{4}$$
$$x = \pm\frac{\sqrt{-3}}{2}$$
$$x = \pm\frac{\sqrt{3}i}{2}$$
$$\left\{\pm 1, \pm\frac{\sqrt{3}i}{2}\right\}$$

47.
$$9x^4 + 11x^2 - 14 = 0$$
$$(9x^2 - 7)(x^2 + 2) = 0$$
$$9x^2 - 7 = 0 \text{ or } x^2 + 2 = 0$$
$$9x^2 = 7 \qquad\qquad x^2 = -2$$
$$x^2 = \frac{7}{9} \qquad\qquad x = \pm\sqrt{-2}$$
$$x = \frac{\pm\sqrt{7}}{3} \qquad\qquad x = \pm\sqrt{2}i$$
$$\left\{\pm\frac{\sqrt{7}}{3}, \pm\sqrt{2}i\right\}$$

49.
$$x^4 - 16 = 0$$

$$(x^2-4)(x^2+4) = 0$$

$$(x-2)(x+2)(x^2+4) = 0$$

$$x-2=0 \text{ or } x+2=0 \text{ or } x^2+4=0$$

$$x = 2 \quad x = -2 \quad x^2 = -4$$

$$x = \pm\sqrt{-4}$$

$$x = \pm 2i$$

$$\{\pm 2, \pm 2i\}$$

51.
$$2x^3 + 54 = 0$$

$$\tfrac{1}{2}(2x^3+54) = \tfrac{1}{2}\cdot 0$$

$$x^3 + 27 = 0$$

$$(x+3)(x^2-3x+9) = 0$$

$$x = -3 \quad \text{or}$$

$$x = \frac{-(-3)\pm\sqrt{(-3)^2-4(1)(9)}}{2(1)}$$

$$= \frac{3\pm\sqrt{9-36}}{2}$$

$$= \frac{3\pm\sqrt{-27}}{2}$$

$$= \frac{3\pm 3\sqrt{3}i}{2} \quad \text{or} \quad \frac{3}{2} \pm \frac{3\sqrt{3}i}{2}$$

$$\{-3, \tfrac{3}{2}\pm\tfrac{3\sqrt{3}i}{2}\}$$

53.
$$2w^3 + 250 = 0$$

$$\tfrac{1}{2}(2w^3+250) = \tfrac{1}{2}\cdot 0$$

$$w^3 + 125 = 0$$

$$(w+5)(w^2-5w+25) = 0$$

$$w = -5 \quad \text{or}$$

$$w = \frac{-(-5)\pm\sqrt{(-5)^2-4(1)(25)}}{2(1)}$$

$$= \frac{5\pm\sqrt{25-100}}{2}$$

$$= \frac{5\pm\sqrt{-75}}{2}$$

$$= \frac{5\pm 5\sqrt{3}i}{2} \quad \text{or} \quad \frac{5}{2} \pm \frac{5\sqrt{3}i}{2}$$

$$\{-5 \ \tfrac{5}{2}\pm\tfrac{5\sqrt{3}i}{2}\}$$

55.
$$u^6 - u^3 = 0$$

$$u^3(u^3-1) = 0$$

$$u^3(u-1)(u^2+u+1) = 0$$

$$u^3=0 \text{ or } u-1=0 \text{ or } u^2+u+1 = 0$$

$$u = 0 \quad u = 1$$

$$u = \frac{-1\pm\sqrt{1^2-4(1)(1)}}{2(1)}$$

$$= \frac{-1\pm\sqrt{-3}}{2}$$

$$= \frac{-1\pm\sqrt{3}i}{2} \quad \text{or} \quad -\frac{1}{2} \pm \frac{\sqrt{3}i}{2}$$

$$\{0,1,-\tfrac{1}{2}\pm\tfrac{\sqrt{3}i}{2}\}$$

57.
$$\tfrac{1}{5}x^4 - 5 = 0$$

$$5(\tfrac{1}{5}x^4-5) = 0$$

$$x^4 - 25 = 0$$

$$(x^2-5)(x^2+5) = 0$$

$$x^2 - 5 = 0 \quad \text{or} \quad x^2 + 5 = 0$$

$$x^2 = 5 \qquad x^2 = -5$$

$$x = \pm\sqrt{5} \qquad x = \pm\sqrt{-5}$$

$$x = \pm\sqrt{5}i$$

$$\{\pm\sqrt{5}, \pm\sqrt{5}i\}$$

59.
$$x^6 - 64 = 0$$

$(x^3-4)(x^3+4) = 0$

$(x-2)(x^2+2x+4)(x+2)(x^2-2x+4) = 0$

$x - 2 = 0$ or $x = \dfrac{-2\pm\sqrt{4-4(1)(4)}}{2}$

$x = 2 \qquad = \dfrac{-2\pm\sqrt{4-16}}{2}$

$\qquad\qquad = \dfrac{-2\pm\sqrt{-12}}{2}$

$\qquad\qquad = \dfrac{-2\pm2\sqrt{3}\,i}{2}$

$\qquad\qquad = -1 \pm\sqrt{3}\,i$

or $x + 2 = 0$ or $x = \dfrac{-(-2)\pm\sqrt{4-4(1)(4)}}{2}$

$x = -2 \qquad = \dfrac{2\pm\sqrt{4-16}}{2}$

$\qquad\qquad = \dfrac{2\pm\sqrt{-12}}{2}$

$\qquad\qquad = \dfrac{2\pm2\sqrt{3}\,i}{2}$

$\qquad\qquad = 1\pm\sqrt{3}\,i$

$\{\pm2,1\pm\sqrt{3}\,i,-1\pm\sqrt{3}\,i\}$

61. $x^3 - 2x^2 + 4x - 8 = 0$

$x^2(x-2) + 4(x-2) = 0$

$(x-2)(x^2+4) = 0$

$x - 2 = 0$ or $x^2 + 4 = 0$

$x = 2 \qquad\qquad x^2 = -4$

$\qquad\qquad\qquad x = \pm\sqrt{-4}$

$\qquad\qquad\qquad x = \pm2i$

$\{2,\pm2i\}$

63. $(x+1)^4 - 5(x+1)^2 + 4 = 0$

$[(x+1)^2-1][(x+1)^2-4] = 0$

$(x+1)^2 - 1 = 0$ or $(x+1)^2 - 4 = 0$

$(x+1)^2 = 1 \qquad\qquad (x+1)^2 = 4$

$x + 1 = \pm1 \qquad\qquad x + 1 = \pm$

$x+1=1$ or $x+1=-1 \qquad x+1=2$ or $x+1=-$

$x = 0 \qquad x = -2 \qquad\quad x = 1 \qquad x = -$

$\{-3,-2,0,1\}$

65. Solution set is $\{4,2,-1\}$

An equation: $(x-4)(x-2)(x+1) = 0$

Problem Set 6.6.

1. $\dfrac{6}{x-2} - \dfrac{3}{x} = 1$

$x(x-2)\left(\dfrac{6}{x-2} -\dfrac{3}{x}\right) = x(x-2)\cdot1$

$6x - 3(x-2) = x(x-2)$

$6x - 3x + 6 = x^2 - 2x$

$3x + 6 = x^2 - 2x$

$0 = x^2 - 5x - 6$

$0 = (x-6)(x+1)$

$x - 6 = 0$ or $x + 1 = 0$

$x = 6 \qquad\qquad x = -1 \quad \{-1,6\}$

3. $\dfrac{2}{x} - 1 = \dfrac{4}{x+3}$

$x(x+3)\left(\dfrac{2}{x}-1\right) = x(x+3)\cdot\dfrac{4}{x+3}$

$2(x+3) - x(x+3) = x\cdot4$

$2x + 6 - x^2 - 3x = 4x$

$6 - x^2 - x = 4x$

$0 = x^2 + 5x - 6$

$0 = (x+6)(x-1)$

$x + 6 = 0$ or $x - 1 = 0$

$x = -6 \qquad\qquad x = 1 \quad \{-6,1\}$

162

$\frac{1}{} + \frac{1}{2t+1} = \frac{6}{5}$

$(t-1)(2t+1)(\frac{1}{t-1} + \frac{1}{2t+1})$

$= 5(t-1)(2t+1)\frac{6}{5}$

$(2t+1)\cdot 1 + 5(t-1)\cdot 1$

$= (t-1)(2t+1)\cdot 6$

$t + 5 + 5t - 5 = 6(2t^2 - t - 1)$

$t = 12t^2 - 6t - 6$

$= 12t^2 - 21t - 6$

$0 = \frac{1}{3}(12t^2 - 21t - 6)$

$= 4t^2 - 7t - 2$

$= (4t+1)(t-2)$

$+ 1 = 0 \quad or \quad t - 2 = 0$

$4t = -1 \qquad t = 2$

$t = -\frac{1}{4} \qquad \{-\frac{1}{4}, 2\}$

$\frac{z^2-5}{+z-20} + \frac{z+1}{z+5} = \frac{z-3}{z-4}$

$\frac{z^2-5}{(z+5)(z-4)} + \frac{z+1}{z+5} = \frac{z-3}{z-4}$

$(z+5)(z-4)[\frac{z^2-5}{(z+5)(z-4)} + \frac{z+1}{z+5}]$

$= (z+5)(z-4)(\frac{z-3}{z-4})$

$- 5 + (z-4)(z+1) = (z+5)(z-3)$

$- 5 + z^2 - 3z - 4$

$= z^2 + 2z - 15$

$z^2 - 3z - 9 = z^2 + 2z - 15$

$- 5z + 6 = 0$

$(z-3)(z-2) = 0$

$z - 3 = 0 \quad or \quad z - 2 = 0$

$z = 3 \qquad z = 2 \quad \{2,3\}$

9. $\frac{z}{z-2} + \frac{2}{z+1} = \frac{7z+1}{z^2-z-2}$

$\frac{z}{z-2} + \frac{2}{z+1} = \frac{7z+1}{(z-2)(z+1)}$

$(z-2)(z+1)(\frac{z}{z-2} + \frac{2}{z+1})$

$= (z-2)(z+1)[\frac{7z+1}{(z-2)(z+1)}]$

$(z+1)z + (z-2)2 = 7z + 1$

$z^2 + z + 2z - 4 = 7z + 1$

$z^2 + 3z - 4 = 7z + 1$

$z^2 - 4z - 5 = 0$

$(z-5)(z+1) = 0$

$z - 5 = 0 \quad or \quad z + 1 = 0$

$z = 5 \qquad z = -1 \quad \{5\}$

-1 is not a solution since $\frac{2}{z+1}$

and $\frac{7z+1}{(z-2)(z+1)}$ are undefined

when $z = -1$.

11. $\frac{x}{x+1} - \frac{2}{1-x} = \frac{8x-4}{x^2-1}$

$\frac{x}{x+1} + \frac{2}{x-1} = \frac{8x-4}{(x-1)(x+1)}$

$(x-1)(x+1)(\frac{x}{x+1} + \frac{2}{x-1})$

$= (x-1)(x+1)[\frac{8x-4}{(x-1)(x+1)}]$

$(x-1)x + (x+1)2 = 8x - 4$

$x^2 - x + 2x + 2 = 8x - 4$

$x^2 + x + 2 = 8x - 4$

$x^2 - 7x + 6 = 0$

$$(x-1)(x-6) = 0$$

$$x - 1 = 0 \quad \text{or} \quad x - 6 = 0$$

$$x = 1 \qquad\qquad x = 6 \quad \{6\}$$

1 is not a solution since $\dfrac{2}{1-x}$ and

$\dfrac{8x-4}{(x-1)(x+1)}$ are undefined when
$x = 1$.

13. $\dfrac{2x^2}{x^2-4x+3} + \dfrac{1}{x-1} = \dfrac{9}{x-3}$

$$\dfrac{2x}{(x-3)(x-1)} + \dfrac{1}{x-1} = \dfrac{9}{x-3}$$

$$(x-3)(x-1)\left[\dfrac{2x^2}{(x-3)(x-1)}+\dfrac{1}{x-1}\right]$$

$$= (x-3)(x-1)\dfrac{9}{x-3}$$

$$2x^2 + (x-3)1 = (x-1)9$$

$$2x^2 + x - 3 = 9x - 9$$

$$2x^2 - 8x + 6 = 0$$

$$\dfrac{1}{2}(2x^2-8x+6) = 0\cdot\dfrac{1}{2}$$

$$x^2 - 4x + 3 = 0$$

$$(x-3)(x-1) = 0$$

$$x - 3 = 0 \quad \text{or} \quad x - 1 = 0$$

$$x = 3 \qquad\qquad x = 1 \quad \emptyset$$

Neither 3 nor 1 are solutions

since $\dfrac{2x^2}{(x-3)(x-1)}$ is undefined
when x is 3 or 1.

15. $\dfrac{2}{x-3} + \dfrac{x^2-1}{x^2-10x+21} = \dfrac{12}{x-7}$

$$\dfrac{2}{x-3} + \dfrac{x^2-1}{(x-3)(x-7)} = \dfrac{12}{x-7}$$

$$(x-3)(x-7)\left[\dfrac{2}{x-3}+\dfrac{x^2-1}{(x-3)(x-7)}\right]$$

$$= (x-3)(x-7)\left(\dfrac{12}{x-7}\right)$$

$$(x-7)2 + (x^2-1) = (x-3)12$$

$$2x - 14 + x^2 - 1 = 12x - 36$$

$$x^2 + 2x - 15 = 12x - 36$$

$$x^2 - 10x + 21 = 0$$

$$(x-3)(x-7) = 0$$

$$x - 3 = 0 \quad \text{or} \quad x - 7 = 0$$

$$x = 3 \qquad\qquad x = 7 \qquad \emptyset$$

Neither 3 nor 7 are solutions

since $\dfrac{x^2-1}{(x-3)(x-7)}$ is unde
when x is 3 or 7.

17. $x^{-2} + 2x^{-1} - 24 = 0$

$$\dfrac{1}{x^2} + \dfrac{2}{x} - 24 = 0$$

$$x^2\left(\dfrac{1}{x^2}+\dfrac{2}{x}-24\right) = x^2\cdot 0$$

$$1 + 2x - 24x^2 = 0$$

$$-1(-24x^2+2x+1) = 0$$

$$24x^2 - 2x - 1 = 0$$

$$(6x+1)(4x-1) = 0$$

$$6x + 1 = 0 \quad \text{or} \quad 4x - 1 = 0$$

$$6x = -1 \qquad\qquad 4x = 1$$

$$x = -\dfrac{1}{6} \qquad\qquad x = \dfrac{1}{4}$$

19. $t^{-4} - 2t^{-2} + 1 = 0$

$$\dfrac{1}{t^4} - \dfrac{2}{t^2} + 1 = 0$$

$$t^4\left(\dfrac{1}{t^4}-\dfrac{2}{t^2}+1\right) = 0$$

$$1 - 2t^2 + t^4 = 0$$

$$t^4 - 2t^2 + 1 = 0$$

$$(t^2-1)^2 = 0$$

$$(t-1)^2(t+1)^2 = 0$$

$$t - 1 = 0 \quad \text{or} \quad t + 1 = 0$$

$$t = 1 \qquad\qquad t = -1 \quad \{-$$

21. x: speed of the ship

	D	R	T
actual	24	x	$\dfrac{24}{x}$
faster	24	x+2	$\dfrac{24}{x+2}$

T

$$\dfrac{24}{x} = \dfrac{24}{x+2} + 1$$

$$x(x+2)\left(\dfrac{24}{x}\right) = x(x+2)\left[\dfrac{24}{x+2}+1\right]$$

$$(x+2)24 + x\cdot 24 + x(x+2)\cdot$$

$$24x + 48 = 24x + x^2 + 2x$$

$$0 = x^2 + 2x - 48$$

$$0 = (x+8)(x-6)$$

$$x + 8 = 0 \quad \text{or} \quad x - 6 = 0$$

$$x = -8 \qquad\qquad x = 6$$

$x \neq -8$ since x must be posi
The ship's speed was 6 kn

23. x: walking speed

	D	R	T
riding	22	x+4	$\frac{22}{x+4}$
walking	1	x	$\frac{1}{x}$

$$\frac{22}{x+4} + \frac{1}{x} = 3$$

$$x(x+4)\left(\frac{22}{x+4}+\frac{1}{x}\right) = 3x(x+4)$$

$$x\cdot 22 + (x+4)\cdot 1 = 3x^2 + 12x$$

$$22x + x + 4 = 3x^2 + 12x$$

$$23x + 4 = 3x^2 + 12x$$

$$0 = 3x^2 - 11x - 4$$

$$0 = (3x+1)(x-4)$$

$$3x + 1 = 0 \quad or \quad x - 4 = 0$$

$$3x = -1 \qquad\qquad x = 4$$

$$x = -\frac{1}{3}$$

$x \neq -\frac{1}{3}$ since x must be positive.

His walking speed is 4 mph.

25. x: number of hours it takes the large pipe to fill alone.

x + 6: number of hours it takes the small pipe to fill alone.

$$\frac{1}{x} + \frac{1}{x+6} = \frac{1}{4}$$

$$4x(x+6)\left(\frac{1}{x}+\frac{1}{x+6}\right) = 4x(x+6)\cdot\frac{1}{4}$$

$$4(x+6) + 4x = x(x+6)$$

$$4x + 24 + 4x = x^2 + 6x$$

$$8x + 24 = x^2 + 6x$$

$$0 = x^2 - 2x - 24$$

$$0 = (x-6)(x+4)$$

$$x - 6 = 0 \quad or \quad x + 4 = 0$$

$$x = 6 \qquad\qquad x = -4$$

$$x + 6 = 12$$

$x \neq -4$ since x must be positive.

It would take the large pipe 6 hrs. and the small pipe 12 hrs.

27. $$\frac{2x}{5} - \frac{2}{x} = \frac{1}{5}$$

$$5x\left(\frac{2x}{5}-\frac{2}{x}\right) = 5x\cdot\frac{1}{5}$$

$$x(2x) - 5(2) = x\cdot 1$$

$$2x^2 - 10 = x$$

$$2x^2 - x - 10 = 0$$

$$(2x-5)(x+2) = 0$$

$$2x - 5 = 0 \quad or \quad x + 2 = 0$$

$$2x = 5 \qquad\qquad x = -2$$

$$x = \frac{5}{2} \qquad\qquad \left\{-2,\frac{5}{2}\right\}$$

29. $$\frac{-4}{3x-1} = 2x + 3$$

$$(3x-1)\left(\frac{-4}{3x-1}\right) = (3x-1)(2x+3)$$

$$-4 = 6x^2 + 7x - 3$$

$$0 = 6x^2 + 7x + 1$$

$$0 = (6x+1)(x+1)$$

$$6x + 1 = 0 \quad or \quad x + 1 = 0$$

$$6x = -1 \qquad\qquad x = -1$$

$$x = -\frac{1}{6} \qquad\qquad \left\{-\frac{1}{6},-1\right\}$$

31. $$\frac{-3}{x} - 1 = \frac{4}{1-x}$$

$$x(1-x)\left(\frac{-3}{x}-1\right) = x(1-x)\left(\frac{4}{1-x}\right)$$

$$(1-x)(-3) - x(1-x) = x\cdot 4$$

$$-3 + 3x - x + x^3 = 4x$$

$$x^2 + 2x - 3 = 4x$$

$$x^2 - 2x - 3 = 0$$

$$(x-3)(x+1) = 0$$

$$x - 3 = 0 \quad \text{or} \quad x + 1 = 0$$

$$x = 3 \qquad\qquad x = -1 \quad \{-1,3\}$$

33. $$\frac{1}{x+1} - \frac{10}{x-2} = \frac{3}{2}$$

$$2(x+1)(x-2)(\frac{1}{x+1} - \frac{10}{x-2})$$

$$= 2(x+1)(x-2)\frac{3}{2}$$

$$2(x-2) - 2(x+1)(10)$$

$$= (x+1)(x-2)(3)$$

$$2x - 4 - 20x - 20 = 3(x^2-x-2)$$

$$-18x - 24 = 3x^2 - 3x - 6$$

$$0 = 3x^2 + 15x + 18$$

$$\frac{1}{3}\cdot 0 = \frac{1}{3}(3x^2+15x+18)$$

$$0 = x^2 + 5 + 6$$

$$0 = (x+2)(x+3)$$

$$x + 2 = 0 \quad \text{or} \quad x + 3 = 0$$

$$x = -2 \qquad\qquad x = -3 \quad \{-3 \ -2\}$$

35. $$\frac{14}{x-2} - \frac{35}{x-5} = \frac{3}{2}$$

$$2(x-2)(x-5)(\frac{14}{x-2} - \frac{35}{x-5})$$

$$= 2(x-2)(x-5)\cdot\frac{3}{2}$$

$$2(x-5)(14) - 2(x-2)(35)$$

$$= (x-2)(x-5)(3)$$

$$28x - 140 - 70x + 180$$

$$= 3(x^2-7x+10)$$

$$-42x = 3x^2 + 21x + 30$$

$$0 = 3x^2 + 21x + 30$$

$$\frac{1}{3}\cdot 0 = \frac{1}{3}(3x^2+21x+30)$$

$$0 = x^2 + 7x + 10$$

$$0 = (x+2)(x+5)$$

$$x + 2 = 0 \quad \text{or} \quad x + 5 = 0$$

$$x = -2 \qquad\qquad x = -5$$

$$\{-2,-5\}$$

37. $$\frac{2}{x^2-1} + \frac{3x+6}{x^2-x-2} = \frac{8}{x^2-3x+2}$$

$$\frac{2}{(x-1)(x+1)} + \frac{3x+6}{(x-2)(x+1)}$$

$$= \frac{8}{(x-1)(x-2)}$$

$$(x-1)(x+1)(x-2)[\frac{2}{(x-1)(x+1)}$$

$$+ \frac{3x+6}{(x-2)(x+1)}]$$

$$= (x-1)(x+1)(x-2)\cdot\frac{8}{(x-1)(x-2)}$$

$$(x-2)(2) + (x-1)(3x+6) = (x+1)8$$

$$2x - 4 + 3x^2 + 3x - 6 = 8x + 8$$

$$3x^2 + 5x - 10 = 8x + 8$$

$$3x^2 - 3x - 18 = 0$$

$$\frac{1}{3}(3x^2-3x-18) = \frac{1}{3}\cdot 0$$

$$x^2 - x - 6 = 0$$

$$(x-3)(x+2) = 0$$

$$x - 3 = 0 \quad \text{or} \quad x + 2 = 0$$

$$x = 3 \qquad\qquad x = -2$$

$$\{-2 \ 3\}$$

39. $$\frac{5}{x+2} - \frac{3}{x-5} = \frac{x^2-8x-6}{x^2-3x-10}$$

$$\frac{5}{x+2} - \frac{3}{x-5} = \frac{x^2-8x-6}{(x-5)(x+2)}$$

166

$(x+2)(x-5)(\frac{5}{x+2}-\frac{3}{x-5})$

$\quad = (x+2)(x-5)[\frac{x^2-8x-6}{(x-5)(x+2)}]$

$(x-5)(5) - (x+2)(3) = x^2 - 8x - 6$

$\quad 5x - 25 - 3x - 6 = x^2 - 8x - 6$

$\qquad\qquad 2x - 31 = x^2 - 8x - 6$

$\quad 0 = x^2 - 10x + 25$

$\quad 0 = (x-5)^2$

$\quad 0 = x - 5$

$\quad 5 = x$

$\emptyset$ since $\frac{3}{x-5}$ and $\frac{x^2-8x-6}{(x-5)(x+2)}$ are

undefined when $x = 5$.

41. $\quad \frac{1}{x} + \frac{5}{3x} = \frac{x+2}{3}$

$\quad 3x(\frac{1}{x}+\frac{5}{3x}) = 3x(\frac{x+2}{3})$

$\qquad 3 + 5 = x(x+2)$

$\qquad\quad 8 = x^2 + 2x$

$\qquad\quad 0 = x^2 + 2x - 8$

$\qquad\quad 0 = (x+4)(x-2)$

$\quad x + 4 = 0 \quad\text{or}\quad x - 2 = 0$

$\qquad x = -4 \qquad\qquad x = 2 \quad \{-4,2\}$

43. $\quad \frac{1}{x} + \frac{x+3}{7} = \frac{5}{7x}$

$\quad 7x(\frac{1}{x}+\frac{x+3}{7}) = 7x\cdot\frac{5}{7x}$

$\quad 7 + x(x+3) = 5$

$\quad 7 + x^2 + 3x = 5$

$x^2 + 3x + 2 = 0$

$(x+1)(x+2) = 0$

$\quad x + 1 = 0 \quad\text{or}\quad x + 2 = 0$

$\qquad x = -1 \qquad\qquad x = -2$

$\hfill \{-2,-1\}$

45. $\quad \frac{2}{x+7} + \frac{16}{x^2+6x-7} + \frac{x}{x-1} = 0$

$\quad \frac{2}{x+7} + \frac{16}{(x+7)(x-1)} + \frac{x}{x-1} = 0$

$\quad (x+7)(x-1)[\frac{2}{x+7}+\frac{16}{(x+7)(x-1)}+\frac{x}{x-1}]$

$\qquad = (x+7)(x-1)\cdot 0$

$\quad 2(x-1) + 16 + x(x+7) = 0$

$\quad 2x - 2 + 16 + x^2 + 7x = 0$

$\qquad\quad x^2 + 9x + 14 = 0$

$\qquad\quad (x+2)(x+7) = 0$

$\quad x + 2 = 0 \quad\text{or}\quad x + 7 = 0$

$\qquad x = -2 \qquad\qquad x = -7 \quad \{-2\}$

-7 is not a solution since $\frac{2}{x+7}$

and $\frac{16}{(x+7)(x-1)}$ are undefined

when $x = -7$.

47. $\quad \frac{1}{5} - \frac{7}{15-5x} = \frac{x^2}{x-3}$

$\quad \frac{1}{5} - \frac{7}{5(3-x)} = \frac{x^2}{x-3}$

$\quad \frac{1}{5} - \frac{7}{-5(x-3)} = \frac{x^2}{x-3}$

$\quad \frac{1}{5} + \frac{7}{5(x-3)} = \frac{x^2}{x-3}$

$\quad 5(x-3)[\frac{1}{5}+\frac{7}{5(x-3)}]$

$\qquad = 5(x-3)(\frac{x^2}{x-3})$

$\quad x - 3 + 7 = 5x^2$

$\qquad x + 4 = 5x^2$

$\qquad\quad 0 = 5x^2 - x - 4$

$\qquad\quad 0 = (5x+4)(x-1)$

$\quad 5x + 4 = 0 \quad\text{or}\quad x - 1 = 0$

$\qquad 5x = -4$

$$x = -\frac{4}{5} \qquad x = 1 \qquad \{-\frac{4}{5}, 1\}$$

49.
$$\frac{2}{t-3} - \frac{t}{2-t} = \frac{2}{t^2-5t+6}$$

$$\frac{2}{t-3} - \frac{t}{2-t} = \frac{2}{(t-2)(t-3)}$$

$$\frac{2}{t-3} - \frac{t}{-(t-2)} = \frac{2}{(t-2)(t-3)}$$

$$\frac{2}{t-3} + \frac{t}{t-2} = \frac{2}{(t-2)(t-3)}$$

$$(t-2)(t-3)\left(\frac{2}{t-3}+\frac{t}{t-2}\right)$$

$$= (t-2)(t-3)\cdot\frac{2}{(t-2)(t-3)}$$

$$2(t-2) + t(t-3) = 2$$

$$2t - 4 + t^2 - 3t = 2$$

$$t^2 - t - 4 = 2$$

$$t^2 - t - 6 = 0$$

$$(t-3)(t+2) = 0$$

$$t - 3 = 0 \quad \text{or} \quad t + 2 = 0$$

$$t = 3 \qquad t = -2 \quad \{-2\}$$

3 is not a solution since $\frac{2}{t-3}$

and $\frac{2}{(t-2)(t-3)}$ are undefined

when t = 3.

51.
$$\frac{1}{x} + \frac{x-3}{x+1} = \frac{16}{x^2+x}$$

$$\frac{1}{x} + \frac{x-3}{x+1} = \frac{16}{x(x+1)}$$

$$x(x+1)\left(\frac{1}{x}+\frac{x-3}{x+1}\right) = x(x+1)\cdot\frac{16}{x(x+1)}$$

$$(x+1) + x(x-3) = 16$$

$$x + 1 + x^2 - 3x = 16$$

$$x^2 - 2x + 1 = 16$$

$$x^2 - 2x - 15 = 0$$

$$(x-5)(x+3) = 0$$

$$x - 5 = 0 \quad \text{or} \quad x + 3 = 0$$

$$x = 5 \qquad x = -3$$

$$\{-3, 5\}$$

53.
$$\frac{1}{x^2} + \frac{1}{3} = \frac{4}{x^2}$$

$$3x^2\left(\frac{1}{x^2}+\frac{1}{3}\right) = 3x^2\cdot\frac{4}{x^2}$$

$$3 + x^2 = 12$$

$$x^2 = 9$$

$$x = \pm 3 \qquad \{\pm 3\}$$

55.
$$\frac{y}{y+5} = \frac{1}{y-3} - \frac{8}{y^2+2y-15}$$

$$\frac{y}{y+5} = \frac{1}{y-3} - \frac{8}{(y+5)(y-3)}$$

$$(y+5)(y-3)\cdot\frac{y}{y+5}$$

$$= (y+5)(y-3)\left[\frac{1}{y-3}-\frac{8}{(y+5)(y-3)}\right]$$

$$(y-3)y = (y+5) - 8$$

$$y^2 - 3y = y + 5 - 8$$

$$y^2 - 3y = y - 3$$

$$y^2 - 4y + 3 = 0$$

$$y - 1 = 0 \quad \text{or} \quad y - 3 = 0$$

$$y = 1 \qquad y = 3 \quad \{1\}$$

3 is not a solution since $\frac{1}{y-3}$

and $\frac{8}{(y+5)(y-3)}$ are undefined

when y = 3.

57.
$$\frac{-2}{x+1} - \frac{5}{3-x} = 1$$

$$\frac{-2}{x+1} - \frac{5}{-(x-3)} = 1$$

$$\frac{-2}{x+1} + \frac{5}{x-3} = 1$$

$$(x+1)(x-3)(\frac{-2}{x+1}+\frac{5}{x-3})$$

$$= (x+1)(x-3)(1)$$

$$(x-3)(-2) + (x+1)(5) = x^2 - 2x - 3$$

$$-2x + 6 + 5x + 5 = x^2 - 2x - 3$$

$$3x + 11 = x^2 - 2x - 3$$

$$0 = x^2 - 5x - 14$$

$$0 = (x-7)(x+2)$$

$$x - 7 = 0 \quad \text{or} \quad x + 2 = 0$$

$$x = 7 \qquad\qquad x = -2 \quad \{-2,7\}$$

59. $\frac{6}{x} + \frac{x}{x+5} = \frac{30}{x^2+5x}$

$$\frac{6}{x} + \frac{x}{x+5} = \frac{30}{x(x+5)}$$

$$x(x+5)(\frac{6}{x}+\frac{x}{x+5}) = x(x+5)\cdot\frac{30}{x(x+5)}$$

$$(x+5)6 + x\cdot x = 30$$

$$6x + 30 + x^2 = 30$$

$$x^2 + 6x = 0$$

$$x(x+6) = 0$$

$$x = 0 \quad \text{or} \quad x + 6 = 0$$

$$x = -6 \qquad \{-6,0\}$$

61. $\frac{t+3}{t-1} + \frac{1}{t+4} = \frac{2t^2+6t+12}{t^2+3t-4}$

$$\frac{t+3}{t-1} + \frac{1}{t+4} = \frac{2t^2+6t+12}{(t-1)(t+4)}$$

$$(t-1)(t+4)(\frac{t+3}{t-1}+\frac{1}{t+4})$$

$$= (t-1)(t+4)[\frac{2t^2+6t+12}{(t-1)(t+4)}]$$

$$(t+4)(t+3) + (t-1) = 2t^2 + 6t + 12$$

$$t^2 + 7t + 12 + t-1 = 2t^2 + 6t + 12$$

$$t^2 + 8t + 11 = 2t^2 + 6t + 12$$

$$0 = t^2 - 2t + 1$$

$$0 = (t-1)^2$$

$$0 = t - 1$$

$$1 = t \qquad\qquad \emptyset$$

1 is not a solution since $\frac{t+3}{t-1}$

and $\frac{2t^2+6t+12}{(t-1)(t+4)}$ are undefined

when $t = 1$.

63. $\frac{1}{t^2-1} + \frac{2t}{2t^2-3t+1} = \frac{1}{2t^2+t-1}$

$$\frac{1}{(t-1)(t+1)} + \frac{2t}{(2t-1)(t-1)}$$

$$= \frac{1}{(2t-1)(t+1)}$$

$$(t-1)(t+1)(2t-1)[\frac{1}{(t-1)(t+1)}$$

$$+ \frac{2t}{(2t-1)(t-1)}]$$

$$= (t-1)(t+1)(2t-1)[\frac{1}{(2t-1)(t+1)}]$$

$$(2t-1) + (t+1)2t = (t-1)$$

$$2t - 1 + 2t^2 + 2t = t - 1$$

$$2t^2 + 4t - 1 = t - 1$$

$$2t^2 + 3t = 0$$

$$t(2t+3) = 0$$

$$t = 0 \quad \text{or} \quad 2t + 3 = 0$$

$$2t = -3$$

$$t = -\frac{3}{2} \qquad \{-\frac{3}{2}, 0\}$$

65. $\frac{18}{s^2+s-6} + \frac{s-1}{s^2+5s+6} = \frac{12}{s^2-4}$

$$\frac{18}{(s+3)(s-2)} + \frac{s-1}{(s+2)(s+3)}$$

$$= \frac{12}{(s-2)(s+2)}$$

$$(s+3)(s-2)(s+2)[\frac{18}{(s+3)(s-2)}$$

$$+ \frac{s-1}{(s+2)(s+3)}]$$

$$= (s+3)(s-2)(s+2)[\frac{12}{(s-2)(s+2)}]$$

$$(s+2)(18) + (s-1)(s-2) = (s+3)(12)$$

$$18s + 36 + s^2 - 3s + 2 = +36$$

$$s^2 + 15s + 38 = 12s + 36$$

$$s^2 + 3s + 2 = 0$$

$$(s+1)(s+2) = 0$$

$$s + 1 = 0 \quad \text{or} \quad s + 2 = 0$$

$$s = -1 \qquad s = -2 \quad \{-1\}$$

-2 is not a solution since

$\frac{s-1}{(s+2)(s+3)}$ and $\frac{12}{(s-2)(s+2)}$

are not defined when s = -2.

67. $\quad \dfrac{1}{x^2-1} + \dfrac{x}{2x^2-3x+1} = \dfrac{1}{2x^2+x-1}$

$$\frac{1}{(x-1)(x+1)} + \frac{x}{(2x-1)(x-1)}$$

$$= \frac{1}{(2x-1)(x+1)}$$

$$(2x-1)(x-1)(x+1)[\frac{1}{(x-1)(x+1)}$$

$$+ \frac{x}{(2x-1)(x-1)}]$$

$$= (2x-1)(x-1)(x+1)[\frac{1}{(2x-1)(x+1)}]$$

$$(2x-1) + (x+1)x = x - 1$$

$$2x - 1 + x^2 + x = x - 1$$

$$x^2 + 3x - 1 = x - 1$$

$$x^2 + 2x = 0$$

$$x(x+2) = 0$$

$$x = 0 \quad \text{or} \quad x + 2 = 0$$

$$x = -2 \qquad \{-2,0\}$$

69. $\quad \dfrac{2}{5y^2-15y-50} + \dfrac{y+1}{y^2-y-6}$

$$= \frac{-8}{5y^2-40y+75}$$

$$\frac{2}{5(y^2-3y-10)} + \frac{y+1}{(y-3)(y+2)}$$

$$= \frac{-8}{5(y^2-8y+15)}$$

$$\frac{2}{5(y-5)(y+2)} + \frac{y+1}{(y-3)(y+2)}$$

$$= \frac{-8}{5(y-3)(y-5)}$$

$$5(y-5)(y+2)(y-3)[\frac{2}{5(y-5)(y+2)}$$

$$+ \frac{y+1}{(y-3)(y+2)}]$$

$$= 5(y-5)(y+2)(y-3)[\frac{-8}{5(y-3)(y-5)}]$$

$$(y-3)2 + 5(y-5)(y+1) = (y+2)(-8)$$

$$2y - 6 + 5(y^2-4y-5) = -8y - 16$$

$$2y - 6 + 5y^2 - 20y - 25 = -8y - 16$$

$$5y^2 - 18y - 31 = -8y - 16$$

$$5y^2 - 10y - 15 = 0$$

$$\frac{1}{5}(5y^2-10y-15) = \frac{1}{5} \cdot 0$$

$$y^2 - 2y - 3 = 0$$

$$(y-3)(y+1) = 0$$

$$y - 3 = 0 \quad \text{or} \quad y + 1 = 0$$

$$y = 3 \qquad y = -1 \quad \{-1\}$$

3 is not a solution since

$\frac{y+1}{(y-3)(y+2)}$ and $\frac{-8}{5(y-3)(y-5)}$

are not defined when $y = 3$.

$$\frac{4}{x^2} + 27 = \frac{21}{x}$$

$$x^2\left(\frac{4}{x^2}+27\right) = x^2\left(\frac{21}{x}\right)$$

$$4 + 27x^2 = 21x$$

$$27x^2 - 21x + 4 = 0$$

$$(9x-4)(3x-1) = 0$$

$$9x - 4 = 0 \quad \text{or} \quad 3x - 1 = 0$$

$$9x = 4 \qquad\qquad 3x = 1$$

$$x = \frac{4}{9} \qquad\qquad x = \frac{1}{3}$$

$$\left\{\frac{1}{3},\frac{4}{9}\right\}$$

71. $x^{-2} - 3x^{-1} - 10 = 0$

$$\frac{1}{x^2} - \frac{3}{x} - 10 = 0$$

$$x^2\left(\frac{1}{x^2}-\frac{3}{x}-10\right) = x^2\cdot 0$$

$$1 - 3x - 10x^2 = 0$$

$$-1(1-3x-10x^2) = -1\cdot 0$$

$$10x^2 + 3x - 1 = 0$$

$$(5x-1)(2x+1) = 0$$

$$5x - 1 = 0 \quad \text{or} \quad 2x + 1 = 0$$

$$5x = 1 \qquad\qquad 2x = -1$$

$$x = \frac{1}{5} \qquad\qquad x = -\frac{1}{2}$$

$$\left\{-\frac{1}{2},\frac{1}{5}\right\}$$

77. $x^{-2} - 10x^{-1} + 25 = 0$

$$\frac{1}{x^2} - \frac{10}{x} + 25 = 0$$

$$x^2\left(\frac{1}{x^2}-\frac{10}{x}+25\right) = x^2\cdot 0$$

$$1 - 10x + 25x^2 = 0$$

$$25x^2 - 10x + 1 = 0$$

$$(5x-1)^2 = 0$$

$$5x - 1 = 0$$

$$5x = 1$$

$$x = \frac{1}{5} \qquad \left\{\frac{1}{5}\right\}$$

73. $2x^{-2} - 17x^{-1} + 21 = 0$

$$\frac{2}{x^2} - \frac{17}{x} + 21 = 0$$

$$x^2\left(\frac{2}{x^2}-\frac{17}{x}+21\right) = x^2\cdot 0$$

$$2 - 17x + 21x^2 = 0$$

$$21x^2 - 17x + 2 = 0$$

$$(7x-1)(3x-2) = 0$$

$$7x - 1 = 0 \quad \text{or} \quad 3x - 2 = 0$$

$$7x = 1 \qquad\qquad 3x = 2$$

$$x = \frac{1}{7} \qquad\qquad x = \frac{2}{3}$$

$$\left\{\frac{1}{7},\frac{2}{3}\right\}$$

79. $2x^{-4} - 11x^{-2} + 9 = 0$

$$\frac{2}{x^4} - \frac{11}{x^2} + 9 = 0$$

$$x^4\left(\frac{2}{x^4}-\frac{11}{x^2}+9\right) = x^4\cdot 0$$

$$2 - 11x^2 + 9x^4 = 0$$

$$9x^4 - 11x^2 + 2 = 0$$

$$(9x^2-2)(x^2-1) = 0$$

$$9x^2 - 2 = 0 \qquad x^2 - 1 = 0$$

$$9x^2 = 2 \qquad\qquad x^2 = 1$$

75. $\qquad 4x^{-2} + 27 = 21x^{-1}$

$$x^2 = \frac{2}{9} \qquad x = \pm 1$$

$$x = \pm\frac{\sqrt{2}}{3} \qquad \{\pm 1, \pm\frac{\sqrt{2}}{3}\}$$

81. x: speed on the bike

	D	R	T
on bike	3	x	$\frac{3}{x}$
walking	6	x-2	$\frac{6}{x-2}$

$T = \frac{D}{R}$

$$\frac{3}{x} = \frac{6}{x-2} - 1$$

$$x(x-2)\frac{3}{x} = x(x-2)[\frac{6}{x-2}-1]$$

$$(x-2)3 = x\cdot 6 - x(x-2)$$

$$3x - 6 = 6x - x^2 + 2x$$

$$3x - 6 = 8x - x^2$$

$$x^2 - 5x - 6 = 0$$

$$(x-6)(x+1) = 0$$

$$x - 6 = 0 \quad \text{or} \quad x + 1 = 0$$

$$x = 6 \qquad x = -1$$

$x \neq -1$ since x must be positive.

His speed on the bike was 6 mph.

83. x: original speed

	D	R	T
no rain	64	x	$\frac{64}{x}$
with rain	10	x-6	$\frac{10}{x-6}$

$T = \frac{D}{R}$

$$\frac{64}{x} + \frac{10}{x-6} = 5$$

$$x(x-6)(\frac{64}{x}+\frac{10}{x-6}) = x(x-6)(5)$$

$$(x-6)(64) + x\cdot 10 = 5x(x-6)$$

$$64x - 384 + 10x = 5x^2 - 30x$$

$$-384 + 74x = 5x^2 - 30x$$

$$0 = 5x^2 - 104x + 384$$

$$0 = (5x-24)(x-16)$$

$$5x - 24 = 0 \quad \text{or} \quad x - 16 = 0$$

$$5x = 24 \qquad\qquad x = 16$$

$$x = \frac{24}{5}$$

$\frac{24}{5}$ is too small to be a solution since $\frac{24}{5} - 6$ would be negative.

Her original speed was 16 mph.

85. x: number of hours for Kathy working alone.

x + 9: number of hours for Jim working alone.

$$\frac{1}{x} + \frac{1}{x+9} = \frac{1}{6}$$

$$6x(x+9)(\frac{1}{x}+\frac{1}{x+9}) = 6x(x+9)\cdot\frac{1}{6}$$

$$6(x+9) + 6x = x(x+9)$$

$$6x + 54 + 6x = x^2 + 9x$$

$$12x + 54 = x^2 + 9x$$

$$0 = x^2 - 3x - 54$$

$$0 = (x-9)(x+6)$$

$$x - 9 = 0 \quad \text{or} \quad x + 6 = 0$$

$$x = 9, \quad x + 9 = 18 \quad x = -6$$

-6 is not a solution since x must be positive.

It would take Kathy 9 hours and Jim 18 hours working alone.

87. $4x^{-4} - 68x^{-2} + 225 = 0$

$$(2x^{-2}-25)(2x^{-2}-9) = 0$$

$$2x^{-2} - 25 = 0 \quad \text{or} \quad 2x^{-2} - 9 = 0$$

$$\frac{2}{x^2} - 25 = 0 \qquad \frac{2}{x^2} - 9 = 0$$

$$x^2\left(\frac{2}{x^2}-25\right) = x^2 \cdot 0 \quad x^2\left(\frac{2}{x^2}-9\right) = x^2 \cdot 0$$

$$2 - 25x^2 = 0 \qquad 2 - 9x^2 = 0$$

$$2 = 25x^2 \qquad\qquad 2 = 9x^2$$

$$\frac{2}{25} = x^2 \qquad\qquad \frac{2}{9} = x^2$$

$$\pm\frac{\sqrt{2}}{5} = x \qquad\qquad \pm\frac{\sqrt{2}}{3} = x$$

$$\left\{\pm\frac{\sqrt{2}}{5}, \pm\frac{\sqrt{2}}{3}\right\}$$

89. $9x^{-4} + 7x^{-2} - 2 = 0$

$$(9x^{-2}-2)(x^{-2}+1) = 0$$

$$9x^{-2} - 2 = 0 \quad \text{or} \quad x^{-2} + 1 = 0$$

$$\frac{9}{x^2} - 2 = 0 \qquad\qquad \frac{1}{x^2} + 1 = 0$$

$$x^2\left(\frac{9}{x^2}-2\right) = x^2 \cdot 0 \quad x^2\left(\frac{1}{x^2}+1\right) = x^2 \cdot 0$$

$$9 - 2x^2 = 0 \qquad\qquad 1 + x^2 = 0$$

$$9 = 2x^2 \qquad\qquad x^2 = -1$$

$$\frac{9}{2} = x^2 \qquad\qquad x = \pm i$$

$$\pm\frac{3}{\sqrt{2}} = x$$

$$\pm\frac{3\sqrt{2}}{\sqrt{2}\sqrt{2}} = x$$

$$\pm\frac{3\sqrt{2}}{2} = x \qquad\qquad \left\{\pm\frac{3\sqrt{2}}{2}, \pm i\right\}$$

91. $16x^{-4} - 8x^{-2} - 15 = 0$

$$\frac{16}{x^4} - \frac{8}{x^2} - 15 = 0$$

$$x^4\left(\frac{16}{x^4}-\frac{8}{x^2}-15\right) = x \cdot 0$$

$$16 - 8x^2 - 15x^4 = 0$$

$$-(16-8x^2-15x^4) = -1 \cdot 0$$

$$15x^4 + 8x^2 - 16 = 0$$

$$(5x^2-4)(3x^2+4) = 0$$

$$5x^2 - 4 = 0 \quad \text{or} \quad 3x^2 + 4 = 0$$

$$5x^2 = 4 \qquad\qquad 3x^2 = -4$$

$$x^2 = \frac{4}{5} \qquad\qquad x^2 = \frac{-4}{3}$$

$$x = \pm\frac{2}{\sqrt{5}} \qquad\qquad x = \pm\sqrt{\frac{-4}{3}}$$

$$x = \pm\frac{2}{\sqrt{5}}\cdot\frac{\sqrt{5}}{\sqrt{5}} \qquad x = \frac{\pm 2i}{\sqrt{3}}\cdot\frac{\sqrt{3}}{\sqrt{3}}$$

$$x = \pm\frac{2\sqrt{5}}{5} \qquad\qquad x = \frac{\pm 2i\sqrt{3}}{3}$$

$$\left\{\pm\frac{2i\sqrt{5}}{5}, \pm\frac{2i\sqrt{2}}{3}\right\}$$

93. $6x^{-2} - x^{-1} = 0$

$$x^{-1}(6x^{-1}-1) = 0$$

$$x^{-1} = 0 \quad \text{or} \quad 6x^{-1} - 1 = 0$$

$$\frac{1}{x} = 0 \qquad\qquad \frac{6}{x} - 1 = 0$$

$$x\left(\frac{1}{x}\right) = x \cdot 0 \qquad x\left(\frac{6}{x}-1\right) = x \cdot 0$$

$$1 = 0 \qquad\qquad 6 - x = 0$$

$$6 = x \quad \{6\}$$

Note: No solution from $x^{-1} = 0$.

95.
$$\frac{3x}{x-1} = \frac{x^2}{1-x}$$

$$\frac{3x}{x-1} = \frac{x^2}{-(x-1)}$$

$$\frac{3x}{x-1} = \frac{-x^2}{x-1}$$

$$(x-1)\frac{3x}{x-1} = (x-1)\frac{-x^2}{x-1}$$

$$3x = -x^2$$

$$x^2 + 3x = 0$$

$$x(x+3) = 0$$

$$x = 0 \quad \text{or} \quad x + 3 = 0$$

$$x = -3 \quad \{-3, 0\}$$

173

97.
$$\frac{5x}{x^2+3x-4} + \frac{x}{x+4} = \frac{x^2}{x-1}$$

$$\frac{5x}{(x+4)(x-1)} + \frac{x}{x+4} = \frac{x^2}{x-1}$$

$$(x+4)(x-1)\left[\frac{5x}{(x+4)(x-1)} + \frac{x}{(x+4)}\right]$$

$$= (x+4)(x-1)\cdot\frac{x^2}{x-1}$$

$$5x + (x-1)x = (x+4)x^2$$

$$5x + x^2 - x = x^3 + 4x^2$$

$$4x + x^2 = x^3 + 4x^2$$

$$0 = x^3 + 3x^2 - 4x$$

$$0 = x(x^2+3x-4)$$

$$0 = x(x+4)(x-1)$$

$$x = 0 \quad \text{or} \quad x + 4 = 0 \quad \text{or} \quad x-1 = 0$$

$$x = -4 \qquad x = 1$$

$$\{0\}$$

Neither −4 nor 1 are solutions since $\frac{5x}{(x+4)(x-1)}$ is undefined when $x = -4$ or $x = 1$.

99.
$$\frac{a-2}{x+2} + \frac{x}{x-1} = \frac{2a^2-a+2}{x^2+x-2}$$

$$\frac{a-2}{x+2} + \frac{x}{x-1} = \frac{2a^2-a+2}{(x+2)(x-1)}$$

$$(x+2)(x-1)\left(\frac{a-2}{x+2} + \frac{x}{x-1}\right)$$

$$= (x+2)(x-1)\frac{2a^2-a+2}{(x+2)(x-1)}$$

$$(x-1)(a-2) + x(x+2) = 2a^2 - a + 2$$

$$(a-2)x - (a-2) + x^2 + 2x$$

$$= 2a^2 - a + 2$$

$$x^2 + 2x + (a-2)x = 2a^2 - a + 2$$
$$+ (a-2)$$

$$x^2 + x(2+a-2) = 2a^2$$

$$x^2 - ax - 2a^2 = 0$$

$$(x-a)(x+2a) = 0$$

$$x - a = 0 \quad \text{or} \quad x + 2a = 0$$

$$x = a \qquad x = -2a$$

$$\{-2a, a\}$$

101. $(x+1)^{-4} - 5(x+1)^{-2} + 4 = 0$

$$[(x+1)^{-2}-1][(x+1)^{-2}-4] = 0$$

$$(x+1)^{-2} - 1 = 0 \quad \text{or} \quad (x+1)^{-2} - 4 = 0$$

$$\frac{1}{(x+1)^2} - 1 = 0 \qquad \frac{1}{(x+1)^2} - 4 = 0$$

$$(x+1)^2\left[\frac{1}{(x+1)^2}-1\right]=(x+1)^2\cdot 0$$

$$(x+1)^2\left[\frac{1}{(x+1)^2}-4\right]=(x+1)^2\cdot 0$$

$$1 - (x+1)^2 = 0$$

$$[1-(x+1)][1+(x+1)]=0 \quad 1-4(x+1)^2 = 0$$

$$(1-x-1)(1+x+1) = 0$$

$$[1-2(x+1)][1+2(x+1)]=0$$

$$(-x)(x+2) = 0 \quad (1-2x-2)(1+2x+2) = 0$$

$$-x = 0 \text{ or } x+2 = 0 \quad (-2x-1)(2x+3) = 0$$

$$x = 0 \qquad x = -2 \quad -2x-1=0 \text{ or } 2x+3=0$$

$$-2x=1 \qquad 2x = -3$$

$$x = -\frac{1}{2} \qquad x = -\frac{3}{2}$$

$$\left\{-2, -\frac{3}{2}, -\frac{1}{2}, 0\right\}$$

103.
$$\frac{2}{3\sqrt{x}} + \frac{\sqrt{x}}{3} = \frac{x^2}{3\sqrt{x}}$$

$$3\sqrt{x}\left(\frac{2}{3\sqrt{x}}+\frac{\sqrt{x}}{3}\right) = 3\sqrt{x}\left(\frac{x^2}{3\sqrt{x}}\right)$$

174

$$2 + \sqrt{x}\sqrt{x} = x^2$$

$$2 + x = x^2$$

$$0 = x^2 - x - 2$$

$$0 = (x-2)(x+1)$$

$$x - 2 = 0 \quad \text{or} \quad x + 1 = 0$$

$$x = 2 \qquad\qquad x = -1 \quad \{-1,2\}$$

105. x: rowing rate in still water

	D	R	T
down	30	x+5	$\frac{30}{x+5}$
back	30	x-5	$\frac{30}{x-5}$

$$T = \frac{D}{R}$$

$$\frac{30}{x+5} + \frac{30}{x-5} = 8$$

$$(x+5)(x-5)\left(\frac{30}{x+5}+\frac{30}{x-5}\right)$$

$$= (x+5)(x-5)(8)$$

$$(x-5)30 + (x+5)30 = 8(x^2-25)$$

$$30x - 150 + 30x + 150 = 8x^2 - 200$$

$$60x = 8x^2 - 200$$

$$0 = 8x^2 - 60x - 200$$

$$\frac{1}{4}\cdot 0 = \frac{1}{4}(8x^2-60x-200)$$

$$0 = 2x^2 - 15x - 50$$

$$0 = (2x+5)(x-10)$$

$$2x + 5 = 0 \quad \text{or} \quad x - 10 = 0$$

$$2x = -5 \qquad\qquad x = 10$$

$$x = -\frac{5}{2}$$

$-\frac{5}{2}$ is not a solution since x must

be positive.

His rowing rate in still water

is 10 mph.

Problem Set 6.7.

1.
$$x = \sqrt{2x^2-3x+2}$$

$$(x)^2 = \left(\sqrt{2x^2-3x+2}\right)^2$$

$$x^2 = 2x^2 - 3x + 2$$

$$0 = x^2 - 3x + 2$$

$$0 = (x-1)(x-2)$$

$$x - 1 = 0 \quad \text{or} \quad x - 2 = 0$$

$$x = 1 \qquad\qquad x = 2$$

Checking 1,

LS: 1

RS: $\sqrt{2(1)^2-3(1)+2} = \sqrt{2-3+2}$

$$= \sqrt{1} = 1$$

1 checks.

Checking 2,

LS: 2

RS: $\sqrt{2(2)^2-3(2)+2} = \sqrt{2\cdot4-6+2}$

$$= \sqrt{8-6+2} = \sqrt{4} = 2$$

2 checks.

{1,2} is the solution set.

3.
$$x - 2 = \sqrt{6-3x}$$

$$(x-2)^2 = \left(\sqrt{6-3x}\right)^2$$

$$x^2 - 4x + 4 = 6 - 3x$$

$$x^2 - x - 2 = 0$$

$$(x-2)(x+1) = 0$$

$$x - 2 = 0 \quad \text{or} \quad x - 1 = 0$$

$$x = 2 \qquad\qquad x = 1$$

Checking 2,

LS: $2 - 2 = 0$

RS: $\sqrt{6-3(2)} = \sqrt{0} = 0$

2 checks.

Checking 1,

LS: $1 - 2 = -1$

RS: $\sqrt{6-3(1)} = \sqrt{6-3} = \sqrt{3}$

1 does not check.

$\{2\}$ is the solution set.

5.
$$x = \sqrt{2x+6} - 3$$

$$x + 3 = \sqrt{2x+6}$$

$$(x+3)^2 = (\sqrt{2x+6})^2$$

$$x^2 + 6x + 9 = 2x + 6$$

$$x^2 + 4x + 3 = 0$$

$$(x+1)(x+3) = 0$$

$$x + 1 = 0 \quad \text{or} \quad x + 3 = 0$$

$$x = -1 \qquad x = -3$$

Checking -1,

LS: -1

RS: $\sqrt{2(-1)+6} - 3$

$= \sqrt{-2+6} - 3$

$= \sqrt{4} - 3$

$= 2 - 3 = -1$

-1 checks.

Checking -3,

LS: -3

RS: $\sqrt{2(-3)+6} - 3$

$= \sqrt{-6+6} - 3$

$= \sqrt{0} - 3 = -1$

-3 checks.

$\{-3,-1\}$ is the solution set.

7.
$$2x - 1 = \sqrt{2x^2+3x-2}$$

$$(2x-1)^2 = (\sqrt{2x^2+3x-2})^2$$

$$4x^2 - 4x + 1 = 2x^2 + 3x - 2$$

$$2x^2 - 7x + 3 = 0$$

$$(2x-1)(x-3) = 0$$

$$2x - 1 = 0 \quad \text{or} \quad x - 3 = 0$$

$$2x = 1 \qquad\qquad x = 3$$

$$x = \frac{1}{2}$$

Checking $\frac{1}{2}$

LS: $2(\frac{1}{2}) - 1 = 1 - 1 = 0$

RS: $\sqrt{2(\frac{1}{2})^2 + 3(\frac{1}{2})-2}$

$= \sqrt{2 \cdot \frac{1}{4}+\frac{3}{2}-2}$

$= \sqrt{\frac{1}{2}+\frac{3}{2}-2}$

$= \sqrt{\frac{4}{2}-2} = \sqrt{2-2} = 0$

$\frac{1}{2}$ checks.

Checking 3,

LS: $2(3) - 1 = 6 - 1 = 5$

RS: $\sqrt{2(3)^2+3(3)-2}$

$= \sqrt{2 \cdot 9+9-2}$

$= \sqrt{18 + 7}$

$= \sqrt{25} = 5$

3 checks.

$\{\frac{1}{2},3\}$ is the solution set.

9.
$$2x + 3 = \sqrt{8+7x-2x^2}$$

$$(2x+3)^2 = (\sqrt{8+7x-2x^2})^2$$

$$4x^2 + 12x + 9 = 8 + 7x - 2x^2$$

$$6x^2 + 5x + 1 = 0$$

$$(2x+1)(3x+1) = 0$$

$$2x + 1 = 0 \quad \text{or} \quad 3x + 1 = 0$$

$$2x = -1 \qquad\qquad 3x = -1$$

$$x = -\frac{1}{2} \qquad\qquad x = -\frac{1}{3}$$

Checking $-\frac{1}{2}$,

LS: $2\left(-\frac{1}{2}\right) + 3$

$\qquad = -1 + 3 = 2$

RS: $\sqrt{8+7\left(-\frac{1}{2}\right)-2\left(-\frac{1}{2}\right)^2}$

$\qquad = \sqrt{8-\frac{7}{2}-\frac{2}{4}} = \sqrt{8-\frac{7}{2}-\frac{1}{2}}$

$\qquad = \sqrt{8-\frac{8}{2}} = \sqrt{4} = 2$

$-\frac{1}{2}$ checks.

Checking $-\frac{1}{3}$,

LS: $2\left(-\frac{1}{3}\right) + 3$

$\qquad = -\frac{2}{3} + 3 = \frac{-2}{9} + \frac{9}{3} = \frac{7}{3}$

RS: $\sqrt{8+7\left(-\frac{1}{3}\right)-2\left(-\frac{1}{3}\right)^2}$

$\qquad = \sqrt{8-\frac{7}{3}-2\left(\frac{1}{9}\right)} = \sqrt{\frac{72}{9}-\frac{21}{9}-\frac{2}{9}}$

$\qquad = \sqrt{\frac{49}{9}} = \frac{7}{3}$

$-\frac{1}{3}$ checks.

$\left\{-\frac{1}{2}, -\frac{1}{3}\right\}$ is the solution set.

11. $\qquad\qquad \sqrt{x-3} - 1 = \sqrt{2x-4}$

$\qquad\qquad \left(\sqrt{x-3})-1\right)^2 = \left(\sqrt{2x-4}\right)^2$

$\left(\sqrt{x-3}\right)^2 - 2\sqrt{x-3} + 1 = 2x - 4$

$$x - 3 - 2\sqrt{x-3} + 1 = 2x - 4$$

$$-2\sqrt{x-3} + x - 2 = 2x - 4$$

$$-2\sqrt{x-3} = x - 2$$

$$\left(-2\sqrt{x-3}\right)^2 = (x-2)^2$$

$$4(x-3) = x^2 - 4x + 4$$

$$4x - 12 = x^2 - 4x + 4$$

$$0 = x^2 - 8x + 16$$

$$0 = (x-4)^2$$

$$0 = x - 4$$

$$4 = x$$

Checking 4,

LS: $\sqrt{4-3} - 1$

$\qquad = \sqrt{1} - 1 = 0$

RS: $\sqrt{2(4)-4}$

$\qquad = \sqrt{8-4} = 2$

$\emptyset$ is the solution set.

13. $\qquad\qquad \sqrt{3x+1} = 1 + \sqrt{2x-1}$

$\qquad \left(\sqrt{3x+1}\right)^2 = \left(1+\sqrt{2x-1}\right)^2$

$\qquad 3x + 1 = 1 + 2\sqrt{2x-1} + \left(\sqrt{2x-1}\right)^2$

$\qquad 3x + 1 = 1 + 2\sqrt{2x-1} + 2x - 1$

$\qquad 3x + 1 = 2x + 2\sqrt{2x-1}$

$\qquad\quad x + 1 = 2\sqrt{2x-1}$

$\qquad (x+1)^2 = \left(2\sqrt{2x-1}\right)^2$

$x^2 + 2x + 1 = 4x - 1$

$x^2 + 2x + 1 = 8x - 4$

$x^2 - 6x + 5 = 0$

$\qquad x - 1 = 0 \quad \text{or} \quad x - 5 = 0$

$\qquad\quad x = 1 \qquad\qquad x = 5$

Checking 1,

LS: $\sqrt{3(1)+1} = \sqrt{4} = 2$

RS: $1 + \sqrt{2(1)-1} = 1 + \sqrt{1}$

$\quad = 2$

1 checks.

Checking 5,

LS: $\sqrt{3(5)+1} = \sqrt{16} = 4$

RS: $1 + \sqrt{2(5)-1} = 1 + \sqrt{9}$

$\quad = 4$

5 checks.

$\{1,5\}$ is the solution set.

15. $\qquad \sqrt{2y-5} = \sqrt{3y+4} - 2$

$\qquad (\sqrt{2y-5})^2 = (\sqrt{3y+4}-2)^2$

$\qquad 2y - 5 = (\sqrt{3y+4})^2 - 4\sqrt{3y+4} + 4$

$\qquad 2y - 5 = 3y + 4 - 4\sqrt{3y+4} + 4$

$\qquad 2y - 5 = 3y + 8 - 4\sqrt{3y+4}$

$\qquad -y - 13 = -4\sqrt{3y+4}$

$\qquad -1(-y-13) = -1(-4\sqrt{3y+4}$

$\qquad y + 13 = 4\sqrt{3y+4}$

$\qquad (y+13)^2 = (16\sqrt{3y+4})^2$

$y^2 + 26y + 169 = 16(3y+4)$

$y^2 + 26y + 169 = 48y + 64$

$y^2 + 22y + 105 = 0$

$\qquad y - 7 = 0 \;$ or $\; y - 15 = 0$

$\qquad\qquad y = 7 \qquad\qquad y = 15$

Checking 7,

LS: $\sqrt{2(y)-5}$

$\qquad = \sqrt{14-5} = \sqrt{9} = 3$

RS: $\sqrt{3(7)+4} - 2$

$\quad = \sqrt{21+4} - 2$

$\quad = \sqrt{25} - 2$

$\quad = 5 - 2 = 3$

7 checks.

Checking 15,

LS: $\sqrt{2(15)-5} = \sqrt{30-5}$

$\quad = \sqrt{25} = 5$

RS: $\sqrt{3(15)+4} - 2$

$\quad = \sqrt{45+4} - 2$

$\quad = \sqrt{49} - 2 = 7 - 2$

$\quad = 5$

15 checks.

$\{7,15\}$ is the solution set.

17. $\qquad \sqrt{5x+21} = 1 - \sqrt{3x+16}$

$\qquad (\sqrt{5x+21})^2 = (1-\sqrt{3x+16})^2$

$\qquad 5x + 21 = 1 - 2\sqrt{3x+16} + 3x + 16$

$\qquad 5x + 21 = 3x + 17 - 2\sqrt{3x+16}$

$\qquad 2x + 4 = -2\sqrt{3x+16}$

$\qquad (2x+4)^2 = (-2\sqrt{3x+16})^2$

$4x^2 + 16x + 16 = 4(3x+16)$

$4x^2 + 16x + 16 = 12x + 64$

$4x^2 + 4x - 48 = 0$

$\frac{1}{4}(4x^2+4x-48) = \frac{1}{4} \cdot 0$

$x^2 + x - 12 = 0$

$(x+4)(x-3) = 0$

$x + 4 = 0 \;$ or $\; x - 3 = 0$

$\qquad x = -4 \qquad\qquad x = 3$

Checking 4, LS: $\sqrt{5(-4)+21}$

$\qquad = \sqrt{-20+21} = \sqrt{1} = 1$

178

RS: $1 - \sqrt{3(-4)+16} = 1 - \sqrt{-12+16}$

$\qquad = 1 - \sqrt{4} = 1 - 2 = -1$

-4 is not a solution.

<u>Checking 3,</u> LS: $\sqrt{5(3)+21} = \sqrt{15+21}$

$\qquad\qquad\qquad = \sqrt{36} = 6$

RS: $1 - \sqrt{3(3)+16} = 1 - \sqrt{25}$

$\qquad\qquad\qquad = 1 - 5 = -4$

3 is not a solution.

$\emptyset$ is the solution set.

19. $\quad x^{1/3} = 2$

$\quad (x^{1/3})^3 = 2^3$

$\qquad\quad x = 8$

8 checks by inspection.

{8} is the solution set.

21. $\sqrt[3]{2x-1} - 3 = 0$

$\qquad \sqrt[3]{2x-1} = 3$

$\quad (\sqrt[3]{2x-1})^3 = 3^3$

$\qquad 2x - 1 = 27$

$\qquad\quad 2x = 28$

$\qquad\qquad x = 14$

Checking 14,

$: \sqrt[3]{2(14)-1} - 3$

$\quad = \sqrt[3]{28-1} - 3$

$\quad = \sqrt[3]{27} - 3$

$\quad = 3 - 3 = 0$

RS: 0

14 checks.

{14} is the solution set.

23. $\quad \sqrt{x+2} = x$

$\quad (\sqrt{x+2})^2 = x^2$

$\qquad x + 2 = x^2$

$0 = x^2 - x - 2$

$0 = (x-2)(x+1)$

$x - 2 = 0 \quad \text{or} \quad x + 1 = 0$

$\quad x = 2 \qquad\qquad x = -1$

Checking 2,

LS: $\sqrt{2+2} = \sqrt{4} = 2$

RS: 2

2 checks.

Checking -1,

LS: $\sqrt{-1+2} = \sqrt{1} = 1$

RS: -1

-1 does not check.

{2} is the solution set.

25. $\quad \sqrt{16x} = x + 3$

$\quad (\sqrt{16x})^2 = (x+3)^2$

$\qquad 16x = x^2 + 6x + 9$

$\qquad 0 = x^2 - 10x + 9$

$\qquad 0 = (x-1)(x-9)$

$x - 1 = 0 \quad \text{or} \quad x - 9 = 0$

$\quad x = 1 \qquad\qquad x = 9$

Checking 1,

LS: $\sqrt{16(1)} = \sqrt{16} = 4$

RS: $1 + 3 = 4$

1 checks.

Checking 9,

LS: $\sqrt{16(9)} = \sqrt{144} = 12$

RS: $9 + 3 = 12$

9 checks.

{1,9} is the solution set.

27. $\sqrt{4-x} = x - 4$

$(\sqrt{4-x})^2 = (x-4)^2$

$4 - x = x^2 - 8x + 16$

$0 = x^2 - 7x + 12$

$0 = (x-3)(x-4)$

$x - 3 = 0$ or $x - 4 = 0$

$x = 3$ $\qquad x = 4$

Checking 3,

LS: $\sqrt{4-3} = \sqrt{1} = 1$

RS: $3 - 4 = -1$

3 does not check.

Checking 4,

LS: $\sqrt{4-4} = \sqrt{0} = 0$

RS: $4 - 4 = 0$

4 checks.

{4} is the solution set.

29. $\sqrt{2x} = x - 4$

$(\sqrt{2x})^2 = (x-4)^2$

$2x = x^2 - 8x + 16$

$0 = x^2 - 10x + 16$

$0 = (x-2)(x-8)$

$x - 2 = 0$ or $x - 8 = 0$

$x = 2$ $\qquad x = 8$

Checking 2,

LS: $\sqrt{2 \cdot 2} = \sqrt{4} = 2$

RS: $2 - 4 = -2$

2 does not check.

Checking 8,

LS: $\sqrt{2 \cdot 8} = \sqrt{16} = 4$

RS: $8 - 4 = 4$

8 checks.

{8} is the solution set.

31. $\sqrt{8x+1} - 2 = x$

$\sqrt{8x+1} = x + 2$

$(\sqrt{8x+1})^2 = (x+2)^2$

$8x + 1 = x^2 + 4x + 4$

$0 = x^2 - 4x + 3$

$0 = (x-1)(x-3)$

$x - 1 = 0$ or $x - 3 = 0$

$x = 1$ $\qquad x = 3$

Checking 1,

LS: $\sqrt{8(1)+1} - 2$

$\qquad = \sqrt{9} - 2 = 3 - 2 = 1$

RS: 1

1 checks.

Checking 3,

LS: $\sqrt{8(3)+1} - 2$

$\qquad = \sqrt{25} - 2 = 5 - 2 = 3$

RS: 3

3 checks.

{1,3} is the solution set.

33. $\sqrt{z+27} - 1 = \sqrt{2z+20}$

$(\sqrt{z+27} - 1)^2 = (\sqrt{2z+20})^2$

$(z+27) - 2\sqrt{z+27} + 1 = 2z + 20$

$$z + 28 - 2\sqrt{z+27} = 2z + 20$$

$$-2\sqrt{z+27} = z - 8$$

$$(-2\sqrt{z+27})^2 = (z-8)^2$$

$$4(z+27) = z^2 - 16z + 64$$

$$4z + 108 = z^2 - 16z + 64$$

$$0 = z^2 - 20z - 44$$

$$0 = (z-22)(z+2)$$

$$z - 22 = 0 \quad \text{or} \quad z + 2 = 0$$

$$z = 22 \qquad z = -2$$

Checking 22,

LS: $\sqrt{22+27} - 1$

$= \sqrt{49} - 1 = 7 - 1 = 6$

RS: $\sqrt{2(22)+20}$

$= \sqrt{64} = 8$

22 does not check.

Checking -2,

LS: $\sqrt{-2+27} - 1$

$= \sqrt{25} - 1 = 5 - 1 = 4$

RS: $\sqrt{2(-2)+20}$

$= \sqrt{-4+20} = \sqrt{16} = 4$

-2 checks.

{-2} is the solution set.

35. $\sqrt{5w} - \sqrt{w-4} = 4$

$$\sqrt{5w} = \sqrt{w-4} + 4$$

$$(\sqrt{5w})^2 = (\sqrt{w-4}+4)^2$$

$$5w = (w-4) + 8\sqrt{w-4} + 16$$

$$5w = w + 12 + 8\sqrt{w-4}$$

$$4w - 12 = 8\sqrt{w-4}$$

$$\frac{1}{4}(4w-12) = \frac{1}{4}(8\sqrt{w-4})$$

$$w - 3 = 2\sqrt{w-4}$$

$$(w-3)^2 = (2\sqrt{w-4})^2$$

$$w^2 - 6w + 9 = 4(w-4)$$

$$w^2 - 6w + 9 = 4w - 16$$

$$w^2 - 10w + 25 = 0$$

$$(w-5)^2 = 0$$

$$w - 5 = 0$$

$$w = 5$$

Checking 5,

LS: $\sqrt{5(5)} - \sqrt{5-4}$

$= \sqrt{25} - \sqrt{1} = 5 - 1 = 4$

5 checks.

{5} is the solution set.

37. $\sqrt{3-2x} - \sqrt{x+4} = 2$

$$\sqrt{3-2x} = 2 + \sqrt{x+4}$$

$$(\sqrt{3-2x})^2 = (2+\sqrt{x+4})^2$$

$$3 - 2x = 4 + 4\sqrt{x+4} + (x+4)$$

$$3 - 2x = x + 8 + 4\sqrt{x+4}$$

$$-5 - 3x = 4\sqrt{x+4}$$

$$(-4-3x)^2 = (4\sqrt{x+4})^2$$

$$25 + 30x + 9x^2 = 16(x+4)$$

$$9x^2 + 30x + 25 = 16x + 64$$

$$9x^2 + 14x - 39 = 0$$

$$(9x-13)(x+3) = 0$$

$$9x - 13 = 0 \quad \text{or} \quad x + 3 = 0$$

$$9x = 13 \qquad x = -3$$

$$x = \frac{13}{9}$$

Checking $\frac{13}{9}$,

LS: $\sqrt{3-2(\frac{13}{9})} - \sqrt{\frac{13}{9}+4}$

$$= \sqrt{3 - \frac{26}{9}} - \sqrt{\frac{13}{9} + \frac{12}{9}}$$

$$= \sqrt{\frac{9}{9} - \frac{26}{9}} - \sqrt{\frac{25}{9}}$$

$$= \frac{\sqrt{-17}}{3} - \frac{5}{3}$$

RS: 2

$\frac{13}{9}$ does not check.

Checking -3,

LS: $\sqrt{3-2(-3)} - \sqrt{-3+4}$

$$= \sqrt{9} - \sqrt{1} = 3 - 1 = 2$$

RS: 2

-3 checks.

{-3} is the solution set.

39. $\sqrt{t+9} = 2 + \sqrt{2t+1}$

$(\sqrt{t+9})^2 = (2+\sqrt{2t+1})^2$

$t + 9 = 4 + 4\sqrt{2t+1} + (2t+1)$

$t + 9 = 2t + 5 + 4\sqrt{2t+1}$

$-t + 4 = 4\sqrt{2t+1}$

$-1(-t+4) = -1(4\sqrt{2t+1})$

$t - 4 = -4\sqrt{2t+1}$

$(t-4)^2 = (-4\sqrt{2t+1})^2$

$t^2 - 8t + 16 = 16(2t+1)$

$t^2 - 8t + 16 = 32t + 16$

$t^2 - 40t = 0$

$t(t-40) = 0$

$t = 0$ or $t - 40 = 0$

$t = 40$

Checking 0,

LS: $\sqrt{0+9} = \sqrt{9} = 3$

RS: $2 + \sqrt{2(0)+1} = 2 + \sqrt{1} = 3$

0 checks.

Checking 40,

LS: $\sqrt{40+9} = \sqrt{49} = 7$

RS: $2 + \sqrt{2(40)+1} = 2 + \sqrt{81}$

$$= 2 + 9 = 11$$

40 does not check.

{0} is the solution set.

41. $\sqrt{z-2} + 2 = \sqrt{2z}$

$\sqrt{z-2} = 2 + \sqrt{2z}$

$(\sqrt{z-2})^2 = (2+\sqrt{2z})^2$

$z - 2 = 4 + 4\sqrt{2z} + 2z$

$-z - 6 = 4\sqrt{2z}$

$-1(-z-6) = -1(4\sqrt{2z})$

$z + 6 = -4\sqrt{2z}$

$(z+6)^2 = (-4\sqrt{2z})^2$

$z^2 + 12z + 36 = 16(2z)$

$z^2 + 12z + 36 = 32z$

$z^2 - 20z + 36 = 0$

$(z-18)(z-2) = 0$

$z - 18 = 0$ or $z - 2 = 0$

$z = 18$ $z = 2$

Checking 18,

LS: $\sqrt{18-2} + 2$

$$= \sqrt{16} + 2 = 4 + 2 = 6$$

RS: $\sqrt{2(18)} = \sqrt{36} = 6$

18 checks.

Checking 2,

LS: $\sqrt{2-2} + 2$

$$= \sqrt{0} + 2 = 0$$

RS: $\sqrt{2 \cdot 2} = \sqrt{4} = 2$

2 checks.

$\{2,18\}$ is the solution set.

43. $\quad \sqrt{2x+1} + 1 = \sqrt{x+4}$

$$(\sqrt{2x+1}+1)^2 = (\sqrt{x+4})^2$$

$$(2x+1)+2\sqrt{2x+1}+1 = (x+4)$$

$$2x + 2 + 2\sqrt{2x+1} = x + 4$$

$$x - 2 = -2\sqrt{2x+1}$$

$$(x-2)^2 = (-2\sqrt{2x+1})^2$$

$$x^2 - 4x + 4 = 4(2x+1)$$

$$x^2 - 4x + 4 = 8x + 4$$

$$x^2 - 12x = 0$$

$$x(x-12) = 0$$

$$x = 0 \quad \text{or} \quad x - 12 = 0$$

$$x = 12$$

Checking 0,

LS: $\sqrt{2(0)+1} + 1$

$$= \sqrt{1} + 1 = 1 + 1 = 2$$

RS: $\sqrt{0+4} = \sqrt{4} = 2$

0 checks.

Checking 12,

LS: $\sqrt{2(12)+1}$

$$= \sqrt{24+1}$$

$$= \sqrt{25+1} = 5 + 1 = 6$$

RS: $\sqrt{12+4} = \sqrt{16} = 4$

12 does not check.

$\{0\}$ is the solution set.

45. $\quad 3\sqrt{x} = 1$

$$(\sqrt[3]{x})^3 = 1^3$$

$$x = 1$$

1 checks by inspection.

$\{1\}$ is the solution set.

47. $\quad (3x+1)^{1/3} = 2$

$$[(3x+1)^{1/3}]^3 = 2^3$$

$$3x + 1 = 8$$

$$3x = 7$$

$$x = \frac{7}{3}$$

Checking $\frac{7}{3}$,

LS: $(3(\frac{7}{3})+1)^{1/3} = (7+1)^{1/3}$

$$= 8^{1/3} = 2$$

RS: 2

$\frac{7}{3}$ checks.

$\{\frac{7}{3}\}$ is the solution set.

49. $\quad \sqrt{x} + \sqrt{x+5} = \sqrt{5x+5}$

$$(\sqrt{x}+\sqrt{x+5})^2 = (\sqrt{5x+5})^2$$

$$x + 2\sqrt{x(x+5)} + x + 5 = 5x + 5$$

$$2x + 5 + 2\sqrt{x(x+5)} = 5x + 5$$

$$2\sqrt{x(x+5)} = 3x$$

$$(2\sqrt{x^2+5x})^2 = (3x)^2$$

$$4(x^2+5x) = 9x^2$$

$$4x^2 + 20x = 9x^2$$

$$0 = 5x^2 - 20x$$

$$0 = 5x(x-4)$$

$$5x = 0 \quad \text{or} \quad x - 4 = 0$$

$$x = 0 \qquad\qquad x = 4$$

Checking 0,

LS: $\sqrt{0} + \sqrt{0+5} = 0 + \sqrt{5} = \sqrt{5}$

RS: $\sqrt{5(0)+5} = \sqrt{0+5} = \sqrt{5}$

0 checks.

Checking 4,

LS: $\sqrt{4} + \sqrt{4+5} = 2 + 3 = 5$

RS: $\sqrt{5(4)} + 5 = \sqrt{25} = 5$

4 checks.

$\{0,4\}$ is the solution set.

51. $\qquad \sqrt{4x+2} = \sqrt{6x+6} - \sqrt{2-2x}$

$(\sqrt{4x+2})^2 = (\sqrt{6x+6} - \sqrt{2-2x})^2$

$4x + 2 = 6x+6 - 2\sqrt{2-2x} + (2-2x)$

$4x + 2$
$= 6x+6 - 2\sqrt{12x-12x^2+12-12x+2-2x}$

$4x + 2 = 4x+8 - 2\sqrt{12-12x^2}$

$2\sqrt{12-12x^2} = 6$

$\frac{1}{2} \cdot 2\sqrt{12-12x^2}) = \frac{1}{2} \cdot 6$

$\sqrt{12-12x^2} = 3$

$(\sqrt{12-12x^2})^2 = 3^2$

$12 - 12x^2 = 9$

$3 = 12x^2$

$\frac{3}{12} = x^2$

$\frac{1}{4} = x^2$

$\pm\frac{1}{2} = x$

Checking $\frac{1}{2}$,

LS: $\sqrt{4(\frac{1}{2})+2}$

$\qquad = \sqrt{2+2} = \sqrt{4} = 2$

RS: $\sqrt{6(\frac{1}{2})+6} - \sqrt{2-2(\frac{1}{2})}$

$\qquad = \sqrt{3+6} - \sqrt{2-1}$

$\qquad = \sqrt{9} - \sqrt{1} = 3 - 1 = 2$

$\frac{1}{2}$ checks.

Checking $-\frac{1}{2}$,

LS: $\sqrt{4(-\frac{1}{2})+2}$

$\qquad = \sqrt{-2+2} = \sqrt{0} = 0$

RS: $\sqrt{6(-\frac{1}{2})+6} - \sqrt{2-2(-\frac{1}{2})}$

$\qquad = \sqrt{-3+6} - \sqrt{2+1}$

$\qquad = \sqrt{3} - \sqrt{3} = 0$

$\frac{1}{2}$ checks.

$\{\pm\frac{1}{2}\}$ is the solution set.

53. $x^{2/3} - x^{1/2} - 2 = 0$

$(x^{1/3}-2)(x^{1/3}+1) = 0$

$x^{1/3} - 2 = 0 \quad$ or $\quad x^{1/3} + 1 = 0$

$\qquad x^{1/3} = 2 \qquad\qquad x^{1/3} = -1$

$\quad (x^{1/3})^3 = 2^3 \qquad\qquad (x^{1/3})^3 = (-1)^3$

$\qquad x = 8 \qquad\qquad\qquad x = -1$

Checking 8,

LS: $8^{2/3} - 8^{1/3} - 2$

$\qquad = (\sqrt[3]{8})^2 - \sqrt[3]{8} - 2$

$\qquad = 2^2 - 2 - 2 = 4 - 4 = 0$

RS: 0

8 checks.

Checking -1,

LS: $(-1)^{2/3} - (-1)^{1/3} - 2$

$\qquad = (\sqrt[3]{-1})^2 - \sqrt[3]{-1}) - 2$

$\qquad = (-1)^2 - (-1) - 2$

$\qquad = 1 + 1 - 2 = 0$

RS: 0

-1 checks.

{-1,8} is the solution set.

55. $x^{2/5} - 2x^{1/5} - 3 = 0$

$(x^{1/5}-3)(x^{1/5}+1) = 0$

$x^{1/5} - 3 = 0$ or $x^{1/5} + 1 = 0$

$\quad\quad x^{1/5} = 3 \quad\quad\quad x^{1/5} = 0$

$\quad (x^{1/5})^5 = 3^5 \quad\quad (x^{1/5})^5 = (-1)^5$

$\quad\quad\quad x = 243 \quad\quad\quad\quad x = -1$

Checking 243,

LS: $243 - 2(243)^{1/5} - 3$

$\quad = (\sqrt[5]{243})^2 - 2\sqrt[5]{243} - 3$

$\quad = 3^2 - 2(3) - 3$

$\quad = 9 - 6 - 3 = 9 - 9 = 0$

RS: 0

243 checks.

Checking -1,

LS: $(-1)^{2/5} - 2(-1)^{1/5} - 3$

$\quad = (\sqrt[5]{-1})^2 - 2(\sqrt[5]{-1}) - 3$

$\quad = (-1)^2 - 2(-1) - 3$

$\quad = 1 + 2 - 3 = 3 - 3 = 0$

-1 checks

{-1,243} is the solution set.

Chapter Review.

1. $12x^2 + 5x - 2 = 0$

$(4x-1)(3x+2) = 0$

$4x - 1 = 0$ or $3x + 2 = 0$

$\quad\quad 4x = 1 \quad\quad\quad 3x = -2$

$\quad\quad x = \frac{1}{4} \quad\quad\quad x = -\frac{2}{3}$

$$\{-\frac{2}{3}, \frac{1}{4}\}$$

3. $x^2 - 7x = 0$

$x(x-7) = 0$

$x = 0$ or $x - 7 = 0$

$\quad\quad\quad\quad x = 7 \quad\quad \{0,7\}$

5. $3x^2 + 4x - 3 = 0$

$a = 3 \quad b = 5 \quad c = -3$

$x = \dfrac{-4 \pm \sqrt{4^2 - 4(3)(-3)}}{2(3)}$

$\quad = \dfrac{-4 \pm \sqrt{16+36}}{6}$

$\quad = \dfrac{-4 \pm \sqrt{52}}{6}$

$\quad = \dfrac{-4 \pm \sqrt{4 \cdot 13}}{6}$

$\quad = \dfrac{-4 \pm 2\sqrt{13}}{6}$

$\quad = \dfrac{-2 \pm \sqrt{13}}{3} \quad\quad \{-\frac{2}{3} \pm \frac{\sqrt{13}}{3}\}$

7. $\dfrac{3}{x-5} + \dfrac{x}{3(x+2)} = \dfrac{5}{x^2-3x-10}$

$\dfrac{3}{x-5} + \dfrac{x}{3(x+2)} = \dfrac{5}{(x-5)(x+2)}$

$3(x+2)(x-5)[\dfrac{3}{x-5} + \dfrac{x}{3(x+2)}]$

$= 3(x+2)(x-5)\dfrac{5}{(x-5)(x-2)}$

$3(x+2)(3) + (x-5)x = 3(5)$

$9(x+2) + x^2 - 5x = 15$

$9x + 18 + x^2 - 5x = 15$

$x^2 + 4x + 18 = 15$

$x^2 + 4x + 3 = 0$

$(x+1)(x+3) = 0$

185

$x + 1 = 0$ or $x + 3 = 0$

$x = -1$ $x = -3$ $\{-3, -1\}$

9. $4x^2 + 12x + 9 = 0$

$(2x+3)^2 = 0$

$2x + 3 = 0$

$2x = -3$

$x = -\dfrac{3}{2}$ $\{-\dfrac{3}{2}\}$

11. $4x^2 - x + 1 = 0$

$a = 4 \quad b = -1 \quad c = 1$

$x = \dfrac{-(-1)\pm\sqrt{(-1)^2-4(4)(1)}}{2(4)}$

$= \dfrac{1\pm\sqrt{1-16}}{8}$

$= \dfrac{1\pm\sqrt{-15}}{8}$

$= \dfrac{1\pm\sqrt{15}i}{8}$ $\{\dfrac{1}{8}\pm\dfrac{\sqrt{15}i}{8}\}$

13. $(3x+2)^2 = 9$

$3x + 2 = \pm 3$

$3x + 2 = 3$ or $3x + 2 = -3$

$3x = 1$ $3x = -5$

$x = \dfrac{1}{3}$ $x = -\dfrac{5}{3}$

$\{-\dfrac{5}{3}, \dfrac{1}{3}\}$

15. $\sqrt{6x+1} - 1 = \sqrt{3x+4}$

$(\sqrt{6x+1}-1)^2 = (\sqrt{3x+4})^2$

$6x+1-2\sqrt{6x+1}+1 = 3x + 4$

$6x + 2 - 2\sqrt{6x+1} = 3x + 4$

$3x - 2 = 2\sqrt{6x+1}$

$(3x-2)^2 = (2\sqrt{6x+1})^2$

$9x^2 - 12x + 4 = 4(6x+1)$

$9x^2 - 12x + 4 = 24x + 4$

$9x^2 - 36x = 0$

$9x(x-4) = 0$

$9x = 0$ or $x - 4 = 0$

$x = 0$ $x = 4$

Checking 0,

$\sqrt{6(0)+1} - 1$

$= \sqrt{0+1} - 1 = \sqrt{1} - 1 = 0$

RS: $\sqrt{3(0)+4} = \sqrt{4} = 2$

0 does not check.

Checking 4,

LS: $\sqrt{6(4)+1} - 1$

$= \sqrt{25-1} = 5 - 1 = 4$

RS: $\sqrt{3(4)+4} = \sqrt{12+4}$

$= \sqrt{16} = 4$

4 checks.

$\{4\}$ is the solution set.

17. $18x^2 + 9x - 5 = 0$

$(6x+5)(3x-1) = 0$

$6x + 5 = 0$ or $3x - 1 = 0$

$6x = -5$ $3x = 1$

$x = \dfrac{-5}{6}$ $x = \dfrac{1}{3}$

$\{-\dfrac{5}{6}, \dfrac{1}{3}\}$

19. $4x^2 - 9 = 0$

$4x^2 = 9$

$x^2 = \dfrac{9}{4}$

$x = \pm\sqrt{\dfrac{9}{4}}$

$$x = \pm \frac{3}{2} \qquad\qquad \left\{\pm\frac{3}{2}\right\}$$

21.
$$\frac{1}{x} + \frac{x+1}{x^2} = \frac{6}{x^3}$$

$$x^3\left(\frac{1}{x} + \frac{x+1}{x^2}\right) = x^3\left(\frac{6}{x^3}\right)$$

$$x^2 + x(x+1) = 6$$

$$x^2 + x^2 + x = 6$$

$$2x^2 + x - 6 = 0$$

$$(2x-3)(x+2) = 0$$

$$2x - 3 = 0 \quad \text{or} \quad x + 2 = 0$$

$$2x = 3 \qquad\qquad x = -2$$

$$x = \frac{3}{2} \qquad\qquad \left\{-2, \frac{3}{2}\right\}$$

23.
$$\frac{3}{x} + \frac{3}{x^2-x} = \frac{x}{1-x}$$

$$\frac{3}{x} + \frac{3}{x(x-1)} = \frac{x}{1-x}$$

$$\frac{3}{x} + \frac{3}{x(x-1)} = \frac{x}{-(x-1)}$$

$$\frac{3}{x} + \frac{3}{x(x-1)} = \frac{-x}{x-1}$$

$$x(x-1)\left[\frac{3}{x} + \frac{3}{x(x-1)}\right] = x(x-1)\left(\frac{-x}{x-1}\right)$$

$$(x-1)(3) + 3 = x(-x)$$

$$3x - 3 + 3 = -x^2$$

$$x^2 + 3x = 0$$

$$x(x+3) = 0$$

$$x = 0 \quad \text{or} \quad x + 3 = 0$$

$$x = -3 \qquad \{-3\}$$

0 is not a solution since $\frac{3}{x}$

and $\frac{3}{x(x-1)}$ are undefined when

$x = 0$.

25.
$$x^3 = \frac{1}{8}$$

$$x^3 - \frac{1}{8} = 0$$

$$\left(x-\frac{1}{2}\right)\left(x^2 + \frac{1}{2}x + \frac{1}{4}\right) = 0$$

$$x - \frac{1}{2} = 0 \quad \text{or} \quad x^2 + \frac{1}{2}x + \frac{1}{4} = 0$$

$$x = \frac{1}{2} \qquad 4\left(x^2 + \frac{1}{2}x + \frac{1}{4}\right) = 4 \cdot 0$$

$$4x^2 + 2x + 1 = 0$$

$$a = 4 \quad b = 2 \quad c = 1$$

$$x = \frac{-2 \pm \sqrt{2^2 - 4(4)(1)}}{2(4)}$$

$$= \frac{-2 \pm \sqrt{4-16}}{8}$$

$$= \frac{-2 \pm \sqrt{-12}}{8}$$

$$= \frac{-2 \pm 2\sqrt{3}\,i}{8}$$

$$= \frac{-1 \pm \sqrt{3}\,i}{4} \qquad \left\{\frac{1}{2}, -\frac{1}{4} \pm \frac{\sqrt{3}}{4}i\right\}$$

27.
$$3x^2 + 8x + 4 = 0$$

$$(3x+2)(x+2) = 0$$

$$3x + 2 = 0 \quad \text{or} \quad x + 2 = 0$$

$$3x = -2 \qquad\qquad x = -2$$

$$x = -\frac{2}{3} \qquad \left\{-2, -\frac{2}{3}\right\}$$

29.
$$\sqrt{x+2} - x = 0$$

$$\sqrt{x+2} = x$$

$$(\sqrt{x+2})^2 = x^2$$

$$x + 2 = x^2$$

$$0 = x^2 - x - 2$$

$$0 = (x-2)(x+1)$$

$$x - 2 = 0 \quad \text{or} \quad x + 1 = 0$$

$$x = 2 \qquad\qquad x = -1$$

Checking 2,

LS: $\sqrt{2+2} - 2 = \sqrt{4} - 2$

$\quad\quad = 2 - 2 = 0$

RS: 0

2 checks.

Checking -1,

LS: $\sqrt{-1+2} - (-1)$

$\quad\quad = \sqrt{1} + 1 = 1 + 1 = 2$

RS: 0

-1 does not check.

$\{2\}$ is the solution set.

31. $3x^2 - x - 2 = 0$

$(3x+2)(x-1) = 0$

$3x + 2 = 0$ or $x - 1 = 0$

$\quad\quad 3x = -2 \quad\quad\quad x = 1$

$\quad\quad x = -\dfrac{2}{3} \quad\quad\quad\quad \{-\dfrac{2}{3}, 1\}$

33. $x^4 - 50x^2 + 49 = 0$

$(x^2-49)(x^2-1) = 0$

$x^2 - 49 = 0$ or $x^2 - 1 = 0$

$\quad\quad x^2 = 49 \quad\quad\quad x^2 = 1$

$\quad\quad x = \pm 7 \quad\quad\quad x = \pm 1$

$\quad\quad\quad\quad\quad\quad\quad\quad \{\pm 1, \pm 7\}$

35. $\quad \sqrt{2x+1} - \sqrt{x} = 1$

$\quad\quad \sqrt{2x+1} = 1 + \sqrt{x}$

$\quad\quad (\sqrt{2x+1})^2 = (1+\sqrt{x})^2$

$\quad\quad 2x + 1 = 1 + 2\sqrt{x} + x$

$\quad\quad\quad x = 2\sqrt{x}$

$\quad\quad\quad x^2 = (2\sqrt{x})^2$

$\quad\quad\quad x^2 = 4x$

$\quad\quad x^2 - 4x = 0$

$x(x-4) = 0$

$x = 0$ or $x - 4 = 0$

$\quad\quad\quad\quad\quad\quad x = 4$

Checking 0,

LS: $\sqrt{2(0)+1} - \sqrt{0}$

$\quad\quad = \sqrt{0+1} - 0 = \sqrt{1} - 0 = 1 - 0$

$\quad\quad = 1$

RS: 1

0 checks.

Checking 4,

LS: $\sqrt{2(4)+1} - \sqrt{4}$

$\quad\quad = \sqrt{9} - \sqrt{4} = 3 - 2 = 1$

RS: 1

4 checks.

$\{0,4\}$ is the solution set.

37. $\sqrt{2x+5} - \sqrt{x-1} = 2$

$\quad\quad \sqrt{2x+5} = 2 + \sqrt{x-1}$

$\quad\quad (\sqrt{2x+5})^2 = (2+\sqrt{x-1})^2$

$\quad\quad 2x + 5 = 4 + 4\sqrt{x-1} + (x-1)$

$\quad\quad 2x + 5 = x + 3 + 4\sqrt{x-1}$

$\quad\quad\quad x + 2 = 4\sqrt{x-1}$

$\quad\quad\quad (x+2)^2 = (4\sqrt{x-1})^2$

$\quad x^2 + 4x + 4 = 16(x-1)$

$\quad x^2 + 4x + 4 = 16x - 16$

$x^2 - 12x + 20 = 0$

$\quad (x-2)(x-10) = 0$

$x - 2 = 0$ or $x - 10 = 0$

$\quad\quad x = 2 \quad\quad\quad\quad x = 10$

Checking 2,

LS: $\sqrt{2(2)+5} - \sqrt{2-1}$

$= \sqrt{9} - \sqrt{1} = 3 - 1 = 2$

RS: 2

2 checks.

Checking 10,

LS: $\sqrt{2(10)+5} - \sqrt{10-1}$

$= \sqrt{25} - \sqrt{9} = 5 - 3 = 2$

RS: 2

10 checks.

{2,10} is the solution set.

39. $\dfrac{3}{x^2+6x+8} + \dfrac{x+4}{x^2+3x+2} = \dfrac{5}{x^2+5x+4}$

$\dfrac{3}{(x+2)(x+4)} + \dfrac{x+4}{(x+2)(x+1)}$

$= \dfrac{5}{(x+1)(x+4)}$

$(x+2)(x+4)(x+1)[\dfrac{3}{(x+2)(x+4)}$

$\qquad + \dfrac{x+4}{(x+2)(x+1)}]$

$= (x+2)(x+4)(x+1)[\dfrac{5}{(x+1)(x+4)}]$

$(x+1)(3) + (x+4)(x+4) = (x+2)(5)$

$3x + 3 + x^2 + 8x + 16 = 5x + 10$

$x^2 + 11x + 19 = 5x + 10$

$x^2 + 6x + 9 = 0$

$(x+3)^2 = 0$

$x + 3 = 0$

$x = -3 \qquad \{-3\}$

41. $5x^2 + 5x + 2 = 0$

$a = 5 \quad b = 5 \quad c = 2$

$x = \dfrac{-5 \pm \sqrt{5^2 - 4(5)(2)}}{2(5)}$

$= \dfrac{-5 \pm \sqrt{25-40}}{10}$

$= \dfrac{-5 \pm \sqrt{-15}}{10}$

$= \dfrac{-5 \pm \sqrt{15}i}{10}$ or $\dfrac{-1}{2} \pm \dfrac{\sqrt{15}i}{10}$

$\{-\dfrac{1}{2} \pm \dfrac{\sqrt{15}i}{10}\}$

43. $\dfrac{1}{x+1} + \dfrac{1}{3} = 2x$

$3(x+1)(\dfrac{1}{x+1}+\dfrac{1}{3}) = 3(x+1)(2x)$

$3(1) + (x+1)(1) = 6x(x+1)$

$3 + x + 1 = 6x^2 + 6x$

$x + 4 = 6x^2 + 6x$

$0 = 6x^2 + 5x - 4$

$0 = (3x+4)(2x-1)$

$3x + 4 = 0 \quad$ or $\quad 2x - 1 = 0$

$3x = -4 \qquad\qquad 2x = 1$

$x = -\dfrac{4}{3} \qquad\qquad x = \dfrac{1}{2}$

$\{-\dfrac{4}{3}, \dfrac{1}{2}\}$

45. $(x^2-2)^2 = 6$

$x - 2 = \pm\sqrt{6}$

$x = 2 \pm\sqrt{6} \qquad \{2\pm\sqrt{6}\}$

47. $\sqrt{2x+7} - \sqrt{x} = 2$

$\sqrt{2x+7} = \sqrt{x} + 2$

$(\sqrt{2x+7})^2 = (\sqrt{x}+2)^2$

$2x + 7 = x + 4\sqrt{x} + 4$

$x + 3 = 4\sqrt{x}$

$(x+3)^2 = (4\sqrt{x})^2$

$$x^2 + 6x + 9 = 16x$$

$$x^2 - 10x + 9 = 0$$

$$(x-1)(x-9) = 0$$

$$x - 1 = 0 \quad \text{or} \quad x - 9 = 0$$

$$x = 1 \qquad\qquad x = 9$$

Checking 1,

LS: $\sqrt{2(1)+7} - \sqrt{1}$

$\qquad = \sqrt{9} - 1 = 3 - 1 = 2$

RS: 2

1 checks.

Checking 9,

LS: $\sqrt{2(9)+7} - \sqrt{9}$

$\qquad = \sqrt{18+7} - 3 = \sqrt{25} - 3 = 2$

RS: 2

9 checks.

$\{1,9\}$ is the solution set.

49. $\quad x^2(x^2-5) - 3(x^2-5) = 0$

$\qquad\qquad (x^2-5)(x^2-3) = 0$

$\quad x^2 - 5 = 0 \quad \text{or} \quad x^2 - 3 = 0$

$\qquad x^2 = 5 \qquad\qquad x^2 = 3$

$\qquad\quad x = \pm\sqrt{5} \qquad\qquad x = \pm\sqrt{3}$

$\qquad\qquad\qquad\qquad\qquad \{\pm\sqrt{3}, \pm\sqrt{5}\}$

51. $\quad (x+3)^2 = -5$

$\quad x + 3 = \pm\sqrt{-5}$

$\quad x + 3 = \pm\sqrt{5}i$

$\qquad x = -3 \pm \sqrt{5}i \qquad \{-3\pm\sqrt{5}i\}$

53. $\quad 16x^4 - 9x^2 - 7 = 0$

$\quad (16x^2-7)(x^2+1) = 0$

$\quad 16x^2 - 7 = 0 \quad \text{or} \quad x^2 + 1 = 0$

$$16x^2 = 7 \qquad\qquad x^2 = -1$$

$$x^2 = \frac{7}{16} \qquad\qquad x = \pm\sqrt{-1}$$

$$x = \pm\sqrt{\frac{7}{16}} \qquad\qquad x = \pm i$$

$$x = \pm\frac{\sqrt{7}}{4} \qquad \{\pm\frac{\sqrt{7}}{4}, \pm i\}$$

55. $\qquad\qquad \dfrac{9}{x-1} + \dfrac{5}{3+x} = 2$

$\quad (x-1)(x+3)\left(\dfrac{9}{x-1} + \dfrac{5}{x+3}\right)$

$\qquad\quad = (x-1)(x+3)(2)$

$\quad (x+3)9 + (x-1)5 = 2(x^2+2x-3)$

$\quad 9x + 27 + 5x - 5 = 2x^2 + 4x - 6$

$\qquad\quad 14x + 22 = 2x^2 + 4x - 6$

$\qquad\qquad\quad 0 = 2x^2 - 10x - 28$

$\qquad\quad \dfrac{1}{2} \cdot 0 = \dfrac{1}{2}(2x^2-10x-28)$

$\qquad\qquad\quad 0 = x^2 - 5x - 14$

$\qquad\qquad\quad 0 = (x-7)(x+2)$

$\quad x - 7 = 0 \quad \text{or} \quad x + 2 = 0$

$\qquad x = 7 \qquad\qquad x = -2$

$\qquad\qquad\qquad\qquad\qquad \{-2,7\}$

57. $\quad (x-7)^2 = -8$

$\quad x - 7 = \pm\sqrt{-8}$

$\quad x - 7 = \pm\sqrt{8}i$

$\quad x - 7 = \pm 2\sqrt{2}i$

$\qquad x = 7 \pm 2\sqrt{2}i \qquad \{7\pm2\sqrt{2}i\}$

59. 1st number: x 2nd number: 17-x

$\quad x(17-x) = -390$

$\quad 17x - x^2 = -390$

$\qquad\quad 0 = x^2 - 17x - 390$

$\qquad\quad 0 = (x-30)(x+13)$

x - 30 = 0   or   x + 13 = 0

x = 30, 17-x = -13 x = -13,

  17 - x = 30

The numbers are -13 and 30.

61. x: length of other leg

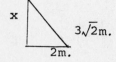

$$x^2 + 2^2 = (3\sqrt{2})^2$$

$$x^2 + 4 = 9 \cdot 2$$

$$x^2 = 14$$

$$x = \pm\sqrt{14}$$

$x \neq -\sqrt{14}$ since x must be positive.

The length of the other leg is $\sqrt{14}$ m.

63. x: speed on the last part of the trip.

	D	R	T
first part	15	x+6	$\frac{15}{x+6}$
last part	12	x	$\frac{12}{x}$

$T = \frac{D}{R}$

$$\frac{15}{x+6} + \frac{12}{x} = 1$$

$$x(x+6)\left(\frac{15}{x+6}+\frac{12}{x}\right) = x(x+6)$$

$$15x + 12(x+6) = x^2 + 6x$$

$$15x + 12x + 72 = x^2 + 6x$$

$$27x + 72 = x^2 + 6x$$

$$0 = x^2 - 21x - 72$$

$$0 = (x-24)(x+3)$$

x - 24 = 0   or   x + 3 = 0

  x = 24   x = -3

$x \neq -3$ since x must be positive.

The speed on the last part of the trip was 24 mph.

65. $(2x+5)^3$ is factored.

67. $16 - (x+1)^2$ is not factored.

$$16 - (x+1)^2 = [4+(x+1)][4-(x+1)]$$
$$= (4+x+1)(4-x-1)$$

69. y(c-d) + x(c-d) is not factored.

$$y(c-3) + x(c-d) = (c-d)(y+x)$$

71. $x^2 - xy + y^2$ has 3 terms.

  x - y is not a factor.

73. x - y(a+b) has 2 terms.

  x - y is not a factor.

75. $\dfrac{-3x^{-2}}{x^{-1}y^3} = \dfrac{-3x}{x^2y^3}$

$$= \frac{-3}{xy^3}$$

77. $a^{-1}b^2(a^{-2}+b) = \dfrac{b^2}{a}\left(\dfrac{1}{a^2}+b\right)$

$$= \frac{b^2}{a^3} + \frac{b^3}{a}$$

79. $\sqrt[5]{a +b^5}$ cannot be simplified.

81. $(3y-1)^3 = (3y)^3 - 3(3y)^2(1)$
$$+ 3(3y)(1)^2 - 1^3$$
$$= 27y^3 - 27y^2 + 9y - 1$$

83. $\dfrac{x(b+c)-y(b+c)}{(b+c)(b-c)} = \dfrac{(b+c)(x-y)}{(b+c)(b-c)}$

$$= \frac{x-y}{b-c}$$

85. $\dfrac{3}{x+4} - \dfrac{x}{x+3}$

$= \dfrac{3(x+3)}{(x+4)(x+3)} - \dfrac{x(x+4)}{(x+4)(x+3)}$

$= \dfrac{3x+9}{(x+4)(x+3)} - \dfrac{x^2+4x}{(x+4)(x+3)}$

$= \dfrac{3x+9-x^2-4x}{(x+4)(x+3)}$

$= \dfrac{-x^2-x+9}{(x+4)(x+3)}$

87. $(1-2i)(1+i)$ is an expression.

$(1-2i)(1+i) = 1 - 2i + i - 2i^2$

$\qquad\qquad = 1 - i - 2(-1)$

$\qquad\qquad = 1 - i + 2$

$\qquad\qquad = 3 - i$

89. $\dfrac{x}{x^2-5x-14} - \dfrac{1}{x-7}$ is an expression.

$\dfrac{x}{x^2-5x-14} - \dfrac{1}{x-7} = \dfrac{x}{(x-7)(x+2)} - \dfrac{1}{x-7}$

$\qquad = \dfrac{x}{(x-7)(x+2)} - \dfrac{x+2}{(x-7)(x+2)}$

$\qquad = \dfrac{x-x-2}{(x-7)(x+2)}$

$\qquad = \dfrac{-2}{(x-7)(x+2)}$

91. $\left|\dfrac{1}{4}(x-3)\right| = 3$ is an equation.

$\dfrac{1}{4}(x-3) = 3$ or $\dfrac{1}{3}(x-3) = -3$

$4[\dfrac{1}{4}(x-3)] = 4\cdot 3$ $4[\dfrac{1}{4}(x-3)] = 4(-3)$

$x - 3 = 12$ $\qquad$ $x - 3 = -12$

$\qquad x = 15$ $\qquad\qquad$ $x = -9$

$\qquad\qquad\qquad\qquad\qquad \{-9,15\}$

93. $\dfrac{3}{5}(x+2)-1 = \dfrac{1}{3}(1-x)$ is an equation.

$\dfrac{3}{5}(x+2) - 1 = \dfrac{1}{3}(1-x)$

$15[\dfrac{3}{5}(x+2)-1] = 15[\dfrac{1}{3}(1-x)]$

$9(x+2) - 15 = 5(1-x)$

$9x + 18 - 15 = 5 - 5x$

$9x + 3 = 5 - 5x$

$14x = 2$

$x = \dfrac{1}{7}$ $\qquad\qquad \{\dfrac{1}{7}\}$

Chapter Test

1. $x^2 - 2x - 3 = 5$

$x^2 - 2x - 8 = 0$

$x - 4 = 0$ or $x + 2 = 0$

$x = 4 \qquad\qquad x = -2 \quad \{-2,4\}$

B.

2. $\dfrac{-3\pm\sqrt{12}}{12} = \dfrac{-3\pm 2\sqrt{3}}{12}$

$\qquad = -\dfrac{3}{12} \pm \dfrac{2\sqrt{3}}{12}$

$\qquad = -\dfrac{1}{4} \pm \dfrac{\sqrt{3}}{6}$

A.

3. $2x^2 - 2x + 3 = 0$

$a = 2 \quad b = -2 \quad c = 3$

$x = \dfrac{-(-2)\pm\sqrt{(-2)^2-4(2)(3)}}{2(2)}$

$\qquad = \dfrac{2\pm\sqrt{4-24}}{4}$

$\qquad = \dfrac{2\pm\sqrt{-20}}{4}$

$\qquad = \dfrac{2\pm\sqrt{20}i}{4}$

$\qquad = \dfrac{2\pm 2\sqrt{5}i}{4}$

192

$$= \frac{1}{2} \pm \frac{\sqrt{5}}{2}i \qquad \{\frac{1}{2} \pm \frac{\sqrt{5}}{2}i\}$$

D.

4.
$$x = \sqrt{7-x} + 1$$
$$x - 1 = \sqrt{7-x}$$
$$(x-1)^2 = (\sqrt{7-x})^2$$
$$x^2 - 2x + 1 = 7 - x$$
$$x^2 - x - 6 = 0$$
$$(x-3)(x+2) = 0$$
$$x - 3 = 0 \quad \text{or} \quad x + 2 = 0$$
$$x = 3 \qquad x = -2$$

Checking 3,

LS: 3

RS: $\sqrt{7-3} + 1 = \sqrt{4} + 1 = 3$

Checking -2,

LS: -2

RS: $\sqrt{7-(-2)} + 1 = \sqrt{9} + 1 = 4$

-2 does not check.

{3} is the solution set.

5.
$$4x^4 - 17x^2 + 4 = 0$$
$$(4x^2-1)(x^2-4) = 0$$
$$4x^2 - 1 = 0 \quad \text{or} \quad x^2 - 4 = 0$$
$$4x^2 = 1 \qquad x^2 = 4$$
$$x^2 = \frac{1}{4} \qquad x = \pm 2$$
$$x = \pm \frac{1}{2} \qquad \{\pm \frac{1}{2}, \pm 2\}$$

C.

6.
$$3x^2 - 4x - 4 = 0$$
$$(3x+2)(x-2) = 0$$
$$3x + 2 = 0 \quad \text{or} \quad x - 2 = 0$$
$$3x = -2 \qquad x = 2$$

$$x = \frac{-2}{3} \qquad \{-\frac{2}{3}, 2\}$$

7.
$$\frac{3}{x+1} + \frac{2}{x+3} = 2$$
$$(x+1)(x+3)(\frac{3}{x+1}+\frac{2}{x+3})$$
$$= (x+1)(x+3)(2)$$
$$(x+3)(3) + (x+1)2 = 2(x^2+4x+3)$$
$$3x + 9 + 2x + 2 = 2x^2 + 8x + 6$$
$$5x + 11 = 2x^2 + 8x + 6$$
$$0 = 2x^2 + 3x - 5$$
$$0 = (2x+5)(x-1)$$
$$2x + 5 = 0 \quad \text{or} \quad x - 1 = 0$$
$$2x = -5 \qquad x = 1$$
$$x = \frac{-5}{2} \qquad \{-\frac{5}{2}, 1\}$$

8.
$$(x-3)^2 = 9$$
$$x - 3 = \pm 3$$
$$x - 3 = 3 \quad \text{or} \quad x - 3 = -3$$
$$x = 6 \qquad x = 0 \quad \{0,6\}$$

9.
$$x^2 = 3x$$
$$x^2 - 3x = 0$$
$$x(x-3) = 0$$
$$x = 0 \quad \text{or} \quad x - 3 = 0$$
$$x = 3 \qquad \{0,3\}$$

10.
$$x^3 - 8 = 0$$
$$(x-2)(x^2+2x+4) = 0$$
$$x - 2 = 0 \quad \text{or} \quad x^2 + 2x + 4 = 0$$
$$x = 2 \qquad a = 1 \ b = 2 \ c = 4$$
$$x = \frac{-2 \pm \sqrt{2^2-4(1)(4)}}{2(1)}$$

193

$$= \frac{-2 \pm \sqrt{4-16}}{2}$$

$$= \frac{-2 \pm \sqrt{-12}}{2}$$

$$= \frac{-2 \pm \sqrt{12}\,i}{2}$$

$$= \frac{-2 \pm 2\sqrt{3}\,i}{2}$$

$$= -1 \pm \sqrt{3}\,i \quad \{2, -1 \pm \sqrt{3}\,i\}$$

11. $\dfrac{1}{x^4} + \dfrac{3}{x^2} - 4 = 0$

$x^4 \left(\dfrac{1}{x^4} + \dfrac{3}{x^2} - 4 \right) = x^4 \cdot 0$

$1 + 3x^2 - 4x^4 = 0$

$-1(1 + 3x^2 - 4x^4) = -1 \cdot 0$

$4x^4 - 3x^2 - 1 = 0$

$(4x^2 + 1)(x^2 - 1) = 0$

$4x^2 + 1 = 0 \quad \text{or} \quad x^2 - 1 = 0$

$4x^2 = -1 \qquad\qquad x^2 = 1$

$x^2 = -\dfrac{1}{4} \qquad\qquad x = \pm 1$

$x = \pm \sqrt{-\dfrac{1}{4}}$

$= \pm \dfrac{1}{2} i \qquad\qquad \{\pm 1, \pm \dfrac{1}{2} i\}$

12. $\sqrt{x+1} + 2 = \sqrt{2x+10}$

$(\sqrt{x+1} + 2)^2 = (\sqrt{2x+10})^2$

$x + 1 + \sqrt{x+1} + 4 = 2x + 10$

$x + 5 + 4\sqrt{x+1} = 2x + 10$

$4\sqrt{x+1} = x + 5$

$(4\sqrt{x+1})^2 = (x+5)^2$

$16(x+1) = x^2 + 10x + 25$

$16x + 16 = x^2 + 10x + 25$

$0 = x^2 - 6x + 9$

$0 = (x-3)^2$

$0 = x - 3$

$3 = x$

Checking 3,

LS: $\sqrt{3+1} + 2$

$= \sqrt{4} + 2 = 2 + 2 = 4$

RS: $\sqrt{2(3)+10} = \sqrt{16} = 4$

3 checks.

$\{3\}$ is the solution set.

13. $3x^2 - 6x - 3 = 0$

$\dfrac{1}{3}(3x^2 - 6x - 3) = \dfrac{1}{3} \cdot 0$

$x^2 - 2x - 1 = 0$

$x^2 - 2x = 1$

$x^2 - 2x + 1 = 1 + 1$

$(x-1)^2 = 2$

$x - 1 = \pm \sqrt{2}$

$x = 1 \pm \sqrt{2} \quad \{1 \pm \sqrt{2}\}$

14. $2x^2 - x - 1 = 0$

$a = 2 \quad b = -1 \quad c = -1$

$d = (-1)^2 - 4(2)(-1)$

$= 1 + 8$

$= 9$

Since d = 9 and 9 is positive, there are two distinct real solutions.

b. two distinct real solutions

15. x: her original speed.

	D	R	T
to Ventura	20	x	$\frac{20}{x}$
to Santa Barbara	30	x-10	$\frac{30}{x-10}$

$$T = \frac{D}{R}$$

$$\frac{20}{x} + \frac{30}{x-10} = 4$$

$$x(x-10)\left(\frac{20}{x} + \frac{30}{x-10}\right) = x(x-10)(4)$$

$$(x-10)(20) + 30x = 4(x^2-10x)$$

$$20x - 200 + 30x = 4x^2 - 40x$$

$$50x - 200 = 4x^2 - 40x$$

$$0 = 4x^2 - 90x + 200$$

$$\frac{1}{2} \cdot 0 = \frac{1}{2}(4x^2 - 90x + 200)$$

$$0 = 2x^2 - 45x + 100$$

$$0 = (2x-5)(x-20)$$

$$2x - 5 = 0 \quad \text{or} \quad x - 20 = 0$$

$$x = \frac{5}{2} \qquad\qquad x = 20$$

$x \neq \frac{5}{2}$ since x - 10 must be positive.

Her original speed was 20 mph.

Problem Set 7.1.

1. $x - 3 \leq 4$

$$x \leq 7$$

$$\{x \mid x \leq 7\}$$

3. $x - 7 \geq 3$

$$x \geq 10$$

$$\{x \mid x \geq 10\}$$

5. $2x + 1 < -5$

$$2x < -6$$

$$x < -3$$

$$\{x \mid x < -3\}$$

7. $-4x \geq 2$

$$x \leq -\frac{2}{4}$$

$$x \leq -\frac{1}{2}$$

$$\{x \mid x \leq -\frac{1}{2}\}$$

9. $6(x-2) \geq 2(x-1)$

$$6x - 12 \geq 2x - 2$$

$$4x \geq 10$$

$$x \geq \frac{10}{4}$$

$$x \geq \frac{5}{2}$$

$$\{x \mid x \geq \frac{5}{2}\}$$

11. $1.1x - 0.5 > 0.7x$

$$-0.5 > -0.4x$$

$$1.25 < x$$

$$x > 1.25$$

$$\{x \mid x > 1.25\}$$

13. $\frac{2}{3}(2x-1) < \frac{1}{6}x + 1$

$6[\frac{2}{3}(2x-1)] < 6(\frac{1}{6}x+1)$

$4(2x-1) < x + 6$

$8x = 4 < x + 6$

$7x < 10$

$x < \frac{10}{7}$

$\{x \mid x < \frac{10}{7}\}$

15. $x + 3 \leq x + 4$

$3 \leq 4$

$\{x \mid x \text{ is a real number}\}$

17. $6x - 2 < 2x - 5$

$4x < -3$

$x < -\frac{3}{4}$

$\{x \mid x < -\frac{3}{4}\}$

19. $7x - 3 \leq 5x - 1$

$2x \leq 2$

$x \leq 1$

$\{x \mid x \leq 1\}$

21. $-4x + 2 > 2x - 4$

$-6x > -6$

$x < 1$

$\{x \mid x < 1\}$

23. x: such a number

$2x + 1 \leq 7$

$2x \leq 6$

$x \leq 3$

All such numbers are 3 or less.

25. width: w length: $w + 4$

$2w + 2(w+4) \leq 72$

$2w + 2w + 8 \leq 72$

$4w + 8 \leq 72$

$4w \leq 64$

$w \leq 16$

The largest width is 16 feet.

27. $x + 7 > 10$

$x > 3$

$\{x \mid x > 3\}$

29. $2 - x \geq 1$

$-x \geq -1$

$x \leq 1$

$\{x \mid x \leq 1\}$

31. $5 - x > 1$

$-x > -4$

$x < 4$

$\{x \mid x < 4\}$

33. $8x < 2x$

$6x < 0$

$x < 0$

$\{x \mid x < 0\}$

35. $\frac{1}{2}x > -5$

$2(\frac{1}{2}x) > 2(-5)$

$x > -10$

$\{x \mid x > -10\}$

37. $6x + 3 \leq 2x - 7$

$\qquad 4x \leq -10$

$\qquad x \leq -\dfrac{10}{4}$

$\qquad x \leq -\dfrac{5}{2}$

$\left\{x \mid x \leq -\dfrac{5}{2}\right\}$

$\xleftarrow{\hspace{3cm}} \quad \underset{-\frac{5}{2}}{\rule{0.4pt}{6pt}} \longrightarrow$

39. $7x - 3 > 2x$

$\qquad -3 > -5x$

$\qquad \dfrac{3}{5} < x$

$\qquad x > \dfrac{3}{5}$

$\left\{x \mid x > \dfrac{3}{5}\right\}$

$\underset{\frac{3}{5}}{\longleftarrow} \longrightarrow$

41. $\dfrac{1}{5}x - \dfrac{1}{3} \leq \dfrac{1}{5} + 2x$

$15\left(\dfrac{1}{5}x - \dfrac{1}{3}\right) \leq 15\left(\dfrac{1}{5} + 2x\right)$

$\qquad 3x - 5 \leq 3 + 30x$

$\qquad -8 \leq 27x$

$\qquad \dfrac{-8}{27} \leq x$

$\qquad x \geq -\dfrac{8}{27}$

$\left\{x \mid x \geq -\dfrac{8}{27}\right\}$

$\underset{\frac{-8}{27}}{\rule{0.4pt}{6pt}} \longrightarrow$

43. $5(x+1) < 2(1-x)$

$\qquad 5x + 5 < 2 - 2x$

$\qquad 7x < -3$

$\qquad x < -\dfrac{3}{7}$

$\left\{x \mid x < -\dfrac{3}{7}\right\}$

$\xleftarrow{\hspace{3cm}} \underset{-\frac{3}{7}}{\rule{0.4pt}{6pt}}$

45. $\dfrac{1}{3}(x+2) > \dfrac{1}{4}(x-2)$

$12\left[\dfrac{1}{3}(x+2)\right] > 12\left[\dfrac{1}{4}(x-2)\right]$

$\qquad 4(x+2) > 3(x-2)$

$\qquad 4x + 8 > 3x - 6$

$\qquad x > -14$

$\{x \mid x > -14\}$

$\underset{-14}{\longleftarrow} \longrightarrow$

47. $\dfrac{x}{7} - \dfrac{1}{3} < \dfrac{x}{3}$

$21\left(\dfrac{x}{7} - \dfrac{1}{3}\right) < 21 \cdot \dfrac{x}{3}$

$\qquad 3x - 7 < 7x$

$\qquad -7 < 4x$

$\qquad -\dfrac{7}{4} < x$

$\qquad x > -\dfrac{7}{4}$

$\left\{x \mid x > -\dfrac{7}{4}\right\}$

$\underset{-\frac{7}{4}}{\longleftarrow} \longrightarrow$

49. $\dfrac{x-3}{6} \leq \dfrac{x}{2} - 1$

$6\left(\dfrac{x-3}{6}\right) \leq 6\left(\dfrac{x}{2} - 1\right)$

$\qquad x - 3 \leq 3x - 6$

$\qquad -2x \leq -3$

$\qquad x \geq \dfrac{3}{2}$

$\left\{x \mid x \geq \dfrac{3}{2}\right\}$

$\underset{\frac{3}{2}}{\rule{0.4pt}{6pt}} \longrightarrow$

51. $\dfrac{1-x}{3} > \dfrac{2}{3}(5-x)$

$3\left(\dfrac{1-x}{3}\right) > 3\left[\dfrac{2}{3}(5-x)\right]$

$\qquad 1 - x > 2(5-x)$

$\qquad 1 - x > 10 - 2x$

$\qquad x > 9$

$\{x \mid x > 9\}$

$\underset{9}{\longleftarrow} \longrightarrow$

53.　$6(y+3) > 2(y-1)$

　　　$6y + 18 > 2y - 2$

　　　　$4y > -20$

　　　　$y > -5$

　　$\{y \mid y > -5\}$
　　　　　　　　　　　　−5

55.　$5(x-3) + 3 \leq -2(2x-4)$

　　$5x - 15 + 3 \leq -4x + 8$

　　　$5x - 12 \leq -4x + 8$

　　　　$9x \leq 20$

　　　　$x \leq \dfrac{20}{9}$

　$\{x \mid x \leq \frac{20}{9}\}$
　　　　　　　　　　$\dfrac{20}{9}$

57.　$3[5-(s+2)] - 2s \geq 6s - 7$

　　$3(5-s-2) - 2s \geq 6s - 7$

　　　$3(-s+3) - 2s \geq 6s - 7$

　　　$-3s + 9 - 2s \geq 6s - 7$

　　　　$-5s + 9 \geq 6s - 7$

　　　　　$-11s \geq -16$

　　　　　　$s \leq \dfrac{16}{11}$

　$\{s \mid s \leq \frac{16}{11}\}$
　　　　　　　　　　$\dfrac{16}{11}$

59.　$\dfrac{3}{4}(y+1) < \dfrac{1}{8}y$

　$8[\frac{3}{4}(y+1)] < 8(\frac{1}{8}y)$

　　　$6(y+1) < y$

　　　$6y + 6 < y$

　　　　$6 < -5y$

　　　$-\dfrac{6}{5} > y$

$y < -\dfrac{6}{5}$

$\{y \mid y < -\frac{6}{5}\}$
　　　　　　$-\dfrac{6}{5}$

61.　$2[3t-5+2(6t-11)] < 10(2t-5)$

　　$2(3t-5+12t-22) < 20t - 50$

　　　$2(15t-27) < 20t - 50$

　　　$30t - 54 < 20t - 50$

　　　　$10t < 4$

　　　　$t < \dfrac{4}{10}$

　　　　$t < \dfrac{2}{5}$

$\{t \mid t < \frac{2}{5}\}$
　　　　　　$\dfrac{2}{5}$

63.　$-3\{-2[(x-5)+2(2x+1)]-1\} \leq 5(x-7)$

　　$-3[-2(x-5+4x+2)-1] \leq 5x - 35$

　　　$-3[-2(5x-3)-1] \leq 5x - 35$

　　　　$-3(-10x+6-1) \leq 5x - 35$

　　　　$-3(-10x+5) \leq 5x - 35$

　　　　$30x - 15 \leq 5x - 35$

　　　　　$25x \leq -20$

　　　　　$x \leq \dfrac{-20}{25}$

　　　　　$x \leq -\dfrac{4}{5}$

$\{x \mid x \leq -\frac{4}{5}\}$
　　　　　　$-\dfrac{4}{5}$

65.　$\dfrac{x}{2} - \dfrac{1}{7} > \dfrac{1}{4}(2x-9)$

　$28(\frac{x}{2}-\frac{1}{7}) > 28[\frac{1}{4}(2x-9)]$

　　$14x - 4 > 7(2x-9)$

　　$14x - 4 > 14x - 63$

198

$$-4 > -63$$

{all reals} ⟵——————⟶

67. $\dfrac{2(x-7)}{3} - \dfrac{3(x-3)}{2} \geq 1 - x$

$\quad 6[\dfrac{2(x-7)}{3} - \dfrac{3(x-3)}{2}] \geq 6(1-x)$

$\quad\quad 4(x-7) - 9(x-3) \geq 6 - 6x$

$\quad\quad 4x - 28 - 9x + 27 \geq 6 - 6x$

$\quad\quad\quad\quad -5x - 1 \geq 6 - 6x$

$\quad\quad\quad\quad\quad\quad x \geq 7$

{x|x≥7} ⊢——————⟶
$\quad\quad\quad\quad\quad\quad 7$

69. $\quad 0 < \dfrac{x-7}{4}$

$\quad\quad 4\cdot 0 < 4(\dfrac{x-7}{4})$

$\quad\quad\quad 0 < x - 7$

$\quad\quad\quad 7 < x$

$\quad\quad\quad x > 7$

{x|x>7} ——(——⟶
$\quad\quad\quad\quad 7$

71. $\quad\quad -5 < \dfrac{3(r-1)}{-2}$

$\quad -2(-5) > -2[\dfrac{3(r-1)}{-2}]$

$\quad\quad\quad 10 > 3(r-1)$

$\quad\quad\quad 10 > 3r - 3$

$\quad\quad\quad 13 > 3r$

$\quad\quad\quad \dfrac{13}{3} > r$

$\quad\quad\quad r < \dfrac{13}{3}$

{r|r<$\frac{13}{3}$} ⟵——)——
$\quad\quad\quad\quad\quad \dfrac{13}{3}$

73. $\quad 0.4x - 20.8 \leq 8.0 - 0.8x$

$\quad\quad\quad 1.2x \leq 28.8$

$\quad\quad\quad\quad x \leq 24$

{x|x≤24} ⟵——]——
$\quad\quad\quad\quad 24$

75. $\quad 0.5 - 10.3x > 4.0x - 28.1$

$\quad\quad\quad -14.3x > -28.6$

$\quad\quad\quad\quad x < 2$

{x|x<2} ⟵——————
$\quad\quad\quad 2$

77. $\quad 2x + 5 > 2(x+3)$

$\quad\quad 2x + 5 > 2x + 6$

$\quad\quad\quad 5 > 6$

∅ ——————————

79. $\quad 3(1-x) \leq 3(x+1) - 6x$

$\quad\quad 3 - 3x \leq 3x + 3 - 6x$

$\quad\quad 3 - 3x \leq -3x + 3$

$\quad\quad\quad 3 \leq 3$

{All reals} ⟵——————⟶

81. x: such a number

$\quad\quad 4x - 2 \leq 10$

$\quad\quad\quad 4x \leq 12$

$\quad\quad\quad x \leq 3$

All such numbers are 3 or less.

83. width: w   length: w + 7

$\quad\quad 2w + 2(w+7) \leq 82$

$\quad\quad 2w + 2w + 14 \leq 82$

$\quad\quad\quad 4w + 14 \leq 82$

$\quad\quad\quad\quad 4w \leq 68$

$\quad\quad\quad\quad\quad w \leq 17$

The largest width is 17 m.

85. $x - 5 < b$
    $x < b + 5$

87. $3x - 2a > b$

    $3x > 2a + b$

    $x > \dfrac{2a+b}{3}$

89. $ax < 5, \quad a > 0$

    $x < \dfrac{5}{a}$

91. $a^2 x + x < b$

    $x(a^2+1) < b$

    $x < \dfrac{b}{a^2+1}$

Problem Set 7.2.

1. $\{x \mid 2<x<3\}$

3. $\{x \mid -\frac{1}{2}<x\leq 0\}$

5. $\{x \mid x<5 \text{ or } x>10\}$

7. $\{x \mid x>5\}$

9. OK

11. Nonsense.

13. Nonsense.

15. $\{x \mid 1<x<2\}$

17. $\{x \mid -1<x\leq 1\}$

19. $\{x \mid x\leq -7 \text{ or } x>-2\}$

21. $\{x \mid x<\frac{7}{4} \text{ and } x>\frac{3}{4}\}$

23. $2 \leq x + 3 \leq 7$

    $-1 \leq x \leq 4 \qquad \{x \mid -1\leq x\leq 4\}$

25. $x < 1$ and $x > -2 \quad \{x \mid -2<x<1\}$

27. $x \geq 4$ or $x < -3 \quad \{x \mid x<-3 \text{ or } x\geq 4\}$

29. $\{x \mid 2<x<3\}$

31. $\{x \mid -3\leq x<2\}$

33. $\{x \mid x<6 \text{ or } x > 11\}$

35. $\{x \mid x<-5 \text{ and } x<-3\}$

37. $\{x \mid x<\frac{5}{3} \text{ or } x\geq\frac{10}{3}\}$

39. $\{x \mid x\leq -3 \text{ or } x>3\}$

41. $\{x \mid 0.5<x\leq 1.5\}$

43. $\{x \mid x\leq -0.16 \text{ and } x>-2.34\}$

45. Nonsense.

47. OK

49. OK

51. $\{x \mid 4\leq x\leq 6\}$

53. $\{x \mid -11<x<-8\}$

55. $\{x \mid x\leq -3 \text{ or } x>3\}$

57. $\{x \mid x<0\}$

59. $\{x \mid x\geq -11\}$

61. $3 \leq 2x + 1 \leq 5$

    $2 \leq 2x \leq 4$

    $1 \leq x \leq 2 \quad \{x \mid 1\leq x\leq 2\}$

63. $-5 \leq 3x - 2 < 7$

$$-3 \leq 3x < 9$$

$$-1 \leq x < 3 \quad \{x \mid -1 \leq x < 3\}$$

65. $4 \leq 1 - x \leq 10$

$$3 \leq -x \leq 9$$

$$-3 \geq x \geq -9 \quad \{x \mid -9 \leq x \leq -3\}$$

67. $5 < \frac{1}{2}x - 2 \leq 8$

$$7 < \frac{1}{2}x \leq 10$$

$$14 < x \leq 20 \quad \{x \mid 14 < x \leq 20\}$$

69. $\frac{1}{2} < 2x - 3 < 3$

$$1 < 4x - 6 < 6$$

$$7 < 4x < 12$$

$$\frac{7}{4} < x < 3 \quad \{x \mid \frac{7}{4} < x < 3\}$$

71. $x < -\frac{3}{2}$ or $x \geq -\frac{1}{2}$

$$\{x \mid x < -\frac{3}{2} \text{ or } x \geq -\frac{1}{2}\}$$

73. $x \leq a$ or $x \geq b$; $a < b$

$$\{x \mid x \leq a \text{ or } x \geq b\}$$

75. $2 \leq x - a \leq 4$

$$2 + a \leq x \leq a + 4 \quad \{x \mid a+2 \leq x \leq a+4\}$$

77. $1 < ax < 3, \quad a < 0$

$$\frac{1}{a} > x > \frac{3}{a} \quad \{x \mid \frac{3}{a} < x < \frac{1}{a}\}$$

79. $\{x \mid x < -1 \text{ or } 1 < x < 2\}$

81. $\{x \mid x \leq -5 \text{ or } 0 < x \leq 3\}$

Problem Set 7.3.

1. $|x-1| < 5$

Find boundary numbers:

$$|x-1| = 5$$

$$x - 1 = 5 \quad \text{or} \quad x - 1 = -5$$

$$x = 6 \qquad\qquad x = -4$$

A   B   C

—————|———————|—————
   -4   6

Test regions: A, $x = -5$

$|-5-1| < 5$ is false.

B, $x = 0$

$|0-1| < 5$ is true.

C $x = 7$

$|7-1| < 5$ is false.

Shade region that tests true

—————(———————)—————
   -4   6

Boundary numbers are not included.

$$\{x \mid -4 < x < 6\}$$

3. $|x+2| \geq 8$

Find boundary numbers:

$$|x+2| = 8$$

$$x + 2 = 8 \quad \text{or} \quad x + 2 = -8$$

$$x = 6 \qquad\qquad x = -10$$

A   B   C

—————|———————|—————
  -10   6

Test regions: A, $x = -11$

$|-11+2| \geq 8$ is true.

B, $x = 0$

$|0+2| \geq 8$ is false.

C, $x = 7$

$|7+2| \geq 8$ is true.

Shade regions that are true

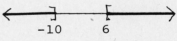

$$-10 \qquad\quad 6$$

Boundary numbers are included.

$\{x \mid x \le -10 \text{ or } x \ge 6\}$

5. $|5x-7| - 2 < 0$

$|5x-7| < 2$

Find boundary numbers:

$|5x-7| = 2$

$5x - 7 = 2 \quad \text{or} \quad 5x - 7 = -2$

$\qquad 5x = 9 \qquad\qquad 5x = 5$

$\qquad x = \dfrac{9}{5} \qquad\qquad x = 1$

Test regions: <u>A</u>, $x = 0$

$|5(0)-7| - 2 < 0$ is false.

<u>B</u>, $x = \dfrac{6}{5}$

$|5(\tfrac{6}{5})-7| - 2 < 0$ is true.

<u>C</u>, $x = 2$

$|5(2)-7| - 2 < 0$ is false.

Shade region that tests true

Boundary numbers are not included.

$\{x \mid 1 < x < \dfrac{9}{5}\}$

7. $|x+1| < |2x+3|$

Find boundary numbers:

$|x+1| = |2x+3|$

$x + 1 = 2x + 3 \quad \text{or} \quad x + 1 = -(2x+3)$

$\quad -x = 2 \qquad\qquad x + 1 = -2x - 3$

$\qquad x = -2 \qquad\qquad\quad 3x = -4$

$\qquad\qquad\qquad\qquad\qquad x = -\dfrac{4}{3}$

Test regions: <u>A</u>, $x = -3$

$|-3+1| < |2(-3)+3|$ is false.

<u>B</u>, $x = -\dfrac{3}{2}$

$|-\dfrac{3}{2}+1| > |2(-\dfrac{3}{2})+3|$ is true.

<u>C</u>, $x = 0$

$|0+1| > |2(0)+3|$ is false.

Shade region that tests true.

Boundary numbers are not included.

$\{x \mid -2 < x < -\dfrac{4}{3}\}$

9. $|2x+3| < |5x-3|$

Find boundary numbers:

$|2x+3| = |5x-3|$

$2x + 3 = 5x - 3 \quad \text{or} \quad 2x + 3$

$\qquad\qquad\qquad\qquad\qquad\qquad = -(5x-3)$

$\quad -3x = -6 \qquad 2x + 3 = -5x + 3$

$\qquad x = 2 \qquad\qquad\quad 7x = 0$

$\qquad\qquad\qquad\qquad\qquad x = 0$

Test regions: <u>A</u>, $x = -1$

$|2(-1)+3| < |5(-1)-3|$ is true.

<u>B</u>, $x = 1$

$|2(1)+3| < |5(1)-3|$ is false.

<u>C</u>, $x = 3$

$|2(3)+3| < |5(3)-3|$ is true.

Shade regions that test true.

$$\xleftarrow{\hspace{1.5cm}} \underset{0 \quad 3}{\overset{\;}{\big|\quad\big|}} \xrightarrow{\hspace{1.5cm}}$$

Boundary numbers are not included.

$\{x \mid x < 0 \text{ or } x > 2\}$

11. $|x-7| \geq 0$

Find boundary number:

$(x-7) = 0$

$x - 7 = 0$

$x = 7$

$$\underset{7}{\overline{\quad\underset{A}{}\;\big|\;\underset{B}{}\quad}}$$

Test regions: $\underline{A}$, $x = 0$

$|0-7| \geq 0$ is true.

$\underline{B}$, $x = 8$

$|8-7| \geq 0$ is true.

Shade regions that test true.

$$\xleftarrow{\hspace{1.5cm}} \underset{7}{\overset{\;}{\big|}} \xrightarrow{\hspace{1.5cm}}$$

Boundary number is included.

$\{x \mid x \text{ is any real number}\}$

13. $|x-5| < -7$

Find boundary numbers:

$|x-5| = -7$ has no solution
  so there are no boundary
  numbers.

$$\overline{\qquad\underset{A}{}\qquad}$$

Test region: $\underline{A}$, $x = 0$

$|0-5| < -7$ is false.

There are no solutions in region A.

$\emptyset$ is the solution set.

15. $|x-7| \leq 5$

$-5 \leq x - 7 \leq 5$

$2 \leq x \leq 12$

17. $\left|2x+\dfrac{1}{2}\right| \geq 7$

$2x + \dfrac{1}{2} \geq 7 \quad$ or $\quad 2x + \dfrac{1}{2} \leq -7$

$4x + 1 \geq 14 \qquad\quad 4x + 1 \leq -14$

$4x \geq 13 \qquad\qquad 4x \leq -15$

$x \geq \dfrac{13}{4} \qquad\qquad x \leq \dfrac{-15}{4}$

19. x: such a number

$|x-(-4)| \leq 2$

$|x+4| \leq 2$

$-2 \leq x + 4 \leq 2$

$-6 \leq x \leq -2$

All such numbers are between -6
  and -2, inclusive.

21. x: such a number

$\left|x-\dfrac{1}{2}\right| < \dfrac{1}{3}$

$-\dfrac{1}{3} < x - \dfrac{1}{2} < \dfrac{1}{3}$

$-2 < 6x - 3 < 2$

$1 < 6x < 5$

$\dfrac{1}{6} < x < \dfrac{5}{6}$

All such numbers are between $\dfrac{1}{6}$
  and $\dfrac{5}{6}$.

23. x: such a number

$|x| > 7$

$x > 7$ or $x < -7$

All such numbers are greater
  than 7 or less than -7.

25. x: such a number

$|x| \leq 3$

$-3 \leq x \leq 3$

All such numbers are between
  -3 and 3, inclusive.

27. $|x| \geq 8$

$x \geq 8$ or $x \leq -8$

$\{x \mid x \geq 8 \text{ or } x \leq -8\}$

29. $|x-3| < 9$

$-9 < x - 3 < 9$

$-6 < x < 12$

$\{x \mid -6 < x < 12\}$

31. $|x+5| \leq 3$

$-3 \leq x + 5 \leq 3$

$-8 \leq x \leq -2$

$\{x \mid -8 \leq x \leq -2\}$

33. $|2x+5| > 7$

$2x + 5 > 7$ or $2x + 5 < -7$

$2x > 2$ $2x < -12$

$x > 1$ or $x < -6$

$\{x \mid x > 1 \text{ or } x < -6\}$

35. $|2x-9| - 1 \leq 0$

$|2x-9| \leq 1$

$-1 \leq 2x - 9 \leq 1$

$8 \leq 2x \leq 10$

$4 \leq x \leq 5$

$\{x \mid 4 \leq x \leq 5\}$

37. $|5x-8| > 9$

$5x - 8 > 9 \text{ or } 5x - 8 < -9$

$5x > 17 \qquad 5x < -1$

$x > \dfrac{17}{5} \qquad x < -\dfrac{1}{5}$

$\{x \mid x < -\dfrac{1}{5} \text{ or } x > \dfrac{17}{5}\}$

39. $|10y+3| - 1 \geq 0$

$|10y+3| \geq 1$

$10y + 3 \geq 1 \text{ or } 10y + 3 \leq -1$

$10y \geq -2 \qquad 10y \leq -4$

$y \geq -\dfrac{2}{10} \qquad y \leq -\dfrac{4}{10}$

$y \geq -\dfrac{1}{5} \text{ or } \qquad y \leq -\dfrac{2}{5}$

$\{y \mid y \leq -\dfrac{2}{5} \text{ or } y \geq -\dfrac{1}{5}\}$

41. $3(|x-1|+3) < 15$

$3|x-1| + 9 < 15$

$3|x-1| < 6$

$|x-1| < 2$

$-2 < x - 1 < 2$

$-1 < x < 3$

$\{x \mid -1 < x < 3\}$

43. $10 \leq 3(4-|x+3|)$

$10 \leq 12 - 3|x+3|$

$-2 \leq -3|x+3|$

$3|x+3| \leq 2$

$|x+3| \leq \dfrac{2}{3}$

$-\dfrac{2}{3} \leq x + 3 \leq \dfrac{2}{3}$

$-\dfrac{11}{3} \leq x \leq -\dfrac{7}{3}$

$\{x \mid -\dfrac{11}{3} \leq x \leq -\dfrac{7}{3}\}$

45. $|t-2.5| < 6.3$

$-6.3 < t - 2.5 < 6.3$

$-3.8 < t < 8.8$

$\{t \mid -3.8 < t < 8.8\}$

47. $|x-2.73| > 6.72$

$x - 2.73 > 6.72 \text{ or } x - 2.73 < -6.7$

$x > 9.45 \qquad x < -3.99$

$\{x \mid x < -3.99 \text{ or } x > 9.45\}$

49. $|\dfrac{2x-1}{3}| \leq 4$

$-4 \leq \dfrac{2x-1}{3} \leq 4$

$-12 \leq 2x - 1 \leq 12$

$-11 \leq 2x \leq 13$

$-\dfrac{11}{2} \leq x \leq \dfrac{13}{2}$

$\{x \mid -\dfrac{11}{2} \leq x \leq \dfrac{13}{2}\}$

51. $|2-x| + 3 \geq 4$

$|2-x| \geq 1$

$2 - x \geq 1 \text{ or } 2 - x \leq -1$

$-x \geq -1 \qquad -x \leq -3$

$x \leq 1 \text{ or } \qquad x \geq 3$

$\{x \mid x \leq 1 \text{ or } x \geq 3\}$

53. $|x+1| \geq 0$

$x + 1 \geq 0 \text{ or } x + 1 \leq 0$

$x \geq -1 \qquad x \leq -1$

$\{x \mid x \text{ is a real number}\}$

55. $|z-3| \leq -5$

Find boundary number:

$|z-3| = -5$ has no solution

so there are no boundary numbers.

A

Test region: <u>A</u>, x = 0

|0-3| $\leq$ -5 is false.

There are no solutions in region A.

∅ is the solution set.

57. |2x+3| $\leq$ -1

Find boundary numbers:

|2x+3| = -1 has no solutions so there are no boundary numbers.

A

Test region: <u>A</u>, x = 0

|2(0)+3| $\leq$ -1 is false.

There are no solutions in region A.

∅ is the solution set.

59. |3x| $\geq$ |x-4|

Find boundary numbers:

|3x| = |x-4|

3x = x - 4   or   3x = -(x-4)

2x = -4   3x = -x + 4

 x = -2   4x = 4

                    x = 1

A   B   C
    -2   1

Test regions: <u>A</u>, x = -3

|3(-3)| $\geq$ |-3-4| is true.

<u>B</u>, x = 0

0| $\geq$ |0-4| is false.

<u>C</u>, x = 2

|3(2)| $\geq$ |2-4| is true.

Shade regions that test true.

    -2   1

{x|x$\leq$-2 or x$\geq$1}

61. |4x+3| $\leq$ |3x+18|

Find boundary numbers:

|4x+3| = |3x+18|

4x + 3 = 3x + 18 or 4x + 3 = -(3x+18)

x = 15   or   4x + 3 = -3x - 18

                        7x = -21

                        x = -3

A   B   C
    -3   15

Test region: <u>A</u>, x = -4

|4(-4)+3| $\leq$ |3(-4)+18| is false.

<u>B</u>, x = 0

|4(0)+3| $\leq$ |3(0)+18| is true.

<u>C</u>, x = 16

|4(16)+3| $\leq$ |3(16)+18| is false.

Shade region that tests true.

    -3   15

{x|-3$\leq$x$\leq$15}

63. |x+1| $\leq$ 3

-3 $\leq$ x + 1 $\leq$ 3

-4 $\leq$ x $\leq$ 2

65. |x| > 4.3

205

$x < -4.3$ or $x > 4.3$

67. $|x+3| < 2$

   $-2 < x + 3 < 2$

   $-5 < x < -1$

69. $|2x-\frac{1}{3}| < 2$

   $-2 < 2x < \frac{1}{3} < 2$

   $-6 < 6x - 1 < 6$

   $-5 < 6x < 7$

   $-\frac{5}{6} < x < \frac{7}{6}$

71. x: such a number

   $|x| < 4$

   $-4 < x < 4$

   Such numbers are between -4 and 4.

73. x: such a number

   $|x| \leq 8$

   $-8 \leq x \leq 8$

   Such numbers are between -8 and 8, inclusive.

75. $|x-1| < 2$

   $-2 < x - 1 < 2$

   $-1 < x < 3$

   Such numbers are between -1 and 3.

77. Prove: $|x| < a$ is equivalent to $-a < x < a$.

   Proof: Assume $a > 0$.

   Find boundary numbers.

   $|x| = a$

   $x = a$ or $x = -a$

   ```
        A     B     C
   ─────────┼───────┼─────────
           -a      a
   ```

Test regions: $\underline{A}$, $x = -a - 1$

$|-a-1| < a$ is false.

$\underline{B}$, $x = 0$

$|0| < a$ is true.

$\underline{C}$, $x = a + 1$

$|a+1| < a$ is false.

Shade region that tests true.

```
   ────────(──────)────────→
          -a      a
```

Boundary numbers are not included.
The solutions is $\{x|-a<x<a\}$
Therefore, $|x| < a$ is equivalent
  to $-a < x < a$.

79. $|x-1| > d$, $d > 0$

   $x - 1 > d$ or $x - 1 < -d$

   $x > d + 1$ $x < 1 - d$

   $\{x|x>d+1$ or $x<1-d\}$

81. $|x-a| > d$, $d < 0$

   Find boundary numbers:

   $|x-a| = d$ has no solution so
     there are no boundary numbers.

   ```
            A
   ──────────────────
   ```

   Test region: $\underline{A}$, $x = 0$

   $|0-a| > d$ is true.

   Shade region that tests true.

   ```
   ←──────────────────→
   ```

   $\{x|x$ is a real number$\}$

83. $|x-a| \geq a$

   $x - a \geq a$ or $x - a \leq -a$

   $x \geq 2a$ or $x \leq 0$
        $\{x|x\leq0$ or $x\geq2a\}$

206

85. $|x-a| > 0$

$x - a > 0$ or $x - a < 0$

$x > a$ or $x < a$

$\{x \mid x \neq a\}$

87. $|x+a| \geq a$

$x + a \geq a$ or $x + a \leq -a$

$x \geq 0$ or $x \leq -2a$

$\{x \mid x \leq -2a \text{ or } x \geq 0\}$

<u>Problem Set 7.4.</u>

1. $(x+1)(x-2) < 0$

Find boundary numbers:

$(x+1)(x-2) = 0$

$x + 1 = 0$ or $x - 2 = 0$

$x = -1$ $x = 2$

-1,2 are boundary numbers.

```
      A       B     C
 ─────────┼─────┼──────────
         -1     2
```

Test regions: <u>A</u>, $x = -2$

$(-2+1)(-2-2) < 0$

$(-1)(-4) < 0$ is false

<u>B</u>, $x = 0$

$(1)(-2) < 0$ is true.

<u>C</u>, $x = 3$

$(3+1)(3-2) < 0$ is false.

Shade region that tests true.

```
 ───────(──────)──────────
        -1      2
```

Boundary numbers are not included.

$\{x \mid -1 < x < 2\}$

3. $(x-3)(x+1) \leq 0$

Find boundary numbers:

$(x-3)(x+1) = 0$

$x - 3 = 0$ or $x + 1 = 0$

$x = 3$ $x = -1$

-1,3 are boundary numbers.

```
      A       B     C
 ─────────┼─────┼──────────
         -1     3
```

Test regions: <u>A</u>, $x = -2$

$(-2-3)(-2+1) \leq 0$

$(-5)(-1) \leq 0$ is false.

<u>B</u>, $x = 0$

$(-3)(1) \leq 0$ is true.

<u>C</u>, $x = 4$

$(4-3)(4+1) \leq 0$ is false.

Shade region that tests true.

```
 ───────[══════]──────────
        -1      3
```

Boundary numbers are included.

$\{x \mid -1 \leq x \leq 3\}$

5. $x(x+2)(x-1) > 0$

Find boundary numbers:

$x(x+2)(x-1) = 0$

$x = 0$ or $x + 2 = 0$ or $x - 1 = 0$

$x = -2$ $x = 1$

```
      A      B      C     D
 ────────┼──────┼─────┼────────
        -2      0     1
```

Test regions: <u>A</u>, $x = -3$

$(-3)(-3+2)(-3-1) > 0$

$(-3)(-1)(-4) > 0$ is false.

$\underline{B}, \ x = -1$

$(-1)(-1+2)(-1-1) > 0$

$(-1)(1)(-2) > 0$ is true.

$\underline{C}, \ x = \frac{1}{2}$

$(\frac{1}{2})(\frac{1}{2}+2)(\frac{1}{2}-1) > 0$

$(\frac{1}{2})(\frac{5}{2})(-\frac{1}{2}) > 0$ is false.

$\underline{D}, \ x = 2$

$(2)(2+2)(2-1) > 0$

$(2)(4)(1) > 0$ is true.

Shade regions that test true.

Boundary numbers are not included.

$\{x \mid -2 < x < 0 \ \text{or} \ x > 1\}$

7. $(x+4)(x-1)(x+3) > 0$

Find boundary numbers:

$(x+4)(x-1)(x+3) = 0$

$x + 4 = 0 \ \text{or} \ x - 1 = 0 \ \text{or} \ x + 3 = 0$

$x = -4 \qquad x = 1 \qquad x = -3$

Test regions: $\underline{A}, \ x = -5$

$(-5+4)(-5-1)(-5+3) > 0$

$(-1)(-6)(-2) > 0$ is false.

$\underline{B}, \ x = -3\frac{1}{2}$

$(-3\frac{1}{2}+4)(-3\frac{1}{2}-1)(-3\frac{1}{2}+3) > 0$

$(\frac{1}{2})(-4\frac{1}{2})(-\frac{1}{2}) > 0$ is true.

$\underline{C}, \ x = 0$

$(4)(-1)(3) > 0$ is false.

$\underline{D}, \ x = 2$

$(2+4)(2-1)(2+3) > 0$

$(6)(1)(5) > 0$ is true.

Shade regions that test true.

Boundary numbers are not included.

$\{x \mid -4 < x < -3 \ \text{or} \ x > 1\}$

9. $x^2 - 4x + 3 < 0$

$(x-1)(x-3) < 0$

Find boundary numbers:

$(x-1)(x-3) = 0$

$x - 1 = 0 \ \text{or} \ x - 3 = 0$

$x = 1 \qquad\qquad x = 3$

Test regions: $\underline{A}, \ x = 0$

$(0-1)(0-3) < 0$

$(-1)(-3) < 0$ is false.

$\underline{B}, \ x = 2$

$(2-1)(2-3) < 0$

$(1)(-1) < 0$ is true.

$\underline{C}, \ x = 4$

$(4-1)(4-3) < 0$

$(3)(1) < 0$ is false.

Shade region that tests true.

Boundary numbers are not included.

$\{x \mid 1 < x < 3\}$

11. $x^2 + 6x < -5$

$x^2 + 6x + 5 < 0$

$(x+1)(x+4) < 0$

Find boundary numbers:

$x + 1 = 0$ or $x + 5 = 0$

$\quad x = -1 \qquad\quad x = -5$

A   B   C

$-5 \qquad -1$

Test regions: $\underline{A}$, $x = -6$

$(-6+1)(-6+5) < 0$

$(-5)(-1) < 0$ is false.

$\underline{B}$, $x = -2$

$(-2+1)(-2+5) < 0$

$(-1)(3) < 0$ is true.

$\underline{C}$, $x = 0$

$(1)(5) < 0$ is false.

Shade region that tests true.

$-5 \qquad -1$

Boundary numbers are not included.

$\{x \mid -5 < x < -1\}$

13. $-x^2 - x + 2 > 0$

Find boundary numbers:

$-x^2 - x + 2 = 0$

$x^2 + x - 2 = 0$

$(x+2)(x-1) = 0$

$x + 2 = 0$ or $x - 1 = 0$

$\quad x = -2 \qquad\quad x = 1$

A   B   C

$-2 \qquad 1$

Test regions: $\underline{A}$, $x = -3$

$-(-3)^2 - (-3) + 2 > 0$

$-9 + 3 + 2 > 0$ is false.

$\underline{B}$, $x = 0$

$0 - 0 + 2 > 0$ is true.

$\underline{C}$, $x = 2$

$-(2)^2 - 2 + 2 > 0$

$-4 + 0 > 0$ is false.

Shade region that test true.

$-2 \qquad 1$

Boundary numbers are not included.

$\{x \mid -2 < x < 1\}$

15. $\dfrac{x-5}{x+5} \geq 0$

-5: free boundary number.

Find other boundary numbers:

$\dfrac{x-5}{x+5} = 0$

$(x+5)\left(\dfrac{x-5}{x+5}\right) = (x+5) - 0$

$x - 5 = 0$

$\quad x = 5$

A   B   C

$-5 \qquad 5$

Test regions: $\underline{A}$, $x = -6$

$\dfrac{-6-5}{-6+5} \geq 0$

$\dfrac{-11}{-1} \geq 0$ is true.

$\underline{B}$, $x = 0$

$\dfrac{-5}{5} > 0$ is false.

$\underline{C}$, $x = 6$

$\dfrac{6-5}{6+5} \geq 0$

$\dfrac{1}{11} \geq 0$ is true.

Shade regions that test true.

$-5 \qquad 5$

-5 not included; 5 included.

$\{x \mid x < -5$ or $x \geq 5\}$

17. $\dfrac{x+5}{x-5} \geq 2$

5: free boundary number.

Find other boundary numbers:

$$\frac{x+5}{x-5} = 2$$

$$(x-5)\left(\frac{x+5}{x-5}\right) = 2(x-5)$$

$$x+5 = 2x - 10$$

$$-x = -15$$

$$x = 15$$

$$\begin{array}{ccc} A & B & C \\ \hline & + & + \\ 5 & & 15 \end{array}$$

Test regions: <u>A</u>, x = 0

$$\frac{0+5}{0-5} \geq 2$$

$$\frac{5}{-5} \geq 2 \text{ is false.}$$

<u>B</u>, x = 10

$$\frac{10+5}{10-5} \geq 2$$

$$\frac{15}{5} \geq 2 \text{ is true.}$$

<u>C</u>, x = 20

$$\frac{20+5}{20-5} \geq 2$$

$$\frac{25}{15} \geq 2 \text{ is false.}$$

Shade region that tests true.

5 not included, 15 included.

$$\{x \mid 5 < x \leq 15\}$$

19. $\dfrac{3}{x+1} > \dfrac{2}{x-1}$

1,-1: free boundary numbers.

Find other boundary numbers:

$$\frac{3}{x+1} = \frac{2}{x-1}$$

$$(x+1)(x-1)\left(\frac{3}{x+1}\right) = (x+1)(x-1)\left(\frac{2}{x-1}\right)$$

$$(x-1)(3) = (x+1)(2)$$

$$3x - 3 = 2x + 2$$

$$x = 5$$

$$\begin{array}{cccc} A & B & C & D \\ \hline & + & + & + \\ & -1 & 1 & 5 \end{array}$$

Test regions: <u>A</u>, x = -2

$$\frac{3}{-2+1} > \frac{2}{-2-1}$$

$$\frac{3}{-1} > \frac{2}{-3} \text{ is false.}$$

<u>B</u>, x = 0

$$\frac{3}{1} > \frac{2}{-1} \text{ is true.}$$

<u>C</u>, x = 2

$$\frac{3}{2+1} > \frac{2}{2-1}$$

$$\frac{3}{3} > \frac{2}{1} \text{ is false.}$$

<u>D</u>, x = 6

$$\frac{3}{6+1} > \frac{2}{6-1}$$

$$\frac{3}{7} > \frac{2}{5} \text{ is true.}$$

Shade regions that test true.

Boundary numbers not included.

$$\{x \mid -1 < x < 1 \text{ or } x > 5\}$$

21. $(x+3)(x+4) < 0$

Find boundary numbers:

$$(x+3)(x+4) = 0$$

$$x + 3 = 0 \quad \text{or} \quad x + 4 = 0$$

$$x = -3 \qquad \qquad x = -4$$

$$\begin{array}{ccc} A & B & D \\ \hline & + & + \\ -4 & & -3 \end{array}$$

Test regions: <u>A</u>, x = -5

$$(-5+3)(-5+4) < 0$$

$$(-2)(-1) < 0 \text{ is false.}$$

<u>B</u>, x = $-3\frac{1}{2}$

$$\left(-3\frac{1}{2}+3\right)\left(-3\frac{1}{2}+4\right) < 0$$

$$\left(-\frac{1}{2}\right)\left(\frac{1}{2}\right) < 0 \text{ is true.}$$

<u>C</u>, x = 0

210

(0+3)(0+4) < 0 is false.

Shade region that tests true.

Boundary numbers not included.

$\{x\,|\,-4<x<-3\}$

23. $(7-x)(x+1) \geq 0$

Find boundary numbers:

$(7-x)(x+1) \geq 0$

7 - x = 0 or x + 1 = 0

   -x = -7   x = -1

    x = 7

Test regions: $\underline{A}$, x = -2

$(7-(-2))(-2+1) \geq 0$

$(9)(-1) \geq 0$ is false.

$\underline{B}$, x = 0

$(7)(1) \geq 0$ is true.

$\underline{C}$, x = 8

$(7-8)(8+1) \geq 0$

$(-1)(9) \geq 0$ is false.

Shade region that tests true.

Boundary numbers are included.

$\{x\,|\,-1\leq x\leq 7\}$

25. $(3x+1)(x-4) < 0$

Find boundary numbers:

$(3x+1)(x-4) = 0$

3x + 1 = 0 or x - 4 = 0

   3x = -1   x = 4

     $x = -\dfrac{1}{3}$

Test regions: $\underline{A}$, x = -1

$(3(-1)+1)(-1-4) < 0$

$(-3+1)(-5) < 0$ is false.

$\underline{B}$, x = 0

$(3(0)+1)(0-4) < 0$

$(3+1)(-4) < 0$ is true.

$\underline{C}$, x = 5

$(3(5)+1)(5-4) < 0$

$(16)(1) < 0$ is false.

Shade region that tests true.

Boundary numbers are not included.

$\{x\,|\,-\dfrac{1}{3}<x<4\}$

27. $(x+1)(x+1) < 0$

Find boundary numbers:

x + 1 = 0

    x = -1

Test regions: $\underline{A}$, x = -2

$(-2+1)(-2+1) < 0$

$(-1)(-1) < 0$ is false.

$\underline{B}$, x = 0

$(0+1)(0+1) < 0$

$(1)(1) < 0$ is false.

There are no solutions in A or B.

Boundary numbers not included.

$\emptyset$ is the solution set.

29. $(5+x)(5+x) \leq 0$

Find boundary numbers:

5 + x = 0

    x = -5

Test regions: $\underline{A}$, x = -6

$(5+-6)(5+-6) \leq 0$

$(-1)(-1) \leq 0$ is false

B, $x = 0$

$(5)(5) \leq 0$ is false.

There are no solutions in A or B.

Boundary number is included.

$\{-5\}$

31. $x^2 - 7x + 6 > 0$

$(x-6)(x-1) > 0$

Find boundary numbers:

$(x-6)(x-1) = 0$

$x - 6 = 0$ or $x - 1 = 0$

$\qquad x = 6 \qquad\qquad x = 1$

```
      A     B      C
 ─────┼─────────┼──────
      1         6
```

Test regions: A, $x = 0$

$(0-6)(0-1) > 0$

$(-6)(-1) > 0$ is true.

B, $x = 2$

$(2-6)(2-1) > 0$

$(-4)(1) > 0$ is false.

C, $x = 7$

$(7-6)(7-1) > 0$

$(1)(6) > 0$ is true.

Shade regions that test true.

```
 ←────)    (────→
      1     6
```

$\{x \mid x<1 \text{ or } x>6\}$

33. $x^2 - 7x > 8$

$x^2 - 7x - 8 > 0$

$(x-8)(x+1) > 0$

Find boundary numbers:

$(x-8)(x+1) = 0$

$x - 8 = 0$ or $x + 1 = 0$

$\qquad x = 8 \qquad\qquad x = -1$

```
     A      B      C
 ────┼──────────┼──────
    -1         8
```

Test regions: A, $x = -2$

$(-2)^2 - 7(-2) - 8 > 0$

$4 + 14 - 8 > 0$ is true.

B, $x = 0$

$0^2 - 7(0) - 8 > 0$

$-8 > 0$ is false.

C, $x = 9$

$9^2 - 7(9) - 8 > 0$

$81 - 63 - 8 > 0$ is true.

Shade regions that test true.

```
 ←───)    (──────→
    -1     8
```

$\{x \mid x^2<-1 \text{ or } x>8\}$

35. $x^2 > 16$

$x^2 - 16 > 0$

$(x-4)(x+4) > 0$

Find boundary numbers:

$(x-4)(x+4) = 0$

$x - 4 = 0$ or $x + 4 = 0$

$\qquad x = 4 \qquad\qquad x = -4$

```
     A      B      C
 ────┼──────────┼──────
    -4         4
```

Test regions: A, $x = -5$

$(-5)^2 > 16$ is true.

B, $x = 0$

$0^2 > 16$ is false.

C, $x = 5$

$5^2 > 16$ is true.

Shade regions that test true.

```
 ←───)    (──────/
    -4     4
```

Boundary numbers are not included.

$\{x \mid x<-4 \text{ or } x>4\}$

37. $-t^2 - 5t \geq 0$

Find boundary numbers:

$-t^2 - 5t = 0$

$-1(-t^2-5t) = -1\cdot 0$

$t^2 + 5t = 0$

$t(t+5) = 0$

$t = 0$ or $t + 5 = 0$

$\qquad\qquad\qquad t = -5$

```
    A      B      C
 ───┼──────┼────────
    -5     0
```

Test regions: $\underline{A}$, $x = -6$

$-(-6)^2 - 5(-6) \geq 0$

$-36 + 30 \geq 0$ is false.

$\underline{B}$, $x = -2$

$-(-2)^2 - 5(-2) \geq 0$

$-4 + 10 \geq 0$ is true.

$\underline{C}$, $x = 1$

$-(1)^2 - 5(1) \geq 0$

$-1 - 5 \geq 0$ is false.

Shade region that tests true.

```
     [━━━━━]
    -5     0
```

Boundary numbers are included.

$\{t \mid -5 \leq t \leq 0\}$

39. $s^2 + 3 < -4s$

$s^2 + 4s + 3 < 0$

Find boundary numbers:

$s^2 + 4s + 3 = 0$

$(s+1)(s+3) = 0$

$s + 1 = 0$ or $s + 3 = 0$

$\quad s = -1 \qquad\qquad s = -3$

```
    A      B      C
 ───┼──────┼────────
    -3     -1
```

Test regions: $\underline{A}$, $x = -4$

$(-4)^2 + 3 < -4(-4)$

$16 + 3$ is false.

$\underline{B}$, $x = -2$

$(-2)^2 + 3 < -4(-2)$

$4 + 3 < 8$ is true.

$\underline{C}$, $x = 0$

$0^2 + 3 < -4(0)$

$3 < 0$ is false.

Shade region that tests true.

```
     (━━━━━)
    -3     -1
```

Boundary numbers are not included.

$\{s \mid -3 < s < -1\}$

41. $5x + 14 \geq x^2$

$-x^2 + 5x + 14 \geq 0$

Find boundary numbers:

$-x^2 + 5x + 14 = 0$

$-1(-x^2+5x+14) = -1\cdot 0$

$x^2 - 5x - 14 = 0$

$(x-7)(x+2) = 0$

$x - 7 = 0$ or $x + 2 = 0$

$\quad x = 7 \qquad\qquad x = -2$

```
    A      B      C
 ───┼──────┼────────
    -2     7
```

Test regions: $\underline{A}$, $x = -3$

$5(-3) + 14 \geq (-3)^2$

$-15 + 14 \geq 9$ is false.

$\underline{B}$, $x = 0$

$5(0) + 14 \geq 0^2$

$14 \geq 0$ is true.

$\underline{C}$, $x = 8$

$5(8) + 14 \geq 8^2$

$40 + 14 \geq 64$ is false.

Shade regions that test true.

```
     [━━━━━]
    -2     7
```

Boundary numbers are included.

$\{x \mid -2 \leq x \leq 7\}$

43. $10x^2 + x - 3 > 0$

$(5x+3)(2x-1) > 0$

Find boundary numbers:

$(5x+3)(2x-1) = 0$

$5x + 3 = 0$ or $2x - 1 = 0$

$5x = -3$ $\qquad$ $2x = 1$

$x = -\dfrac{3}{5}$ $\qquad$ $x = \dfrac{1}{2}$

```
    A      B      C
 ───┼──────┼──────────
   -3/5   1/2
```

Test regions: <u>A</u>, $x = -1$

$10(-1)^2 + (-1) - 3 > 0$

$10 - 4 > 0$ is true.

<u>B</u>, $x = 0$

$10(0)^2 + 0 - 3 > 0$

$-3 > 0$ is false.

<u>C</u>, $x = 1$

$10(1)^2 + 1 - 3 > 0$

$11 - 3 > 0$ is true.

Shade regions that are true.

```
◄─────)      (─────►
    -3/5    1/2
```

Boundary numbers are not included.

$\{x \mid x < -\dfrac{3}{5}$ or $x > \dfrac{1}{2}\}$

45. $21x^2 + 19x - 12 \leq 0$

Find boundary numbers:

$(7x-3)(3x+4) \leq 0$

$7x - 3 = 0$ or $3x + 4 = 0$

$7x = 3$ $\qquad$ $3x = -4$

$x = \dfrac{3}{7}$ $\qquad$ $x = -\dfrac{4}{3}$

```
    A      B      C
 ───┼──────┼──────────
   -4/3    3/7
```

Test regions: <u>A</u>, $x = -2$

$21(-2)^2 + 19(-2) - 12 \leq 0$

$21(4) - 38 - 12 \leq 0$

$84 - 50 \leq 0$ is false.

<u>B</u>, $x = 0$

$21(0)^2 + 19(0) - 12 \leq 0$

$0 + 0 - 12 \leq 0$ is true.

<u>C</u>, $x = 1$

$21(1)^2 + 19(1) - 12 \leq 0$

$21 + 19 - 12 \leq 0$ is false.

Shade region that tests true.

```
    [──────]
   -4/3    3/7
```

Boundary numbers are included.

$\{x \mid -\dfrac{4}{3} \leq x \leq \dfrac{3}{7}\}$

47. $12x^2 + 5x - 2 < 0$

Find boundary numbers:

$12x^2 + 5x - 2 = 0$

$(4x-1)(3x+2) = 0$

$4x - 1 = 0$ or $3x + 2 = 0$

$4x = 1$ $\qquad$ $3x = -2$

$x = \dfrac{1}{4}$ $\qquad$ $x = -\dfrac{2}{3}$

```
    A      B      C
 ───┼──────┼──────────
   -2/3    1/4
```

Test regions: <u>A</u>, $x = -1$

$12(-1)^2 + 5(-1) - 2 \leq 0$

$12 - 5 - 2 \leq 0$ is false.

<u>B</u>, $x = 20$

$12(0)^2 + 5(0) - 2 \leq 0$

$0 + 0 - 2 \leq 0$ is true.

<u>C</u>, $x = 1$

$12(1)^2 + 5(1) - 2 \leq 0$

$12 + 5 - 2 \leq 0$ is false.

Shade region that tests true.

```
    (──────)
   -2/3    1/4
```

214

Boundary numbers are not included.

$\{x \mid -\frac{2}{3} < x < \frac{1}{4}\}$

49. $10x^2 - 21x - 49 < 0$

Find boundary numbers:

$(5x+7)(2x-7) = 0$

$5x + 7 = 0$ or $2x - 7 = 0$

$5x = -7$ $\qquad$ $2x = 7$

$x = -\frac{7}{5}$ $\qquad$ $x = \frac{7}{2}$

```
        A       B       C
 ───────────┼───────┼───────────
          -7/5     7/2
```

Test regions: <u>A</u>, $x = -2$

$10(-2)^2 - 21(-2) - 49 < 0$

$10(4) + 42 - 49 < 0$ is false.

<u>B</u>, $x = 0$

$10(0)^2 - 21(0) - 49 < 0$

$0 + 0 - 49 < 0$ is true.

<u>C</u>, $x = 4$

$10(4)^2 - 21(4) - 49 < 0$

$10(16) - 84 - 49 < 0$ is false.

Shade region that tests true.

```
     (───────────)
   -7/5         7/2
```

Boundary numbers are not included.

$\{x \mid -\frac{7}{5} < x < \frac{7}{2}\}$

51. $(x-7)(x+3)(x-1) \geq 0$

Find boundary numbers:

$(x-7)(x+3)(x-1) = 0$

$x-7 = 0$ or $x+3 = 0$ or $x-1 = 0$

$x = 7$ $\qquad$ $x = -3$ $\qquad$ $x = 1$

```
      A     B     C     D
 ─────────┼─────┼─────┼─────
         -3     1     7
```

Test regions: <u>A</u>, $x = -4$

$(-4-7)(-4+3)(-4-1) \geq 0$

$(-11)(-1)(-5) \geq 0$ is false.

<u>B</u>, $x = 0$

$(-7)(3)(-1) \geq$ is true.

<u>C</u>, $x = 2$

$(2-7)(2+3)(2-1) \geq 0$

$(-5)(5)(1) \geq 0$ is false.

<u>D</u>, $x = 8$

$(8-7)(8+3)(8-1) \geq 0$

$(1)(11)(7) \geq 0$ is true.

Shade regions that test true.

```
    ┌───────┐   ┌──────→
 ───┼───────┼───┼────────
   -3       1   7
```

Boundary numbers are included.

$\{x \mid -3 \leq x \leq 1 \text{ or } x \geq 7\}$

53. $x(x+1)(x-1) > 0$

Find boundary numbers:

$x(x+1)(x-1) = 0$

$x = 0$ or $x + 1 = 0$ or $x - 1 = 0$

$\qquad\qquad x = -1$ $\qquad$ $x = 1$

```
      A     B     C     D
 ─────────┼─────┼─────┼─────
         -1     0     1
```

Test regions: <u>A</u>, $x = -2$

$(-2)(-2+1)(-2-1) > 0$

$(-2)(-1)(-3) > 0$ is false.

<u>B</u>, $x = -\frac{1}{2}$

$(-\frac{1}{2})(-\frac{1}{2}+1)(-\frac{1}{2}-1) > 0$

$(-\frac{1}{2})(\frac{1}{2})(-\frac{3}{2}) > 0$ is true.

<u>C</u>, $x = \frac{1}{2}$

$(\frac{1}{2})(\frac{1}{2}+1)(\frac{1}{2}-1) > 0$

$(\frac{1}{2})(\frac{3}{2})(-\frac{1}{2}) > 0$ is false.

<u>D</u>, $x = 2$

$(2)(2+1)(2-1) > 0$

$(2)(3)(1) > 0$ is true.

Shade regions that test true.

```
    (───────)   (──→
 ───┼───────┼───┼────
   -1       0   1
```

Boundary numbers are not

included.

$\{x \mid -1 < x < 0 \text{ or } x > 1\}$

55. $x^3 - 4x \geq 0$

Find boundary numbers:

$x^3 - 4x = 0$

$x(x^2 - 4) = 0$

$x(x-2)(x+2) = 0$

$x = 0 \text{ or } x - 2 = 0 \text{ or } x + 2 = 0$

$\qquad\qquad\quad x = 2 \qquad\quad x = -2$

```
    A      B      C      D
----+------+------+---------
   -2      0      2
```

Test regions: $\underline{A}$, $x = -3$

$(-3)^3 - 4(-3) \geq 0$

$-27 + 12 \geq 0$ is false.

$\underline{B}$, $x = -1$

$(-1)^3 - 4(-1) \geq 0$

$-1 + 4 \geq 0$ is true.

$\underline{C}$, $x = 1$

$(1)^3 - 4(1) \geq 0$

$1 - 4 \geq 0$ is false.

$\underline{D}$, $x = 3$

$(3)^3 - 4(3) \geq 0$

$27 - 12 \geq 0$ is true.

Shade regions that test true.

```
---[------]---[------->
  -2      0    2
```

Boundary numbers are included.

$\{x \mid -2 \leq x \leq 0 \text{ or } x \geq 2\}$

57. $\dfrac{x+1}{x-1} > 0$

1: free boundary number

Find other boundary numbers:

$\dfrac{x+1}{x-1} = 0$

$(x-1)\left(\dfrac{x+1}{x-1}\right) = (x-1)(0)$

$x + 1 = 0$

$\qquad x = -1$

```
    A      B      C
----+------+---------
   -1      1
```

Test regions: $\underline{A}$, $x = -2$

$\dfrac{-2+1}{-2-1} > 0$

$\dfrac{-1}{-3} > 0$ is true.

$\underline{B}$, $x = 0$

$\dfrac{0+1}{0-1} > 0$

$\dfrac{1}{-1} > 0$ is false.

$\underline{C}$, $x = 2$

$\dfrac{2+1}{2-1} > 0$

$\dfrac{3}{1} > 0$ is true.

Shade regions that test true.

```
<------)    (------->
     -1      1
```

Boundary numbers are not included.

$\{x \mid x < -1 \text{ or } x > 1\}$

59. $\dfrac{x-4}{x-5} \geq 0$

5: free boundary number

Find other boundary numbers.

$\dfrac{x-4}{x-5} = 0$

$(x-5)\left(\dfrac{x-4}{x-5}\right) = (x-5)(0)$

$x - 4 = 0$

$\qquad x = 4$

```
  A      B      C
--+------+------
  4      5
```

Test regions: $\underline{A}$, $x = 0$

$\dfrac{0-4}{0-5} \geq 0$

$\dfrac{-4}{-5} \geq 0$ is true.

$\underline{B}$, $x = 4\frac{1}{2}$

$\dfrac{4\frac{1}{2}-4}{4\frac{1}{2}-5} \geq 0$

$\dfrac{\frac{1}{2}}{-\frac{1}{2}} \geq 0$ is false.

$\underline{C}$, $x = 6$

$\dfrac{6-4}{6-5} \geq 0$

$\frac{2}{1} \geq 0$ is true.

Shade regions that test true.

$\{x \mid x \leq 4 \text{ or } x > 5\}$

61. $\frac{x+2}{x} < 0$

0: free boundary number

Find other boundary numbers:

$\frac{x+2}{x} = 0$

$x\left(\frac{x+2}{x}\right) = x \cdot 0$

$x + 2 = 0$

$x = -2$

Test regions: A, x = -3

$\frac{-3+2}{-3} < 0$

$\frac{-1}{-3} < 0$ is false.

B, x = -1

$\frac{-1+2}{-1} < 0$

$\frac{1}{-1} < 0$ is true.

C, x = 1

$\frac{1+2}{1} < 0$

$\frac{3}{1} < 0$ is false.

Shade region that tests true.

$\{x \mid -2 < x < 0\}$

63. $\frac{r-5}{r+2} \leq 2$

-2: free boundary number

Find other boundary numbers:

$\frac{r-5}{r+2} = 2$

$(r+2)\left(\frac{r-5}{r+2}\right) = (r+2)(2)$

$r - 5 = 2(r+2)$

$r - 5 = 2r + 4$

$-r = 9$

$r = -9$

Test regions: A, x = -10

$\frac{-10-5}{-10+2} \leq 2$

$\frac{-15}{-8} \leq 2$ is true.

B, x = -3

$\frac{-3-5}{-3+2} \leq 2$

$\frac{-8}{-1} \leq 2$ is false.

C, x = 0

$\frac{0-5}{0+2} \leq 2$

$\frac{-5}{2} \leq 2$ is true.

Shade regions that test true.

-9 is included; -2 is not included.

$\{r \mid r \leq -9 \text{ or } r > -2\}$

65. $\frac{2x+3}{x+4} \geq 1$

-4: free boundary number

Find other boundary numbers:

$\frac{2x+3}{x+4} = 1$

$(x+4)\left(\frac{2x+3}{x+4}\right) = (x+4)(1)$

$2x + 3 = x + 4$

$x = 1$

Test regions: A, x = -5

$\frac{2(-5)+3}{-5+4} \geq 1$

$\frac{-10+3}{-1} \geq 1$

$\frac{-7}{-1} \geq 1$ is true.

B, x = 0

217

$$\frac{2(0)+3}{0+4} \geq 1$$

$\frac{3}{4} \geq 1$ is false.

$\underline{C}$, x = 2

$$\frac{2(2)+3}{-2+4} \geq 1$$

$\frac{7}{2} \geq 1$ is true.

Shade regions that test true.

-4 is not included; 1 is included.

$\{x|x<-4 \text{ or } x \geq 1\}$

67. $\frac{1}{x-1} \leq \frac{1}{x+1}$

1,-1: free boundary numbers.

Find other boundary numbers:

$\frac{1}{x-1} = \frac{1}{x+1}$

$(x-1)(x+1)(\frac{1}{x-1}) = (x-1)(x+1)(\frac{1}{x+1})$

$x + 1 = x - 1$

$1 = -1$

Equation has no solution.

Test regions: $\underline{A}$, x = -2

$\frac{1}{-2-1} \leq \frac{1}{-2+1}$

$\frac{1}{-3} \leq \frac{1}{-1}$ is false.

$\underline{B}$, x = 0

$\frac{1}{0-1} \leq \frac{1}{0+1}$

$-1 \leq 1$ is true.

$\underline{C}$, x = 2

$\frac{1}{2-1} \leq \frac{1}{2+1}$

$1 \leq \frac{1}{3}$ is false.

Shade regions that test true.

Boundary numbers are not included.

$\{x|-1<x<1\}$

69. 1st: x 2nd: x + 1

x(x+1) $\leq$ 2

$x^2 + x - 2 \leq 0$

Find boundary numbers:

$x^2 + x - 2 = 0$

$(x+2)(x-1) = 0$

x + 2 = 0 or x - 1 = 0

x = -2   x = 1

Test regions: $\underline{A}$, x = -3

$(-3)(-3+1) \leq 2$

$(-3)(-2) \leq 2$ is false.

$\underline{B}$, x = 0

$0(0+1) \leq 2$

$0(1) \leq 2$ is true.

$\underline{C}$, x = 2

$(2)(2+1) \leq 2$

$2(3) \leq 2$ is false.

Shade region that tests true.

x = -2,-1,0,1

x + 1 = -1,0,1,2

The integers are -2 and -1, -1
and 0, 0 and 1, and 1 and 2.

71. x: such a number

$\frac{1}{x+1} < 0$

-1: free boundary number

Find other boundary numbers:

$\frac{1}{x+1} = 0$

$(x+1)(\frac{1}{x+1}) = (x+1)(0)$

1 = 0

Equation has no solution.

Test regions: $\underline{A}$, x = -2

218

$\frac{1}{-2+1} < 0$

$\frac{1}{-1} <$ is true.

$\underline{B}$, $x = 0$

$\frac{1}{0+1} < 0$ is false.

Shade region that tests true.

$\longleftarrow\!\!\!\!\longrightarrow$
$\qquad$ -1

Boundary number not included.

All such numbers are less than -1.

73. x: length

$x^2 < 10,000$

Find boundary numbers:

$x^2 = 10,000$

$x^2 - 10,000 = 0$

$(x-100)(x+100) = 0$

$x - 100 = 0$ or $x + 100 = 0$

$\qquad x = 100 \qquad\qquad x = -100$

```
    A       B    C
 ———————+————+————+———
      -100  0  100
```

No need to test A since x must be positive.

Test regions: $\underline{B}$, $x = 50$

$(50)^2 < 10,000$ is true.

$\underline{C}$, $x = 101$

$(101)^2 < 10,000$ is false.

Shade region that tests true.

```
 ———+———(————————)———
  -100   0    100
```

The length must be less than 100 yards (but greater than zero.)

75. x: such a number

$\frac{x+1}{x-1} \geq 0$

1: free boundary number

Find other boundary numbers:

$\frac{x+1}{x-1} = 0$

$(x-1)\left(\frac{x+1}{x-1}\right) = (x-1)(0)$

$x + 1 = 0$

$x = -1$

```
    A       B    C
 ———————+————+————+———
      -1       1
```

Test regions: $\underline{A}$, $x = -2$

$\frac{-2+1}{-2-1} \geq 0$

$\frac{-1}{-3} \geq 0$ is true.

$\underline{B}$, $x = 0$

$\frac{0+1}{0-1} \geq 0$

$-1 \geq 0$ is false.

$\underline{C}$, $x = 2$

$\frac{2+1}{2-1} \geq 0$

$\frac{3}{1} \geq 0$ is true.

Shade regions that test true.

```
 ←————]———(—————————→
     -1    1
```

All such numbers are less than or equal to -1 or greater than 1.

77. $x^2 + x + 1 \geq 0$

Find boundary numbers:

$x^2 + x + 1 = 0$ has no real solutions so there are no boundary numbers.

```
 ——————————————————————
           A
```

Test region: $\underline{A}$, $x = 0$

$0^2 + 0 + 1 \geq 0$ is true.

Shade region that tests true.

$\longleftarrow\!\!\!\!\!\!\!\longrightarrow$

$\{x \mid x$ is a real number$\}$

79. $x(x-1)^2 < 0$

Find boundary numbers:

$x(x-1)^2 = 0$

$x = 0$ or $(x-1)^2 = 0$

$\qquad\qquad\qquad x - 1 = 0$

$\qquad\qquad\qquad\qquad x = 1$

```
    A       B    C
 ———————+————+————+———
        0       1
```

Test regions: $\underline{A}$, $x = -1$

$(-1)(-1-1)^2 < 0$

$(-1)(-2)^2 < 0$ is true.

$\underline{B}$, $x = \frac{1}{2}$

$(\frac{1}{2})(\frac{1}{2}-1)^2 < 0$

$(\frac{1}{2})(-\frac{1}{2})^2 < 0$ is false.

$\underline{C}$, $x = 2$

$(2)(2-1)^2 < 0$ is false.

Shade regions that test true.

Boundary numbers not included.

$\{x \mid x < 0\}$

81. $\dfrac{(x+2)(x-1)}{(x+3)(x-7)} \leq 0$

$-5, 7$: Free boundary numbers.

Find other boundary numbers:

$\dfrac{(x+2)(x-1)}{(x+5)(x-7)} = 0$

$(x+4)(x-7)[\dfrac{(x+2)(x-1)}{(x+5)(x-7)}]$

$\quad = (x+5)(x-7)(0)$

$(x+2)(x-1) = 0$

$x + 2 = 0 \quad$ or $\quad x - 1 = 0$

$\quad x = -2 \qquad\qquad x = 1$

Test regions: $\underline{A}$, $x = -6$

$\dfrac{(-6+2)(-6-1)}{(-6+5)(-6-7)} \leq 0$

$\dfrac{(-4)(-7)}{(-1)(-13)} \leq 0$ is false.

$\underline{B}$, $x = -3$

$\dfrac{(-3+2)(-3-1)}{(-3+5)(-3-7)} \leq 0$

$\dfrac{(-1)(-4)}{(2)(-10)} \leq 0$ is true.

$\underline{C}$, $x = 0$

$\dfrac{(0+2)(0-1)}{(0+5)(0-7)} \leq 0$

$\dfrac{(2)(-1)}{(5)(7)} \leq 0$ is false.

$\underline{D}$, $x = 2$

$\dfrac{(2+2)(2-1)}{(2+5)(2-7)} \leq 0$

$\dfrac{(4)(1)}{(7)(-5)} \leq 0$ is true.

$\underline{E}$, $x = 8$

$\dfrac{(8+2)(8-1)}{(8+5)(8-7)} \leq 0$

$\dfrac{(10)(7)}{(13)(1)} \leq 0$ is false

Shade regions that test true.

-5 and 7 are not included; -2 and 1 are included.

$\{x \mid -5 < x \leq -2 \text{ or } 1 \leq x < 7\}$

83. $\dfrac{x-a}{x-b} \leq 0 \quad a < 0, \; b > 0$

b: free boundary number

Find other boundary numbers:

$\dfrac{x-a}{x-b} = 0$

$(x-b)(\dfrac{x-a}{x-b}) = (x-b)(0)$

$x - a = 0$

$\quad x = a$

Test regions: $\underline{A}$, $x = a - 1$

$\dfrac{(a-1)-a}{(a-1)-b} \leq 0$

$\dfrac{-1}{\text{negative value}} \leq 0$ is false

$\underline{B} \quad x = 0$

$\dfrac{0-a}{0-b} \leq 0$

$\dfrac{a}{b}$ is negative, so $\dfrac{a}{b} \leq 0$ is true.

$\underline{C}$, $x = b + 1$

$\dfrac{(b+1)-a}{(b+1)-b} \leq 0$

$\dfrac{\text{positive value}}{1} \leq 0$ is false.

Shade region that tests true.

a is included; b is not included.

$\{x \mid a \leq x < b\}$

Chapter Review.

1. $2x - 3 \leq 5$

    $2x \leq 8$

    $x \leq 4$

3. $|x+16| > 8$

    $x + 16 > 8$ or $x + 16 < -8$

    $x > -8$ $\qquad$ $x < -24$

5. $\dfrac{x-7}{x+5} > 0$

    -5: free boundary number

    Find other boundary numbers:

    $\dfrac{x-7}{x+5} = 0$

    $(x+5)(\dfrac{x-7}{x+5}) = (x+5)(0)$

    $x - 7 = 0$

    $x = 7$

    Test regions: $\underline{A}$, $x = -6$

    $\dfrac{-6-7}{-6+5} > 0$ is true.

    $\underline{B}$, $x = 0$

    $\dfrac{0-7}{0+5} > 0$ is false.

    $\underline{C}$, $x = 8$

    $\dfrac{8-7}{8+5} > 0$ is true.

    Shade regions that test true.

    Boundary numbers are not included.

7. $x \geq 5$ or $2x - 1 \leq 3$

    $\qquad\qquad 2x \leq 4$

    $\qquad\qquad x \leq 2$

9. $|2x-3| \leq 3$

    $-3 \leq 2x - 3 \leq 3$

    $0 \leq 2x \leq 6$

    $0 \leq x \leq 3$

11. $x^2 - 3x \leq 10$

    Find boundary numbers:

    $x^2 - 3x - 10 = 0$

    $(x-5)(x+2) = 0$

    $x - 5 = 0$ or $x + 2 = 0$

    $x = 5$ $\qquad$ $x = -2$

    Test regions: $\underline{A}$, $x = -3$

    $(-3)^2 - 3(-3) \leq 10$

    $9 + 9 \leq 10$ is false

    $\underline{B}$, $x = 0$

    $0^2 - 3(0) \leq 10$ is true.

    $\underline{C}$, $x = 6$

    $6^2 - 3(6) \leq 10$

    $36 - 18 \leq 10$ is false.

    Shade region that tests true.

    Boundary numbers included.

13. $\dfrac{1}{2}x - \dfrac{3}{4} < \dfrac{1}{4}x + 1$

    $4(\dfrac{1}{2}x-\dfrac{3}{4}) < 4(\dfrac{1}{4}x+1)$

    $2x - 3 < x + 4$

    $x < 7$

15. $\dfrac{x-3}{x+2} \leq 6$

    -2: free boundary number

    Find other boundary numbers:

    $\dfrac{x-3}{x+2} = 6$

    $(x+2)(\dfrac{x-3}{x+2}) = 6(x+2)$

    $x - 3 = 6x + 12$

$-5x = 15$

$x = -3$

$$\begin{array}{ccc} A & B & C \\ \hline & | & | \\ -3 & -2 & \end{array}$$

Test regions: $\underline{A}$, $x = -4$

$\dfrac{-4-3}{-4+2} \le 6$

$\dfrac{-7}{-2} \le 6$ is true.

$\underline{B}$, $x = -2\dfrac{1}{2}$

$\dfrac{-2^{1/2}-3}{-2^{1/2}+2} \le 6$

$\dfrac{-5^{1/2}}{-\frac{1}{2}} \le 6$ is false.

$\underline{C}$, $x = 0$

$\dfrac{0-3}{0+2} \le 6$

$\dfrac{-3}{2} \le 6$ is true.

Shade regions that test true.

$$\xleftarrow{\quad\bullet\quad}\;(\;\longrightarrow$$
$$\begin{array}{cc} -3 & -2 \end{array}$$

-3 is included; -2 is not included.

17. $|x-1.5| < 4.6$

$-4.6 < x - 1.5 < 4.6$

$-3.1 < x < 6.1$

$$\underset{-3.1 \quad 6.1}{(\text{————})}$$

19. $2x + 1 < 5$ and $x + 2 > 5$

$\qquad 2x < 4 \qquad\qquad x > 3$

$\qquad x < 2$ and $\qquad x > 3$

There are no numbers less than 2 <u>and</u> greater than 3.

Graph of solution: _____

$\emptyset$

21. $\dfrac{x-1.4}{x+2.3} \le 0$

-2.3: free boundary number

Find other boundary numbers:

$\dfrac{x-1.4}{x+2.3} = 0$

$(x+2.3)\left(\dfrac{x-1.4}{x+2.3}\right) = (x+2.3)(0)$

$x - 1.4 = 0$

$\qquad x = 1.4$

$$\begin{array}{ccc} A & B & C \\ \hline & | & | \\ -2.3 & 1.4 & \end{array}$$

Test regions: $\underline{A}$, $x = -3$

$\dfrac{-3-1.4}{-2+2.3} \le 0$ is false.

$\underline{B}$, $x = 0$

$\dfrac{0-1.4}{0+2.3} \le 0$ is true.

$\underline{C}$, $x = 2$

$\dfrac{2-1.4}{2+2.3} \le 0$ is false

Shade region that tests true.

$$\underset{-2.3 \quad 1.4}{(\text{————}]}$$

-2.3 is not included; 1.4 is included.

23. x: such a number

$2x - 5 \le 17$

$\qquad 2x \le 22$

$\qquad x \le 11$

Such numbers are 11 or less.

25. s: length of a side

$4s \le 100$

$\quad s \le 25$

The length of a side is 25 feet. or less.

27. x: 5th test grade

$\dfrac{75+86+88+62+x}{5} \le 80$

$5\left(\dfrac{311+x}{5}\right) \le (5)(80)$

$311 + x \le 400$

$\qquad x \le 89$

She must score at least 89.

29. $(a-2)^3$ is factored.

31. $(x-y)^2 - 4 = [(x-y)-2][(x-y)+2]$

= (x-y-2)(x-y+2)

33. a^2bc is factored.

35. $\sqrt{x}(1+\sqrt{x})$ is factored.

37. $x^2 - 25$ has two terms.

$x^2 - 25 = (x-5)(x+5)$

$x^2 - 25$ has $x - 5$ as a factor.

39. $a(x-5) - b(5-x)$ has two terms.

$a(x-5) - b(5-x)$

$= a(x-5) - b[-(x-5)]$

$= a(x-5) + b(x-5)$

$= (x-5)(a+b)$

$a(x-5) - b(5-x)$ has $x - 5$ as a factor.

41. $\sqrt{a^3+b^3}$ will not simplify.

43. $-2x^{-1} = \dfrac{-2}{x}$

45. $\dfrac{(27a^3b^3)^{-1/3}}{(8a^{-2}b^3)^{-1/3}} = \dfrac{27^{-1/3}a^{-1}b^{-1}}{8^{-1/3}a^{2/3}b^{-1}}$

$= \dfrac{8^{1/3}}{27^{1/3} \cdot a \cdot a^{2/3}}$

$= \dfrac{2}{3a^{5/3}}$

47. $(3+2x)^3 = 3^3 + 3(3)^2(2x)$

$+ 3(3)(2x)^2 + (2x)^3$

$= 27 + 54x + 36x^2 + 8x^3$

49. $\dfrac{(a+b)+x(a+b)}{(a+b)} = \dfrac{(a+b)(1+x)}{(a+b)}$

$= 1 + x$ or $x + 1$

51. $\dfrac{x}{x+1} = \dfrac{2}{x+2}$

$(x+1)(x+2)(\dfrac{x}{x+1}) = (x+1)(x+2)(\dfrac{2}{x+2})$

$(x+2)x = (x+1)2$

$x^2 + 2x = 2x + 2$

$x^2 = 2$

$x = \pm\sqrt{2}$ $\quad\quad\quad \{\pm\sqrt{2}\}$

53. $2x - 5 = x - 3(4-x)$ Equation

$2x - 5 = x - 12 + 3x$

$2x - 5 = 4x - 12$

$-2x = -7$

$x = \dfrac{7}{2}$ $\quad\quad \{\dfrac{7}{2}\}$

55. $x^2 - 2x - 3 = 0$ Equation

$(x-3)(x+1) = 0$

$x - 3 = 0$ or $x + 1 = 0$

$x = 3 \quad\quad\quad x = -1$ $\quad \{-1,3\}$

57. $2\sqrt{x} + 3 = x$ Equation

$2\sqrt{x} = x - 3$

$(2\sqrt{x})^2 = (x-3)^2$

$4x = x^2 - 6x + 9$

$0 = x^2 - 10x + 9$

$0 = (x-1)(x-9)$

$x - 1 = 0$ or $x - 9 = 0$

$x = 1 \quad\quad\quad x = 9$

Checking 1,

LS: $2\sqrt{1} + 3 = 2 + 3 = 5$

RS: 1

1 does not check.

Checking 9,

LS: $2\sqrt{9} + 3 = 2 \cdot 3 + 3 = 9$

RS: 9

9 checks. $\quad\quad\quad \{9\}$

59. $x^2 < 4$ Inequality

$x^2 - 4 < 0$

Find boundary numbers:

$x^2 - 4 = 0$

$(x-2)(x+2) = 0$

$x - 2 = 0$ or $x + 2 = 0$

$x = 2$ $\qquad x = -2$

$$\begin{array}{ccc} A & B & C \\ \hline & | & | \\ & -2 & 2 \end{array}$$

Test regions: $\underline{A}$, $x = -3$

$(-3)^2 < 4$ is false.

$\underline{B}$, $x = 0$

$0^2 < 4$ is true.

$\underline{C}$, $x = 3$

$(3)^2 < 4$ is false.

Shade region that tests true.

$$\begin{array}{cc} (&) \\ \hline -2 & 2 \end{array}$$

Boundary numbers are not included.

$\{x \mid -2 < x < 2\}$

61. $\dfrac{x+y}{y-x} - \dfrac{(x+y)^2}{x^2-y^2} = \dfrac{x+y}{-(x-y)} - \dfrac{(x+y)^2}{(x-y)(x+y)}$

$= \dfrac{-(x+y)}{(x-y)} - \dfrac{(x+y)^2}{(x-y)(x+y)}$

$= \dfrac{-(x+y)^2}{(x-y)(x+y)} - \dfrac{(x+y)^2}{(x-y)(x+y)}$

$= \dfrac{-2(x+y)^2}{(x-y)(x+y)}$

$= \dfrac{-2(x+y)}{x-y}$

$= \dfrac{-2(x+y)}{-(y-x)}$

$= \dfrac{2(x+y)}{y-x}$ or $\dfrac{2x+2y}{y-x}$

Chapter Test.

1. Graph of $\{x \mid 1 < x < 3\}$:

$$\begin{array}{cc} (&) \\ \hline 1 & 3 \end{array}$$

   B.

2.
$$\begin{array}{ccc} &] & (\\ \hline -5 & 0 & 3 \end{array}$$
is

$\{x \mid x < -5$ or $0 < x \leq 3\}$

   A.

3. $\dfrac{x-3}{6} \leq \dfrac{x}{2} - 1$

$6\left(\dfrac{x-3}{6}\right) \leq 6\left(\dfrac{x}{2} - 1\right)$

$x - 3 \leq 3x - 6$

$-2x \leq -3$

$x \geq \dfrac{3}{2}$

$\{x \mid x \geq \dfrac{3}{2}\}$

   C.

4. Solution set for $|x+3| < 0$ is $\emptyset$.

   C.

5. $(x+2)(x+3) = 0$

$x + 2 = 0$ or $x + 3 = 0$

$x = -2$ $\qquad x = -3$ $\quad \{-3, -2\}$

   A.

6. $\dfrac{x-1}{x+2} < 0$

-2: free boundary number

Find other boundary numbers.

$\dfrac{x-1}{x+2} = 0$

$(x+2)\left(\dfrac{x-1}{x+2}\right) = (x+2)(0)$

$x - 1 = 0$

$x = 1$

$$\begin{array}{ccc} A & B & C \\ \hline & | & | \\ & -2 & 1 \end{array}$$

Test regions: $\underline{A}$, $x = -3$

$\dfrac{-3-1}{-3+2} < 0$ is false.

$\underline{B}$, $x = 0$

$\dfrac{0-1}{0+2} < 0$ is true.

$\underline{C}$, $x = 2$

$\dfrac{2-1}{2+2} < 0$ is false.

Shade region that tests true.

$$\begin{array}{cc} (&) \\ \hline -2 & 1 \end{array}$$

Boundary numbers are not included.

$\{x|-2<x<1\}$

7. $x(x-2)(x+3) > 0$

Find boundary numbers:

$x(x-2)(x+3) = 0$

$x = 0$ or $x-2 = 0$ or $x+3 = 0$

$\qquad\qquad\quad x = 2 \qquad x = -3$

```
        A       B       C       D
    ────┼───────┼───────┼──────────
       -3       0       2
```

Test regions: $\underline{A}$, $x = -4$

$(-4)(-4-2)(-4+3) > 0$

$(-4)(-6)(-1) > 0$ is false.

$\underline{B}$, $x = -1$

$(-1)(-1-2)(-1+3) > 0$

$(-1)(-3)(2) > 0$ is true.

$\underline{C}$, $x = 1$

$(1)(1-2)(1+3) > 0$

$(1)(-1)(4) > 0$ is false.

$\underline{D}$, $x = 3$

$(3)(3-2)(3+3) > 0$

$(3)(1)(6) > 0$ is true.

Shade regions that test true.

```
    ────(───────)───(────────→
       -3       0   2
```

Boundary numbers are not included.
$\{x|-3<x<0 \text{ or } x>2\}$

8. $\dfrac{x-3}{x+1} \geq 2$

-1: free boundary number.

Find other boundary numbers

$\dfrac{x-3}{x+1} = 2$

$(x+1)\left(\dfrac{x-3}{x+1}\right) = 2(x+1)$

$x - 3 = 2x + 2$

$\quad -x = 5$

$\quad\ \ x = -5$

```
        A       B       C
    ────┼───────┼──────────
       -5      -1
```

Test regions: $\underline{A}$, $x = -6$

$\dfrac{-6-3}{-6+1} \geq 2$

$\dfrac{-9}{-5} \geq 2$ is false.

$\underline{B}$, $x = -2$

$\dfrac{-2-3}{-2+1} \geq 2$

$\dfrac{-5}{-1} \geq 2$ is true.

$\underline{C}$, $x = 0$

$\dfrac{0-3}{0+1} \geq 2$ is false.

Shade regions that test true.

```
    ───────[━━━━━━━━→
          -5      -1
```

-5 is included, -1 is not included.

$\{x|-5\leq x<-1\}$

9. $x^2 + 2x \leq -1$

$x^2 + 2x + 1 \leq 0$

Find boundary numbers:

$x^2 + 2x + 1 = 0$

$(x+1)^2 = 0$

$x + 1 = 0$

$\quad x = -1$

```
        A       B
    ────────┼───────
           -1
```

Test regions: $\underline{A}$, $x = -2$

$(-2)^2 + 2(-2) \leq -1$

$4 - 4 \leq -1$ is false.

$\underline{B}$, $x = 0$

$0^2 + 2(0) \leq -1$

$0 \leq -1$ is false.

Only -1 is a solution.

$\{-1\}$

10. $1 - 2x + 2(x-7) < 3x$

$1 - 2x + 2x - 14 < 3x$

$\qquad\qquad\quad -13 < 3x$

$\qquad\qquad\ \dfrac{-13}{3} < x$

$\{x|x>\dfrac{-13}{3}\}$

225

11. $\frac{1-x}{x} \geq 0$

0: free boundary number

Find other boundary numbers:

$\frac{1-x}{x} = 0$

$x(\frac{1-x}{x}) = x \cdot 0$

$1 - x = 0$

$\quad -x = -1$

$\quad\quad x = 1$

```
  A     B     C
——+———————+———————
  0     1
```

Test regions: $\underline{A}$, $x = -1$

$\frac{1-(-1)}{-1} \geq 0$ is false.

$\underline{B}$, $x = \frac{1}{2}$

$\frac{1-1/2}{1/2} \geq 0$ is true.

$\underline{C}$, $x = 2$

$\frac{1-2}{2} \geq 0$ is false

Shade region that tests true.

```
——————(———————]—————
      0       1
```

0 is not included; 1 is included.

$\{x \mid 0 < x \leq 1\}$

12. $2x^2 + 3x - 2 < 0$

Find boundary numbers:

$2x^2 + 3x - 2 = 0$

$(2x-1)(x+2) = 0$

$2x - 1 = 0 \quad$ or $\quad x + 2 = 0$

$\quad 2x = 1 \quad\quad\quad\quad x = -2$

$\quad\quad x = \frac{1}{2}$

```
     A      B      C
————————+——————+————————
       -2      1
                2
```

Test regions: $\underline{A}$, $x = -3$

$2(-3)^2 + 3(-2) - 2 < 0$

$18 - 9 - 2 < 0$ is false.

$\underline{B}$, $x = 0$

$2(0)^2 + 3(0) - 2 < 0$

$0 + 0 - 2 < 0$ is true.

$\underline{C}$, $x = 1$

$2(1)^2 + 3(1) - 2 < 0$

$2 + 3 - 2 < 0$ is false.

Shade region that tests true.

```
——————(———————)—————
      -2      1
               2
```

Boundary numbers are not included.

$\{x \mid -2 < x < \frac{1}{2}\}$

13. $|3x+1| > 10$

$3x + 1 > 10 \quad$ or $\quad 3x + 1 < -10$

$\quad 3x > 9 \quad\quad\quad\quad\quad 3x < -11$

$\quad\quad x > \frac{9}{3}$ or 3 $\quad\quad\quad x < -\frac{11}{3}$

$\{x \mid x < -\frac{11}{3}$ or $x > 3\}$

14. $(x+3)(x+1)(x-2) \leq 0$

Find boundary numbers:

$(x+3)(x+1)(x-2) = 0$

$x+3 = 0$ or $x+1 = 0$ or $x-2 = 0$

$\quad x = -3 \quad\quad\quad x = -1 \quad\quad\quad x = 2$

```
  A        B        C        D
——+————————+————————+————————+——
 -3       -1        2
```

Test regions: $\underline{A}$, $x = -4$

$(-4+3)(-4+1)(-4-2) \leq 0$

$(-1)(-3)(-6) \leq 0$ is true.

$\underline{B}$, $x = -2$

$(-2+3)(-2+1)(-2-2) \leq 0$

$(1)(-1)(-4) \leq 0$ is false.

$\underline{C}$, $x = 0$

$(0+3)(0+1)(0-2) \leq 0$

$(3)(1)(-2) \leq 0$ is true.

$\underline{D}$, $x = 3$

$(3+3)(3+1)(3-2) \leq 0$

$(6)(4)(1) \leq 0$ is false.

Shade regions that test true.

CHAPTER 8

Boundary numbers are included.

$\{x \mid x < -3 \text{ or } -1 \leq x \leq 2\}$

15. $\dfrac{1}{x+2} \leq \dfrac{2}{x-1}$

-2.1: free boundary numbers.

Find boundary numbers:

$\dfrac{1}{x+2} = \dfrac{2}{x-1}$

$(x+2)(x-1)\left(\dfrac{1}{x+2}\right) = (x+2)(x-1)\left(\dfrac{2}{x-1}\right)$

$(x-1)(1) = (x+2)(2)$

$x - 1 = 2x + 4$

$-x = 5$

$x = -5$

Test regions: <u>A</u>, x = -6

$\dfrac{1}{-6+2} \leq \dfrac{2}{-6-1}$

$\dfrac{1}{-4} \leq \dfrac{2}{-7}$ is false.

<u>B</u>, x = -4

$\dfrac{1}{-4+2} \leq \dfrac{2}{-4-1}$

$\dfrac{1}{-2} \leq \dfrac{2}{-5}$ is true.

<u>C</u>, x = 0

$\dfrac{1}{2} \leq \dfrac{2}{-1}$ is false.

<u>D</u>, x = 2

$\dfrac{1}{2+2} \leq \dfrac{2}{2-1}$

$\dfrac{1}{4} \leq 2$ is true.

Shade regions that test true.

-5 is included; -2 and 1 are not included.

$\{x \mid -5 \leq x < -2 \text{ or } x > 1\}$

1. (2,5) in I.

3. (11,-1) in IV.

5. (-3,0) on x-axis.

7. (2.4,-0.01) in IV.

9. (0,0) on x and y-axis.

11.
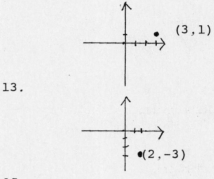

13.
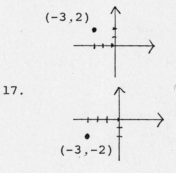

15.

17.

19.
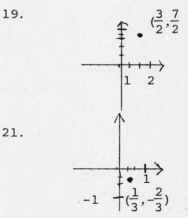

21.

23.

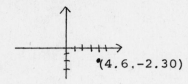

(4.6,-2.30)

25. (8,6) and (5,2)

$$d = \sqrt{(8-5)^2 + (6-2)^2}$$

$$= \sqrt{3^2 + 4^2}$$

$$= \sqrt{9+16}$$

$$= \sqrt{25}$$

$$= 5$$

27. (-7,3) and (1,-3)

$$d = \sqrt{(-7-1)^2 + [3-(-3)]^2}$$

$$= \sqrt{(-8)^2 + 6^2}$$

$$= \sqrt{64+36}$$

$$= \sqrt{100}$$

$$= 10$$

29. (-5,1), (-5,14)

$$d = \sqrt{[-5-(-5)]^2 + (1-14)^2}$$

$$= \sqrt{0^2 + (-13)^2}$$

$$= \sqrt{169}$$

$$= 13$$

31. (-1,-2) and (-3,-4)

$$d = \sqrt{[(-1)-(-3)]^2 + [(-2)-(-4)]^2}$$

$$= \sqrt{2^2 + (2)^2}$$

$$= \sqrt{4+4}$$

$$= \sqrt{8}$$

$$= 2\sqrt{2}$$

33. (7,0) and (0,7)

$$d = \sqrt{(7-0)^2 + (0-7)^2}$$

$$= \sqrt{7^2 + 7^2}$$

$$= \sqrt{49+49}$$

$$= \sqrt{98} = \sqrt{2 \cdot 49}$$

$$= 7\sqrt{2}$$

35. $(\frac{1}{2},\frac{5}{2})$ and $(\frac{3}{2},\frac{1}{2})$

$$d = \sqrt{(\frac{1}{2}-\frac{3}{2})^2 + (\frac{5}{2}-\frac{1}{2})^2}$$

$$= \sqrt{(\frac{-2}{2})^2 + (\frac{4}{2})^2}$$

$$= \sqrt{(-1)^2 + 2^2}$$

$$= \sqrt{1+4}$$

$$= \sqrt{5}$$

37. $(\frac{1}{2},\frac{1}{6})$ and $(\frac{1}{3},1)$

$$d = \sqrt{(\frac{1}{2}-\frac{1}{3})^2 + (\frac{1}{6}-1)^2}$$

$$= \sqrt{(\frac{3-2}{6})^2 + (\frac{1-6}{6})^2}$$

$$= \sqrt{(\frac{1}{6})^2 + (\frac{-5}{6})^2}$$

$$= \sqrt{\frac{1}{36} + \frac{25}{36}}$$

$$= \sqrt{\frac{26}{36}}$$

$$= \frac{\sqrt{26}}{6}$$

39. (5,1) and (-3,-1)

$$x = \frac{5+-3}{2} \qquad y = \frac{1+-1}{2}$$

$$= \frac{2}{2} \qquad\qquad = \frac{0}{2}$$

$$= 1 \qquad\qquad = 0$$

(1,0) is the midpoint.

41. (11,8) and (3,2)

$$d = \sqrt{(11-3)^2+(8-2)^2}$$

$$= \sqrt{8^2+6^2}$$

$$= \sqrt{64+36}$$

$$= \sqrt{100}$$

$$= 10$$

43. (2,3) and (14,8)

$$d = \sqrt{(2-14)^2+(3-8)^2}$$

$$= \sqrt{(-12)^2+(-5)^2}$$

$$= \sqrt{144+25}$$

$$= \sqrt{169}$$

$$= 13$$

45. (10,2) and (2,2)

$$d = \sqrt{(10-2)^2+(2-2)^2}$$

$$= \sqrt{8^2+0^2}$$

$$= \sqrt{64}$$

$$= 8$$

47. (2,3) and (-4,6)

$$d = \sqrt{[2-(-4)]^2+(3-6)^2}$$

$$= \sqrt{6^2+(-3)^2}$$

$$= \sqrt{36+9}$$

$$= \sqrt{45}$$

$$= 3\sqrt{5}$$

49. (-2,-3), (1,1)

$$d = \sqrt{(-2-1)^2+(-3-1)^2}$$

$$= \sqrt{(-3)^2+(-4)^2}$$

$$= \sqrt{9+16}$$

$$= \sqrt{25}$$

$$= 5$$

51. (-5,12) and (-4,11)

$$d = \sqrt{[-5-(-4)]^2+(12-11)^2}$$

$$= \sqrt{(-1)^2+(1)^2}$$

$$= \sqrt{1+1}$$

$$= \sqrt{2}$$

53. (-2,1) and (-2,10)

$$d = \sqrt{[-2-(-2)]^2+(1-10)^2}$$

$$= \sqrt{0^2+(-9)^2}$$

$$= \sqrt{81}$$

$$= 9$$

55. (-4,-7) and (5,-6)

$$d = \sqrt{(-4-5)^2+[-7-(-6)]^2}$$

$$= \sqrt{(-9)^2+(-1)^2}$$

$$= \sqrt{81+1}$$

$$= \sqrt{82}$$

57. (0,7) and (-7,0)

$$d = \sqrt{[0-(-7)]^2+(7-0)^2}$$

$$= \sqrt{7^2+y^2}$$

$$= \sqrt{49+49}$$

$$= \sqrt{98}$$

$$= 7\sqrt{2}$$

59. $(\frac{7}{2},\frac{3}{2})$ and $(-\frac{5}{2},\frac{1}{2})$

$$d = \sqrt{[\frac{7}{2}-(-\frac{5}{2})]^2+(\frac{3}{2}-\frac{1}{2})^2}$$

$$= \sqrt{(\frac{12}{2})^2 + (\frac{2}{2})^2}$$

$$= \sqrt{6^2 + 1^2}$$

$$= \sqrt{36 + 1}$$

$$= \sqrt{37}$$

61. $(\frac{1}{3}, \frac{1}{3})$ and $(\frac{1}{4}, -\frac{1}{4})$

$$d = \sqrt{(\frac{1}{3} - \frac{1}{4})^2 + [\frac{1}{3} - (-\frac{1}{4})]^2}$$

$$= \sqrt{(\frac{4-3}{12})^2 + (\frac{4+3}{12})^2}$$

$$= \sqrt{(\frac{1}{12})^2 + (\frac{7}{12})^2}$$

$$= \sqrt{\frac{1}{144} + \frac{49}{144}}$$

$$= \sqrt{\frac{50}{144}}$$

$$= \frac{5\sqrt{2}}{12}$$

63. $(-5, -4)$ and $(-1, -10)$

$$x = \frac{-5 + -1}{2} \qquad y = \frac{-4 + -10}{2}$$

$$= \frac{-6}{2} \qquad\qquad = \frac{-14}{2}$$

$$= -3 \qquad\qquad = -7$$

$(-3, -7)$ is the midpoint.

65. (a,b) in I since $(+,+)$ in I.

67. (c,b) in II since $(-,+)$ in II.

69. $(-a,c)$ in III since $(-,-)$ in III.

71. $(-b,-a)$ in III since $(-,-)$ in III.

73. $(-c,-d)$ in I since $(+,+)$ in I.

75. $(-d,0)$ on x axis.

77. P_1: $(2,1)$ P_2: $(-2,-1)$ P_3: $(0,0)$

d_1 (for P_1 and P_2,

$$= \sqrt{[2 - (-2)]^2 + [1 - (-1)]^2}$$

$$= \sqrt{4^2 + 2^2}$$

$$= \sqrt{16 + 4}$$

$$= \sqrt{20}$$

$$= 2\sqrt{5}$$

d_2 (for P_2 and P_3)

$$= \sqrt{(-2-0)^2 + (-1-0)^2}$$

$$= \sqrt{(-2)^2 + (-1)^2}$$

$$= \sqrt{4 + 1}$$

$$= \sqrt{5}$$

d_3 (for P_1 and P_3)

$$= \sqrt{(2-0)^2 + (1-0)^2}$$

$$= \sqrt{2^2 + 1^2}$$

$$= \sqrt{5}$$

Since $d_2 + d_3 = d_1$, P_1, P_2, and P_3 are collinear.

79. P_1: $(-1,1)$ P_2: $(-2,5)$ P_3: $(4,2)$

d_1 (for P_1 and P_2)

$$= \sqrt{[-1 - (-2)]^2 + (1-5)^2}$$

$$= \sqrt{1^2 + (-4)^2}$$

$$= \sqrt{1 + 16}$$

$$= \sqrt{17}$$

d_2 (for P_2 and P_3)

$$= \sqrt{(-2-4)^2 + (5-2)^2}$$

$$= \sqrt{(-6)^2 + 3^2}$$

$$= \sqrt{36 + 9}$$

$$= \sqrt{45}$$

$$= 3\sqrt{5}$$

d_3 (for P_1 and P_3)

$$= \sqrt{(-1-4)^2 + (1-2)^2}$$
$$= \sqrt{(-5)^2 + (-1)^2}$$
$$= \sqrt{25+1}$$
$$= \sqrt{26}$$

It is not a right triangle because
$$(d_1)^2 + (d_3)^2 \neq (d_2)^2,$$

i.e., the lengths of the sides do not satisfy the Pythagorean Theorem.

Problem Set 8.2.

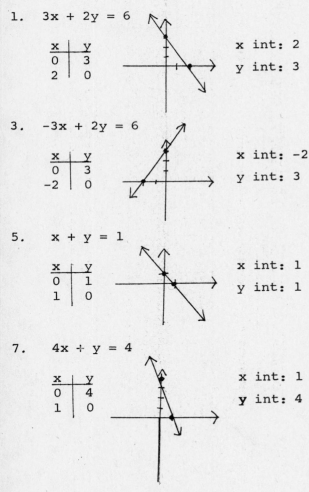

1. $3x + 2y = 6$

x	y
0	3
2	0

x int: 2
y int: 3

3. $-3x + 2y = 6$

x	y
0	3
-2	0

x int: -2
y int: 3

5. $x + y = 1$

x	y
0	1
1	0

x int: 1
y int: 1

7. $4x + y = 4$

x	y
0	4
1	0

x int: 1
y int: 4

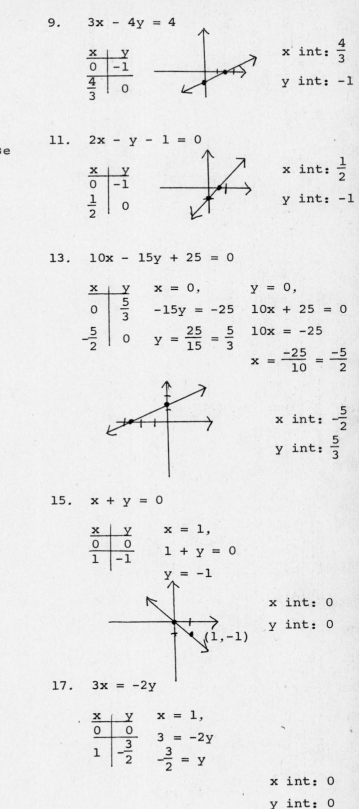

9. $3x - 4y = 4$

x	y
0	-1
$\frac{4}{3}$	0

x int: $\frac{4}{3}$
y int: -1

11. $2x - y - 1 = 0$

x	y
0	-1
$\frac{1}{2}$	0

x int: $\frac{1}{2}$
y int: -1

13. $10x - 15y + 25 = 0$

x	y
0	$\frac{5}{3}$
$-\frac{5}{2}$	0

$x = 0,$ $-15y = -25$ $y = \frac{25}{15} = \frac{5}{3}$

$y = 0,$ $10x + 25 = 0$ $10x = -25$ $x = \frac{-25}{10} = \frac{-5}{2}$

x int: $-\frac{5}{2}$
y int: $\frac{5}{3}$

15. $x + y = 0$

x	y
0	0
1	-1

$x = 1,$
$1 + y = 0$
$y = -1$

x int: 0
y int: 0

$(1,-1)$

17. $3x = -2y$

x	y
0	0
1	$-\frac{3}{2}$

$x = 1,$
$3 = -2y$
$-\frac{3}{2} = y$

x int: 0
y int: 0

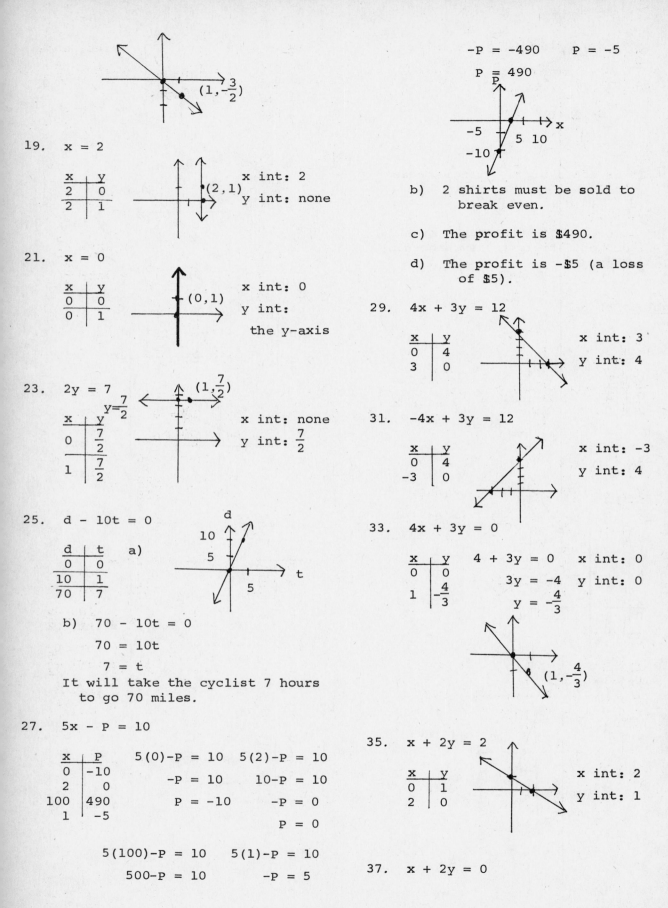

$(1, -\frac{3}{2})$

$-P = -490 \qquad P = -5$

$P = 490$

19. $x = 2$

x	y
2	0
2	1

$(2,1)$

x int: 2
y int: none

b) 2 shirts must be sold to break even.

c) The profit is $490.

d) The profit is -$5 (a loss of $5).

21. $x = 0$

x	y
0	0
0	1

$(0,1)$

x int: 0
y int: the y-axis

29. $4x + 3y = 12$

x	y
0	4
3	0

x int: 3
y int: 4

23. $2y = 7$

$y = \frac{7}{2}$

x	y
0	$\frac{7}{2}$
1	$\frac{7}{2}$

$(1, \frac{7}{2})$

x int: none
y int: $\frac{7}{2}$

31. $-4x + 3y = 12$

x	y
0	4
-3	0

x int: -3
y int: 4

25. $d - 10t = 0$

d	t
0	0
10	1
70	7

a)

b) $70 - 10t = 0$

$70 = 10t$

$7 = t$

It will take the cyclist 7 hours to go 70 miles.

33. $4x + 3y = 0$

x	y
0	0
1	$-\frac{4}{3}$

$4 + 3y = 0$ x int: 0

$3y = -4$ y int: 0

$y = -\frac{4}{3}$

$(1, -\frac{4}{3})$

27. $5x - P = 10$

x	P
0	-10
2	0
100	490
1	-5

$5(0)-P = 10 \qquad 5(2)-P = 10$

$-P = 10 \qquad\quad 10-P = 10$

$P = -10 \qquad\quad -P = 0$

$\qquad\qquad\qquad P = 0$

$5(100)-P = 10 \qquad 5(1)-P = 10$

$500-P = 10 \qquad\qquad -P = 5$

35. $x + 2y = 2$

x	y
0	1
2	0

x int: 2
y int: 1

37. $x + 2y = 0$

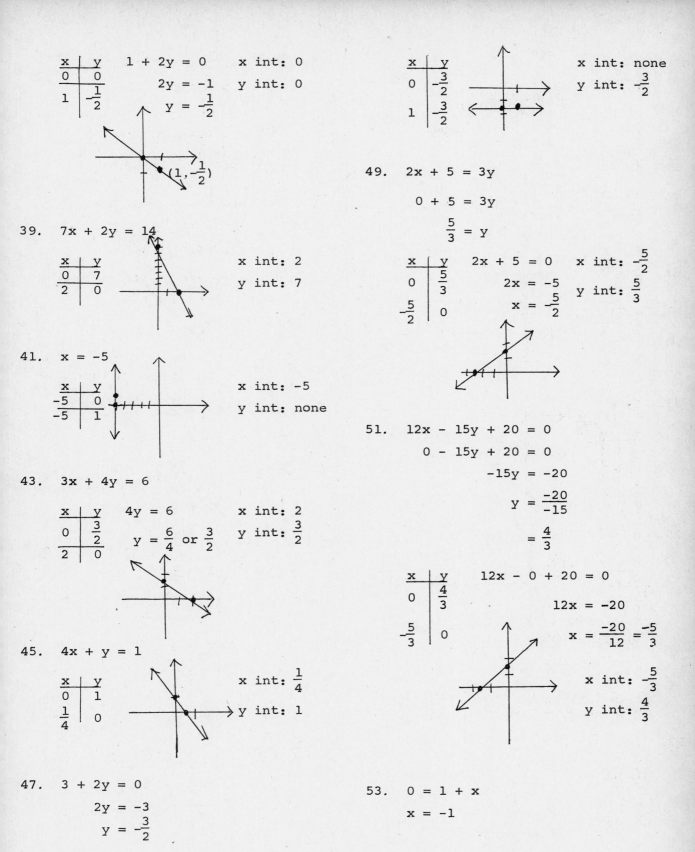

x	y
0	0
1	$-\frac{1}{2}$

$1 + 2y = 0$

$2y = -1$

$y = -\frac{1}{2}$

x int: 0

y int: 0

$(1, -\frac{1}{2})$

x	y
0	$-\frac{3}{2}$
1	$-\frac{3}{2}$

x int: none

y int: $-\frac{3}{2}$

39. $7x + 2y = 14$

x	y
0	7
2	0

x int: 2

y int: 7

49. $2x + 5 = 3y$

$0 + 5 = 3y$

$\frac{5}{3} = y$

x	y
0	$\frac{5}{3}$
$-\frac{5}{2}$	0

$2x + 5 = 0$

$2x = -5$

$x = -\frac{5}{2}$

x int: $-\frac{5}{2}$

y int: $\frac{5}{3}$

41. $x = -5$

x	y
-5	0
-5	1

x int: -5

y int: none

51. $12x - 15y + 20 = 0$

$0 - 15y + 20 = 0$

$-15y = -20$

$y = \frac{-20}{-15}$

$= \frac{4}{3}$

43. $3x + 4y = 6$

x	y
0	$\frac{3}{2}$
2	0

$4y = 6$

$y = \frac{6}{4}$ or $\frac{3}{2}$

x int: 2

y int: $\frac{3}{2}$

x	y
0	$\frac{4}{3}$
$-\frac{5}{3}$	0

$12x - 0 + 20 = 0$

$12x = -20$

$x = \frac{-20}{12} = \frac{-5}{3}$

x int: $-\frac{5}{3}$

y int: $\frac{4}{3}$

45. $4x + y = 1$

x	y
0	1
$\frac{1}{4}$	0

x int: $\frac{1}{4}$

y int: 1

47. $3 + 2y = 0$

$2y = -3$

$y = -\frac{3}{2}$

53. $0 = 1 + x$

$x = -1$

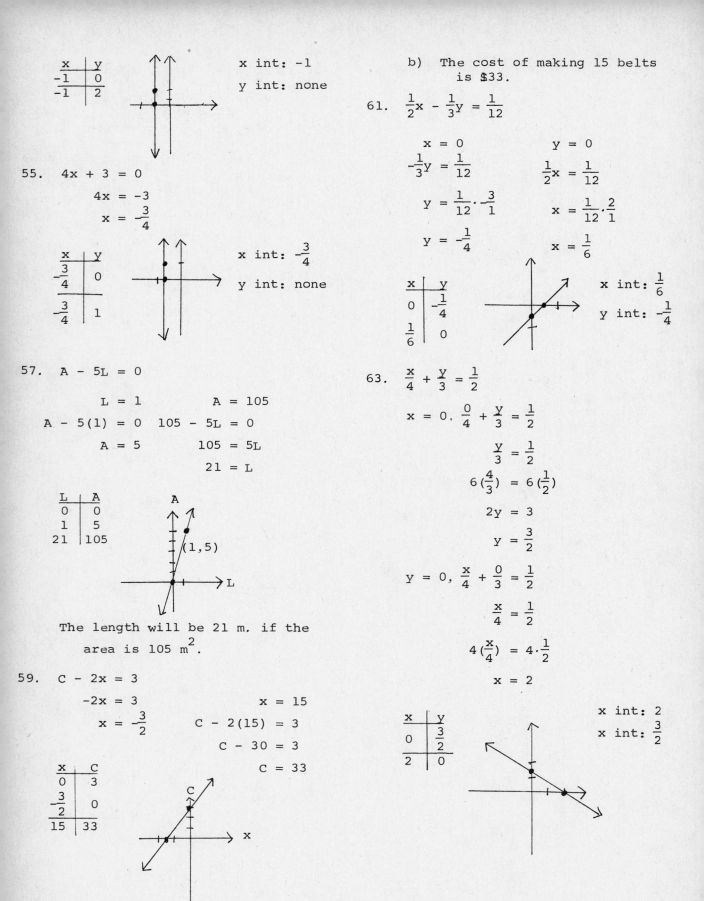

x	y
-1	0
-1	2

x int: -1

y int: none

55. $4x + 3 = 0$

$$4x = -3$$

$$x = -\frac{3}{4}$$

x	y
$-\frac{3}{4}$	0
$-\frac{3}{4}$	1

x int: $-\frac{3}{4}$

y int: none

57. $A - 5L = 0$

$$L = 1 \qquad A = 105$$

$$A - 5(1) = 0 \qquad 105 - 5L = 0$$

$$A = 5 \qquad 105 = 5L$$

$$21 = L$$

L	A
0	0
1	5
21	105

$(1,5)$

The length will be 21 m. if the
area is 105 m^2.

59. $C - 2x = 3$

$$-2x = 3 \qquad\qquad x = 15$$

$$x = -\frac{3}{2} \qquad C - 2(15) = 3$$

$$C - 30 = 3$$

$$C = 33$$

x	C
0	3
$-\frac{3}{2}$	0
15	33

b) The cost of making 15 belts
is $33.

61. $\frac{1}{2}x - \frac{1}{3}y = \frac{1}{12}$

$x = 0$ $y = 0$

$-\frac{1}{3}y = \frac{1}{12}$ $\frac{1}{2}x = \frac{1}{12}$

$y = \frac{1}{12}\cdot\frac{3}{1}$ $x = \frac{1}{12}\cdot\frac{2}{1}$

$y = -\frac{1}{4}$ $x = \frac{1}{6}$

x	y
0	$-\frac{1}{4}$
$\frac{1}{6}$	0

x int: $\frac{1}{6}$

y int: $-\frac{1}{4}$

63. $\frac{x}{4} + \frac{y}{3} = \frac{1}{2}$

$x = 0$, $\frac{0}{4} + \frac{y}{3} = \frac{1}{2}$

$$\frac{y}{3} = \frac{1}{2}$$

$$6\left(\frac{4}{3}\right) = 6\left(\frac{1}{2}\right)$$

$$2y = 3$$

$$y = \frac{3}{2}$$

$y = 0$, $\frac{x}{4} + \frac{0}{3} = \frac{1}{2}$

$$\frac{x}{4} = \frac{1}{2}$$

$$4\left(\frac{x}{4}\right) = 4\cdot\frac{1}{2}$$

$$x = 2$$

x	y
0	$\frac{3}{2}$
2	0

x int: 2

x int: $\frac{3}{2}$

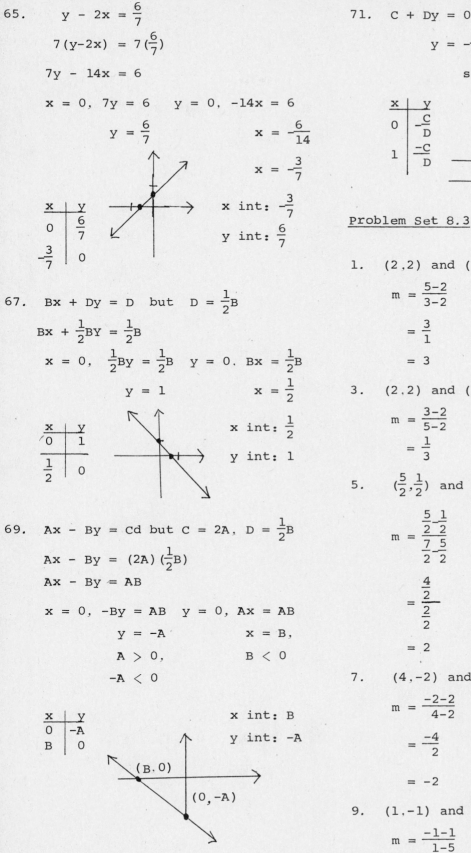

65.　　$y - 2x = \dfrac{6}{7}$

　　　$7(y-2x) = 7\left(\dfrac{6}{7}\right)$

　　　$7y - 14x = 6$

　　　$x = 0,\ 7y = 6$　　$y = 0,\ -14x = 6$

　　　　　$y = \dfrac{6}{7}$　　　　　$x = -\dfrac{6}{14}$

　　　　　　　　　　　　　　$x = -\dfrac{3}{7}$

x	y
0	$\dfrac{6}{7}$
$-\dfrac{3}{7}$	0

x int: $-\dfrac{3}{7}$

y int: $\dfrac{6}{7}$

67.　$Bx + Dy = D$　but　$D = \dfrac{1}{2}B$

　　$Bx + \dfrac{1}{2}BY = \dfrac{1}{2}B$

　　$x = 0,\ \dfrac{1}{2}By = \dfrac{1}{2}B$　$y = 0.\ Bx = \dfrac{1}{2}B$

　　　　　$y = 1$　　　　　　$x = \dfrac{1}{2}$

x	y
0	1
$\dfrac{1}{2}$	0

x int: $\dfrac{1}{2}$

y int: 1

69.　$Ax - By = Cd$　but　$C = 2A,\ D = \dfrac{1}{2}B$

　　$Ax - By = (2A)\left(\dfrac{1}{2}B\right)$

　　$Ax - By = AB$

　　$x = 0,\ -By = AB$　$y = 0,\ Ax = AB$

　　　　　$y = -A$　　　　　$x = B,$

　　　　　$A > 0,$　　　　　$B < 0$

　　　　　$-A < 0$

x	y
0	-A
B	0

x int: B

y int: -A

(B,0)

(0,-A)

71.　$C + Dy = 0$

　　　　$y = -\dfrac{C}{D},\ C > 0$ and $D < 0$

　　　　　so $-\dfrac{C}{D}$ is positive.

x	y
0	$-\dfrac{C}{D}$
1	$\dfrac{-C}{D}$

$\left(1, -\dfrac{C}{D}\right)$

x int: none

y int: $-\dfrac{C}{D}$

<u>Problem Set 8.3.</u>

1.　(2,2) and (3,5)

　　$m = \dfrac{5-2}{3-2}$

　　　$= \dfrac{3}{1}$

　　　$= 3$

3.　(2,2) and (5,3)

　　$m = \dfrac{3-2}{5-2}$

　　　$= \dfrac{1}{3}$

5.　$\left(\dfrac{5}{2}, \dfrac{1}{2}\right)$ and $\left(\dfrac{7}{2}, \dfrac{5}{2}\right)$

　　$m = \dfrac{\dfrac{5}{2} - \dfrac{1}{2}}{\dfrac{7}{2} - \dfrac{5}{2}}$

　　　$= \dfrac{\dfrac{4}{2}}{\dfrac{2}{2}}$

　　　$= 2$

7.　(4,-2) and (2,2)

　　$m = \dfrac{-2-2}{4-2}$

　　　$= \dfrac{-4}{2}$

　　　$= -2$

9.　(1,-1) and (5,1)

　　$m = \dfrac{-1-1}{1-5}$

$= \dfrac{-2}{-4}$

$= \dfrac{1}{2}$

11. $(-1,4)$ and $(4,6)$

$m = \dfrac{4-6}{-1-4}$

$= \dfrac{-2}{-5}$

$= \dfrac{2}{5}$

13. $(-7,4)$ and $(-3,2)$

$m = \dfrac{4-2}{-7-(-3)}$

$= \dfrac{2}{-4}$

$= -\dfrac{1}{2}$

15. $(-9,1)$ and $(-1 -9)$

$m = \dfrac{1-(-9)}{-9-(-1)}$

$= \dfrac{10}{-8}$

$= -\dfrac{5}{4}$

17. $(-2,-6)$ and $(-4,-1)$

$m = \dfrac{-6-(-1)}{-2-(-4)}$

$= \dfrac{-5}{2}$ or $-\dfrac{5}{2}$

19. $(0,-9)$ and $(-4,0)$

$m = \dfrac{-9-0}{0-(-4)}$

$= \dfrac{-9}{4}$ or $-\dfrac{9}{4}$

21. $(-2,3)$ and $(-5,3)$

$m = \dfrac{3-3}{-2-(-5)}$

$= \dfrac{0}{3}$

$= 0$

23. $(-2,0)$ and $(0,0)$

$m = \dfrac{0-0}{-2-0}$

$= \dfrac{0}{-2}$

$= 0$

25. $(-3,-6)$ and $(-3,-8)$

$m = \dfrac{-6-(-8)}{-3-(-3)}$

$= \dfrac{2}{0}$ is undefined

No slope.

27. $x - y = 1$

$x = 0$ $-y = 1$ $y = 0,\ x = 1$

$y = -1$

Using $(0,-1)$ and $(1,0)$,

$m = \dfrac{-1-0}{0-1}$

$= \dfrac{-1}{-1}$

$= 1$

29. $2x + 3y = 6$

$x = 0$ $3y = 6$ $y = 0$ $2x = 6$

$y = 2$ $x = 3$

Using $(0,2)$ and $(3,0)$,

$m = \dfrac{2-0}{0-3}$

$= \dfrac{2}{-3}$ or $-\dfrac{2}{3}$

31. $4x - y = 0$

$x = 0$ $-y = 0$ $x = 1$ $4 - y = 0$

$y = 0$ $-y = -4$

$y = 4$

Using $(0,0)$ and $(1,4)$,

$m = \dfrac{4-0}{1-0}$

$= \dfrac{4}{1}$

$= 4$

33. $y = 4$, graph is a horizontal line so $m = 0$.

35. $4 + 3y = 0$

$y = -\dfrac{4}{3}$, graph is a horizontal line so $m = 0$.

37. ℓ_1: $(0,-2)$ and $(-4,-5)$

$m_1 = \dfrac{-2-(-5)}{0-(-4)}$

$= \dfrac{3}{4}$

$\ell_2 \perp \ell_1$ so $m_2 = -\dfrac{1}{m_1}$

$m_2 = -\dfrac{1}{\frac{3}{4}}$

$= -\dfrac{4}{3}$

39. ℓ_1: $(2,-3)$ and $(7,-3)$

$m_1 = \dfrac{-3-(-3)}{2-7}$

$= \dfrac{0}{-5}$

$= 0$

$\ell_2 \perp \ell_1$ so $m_2 = -\dfrac{1}{m_1}$

$m_2 = \dfrac{1}{0}$ is undefined

ℓ_2 has no slope.

41. $2x - 5y = 20$

$x = 0$ $-5y = 20$ $y = 0$ $2x = 20$

$y = -4$ $x = 10$

Using $(0,-4)$ and $(10,0)$ on ℓ_1:

$m_1 = \dfrac{-4-0}{0-10}$

$= \dfrac{-4}{-10}$

$= \dfrac{2}{5}$

$\ell_2 \parallel \ell_1$, so $m_2 = m_1$

$m_2 = \dfrac{2}{5}$

43. $(4,4)$ and $(5,2)$

$m = \dfrac{4-2}{4-5}$

$= \dfrac{2}{-1}$

$= -2$

45. $(4,5)$ and $(2,4)$

$m = \dfrac{5-4}{4-2}$

$= \dfrac{1}{2}$

47. $(1,-2)$ and $(4,4)$

$m = \dfrac{-2-4}{1-4}$

$= \dfrac{-6}{-3}$

$= 2$

49. $(-2,3)$ and $(1,5)$

$m = \dfrac{3-5}{-2-1}$

$= \dfrac{-2}{-3}$

$= \dfrac{2}{3}$

51. $(-2,2)$ and $(-5,6)$

$m = \dfrac{6-2}{-5-(-2)}$

$= \dfrac{4}{-3}$ or $-\dfrac{4}{3}$

53. $(-6,5)$ and $(6,-4)$

$m = \dfrac{5-(-4)}{-6-6}$

$= \dfrac{9}{-12}$ or $-\dfrac{3}{4}$

55. $(1,3)$ and $(5,3)$

$m = \dfrac{3-3}{1-5}$

$= \dfrac{0}{-4}$

$= 0$

57. $(-5,-5)$ and $(-2,-7)$

$$m = \frac{-5-(-7)}{-5-(-2)}$$

$$= \frac{2}{-3} \text{ or } -\frac{2}{3}$$

59. $(-2,-4)$ and $(-5,-4)$

$$m = \frac{-4-(-4)}{-2-(-5)}$$

$$= \frac{0}{3}$$

$$= 0$$

61. $(0,-3)$ and $(0,0)$

$$m = \frac{-3-0}{0-0}$$

$$= \frac{-3}{0} \text{ is undefined}$$

No slope.

63. $(-\frac{1}{2},\frac{2}{3})$ and $(\frac{1}{2},\frac{5}{3})$

$$m = \frac{\frac{2}{3}-\frac{5}{3}}{-\frac{1}{2}-\frac{1}{2}}$$

$$= \frac{\frac{-3}{3}}{\frac{-2}{2}}$$

$$= \frac{-1}{-1}$$

$$= 1$$

65. $(-\frac{2}{3}, -\frac{5}{3})$ and $(\frac{1}{6}, -\frac{1}{3})$

$$m = \frac{\frac{-5}{3}-(-\frac{1}{3})}{-\frac{2}{3}-\frac{1}{6}}$$

$$= \frac{\frac{-4}{3}}{\frac{-4-1}{6}}$$

$$= \frac{\frac{-4}{3}}{\frac{-5}{6}}$$

$$= -\frac{4}{3} \cdot -\frac{6}{5}$$

$$= \frac{8}{5}$$

67. $(\frac{5}{2},\frac{1}{6})$ and $(2,\frac{2}{3})$

$$m = \frac{\frac{1}{6}-\frac{2}{3}}{\frac{5}{2}-2}$$

$$= \frac{\frac{1-4}{6}}{\frac{5-4}{2}}$$

$$= \frac{\frac{-3}{6}}{\frac{1}{2}}$$

$$= -\frac{1}{2} \cdot \frac{2}{1}$$

$$= -1$$

69. $(-\frac{3}{4},-2)$ and $(\frac{1}{2},\frac{1}{2})$

$$m = \frac{-2-\frac{1}{2}}{-\frac{3}{4}-\frac{1}{2}}$$

$$= \frac{\frac{-4-1}{2}}{\frac{-3-2}{4}}$$

$$= \frac{\frac{-5}{2}}{\frac{-5}{4}}$$

$$= \frac{-5}{2} \cdot -\frac{4}{5}$$

$$= 2$$

71. $(\frac{1}{5},\frac{1}{5})$ and $(\frac{1}{4},\frac{1}{3})$

$$m = \frac{\frac{1}{5}-\frac{1}{3}}{\frac{1}{5}-\frac{1}{4}}$$

$$= \frac{\frac{3-5}{15}}{\frac{4-5}{20}}$$

$$= \frac{\frac{-2}{15}}{\frac{-1}{20}}$$

$$= \frac{-2}{15} \cdot -\frac{20}{1}$$

$$= \frac{8}{3}$$

73. $2x - y = 6$

$x = 0$ $-y = 6$ $y = 0$ $2x = 6$

  $y = -6$ $x = 3$

Using $(0,-6)$ and $(3,0)$

$m = \dfrac{-6-0}{0-3}$

$= \dfrac{-6}{-3}$

$= 2$

75. $x - 2y = 8$

$x = 0$ $-2y = 8$ $y = 0$ $x = 8$

    $y = -4$

Using $(0,-4)$ and $(8,0)$

$m = \dfrac{-4-0}{0-8}$

$= \dfrac{-4}{-8}$

$= \dfrac{1}{2}$

77. $3x + 5y = 0$

$x = 0$ $5y = 0$ $x = 1$ $3+5y = 0$

    $y = 0$ $5y = -3$

          $y = -\dfrac{3}{5}$

Using $(0,0)$ and $(1,-\dfrac{3}{5})$,

$m = \dfrac{-\dfrac{3}{5}-0}{1-0}$

$= -\dfrac{3}{5}$

79. $11 - 5y$

$y = \dfrac{11}{5}$, graph is a horizontal line
  so $m = 0$

81. ℓ_1: $(1,6)$ and $(-1,3)$

$m_1 = \dfrac{6-3}{1-(-1)}$

$= \dfrac{3}{2}$

$\ell_1 \parallel \ell_2$ $m_2 = m_1 = \dfrac{3}{2}$

83. ℓ_1: $(5,-9)$ and $(5,-3)$

$m_1 = \dfrac{-9-(-3)}{5-5}$

$= \dfrac{-6}{0}$

m_1 is undefined; no slope

$\ell_1 \parallel \ell_2$, $m_2 = m_1 =$ no slope.

85. $2x - 3y = 24$

$x = 0$ $-3y = 24$ $y = 0$ $2x = 24$

      $y = -8$ $x = 12$

Using $(0,-8)$ and $(12,0)$,

$m_1 = \dfrac{-8-0}{0-12}$

$= \dfrac{-8}{-12}$

$= \dfrac{2}{3}$

$\ell_1 \perp \ell_2$ so $m_2 = -\dfrac{1}{m_1}$

$= \dfrac{-1}{\dfrac{2}{3}}$

$= -\dfrac{3}{2}$

87. $y = 3x + 3$

$x = 0$ $y = 3$ $y = 0$

        $3x = -3$

        $x = -1$

Using $(0,3)$ and $(-1,0)$,

$m = \dfrac{3-0}{0-(-1)}$

$= 3$

89. $y = 3x + Q$

$x = 0$ $y = Q$ $y = 0$ $3x+Q = 0$

        $3x = -Q$

        $x = \dfrac{-Q}{3}$

Using $(0,Q)$ and $(-\dfrac{Q}{3},0)$,

$m = \dfrac{Q-0}{0-(-\dfrac{Q}{3})}$

$$= \frac{Q}{\frac{Q}{3}}$$

$$= \frac{Q}{1} \cdot \frac{3}{Q} = 3$$

91. $y = Px + Q$

$x = 0 \quad y = Q \quad y = 0 \quad Px+Q = 0$

$$Px = -Q$$

$$x = -\frac{Q}{P}$$

Using $(0,Q)$ and $(-\frac{Q}{P}, 0)$,

$$m = \frac{Q-0}{0-(-\frac{Q}{P})}$$

$$= \frac{Q}{\frac{Q}{P}}$$

$$= Q \cdot \frac{P}{Q}$$

$$= P$$

93. $5x - y = 7$

$$-y = -5x + 7$$

$$y = 5x - 7$$

$$m = 5$$

95. $4x - 2 = 5y$

$$\frac{4}{5}x - \frac{2}{5} = y$$

$$m = \frac{4}{5}$$

Problem Set 8.4.

1. $2x + 3y = 6$

$$3y = -2x + 6$$

$$y = -\frac{2}{3}x + 2$$

$$m = -\frac{2}{3}$$

3. $x + 7y = 14$

$$7y = -x + 14$$

$$y = -\frac{1}{7}x + 2$$

$$m = -\frac{1}{7}$$

5. $5x - y = 7$

$$-y = -5x + 7$$

$$y = 5x - 7$$

$$m = 5$$

7. $4x - 7y = 0$

$$-7y = -4x$$

$$y = \frac{-4}{-7}x$$

$$y = \frac{4}{7}x$$

$$m = \frac{4}{7}$$

9. $y = x$

$$m = 1$$

11. $y = -x + 1$

$$m = -1 \quad b = 1$$

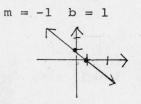

13. $y = -\frac{1}{3}x + \frac{5}{3}$

$$m = -\frac{1}{3} \quad b = \frac{5}{3}$$

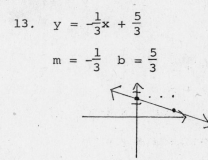

15. $y = -4x$

$$m = -4 \quad b = 0$$

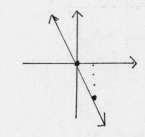

17. $(-1,1)$ $m = 2$

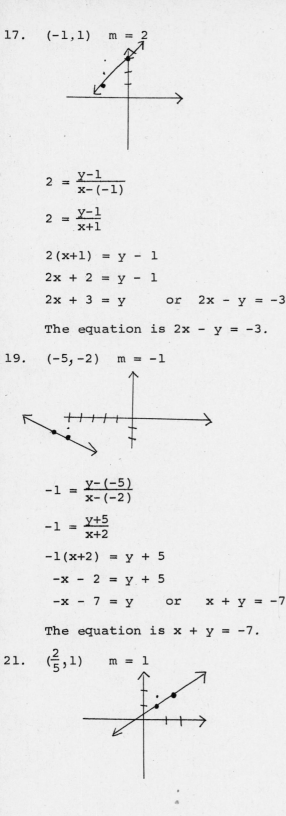

$2 = \dfrac{y-1}{x-(-1)}$

$2 = \dfrac{y-1}{x+1}$

$2(x+1) = y - 1$

$2x + 2 = y - 1$

$2x + 3 = y$ or $2x - y = -3$

The equation is $2x - y = -3$.

19. $(-5,-2)$ $m = -1$

$-1 = \dfrac{y-(-5)}{x-(-2)}$

$-1 = \dfrac{y+5}{x+2}$

$-1(x+2) = y + 5$

$-x - 2 = y + 5$

$-x - 7 = y$ or $x + y = -7$

The equation is $x + y = -7$.

21. $(\frac{2}{5},1)$ $m = 1$

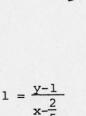

$1 = \dfrac{y-1}{x-\frac{2}{5}}$

$x - \dfrac{2}{5} = y - 1$

$5(x-\frac{2}{5}) = 5(y-1)$

$5x - 2 = 5y - 5$

$5x + 3 = 5y$ or $5x - 5y = -3$

The equation is $5x - 5y = -3$.

23. $(-1,4)$ and $(2,3)$

$m = \dfrac{4-3}{-1-2}$

$= \dfrac{1}{-3}$ or $-\dfrac{1}{3}$

Using $(2,3)$

$y - 3 = -\dfrac{1}{3}(x-2)$

$3(y-3) = 3[-\dfrac{1}{3}(x-2)]$

$3y - 9 = -1(x-2)$

$3y - 9 = -x + 2$

$x + 3y = 11$

The equation is $x + 3y = 11$.

25. $(0,-2)$ and $(5,0)$

$m = \dfrac{-2-0}{0-5}$

$= \dfrac{-2}{-5}$ or $\dfrac{2}{5}$

Using $(5,0)$

$y - 0 = \dfrac{2}{5}(x-5)$

$5(y) = 5[\dfrac{2}{5}(x-5)]$

$5y = 2(x-5)$

$5y = 2x - 10$

$10 = 2x - 5y$

The equation is $2x - 5y = 10$.

27. $(-1,-2)$ and $(-6,-9)$

$m = \dfrac{-2-(-9)}{-1-(-6)}$

$= \dfrac{7}{5}$

Using $(-1,-2)$,

241

$$y - (-2) = \frac{7}{5}[x-(-1)]$$

$$5(y+2) = [\frac{7}{5}(x+1)]$$

$$5y + 10 = 7(x+1)$$

$$5y + 10 = 7x + 7$$

$$3 = 7x - 5y$$

The equation is 7x - 5y = 3.

29. m = -1   x int: -3

Through (-3,0)
Using pt.-slope form:

$$y - 0 = -1[x-(-3)]$$

$$y = -(x+3)$$

$$y = -x - 3$$

$$x + y = -3$$

The equation is x + y = -3.

31. Through (1,-5), ll to y = 6x - 5

m = 6

Using pt.-slope form:

$$y - (-5) = 6(x-1)$$

$$y + 5 = 6x - 6$$

$$6x - y = 11$$

The equation is 6x - y = 11.

33. Through (-7,0), ll to 4x - 2y = 3

$$4x - 2y = 3$$

$$-2y = -4x + 3$$

$$y = 2x - \frac{3}{2} \quad \text{so } m = 2$$

Using pt.-slope form:

$$y - 0 = 2[x-(-7)]$$

$$y = 2(x+7)$$

$$y = 2x + 14$$

$$2x - y = -14$$

The equation is 2x - y = -14.

35. Through (-4,-1), ll to x-axis

m = 0

$$y = -1$$

The equation is y = -1.

37. Through (32,0) and (212,100)

$$m = \frac{100-0}{212-32}$$

$$= \frac{100}{180}$$

$$= \frac{5}{9}$$

Using (32,0),

$$C - 0 = \frac{5}{9}(F-32)$$

$$C = \frac{5}{9}(F-32)$$

The equation is $C = \frac{5}{9}(F-32)$.

39. 3x + 4y = 12

a)

x	y
0	3
4	0

$$m = \frac{3-0}{0-4}$$

$$= \frac{3}{-4} \quad \text{or} \quad -\frac{3}{4}$$

b) 3x + 4y = 12

$$4y = -3x + 12$$

$$y = -\frac{3}{4}x + 12 \text{ so } m = -\frac{3}{4}$$

41. x + 5y = 10

a)

x	y
0	2
10	0

$$m = \frac{2-0}{0-10}$$

$$= \frac{2}{-10} \quad \text{or} \quad -\frac{1}{5}$$

b) x + 5y = 10

$$5y = -x + 10$$

$$y = -\frac{1}{5}x + 2 \quad \text{so} \quad m = -\frac{1}{5}$$

43. 4x - y = 7

a)

x	y
0	-7
$\frac{7}{4}$	0

$$m = \frac{-7-0}{0-\frac{7}{4}}$$

$$= \frac{-7}{\frac{-7}{4}}$$

$$= -7 - \frac{4}{7}$$

$$= 4$$

b) $4x - y = 7$

$$-y = -4x + 7$$

$$y = 4x - 7 \quad \text{so} \quad m = 4$$

45. $3x + 7y = 0$

a)

x	y
0	0
1	$-\frac{3}{7}$

$$m = \frac{-\frac{3}{7}-0}{1-0}$$

$$= -\frac{3}{7}$$

b) $3x + 7y = 0$

$$7y = -3x$$

$$y = -\frac{3}{7}x \quad \text{so} \quad m = -\frac{3}{7}$$

47. $y + 9 = 0$

a)

x	y
0	-9
1	-9

$$m = \frac{9--9}{0-1}$$

$$= 0$$

b) $y + 9 = 0$

$$y = -9$$

$$y = 0 \cdot x - 9 \quad m = 0$$

49. $y = -x - 1$

$m = -1$

y int = -1

51. $y = -\frac{1}{2}x + \frac{3}{2}$

$m = -\frac{1}{2}$

y int: $\frac{3}{2}$

53. $y = 4x$

$m = 4$

y int: 0

55. Through $(1,-1)$, $m = -2$

$$y - (-1) = -2(x-1)$$

$$y + 1 = -2x+2$$

$$2x + y = 1$$

The equation is $2x + y = 1$.

57. Through $(-4,-3)$ $m = 1$

$$y - (-3) = 1[x-(-4)]$$

$$y + 3 = x + 4$$

$$x - y = -1$$

The equations is $x - y = -1$.

59. Through $(\frac{2}{3},\frac{3}{5})$, $m = 1$

$$y - \frac{3}{5} = 1(x-\frac{2}{3})$$

$$15(y-\frac{3}{5}) = 15(x-\frac{2}{3})$$

$$15y - 9 = 15x - 10$$

$$15x - 15y = 1$$

The equation is $15x - 15y = 1$

61. Through $(-2,3)$ and $(1,4)$

$m = \dfrac{3-4}{-2-1}$

$\quad = \dfrac{-1}{-3}$ or $\dfrac{1}{3}$

Using $(1,4)$ and $m = \dfrac{1}{3}$,

$y - 4 = \dfrac{1}{3}(x-1)$

$3(y-4) = 3[\dfrac{1}{3}(x-1)]$

$3y - 12 = x - 1$

$x - 3y = -11$

The equation is $x - 3y = -11$.

63. Through $(0,2)$ and $(-5,0)$

$m = \dfrac{2-0}{0-(-5)}$

$\quad = \dfrac{2}{5}$

Using $(0,2)$ and $m = \dfrac{2}{5}$

$y - 2 = \dfrac{2}{5}(x-0)$

$y - 2 = \dfrac{2}{5}x$

$5(y-2) = 5(\dfrac{2}{5}x)$

$5y - 10 = 2x$

$2x - 5y = -10$

The equation is $2x - 5y = -10$.

65. Through $(-2,-3)$ $(-5,-6)$

$m = \dfrac{-3-(-6)}{-2-(-5)}$

$\quad = \dfrac{3}{3}$

$\quad = 1$

Using $(-2,-3)$ and $m = 1$

$y - (-3) = 1[x-(-2)]$

$y + 3 = x + 2$

$x - y = 1$

The equation is $x - y = 1$.

67. $m = 1$ $\quad$ x int: $-\dfrac{1}{2}$

Using $m = 1$ and $(-\dfrac{1}{2}, 0)$,

$y - 0 = 1[x-(-\dfrac{1}{2})]$

$y = x + \dfrac{1}{2}$

$2(y) = 2(x+\dfrac{1}{2})$

$2y = 2x + 1$

$2x - 2x = -1$

The equation is $2x - 2y = -1$

69. Through $(-1,4)$, $||$ to $y = 4x - 3$

Using $m = 4$ and $(-1,4)$

$y - 4 = 4[x-(-1)]$

$y - 4 = 4x + 4$

$4x - y = -8$

The equation is $4x - y = -8$.

71. Through $(0 -7)$, $||$ to $5x - 3y = 13$

$5x - 3y = 13$

$-3y = -5x + 13$

$y = \dfrac{5}{3}x - \dfrac{13}{3}$

Using $(0,-7)$ so y intercept is -7
and $m = \dfrac{5}{3}$,

$y = \dfrac{5}{3}x - 7$

$3y = 3(\dfrac{5}{3}x-7)$

$3y = 5x - 21$

$5x - 37 = 21$

The equation is $5x - 3y = 21$.

73. Through $(2,-3)$ $||$ to y-axis.

Using $(2,-3)$, line is vertical.

$x = 2$

75. Through $(0,0)$, $\perp$ to $x = -y$

$x = -y$ so $y = -x$ and $m_1 = -1$

Using $(0,0)$ and $m_2 = \dfrac{1}{-1}$

$\quad = 1$

$y - 0 = 1(x-0)$

$y = x$

$x - y = 0$

The equation of the line is $x - y$
$= 0$.

77. Through $(2,0)$, $\perp$ to line containing $(-5,3)$ and $(3,3)$

$$m = \frac{3-3}{-5-3}$$

$$= \frac{0}{-8}$$

$$= 0$$

Line is horizontal; through $(2,0)$.

$y = 0$

The equation of the line is $y = 0$.

79. y int: $||$ and $\perp$ to $4x - y = 0$

$4x - y = 0$

$-y = -4x$

$y = 4x$

$m_1 = 4$ so $m_2 = -\frac{1}{4}$

Using $(0,11)$ and $m_2 = -\frac{1}{4}$

$$y - 11 = -\frac{1}{4}(x-0)$$

$$y(y-11) = 4[-\frac{1}{4}(x)]$$

$4y - 44 = -x$

$x + 4y = 44$

The equation is $x + 4y = 44$.

81. Through $(1,2.9)$, $(5,4.5)$

$$m = \frac{2.9-4.5}{1-5}$$

$$= \frac{-1.6}{-4}$$

$$= 0.4$$

Using $(1,2.9)$ and $m = 0.4$

$s - 2.9 = 0.4(t-1)$

$10(s-2.9) = 10[0.4(t-1)]$

$10s - 29 = 4(t-1)$

$10s - 29 = 4t - 4$

$4t - 10s = -25$

The equation is $4t - 10s = -25$.

When $t = 10$,

$4(10) - 10s = -25$

$-10s = -65$

$$x = \frac{-65}{-10}$$

$$= 6.5$$

The sales will be $6.5 billion in 10 years.

83. Through (p,q), $\perp$ to $px + qy = c$

$px + qy = c$ $\qquad m_1 = -\frac{p}{q}$

$qy = -px + c$ $\qquad m_2 = \frac{-1}{-\frac{p}{q}}$

$y = \frac{-p}{q}x + \frac{c}{q}$

$\qquad\qquad\qquad = \frac{q}{p}$

Using (p,q) and $m_2 = \frac{q}{p}$

$$y - q = \frac{8}{p}(x-p)$$

$$p(y-q) = p[\frac{q}{p}(x-p)]$$

$py - pq = qx - pq$

$qx - py = 0$

The equation is $qx - py = 0$

85. $2x + 3y = 6$

$$\frac{2x}{6} + \frac{3y}{6} = \frac{6}{6}$$

$$\frac{x}{3} + \frac{y}{2} = 1$$

The x intercept is 3; the y intercept is 2.

87. $2x + 3y = 1$

$$\frac{x}{\frac{1}{2}} + \frac{y}{\frac{1}{3}} = 1$$

The x intercept is $\frac{1}{2}$; the y intercept is $\frac{1}{3}$.

89. $3x = 5$

$$\frac{3x}{5} = 1$$

$$\frac{x}{\frac{5}{3}} = 1$$

The x-intercept is $\frac{5}{3}$; no y-intercept.

Problem Set 8.5.

1. $A = Kr^2$

3. $V = Kr^3$

5. $u = \dfrac{Kv}{w}$

7. $x = Ky^2$

    $x = 12$ when $y = 2$

    $12 = K(2)^2$

    $12 = 4K$

    $K = 3$

    $x = ?$ when $y = 5$

    $x = 3(5)^2$

    $x = 75$

9. $s = Kt^2g$

    $s = 36$ when $t = 2$, $g = 3$

    $36 = K(2)^2(3)$

    $36 = K(4)(3)$

    $36 = 12K$

    $3 = K$

    $s = ?$ when $t = \sqrt{2}$, $g = 32.2$

    $s = 3(\sqrt{2})^2(32.2)$

    $x = 193.2$

11. $F = Kd$

    $F = 10$ when d is 5

    $10 = K(5)$

    $2 = K$

    $F = ?$ when d is 10

    $F = 2(10)$

    $\quad = 20$

    It will require 20 lbs.of force.

13. $d = Kt^2$

    $d = 64.4$ when $t = 2$

    $\quad 64.4 = K(2)^2$

$64.4 = 4K$

$16.1 = K$

$d = ?$ when $t = 3$

$d = 16.1(3)^2$

$d = 144.9$

It will have fallen 144.9 ft.

15. $P = K\sqrt{L}$

    $P = \dfrac{1}{2}$ when $L = 16$

    $\dfrac{1}{2} = K\sqrt{16}$

    $\dfrac{1}{2} = 4K$

    $2(\dfrac{1}{2}) = 2(4K)$

    $1 = 8K$

    $\dfrac{1}{8} = K$

    $L = ?$ when $P = \dfrac{1}{4}$

    $\dfrac{1}{4} = \dfrac{1}{8}\sqrt{L}$

    $8(\dfrac{1}{4}) = 8(\dfrac{1}{8}\sqrt{L})$

    $2 = \sqrt{L}$

    $(2)^2 = (\sqrt{L})^2$

    $4 = L$

Checking 4,

LS: $\dfrac{1}{4}$

RS: $\dfrac{1}{8}\sqrt{4}$

$\quad = \dfrac{1}{8} \cdot 2$

$\quad = \dfrac{1}{4}$

4 checks.

The length of the pendulum is 4 in.

17. $S = Kv$

19. $V = K\ell wh$

21. $h = \dfrac{K\sqrt{g}}{d}$

23. $x = \dfrac{K}{y^2}$

    $x = 2$ when $y = 3$

      $2 = \dfrac{K}{3^2}$

    $9(2) = 9\left(\dfrac{K}{9}\right)$

      $18 = K$

    $x = ?$ when $y = 5$

    $x = \dfrac{18}{5^2}$

    $x = \dfrac{18}{25}$

25. $N = \dfrac{KL^2}{M^3}$

    $N = 9$ when $L = \sqrt{3}$, $M = 2$

      $9 = \dfrac{K(\sqrt{3})^2}{2^3}$

      $9 = \dfrac{3K}{8}$

    $8(9) = 8\left(\dfrac{3K}{8}\right)$

      $72 = 3K$

      $24 = K$

    $N = ?$ when $L = \dfrac{\sqrt{2}}{2}$ $M = \dfrac{3}{2}$

    $N = \dfrac{24\left(\dfrac{\sqrt{2}}{2}\right)^2}{\left(\dfrac{3}{2}\right)^3}$

    $= \dfrac{24\left(\dfrac{2}{4}\right)}{\dfrac{27}{8}}$

    $= 24\left(\dfrac{1}{2}\right)\left(\dfrac{8}{27}\right)$

    $= \dfrac{32}{9}$

  N is $\dfrac{32}{9}$.

27. $m_1 = \dfrac{K}{m_2}$

    $m_1 = \dfrac{2}{3}$ when $m_2 = -\dfrac{3}{2}$

    $\dfrac{2}{3} = \dfrac{K}{-\dfrac{3}{2}}$

    $-\dfrac{3}{2}\left(\dfrac{2}{3}\right) = -\dfrac{3}{2}\left(\dfrac{K}{-\dfrac{3}{2}}\right)$

      $-1 = K$

    $m_2 = ?$ when $m_1 = -\dfrac{3}{4}$

    $m_1 = \dfrac{-1}{-\dfrac{3}{4}}$

      $= -1 \cdot -\dfrac{4}{3}$

      $= \dfrac{4}{3}$

  The slope of the line is $\dfrac{4}{3}$.

29. $F = Kd$

    $F = 5$ when $d = 2$

      $5 = K(2)$

      $\dfrac{5}{2} = K$

    $F = ?$ when $d = 1$

    $F = \dfrac{5}{2}(1)$

    $= \dfrac{5}{2}$

  It will require $\dfrac{5}{2}$ lbs. of force.

Chapter Review.

1. $(1,1)$ and $(5,4)$

    $d = \sqrt{(1-5)^2 + (1-4)^2}$

      $= \sqrt{(-4)^2 + (-3)^2}$

      $= \sqrt{16+9}$

      $= \sqrt{25}$

      $= 5$

    $x = \dfrac{1+5}{2}$ $y = \dfrac{1+4}{2}$

      $= \dfrac{6}{2}$ $= \dfrac{5}{2}$

      $= 3$

The distance is 5; the midpoint is $(3,\frac{5}{2})$.

3. (2.1) and (1,3)

$$d = \sqrt{(2-1)^2+(1-3)^2}$$

$$= \sqrt{1^2+(-2)^2}$$

$$= \sqrt{1+4}$$

$$= \sqrt{5}$$

$$x = \frac{2+1}{2} \qquad y = \frac{1+3}{2}$$

$$= \frac{3}{2} \qquad\qquad = \frac{4}{2}$$

$$\qquad\qquad\qquad = 2$$

The distance is $\sqrt{5}$, the midpoint is $(\frac{3}{2},2)$.

5. (8,-3) and (9,-2)

$$d = \sqrt{(8-9)^2+[-3-(-2)]^2}$$

$$= \sqrt{(-1)^2+(-1)^2}$$

$$= \sqrt{1+1}$$

$$= \sqrt{2}$$

$$x = \frac{8+9}{2} \qquad y = \frac{-3+-2}{2}$$

$$= \frac{17}{2} \qquad\qquad = \frac{-5}{2}$$

The distance is $\sqrt{2}$, the midpoint is $(\frac{17}{2}, -\frac{5}{2})$.

7. 2x + 3y = 12

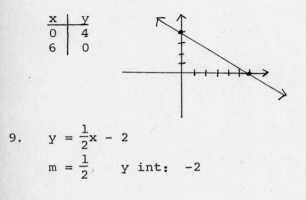

x	y
0	4
6	0

9. $y = \frac{1}{2}x - 2$

$m = \frac{1}{2}$ y int: -2

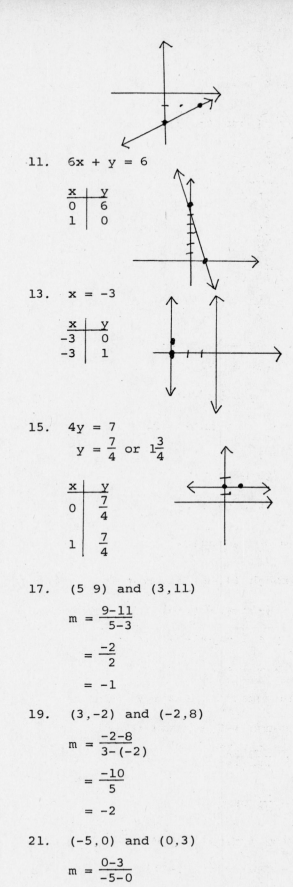

11. 6x + y = 6

x	y
0	6
1	0

13. x = -3

x	y
-3	0
-3	1

15. 4y = 7

$y = \frac{7}{4}$ or $1\frac{3}{4}$

x	y
0	$\frac{7}{4}$
1	$\frac{7}{4}$

17. (5 9) and (3,11)

$$m = \frac{9-11}{5-3}$$

$$= \frac{-2}{2}$$

$$= -1$$

19. (3,-2) and (-2,8)

$$m = \frac{-2-8}{3-(-2)}$$

$$= \frac{-10}{5}$$

$$= -2$$

21. (-5,0) and (0,3)

$$m = \frac{0-3}{-5-0}$$

$$= \frac{-3}{-5}$$

$$= \frac{3}{5}$$

23. $(-\frac{4}{3}, \frac{1}{2})$ and $(\frac{1}{3}, -\frac{5}{2})$

$$m = \frac{\frac{1}{2} - (-\frac{5}{2})}{-\frac{4}{3} - \frac{1}{3}}$$

$$= \frac{\frac{6}{2}}{\frac{-5}{3}}$$

$$= \frac{3}{1} \cdot -\frac{3}{5}$$

$$= -\frac{9}{5}$$

25. $2x - 3y = 6$

$$-3y = -2x + 6$$

$$y = \frac{2}{3}x - 2$$

$m = \frac{2}{3}$ y int: -2

27. $2y + 3 = 0$

$$2y = -3$$

$$y = 0x + -\frac{3}{2}$$

$m = 0$ y int: $-\frac{3}{2}$

29. Through $(4,-2)$ and $m = -1$

$$y - (-2) = -1(x-4)$$

$$y + 2 = -x + 4$$

$$x + y = 2$$

The equation is $x + y = 2$.

31. Through $(-9,-6)$ and $(-2,-1)$

$$m = \frac{-6-(-1)}{-9-(-2)}$$

$$= \frac{-5}{-7} \text{ or } \frac{5}{7}$$

Using $(-9,-6)$ and $m = \frac{5}{7}$

$$y - (-6) = \frac{5}{7}[x-(-9)]$$

$$y + 6 = \frac{5}{7}(x+9)$$

$$7(y+6) = 7[\frac{5}{7}(x+9)]$$

$$7y + 42 = 5(x+9)$$

$$7y + 42 = 5x + 45$$

$$5x - 7y = -3$$

The equation is $5x - 7y = -3$.

33. Through $(1,-7)$, $||$ to $2x + 3y = 4$

$$2x + 3y = 4$$

$$3y = -2x + 4$$

$$y = \frac{-2}{3}x + \frac{4}{3}$$

$$m = -\frac{2}{3}$$

Using $(1,-7)$ and $m = -\frac{2}{3}$

$$y - (-7) = -\frac{2}{3}(x-1)$$

$$y + 7 = -\frac{2}{3}(x-1)$$

$$3(y+7) = 3[-\frac{2}{3}(x-1)]$$

$$3y + 21 = -2(x-1)$$

$$3y + 21 = -2x + 2$$

$$2x + 3y = -19$$

The equation is $2x + 3y = -19$.

35. Through $(3,1)$, $\perp$ to $3x = 4y$

$$3x = 4y$$

$$y = \frac{3}{4}x$$

$$m_1 = \frac{3}{4} \text{ so } m_2 = \frac{-1}{\frac{3}{4}}$$

$$= -\frac{4}{3}$$

Using $(3,1)$ and $m_2 = -\frac{4}{3}$

$$y - 1 = -\frac{4}{3}(x-3)$$

$$3(y-1) = 3[-\frac{4}{3}(x-3)]$$

$$3y - 3 = -4(x-3)$$

$$3y - 3 = -4x + 12$$

$$4x + 3y = 15$$

The equation is $4x + 3y = 15$.

37. $u = Kv$

   $u = 8$ when $v = 4$

   $8 = K(4)$

   $K = 2$

   $u = ?$ when $v = 12$

   $u = 2v$

   $u = 2(12)$

   $= 24$

39. $F = \dfrac{K}{d^2}$

   $F = 50$ when $d = 12$

   $50 = \dfrac{K}{(12)^2}$

   $7200 = K$

   $F = \dfrac{7200}{d^2}$

   $F = ?$ when $d = 20$

   $F = \dfrac{7200}{(20)^2}$

   $= \dfrac{7200}{400}$

   $= 18$

   The force is 18 units.

41. $27 + a^3 = (3+a)(9-3a+a^2)$

43. $(q+r)^2$ is factored.

45. $(f-g)^2 - g = [(f-g)-3][(f-g]+3]$

   $= (f-g-3)(f-g+3)$

47. $y^3 - 7$ has two terms.

   $y - 7$ is not a factor.

49. $2y^2 - 11y - 21$ has three terms.

   $2y^2 - 11y - 21 = (2y+3)(y-7)$

   $y - 7$ is a factor.

51. $9^{-2} = \dfrac{1}{9^2}$

   $= \dfrac{1}{81}$

53. $(-9)^2 = -9 \cdot -9$

   $= 81$

55. $\sqrt{x^2-4}$ will not simplify.

57. $(a^{2/3}b^{3/2})^6 = (a^{2/3})^6 \cdot (b^{3/2})^6$

   $= a^4 b^9$

59. $\dfrac{x^2+y^2}{x^2-y^2}$ will not reduce.

61. $\dfrac{x}{x-1} - \dfrac{3}{1-x} = \dfrac{x}{x-1} - \dfrac{3}{-(x-1)}$

   $= \dfrac{x}{x-1} + \dfrac{3}{x-1}$

   $= \dfrac{x+3}{x-1}$

63. $\dfrac{\dfrac{3}{x^2-1}}{\dfrac{1}{x+1}-\dfrac{1}{x-1}} = \dfrac{\dfrac{3}{(x+1)(x-1)}}{\dfrac{1}{x+1}-\dfrac{1}{x-1}}$

   $= \dfrac{(x+1)(x-1)[\dfrac{3}{(x+1)(x-1)}]}{(x+1)(x-1)(\dfrac{1}{x+1}-\dfrac{1}{x-1})}$

   $= \dfrac{3}{(x-1)-(x+1)}$

   $= \dfrac{3}{x-1-x-1}$

   $= \dfrac{3}{-2}$ or $-\dfrac{3}{2}$

65. Expression

   $\dfrac{s-5}{2s-12} + \dfrac{s-4}{12-2s} = \dfrac{s-5}{2(s-6)} + \dfrac{s-4}{2(6-s)}$

   $= \dfrac{s-5}{2(s-6)} + \dfrac{s-4}{-2(s-6)}$

   $= \dfrac{s-5}{2(s-6)} - \dfrac{s-4}{2(s-6)}$

   $= \dfrac{s-6-(s-4)}{2(s-6)}$

   $= \dfrac{s-5-s+4}{2(s-6)}$

   $= \dfrac{-1}{2(s-6)}$ or $\dfrac{-1}{2s-12}$

67. $6x^2 - 5x < 6$

Find boundary numbers:

$6x^2 - 5x = 6$

$6x^2 - 5x - 6 = 0$

$(3x+2)(2x-3) = 0$

$3x + 2 = 0$ or $2x - 3 = 0$

$x = -\dfrac{2}{3}$ $\qquad$ $x = \dfrac{3}{2}$

Test regions: $\underline{A}$. $x = -1$

$6(-1)^2 - 5(-1) < 6$

$6 + 5 < 6$ is false.

$\underline{B}$, $x = 0$

$6(0)^2 - 5(0) < 6$

$0 - 0 < 6$ is true.

$\underline{C}$, $x = 2$

$6(2)^2 - 5(2) < 6$

$6(4) < 10 < 6$ is false.

Shade region that test true.

$\{x \mid -\dfrac{2}{3} < x < \dfrac{3}{2}\}$

69. $x^4 - 3x^2 - 4 = 0$

$(x^2-4)(x^2+1) = 0$

$x^2 - 4 = 0$ or $x^2 + 1 = 0$

$x^2 = 4$ $\qquad$ $x^2 = -1$

$x = \pm 2$ $\qquad$ $x = \pm i$

$\{\pm 2 \ \pm i\}$

Chapter Test.

1. $(2,-3)$ and $(-1,5)$

$d = \sqrt{[2-(-1)]^2 + [(-3)-5]^2}$

$= \sqrt{3^2 + (-8)^2}$

$= \sqrt{9+64}$

$= \sqrt{73}$

B.

2. $(5,-1)$ and $(2,4)$

$m = \dfrac{-1-4}{5-2}$

$= \dfrac{-5}{3}$

C.

3. Through $(3,7)$, $m = -\dfrac{2}{3}$

$y - 7 = -\dfrac{2}{3}(x-3)$

$3(y-7) = 3[-\dfrac{2}{3}(x-3)]$

$3y - 21 = -2(x-3)$

$3y - 21 = -2x + 6$

$2x + 3y = 27$

A.

4. Through $(0,0)$, $\perp$ to $3x - 4y = -1$

$3x - 4y = -1$

$-4y = -3x - 1$

$y = \dfrac{3}{4}x + \dfrac{1}{4}$

$m_2 = \dfrac{3}{4}$

$m_1 = -\dfrac{1}{\frac{3}{4}}$

$= \dfrac{-4}{3}$

Using $(0,0)$ and $m_1 = \dfrac{-4}{3}$

$y - 0 = \dfrac{-4}{3}(x-0)$

$y = \dfrac{-4}{3}x$

$-3(y) = -3(\dfrac{-4}{3}x)$

$-3y = 4x$

$4x + 3y = 0$

B.

251

5. $y = -3$ or $y = 0 \cdot x - 3$

    $m = 0$

    C.

6. $x = \dfrac{Kyz}{w^2}$

    C.

7. $x + 2y = 2$

x	y
0	1
2	0

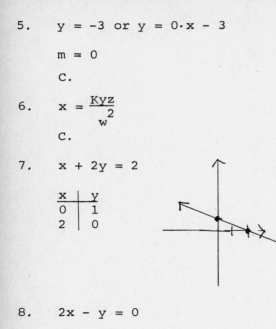

8. $2x - y = 0$

x	y
0	0
1	2

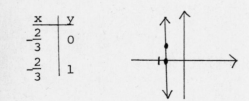

9. $x = -\dfrac{2}{3}$

x	y
$-\dfrac{2}{3}$	0
$-\dfrac{2}{3}$	1

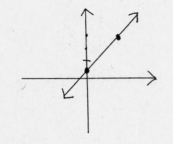

10. $y = \dfrac{3}{2}x + \dfrac{1}{2}$

    $m = \dfrac{3}{2}$ y int: $\dfrac{1}{2}$

11. Through $(-1,0)$

    $\parallel$ to line containing $(1,2)$ and $(3,4)$

    $m = \dfrac{2-4}{1-3}$

    $= \dfrac{-2}{-2}$

    $= 1$

    Using $(-1,0)$ and $m = 1$

    $y - 0 = 1[x-(-1)]$

    $y = x + 1$

    The equation is $x - y = -1$.

12. $\perp$ to x axis through $(-2,-3)$.
    Vertical line so no slope.
    The equation is $x = -2$.

13. $(5,-6)$ and $(-7,-1)$

    $d = \sqrt{[-6-(-1)]^2+[5-(-7)]^2}$

    $= \sqrt{(-5)^2+(12)^2}$

    $= \sqrt{25+144}$

    $= \sqrt{169}$

    $= 13$

14. $(5,-6)$ and $(-7,-1)$

    $x = \dfrac{5+-7}{2}$ $y = \dfrac{-6+-1}{2}$

    $= \dfrac{-2}{2}$ $= \dfrac{-7}{2}$

    $= -1$

    The midpoint is $(-1, -\dfrac{7}{2})$

15. Through $(3,0)$ and $(0,2)$

    $m = \dfrac{0-2}{3-0}$

    $= -\dfrac{2}{3}$

16. $5x + 3y = 7$

    $3y = -5x + 7$

$$y = \frac{-5}{3}x + \frac{7}{3}$$

$m = -\frac{5}{3}$ y int: $\frac{7}{3}$

17. $x = \frac{K\sqrt{y}}{z^2}$

$x = 6, \quad y = 9, \quad z = 2$

$6 = \frac{K\sqrt{9}}{(2)^2}$

$6 = \frac{3K}{4}$

$4(6) = 4\left(\frac{3K}{4}\right)$

$24 = 3K$

$8 = K$

$x = ?$ when $y = 16$, $z = 4$

$x = \frac{8\sqrt{y}}{z^2}$

$x = \frac{8\sqrt{16}}{(4)^2}$

$= \frac{8 \cdot 4}{16}$

$= \frac{32}{16}$

$= 2$

CHAPTER 9

Problem Set 9.1.

1. $\begin{cases} x - 2y = 0 \\ 2x + y = 5 \end{cases}$

$x = 2y$

So, $2(2y) + y = 5$

$4y + y = 5$

$5y = 5$

$y = 1$

$x = 2(1)$

$= 2$ $\{(2,1)\}$

3. $\begin{cases} 2x - y = 0 \\ x + 4y = 9 \end{cases}$

$x = 9 - 4y$

So, $2(9-4y) - y = 0$

$18 - 8y - y = 0$

$18 - 9y = 0$

$18 = 9y$

$2 = y$

$x = 9 - 4(2)$

$= 9 - 8$

$= 1$ $\{(1,2)\}$

5. $\begin{cases} 2x - 5y = 4 \\ 3x - 2y = -5 \end{cases}$

$2x - 5y = 4$

$2x = 4 + 5y$

$x = 2 + \frac{5}{2}y$

So, $3(2+\frac{5}{2}y) - 2y = -5$

$6 + \frac{15}{2}y - 2y = -5$

$6 + \frac{15}{2}y - \frac{4}{2}y = -5$

$6 + \frac{11}{2}y = -5$

$\frac{11}{2}y = -11$

$$2\left(\frac{11}{2}y\right) = 2(-11)$$

$$11y = -22$$

$$y = -2$$

$$x = 2 + \frac{5}{2}(-2)$$

$$= 2 + -5$$

$$= -3 \qquad \{(-3,-2)\}$$

7. $\begin{cases} x + y = 4 \\ 3x + 3y = 12 \end{cases}$

$$x = 4 - y$$

So, $3(4-y) + 3y = 12$

$$12 - 3y + 3y = 12$$

$$12 = 12 \quad \{(x,y) \mid x+y=4\}$$

9. $\begin{cases} \frac{1}{3}x - \frac{7}{4}y = 1 \\ 4x - 9y = 6 \end{cases}$

$$\frac{1}{3}x - \frac{3}{4}y = 1$$

$$12\left(\frac{1}{3}x - \frac{3}{4}y\right) = 12 \cdot 1$$

$$4x - 9y = 12$$

$$4x = 9y + 12$$

$$x = \frac{9}{4}y + 3$$

So, $4\left(\frac{9}{4}y+3\right) - 9y = 6$

$$9y + 12 - 9y = 6$$

$$12 = 6 \qquad \emptyset$$

11. $\begin{cases} x^2 - y = -1 \\ x - y = -1 \end{cases}$

$$x = y - 1$$

So $(y-1)^2 - y = -1$

$$y^2 - 2y + 1 - y = -1$$

$$y^2 - 3y + 2 = 0$$

$$(y-1)(y-2) = 0$$

$$y - 1 = 0 \text{ or } y - 2 = 0$$

$$y = 1 \text{ or } \qquad y = 2$$

$$y = 1, \qquad x = 1 - 1$$

$$= 0$$

$$y = 2 \qquad\qquad x = 2-1$$

$$= 1$$

$$\{(0,1),(1,2)\}$$

13. $\begin{cases} x + y = 1 \\ x - y = 3 \end{cases}$

$$\begin{array}{l} x + y = 1 \\ \underline{x - y = 3} \\ 2x \quad\;\; = 4 \end{array}$$

$$x = 2, \quad 2 - y = 3$$

$$-y = 1$$

$$y = -1 \qquad \{(2,-1)\}$$

15. $\begin{cases} 2x - y = -5 \\ 3x + 2y = 3 \end{cases}$

$$\begin{array}{l} 4x - 2y = -10 \\ \underline{3x + 2y = \quad 3} \\ 7x \qquad\;\; = -7 \end{array}$$

$$x = -1, \quad 2(-1) - y = -5$$

$$-2 - y = -5$$

$$-y = -3$$

$$y = 3 \quad \{(-1,3)\}$$

17. $\begin{cases} 3x + 2y = 5 \\ 6x - y = 0 \end{cases}$

$$\begin{array}{l} 3x + 2y = 5 \\ \underline{12x - 2y = 0} \\ 15x \qquad = 5 \end{array}$$

$$x = \frac{5}{15} \text{ or } \frac{1}{3}, \quad 3\left(\frac{1}{3}\right) + 2y = 5$$

$$1 + 2y = 5$$

$$2y = 4$$

$$y = 2$$

$$\left\{\left(\frac{1}{3},2\right)\right\}$$

19. $\begin{cases} 2x + 3y = 5 \\ 3x - 2y = 1 \end{cases}$

$$\begin{array}{l} 6x + 9y = 15 \\ \underline{-6x + 4y = -2} \\ 13y = 13 \end{array}$$

$$y = 1, \quad 2x + 3(1) = 5$$

$$2x + 3 = 5$$
$$2x = 2$$
$$x = 1 \quad \{(1,1)\}$$

21. $\begin{cases} 5x - 2y = 0 \\ 7x - 3y = -1 \end{cases}$

$$15x - 6y = 0$$
$$\underline{-14x + 6y = 2}$$
$$x = 2, \quad 5(2) - 2y = 0$$
$$-2y = -10$$
$$y = 5$$
$$\{(2,5)\}$$

23. $\begin{cases} \dfrac{4}{7}x - \dfrac{3}{5}y = 0 \\ -\dfrac{2}{5}x + \dfrac{1}{7}y = 0 \end{cases}$

$$35\left(\dfrac{4}{7}x - \dfrac{3}{5}y\right) = 35 \cdot 0$$
$$20x - 21y = 0$$
$$35\left(-\dfrac{2}{5}x + \dfrac{1}{7}y\right) = 35 \cdot 0$$
$$-14x + 5y = 0$$
$$5(20x - 21y) = 5 \cdot 0$$
$$21(-14x + 5y) = 14 \cdot 0$$

$$100x - 105y = 0$$
$$\underline{-294x + 105y = 0}$$
$$-194x \qquad = 0$$
$$x = 0 \quad \dfrac{4}{7}(0) - \dfrac{3}{5}y = 0$$
$$-\dfrac{3}{5}y = 0$$
$$y = 0$$
$$\{(0,0)\}$$

25. $\begin{cases} 6x - 4y = 23 \\ -9x + 6y = 12 \end{cases}$

$$36x - 24y = 128$$
$$\underline{-36x + 24y = 48}$$
$$0 = 186 \qquad \varnothing$$

27. $\begin{cases} \dfrac{2}{3}x + 8y = \dfrac{6}{7} \\ \dfrac{3}{4}x + 9y = 3 \end{cases}$

$$21\left(\dfrac{2}{3}x + 8y\right) = 21 \cdot \dfrac{6}{7}$$

$$14x + 168y = 18$$
$$4\left(\dfrac{3}{4}x + 9y\right) = 4 \cdot 3$$
$$3x + 36y = 12$$
$$-3(14x + 168y) = -3 \cdot 18$$
$$-42x - 504y = -54$$
$$14(3x + 36y) = 14 \cdot 12$$
$$42x + 504y = 168$$

$$42x + 504y = 168$$
$$\underline{-42x - 504y = -54}$$
$$0 = 114 \qquad \varnothing$$

29. x: 1st number   y: 2nd number

$\begin{cases} x - y = 18 \\ x + y = 0 \end{cases}$

$$x - y = 18$$
$$\underline{x + y = 0}$$
$$2x \quad = 18$$
$$x = 9, \quad 9 - y = 18$$
$$-y = 9$$
$$y = -9$$

The numbers are 9 and -9.

31. $\begin{cases} x + 2y = 5 \\ 2x - y = 0 \end{cases}$

$$x = 5 - 2y$$

$$\text{So, } 2(5 - 2y) - y = 0$$
$$10 - 4y - y = 0$$
$$10 - 5y = 0$$
$$10 = 5y$$
$$2 = y$$

$$x = 5 - 2(2)$$
$$= 5 - 4$$
$$= 1 \qquad \{(1,2)\}$$

33. $\begin{cases} 2x + y = 5 \\ x - 4y = -2 \end{cases}$

$$x = -2 + 4y$$

$$\text{So, } 2(-2 + 4y) + y = 5$$

$$-4 + 8y + y = 5$$
$$-4 + 9y = 5$$
$$9y = 9$$
$$y = 1$$

$$x = -2 + 4(1)$$
$$= -2 + 4$$
$$= 2 \qquad \{(2,1)\}$$

35. $\begin{cases} 2x + 5y = -10 \\ 3x - 2y = 4 \end{cases}$

$$2x = -5y - 10$$
$$x = \frac{-5}{2} - 5$$
So, $3(-\frac{5}{2}y-5) - 2y = 4$
$$-\frac{15}{2}y - 15 - 2y = 4$$
$$2(-\frac{15}{2}y-15-2y) = 2(4)$$
$$-15y - 30 - 4y = 8$$
$$-19y - 30 = 8$$
$$-19y = 38$$
$$y = -2$$
$$2x + 5(-2) = -10$$
$$2x + -10 = -10$$
$$2x = 0$$
$$x = 0 \qquad \{(0,-2)\}$$

37. $\begin{cases} 4x - 5y = -8 \\ 2x + 3y = 7 \end{cases}$

$$2x + 3y = 7$$
$$2x = -3y + 7$$
$$x = -\frac{3}{2}y + \frac{7}{2}$$
So, $4(-\frac{3}{2}y+\frac{7}{2}) - 5y = -8$
$$-6y + 14 - 5y = -8$$
$$-11y + 14 = -8$$
$$-11y = -22$$
$$y = 2$$

$$2x + 3(2) = 7$$
$$2x + 6 = 7$$

$$2x = 1$$
$$x = \frac{1}{2} \qquad \{(\frac{1}{2},2)\}$$

39. $\begin{cases} 4x + 6y = 1 \\ 2x + 3y = 2 \end{cases}$

$$2x + 3y = 2$$
$$2x = -3y + 2$$
$$x = -\frac{3}{2}y + 1$$
So, $4(-\frac{3}{2}y+1) + 6y = 1$
$$-6y + 4 + 6y = 1$$
$$4 = 1 \qquad \emptyset$$

41. $\begin{cases} 2x + 6y = 9 \\ 4x + y = 7 \end{cases}$

$$y = -4x + 7$$
So, $2x + 6(-4x+7) = 9$
$$2x - 24x + 42 = 9$$
$$-22x = -33$$
$$x = \frac{-33}{-22} \text{ or } \frac{3}{2}$$

$$2(\frac{3}{2}) + 6y = 9$$
$$3 + 6y = 9$$
$$6y = 6$$
$$y = 1 \qquad \{(\frac{3}{2},1)\}$$

43. $\begin{cases} 2x - y = 4 \\ 6x - 3y = 8 \end{cases}$

$$2x - y = 4$$
$$-y = -2x + 4$$
$$y = 2x - 4$$

So, $6x - 3(2x-4) = 8$
$$6x - 6x + 12 = 8$$
$$12 = 8 \qquad \emptyset$$

45. $\begin{cases} x - 2y = 0 \\ 3x - 4y = 0 \end{cases}$

$$x - 2y = 0$$

$x = 2y$

So, $3(2y) - 4y = 0$

$6y - 4y = 0$

$2y = 0$

$y = 0$

$x - 2(0) = 0$

$x - 0 = 0$

$x = 0 \qquad \{(0,0)\}$

47. $\begin{cases} x + y = 3 \\ xy = 2 \end{cases}$

$x + y = 3$

$x = 3 - y$

So, $(3-y)y = 2$

$3y - y^2 = 2$

$0 = y^2 - 3y + 2$

$0 = (y-1)(y-2)$

$y - 1 = 0$ or $y - 2 = 0$

$y = 1 \qquad y = 2$

$x + 1 = 3 \qquad x + 2 = 3$

$x = 2 \qquad x = 1$

$\{(1,2),(2,1)\}$

49. $\begin{cases} 2x - y = 7 \\ 3x + y = 8 \end{cases}$

$\begin{array}{l} 2x - y = 7 \\ \underline{3x + y = 8} \\ 5x \quad\;\; = 15 \end{array}$

$x = 3$

$2(3) - y = 7$

$6 - y = 7$

$-y = 1$

$y = -1 \qquad \{(3,-1)\}$

51. $\begin{cases} 3x + y = 5 \\ 4x - 2y = 10 \end{cases}$

$2(3x+y) = 2 \cdot 5$

$6x + 2y = 10$

So, $\begin{array}{l} 4x - 2y = 10 \\ \underline{6x + 2y = 10} \\ 10x \qquad = 20 \end{array}$

$x = \;\; 2$

$3(2) + y = 5$

$6 + y = 5$

$y = -1 \qquad \{(2,-1)\}$

53. $\begin{cases} 2x - 3y = -5 \\ 3x + y = -2 \end{cases}$

$3(3x+y) = 3 \cdot -2$

$9x + 3y = -6$

So, $\begin{array}{l} 2x - 3y = -5 \\ \underline{9x + 3y = -6} \\ 11x \qquad = -11 \end{array}$

$x = -1$

$2(-1) - 3y = -5$

$-2 - 3y = -5$

$-3y = -3$

$y = 1 \qquad \{(-1,1)\}$

55. $\begin{cases} 2x - 3y = -3 \\ 3x + 2y = 15 \end{cases}$

$2(2x-3y) = 2 \cdot -3$

$4x - 6y = -6$

$3(3x+2y) = 3 \cdot 15$

$9x + 6y = 45$

So, $\begin{array}{l} 4x - 6y = -6 \\ \underline{9x + 6y = 45} \\ 13x \qquad = 39 \end{array}$

$x = 3$

$2(3) - 3y = -3$

$6 - 3y = -3$

$-3y = -9$

$y = 3 \qquad \{(3,3)\}$

57. $\begin{cases} 7x + 4y = -1 \\ 9x - 6y = -5 \end{cases}$

$3(7x+4y) = 3 \cdot -1$

$21x + 12y = -3$

$2(9x-6y) = 2 \cdot -5$

$18x - 12y = -10$

So, $21x + 12y = -3$

$\underline{18x - 12y = -10}$

$39x \quad\quad = -13$

$x = -\dfrac{13}{39}$ or $-\dfrac{1}{3}$

$9(-\dfrac{1}{3}) - 6y = -5$

$-3 - 6y = -5$

$-6y = -2$

$y = \dfrac{-2}{-6}$ or $\dfrac{1}{3}$

$\{(-\dfrac{1}{3}, \dfrac{1}{3})\}$

59. $\begin{cases} 5x - 2y = 0 \\ 3x - 7y = 0 \end{cases}$

$3(5x-2y) = 3 \cdot 0$

$15x - 6y = 0$

$-5(3x-7y) = -5 \cdot 0$

$15x + 35y = 0$

So, $15x - 6y = 0$

$\underline{-15x + 35y = 0}$

$29y = 0$

$y = 0$

$5x - 2(0) = 0$

$5x - 0 = 0$

$5x = 0$

$x = 0 \qquad\qquad \{(0,0)\}$

61. $\begin{cases} 3x + 4y = 0 \\ 4x + 3y = 0 \end{cases}$

$4(3x+4y) = 4 \cdot 0$

$12x + 16y = 0$

$-3(4x+3y) = -3 \cdot 0$

$-12x - 9y = 0$

So, $12x + 16y = 0$

$\underline{-12x - 9y = 0}$

$7y = 0$

$y = 0$

$3x + 4(0) = 0$

$3x + 0 = 0$

$3x = 0$

$x = 0 \qquad\qquad \{(0,0)\}$

63. $\begin{cases} 6x - 5y = 6 \\ 9x + 7y = -20 \end{cases}$

$7(6x-5y) = 7 \cdot 6$

$42x - 35y = 42$

$5(9x+7y) = 5 \cdot -20$

$45x + 35y = -100$

So, $42x - 35y = 42$

$\underline{45x + 35y = -100}$

$87x \quad\quad = -58$

$x = \dfrac{-58}{87}$ or $-\dfrac{2}{3}$

$6(-\dfrac{2}{3}) - 5y = 6$

$-4 - 5y = 6$

$-5y = 10$

$y = -2 \qquad \{(-\dfrac{2}{3}, -2)\}$

65. $\begin{cases} -4x + 15y = -2 \\ 12x + 5y = -4 \end{cases}$

$3(-4x+15y) = 3 \cdot -2$

$-12x + 45y = -6$

So, $-12x + 45y = -6$

$\underline{12x + 5y = -4}$

$50y = -10$

$y = \dfrac{-10}{50}$ or $-\dfrac{1}{5}$

$-4x + 15(-\dfrac{1}{5}) = -2$

$-4x + -3 = -2$

$-4x = 1$

$x = \dfrac{1}{-4} \qquad \{(-\dfrac{1}{4}, -\dfrac{1}{5})\}$

67. $\begin{cases} 3x - 4y = 5 \\ 4x - 7y = 9 \end{cases}$

$4(3x-4y) = 4 \cdot 5$

$12x - 16y = 20$

$-3(4x-7y) = -3 \cdot 9$

$-12x + 21y = -27$

So, $12x - 16y = 20$

$\underline{-12x + 21y = -27}$

$5y = -7$

$y = -\dfrac{7}{5}$

$3x - 4(-\dfrac{7}{5}) = 5$

$3x + \dfrac{28}{5} = 5$

$5(3x+\dfrac{28}{5}) = 5 \cdot 5$

$15x + 28 = 25$

$15x = -3$

$x = -\dfrac{3}{15} \text{ or } -\dfrac{1}{5}$

$\{(-\dfrac{1}{5}, -\dfrac{7}{5})\}$

69. $\begin{cases} 17x - 11y = -1 \\ -34x + 22y = 2 \end{cases}$

$2(17x-11y) = 2 \cdot -1$

$34x - 22y = -2$

So, $34x - 22y = -2$

$\underline{-34x + 22y = 2}$

$0 = 0$

$\{(x,y) \mid 17x-11y=-1\}$

71. $\begin{cases} \dfrac{1}{5}x - \dfrac{2}{3}y = \dfrac{1}{15} \\ \dfrac{3}{4}x - \dfrac{5}{6}y = \dfrac{1}{3} \end{cases}$

$-15(\dfrac{1}{5}x-\dfrac{2}{3}y) = -15 \cdot \dfrac{1}{15}$

$-3x + 10y = -1$

$12(\dfrac{3}{4}x-\dfrac{5}{6}y) = 12 \cdot \dfrac{1}{3}$

$9x - 10y = 4$

So, $-3x + 10y = -1$

$\underline{9x - 10y = 4}$

$6x = 3$

$x = \dfrac{3}{6} \text{ or } \dfrac{1}{2}$

$\dfrac{1}{5}(\dfrac{1}{2}) - \dfrac{2}{3}y = \dfrac{1}{15}$

$\dfrac{1}{10} - \dfrac{2}{3}y = \dfrac{1}{15}$

$30(\dfrac{1}{10} - \dfrac{2}{3}y) = 30 \cdot \dfrac{1}{15}$

$3 - 20y = 2$

$-20y = -1$

$y = \dfrac{-1}{-20} = \dfrac{1}{20} \quad \{(\dfrac{1}{2}, \dfrac{1}{20})\}$

73. $\begin{cases} \dfrac{2}{7}x + \dfrac{2}{5}y = \dfrac{3}{7} \\ \dfrac{3}{5}x + \dfrac{7}{3}y = \dfrac{5}{2} \end{cases}$

$35(\dfrac{2}{7}x+\dfrac{2}{5}y) = 35 \cdot \dfrac{3}{7}$

$10x + 14y = 15$

$30(\dfrac{3}{5}x+\dfrac{7}{3}y) = 30 \cdot \dfrac{5}{2}$

$18x + 70y = 75$

$-5(10x+14y) = -5 \cdot 15$

$-50x-70y = -75$

So, $18x + 70y = 75$

$\underline{-50x - 70y = -75}$

$-32x = 0$

$x = 0$

$\dfrac{2}{7}(0) + \dfrac{2}{5}y = \dfrac{3}{7}$

$\dfrac{2}{5}y = \dfrac{3}{7}$

$35(\dfrac{2}{5}y) = 35(\dfrac{3}{7})$

$14y = 15$

$y = \dfrac{15}{14} \quad \{(0, \dfrac{15}{14})\}$

75. $\begin{cases} \dfrac{3}{8}x - \dfrac{1}{9}y = 0 \\ \dfrac{9}{2}x - \dfrac{5}{3}y = 0 \end{cases}$

$-72(\dfrac{3}{8}x-\dfrac{1}{9}y) = -72 \cdot 0$

$$-27x + 8y = 0$$

$$6\left(\tfrac{9}{2}x - \tfrac{5}{3}y\right) = 6 \cdot 0$$

$$27x - 10y = 0$$

So,
$$-27x + 8y = 0$$
$$\underline{27x - 10y = 0}$$
$$-2y = 0$$
$$y = 0$$

$$\tfrac{3}{8}x - \tfrac{1}{9}(0) = 0$$

$$\tfrac{3}{8}x = 0$$

$$x = 0 \qquad \{(0,0)\}$$

77. $\begin{cases} 3x^2 - 2y^2 = 4 \\ 2x - y^2 = 0 \end{cases}$

$$-2(2x - y^2) = 0 \cdot -2$$

$$-4x + 2y^2 = 0$$
$$\underline{3x^2 \qquad - 2y^2 = 4}$$
$$3x^2 - 4x \qquad = 4$$

$$3x^2 - 4x - 4 = 0$$

$$(3x+2)(x-2) = 0$$

$$3x + 2 = 0 \quad \text{or} \quad x - 2 = 0$$
$$x = -\tfrac{2}{3} \qquad\qquad x = 2$$

$$2\left(-\tfrac{2}{3}\right) - y^2 = 0 \quad 2(2) - y^2 = 0$$

$$-\tfrac{4}{3} = y^2 \qquad\quad 4 - y^2 = 0$$

No solution $\qquad\qquad y^2 = 4$

$$y = \pm 2$$

$$\{(2,-2),(2,2)\}$$

79. $\begin{cases} x^2 + y^2 = 1 \\ x^2 - y = 1 \end{cases}$

$$x^2 - y = 1$$

$$-y = 1 - x^2$$

$$y = -(1-x^2) \quad \text{or} \quad x^2 - 1$$

So, $x^2 + (x^2-1)^2 = 1$

$$x^2 + x^4 - 2x^2 + 1 = 1$$

$$x^4 - x^2 + 1 = 1$$

$$x^4 - x^2 = 0$$

$$x^2(x^2-1) = 0$$

$$x^2 = 0 \quad \text{or} \quad x^2 - 1 = 0$$

$$x = 0 \qquad\qquad x^2 = 1$$

$$x = \pm 1$$

$$0^2 - y = 1 \quad 1^2 - y = 1 \quad (-1)^2 - y = 1$$

$$-y = 1 \qquad 1 - y = 1 \qquad 1 - y = 1$$

$$y = -1 \quad\; -y = 0 \qquad\quad -y = 0$$

$$y = 0 \qquad\qquad y = 0$$

$$\{(0,-1),(1,0)\ (-1,0)\}$$

81. x: larger number   y: smaller number

$$x - y = 2$$

$$3x + 5y = 94$$

$$5(x-y) = 5 \cdot 2$$

$$5x - 5y = 10$$

So,
$$5x - 5y = 10$$
$$\underline{3x + 5y = 94}$$
$$8x \qquad = 104$$
$$x = 13$$

$$13 - y = 2$$

$$-y = -11$$

$$y = 11$$

The numbers are 11 and 13.

83. x: 1st number   y: 2nd number

other number: $2\left(\tfrac{x+y}{3}\right)$ or $x + y$

$$x + y + (x+y) = 68$$

$$x - y = 20$$

$$2x + 2y = 68$$

$$2(x-y) = 2(20)$$

$$2x + 2y = 68$$
$$\underline{2x - 2y = 40}$$
$$4x \qquad = 108$$

$$x = 27$$

$$x - y = 20$$

$$27 - y = 20$$

$$-y = -7$$
$$y = 7$$

$$x + y = 34$$

The numbers are 7, 27, and 34.

85. $\begin{cases} \dfrac{3}{x} + \dfrac{4}{4} = 5 \\ \dfrac{6}{x} + \dfrac{5}{4} = 7 \end{cases}$

Let $u = \dfrac{1}{x}$ and $v = \dfrac{1}{y}$

$$3u + 4v = 5$$
$$6u + 5v = 7$$

$$-2(3u+4v) = -2 \cdot 5$$
$$-6u - 8v = -10$$

$$-6u - 8v = -10$$
$$\underline{6u + 5v = 7}$$
$$-3v = -3$$
$$v = 1$$

$$3u + 4(1) = 5$$
$$3u = 1$$
$$u = \dfrac{1}{3}$$

$v = 1$ and $y = \dfrac{1}{v}$ so $y = 1$

$u = \dfrac{1}{3}$ and $x = \dfrac{1}{u}$ so $x = 3$ $\{(3,1)\}$

Problem Set 9.2.

1. $\begin{cases} x + y + z = 6 \\ x + 2y - z = 2 \\ 2x - 2y + z = 1 \end{cases}$

$\begin{array}{ll} x + y + z = 6 & x + 2y - z = 2 \\ \underline{x + 2y - z = 2} & \underline{2x - 2y + z = 1} \\ 2x + 3y \quad\;\; = 8 & 3x \qquad\quad = 3 \\ & \qquad\quad\; x = 1 \end{array}$

$$2(1) + 3y = 8$$
$$3y = 6$$
$$y = 2$$

$$1 + 2 + z = 6$$

$$z = 3 \qquad \{(1,2,3)\}$$

3. $\begin{cases} 2x - y + 2z = 2 \\ -2x + 3y + 4z = 10 \\ -2x + y - z = 0 \end{cases}$

$\begin{array}{ll} 2x - y + 2z = 2 & 2x - y + 2z = 2 \\ \underline{-2x +3y + 4z = 10} & \underline{-2x + y - z = 0} \\ 2y + 6z = 12 & z = 2 \end{array}$

$$2y + 6(2) = 12$$
$$2y = 0$$
$$y = 0$$

$$2x - 0 + 2(2) = 2$$
$$2x + 4 = 2$$
$$2x = -2$$
$$x = -2 \quad \{(-1,0,2)\}$$

5. $\begin{cases} x + 2y + 3z = 1 \\ 2x - 2y - 3z = -1 \\ 3x + y + 6z = 2 \end{cases}$

$\begin{array}{l} x + 2y + 3z = 1 \\ \underline{2x - 2y - 3z = -1} \\ 3x \qquad\qquad\; = 0 \\ \qquad\quad x = 0 \end{array}$

$$2(3x+y+6z) = 2 \cdot 2$$
$$6x + 2y + 12z = 4$$
$$\underline{2x - 2y - 3z = -1}$$
$$8x + \qquad 9z = 3$$

$$8(0) + 9z = 3$$
$$9z = 3$$
$$z = \dfrac{3}{9} \text{ or } \dfrac{1}{3}$$

$$0 + 2y + 3(\tfrac{1}{3}) = 1$$
$$2y + 1 = 1$$
$$2y = 0$$
$$y = 0 \quad \{(0,0,\tfrac{1}{3})\}$$

7. $\begin{cases} 3x + 3y - z = 5 \\ x + y + z = 5 \\ -2x - 2y + z = -3 \end{cases}$

$$3x + 3y - z = 5 \qquad 3x + 3y - z = 5$$
$$\underline{x + y + z = 5} \qquad \underline{-2x - 2y + z = -3}$$
$$4x + 4y = 10 \qquad x + y = 2$$
$$-4(x+y) = -4 \cdot 2$$

$$4x + 4y = 10$$
$$\underline{-4x - 4y = -8}$$
$$0 = 2 \qquad\qquad \emptyset$$

9. $\begin{cases} 3x - 5y - 2z = 9 \\ x - y + 2z = 1 \\ 2x - 3y = 1 \end{cases}$

$$3x - 5y - 2z = 9 \qquad -2(2x-3y) = -2 \cdot 1$$
$$\underline{x - y + 2z = 1} \qquad\qquad -4x + 6y = -2$$
$$4x - 6y = 10$$

$$4x - 6y = 10$$
$$\underline{-4x + 6y = -2}$$
$$0 = 8 \qquad\qquad \emptyset$$

11. $\begin{cases} x + y + z = 6 \\ x + 2y + z = 9 \\ 2x + 2y - z = 6 \end{cases}$

$$x + y + z = 6 \qquad x + 2y + z = 9$$
$$\underline{2x + 2y - z = 6} \qquad \underline{2x + 2y - z = 6}$$
$$3x + 3y = 12 \qquad 3x + 4y = 15$$

$$-1(3x+4y) = -1 \cdot 15$$

$$-3x - 4y = -15$$
$$\underline{3x + 3y = 12}$$
$$-y = -3$$
$$y = 3$$

$$3x + 3(3) = 12$$
$$3x = 3$$
$$x = 1$$

$$1 + 3 + z = 6$$
$$z = 2 \qquad\qquad \{(1,3,2)\}$$

13. $\begin{cases} 3x + y + 2z = 10 \\ -3x - 2y + 4z = -11 \\ 2y + z = 2 \end{cases}$

$$3x + y + 2z = 10$$
$$\underline{-3x - 2y + 4z = -11}$$
$$-y + 6z = -1$$

$$2(-y+6z) = 2(-1)$$
$$-2y + 12z = -2$$
$$\underline{2y + z = 2}$$
$$13z = 0$$
$$z = 0$$

$$2y + 6(0) = 2$$
$$2y = 2$$
$$y = 1$$

$$3x + 1 + 2(0) = 10$$
$$3x = 9$$
$$x = 3 \qquad \{(3,1,0)\}$$

15. $\begin{cases} 3x + 3y - z = 3 \\ 5x + y + 3z = 1 \\ 2x + 4y - 3z = 4 \end{cases}$

$$5x + y + 3z = 1$$
$$\underline{2x + 4y - 3z = 4}$$
$$7x + 5y = 5$$

$$3(3x+3y-z) = 3 \cdot 3$$
$$9x + 9y - 3z = 9$$
$$\underline{5x + y + 3z = 1}$$
$$14x + 10y = 10$$

$$-2(7x+5y) = -2(5)$$

$$-14x - 10y = -10$$
$$\underline{14x + 10y = 10}$$
$$0 = 0$$

Dependent system.

17. $\begin{cases} 2x + 2y - z = 1 \\ x + 2y - 3z = 4 \\ 5x + 6y - 5z = 3 \end{cases}$

$$-3(2x+2y-z) = -3 \cdot 1$$

$$-6x - 6y + 3z = -3$$
$$\underline{5x + 6y - 5z = 3}$$
$$-x - 2z = 0$$

$$-3(x+2y-3z) = -3\cdot 4$$

$$-3x - 6y + 9z = -12$$
$$\underline{5x + 6y - 5z = 3}$$
$$2x +   4z = -9$$

$$2(-x-2z) = 2\cdot 0$$

$$-2x - 4z = 0$$
$$\underline{2x + 4z = -9}$$
$$\ 0 = -9 \qquad \emptyset$$

19. $\begin{cases} 3x + y - z = 8 \\ 2x - y + 2z = 3 \\ x + 2y - 3z = 5 \end{cases}$

$$3x + y - z = 8$$
$$\underline{2x - y + 2z = 3}$$
$$5x + z = 11$$

$$2(2x-y+2z) = 2\cdot 3$$

$$4x - 2y + 4z = 6$$
$$\underline{x + 2y - 3z = 5}$$
$$5x + z = 11$$

$$-(5x+z) = -11$$

$$-5x - z = -11$$
$$\underline{5x + z = 11}$$
$$\ 0 = 0$$

Dependent system.

21. $\begin{cases} 2x - 3y - 10z = 4 \\ 4x \ - 5z = 3 \\ \ 6y + 5z = -3 \end{cases}$

$$2(2x-3y-10z) = 2\cdot 4$$

$$4x - 6y - 20z = 8$$
$$\underline{\ 6y + 5z = -3}$$
$$4x - 15z = 5$$

$$-1(4x-15z) = -1\cdot 5$$

$$-4x + 15z = -5$$
$$\underline{4x - 5z = 3}$$
$$\ 10z = -2$$

$$z = \frac{-2}{10} \quad \text{or} \quad -\frac{1}{5}$$

$$4x - 5\left(-\frac{1}{5}\right) = 3$$

$$4x + 1 = 3$$

$$4x = 2$$

$$x = \frac{2}{4} \quad \text{or} \quad \frac{1}{2}$$

$$2\left(\frac{1}{2}\right) - 3y - 10\left(-\frac{1}{5}\right) = 4$$

$$1 - 3y + 2 = 4$$

$$-3y = 1$$

$$y = -\frac{1}{3}$$

$$\left\{ \left(\frac{1}{2}, -\frac{1}{3}, -\frac{1}{5}\right) \right\}$$

23. $\begin{cases} 2x + 6y \ = 5 \\ \ 3y - z = 2 \\ -3x \ - 3z = 1 \end{cases}$

$$-2(3y-z) = -2\cdot 2$$

$$- 6y + 2z = -4$$
$$\underline{2x + 6y \ = 5}$$
$$2x \ + 2z = 1$$

$$3(2x+2z) = 3\cdot 1$$

$$6x + 6z = 3$$
$$2(-3x-3z) = 2\cdot 1$$

$$-6x - 6z = 2$$
$$\underline{6x + 6z = 3}$$
$$\ 0 = 5 \qquad \emptyset$$

25. $\begin{cases} 2x - 3y \ = 6 \\ \ - 2y - 3z = 4 \\ 3x \ - 2z = 0 \end{cases}$

$$-2(2x-3y) = -2\cdot 6$$

$$-4x + 6y \ = -12$$
$$\underline{\ - 6y - 9z = 12}$$
$$-4x - 9z = 0$$

$$3(-2y-3z) = 3\cdot 4$$

$$-6y - 9z = 12$$

$$3(-4x-9z) = 3\cdot 0$$

$$4(3x-2z) = 4 \cdot 0$$
$$12x - 8z = 0$$
$$-12x - 27z = 0$$
$$\underline{12x - 8z = 0}$$
$$-35z = 0$$
$$z = 0$$
$$3x - 2(0) = 0$$
$$3x = 0$$
$$x = 0$$
$$2(0) - 3y = 6$$
$$-3y = 6$$
$$y = -2 \qquad \{(0,-2,0)\}$$

27. $\begin{cases} x + y - z = -8 \\ 4x + 5y - 6z = -2 \\ 2x + 3y - 4z = 14 \end{cases}$

$$-4(x+y-z) = -4 \cdot -8$$

$$-4x - 4y + 4z = 32$$
$$\underline{4x + 5y - 6z = -2}$$
$$y - 2z = 30$$

$$-2(x+y-z) = -2 \cdot -8$$

$$-2x - 2y + 2z = 16$$
$$\underline{2x + 3y - 4z = 14}$$
$$y - 2z = 30$$

$$-(y-2z) = -1.30$$

$$-y + 2z = -30$$
$$\underline{y - 2z = 30}$$
$$0 = 0$$

Dependent system.

29. $\begin{cases} 2x + 4y - z = 3 \\ x + y \quad\;\; = 1 \\ 2x + 3y + z = 2 \end{cases}$

$$2x + 4y - z = 3$$
$$\underline{2x + 3y + z = 2}$$
$$4x + 7y = 5$$

$$-4(x+y) = -4 \cdot 1$$

$$-4x - 4y = -4$$

$$4x + 7y = 5$$
$$\underline{-4x - 4y = -4}$$
$$3y = 1$$
$$y = \frac{1}{3}$$

$$x + \frac{1}{3} = 1$$
$$x = \frac{2}{3}$$
$$2\left(\frac{2}{3}\right) + 4\left(\frac{1}{3}\right) - z = 3$$
$$\frac{4}{3} + \frac{4}{3} - z = 3$$
$$\frac{8}{3} - z = 3$$
$$3\left(\frac{8}{3} - z\right) = 3 \cdot 3$$
$$8 - 3z = 9$$
$$-3z = 1$$
$$z = -\frac{1}{3}$$
$$\left\{ \left(\frac{2}{3}, \frac{1}{3}, -\frac{1}{3}\right) \right\}$$

31. $\begin{cases} 3x - 2y - z = 4 \\ x + 4y + 2z = -1 \\ 2x - 4y - 3z = 6 \end{cases}$

$$x + 4y + 2z = -1$$
$$\underline{2x - 4y - 3z = 6}$$
$$3x - \quad z = 5$$

$$2(3x-2y-z) = 2 \cdot 4$$

$$6x - 4y - 2z = 8$$
$$\underline{x + 4y + 2z = -1}$$
$$7x \qquad\quad = 7$$
$$x = 1$$

$$3(1) - z = 5$$
$$-z = 2$$
$$z = -2$$

$$3(1) - 2y - (-2) = 4$$
$$3 - 2y + 2 = 4$$
$$-2y + 5 = 4$$
$$-2y = -1$$
$$y = \frac{1}{2} \qquad \left\{\left(1, \frac{1}{2}, -2\right)\right\}$$

33. x: 1st number   y: 2nd number

z: 3rd number

$$\begin{cases} x + y \quad\;\; = 6 \\ x + \quad\; z = 7 \\ x + y + z = 12 \end{cases}$$

$-1(x+y) = -1\cdot 6$

$-x - y = -6$

$\quad\; -x - y \qquad = -6$

$\quad\;\; \underline{x + y + z = 12}$

$\qquad\qquad\quad z = 6$

$x + 6 = 7$

$\quad\; x = 1$

$1 + y + 6 = 12$

$\quad y + 7 = 12$

$\qquad\quad y = 5$

The numbers are 1, 5, and 6.

35. x: 1st number   y: 2nd number

z: 3rd number

$$\begin{cases} x + y \quad\;\; = 1 \\ x + \quad\; z = 8 \\ x + y + z = 6 \end{cases}$$

$-1(x+y) = -1\cdot 1$

$-x - y = -1$

$\quad -x - y \qquad = -1$

$\quad\; \underline{x + y + z = 6}$

$\qquad\qquad\; z = 5$

$x + 5 = 8$

$\quad\; x = 3$

$3 + y + 5 = 6$

$\quad y + 8 = 6$

$\qquad\quad y = -2$

The numbers are 3, -2, and 5.

37. $x + y + z + w = 2$

$\quad x - y + 2z \qquad = -1$

$\qquad 2y + 3z - 3w = -9$

$2x - 3y \qquad\; + 2w = 6$

Eliminate y,

$x + y + \; z + w = 2$

$\underline{x - y + 2z \qquad = -1}$

$2x + \qquad 3z + w = 1$

Eliminate y again,

$-2(x+y+z+w) = -2\cdot 2$

$-2x - 2y - 2z - 2w = -4$

$\underline{\qquad\;\; 2y - 3z - 3w = -9}$

$-2x + \qquad\;\; z - 5w = -13$

Now eliminate x,

$\quad 2x + 3z + \; w = 1$

$\underline{-2x + \; z - 5w = -13}$

$\qquad\; 4z - 4w = -12$

$\quad \frac{1}{4}(4z-4w) = \frac{1}{4}\cdot -12$

$\qquad\quad z - w = -3$

Eliminate y,

$2(x-y+2z) = 2\cdot -1$

$2x - 2y + 4z \qquad\quad = -2$

$\underline{\qquad\; 2y + 3z - 3w = -9}$

$2x + \qquad 7z - 3w \; = -11$

Eliminate y again,

$3(x+y+z+w) = 3\cdot 2$

$3x + 3y + 3z + 3w = 6$

$\underline{2x - 3y \qquad\;\; + 2w = 6}$

$5x + \qquad 3z + 5w = 12$

Now eliminate x,

$-5(2x+7z-3w) = -5\cdot -11$

$-10x - 35z + 15w = 55$

$2(5x+3z+5w) = 2\cdot 12$

265

$$10x + 6z + 10w = 24$$
$$\underline{-10x - 35z + 15w = 55}$$
$$-29z + 25w = 79$$

Now solve,

$$\begin{cases} z - w = -3 \\ -29z + 25w = 79 \end{cases}$$

Eliminate w,

$$25(z-w) = 25 \cdot -3$$

$$25z - 25w = -75$$
$$\underline{-29z + 25w = 79}$$
$$-\ 4z = 4$$
$$z = -1$$

$$-1 - w = -3$$
$$-w = -2$$
$$w = 2$$

$$2x + 7(-1) - 3(2) = -11$$
$$2x - 7 - 6 = -11$$
$$2x - 13 = -11$$
$$2x = 2$$
$$x = 1$$

$$1 + y - 1 + 2 = 2$$
$$y + 2 = 2$$
$$y = 0 \qquad \{(1,0,-1,2)\}$$

39. $$\begin{cases} x + 2y - z = 2 \\ 2x + z + w = 9 \\ y - w = -2 \\ 3x + 4y = 11 \end{cases}$$

Eliminate z,

$$x + 2y - z = 2$$
$$\underline{2x + z + w = 9}$$
$$3x + 2y + w = 11$$

Eliminate x,

$$-(3x+4y) = -11$$

$$-3x - 4y -11$$
$$\underline{3x + 2y + w = 11}$$
$$2y + w = 0$$

Now solve,

$$\begin{cases} y - w = -2 \\ -2y + w = 0 \end{cases}$$

$$y - w = -2$$
$$\underline{-2y + w = 0}$$
$$-y = -2$$
$$y = 2$$

$$2 - w = -2$$
$$-w = -4$$
$$w = 4$$

$$3x + 4(2) = 11$$
$$3x + 8 = 11$$
$$3x = 3$$
$$x = 1$$

$$1 + 2(2) - z = 2$$
$$5 - z = 2$$
$$-z = -3$$
$$z = 3 \qquad \{(1,2,3,4)\}$$

Problem Set 9.3.

1.   x: number of liters of 17% sauce.

      y: number of liters of 30% sauce.

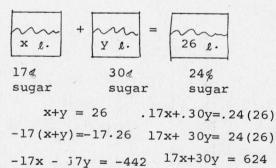

17%   30%   24%
sugar   sugar   sugar

$$x+y = 26 \qquad .17x+.30y=.24(26)$$
$$-17(x+y)=-17 \cdot 26 \quad 17x+ 30y= 24(26)$$
$$-17x - 17y = -442 \quad 17x+30y = 624$$
$$\underline{17x + 30y = 624}$$
$$13y = 182$$
$$y = 14$$

$$x + 14 = 26$$
$$x = 12$$

266

She should mix 12 ℓ. of 17% sauce
and 14 ℓ of 30% sauce.

3. x: price of a head of lettuce.

   y: price of a pound of tomatoes.

$$\begin{cases} 3x + 2y = 405 \\ 2x + 3y = 435 \end{cases}$$

$-2(3x+2y)=-2(405)$ $3(2x+3y)=3 \cdot 435$

$6x + 9y = 1305$

$-6x - 4y = -810$
$\underline{6x + 9y = 1305}$
$5y = 495$
$y = 99$

$3x + 2(99) = 405$

$3x + 198 = 405$

$3x = 207$

$x = 69$

The lettuce is 69¢ per head and
the tomatoes are 99¢ per pound.

5. x: one side y: other side

$$\begin{cases} 2x + 2y = 54 \\ \ x = 2y - 3 \end{cases}$$

$2(2y-3) + 2y = 54$

$4y - 6 + 2y = 54$

$6y - 6 = 54$

$6y = 60$

$y = 10$

$x = 2(10) - 3$

$x = 20 - 3$

$ = 17$

The dimensions of the lawn are
10 m. by 17m.

7. x: speed of the boat in still
     water.

   y: speed of the current

	D	R	T
down-stream	24	x+y	3
upstream	10	x−y	5

$3(x+y) = 24$

$5(x-y) = 10$

$3x + 3y = 24$ $5x - 5y = 10$

$5(3x+3y)=5 \cdot 24$ $3(5x-5y)=3 \cdot 10$

$15x-15y=30$

$15x + 15y = 120$
$\underline{15x - 15y = 30}$
$30x = 150$
$x = 5$

$3(5+y) = 24$

$15 + 3y = 24$

$3y = 9$

$y = 3$

The speed of the boat in still
water is 5 mph. The speed of
the current is 3 mph.

9. F: hours for Frank to mow,
     working alone.

   J: hours for Jack to mow,
     working alone.

$$\begin{cases} \dfrac{1}{F} + \dfrac{1}{J} = \dfrac{1}{4} \\ \dfrac{3}{F} + \dfrac{6}{J} = 1 \end{cases}$$

Let $x = \dfrac{1}{F}$, $y = \dfrac{1}{J}$

$x + y = \dfrac{1}{4}$

$3x + 6y = 1$

$-12(x+y) = -12 \cdot \dfrac{1}{4}$ $4(3x+6y) = 4 \cdot 1$

$12x + 24y = 4$

$-12x - 12y = -3$
$\underline{12x + 24y = 4}$
$12y = 1$
$y = \dfrac{1}{12}$

$$x + \frac{1}{12} = \frac{1}{4}$$

$$x = \frac{1}{4} - \frac{1}{12}$$

$$= \frac{3}{12} - \frac{1}{12}$$

$$= \frac{2}{12}$$

$$= \frac{1}{6}$$

$x = \frac{1}{6}$ so $F = 6$ $y = \frac{1}{12}$ so $J = 12$

It would take Frank 6 hours and Jack 12 hours working alone.

11.   x: 1st number   y: 2nd number

$$\begin{cases} x + y = 19 \\ x^2 + y^2 = 185 \end{cases}$$

$$x = 19 - y$$

$$(19-y)^2 + y^2 = 185$$
$$361 - 38y + y^2 + y^2 = 185$$
$$2y^2 - 38y + 361 = 185$$
$$2y^2 - 38y + 176 = 0$$
$$\frac{1}{2}(2y^2 - 38y + 176) = \frac{1}{2} \cdot 0$$
$$y^2 - 19y + 88 = 0$$
$$(y-8)(y-11) = 0$$

$y - 8 = 0$ or $y - 11 = 0$

$y = 8$ $y = 11$

$x = 11$ $x = 8$

The numbers are 8 and 11.

13.   x: price per pound for grapes
y: price per lemon

$$\begin{cases} 3x + 6y = 357 \\ 2x + 5y = 248 \end{cases}$$

$-2(3x+6y) = -2 \cdot 357$ $3(2x+5y) = 3 \cdot 248$
$$6x + 15y = 744$$

$$\begin{array}{r} -6x - 12y = -714 \\ \underline{6x + 15y = 744} \\ 3y = 30 \\ y = 10 \end{array}$$

$$3x + 6(10) = 357$$
$$3x + 60 = 357$$
$$3x = 297$$
$$x = 99$$

The grapes are 99¢ per pound and the lemons are 10¢ each.

15.   T: hours for Tom working alone.
R: hours for Randy working alone.

$$\begin{cases} 1 \text{ hr. } 12 \text{ min.} = 1\frac{12}{60} = 1\frac{1}{5} \text{ or } \frac{6}{5} \text{ hrs.} \\ 1 \text{ hr. } 48 \text{ min.} = 1\frac{48}{60} = 1\frac{4}{5} \text{ or } \frac{9}{5} \text{ hrs.} \\ 18 \text{ min.} = \frac{18}{60} = \frac{3}{10} \text{ hrs.} \end{cases}$$

$$\frac{1}{T} + \frac{1}{R} = \frac{1}{\frac{6}{5}}$$

$$\frac{\frac{9}{5}}{T} + \frac{\frac{3}{10}}{R} = 1$$

Let $x = \frac{1}{T}$ and $y = \frac{1}{R}$

$x + y = \frac{5}{6}$ $6(x+y) = 6 \cdot \frac{5}{6}$

$\frac{9}{5}x + \frac{3}{10}y = 1$ $6x + 6y = 5$

$$10\left(\frac{9}{5}x + \frac{3}{10}y\right) = 10 \cdot 1$$

$$18x + 3y = 10$$

$$\begin{array}{r} 18x + 3y = 10 \\ \underline{-18x - 18y = -15} \\ -15y = -5 \end{array}$$

$$y = \frac{-5}{-15} \text{ or } \frac{1}{3}$$

$$x + \frac{1}{3} = \frac{5}{6}$$

$$6\left(x+\frac{1}{3}\right) = 6 \cdot \frac{5}{6}$$

$$6x + 2 = 5$$

$$6x = 3$$

$$x = \frac{3}{6} \text{ or } \frac{1}{2}$$

$x = \frac{1}{2}$ so $T = 2$, $y = \frac{1}{3}$ so $R = 3$.

It would take Tom 2 hours and Randy 3 hours working alone.

17. x: width   y: length

$$\begin{cases} y = 4x \\ 2x + 2y = 1200 \end{cases}$$

$$2x + 2(4x) = 1200$$
$$2x + 8x = 1200$$
$$10x = 1200$$
$$x = 120$$
$$y = 4(120)$$
$$= 480$$

The pasture would be 120 ft. by 480 ft.

19. x: Bill's walking speed.

y: Carolyn's walking speed.

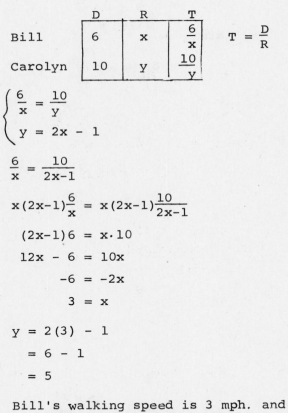

	D	R	T
Bill	6	x	$\frac{6}{x}$
Carolyn	10	y	$\frac{10}{y}$

$T = \frac{D}{R}$

$$\begin{cases} \frac{6}{x} = \frac{10}{y} \\ y = 2x - 1 \end{cases}$$

$$\frac{6}{x} = \frac{10}{2x-1}$$

$$x(2x-1)\frac{6}{x} = x(2x-1)\frac{10}{2x-1}$$

$$(2x-1)6 = x \cdot 10$$
$$12x - 6 = 10x$$
$$-6 = -2x$$
$$3 = x$$

$$y = 2(3) - 1$$
$$= 6 - 1$$
$$= 5$$

Bill's walking speed is 3 mph. and Carolyn's walking speed is 5 mph.

21. x: length of shortest side.

y: length of other sides.

$$\begin{cases} x = y - 3 \\ x + 2y = 48 \end{cases}$$

$$(y-3) + 2y = 48$$
$$3y - 3 = 48$$
$$3y = 51$$
$$y = 17$$
$$x = 17 - 3 = 14$$

The lengths of the sides are 14 inches, 17 inches, and 17 inches.

23. x: length   y: width

$$\begin{cases} xy = 216 \\ 2x + 2y = 60 \end{cases}$$

$$x = \frac{216}{y}$$

$$2\left(\frac{216}{y}\right) + 2y = 60$$

$$\frac{432}{y} + 2y = 60$$

$$y\left(\frac{432}{y}+2y\right) = y \cdot 60$$

$$432 + 2y^2 = 60y$$

$$2y^2 - 60y + 432 = 0$$

$$\frac{1}{2}(2y^2-60y+432) = \frac{1}{2} \cdot 0$$

$$y^2 - 30y + 216 = 0$$

$$(y-12)(y-18) = 0$$

$$y - 12 = 0 \quad \text{or} \quad y - 18 = 0$$

$$y = 12 \qquad\qquad y = 18$$

$$x = \frac{216}{12} \qquad\qquad x = \frac{216}{18}$$

$$x = 18 \qquad\qquad x = 12$$

The dimensions are 12 inches by 18 inches.

25. x: hours for $\frac{1}{4}$" pipe to empty the tank working alone, drain closed.

y: hours for $\frac{1}{2}$" pipe to empty the tank, working alone, drain closed

z: hours for drain to empty the tank. working alone.

$$40 \text{ min.} = \frac{40}{60} = \frac{2}{3} \text{ hrs.;}$$

12 min. $= \dfrac{12}{60} = \dfrac{1}{5}$ hrs.

$$\begin{cases} \dfrac{1}{x} + \dfrac{1}{y} = \dfrac{1}{\frac{1}{5}} \\[2mm] \dfrac{1}{y} - \dfrac{1}{2} = \dfrac{2}{3} \\[2mm] \dfrac{1}{x} - \dfrac{1}{2} = \dfrac{1}{2} \end{cases}$$

Let $A = \dfrac{1}{x}$, $B = \dfrac{1}{y}$, $C = \dfrac{1}{z}$

$A + B = 5$

$B - C = \dfrac{3}{2}$ $-(B-C) = -\dfrac{3}{2}$

$A - C = \dfrac{1}{2}$

$\begin{array}{l} A + B \qquad = 5 \\ \underline{\quad -B + C = -\dfrac{3}{2}} \\ A + \quad\; C = \dfrac{7}{2} \end{array}$

$\begin{array}{l} A + C = \dfrac{7}{2} \\ \underline{A - C = \dfrac{1}{2}} \\ 2A \quad\;\; = \dfrac{8}{2} \text{ or } 4 \end{array}$

$A = 2$

$2 - C = \dfrac{1}{2}$

$-C = \dfrac{1}{2} - 2$

$-C = -\dfrac{3}{2}$

$C = \dfrac{3}{2}$

So $z = \dfrac{2}{3}$ hrs or 40 minutes.

It takes the open drain 40 minutes to empty a full tank with the other pipes closed.

27. x: 1st number   y: 2nd number

z: 3rd number   w: 4th number

$$\begin{cases} x + y + z + w = 11 \\ 2x + \qquad z \qquad\; = 2 \\ 3x + \qquad 2z \qquad = 5 \\ \qquad 3y + \qquad 2w = 17 \end{cases}$$

Eliminate z,

$$\begin{cases} 2x + z = 2 \\ 3x + 2z = 5 \end{cases}$$

$-2(2x+z) = -2 \cdot 2$

$\begin{array}{l} -4x - 2z = -4 \\ \underline{3x - 2z = 5} \\ -\;x \qquad\;\; = 1 \\ \qquad\quad x = -1 \end{array}$

$2(-1) + z = 2$

$-2 + z = 2$

$z = 4$

$x = -1$, $z = 4$ so

$-1 + y + 4 + w = 11$

$y + w = 8$

Eliminate w,

$$\begin{cases} y + w = 8 \\ 3y + 2w = 17 \end{cases}$$

$-2(w+w) = -2 \cdot 8$

$\begin{array}{l} -2y - 2w = -16 \\ \underline{3y + 2w = 17} \\ y \qquad\quad = 1 \end{array}$

$1 + w = 8$

$w = 7$

The numbers are $-1, 1, 4,$ and 7.

Problem Set 9.4.

1. $x - y < 2$

Boundary line: $x - y = 2$ (not included).

x	y
0	-2
2	0

Test $(0,0)$

$0 - 0 < 2$ is true.

Shade region.

Test $(3,0)$

$3 - 0 < 2$ is false.

Do not shade region.

3. $y - \frac{1}{2}x > 4$

Boundary line: $y - \frac{1}{2}x = 4$ (not included).

x	y
0	4
-8	0

$-\frac{1}{2}x = 4$

$x = -8$

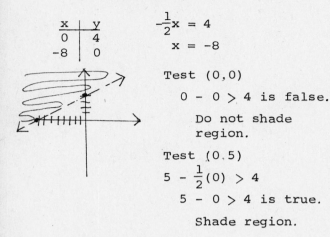

Test (0,0)

$0 - 0 > 4$ is false.

Do not shade region.

Test (0,5)

$5 - \frac{1}{2}(0) > 4$

$5 - 0 > 4$ is true.

Shade region.

5. $x - y \le 0$

Boundary line: $x - y = 0$ (include).

x	y
0	0
1	1

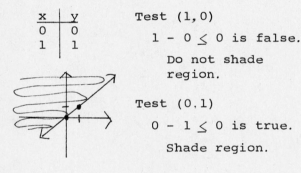

Test (1,0)

$1 - 0 \le 0$ is false.

Do not shade region.

Test (0,1)

$0 - 1 \le 0$ is true.

Shade region.

7. $x \ge 3$

Boundary line: $x = 3$ (included).

x	y
3	0
3	1

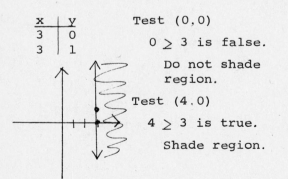

Test (0,0)

$0 \ge 3$ is false.

Do not shade region.

Test (4,0)

$4 \ge 3$ is true.

Shade region.

9. $y \le -1$

Boundary line: $y = -1$ (included).

x	y
0	-1
1	-1

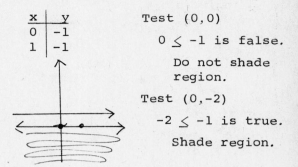

Test (0,0)

$0 \le -1$ is false.

Do not shade region.

Test (0,-2)

$-2 \le -1$ is true.

Shade region.

11. $x + y < 3$

Boundary line: $x + y = 3$ (not included).

x	y
0	3
3	0

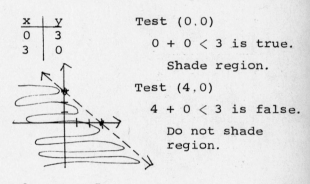

Test (0,0)

$0 + 0 < 3$ is true.

Shade region.

Test (4,0)

$4 + 0 < 3$ is false.

Do not shade region.

13. $3x + y \le 5$

Boundary line: $3x + y = 5$ (included).

x	y
0	5
$\frac{5}{3}$	0

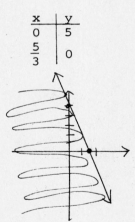

Test (0,0)

$0 + 0 \le 5$ is true.

Shade region.

Test (2,0)

$3(2) + 0 \le 5$ is false.

Do not shade region.

15. $x + y \geq 0$

Boundary line: $x + y = 0$ (included).

x	y
0	0
1	-1

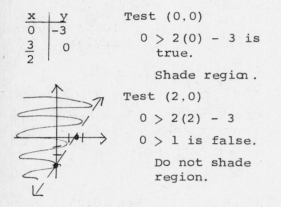

Test (1,0)

$1 + 0 \geq 0$ is true.

Shade region.

Test (0,-1)

$0 + (-1) \geq 0$ is false.

Do not shade region.

17. $y > 2x - 3$

Boundary line: $y = 2x - 3$ (not included).

x	y
0	-3
$\frac{3}{2}$	0

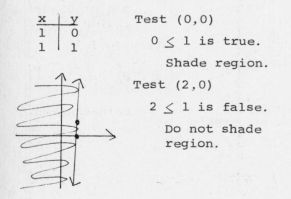

Test (0,0)

$0 > 2(0) - 3$ is true.

Shade region.

Test (2,0)

$0 > 2(2) - 3$

$0 > 1$ is false.

Do not shade region.

19. $x \leq 1$

Boundary line: $x = 1$ (included).

x	y
1	0
1	1

Test (0,0)

$0 \leq 1$ is true.

Shade region.

Test (2,0)

$2 \leq 1$ is false.

Do not shade region.

21. $y < 3x + 4$

Boundary line: $y = 3x + 4$ (not included).

x	y
0	4
$-\frac{4}{3}$	0

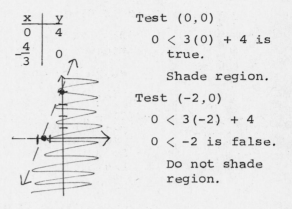

Test (0,0)

$0 < 3(0) + 4$ is true.

Shade region.

Test (-2,0)

$0 < 3(-2) + 4$

$0 < -2$ is false.

Do not shade region.

23. $x > 0$

Boundary line: $x = 0$ (not included).

x	y
0	0
0	1

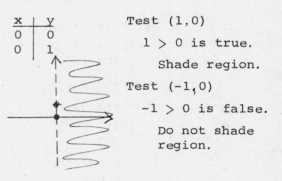

Test (1,0)

$1 > 0$ is true.

Shade region.

Test (-1,0)

$-1 > 0$ is false.

Do not shade region.

25. $2x - 3y \leq 4$

Boundary line: $2x - 3y = 4$ (included).

x	y
0	$-\frac{4}{3}$
2	0

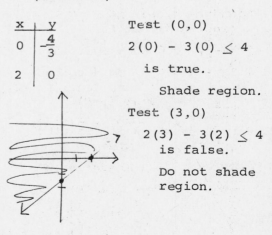

Test (0,0)

$2(0) - 3(0) \leq 4$ is true.

Shade region.

Test (3,0)

$2(3) - 3(2) \leq 4$ is false.

Do not shade region.

27. $3x - 2y \leq 5$

Boundary line: $3x - 2y = 5$ (included)

x	y
0	$\frac{5}{2}$
$\frac{5}{3}$	0

Test (0,0)

$3(0) - 2(0) \leq 5$ is true.

Shade region.

Test (2,0)

$3(2) - 2(0) \leq 5$ is false.

Do not shade region.

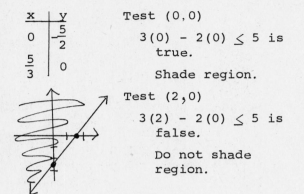

29. $3x - y < 6$

Boundary line: $3x - y = 6$ (not included).

x	y
0	-6
2	0

Test (0,0)

$3(0) - 0 < 6$ is true.

Shade region.

Test (3,0)

$3(3) - 0 < 6$ is false.

Do not shade region.

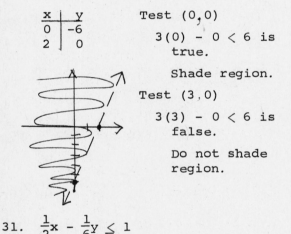

31. $\frac{1}{2}x - \frac{1}{6}y \leq 1$

Boundary line: $\frac{1}{2}x - \frac{1}{6}y = 1$ (included).

$6(\frac{1}{2}x - \frac{1}{6}y) = 6 \cdot 1$

$3x - y = 6$

x	y
0	-6
2	0

Test (0,0)

$\frac{1}{2}(0) - \frac{1}{6}(0)$, is true.

Shade region.

Test (4, 10)

$\frac{1}{2}(4) - \frac{1}{6}(0) \leq 1$

$2 - 0 \leq 1$ is false.

Do not shade region.

33. $2.4x - 3.2y \geq 0$

Boundary line: $2.4x - 3.2y \geq 0$ (included)

$10(2.4x - 3.2y) = 10 \cdot 0$

$24x - 32y = 0$

x	y
0	0
4	3

Test (1,0)

$2.4(1) - 3.2(0) \geq 0$ is true.

Shade region.

Test (0,1)

$2.4(0) - 3.2(1) \geq 0$ is false.

Do not shade region.

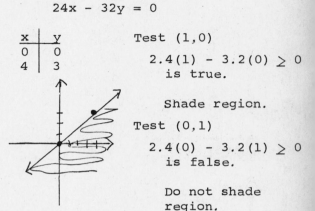

35. $3y - 6 \geq 0$

Boundary line: $3y - 6 = 0$ (included).

$3y = 6$

$y = 2$

x	y
0	2
1	2

Test (0,0)

$3(0) - 6 \geq$ is is false.

Do not shade region.

Test (0,3)

$3(3) - 6 \geq 0$ is is true.

Shade region.

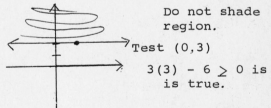

37. $y - \frac{1}{3}x < \frac{4}{3}$

Boundary line: $y - \frac{1}{3}x = \frac{4}{3}$ (not included).

x	y
0	$\frac{4}{3}$
-4	0

$0 - \frac{1}{3}x = \frac{4}{3}$

$3(-\frac{1}{3}x) = 3(\frac{4}{3})$

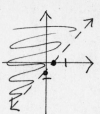

$-x = 4$

$x = -4$

Test $(0,0)$

$0 - \frac{1}{3}(0) < \frac{4}{3}$ is true.

Shade region.

Test $(0,2)$

$2 - \frac{1}{3}(0) < \frac{4}{3}$ is false.

Do not shade region.

39. $\frac{1}{4}x - \frac{1}{2}y < 2$

Boundary line: $\frac{1}{4}x - \frac{1}{2}y = 2$ (not included).

$4(\frac{1}{4}x - \frac{1}{2}y) = 4 \cdot 2$

$x - 2y = 8$

x	y
0	-4
8	0

Test $(0,0)$

$\frac{1}{4}(0) - \frac{1}{2}(0) < 2$ is true.

Shade region.

Test $(0,-6)$

$\frac{1}{4}(0) - \frac{1}{2}(-6) < 2$

$0 + 3 < 2$ is false.

Do not shade region.

41. $2.1x - 1.2y < 1.1$

Boundary line: $2.1x - 1.2y = 1.1$ (not included)

$10(2.1x - 1.2y) = 10(1.1)$

$21x - 12y = 11$

x	y
0	$-\frac{11}{12}$
$\frac{11}{21}$	0

Test $(0,0)$

$2.1(0) - 1.2(0) < 1.1$ is true.

Shade region.

Test $(1,0)$

$2.1(1) - 1.2(0) <$

1.1 is false.

Do not shade region.

43. $3x \leq 6$

Boundary line: $3x = 6$ (included).

$x = 2$

x	y
2	0
2	1

Test $(0,0)$

$3(0) \leq 6$ is true.

Shade region.

Test $(3,0)$

$3(3) \leq 6$ is false.

Do not shade region.

45. $6x - y > 2$

Boundary line: $6x - y = 2$ (not included).

x	y
0	-2
$\frac{1}{3}$	0

Test $(0,0)$

$6(0) - 0 > 2$

$0 - 0 > 2$ is false.

Do not shade region.

Test $(1,0)$

$6(1) - 0 > 2$ is true.

Shade region.

47. $y \leq mx$ $m > 0$

Boundary line: $y = mx$ (included).

x	y
0	0
1	m

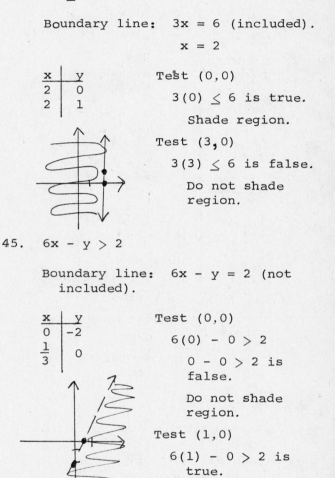

Test $(0,1)$

$1 \leq m(0)$

$1 \leq 0$ is false.

Do not shade region.

Test $(1,0)$

$0 \leq m(1)$ is true.

Shade region.

49. $y \leq mx + b$, $m > 0$, $b > 0$

Boundary line: $y = mx + b$ (included).

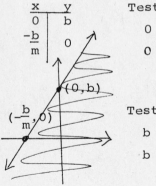

x	y
0	b
$-\frac{b}{m}$	0

Test $(0,0)$

$0 \leq m(0) + b$

$0 \leq b$ is true since $b > 0$.

Shade region.

Test $(0, b+1)$

$b + 1 \leq m(0) + b$

$b + 1 \leq b$ is false since $b > 0$.

Do not shade region.

51. $y > mx + b$, $m < 0$, $b > 0$

Boundary line: $y = mx + b$ (not included).

$(-\frac{b}{m} > 0$ since $m < 0$ and $b > 0)$

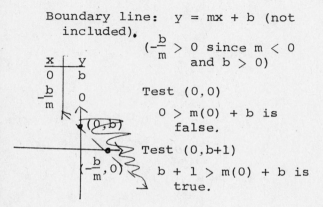

x	y
0	b
$-\frac{b}{m}$	0

Test $(0,0)$

$0 > m(0) + b$ is false.

Test $(0, b+1)$

$b + 1 > m(0) + b$ is true.

53. $y \leq a$, $a > 0$

Boundary line: $y = a$ (included).

x	y
0	a
1	a

Test $(0,0)$

$0 \leq a$ is true since $a > 0$.

Shade region.

Test $(0, a+1)$

$a + 1 < a$ is false.

Do not shade region.

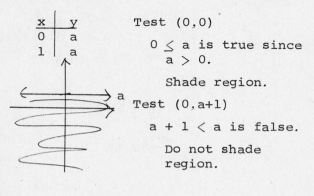

55. $x \geq a$, $a > 0$

Boundary line: $x = a$ (included).

x	y
a	0
a	1

Test $(0,0)$

$0 \geq a$ is false.

Do not shade region.

Test $(a+1, 0)$

$a + 1 \geq a$ is true.

Shade region.

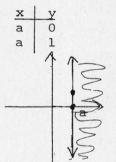

Problem Set 9.5.

1. $\begin{cases} x - y \leq 4 \\ x + y \geq 2 \end{cases}$

Boundary line 1: $x - y = 4$ (included).

x	y
0	-4
4	0

Test $(0,0)$

$0 - 0 \leq 4$ is true.

Region in soln. set.

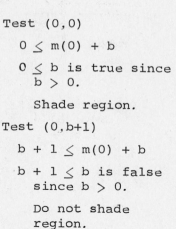

Boundary line 2: $x + y = 2$ (included).

x	y
0	2
2	0

Test $(0,0)$

$0 + 0 = 2$ is false.

Region not in soln. set.

3. $\begin{cases} x + y \leq 0 \\ x - y > 0 \end{cases}$

Boundary line 1: $x + y = 0$ (included).

x	y
0	0
1	-1

Test $(1,0)$

$1 + 0 \leq 0$ is false.

Region not in soln. set.

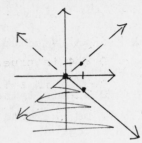

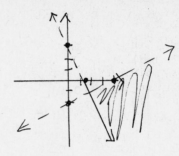

Boundary line 2: x - y = 0 (not included).

x	y
0	0
1	1

Test (1,0)

1 - 0 > 0 is true.

Region in soln. set.

5. $\begin{cases} 3x - y < 1 \\ x + 2y > 5 \end{cases}$

Boundary line 1: 3x - y = 1 (not included).

x	y
0	-1
$\frac{1}{3}$	0

Test (0,0)

3(0) - 0 < 1 is true.

Region in soln. set.

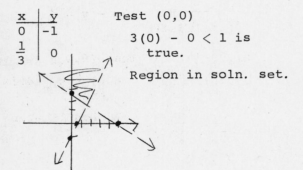

Boundary line 2: x + 2y = 5

x	y
0	$\frac{5}{2}$
5	0

Test (0,0)

0 + 2(0) > 5 is false.

Region not in soln. set.

7. $\begin{cases} 2x + y \geq 3 \\ x - 2y > 4 \end{cases}$

Boundary line 1: 2x + y = 3 (included).

x	y
0	3
$\frac{3}{2}$	0

Test (0,0)

0 + 0 ≥ 3 is false.

Region not in soln. set.

Boundary line 2: x - 2y = 4 (not included)

x	y
0	-2
4	0

Test (0,0)

0 - 2(0) > 4 is false.

Region not in soln. set.

9. $\begin{cases} x - y \geq -2 \\ x + y \leq 2 \\ x - 2y \leq -2 \end{cases}$

Boundary line 1: x - y = -2 (included).

x	y
0	2
-2	0

Test (0,0)

0 - 0 ≥ -2 is true.

Region in soln. set.

Boundary line 2: x + y = 2 (included).

x	y
0	2
2	0

Test (0,0)

0 + 0 ≤ 2 is true.

Region in soln. set.

Boundary line 3: x - 2y ≤ -2 (included).

x	y
0	1
-2	0

Test (0,0)

0 - 2(0) ≤ -2 is false.

Region not in soln. set.

11. $\begin{cases} x - \frac{1}{3}y \le -1 \\ 3x + y \ge -9 \end{cases}$

Boundary line 1: $x - \frac{1}{3}y$ (included).

x	y
0	3
-1	0

Test (0,0)

$0 - \frac{1}{3}(0) \le -1$

$0 \le -1$ is false.

Region not in soln. set.

Boundary line 2: $3x + y = -9$ (included).

x	y
0	-9
-3	0

Test (0,0)

$3(0) + 0 \ge -9$ is true.

Region is in soln. set.

13. $\begin{cases} x \ge 0 \\ y \ge 0 \end{cases}$

Boundary line 1: $x = 0$ (included).

x	y
0	1
0	2

Test (1,0)

$1 \ge 0$ is true.

Region is in soln. set.

Boundary line 2: $y = 0$ (included).

Test (1,1)

$1 \ge 0$

Region is in soln. set.

15. $\begin{cases} x < 4 \\ y > 2 \end{cases}$

Boundary line $x = 4$ (not

included).

x	y
4	0
4	1

Test (0,0)

$0 < 4$ is true.

Region in soln. set.

Boundary line 2: $y = 2$ (not included).

x	y
0	2
1	2

Test (0,0)

$0 > 2$ is false.

Region not in soln. set.

17. $\begin{cases} 2x - y \le 4 \\ 2x - y \ge 5 \end{cases}$

Boundary line: $2x - y = 4$ (included).

x	y
0	-4
2	0

Test (0,0)

$2(0) - 0 \le 4$ is true.

Region in soln. set.

Boundary line 2: $2x - y = 5$ (included).

x	y
0	-5
$\frac{5}{2}$	0

Test (0,0)

$2(0) - 0 \ge 5$ is false.

Region not in soln. set.

19. $\begin{cases} x + 3y \ge 6 \\ 2x + 6y \le 4 \end{cases}$

Boundary line 1: $x + 3y = 6$ (included).

x	y
0	2
6	0

Test (0,0)

$0 + 3(0) \ge 6$ is false.

Region not in the

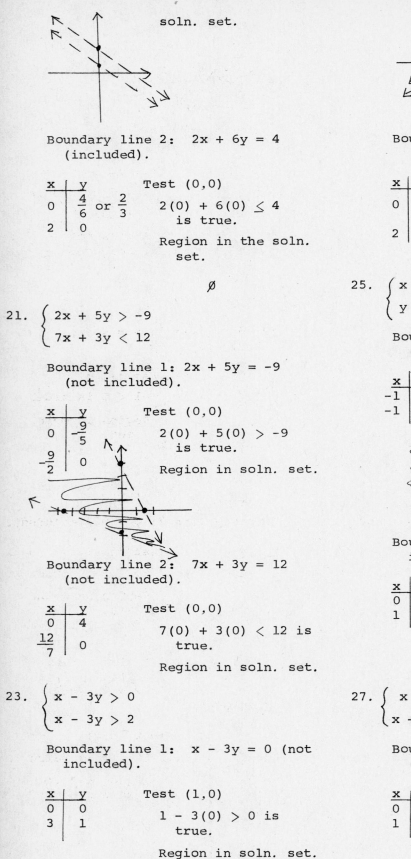
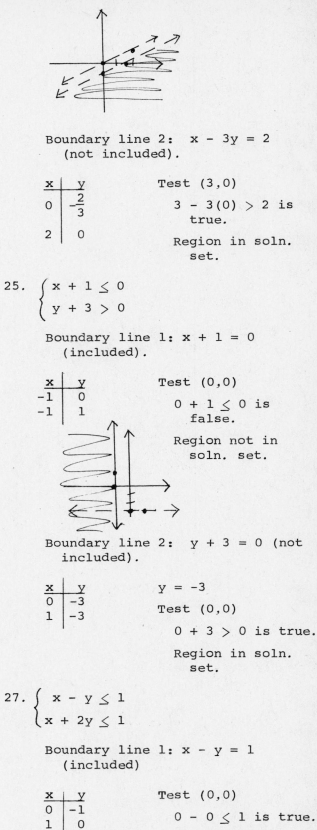

soln. set.

Boundary line 2: $2x + 6y = 4$ (included).

x	y
0	$\frac{4}{6}$ or $\frac{2}{3}$
2	0

Test (0,0)

$2(0) + 6(0) \leq 4$ is true.

Region in the soln. set.

$\emptyset$

21. $\begin{cases} 2x + 5y > -9 \\ 7x + 3y < 12 \end{cases}$

Boundary line 1: $2x + 5y = -9$ (not included).

x	y
0	$-\frac{9}{5}$
$-\frac{9}{2}$	0

Test (0,0)

$2(0) + 5(0) > -9$ is true.

Region in soln. set.

Boundary line 2: $7x + 3y = 12$ (not included).

x	y
0	4
$\frac{12}{7}$	0

Test (0,0)

$7(0) + 3(0) < 12$ is true.

Region in soln. set.

23. $\begin{cases} x - 3y > 0 \\ x - 3y > 2 \end{cases}$

Boundary line 1: $x - 3y = 0$ (not included).

x	y
0	0
3	1

Test (1,0)

$1 - 3(0) > 0$ is true.

Region in soln. set.

Boundary line 2: $x - 3y = 2$ (not included).

x	y
0	$-\frac{2}{3}$
2	0

Test (3,0)

$3 - 3(0) > 2$ is true.

Region in soln. set.

25. $\begin{cases} x + 1 \leq 0 \\ y + 3 > 0 \end{cases}$

Boundary line 1: $x + 1 = 0$ (included).

x	y
-1	0
-1	1

Test (0,0)

$0 + 1 \leq 0$ is false.

Region not in soln. set.

Boundary line 2: $y + 3 = 0$ (not included).

x	y
0	-3
1	-3

$y = -3$

Test (0,0)

$0 + 3 > 0$ is true.

Region in soln. set.

27. $\begin{cases} x - y \leq 1 \\ x + 2y \leq 1 \end{cases}$

Boundary line 1: $x - y = 1$ (included)

x	y
0	-1
1	0

Test (0,0)

$0 - 0 \leq 1$ is true.

Region in soln. set.

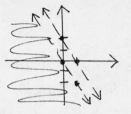

Boundary line 2: x + 2y = 1
(included)

x	y
0	$\frac{1}{2}$
1	0

Test (0,0)

$0 + 2(0) \leq 1$ is
true.

Region in soln. set.

29. $\begin{cases} x - 2y \leq 3 \\ 2x - 4y > 1 \end{cases}$

Boundary line 1: x - 2y = 3
(included).

x	y
0	$-\frac{3}{2}$
3	0

Test (0,0)

$0 - 2(0) \leq 3$ is
true.

Region in soln. set.

Boundary line 2: 2x - 4y = 1 (not
included).

x	y
0	$-\frac{1}{4}$
$\frac{1}{2}$	0

Test (0,0)

$2(0) - 4(0) > 1$
is false.

Region not in soln.
set.

31. $\begin{cases} 2x + y < 2 \\ x + \frac{1}{2}y < 0 \end{cases}$

Boundary line 1: 2x + y = 2 (not
included).

x	y
0	2
1	0

Test (0,0)

$2(0) + 0 < 2$ is
true.

Region in soln. set.

Boundary line 2: $x + \frac{1}{2}y = 0$ (not
included).

x	y
0	0
1	-2

Test (1,0)

$1 + \frac{1}{2}(0) < 0$ is
false.

Region not in
soln set.

33. $\begin{cases} x < 0 \\ y \leq 0 \end{cases}$

Boundary line 1: x = 0 (not
included)

x	y
0	0
0	2

Test (-1,1)

$-1 < 0$ is true.

Region in soln.
set.

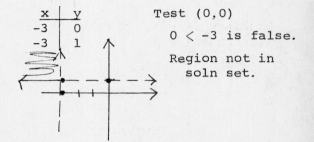

Boundary line 2: y = 0 (included).

x	y
0	0
2	0

Test (1,-1)

$-1 \leq 0$ is true

Region in soln.
set.

35. $\begin{cases} x < -3 \\ y \geq 1 \end{cases}$

Boundary line 1: x = -3 (not
included).

x	y
-3	0
-3	1

Test (0,0)

$0 < -3$ is false.

Region not in
soln set.

Boundary line 2: $y = 1$ (included).

x	y
0	1
1	1

Test (0,0)

$0 \geq 1$ is false.

Region not in soln. set.

37. $\begin{cases} \frac{1}{2}x - y > 5 \\ x + 2y < 14 \end{cases}$

Boundary line 1: $\frac{1}{2}x - y = 5$ (not included).

x	y
0	-5
10	0

Test (0,0)

$\frac{1}{2}(0) - 0 > 5$ is false.

Region is not in soln. set.

Boundary line 2: $x + 2y = 14$ (not included).

x	y
0	7
14	0

Test (0,0)

$0 + 2(0) < 14$ is true.

Region in soln. set.

39. $\begin{cases} 3x + 2y < 6 \\ 3x + 2y \geq 1 \end{cases}$

Boundary line 1: $3x + 2y = 6$ (not included).

x	y
0	3
2	0

Test (0,0)

$2(0) + 2(0) < 6$ is true.

Region in soln. set.

Boundary line 2: $3x + 2y = 1$ (included).

x	y
0	$\frac{1}{2}$
$\frac{1}{3}$	0

Test (0,0)

$3(0) + 2(0) \geq 1$ is false.

Region not in soln. set.

41. $\begin{cases} x - y > -3 \\ x - 2y \leq 0 \\ 3x + y \leq 3 \end{cases}$

Boundary line 1: $x - y = -3$ (not included).

x	y
0	3
-3	0

Test (0,0)

$0 - 0 > -3$ is true.

Region in soln. set.

Boundary line 2: $x - 2y = 0$ (included).

x	y
0	0
2	1

Test (0,1)

$0 - 2(1) \leq 0$ is true.

Region in soln. set.

Boundary line 3: $3x + y = 3$ (included).

x	y
0	3
1	0

Test (0,0)

$3(0) + 0 \leq 3$ is true.

Region in soln. set.

43. C: pounds of cashews

P: pounds of peanuts

$\begin{cases} C + 2P \leq 30 \\ 2C + P \leq 40 \\ P \geq 0 \\ C \geq 0 \end{cases}$

Boundary line 1: $C + 2P = 30$ (included).

C	P
0	15
30	0	P

Test (0,0)

$0 + 2(0) \leq 30$ is true.

Region in soln. set.

Boundary line 2: $2C + P \leq 40$ (included).

C	P
0	40
20	0

Test (0,0)

$2(0) + 0 \leq 40$ is true.

Region in soln. set.

Boundary line 3: $P = 0$ (included).

$P = 0$ is C axis

Test (1,1)

$1 \geq 0$ is true.

Region in soln. set.

Boundary line 4: $C = 0$ (included).

$C = 0$ is P axis.

Test (1,1)

$1 \geq 0$ is true.

Region in soln. set.

45. $\begin{cases} y \leq mx; \quad m > 0 \\ y < nx; \quad n < 0 \end{cases}$

Boundary line 1: $y = mx$, $m > 0$ (included).

x	y
0	0
1	m

Test (1,0)

$0 \leq m(1)$ is true.

Region in soln. set.

Boundary line 2: $y = nx$, $n < 0$ (not included).

x	y
0	0
1	n

Test (0,-1)

$-1 < 0(n)$ is true.

Region in soln. set.

47. $\begin{cases} y < a; \quad a > 0 \\ x < b; \quad b > 0 \end{cases}$

Boundary line 1: $y = a$, $a > 0$ (not included).

x	y
0	a
1	a

Test (0,0)

$0 < a$ is true.

Region in soln. set.

Boundary line 2: $x = b$, $b > 0$ (not included).

x	y
b	0
b	1

Test (0,0)

$0 < b$ is true.

Region in soln. set.

Problem Set 9.6.

1. $\begin{vmatrix} 1 & 2 \\ 2 & 5 \end{vmatrix} = 1 \cdot 5 - 2 \cdot 2$

$= 5 - 4$

$= 1$

3. $\begin{vmatrix} 3 & 2 \\ 6 & 4 \end{vmatrix} = 3 \cdot 4 - 2 \cdot 6$

$= 12 - 12$

$= 0$

5. $\begin{vmatrix} 3 & 5 \\ -2 & 4 \end{vmatrix} = 3 \cdot 4 - (-2)(5)$

$= 12 - (-10)$

$= 22$

7. Expand about first row:

$\begin{vmatrix} 1 & 1 & 2 \\ 2 & 3 & 1 \\ 1 & -1 & 1 \end{vmatrix} = 1 \begin{vmatrix} 3 & 1 \\ -1 & 1 \end{vmatrix} - 1 \begin{vmatrix} 2 & 1 \\ 1 & 1 \end{vmatrix}$

$+ 2 \begin{vmatrix} 2 & 3 \\ 1 & -1 \end{vmatrix}$

281

$$= 1[3 \cdot 1 - 1 \cdot (-1)] - 1(2 \cdot 1 - 1 \cdot 1)$$
$$+ 2[2(-1) - 3 \cdot 1]$$
$$= (3+1) - (2-1) + 2(-2-3)$$
$$= 4 - 1 + 2(-5)$$
$$= 3 - 10$$
$$= -7$$

9. Expand about second row:

$$\begin{vmatrix} 4 & 2 & 1 \\ 0 & 0 & 3 \\ 3 & 5 & 3 \end{vmatrix} = -0 + 0 - 3 \begin{vmatrix} 4 & 2 \\ 3 & 5 \end{vmatrix}$$
$$= -3(4 \cdot 5 - 2 \cdot 3)$$
$$= -3(20 - 6)$$
$$= -3(14)$$
$$= -42$$

11. Expand about first column:

$$\begin{vmatrix} 0 & 1 & 0 \\ 0 & 0 & 1 \\ 2 & 0 & 0 \end{vmatrix} = 0 - 0 + 2 \begin{vmatrix} 1 & 0 \\ 0 & 1 \end{vmatrix}$$
$$= 2(1 \cdot 1 - 0 \cdot 0)$$
$$= 2 \cdot 1$$
$$= 2$$

13. $\begin{cases} x + y = 1 \\ x - y = 3 \end{cases}$

$$x = \frac{\begin{vmatrix} 1 & 1 \\ 3 & -1 \end{vmatrix}}{\begin{vmatrix} 1 & 1 \\ 1 & -1 \end{vmatrix}} = \frac{1 \cdot (-1) - 1 \cdot 3}{1 \cdot (-1) - (1 \cdot 1)}$$
$$= \frac{-1 - 3}{-1 - 1}$$
$$= \frac{-4}{-2}$$
$$= 2$$

$$y = \frac{\begin{vmatrix} 1 & 1 \\ 1 & 3 \end{vmatrix}}{\begin{vmatrix} 1 & 1 \\ 1 & -1 \end{vmatrix}} = \frac{1 \cdot 3 - 1 \cdot 1}{-2}$$
$$= \frac{3 - 1}{-2}$$
$$= \frac{2}{-2}$$
$$= -1$$

$\{(2,-1)\}$

15. $\begin{cases} 2x - y = -5 \\ 3x + 2y = 3 \end{cases}$

$$x = \frac{\begin{vmatrix} -5 & -1 \\ 3 & 2 \end{vmatrix}}{\begin{vmatrix} 2 & -1 \\ 3 & 2 \end{vmatrix}} = \frac{(-5) \cdot 2 - (-1) \cdot 3}{2 \cdot 2 - (-1) \cdot 3}$$
$$= \frac{-10 - (-3)}{4 - (-3)}$$
$$= \frac{-7}{7}$$
$$= -1$$

$$y = \frac{\begin{vmatrix} 2 & -5 \\ 3 & 3 \end{vmatrix}}{\begin{vmatrix} 2 & -1 \\ 3 & 2 \end{vmatrix}} = \frac{2 \cdot 3 - (-5) \cdot 3}{7}$$
$$= \frac{6 - (-15)}{7}$$
$$= \frac{6 + 15}{7}$$
$$= \frac{21}{7}$$
$$= 3$$

$\{(-1,3)\}$

17. $\begin{cases} 3x + 2y = 5 \\ 6x - y = 0 \end{cases}$

$$x = \frac{\begin{vmatrix} 5 & 2 \\ 0 & -1 \end{vmatrix}}{\begin{vmatrix} 3 & 2 \\ 6 & -1 \end{vmatrix}} = \frac{5 \cdot (-1) - 2 \cdot 0}{3 \cdot (-1) - 2 \cdot 6}$$
$$= \frac{-5}{-3 - 12}$$
$$= \frac{-5}{-15} \text{ or } \frac{1}{3}$$

$$y = \frac{\begin{vmatrix} 3 & 5 \\ 6 & 0 \end{vmatrix}}{\begin{vmatrix} 3 & 2 \\ 6 & -1 \end{vmatrix}} = \frac{3 \cdot 0 - 5 \cdot 6}{-15}$$
$$= \frac{-30}{-15} \text{ or } 2$$

$\{(\frac{1}{3},2)\}$

19. $\begin{cases} x + y + z = 6 \\ x + 2y - z = 2 \\ 2x - 2y + z = 1 \end{cases}$

$$x = \frac{\begin{vmatrix} 6 & 1 & 1 \\ 2 & 2 & -1 \\ 1 & -2 & 1 \end{vmatrix}}{\begin{vmatrix} 1 & 1 & 1 \\ 1 & 2 & -1 \\ 2 & -2 & 1 \end{vmatrix}}$$

$$= \frac{6\begin{vmatrix} 2 & -1 \\ -2 & 1 \end{vmatrix} - 2\begin{vmatrix} 1 & 1 \\ -2 & 1 \end{vmatrix} + 1\begin{vmatrix} 1 & 1 \\ 2 & -1 \end{vmatrix}}{1\begin{vmatrix} 2 & -1 \\ -2 & 1 \end{vmatrix} - 1\begin{vmatrix} 1 & 1 \\ -2 & 1 \end{vmatrix} + 2\begin{vmatrix} 1 & 1 \\ 2 & -1 \end{vmatrix}}$$

$$= \frac{6[2 \cdot 1 - (-1)(-2)] - 2[1 \cdot 1 - 1 \cdot (-2)]}{1[2 \cdot 1 - (-1)(-2)] - 1[1 \cdot 1 - 1 \cdot (-2)]}$$

$$\frac{+1[1 \cdot (-1) - 1 \cdot 2]}{+2[1 \cdot (-1) - 1 \cdot 2]}$$

$$= \frac{6(2-2) - 2(1+2) + (-1-2)}{1(2-2) - (1+2) + 2(-1-2)}$$

$$= \frac{6(0) - 2(3) - 3}{0 - 3 + 2(-3)}$$

$$= \frac{0 - 6 - 3}{0 - 3 - 6}$$

$$= \frac{-9}{-9} \text{ or } 1$$

$$y = \frac{\begin{vmatrix} 1 & 6 & 1 \\ 1 & 2 & -1 \\ 2 & 1 & 1 \end{vmatrix}}{\begin{vmatrix} 1 & 1 & 1 \\ 1 & 2 & -1 \\ 2 & -2 & 1 \end{vmatrix}}$$

$$= \frac{1\begin{vmatrix} 2 & -1 \\ 1 & 1 \end{vmatrix} - 1\begin{vmatrix} 6 & 1 \\ 1 & 1 \end{vmatrix} + 2\begin{vmatrix} 6 & 1 \\ 2 & -1 \end{vmatrix}}{-9}$$

$$= \frac{1[2 - 1 \cdot (-1)] - 1(6 \cdot 1 - 1 \cdot 1) + 2[6 \cdot (-1) - 1 \cdot 2]}{-9}$$

$$= \frac{(2+1) - (6-1) + 2[(-6) - 2]}{-9}$$

$$= \frac{3 - 5 + -16}{-9}$$

$$= \frac{-18}{-9} \text{ or } 2$$

$$z = \frac{\begin{vmatrix} 1 & 1 & 6 \\ 1 & 2 & 2 \\ 2 & -2 & 1 \end{vmatrix}}{\begin{vmatrix} 1 & 1 & 1 \\ 1 & 2 & -1 \\ 2 & -2 & 1 \end{vmatrix}}$$

$$= \frac{1\begin{vmatrix} 2 & 2 \\ -2 & 1 \end{vmatrix} - 1\begin{vmatrix} 1 & 6 \\ -2 & 1 \end{vmatrix} + 2\begin{vmatrix} 1 & 6 \\ 2 & 2 \end{vmatrix}}{-9}$$

$$= \frac{[2 \cdot 1 - 2(-2)] - [1 \cdot 1 - 6(-2)] + 2(1 \cdot 2 - 6 \cdot 2)}{-9}$$

$$= \frac{(2+4) - (1+12) + 2(2-12)}{-9}$$

$$= \frac{6 - 13 - 20}{-9}$$

$$= \frac{-27}{-9} \text{ or } 3$$

$\{(1,2,3)\}$

21. $\begin{cases} 2x - y + 2z = 2 \\ -2x + 3y + 4z = 10 \\ -2x + y - z = 0 \end{cases}$

$$x = \frac{\begin{vmatrix} 2 & -1 & 2 \\ 10 & 3 & 4 \\ 0 & 1 & -1 \end{vmatrix}}{\begin{vmatrix} 2 & -1 & 2 \\ -2 & 3 & 4 \\ -2 & 1 & -1 \end{vmatrix}}$$

$$= \frac{2\begin{vmatrix} 3 & 4 \\ 1 & -1 \end{vmatrix} - 10\begin{vmatrix} -1 & 2 \\ 1 & -1 \end{vmatrix} + 0}{2\begin{vmatrix} 3 & 4 \\ 1 & -1 \end{vmatrix} - (-2)\begin{vmatrix} -1 & 2 \\ 1 & -1 \end{vmatrix} + (-2)\begin{vmatrix} -1 & 2 \\ 2 & 4 \end{vmatrix}}$$

$$= \frac{2[3(-1) - 4 \cdot 1] - 10[(-1)(-1) - 2 \cdot 1]}{2[3 \cdot (-1) - 4 \cdot 1] + 2[(-1)(-1) - 2 \cdot 1]}$$

$$\frac{}{-2[(-1) \cdot 4 - 2 \cdot 3]}$$

$$= \frac{2(-3-4) - 10(1-2)}{2(-3-4) + 2(1-2) - 2(-4-6)}$$

$$= \frac{2(-7) - 10(-1)}{2(-7) + 2(-1) - 2(-10)}$$

$$= \frac{-14 + 10}{-14 - 2 + 20}$$

$$= \frac{-4}{4} \text{ or } -1$$

$$y = \frac{\begin{vmatrix} 2 & 2 & 2 \\ -2 & 10 & 4 \\ -2 & 0 & -1 \end{vmatrix}}{\begin{vmatrix} 2 & -1 & 2 \\ -2 & 3 & 4 \\ -2 & 1 & -1 \end{vmatrix}}$$

$$= \frac{-2\begin{vmatrix} -2 & 4 \\ -2 & -1 \end{vmatrix} + 10\begin{vmatrix} 2 & 2 \\ -2 & -1 \end{vmatrix} - 0}{4}$$

$$= \frac{-2[(-2)(-1)-(-2)4]+10[2(-1)-2(-2)]}{4}$$

$$= \frac{-2(2+8)+10(-2+4)}{4}$$

$$= \frac{-2(10)+10(2)}{4}$$

$$= \frac{0}{4} \text{ or } 0$$

$$z = \frac{\begin{vmatrix} 2 & -1 & 2 \\ -2 & 3 & 10 \\ -2 & 1 & 0 \end{vmatrix}}{\begin{vmatrix} 2 & -1 & 2 \\ -2 & 3 & 4 \\ -2 & 1 & -1 \end{vmatrix}}$$

$$= \frac{2\begin{vmatrix} -2 & 3 \\ -2 & 1 \end{vmatrix} - 10\begin{vmatrix} 2 & -1 \\ -2 & 1 \end{vmatrix} + 0}{4}$$

$$= \frac{2[(-2)1-3(-2)]-10[2\cdot1-(-1)(-2)]}{4}$$

$$= \frac{2(-2+6)-10(2-2)}{4}$$

$$= \frac{2(4)-10(0)}{4}$$

$$= \frac{8}{4} \text{ or } 2$$

$$\{(-1,0,2)\}$$

23. $\begin{vmatrix} 2 & 1 \\ 5 & 3 \end{vmatrix} = 2 \cdot 3 - 1 \cdot 5$

$\qquad = 6 - 5$

$\qquad = 1$

25. $\begin{vmatrix} 2 & 6 \\ 3 & 9 \end{vmatrix} = 2 \cdot 9 - 3 \cdot 6$

$\qquad = 18 - 18$

$\qquad = 0$

27. $\begin{vmatrix} 4 & 5 \\ -3 & 3 \end{vmatrix} = 4 \cdot 3 - 5 \cdot (-3)$

$\qquad = 12 + 15$

$= 27$

29. $\begin{vmatrix} 2 & 1 & 1 \\ 1 & 3 & -1 \\ 1 & -2 & 4 \end{vmatrix}$

$$= 2\begin{vmatrix} 3 & -1 \\ -2 & 4 \end{vmatrix} - 1\begin{vmatrix} 1 & -1 \\ 1 & 4 \end{vmatrix} + 1\begin{vmatrix} 1 & 3 \\ 1 & -2 \end{vmatrix}$$

$$= 2[3\cdot4-(-1)(-2)] - [1\cdot4-(-1)(1)]$$

$$\qquad\qquad + [1\cdot(-2)-1\cdot3]$$

$$= 2(12-2) - (4+1) + (-2-3)$$

$$= 2(10) - 5 + (-5)$$

$$= 20 + 10$$

$$= 10$$

31. $\begin{vmatrix} 1 & 2 & 0 \\ -1 & -1 & 0 \\ 3 & 4 & 2 \end{vmatrix} = 0 - 0 + 2\begin{vmatrix} 1 & 2 \\ -1 & -1 \end{vmatrix}$

$$= 2[1\cdot(-1)-2(-1)]$$

$$= 2(-1+2)$$

$$= 2(1)$$

$$= 2$$

33. $\begin{vmatrix} 2 & 0 \\ 0 & -3 \end{vmatrix} = 2 \cdot (-3) - 0 \cdot 0$

$$= -6$$

35. Expand about first row:

$\begin{vmatrix} 3 & 3 & 4 \\ 2 & 2 & 1 \\ 1 & 1 & 3 \end{vmatrix}$

$$= 3\begin{vmatrix} 2 & 1 \\ 1 & 3 \end{vmatrix} - 3\begin{vmatrix} 2 & 1 \\ 1 & 3 \end{vmatrix} + 4\begin{vmatrix} 2 & 2 \\ 1 & 1 \end{vmatrix}$$

$$= 3(2\cdot3-1\cdot1) - 3(2\cdot3-1\cdot1)$$

$$\qquad\qquad + 4(2\cdot1-2\cdot1)$$

$$= 3(6-1) - 3(6-1) + 4(0)$$

$$= 3(5) - 3(5) + 0$$

$$= 0$$

37. Expand about first column:

$$\begin{vmatrix} -2 & 3 & 5 \\ 4 & 2 & 3 \\ 7 & -3 & 2 \end{vmatrix}$$

$$= -2\begin{vmatrix} 2 & 3 \\ -3 & 2 \end{vmatrix} -4\begin{vmatrix} 3 & 5 \\ -3 & 2 \end{vmatrix} +7\begin{vmatrix} 3 & 5 \\ 2 & 3 \end{vmatrix}$$

$$= -2[2\cdot2-3\cdot(-3)] - 4[3\cdot2-5(-3)] + 7(3\cdot3-5\cdot2)$$

$$= -2(4+9) - 4(6+15) + 7(-1)$$

$$= -2(13) - 4(21) + -7$$

$$= -26 - 84 - 7$$

$$= -117$$

39. $\begin{vmatrix} 4 & 0 \\ 2 & -6 \end{vmatrix} = 4\cdot(-6) - 0\cdot2$

$$= -24$$

41. $\begin{cases} 3x + 4y = 0 \\ 4x + 3y = 0 \end{cases}$

$$x = \frac{\begin{vmatrix} 0 & 4 \\ 0 & 3 \end{vmatrix}}{\begin{vmatrix} 3 & 4 \\ 4 & 3 \end{vmatrix}} = \frac{0\cdot3-4\cdot0}{9-16}$$

$$= \frac{0}{-7} = 0$$

$$y = \frac{\begin{vmatrix} 3 & 0 \\ 4 & 0 \end{vmatrix}}{\begin{vmatrix} 3 & 4 \\ 4 & 3 \end{vmatrix}} = \frac{3\cdot0-0\cdot4}{-7}$$

$$= \frac{0}{-7} = 0$$

$\{(0,0)\}$

43. $\begin{cases} 6x - 5y = 6 \\ 9x + 7y = -20 \end{cases}$

$$x = \frac{\begin{vmatrix} 6 & -5 \\ -20 & 7 \end{vmatrix}}{\begin{vmatrix} 6 & -5 \\ 9 & 7 \end{vmatrix}} = \frac{6\cdot7-(-5)(-20)}{6\cdot7-(-5)(9)}$$

$$= \frac{42-100}{42+45}$$

$$= \frac{-58}{87} \text{ or } -\frac{2}{3}$$

$$y = \frac{\begin{vmatrix} 6 & 6 \\ 7 & -20 \end{vmatrix}}{\begin{vmatrix} 6 & -5 \\ 9 & 7 \end{vmatrix}} = \frac{6\cdot(-20)-6\cdot9}{87}$$

$$= \frac{-120-54}{87}$$

$$= \frac{-174}{87} \text{ or } -2$$

$\{(-\frac{2}{3},-2)\}$

45. $\begin{cases} -4x + 15y = -2 \\ 12x + 6y = -4 \end{cases}$

$$x = \frac{\begin{vmatrix} -2 & 15 \\ -4 & 5 \end{vmatrix}}{\begin{vmatrix} -4 & 15 \\ 12 & 5 \end{vmatrix}} = \frac{(-2)\cdot5-15\cdot(-4)}{(-4)5-15\cdot12}$$

$$= \frac{-10-(-60)}{-20-180}$$

$$= \frac{-10+60}{-200}$$

$$= \frac{50}{-200} \text{ or } -\frac{1}{4}$$

$$y = \frac{\begin{vmatrix} -4 & -2 \\ 12 & -4 \end{vmatrix}}{\begin{vmatrix} -4 & 15 \\ 12 & 5 \end{vmatrix}} = \frac{(-4)(-4)-(-2)\cdot12}{-200}$$

$$= \frac{16+24}{-200}$$

$$= \frac{40}{-200} \text{ or } -\frac{1}{5}$$

$\{(-\frac{1}{4},-\frac{1}{5})\}$

47. $\begin{cases} 3x - 4y = 5 \\ 4x - 7y = 9 \end{cases}$

$$x = \frac{\begin{vmatrix} 5 & -4 \\ 9 & -7 \end{vmatrix}}{\begin{vmatrix} 3 & -4 \\ 4 & -7 \end{vmatrix}} = \frac{5\cdot(-7)-(-4)\cdot9}{3\cdot(-7)-(-4)(4)}$$

$$= \frac{-35+36}{-21+16}$$

$$= \frac{1}{-5} \text{ or } -\frac{1}{5}$$

$$y = \frac{\begin{vmatrix} 3 & 5 \\ 4 & 9 \end{vmatrix}}{\begin{vmatrix} 3 & -4 \\ 4 & -7 \end{vmatrix}} = \frac{3\cdot9-5\cdot4}{-5}$$

$$= \frac{27-20}{-5}$$

$$= \frac{7}{-5} \text{ or } -\frac{7}{5}$$

$\{(-\frac{1}{5},-\frac{7}{5})\}$

49. $\begin{cases} 17x - 11y = -1 \\ -34x + 22y = 2 \end{cases}$

Since $\begin{vmatrix} 17 & -11 \\ -34 & 22 \end{vmatrix} = 17(22)$

$\qquad\qquad\qquad\qquad\quad -(-11)(-34)$

$\qquad\qquad\qquad\quad = 374 - 374$

$\qquad\qquad\qquad\quad = 0$

Cramer's Rule does not apply.

51. $\begin{cases} \dfrac{1}{5}x - \dfrac{2}{3}y = \dfrac{1}{15} \\ \dfrac{3}{4}x - \dfrac{5}{6}y = \dfrac{1}{3} \end{cases}$

$x = \dfrac{\begin{vmatrix} \frac{1}{15} & -\frac{2}{3} \\ \frac{1}{3} & -\frac{5}{6} \end{vmatrix}}{\begin{vmatrix} \frac{1}{5} & -\frac{2}{3} \\ \frac{3}{4} & -\frac{5}{6} \end{vmatrix}} = \dfrac{\frac{1}{15}\cdot(-\frac{5}{6})-(-\frac{2}{3})(\frac{1}{3})}{(\frac{1}{5})(-\frac{5}{6})-(-\frac{2}{3})(\frac{3}{4})}$

$= \dfrac{-\frac{1}{18}+\frac{2}{9}}{-\frac{1}{6}+\frac{1}{2}} = \dfrac{\frac{-1+4}{18}}{\frac{-1+3}{6}}$

$= \dfrac{\frac{3}{18}}{\frac{2}{6}} = \dfrac{1}{6}\cdot\dfrac{3}{1} = \dfrac{3}{6} \text{ or } \dfrac{1}{2}$

$y = \dfrac{\begin{vmatrix} \frac{1}{5} & \frac{1}{15} \\ \frac{3}{4} & \frac{1}{3} \end{vmatrix}}{\begin{vmatrix} \frac{1}{5} & -\frac{2}{3} \\ \frac{3}{4} & -\frac{5}{6} \end{vmatrix}} = \dfrac{(\frac{1}{5})(\frac{1}{3})-(\frac{1}{15})(\frac{3}{4})}{\frac{1}{3}}$

$= \dfrac{\frac{1}{15}-\frac{1}{20}}{\frac{1}{3}}$

$= \dfrac{\frac{4-3}{60}}{\frac{1}{3}} = \dfrac{1}{60}\cdot\dfrac{3}{1}$

$= \dfrac{3}{60} \text{ or } \dfrac{1}{20}$

$\{(\dfrac{1}{2},\dfrac{1}{20})\}$

53. $\begin{cases} x + y + z = 6 \\ x + 2y + 2 = 9 \\ 2x + 2y - z = 6 \end{cases}$

$x = \dfrac{\begin{vmatrix} 6 & 1 & 1 \\ 9 & 2 & 1 \\ 6 & 2 & -1 \end{vmatrix}}{\begin{vmatrix} 1 & 1 & 1 \\ 1 & 2 & 1 \\ 2 & 2 & -1 \end{vmatrix}}$

$= \dfrac{6\begin{vmatrix} 2 & 1 \\ 2 & -1 \end{vmatrix}-1\begin{vmatrix} 9 & 1 \\ 6 & -1 \end{vmatrix}+1\begin{vmatrix} 9 & 2 \\ 6 & 2 \end{vmatrix}}{1\begin{vmatrix} 2 & 1 \\ 2 & -1 \end{vmatrix}-1\begin{vmatrix} 1 & 1 \\ 2 & -1 \end{vmatrix}+1\begin{vmatrix} 1 & 2 \\ 2 & 2 \end{vmatrix}}$

$= \dfrac{6[2\cdot(-1)-1\cdot2]-1[9\cdot(-1)-1\cdot6]+1[9\cdot2-2\cdot6]}{1[2\cdot(-1)-1\cdot2]-1[1\cdot(-1)-1\cdot2]+1(1\cdot2-2\cdot2)}$

$= \dfrac{6(-2-2)-(-9-6)+(18-12)}{(-2-2)-(-1-2)+(2-4)}$

$= \dfrac{6(-4)-(-15)+6}{-4-(-3)+(-2)}$

$= \dfrac{-24+15+6}{-4+3-2}$

$= \dfrac{-3}{-3} \text{ or } 1$

$y = \dfrac{\begin{vmatrix} 1 & 6 & 1 \\ 1 & 9 & 1 \\ 2 & 6 & -1 \end{vmatrix}}{\begin{vmatrix} 1 & 1 & 1 \\ 1 & 2 & 1 \\ 2 & 2 & -1 \end{vmatrix}}$

$= \dfrac{1\begin{vmatrix} 9 & 1 \\ 6 & -1 \end{vmatrix}-1\begin{vmatrix} 6 & 1 \\ 6 & -1 \end{vmatrix}+2\begin{vmatrix} 6 & 1 \\ 9 & 1 \end{vmatrix}}{-3}$

$= \dfrac{[9\cdot(-1)-1\cdot6]-[6\cdot(-1)-1\cdot6]+2(6\cdot1-1\cdot9)}{-3}$

$= \dfrac{(-9-6)-(-6-6)+2(6-9)}{-3}$

$= \dfrac{-15+12-6}{-3}$

$= \dfrac{-9}{-3} \text{ or } 3$

$z = \dfrac{\begin{vmatrix} 1 & 1 & 6 \\ 1 & 2 & 9 \\ 2 & 2 & 6 \end{vmatrix}}{\begin{vmatrix} 1 & 1 & 1 \\ 1 & 2 & 1 \\ 2 & 2 & -1 \end{vmatrix}}$

$= \dfrac{1\begin{vmatrix} 2 & 9 \\ 2 & 6 \end{vmatrix}-1\begin{vmatrix} 1 & 6 \\ 2 & 6 \end{vmatrix}+2\begin{vmatrix} 1 & 6 \\ 2 & 9 \end{vmatrix}}{-3}$

$= \dfrac{(2\cdot6-9\cdot2)-(1\cdot6-2\cdot6)+2(1\cdot9-6\cdot2)}{-3}$

$$= \frac{(12-18)(6-12)+2(9-12)}{-3}$$

$$= \frac{-6+6-6}{-3}$$

$$= \frac{-6}{-3} \text{ or } 2$$

$$\{(1,3,2)\}$$

55. $\begin{cases} 3x + y + 2z = 10 \\ -3x - 2y + 4z = -11 \\ 2y + z = 2 \end{cases}$

$$x = \frac{\begin{vmatrix} 10 & 1 & 2 \\ -11 & -2 & 4 \\ 2 & 2 & 1 \end{vmatrix}}{\begin{vmatrix} 3 & 1 & 2 \\ -3 & -2 & 4 \\ 0 & 2 & 1 \end{vmatrix}}$$

$$= \frac{10 \begin{vmatrix} -2 & 4 \\ 2 & 1 \end{vmatrix} -1 \begin{vmatrix} -11 & 4 \\ 2 & 1 \end{vmatrix} +2 \begin{vmatrix} -11 & -2 \\ 2 & 2 \end{vmatrix}}{0-2 \begin{vmatrix} 3 & 2 \\ -3 & 4 \end{vmatrix} +1 \begin{vmatrix} 3 & 1 \\ -3 & -2 \end{vmatrix}}$$

$$= \frac{\begin{array}{l} 10[(-2)(1)-4\cdot 2]-[(-11)\cdot 1-4\cdot 2] \\ +2[(-11)\cdot 2-(-2)\cdot 2] \end{array}}{-2[3\cdot 4-2(-3)]+[3\cdot(-2)-1\cdot(-3)]}$$

$$= \frac{10(-2-8)-(-11-8)+2(-22+4)}{-2(12+6)+(-6+3)}$$

$$= \frac{-100+19-36}{-36-3}$$

$$= \frac{-117}{-39} \text{ or } 3$$

$$y = \frac{\begin{vmatrix} 3 & 10 & 2 \\ -3 & -11 & 4 \\ 0 & 2 & 1 \end{vmatrix}}{\begin{vmatrix} 3 & 1 & 2 \\ -3 & -2 & 4 \\ 0 & 2 & 1 \end{vmatrix}}$$

$$= \frac{3 \begin{vmatrix} -11 & 4 \\ 2 & 1 \end{vmatrix} -(-3) \begin{vmatrix} 10 & 2 \\ 2 & 1 \end{vmatrix} +0}{-39}$$

$$= \frac{3[(-11)\cdot 1-4\cdot 2]+3(10\cdot 1-2\cdot 2)}{-39}$$

$$= \frac{3(-11-8)+3(10-4)}{-39}$$

$$= \frac{3(-19)+3(6)}{-39}$$

$$= \frac{-57+18}{-39}$$

$$= \frac{-39}{-39} \text{ or } 1$$

$$z = \frac{\begin{vmatrix} 3 & 1 & 10 \\ -3 & -2 & -11 \\ 0 & 2 & 2 \end{vmatrix}}{\begin{vmatrix} 3 & 1 & 2 \\ -3 & -2 & 4 \\ 0 & 2 & 1 \end{vmatrix}}$$

$$= \frac{3 \begin{vmatrix} -2 & -11 \\ 2 & 2 \end{vmatrix} -(-3) \begin{vmatrix} 1 & 10 \\ 2 & 2 \end{vmatrix} +0}{-39}$$

$$= \frac{3[(-2)\cdot 2-(-11)(2)]+3(1\cdot 2-10\cdot 2)}{-39}$$

$$= \frac{3(-4+22)+3(-18)}{-39}$$

$$= \frac{3(18)+3(-18)}{-39}$$

$$= \frac{0}{39} \text{ or } 0$$

$$\{(3,1,0)\}$$

57. $\begin{cases} 3x + 3y - z = 3 \\ 5x + y + 3z = 1 \\ 2x + 4y - 3z = 4 \end{cases}$

Since $\begin{vmatrix} 3 & 3 & -1 \\ 5 & 1 & 3 \\ 2 & 4 & -3 \end{vmatrix}$

$$= 3 \begin{vmatrix} 1 & 3 \\ 4 & -3 \end{vmatrix} -3 \begin{vmatrix} 5 & 3 \\ 2 & -3 \end{vmatrix} +(-1) \begin{vmatrix} 5 & 1 \\ 2 & 4 \end{vmatrix}$$

$$= 3[1\cdot(-3)-3\cdot 4] - 3[5\cdot(-3)-2\cdot 3] \\ - 1(5\cdot 4-2\cdot 1)$$

$$= 3(-3-12) - 3(-15-6) - (20-2)$$

$$= 3(-15) - 3(-21) - 18$$

$$= -45 + 63 - 18$$

$$= 0$$

Cramer's Rule does not apply.

59. $\begin{cases} 2x + 2y - z = 1 \\ x + 2y - 3z = 4 \\ 5x + 6y - 5z = 3 \end{cases}$

Since

$$\begin{vmatrix} 2 & 2 & -1 \\ 1 & 2 & -3 \\ 5 & 6 & -5 \end{vmatrix}$$

$$= 2\begin{vmatrix} 2 & -3 \\ 6 & -5 \end{vmatrix} - 1\begin{vmatrix} 2 & -1 \\ 6 & -5 \end{vmatrix} + 5\begin{vmatrix} 2 & -1 \\ 2 & -3 \end{vmatrix}$$

$$= 2[2(-5)-(-3)\cdot 6] - [2(-5)-(-1)\cdot 6]$$
$$\qquad + 5[2\cdot(-3)-(-1)\cdot 2]$$

$$= 2(-10+18) - (-10+6) + 5(-6+2)$$

$$= 2(8) + 4 + 5(-4)$$

$$= 16 + 4 - 20$$

$$= 0$$

Cramer's Rule does not apply.

61. Expand about column 2:

$$\begin{vmatrix} 1 & 1 & 2 & 1 \\ 2 & 1 & 0 & -3 \\ -2 & 0 & 1 & 2 \\ 4 & 0 & 5 & 1 \end{vmatrix}$$

$$= -1\begin{vmatrix} 2 & 0 & -3 \\ -2 & 1 & 2 \\ 4 & 5 & 1 \end{vmatrix} + 1\begin{vmatrix} 1 & 2 & 1 \\ -2 & 1 & 2 \\ 4 & 5 & 1 \end{vmatrix} - 0 + 0$$

$$= -1(-0+1\begin{vmatrix} 2 & -3 \\ 4 & 1 \end{vmatrix} - 5\begin{vmatrix} 2 & -3 \\ -2 & 2 \end{vmatrix})$$

$$\quad + 1(1\begin{vmatrix} 1 & 2 \\ 5 & 1 \end{vmatrix} - 2\begin{vmatrix} -2 & 2 \\ 4 & 1 \end{vmatrix} + 1\begin{vmatrix} -2 & 1 \\ 4 & 5 \end{vmatrix})$$

$$= -1\{[2\cdot 1-(-3)\cdot 4]$$
$$\qquad -5[2\cdot 2-(-3)(-2)]\}$$
$$\quad + (1\cdot 1-2\cdot 5) - 2[(-2)(1)-2\cdot 4]$$
$$\quad + [(-2)(5)-1\cdot 4]$$

$$= -1\{(2+12)-5(4-6)\} + (1-10)$$
$$\quad - 2(-2-8) + (-10-4)$$

$$= -1[14+10] - 9 + 20 - 14$$

$$= -24 - 9 + 20 - 14$$

$$= -27$$

63. $$\begin{vmatrix} 1 & 1 & 0 & 0 & 0 \\ 0 & 2 & 2 & 0 & 0 \\ 0 & 0 & 3 & 3 & 0 \\ 0 & 0 & 0 & 4 & 4 \\ 5 & 0 & 0 & 0 & 5 \end{vmatrix}$$

$$= 1\begin{vmatrix} 2 & 2 & 0 & 0 \\ 0 & 3 & 3 & 0 \\ 0 & 0 & 4 & 4 \\ 0 & 0 & 0 & 5 \end{vmatrix} - 1\begin{vmatrix} 0 & 2 & 0 & 0 \\ 0 & 3 & 3 & 0 \\ 0 & 0 & 4 & 4 \\ 5 & 0 & 0 & 5 \end{vmatrix}$$

$$+ 0 - 0 + 0$$

$$= 2\begin{vmatrix} 3 & 3 & 0 \\ 0 & 4 & 4 \\ 0 & 0 & 5 \end{vmatrix} - 0 + 0 - 0$$

$$- (0-0+0-5\begin{vmatrix} 2 & 0 & 0 \\ 3 & 3 & 0 \\ 0 & 4 & 4 \end{vmatrix})$$

$$= 2[3\begin{vmatrix} 4 & 4 \\ 0 & 5 \end{vmatrix} - 0+0] + 5[2\begin{vmatrix} 3 & 0 \\ 4 & 4 \end{vmatrix} - 0+0]$$

$$= 6(4\cdot 5-4\cdot 0) + 10(3\cdot 4-0\cdot 4)$$

$$= 6(20 + 10(12)$$

$$= 120 + 120$$

$$= 240$$

65. $\begin{cases} x - 2y - z + 2w = -2 \\ 2x - y + z - w = 0 \\ -x + 3y \quad - w = 4 \\ 5x - 3y \qquad = -4 \end{cases}$

$$x = \frac{\begin{vmatrix} -2 & -2 & -1 & 2 \\ 0 & -1 & 1 & -1 \\ 4 & 3 & 0 & -1 \\ -4 & -3 & 0 & 0 \end{vmatrix}}{\begin{vmatrix} 1 & -2 & -1 & 2 \\ 2 & -1 & 1 & -1 \\ -1 & 3 & 0 & -1 \\ 5 & -3 & 0 & 0 \end{vmatrix}}$$

$$= \frac{-1\begin{vmatrix} 0 & -1 & -1 \\ 4 & 3 & -1 \\ -4 & -3 & 0 \end{vmatrix} - 1\begin{vmatrix} -2 & -2 & 2 \\ 4 & 3 & -1 \\ -4 & -3 & 0 \end{vmatrix} + 0-0}{-1\begin{vmatrix} 2 & -1 & -1 \\ -1 & 3 & -1 \\ 5 & -3 & 0 \end{vmatrix} - 1\begin{vmatrix} 1 & -2 & 2 \\ -1 & 3 & -1 \\ 5 & -3 & 0 \end{vmatrix} + 0-0}$$

$$= \frac{-1[0-(-1)\begin{vmatrix} 4 & -1 \\ -4 & 0 \end{vmatrix} + (-1)\begin{vmatrix} 4 & 3 \\ -4 & -3 \end{vmatrix}]}{-1[-1\begin{vmatrix} -1 & 3 \\ 5 & -3 \end{vmatrix} - (-1)\begin{vmatrix} 2 & -1 \\ 5 & -3 \end{vmatrix} + 0]}$$

$$= \frac{-1[2\begin{vmatrix} 4 & 3 \\ -4 & -3 \end{vmatrix} - (-1)\begin{vmatrix} -2 & -2 \\ -4 & -3 \end{vmatrix} + 0]}{-1[2\begin{vmatrix} -1 & 3 \\ 5 & -3 \end{vmatrix} - (-1)\begin{vmatrix} 1 & -2 \\ 5 & -3 \end{vmatrix} + 0]}$$

288

$$= \frac{-1\{[4\cdot 0-(-1)(-4)]-1[4(-3)-3(-4)]\}}{-1\{-1[(-1)(-3)-3\cdot 5]+[2(-3)-(-1)\cdot 5])}$$

$$\frac{-1\{2[4\cdot(-3)-3(-4)]+[(-2)(-3)-(-2)(-4)]\}}{-\{2[(-1)(-3)-3\cdot 5]+[1(-3)-(-2)(5)]\}}$$

$$= \frac{-1[(0-4)-(-12+12)]-1[(-12+12)+(6-8)]}{-1[-1(3-15)+(-6+5)]-[2(3-15)+(-3+10)]}$$

$$= \frac{-1(-4)-(-2)}{-(12-1)-(-24+7)}$$

$$= \frac{4+2}{-11-(-17)}$$

$$= \frac{6}{6} \text{ or } 1$$

$$y = \frac{\begin{vmatrix} 1 & -2 & -1 & 2 \\ 2 & 0 & 1 & -1 \\ -1 & 4 & 0 & -1 \\ 5 & -4 & 0 & 0 \end{vmatrix}}{\begin{vmatrix} 1 & -2 & -1 & 2 \\ 2 & -1 & 1 & -1 \\ -1 & 3 & 0 & -1 \\ 5 & -3 & 0 & 0 \end{vmatrix}}$$

$$y = \frac{-1\begin{vmatrix} 2 & 0 & -1 \\ -1 & 4 & -1 \\ 5 & -4 & 0 \end{vmatrix} -1\begin{vmatrix} 1 & -2 & 2 \\ -1 & 4 & -1 \\ 5 & -4 & 0 \end{vmatrix} +0-0}{6}$$

$$= \frac{-1[-0+4\begin{vmatrix} 2 & -1 \\ 5 & 0 \end{vmatrix}-(-4)\begin{vmatrix} 2 & -1 \\ -1 & -1 \end{vmatrix}]}{}$$

$$\frac{-1[2\begin{vmatrix} -1 & 4 \\ 5 & 4 \end{vmatrix}-(-1)\begin{vmatrix} 1 & -2 \\ 5 & -4 \end{vmatrix}+0]}{6}$$

$$= \frac{-1\{4[2\cdot 0-(-1)(5)]+4[2(-1)-(-1)(-1)]\}}{}$$

$$\frac{-\{2[(-1)(-4)-4\cdot 5]+[1\cdot(-4)-(-2)\cdot 5]+0\}}{6}$$

$$= \frac{-[4(5)+4(-3)]-[2(-16)+6]}{6}$$

$$= \frac{-(20-12)-(-32+6)}{6}$$

$$= \frac{-8-(-26)}{6}$$

$$= \frac{18}{6} \text{ or } 3$$

$$z = \frac{\begin{vmatrix} 1 & -2 & -2 & 2 \\ 2 & -1 & 0 & -1 \\ -1 & 3 & 4 & -1 \\ 5 & -3 & -4 & 0 \end{vmatrix}}{\begin{vmatrix} 1 & -2 & -1 & 2 \\ 2 & -1 & -1 & -1 \\ -1 & 3 & 0 & -1 \\ 5 & -3 & 0 & 0 \end{vmatrix}}$$

$$= \frac{-2\begin{vmatrix} 2 & -1 & -1 \\ -1 & 3 & -1 \\ 5 & -3 & 0 \end{vmatrix}-0+4\begin{vmatrix} 1 & -2 & 2 \\ 2 & -1 & -1 \\ 5 & -3 & 0 \end{vmatrix}}{}$$

$$\frac{-(-4)\begin{vmatrix} 1 & -2 & 2 \\ 2 & -1 & -1 \\ -1 & 3 & -1 \end{vmatrix}}{6}$$

$$= \frac{-2[-1\begin{vmatrix} -1 & 3 \\ 5 & -3 \end{vmatrix}-(-1)\begin{vmatrix} 2 & -1 \\ 5 & -3 \end{vmatrix}+0]}{}$$

$$+4[2\begin{vmatrix} 2 & -1 \\ 5 & -3 \end{vmatrix}-(-1)\begin{vmatrix} 1 & -2 \\ 5 & -3 \end{vmatrix}+0]$$

$$\frac{+4[1\begin{vmatrix} -1 & -1 \\ 3 & -1 \end{vmatrix}-2\begin{vmatrix} -2 & 2 \\ 3 & -1 \end{vmatrix}+(-1)\begin{vmatrix} -2 & 2 \\ -1 & -1 \end{vmatrix}]}{6}$$

$$= \frac{-2\{-1[(-1)(-3)-3\cdot 5]+[2(-3)-(-1)(5)]\}}{}$$

$$+4\{2[2(-3)-(-1)(5)]+[1(-3)-(-2)(5)]\}$$

$$+4\{[(-1)(-1)-(-1)(3)]-2[(-2)(-1)-2\cdot 3]$$

$$\frac{-[(-2)(-1)-2(-1)]\}}{6}$$

$$= \frac{-2[-(3-15)+(-6+5)]+4[2(-6+5)+(-3+10)]}{}$$

$$\frac{+4[(1+3)-2(2-6)-(2+2)]}{6}$$

$$= \frac{-2(12-1)+4(-2+7)+4(4+8-4)}{6}$$

$$= \frac{-22+20+32}{6}$$

$$= \frac{30}{6} \text{ or } 5$$

$$w = \frac{\begin{vmatrix} 1 & -2 & -1 & -2 \\ 2 & -1 & 1 & 0 \\ -1 & 3 & 0 & 4 \\ 5 & -3 & 0 & -4 \end{vmatrix}}{\begin{vmatrix} 1 & -2 & -1 & 2 \\ 2 & -1 & 1 & -1 \\ -1 & 3 & 0 & -1 \\ 5 & -3 & 0 & 0 \end{vmatrix}}$$

$$= \frac{-1\begin{vmatrix} 2 & -1 & 0 \\ -1 & 3 & 4 \\ 5 & -3 & -4 \end{vmatrix} -1\begin{vmatrix} 1 & -2 & -2 \\ -1 & 3 & 4 \\ 5 & -3 & -4 \end{vmatrix} +0-0}{6}$$

$$= \frac{-1[0-4\begin{vmatrix} 2 & -1 \\ 5 & -3 \end{vmatrix} +(-4)\begin{vmatrix} 2 & -1 \\ -1 & 3 \end{vmatrix}]}{6}$$

$$\frac{-[1\begin{vmatrix} 3 & 4 \\ -3 & -4 \end{vmatrix} -(-1)\begin{vmatrix} -2 & -2 \\ -3 & -4 \end{vmatrix} +5\begin{vmatrix} -2 & -2 \\ 3 & 4 \end{vmatrix}]}{6}$$

$$= \frac{-1\{-4[2(-3)-(-1)\cdot 5]-4[2\cdot 3-(-1)(-1)]\}}{}$$

$$\frac{-\{[3\cdot(-4)-4(-3)]+[(-2)(-4-(-2)(-3)]}{}$$

$$\frac{+5[(-2)(4)-(-2)\cdot 3]\}}{6}$$

$$= \frac{-1[-4(-6+5)-4(6-1)]}{}$$

$$\frac{-[(-12+12)+(8-6)+5(-8+6)]}{6}$$

$$= \frac{-(4-20)-(0+2-10)}{6}$$

$$= \frac{-(-16)-(-8)}{6}$$

$$= \frac{16+8}{6}$$

$$= \frac{24}{6} \text{ or } 4$$

$$\{(1,3,5,4)\}$$

Problem Set 9.7:

1. $\begin{cases} 2x + 3y = -4 \\ 5x - 6y = 1 \end{cases}$ $\begin{bmatrix} 2 & 3 & | & -4 \\ 5 & -6 & | & 1 \end{bmatrix}$

3. $\begin{cases} 2x - 3y + 4z = 1 \\ 5x - y + z = 0 \\ 7x + 6y - 2z = 5 \end{cases}$ $\begin{bmatrix} 2 & -3 & 4 & | & 1 \\ 5 & -1 & 1 & | & 0 \\ 7 & 6 & -2 & | & 5 \end{bmatrix}$

5. $\begin{cases} x + 2y = z \\ -x - 11 = y \\ y - 13 = \frac{1}{2} \end{cases}$ $\begin{cases} x + 2y - z = 0 \\ -x - y = 11 \\ y -4z = 13 \end{cases}$

$$\begin{bmatrix} 1 & 2 & -1 & | & 0 \\ -1 & -1 & 0 & | & 11 \\ 0 & 1 & -4 & | & 13 \end{bmatrix}$$

7. $\begin{bmatrix} 1 & 2 & | & 4 \\ 9 & -8 & | & -1 \end{bmatrix}$ $\begin{cases} x + 2y = 4 \\ 9x - 8y = -1 \end{cases}$

9. $\begin{bmatrix} 1 & 0 & 0 & | & 5 \\ 0 & 1 & 0 & | & -3 \\ 0 & 0 & 1 & | & -2 \end{bmatrix}$ $\begin{cases} x = 5 \\ y = -3 \\ z = -2 \end{cases}$

11. $\begin{cases} x + 3y = 7 \\ -2x + y = 0 \end{cases}$ $\begin{bmatrix} 1 & 3 & | & 7 \\ -2 & 1 & | & 0 \end{bmatrix}$

$\begin{bmatrix} 1 & 3 & | & 7 \\ -2 & 1 & | & 0 \end{bmatrix}$ $\xrightarrow[\text{by 2 and add to row 2}]{\text{multiply row 1}}$ $\begin{bmatrix} 1 & 3 & | & 7 \\ 0 & 7 & | & 14 \end{bmatrix}$

$\xrightarrow[\text{2 by } \frac{1}{7}]{\text{multiply row}}$ $\begin{bmatrix} 1 & 3 & | & 7 \\ 0 & 1 & | & 2 \end{bmatrix}$

So, $x + 3y = 7$

$y = 2$

$x + 6 = 7$

$x = 1$ $\{(1,2)\}$

13. $\begin{cases} 2x + 4y = 2 \\ 3x + 7y = 1 \end{cases}$ $\begin{bmatrix} 2 & 4 & | & 2 \\ 3 & 7 & | & 1 \end{bmatrix}$

$\begin{bmatrix} 2 & 4 & | & 2 \\ 3 & 7 & | & 1 \end{bmatrix}$ $\xrightarrow[\text{by } \frac{1}{2}]{\text{multiply row 1}}$ $\begin{bmatrix} 1 & 2 & | & 1 \\ 3 & 7 & | & 1 \end{bmatrix}$

$\xrightarrow[\text{and add to row 2}]{\text{multiply row 1 by -3}}$ $\begin{bmatrix} 1 & 2 & | & 1 \\ 0 & 1 & | & -2 \end{bmatrix}$

So, $x + 2y = 1$

$y = -2$

$x + 2(-2) = 1$

$x = 5$ $\{(5,-2)\}$

15. $\begin{cases} x + 2y + 2z = 3 \\ 2x + 3y + 6z = 2 \\ -x + y + z = 0 \end{cases}$ $\begin{bmatrix} 1 & 2 & 2 & | & 3 \\ 2 & 3 & 6 & | & 2 \\ -1 & 1 & 1 & | & 0 \end{bmatrix}$

$\begin{bmatrix} 1 & 2 & 2 & | & 3 \\ 2 & 3 & 6 & | & 2 \\ -1 & 1 & 1 & | & 0 \end{bmatrix}$ $\xrightarrow[\text{by 2 and add to row 2}]{\text{multiply row 3}}$ $\begin{bmatrix} 1 & 2 & 2 & | & 3 \\ 0 & 5 & 8 & | & 2 \\ -1 & 1 & 1 & | & 0 \end{bmatrix}$

$\xrightarrow[\text{to row 3}]{\text{add row 1}}$ $\begin{bmatrix} 1 & 2 & 2 & | & 3 \\ 0 & 5 & 8 & | & 2 \\ 0 & 3 & 3 & | & 3 \end{bmatrix}$

$\xrightarrow[\text{row 3}]{\text{Exchange row 2}}$ $\begin{bmatrix} 1 & 2 & 2 & | & 3 \\ 0 & 3 & 3 & | & 3 \\ 0 & 5 & 8 & | & 2 \end{bmatrix}$

$\xrightarrow[\text{by } \frac{1}{3}]{\text{multiply row 2}}$ $\begin{bmatrix} 1 & 2 & 2 & | & 3 \\ 0 & 1 & 1 & | & 1 \\ 0 & 5 & 8 & | & 2 \end{bmatrix}$

$\xrightarrow[\substack{-5 \text{ and add to row} \\ 3}]{\text{multiply row 2 by}}$ $\begin{bmatrix} 1 & 2 & 2 & | & 3 \\ 0 & 1 & 1 & | & 1 \\ 0 & 0 & 3 & | & -3 \end{bmatrix}$

$\xrightarrow[\text{by } \frac{1}{3}]{\text{multiply row 3}}$ $\begin{bmatrix} 1 & 2 & 2 & | & 3 \\ 0 & 1 & 1 & | & 1 \\ 0 & 0 & 1 & | & -1 \end{bmatrix}$

$x + 2y + 2z = 3$
$y + z = 1$
$z = -1$

$y - 1 = 1$
$y = 2$

$x + 4 + 2(-1) = 3$
$x + 2 = 3$
$x = 1$ $\qquad \{(1,2,-1)\}$

17. $\begin{cases} 3x + 2y = 5 \\ 6x - 5y = 3 \end{cases}$ $\begin{bmatrix} 3 & 2 & | & 5 \\ 6 & -5 & | & 3 \end{bmatrix}$

19. $\begin{cases} 3x - 2y + 5z = 4 \\ 2x + 3y - z = 0 \\ x - y - 2z = 1 \end{cases}$ $\begin{bmatrix} 3 & -2 & 5 & | & 4 \\ 2 & 3 & -1 & | & 0 \\ 1 & -1 & -2 & | & 1 \end{bmatrix}$

21. $\begin{cases} x + 3z = 2y \\ -x - 10 = z \\ y + 3 = 4x - z \end{cases}$ $\begin{cases} x - 2y + 3z = 0 \\ -x - \quad z = 10 \\ -4x + y + z = -3 \end{cases}$

$\begin{bmatrix} 1 & -2 & 3 & | & 0 \\ -1 & 0 & -1 & | & 10 \\ -4 & 1 & 1 & | & -3 \end{bmatrix}$

23. $\begin{bmatrix} 2 & 1 & | & 3 \\ 6 & -5 & | & 11 \end{bmatrix}$ $\begin{cases} 2x + y = 3 \\ 6x - 5y = 11 \end{cases}$

25. $\begin{bmatrix} 0 & 0 & 1 & | & -3 \\ 0 & 1 & 0 & | & 4 \\ 1 & 0 & 0 & | & 2 \end{bmatrix}$ $\begin{cases} x = -3 \\ y = 4 \\ z = 2 \end{cases}$

27. $\begin{cases} x - 2y = -1 \\ -3x + 8y = 5 \end{cases}$ $\begin{bmatrix} 1 & -2 & | & -1 \\ -3 & 8 & | & 5 \end{bmatrix}$

$\begin{bmatrix} 1 & -2 & | & -1 \\ -3 & 8 & | & 5 \end{bmatrix}$ $\xrightarrow[\substack{\text{by 3 and add to} \\ \text{row 2}}]{\text{multiply row 1}}$ $\begin{bmatrix} 1 & -2 & | & -1 \\ 0 & 2 & | & 2 \end{bmatrix}$

$\xrightarrow[\text{by } \frac{1}{2}]{\text{multiply row 2}}$ $\begin{bmatrix} 1 & -2 & | & -1 \\ 0 & 1 & | & 1 \end{bmatrix}$

$x - 2y = -1$
$y = 1$

$x - 2 = -1$
$x = 1$ $\qquad \{(1,1)\}$

29. $\begin{cases} 3x - 9y = 3 \\ 2x - 5y = 4 \end{cases}$ $\begin{bmatrix} 3 & -9 & | & 3 \\ 2 & -5 & | & 4 \end{bmatrix}$

$\begin{bmatrix} 3 & -4 & | & 3 \\ 2 & -5 & | & 4 \end{bmatrix}$ $\xrightarrow[\text{by } \frac{1}{3}]{\text{multiply row 1}}$ $\begin{bmatrix} 1 & -3 & | & 1 \\ 2 & -5 & | & 4 \end{bmatrix}$

$\xrightarrow[\substack{-2 \text{ and add to row 2}}]{\text{multiply row 1 by}}$ $\begin{bmatrix} 1 & -3 & | & 1 \\ 0 & 1 & | & 2 \end{bmatrix}$

$x - 3y = 1$
$y = 2$

$x - 6 = 1$
$x = 7$ $\qquad \{(7,2)\}$

31. $\begin{cases} x + 3y - 2z = 1 \\ 2x + 5y - 2z = 6 \\ -2x - 4y + 3z = -1 \end{cases}$ $\begin{bmatrix} 1 & 3 & -2 & | & 1 \\ 2 & 5 & -2 & | & 6 \\ -2 & -4 & 3 & | & -1 \end{bmatrix}$

$\begin{bmatrix} 1 & 3 & -2 & | & 1 \\ 2 & 5 & -2 & | & 6 \\ -2 & -4 & 3 & | & -1 \end{bmatrix}$ $\xrightarrow[\text{to row 2}]{\text{add row 3}}$ $\begin{bmatrix} 1 & 3 & -2 & | & 1 \\ 0 & 1 & 1 & | & 5 \\ -2 & -4 & 3 & | & -1 \end{bmatrix}$

$\xrightarrow[\substack{\text{by 2 and add} \\ \text{to row 3}}]{\text{multiply row 1}}$ $\begin{bmatrix} 1 & 3 & -2 & | & 1 \\ 0 & 1 & 1 & | & 5 \\ 0 & 2 & -1 & | & 1 \end{bmatrix}$

$$\xrightarrow[\substack{\text{-3 and add to row} \\ 1}]{\text{multiply row 2 by}} \begin{bmatrix} 1 & 0 & -5 & | & -14 \\ 0 & 1 & 1 & | & 5 \\ 0 & 2 & -1 & | & 1 \end{bmatrix}$$

$$\xrightarrow[\substack{\text{-2 and add to row} \\ 3}]{\text{multiply row 2 by}} \begin{bmatrix} 1 & 0 & -5 & | & -14 \\ 0 & 1 & 1 & | & 5 \\ 0 & 0 & -3 & | & -9 \end{bmatrix}$$

$$\xrightarrow[\text{by} -\frac{1}{3}]{\text{multiply row 3}} \begin{bmatrix} 1 & 0 & -5 & | & -14 \\ 0 & 1 & 1 & | & 5 \\ 0 & 0 & 1 & | & 3 \end{bmatrix}$$

$x - 5z = -14$

$\quad y + z = 5$

$\qquad z = 3$

$y + 3 = 5$

$\quad y = 2$

$x - 5(3) = -14$

$\quad x - 15 = -14$

$\qquad x = 1 \qquad \{(1,2,3)\}$

33. $\begin{cases} 2x - 6y + 4z = 0 \\ 3x + y - 4z = 10 \\ 4x + 3y - 9x = 13 \end{cases}$ $\begin{bmatrix} 2 & -6 & 4 & | & 0 \\ 3 & 1 & -4 & | & 10 \\ 4 & 3 & -9 & | & 13 \end{bmatrix}$

$\begin{bmatrix} 2 & -6 & 4 & | & 0 \\ 3 & 1 & -4 & | & 10 \\ 4 & 3 & -9 & | & 13 \end{bmatrix} \xrightarrow[\text{row 1 by } \frac{1}{2}]{\text{multiply}} \begin{bmatrix} 1 & -3 & 2 & | & 0 \\ 3 & 1 & -4 & | & 10 \\ 4 & 3 & -9 & | & 13 \end{bmatrix}$

$$\xrightarrow[\substack{\text{-3 and add to row} \\ 2}]{\text{multiply row 1 by}} \begin{bmatrix} 1 & -3 & 2 & | & 0 \\ 0 & 10 & -10 & | & 10 \\ 4 & 3 & -9 & | & 13 \end{bmatrix}$$

$$\xrightarrow[\substack{\text{-4 and add to row} \\ 3}]{\text{multiply row 1 by}} \begin{bmatrix} 1 & -3 & 2 & | & 0 \\ 0 & 10 & -10 & | & 10 \\ 0 & 15 & -17 & | & 13 \end{bmatrix}$$

$$\xrightarrow[\text{by} \frac{1}{10}]{\text{multiply row 2}} \begin{bmatrix} 1 & -3 & 2 & | & 0 \\ 0 & 1 & -1 & | & 1 \\ 0 & 15 & -17 & | & 13 \end{bmatrix}$$

$$\xrightarrow[\text{3 and add to row 1}]{\text{multiply row 2 by}} \begin{bmatrix} 1 & 0 & -1 & | & 3 \\ 0 & 1 & -1 & | & 1 \\ 0 & 15 & -17 & | & 13 \end{bmatrix}$$

$$\xrightarrow[\substack{\text{-15 and add to row} \\ 3}]{\text{multiply row 2 by}} \begin{bmatrix} 1 & 0 & -1 & | & 3 \\ 0 & 1 & -1 & | & 1 \\ 0 & 0 & -2 & | & -2 \end{bmatrix}$$

$$\xrightarrow[\text{by} -\frac{1}{2}]{\text{multiply row 3}} \begin{bmatrix} 1 & 0 & -1 & | & 3 \\ 0 & 1 & -1 & | & 1 \\ 0 & 0 & 1 & | & 1 \end{bmatrix}$$

$x - z = 3$

$y - z = 1$

$\quad z = 1$

$y - 1 = 1$

$\quad y = 2$

$x - 1 = 3$

$\quad x = 4 \qquad \{(4,2,1)\}$

35. $\begin{cases} 3x + 9y - 6z = -15 \\ 2x + 3y + 2z = 2 \\ 5x + 8y + 14z = 13 \end{cases}$ $\begin{bmatrix} 3 & 9 & -6 & | & -15 \\ 2 & 3 & 2 & | & 2 \\ 5 & 8 & 14 & | & 13 \end{bmatrix}$

$\begin{bmatrix} 3 & 9 & -6 & | & -15 \\ 2 & 3 & 2 & | & 2 \\ 5 & 8 & 14 & | & 13 \end{bmatrix} \xrightarrow[\text{by } \frac{1}{3}]{\text{multiply row 1}} \begin{bmatrix} 1 & 3 & -2 & | & -5 \\ 2 & 3 & 2 & | & 2 \\ 5 & 8 & 14 & | & 13 \end{bmatrix}$

$$\xrightarrow[\substack{\text{-2 and add to row} \\ 2}]{\text{multiply row 1 by}} \begin{bmatrix} 1 & 3 & -2 & | & -5 \\ 0 & -3 & 6 & | & 12 \\ 5 & 8 & 14 & | & 13 \end{bmatrix}$$

$$\xrightarrow[\substack{\text{-5 and add to row} \\ 3}]{\text{multiply row 1 by}} \begin{bmatrix} 1 & 3 & -2 & | & -5 \\ 0 & -3 & 6 & | & 12 \\ 0 & -7 & 24 & | & 38 \end{bmatrix}$$

$$\xrightarrow[\text{by} -\frac{1}{3}]{\text{multiply row 2}} \begin{bmatrix} 1 & 3 & -2 & | & -5 \\ 0 & 1 & -2 & | & -4 \\ 0 & -7 & 24 & | & 38 \end{bmatrix}$$

$$\xrightarrow[\text{7 and add to row 3}]{\text{multiply row 2 by}} \begin{bmatrix} 1 & 3 & -2 & | & -5 \\ 0 & 1 & -2 & | & -4 \\ 0 & 0 & 10 & | & 10 \end{bmatrix}$$

$$\xrightarrow[\text{by} \frac{1}{10}]{\text{multiply row 3}} \begin{bmatrix} 1 & 3 & -2 & | & -5 \\ 0 & 1 & -2 & | & -4 \\ 0 & 0 & 1 & | & 1 \end{bmatrix}$$

$x + 3y - 2z = -5$

$\quad y - 2z = -4$

$\qquad z = 1$

$$y - 2(1) = -4$$
$$y - 2 = -4$$
$$y = -2$$

$$x + 3(-2) - 2(1) = -5$$
$$x - 6 - 2 = -5$$
$$x - 8 = -5$$
$$x = 3 \quad \{(3,-2,1)\}$$

37. $\begin{cases} 3x + 4y = 0 \\ 4x + 3y = 0 \end{cases}$ $\begin{bmatrix} 3 & 4 & | & 0 \\ 4 & 3 & | & 0 \end{bmatrix}$

$\begin{bmatrix} 3 & 4 & | & 0 \\ 4 & 3 & | & 0 \end{bmatrix}$ $\xrightarrow[\text{by } \frac{1}{3}]{\text{multiply row 1}}$ $\begin{bmatrix} 1 & \frac{4}{3} & | & 0 \\ 4 & 3 & | & 0 \end{bmatrix}$

$$\frac{-16}{3} + \frac{9}{3} = \frac{-7}{3}$$

$\xrightarrow[\substack{-4 \text{ and add to row} \\ 2}]{\text{multiply row 1 by}}$ $\begin{bmatrix} 1 & \frac{4}{3} & | & 0 \\ 0 & -\frac{7}{3} & | & 0 \end{bmatrix}$

$\xrightarrow[\text{by } -\frac{3}{7}]{\text{multiply row 2}}$ $\begin{bmatrix} 1 & \frac{4}{3} & | & 0 \\ 0 & 1 & | & 0 \end{bmatrix}$

$$x + \frac{4}{3}y = 0$$
$$y = 0$$

$$x + \frac{4}{3}(0) = 0$$
$$x = 0 \quad \{(0,0)\}$$

39. $\begin{cases} 6x - 5y = 6 \\ 9x + 7y = -20 \end{cases}$ $\begin{bmatrix} 6 & -5 & | & 6 \\ 9 & 7 & | & -20 \end{bmatrix}$

$\begin{bmatrix} 6 & -5 & | & 6 \\ 9 & 7 & | & -20 \end{bmatrix}$ $\xrightarrow[\text{by } \frac{1}{6}]{\text{multiply row 1}}$ $\begin{bmatrix} 1 & -\frac{5}{6} & | & 1 \\ 9 & 7 & | & -20 \end{bmatrix}$

$$\frac{45}{6} + \frac{42}{6} = \frac{87}{6} \text{ or } \frac{29}{2}$$

$\xrightarrow[\substack{-9 \text{ and add to row} \\ 2}]{\text{multiply row 1 by}}$ $\begin{bmatrix} 1 & -\frac{5}{6} & | & 1 \\ 0 & \frac{29}{2} & | & -29 \end{bmatrix}$

$\xrightarrow[\text{by } \frac{2}{29}]{\text{multiply row 2}}$ $\begin{bmatrix} 1 & -\frac{5}{6} & | & 1 \\ 0 & 1 & | & -2 \end{bmatrix}$

$$x - \frac{5}{6}y = 1$$
$$y = -2$$
$$x - \frac{5}{6}(-2) = 1$$
$$x + \frac{5}{3} = 1$$
$$x = 1 - \frac{5}{3} \text{ or } -\frac{2}{3}$$

$$\left\{\left(-\frac{2}{3}, -2\right)\right\}$$

41. $\begin{cases} -4x + 15y = -2 \\ 12x + 5y = -4 \end{cases}$ $\begin{bmatrix} -4 & 15 & | & -2 \\ 12 & 5 & | & -4 \end{bmatrix}$

$\begin{bmatrix} -4 & 15 & | & -2 \\ 12 & 5 & | & -4 \end{bmatrix}$ $\xrightarrow[\text{by } -\frac{1}{4}]{\text{multiply row 1}}$ $\begin{bmatrix} 1 & -\frac{15}{4} & | & \frac{1}{2} \\ 12 & 5 & | & -4 \end{bmatrix}$

$$-12 \cdot \frac{-15}{4} = 45$$
$$45 + 5 = 50$$

$\xrightarrow[\substack{12 \text{ and add to row} \\ 2}]{\text{multiply row 1 by}}$ $\begin{bmatrix} 1 & -\frac{15}{4} & | & \frac{1}{2} \\ 0 & 50 & | & -10 \end{bmatrix}$

$\xrightarrow[\text{by } \frac{1}{50}]{\text{multiply row 2}}$ $\begin{bmatrix} 1 & -\frac{15}{4} & | & \frac{1}{2} \\ 0 & 1 & | & -\frac{1}{5} \end{bmatrix}$

$$x - \frac{15}{4}y = \frac{1}{2}$$
$$y = -\frac{1}{5}$$

$$x - \frac{15}{4}\left(-\frac{1}{5}\right) = \frac{1}{2}$$
$$x + \frac{3}{4} = \frac{1}{2}$$
$$x = -\frac{1}{4} \quad \left\{\left(-\frac{1}{4}, -\frac{1}{5}\right)\right\}$$

43. $\begin{cases} 3x - 4y = 5 \\ 4x - 7y = 9 \end{cases}$ $\begin{bmatrix} 3 & -4 & | & 5 \\ 4 & -7 & | & 9 \end{bmatrix}$

$\begin{bmatrix} 3 & -4 & | & 5 \\ 4 & -7 & | & 9 \end{bmatrix}$ $\xrightarrow[\text{by } \frac{1}{3}]{\text{multiply row 1}}$ $\begin{bmatrix} 1 & -\frac{4}{3} & | & \frac{5}{3} \\ 4 & -7 & | & 9 \end{bmatrix}$

$\xrightarrow[\substack{-4 \text{ and add to row} \\ 2}]{\text{multiply row 1 by}}$ $\begin{bmatrix} 1 & -\frac{4}{3} & | & \frac{5}{3} \\ 0 & -\frac{5}{3} & | & \frac{7}{3} \end{bmatrix}$

$$\frac{16}{3} + -7 = -\frac{5}{3}$$

$$-\frac{20}{3} + 9 = \frac{7}{3}$$

$$\xrightarrow[\text{by } -\frac{3}{5}]{\text{multiply row 2}} \begin{bmatrix} 1 & -\frac{4}{3} & \bigg| & \frac{5}{3} \\ 0 & 1 & \bigg| & -\frac{7}{5} \end{bmatrix}$$

$$x - \frac{4}{3}y = \frac{5}{3}$$
$$y = -\frac{7}{5}$$

$$x - \frac{4}{3}(-\frac{7}{5}) = \frac{5}{3}$$
$$x + \frac{28}{15} = \frac{5}{3}$$
$$x = \frac{5}{3} - \frac{28}{15}$$
$$= \frac{25}{15} - \frac{28}{15}$$
$$= \frac{-3}{15} \text{ or } -\frac{1}{5} \qquad \{(-\frac{1}{5}, \frac{-7}{5})\}$$

45. $\begin{cases} 17x - 11y = -1 \\ -34x + 22y = 2 \end{cases}$ $\begin{bmatrix} 17 & -11 & \big| & -1 \\ -34 & 22 & \big| & 2 \end{bmatrix}$

$$\begin{bmatrix} 17 & -11 & \big| & -1 \\ -34 & 22 & \big| & 2 \end{bmatrix} \xrightarrow[\text{by } \frac{1}{17}]{\text{multiply row 1}} \begin{bmatrix} 1 & -\frac{11}{17} & \big| & -\frac{1}{17} \\ -34 & 22 & \big| & 2 \end{bmatrix}$$

$$\xrightarrow[\substack{34 \text{ and add to row} \\ 2}]{\text{multiply row 1 by}} \begin{bmatrix} 1 & -\frac{11}{17} & \big| & -\frac{1}{17} \\ 0 & 0 & \big| & 0 \end{bmatrix}$$

Dependent system

$$\{(x,y) \mid 17x-11y=-1\}$$

47. $\begin{cases} \frac{1}{5}x - \frac{2}{3}y = \frac{1}{15} \\ \frac{3}{4}x - \frac{5}{6}y = \frac{1}{3} \end{cases}$ $\begin{bmatrix} \frac{1}{5} & -\frac{2}{3} & \big| & \frac{1}{15} \\ \frac{3}{4} & -\frac{5}{6} & \big| & \frac{1}{3} \end{bmatrix}$

$$\begin{bmatrix} \frac{1}{5} & -\frac{2}{3} & \big| & \frac{1}{15} \\ \frac{3}{4} & -\frac{5}{6} & \big| & \frac{1}{3} \end{bmatrix} \xrightarrow[\text{by } 5]{\text{multiply row 1}} \begin{bmatrix} 1 & -\frac{10}{3} & \big| & \frac{1}{3} \\ \frac{3}{4} & -\frac{5}{6} & \big| & \frac{1}{3} \end{bmatrix}$$

$$\frac{-10}{3} - \frac{3}{4} = \frac{5}{2}$$

$$\frac{5}{2} + \frac{-5}{6} = \frac{15-5}{6} = \frac{10}{6} = \frac{5}{3}$$

$$-\frac{3}{4} \cdot \frac{1}{3} = \frac{-1}{4}$$

$$\frac{-1}{4} + \frac{1}{3} = \frac{-3}{12} + \frac{4}{12} = \frac{1}{12}$$

$$\xrightarrow[\substack{-\frac{3}{4} \text{ and add to row} \\ 2}]{\text{multiply row 1 by}} \begin{bmatrix} 1 & -\frac{10}{3} & \big| & \frac{1}{3} \\ 0 & \frac{5}{3} & \big| & \frac{1}{12} \end{bmatrix}$$

$$\xrightarrow[\text{by } \frac{3}{5}]{\text{multiply row 2}} \begin{bmatrix} 1 & -\frac{10}{3} & \big| & \frac{1}{3} \\ 0 & 1 & \big| & \frac{1}{20} \end{bmatrix}$$

$$x + \frac{-10}{3}y = \frac{1}{3}$$
$$y = \frac{1}{20}$$

$$x + \frac{-10}{3}(\frac{1}{20}) = \frac{1}{3}$$
$$x + -\frac{1}{6} = \frac{1}{3}$$
$$x = \frac{1}{3} + \frac{1}{6} = \frac{2+1}{6}$$
$$= \frac{3}{6} \text{ or } \frac{1}{2} \qquad \{(\frac{1}{2}, \frac{1}{20})\}$$

49. $\begin{cases} x + y + z = 6 \\ x + 2y + z = 9 \\ 2x + 2y - z = 6 \end{cases}$ $\begin{bmatrix} 1 & 1 & 1 & \big| & 6 \\ 1 & 2 & 1 & \big| & 9 \\ 2 & 2 & -1 & \big| & 6 \end{bmatrix}$

$$\begin{bmatrix} 1 & 1 & 1 & \big| & 6 \\ 1 & 2 & 1 & \big| & 9 \\ 2 & 2 & -1 & \big| & 6 \end{bmatrix} \xrightarrow[\substack{\text{by } -1 \text{ and add} \\ \text{to row } 2}]{\text{multiply row 1}} \begin{bmatrix} 1 & 1 & 1 & \big| & 6 \\ 0 & 1 & 0 & \big| & 3 \\ 2 & 2 & -1 & \big| & 6 \end{bmatrix}$$

$$\xrightarrow[\substack{-2 \text{ and add to row} \\ 3}]{\text{multiply row 1 by}} \begin{bmatrix} 1 & 1 & 1 & \big| & 6 \\ 0 & 1 & 0 & \big| & 3 \\ 0 & 0 & -3 & \big| & -6 \end{bmatrix}$$

$$\xrightarrow[\text{by } -\frac{1}{3}]{\text{multiply row 3}} \begin{bmatrix} 1 & 1 & 1 & \big| & 6 \\ 0 & 1 & 0 & \big| & 3 \\ 0 & 0 & 1 & \big| & 2 \end{bmatrix}$$

$$x + y + z = 6$$
$$y = 3$$
$$z = 2$$

$$x + 3 + 2 = 6$$
$$x = 1 \qquad \{(1,3,2)\}$$

51. $\begin{cases} 3x + y + 2z = 10 \\ -3x - 2y + 4z = -11 \\ 2y + z = 2 \end{cases}$ $\begin{bmatrix} 3 & 1 & 2 & \big| & 10 \\ -3 & -2 & 4 & \big| & -11 \\ 0 & 2 & 1 & \big| & 2 \end{bmatrix}$

$$\begin{bmatrix} 3 & 1 & 2 & | & 10 \\ -3 & -2 & 4 & | & -11 \\ 0 & 2 & 1 & | & 2 \end{bmatrix} \xrightarrow[\text{1 by } \frac{1}{3}]{\text{multiply row}} \begin{bmatrix} 1 & \frac{1}{3} & \frac{2}{3} & | & \frac{10}{3} \\ -3 & -2 & 4 & | & -11 \\ 0 & 2 & 1 & | & 2 \end{bmatrix}$$

$$\xrightarrow[\substack{\text{3 and add to row} \\ 2}]{\text{multiply row 1 by}} \begin{bmatrix} 1 & \frac{1}{3} & \frac{2}{3} & | & \frac{10}{3} \\ 0 & -1 & 6 & | & -1 \\ 0 & 2 & 1 & | & 2 \end{bmatrix}$$

$$\xrightarrow[\text{by } -1]{\text{multiply row 2}} \begin{bmatrix} 1 & \frac{1}{3} & \frac{2}{3} & | & \frac{10}{3} \\ 0 & 1 & -6 & | & 1 \\ 0 & 2 & 1 & | & 2 \end{bmatrix}$$

$$\xrightarrow[\substack{-2 \text{ and add to row} \\ 3}]{\text{multiply row 2 by}} \begin{bmatrix} 1 & \frac{1}{3} & \frac{2}{3} & | & \frac{10}{3} \\ 0 & 1 & -6 & | & 1 \\ 0 & 0 & 13 & | & 0 \end{bmatrix}$$

$$x + \frac{1}{3}y + \frac{2}{3}z = \frac{10}{3}$$
$$y - 6z = 1$$
$$13z = 0$$
$$z = 0$$

$$y - 6(0) = 1$$
$$y = 1$$

$$x + \frac{1}{3}(1) + \frac{2}{3}(0) = \frac{10}{3}$$
$$x + \frac{1}{3} = \frac{10}{3}$$
$$x = \frac{9}{3} \text{ or } 3$$

$$\{(3,1,0)\}$$

53. $\begin{cases} 3x + 3y - z = 3 \\ 5x + y + 3z = 1 \\ 2x + 4y - 3z = 4 \end{cases}$ $\begin{bmatrix} 3 & 3 & -1 & | & 3 \\ 5 & 1 & 3 & | & 1 \\ 2 & 4 & -3 & | & 4 \end{bmatrix}$

$$\begin{bmatrix} 3 & 3 & -1 & | & 3 \\ 5 & 1 & 3 & | & 1 \\ 2 & 4 & -3 & | & 4 \end{bmatrix} \xrightarrow[\substack{\text{by } -1 \text{ and add} \\ \text{to row 1}}]{\text{multiply row 3}} \begin{bmatrix} 1 & -1 & 2 & | & -1 \\ 5 & 1 & 3 & | & 1 \\ 2 & 4 & -3 & | & 4 \end{bmatrix}$$

$$\xrightarrow[\substack{\text{Also, multiply row 1} \\ \text{by } -2 \text{ and add to} \\ \text{row 3}}]{\substack{\text{multiply row 1 by} \\ -5 \text{ and add to row 2}}} \begin{bmatrix} 1 & -1 & 2 & | & 1 \\ 0 & 6 & -7 & | & 6 \\ 0 & 6 & -7 & | & 6 \end{bmatrix}$$

$$\xrightarrow[\substack{-1 \text{ and add to row} \\ 3}]{\text{multiply row 2 by}} \begin{bmatrix} 1 & -1 & 2 & | & 1 \\ 0 & 6 & -7 & | & 6 \\ 0 & 0 & 0 & | & 0 \end{bmatrix}$$

Row 3 indicates the system is dependent.

55. $\begin{cases} 2x + 2y - z = 1 \\ x + 2y - 3z = 4 \\ 5x + 6y - 5z = 3 \end{cases}$ $\begin{bmatrix} 2 & 2 & -1 & | & 1 \\ 1 & 2 & -3 & | & 4 \\ 5 & 6 & -5 & | & 3 \end{bmatrix}$

$$\begin{bmatrix} 2 & 2 & -1 & | & 1 \\ 1 & 2 & -3 & | & 4 \\ 5 & 6 & -5 & | & 3 \end{bmatrix} \xrightarrow[\text{and row 2}]{\text{exchange row 1}} \begin{bmatrix} 1 & 2 & -3 & | & 4 \\ 2 & 2 & -1 & | & 1 \\ 5 & 6 & -5 & | & 3 \end{bmatrix}$$

$$\xrightarrow[\substack{-2 \text{ and add to row} \\ 2}]{\text{multiply row 1 by}} \begin{bmatrix} 1 & 2 & -3 & | & 4 \\ 0 & -2 & 5 & | & -7 \\ 5 & 6 & -5 & | & 3 \end{bmatrix}$$

$$\xrightarrow[\substack{-5 \text{ and add to row} \\ 3}]{\text{multiply row 1 by}} \begin{bmatrix} 1 & 2 & -3 & | & 4 \\ 0 & -2 & 5 & | & -7 \\ 0 & -4 & 10 & | & -17 \end{bmatrix}$$

$$\xrightarrow[\text{by } -\frac{1}{2}]{\text{multiply row 2}} \begin{bmatrix} 1 & 2 & -3 & | & 4 \\ 0 & 1 & -\frac{5}{2} & | & \frac{7}{2} \\ 0 & -4 & 10 & | & -17 \end{bmatrix}$$

$$\xrightarrow[\substack{4 \text{ and add to row} \\ 3}]{\text{multiply row 2 by}} \begin{bmatrix} 1 & 2 & -3 & | & 4 \\ 0 & 1 & -\frac{5}{2} & | & \frac{7}{2} \\ 0 & 0 & 0 & | & -3 \end{bmatrix}$$

Row three indicates the system is inconsistent.

The solution set is $\emptyset$.

57. $\begin{cases} x + y + z + w = 2 \\ x - y + 2z = -1 \\ 2y + 3z - 3w = -9 \\ 2x - 3y + 2w = 6 \end{cases}$

$$\begin{bmatrix} 1 & 1 & 1 & 1 & | & 2 \\ 1 & -1 & 2 & 0 & | & -1 \\ 0 & 2 & 3 & -3 & | & -9 \\ 2 & -3 & 0 & 2 & | & 6 \end{bmatrix}$$

$$\begin{bmatrix} 1 & 1 & 1 & 1 & \Big| & 2 \\ 1 & -1 & 2 & 0 & \Big| & -1 \\ 0 & 2 & 3 & -3 & \Big| & -9 \\ 2 & -3 & 0 & 2 & \Big| & 6 \end{bmatrix} \xrightarrow[\substack{\text{also,} \\ \text{multiply row} \\ 1 \text{ by } -2 \text{ and} \\ \text{add to row 4}}]{\substack{\text{multiply} \\ \text{row 1 by} \\ -1 \text{ and add} \\ \text{to row 2}}} \begin{bmatrix} 1 & 1 & 1 & 1 & \Big| & 2 \\ 0 & -2 & 1 & -1 & \Big| & -3 \\ 0 & 2 & 3 & -3 & \Big| & -9 \\ 0 & -5 & -2 & 0 & \Big| & 2 \end{bmatrix}$$

$$\xrightarrow[\text{by } -\frac{1}{2}]{\text{multiply row 2}} \begin{bmatrix} 1 & 1 & 1 & 1 & \Big| & 2 \\ 0 & 1 & -\frac{1}{2} & \frac{1}{2} & \Big| & \frac{3}{2} \\ 0 & 2 & 3 & -3 & \Big| & -9 \\ 0 & -5 & -2 & 0 & \Big| & 2 \end{bmatrix}$$

$$\xrightarrow[\substack{\text{Also, multiply row} \\ 2 \text{ by 5 and add to} \\ \text{row 4.}}]{\substack{\text{multiply row 2 by} \\ -2 \text{ and add to row} \\ 3}} \begin{bmatrix} 1 & 1 & 1 & 1 & \Big| & 2 \\ 0 & 1 & -\frac{1}{2} & -\frac{1}{2} & \Big| & \frac{3}{2} \\ 0 & 0 & 4 & -4 & \Big| & -12 \\ 0 & 0 & -\frac{9}{2} & \frac{5}{2} & \Big| & \frac{19}{2} \end{bmatrix}$$

$$-\frac{5}{2} - 2 = \frac{-5-4}{2} = \frac{-9}{2}$$

$$\frac{15}{2} + 2 = \frac{15+4}{2} = \frac{19}{2}$$

$$\xrightarrow[\text{by } \frac{1}{4}]{\text{multiply row 3}} \begin{bmatrix} 1 & 1 & 1 & 1 & \Big| & 2 \\ 0 & 1 & -\frac{1}{2} & \frac{1}{2} & \Big| & \frac{3}{2} \\ 0 & 0 & 1 & -1 & \Big| & -3 \\ 0 & 0 & -\frac{9}{2} & \frac{5}{2} & \Big| & \frac{19}{2} \end{bmatrix}$$

$$\xrightarrow[\substack{\text{by } \frac{9}{2} \text{ and add to} \\ \text{row 4}}]{\text{multiply row 3}} \begin{bmatrix} 1 & 1 & 1 & 1 & \Big| & 2 \\ 0 & 1 & -\frac{1}{2} & \frac{1}{2} & \Big| & \frac{3}{2} \\ 0 & 0 & 1 & -1 & \Big| & -3 \\ 0 & 0 & 0 & -2 & \Big| & -4 \end{bmatrix}$$

$$-\frac{9}{2} + \frac{5}{2} = \frac{-4}{2} = -2$$

$$\frac{-27}{2} + \frac{19}{2} = \frac{-8}{2} = -4$$

$$\xrightarrow[\text{by } -\frac{1}{2}]{\text{multiply row 4}} \begin{bmatrix} 1 & 1 & 1 & 1 & \Big| & 2 \\ 0 & 1 & -\frac{1}{2} & \frac{1}{2} & \Big| & \frac{3}{2} \\ 0 & 0 & 1 & -1 & \Big| & -3 \\ 0 & 0 & 0 & 1 & \Big| & 2 \end{bmatrix}$$

$$x + y + z + w = 2$$
$$y - \frac{1}{2}z + \frac{1}{2}w = \frac{3}{2}$$
$$z - w = -3$$

$$w = 2$$
$$z - 2 = -3$$
$$z = -1$$
$$y + \frac{1}{2} + \frac{1}{2}(2) = \frac{3}{2}$$
$$y + \frac{3}{2} = \frac{3}{2}$$
$$y = 0$$
$$x + 0 - 1 + 2 = 2$$
$$x + 1 = 2$$
$$x = 1 \qquad \{(1,0,-1,2)\}$$

59. $\begin{cases} x + 2y - z & = 2 \\ 2x & + z + w = 9 \\ & y & - w = -2 \\ 3x + 4y & = 11 \end{cases}$

$$\begin{bmatrix} 1 & 2 & -1 & 0 & \Big| & 2 \\ 2 & 0 & 1 & 1 & \Big| & 9 \\ 0 & 1 & 0 & -1 & \Big| & -2 \\ 3 & 4 & 0 & 0 & \Big| & 11 \end{bmatrix}$$

$$\begin{bmatrix} 1 & 2 & -1 & 0 & \Big| & 2 \\ 2 & 0 & 1 & 1 & \Big| & 9 \\ 0 & 1 & 0 & -1 & \Big| & -2 \\ 3 & 4 & 0 & 0 & \Big| & 11 \end{bmatrix} \xrightarrow[\substack{\text{Also,} \\ \text{multiply} \\ \text{row 1 by} \\ -3 \text{ and add} \\ \text{to row 4}}]{\substack{\text{multiply} \\ \text{row 1 by} \\ -2 \text{ and add} \\ \text{to row 2}}} \begin{bmatrix} 1 & 2 & -1 & 0 & \Big| & 2 \\ 0 & -4 & 3 & 1 & \Big| & 5 \\ 0 & 1 & 0 & -1 & \Big| & -2 \\ 0 & -2 & 3 & 0 & \Big| & 5 \end{bmatrix}$$

$$\xrightarrow[\text{and row 3}]{\text{exchange row 2}} \begin{bmatrix} 1 & 2 & -1 & 0 & \Big| & 2 \\ 0 & 1 & 0 & -1 & \Big| & -2 \\ 0 & -4 & 3 & 1 & \Big| & 5 \\ 0 & -2 & 3 & 0 & \Big| & 5 \end{bmatrix}$$

Multiply row 2 by -2 and add to row 1. Also, multiply row 2 by 4 and add to row 3

$$\xrightarrow[\substack{\text{Also, multiply} \\ \text{row 2 by 2 and} \\ \text{add to row 4}}]{} \begin{bmatrix} 1 & 0 & -1 & 2 & \Big| & 6 \\ 0 & 1 & 0 & -1 & \Big| & -2 \\ 0 & 0 & 3 & -3 & \Big| & -3 \\ 0 & 0 & 3 & -2 & \Big| & 1 \end{bmatrix}$$

$$\xrightarrow[\text{by } \frac{1}{3}]{\text{Multiply row 3}} \begin{bmatrix} 1 & 0 & -1 & 2 & \Big| & 6 \\ 0 & 1 & 0 & -1 & \Big| & -2 \\ 0 & 0 & 1 & -1 & \Big| & -1 \\ 0 & 0 & 3 & -2 & \Big| & 1 \end{bmatrix}$$

Multiply row 3 by
───────────────────→
-3 and add to row
4

$$\begin{bmatrix} 1 & 0 & -1 & 2 & | & 6 \\ 0 & 1 & 0 & -1 & | & -2 \\ 0 & 0 & 1 & -1 & | & -1 \\ 0 & 0 & 0 & 1 & | & 4 \end{bmatrix}$$

$x - z + 2w = 6$

$y - w = -2$

$z - w = -1$

$w = 4$

$z - 4 = -1$ $x - 3 + 2(4) = 6$

$z = 3$ $x - 3 + 8 = 6$

$y - 4 = -2$ $x + 5 = 6$

$y = 2$ $x = 1$

$\{(1,2,3,4)\}$

Review.

1. $\begin{cases} 2x + y = 4 \\ 3x - 2y = -1 \end{cases}$

$y = 4 - 2x$

So, $3x - 2(4-2x) = -1$

$3x - 8 + 4x = -1$

$7x - 8 = -1$

$7x = 7$

$x = 1$

$2(1) + y = 4$

$y = 2$ $\{(1,2)\}$

3. $\begin{cases} 5x + 3y = 1 \\ 7x + 2y = 8 \end{cases}$

$2y = 8 - 7x$

$y = 4 - \dfrac{7}{2}x$

So, $5x + 3(4 - \dfrac{7}{2}x) = 1$

$5x + 12 - \dfrac{21}{2}x = 1$

$2(5x + 12 - \dfrac{21}{2}x) = 2 \cdot 1$

$10x + 24 - 21x = 2$

$-11x + 24 = 2$

$-11x = -22$

$x = 2$

$5(2) + 3y = 1$

$3y = -9$

$y = -3$ $\{(2,-3)\}$

5. $\begin{cases} x^2 - 4y^2 = 9 \\ x - y = 3 \end{cases}$

$x = y + 3$

So, $(y+3)^2 - 4y^2 = 9$

$y^2 + 6y + 9 - 4y^2 = 9$

$-3y^2 + 6y = 0$

$-3y(y-2) = 0$

$-3y = 0$ or $y - 2 = 0$

$y = 0$ $y = 2$

$x - 0 = 3$ $x - 2 = 3$

$x = 3$ $x = 5$

$\{(3,0),(5,2)\}$

7. $\begin{cases} x + 2y = 2 \\ x - 2y = 6 \end{cases}$

$x + 2y = 2$
$\underline{x - 2y = 6}$
$2x \qquad = 8$

$x = 4$

$4 + 2y = 2$

$2y = -2$

$y = -1$ $\{(4,-1)\}$

9. $\begin{cases} 2x + 3y = 15 \\ 2x - 7y = 5 \end{cases}$

$-1(2x+3y) = -1 \cdot 15$

So, $-2x - 3y = -15$
$\underline{2x - 7y = \qquad 5}$
$-10y = -10$

$y = 1$

$2x + 3(1) = 15$

$2x + 3 = 15$

297

$$2x = 12$$
$$x = 6 \qquad \{(6,1)\}$$

11. $\begin{cases} 5x + 6y = -3 \\ -4x + 9y = 7 \end{cases}$

$$4(5x+6y) = 4 \cdot -3$$
$$20x + 24y = -12$$
$$5(-4x+9y) = 5 \cdot 7$$
$$-20x + 45y = 35$$

So, $20x + 24y = -12$
$$\underline{-20x + 45y = 35}$$
$$69y = 23$$
$$y = \frac{23}{69} \text{ or } \frac{1}{3}$$

$$5x + 6(\tfrac{1}{3}) = -3$$
$$5x + 2 = -3$$
$$5x = -5$$
$$x = -1 \qquad \{(-1,\tfrac{1}{3})\}$$

13. $\begin{cases} 24x - 18y = -1 \\ 6x - 10y = -3 \end{cases}$

$$-4(6x-10y) = -4 \cdot -3$$

So, $-24x + 40y = 12$
$$\underline{24x - 18y = -1}$$
$$22y = 11$$
$$y = \frac{11}{22} \text{ or } \frac{1}{2}$$

$$24x - 18(\tfrac{1}{2}) = -1$$
$$24x - 9 = -1$$
$$24x = 8$$
$$x = \frac{8}{24} \text{ or } \frac{1}{3} \quad \{(\tfrac{1}{3},\tfrac{1}{2})\}$$

15. $\begin{cases} 5x + 4y = 2 \\ 10x + 12y = 5 \end{cases}$

$$-3(5x+4y) = -3 \cdot 2$$

So, $-15x - 12y = -6$
$$\underline{10x + 12y = 5}$$
$$-5x = -1$$
$$x = \frac{1}{5}$$

$$5(\tfrac{1}{5}) + 4y = 2$$
$$1 + 4y = 2$$
$$4y = 1$$
$$y = \frac{1}{4} \qquad \{(\tfrac{1}{5},\tfrac{1}{4})\}$$

17. $\begin{cases} x - 2y + z = 2 \\ x + y + z = 8 \\ x - y - z = 2 \end{cases}$

$$x - 2y + z = 2$$
$$\underline{x - y - z = 2}$$
$$2x - 3y = 4$$

$$x + y + z = 8$$
$$\underline{x - y - z = 2}$$
$$2x = 10$$
$$x = 5$$

$$2(5) - 3y = 4$$
$$10 - 3y = 4$$
$$-3y = -6$$
$$y = \frac{-6}{-3} \text{ or } 2$$

$$5 + 2 + z = 8$$
$$7 + z = 8$$
$$z = 1 \qquad \{(5,2,1)\}$$

19. $\begin{cases} 2x + 3y + 5z = 0 \\ x - 2y - z = 0 \\ 3x + 2y - 2z = 0 \end{cases}$

$$-2(x-2y-z) = -2 \cdot 0$$

$$-2x + 4y + 2z = 0$$
$$\underline{2x + 3y + 5z = 0}$$
$$7y + 7z = 0$$

$$-3(x-2y-z) = -3 \cdot 0$$

$$-3x + 6y + 3z = 0$$
$$\underline{3x + 2y - 2z = 0}$$
$$8y + z = 0$$

$$-7(8y+z) = -7 \cdot 0$$

$$-56y - 7z = 0$$
$$\underline{7y + 7z = 0}$$
$$-49y = 0$$

$$y = 0$$

$$8(0) + z = 0$$

$$z = 0$$

$$x - 2(0) - 0 = 0$$

$$x = 0 \qquad \{(0,0,0)\}$$

21. $\begin{cases} 2x + 5y - z = -6 \\ x - y + 3z = 18 \\ 2x - 3y - 2z = -12 \end{cases}$

$$-(2x+5y-z) = -1 \cdot -6$$

$$\begin{array}{r} -2x - 5y + z = 6 \\ 2x + 3y - 2z = -12 \\ \hline -2y - z = -6 \end{array}$$

$$-2(x-y+3z) = -2 \cdot 18$$

$$\begin{array}{r} -2x + 2y - 6z = -36 \\ 2x + 3y - 2z = -12 \\ \hline 5y - 8z = -48 \end{array}$$

$$-8(2y-z) = -8 \cdot -6$$

$$\begin{array}{r} -16y + 8z = 48 \\ 5y - 8z = -48 \\ \hline -11y = 0 \end{array}$$

$$y = 0$$

$$5(0) - 8z = -48$$

$$-8z = -48$$

$$z = 6$$

$$x - 0 + 3(6) = 18$$

$$x + 18 = 18$$

$$x = 0 \qquad \{(0,0,6)\}$$

23. $\begin{cases} x + 3y + z = 1 \\ 2x + y + 2z = 2 \\ 3x - y + 2z = 0 \end{cases}$

$$\begin{array}{r} 2x + y + 2z = 2 \\ 3x - y + 2z = 0 \\ \hline 5x + 4z = 2 \end{array}$$

$$3(3x-y+2z) = 3 \cdot 0$$

$$9x - 3y + 6z = 0$$
$$\underline{x + 3y + z = 1}$$
$$10x \qquad + 7x = 1$$

$$-2(5x+4z) = -2 \cdot 2$$

$$\begin{array}{r} -10x - 8z = -4 \\ 10x + 7z = 1 \\ \hline -z = -3 \end{array}$$

$$z = 3$$

$$5x + 4(3) = 2$$

$$5x + 12 = 2$$

$$5x = -10$$

$$x = -2$$

$$-2 + 3y + 3 = 1$$

$$3y + 1 = 1$$

$$3y = 0$$

$$y = 0 \qquad \{(-2,0,3)\}$$

25. $\begin{cases} x - y + 3z = 6 \\ 2x + y - z = -3 \\ 3x - 2y + z = -4 \end{cases}$

$$\begin{array}{r} x - y + 3z = 6 \\ 2x + y - z = -3 \\ \hline 3x + 2z = 3 \end{array}$$

$$2(2x+y-z) = 2 \cdot -3$$

$$\begin{array}{r} 4x + 2y - 2z = -6 \\ 3x - 2y + z = -4 \\ \hline 7x - z = -10 \end{array}$$

$$2(7x-z) = 2 \cdot -10$$

$$\begin{array}{r} 14x - 2z = -20 \\ 3x + 2z = 3 \\ \hline 17x = -17 \end{array}$$

$$x = -1$$

$$7(-1) - z = -10$$

$$-7 - z = -10$$

$$-z = -3$$

$$z = 3$$

$$-1 - y + 3(3) = 6$$

$$-y + 8 = 6$$

$$-y = -2$$
$$y = 2 \qquad \{(-1,2,3)\}$$

27. c: price per pound for cantaloupes.

h: price per pound for honeydew

w: price per pound for water-
melon

$$\begin{cases} 3c + 4h + w = 1192 \\ c + h + w = 477 \\ c + 2w = 517 \end{cases}$$

$$-4(c+h+w) = -4 \cdot 477$$

$$\begin{array}{r} -4c - 4h - 4w = -1908 \\ 3c + 4h + w = 1192 \\ \hline -c - 3w = -716 \\ c + 2w = 517 \\ \hline -w = -199 \\ w = 199 \end{array}$$

$$c + 2(199) = 517$$
$$c + 398 = 517$$
$$c = 119$$

$$119 + h + 199 = 477$$
$$h + 318 = 477$$
$$h = 159$$

Cantaloupes are $1.19; honeydews
are $1.59; watermelons are
$1.99.

29. x: 1st number   y: 2nd number

$$\begin{cases} x^2 + y^2 = 58 \\ x - y = 10 \\ x = y + 10 \end{cases}$$

$$(y+10)^2 + y^2 = 58$$
$$y^2 + 20y + 100 + y^2 = 58$$
$$2y^2 + 20y + 100 = 58$$
$$2y^2 + 20y + 42 = 0$$
$$\frac{1}{2}(2y^2 + 20y + 42) = \frac{1}{2} \cdot 0$$

$$y^2 + 10y + 21 = 0$$
$$(y+3)(y+7) = 0$$

$$y + 3 = 0 \quad \text{or} \quad y + 7 = 0$$
$$y = -3 \qquad\qquad y = -7$$
$$x - (-3) = 10 \qquad x - (-7) = 10$$
$$x + 3 = 10 \qquad\quad x + 7 = 10$$
$$x = 7 \qquad\qquad\quad x = 3$$

One such pair of numbers is -3
and 7. Another pair is 3 and
-7.

31. $x + 2y \geq 3$

Boundary line: $x + 2y = 3$
(included).

x	y
0	$\frac{3}{2}$
3	0

Test (0,0)

$0 + 2(0) \geq 3$

$0 \geq 3$ is false.

Do not shade
region.

Test (0,2)

$0 + 2(2) \geq 3$

$4 \geq 3$ is true.

Shade region.

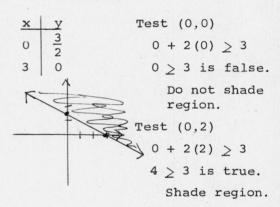

33. $x - y < 0$

Boundary line: $x - y = 0$ (not
included).

x	y
0	0
1	1

Test (1,0)

$1 - 0 < 0$ is false.

Do not shade
region.

Test (0,1)

$0 - 1 < 0$ is true.

Shade region.

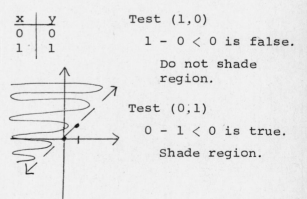

35. $y < 3x - 2$

Boundary line: $y = 3x - 2$ (not included).

x	y
0	-2
$\frac{2}{3}$	0

Test (0,0)

$0 < 3(0) < 2$ is false.

Do not shade region.

Test (1,0)

$0 < 3(1) - 2$ is true.

Shade region.

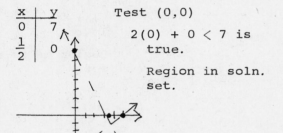

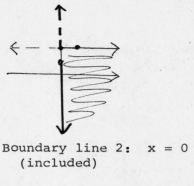

Boundary line 2: $x = 0$ (included)

y axis

x	y
0	1
0	2

Test (1,2)

$2 \geq 0$ is true.

Region in soln. set.

37. $\begin{cases} 2x + y < 7 \\ x - y > 5 \end{cases}$

Boundary line 1: $2x + y = 7$ (not included).

x	y
0	7
$\frac{1}{2}$	0

Test (0,0)

$2(0) + 0 < 7$ is true.

Region in soln. set.

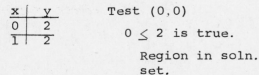

Boundary line 2: $x - y = 5$ (not included).

x	y
0	-5
5	0

Test (0,0)

$0 - 0 > 5$ is false.

Region not in soln. set.

39. $\begin{cases} y \leq 2 \\ x \geq 0 \end{cases}$

Boundary line 1: $y = 2$ (included).

x	y
0	2
1	2

Test (0,0)

$0 \leq 2$ is true.

Region in soln. set.

41. $2x \leq y + 3$

Boundary line: $2x = y + 3$ (included).

x	y
0	-3
$\frac{3}{2}$	0

Test (0,0)

$2(0) < 0 + 3$ is true.

Shade region.

Test (2,-2)

$2(2) \leq -2 + 3$ is false.

Region not in solution set.

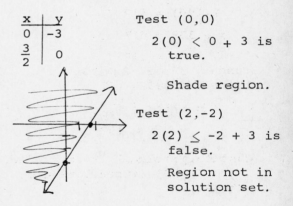

43. $y < 2x$

Boundary line: $y = 2x$ (not included)

x	y
0	0
1	2

Test (1,0)

$1 < 2(0)$ is true.

Shade region.

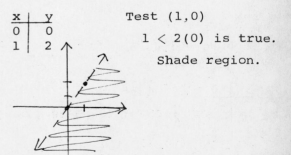

301

45. $\begin{cases} x - y > 7 \\ x - y < 5 \end{cases}$

Boundary line 1: $x - y = 7$ (not included).

x	y
0	-7
7	0

Test (0,0)

$\quad 0 - 0 > 7$ is false.

Region not in soln. set.

Boundary line 2: $x - y = 5$ (not included).

x	y
0	-5
5	0

Test (0,0)

$\quad 0 - 0 < 5$ is true.

Region in soln. set.

$\emptyset$

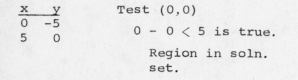

47. $2x - 3y \leq 4$

Boundary line: $2x - 3y = 4$ (included).

x	y
0	$-\frac{4}{3}$
2	0

Test (0,0)

$\quad 2(0) - 3(0) \leq 4$ is true.

Shade region.

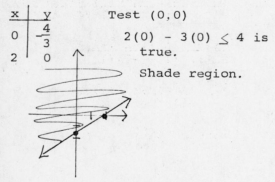

49. $5x - 7y > 0$

Boundary line $5x - 7y = 0$ (not included).

x	y
0	0
$\frac{7}{5}$	1

Test (1,0)

$\quad 5(1) - 7(0) > 0$ is true.

Shade region.

51. $\frac{1}{2}x - y < 1$

Boundary line: $\frac{1}{2}x - y = 1$ (not included).

x	y
0	-1
2	0

Test (0,0)

$\quad \frac{1}{2}(0) - 0 < 1$ is true.

Shade region.

53. $\begin{cases} 2x - 5y \leq 5 \\ 4x - 10y \leq 0 \end{cases}$

Boundary line 1: $2x - 5y = 5$ (included).

x	y
0	-1
$\frac{5}{2}$	0

Test (0,0)

$\quad 2(0) - 5(0) \leq 5$ is true.

Region is soln. set.

Boundary line 2: $4x - 10y = 0$ (included)

x	y
0	0
1	$\frac{2}{5}$

$4(1) - 10y = 0$

$\quad -10y = -4$

$\quad\quad y = \frac{-4}{-10}$

$\quad\quad$ or $\frac{2}{5}$

Test (0,1)

$\quad 4(0) - 10(1) \leq 0$ is true.

Region in soln. set.

55. $\begin{cases} 3x + y = 1 \\ 4x + y = -1 \end{cases}$

$$x = \frac{\begin{vmatrix} 1 & 1 \\ -1 & 1 \end{vmatrix}}{\begin{vmatrix} 3 & 1 \\ 4 & 1 \end{vmatrix}} = \frac{1 \cdot 1 - 1 \cdot (-1)}{3 \cdot 1 - 4 \cdot 1}$$

$$= \frac{1+1}{3-4}$$

$$= \frac{2}{-1} \text{ or } -2$$

$$y = \frac{\begin{vmatrix} 3 & 1 \\ 4 & -1 \end{vmatrix}}{\begin{vmatrix} 3 & 1 \\ 4 & 1 \end{vmatrix}} = \frac{3 \cdot (-1) - 1 \cdot 4}{-1}$$

$$= \frac{-3-4}{-1}$$

$$= \frac{-7}{-1} \text{ or } 7 \qquad \{(-2,7)\}$$

57. $\begin{cases} 2x - 3y = -5 \\ 3x + 2y = -1 \end{cases}$

$$x = \frac{\begin{vmatrix} -5 & -3 \\ -1 & 2 \end{vmatrix}}{\begin{vmatrix} 2 & -3 \\ 3 & 2 \end{vmatrix}} = \frac{-5 \cdot 2 - (-3)(-1)}{2 \cdot 2 - (-3)(3)}$$

$$= \frac{-10-3}{4 - -9}$$

$$= \frac{-13}{13} \text{ or } -1$$

$$y = \frac{\begin{vmatrix} 2 & -5 \\ 3 & -1 \end{vmatrix}}{\begin{vmatrix} 2 & -3 \\ 3 & 2 \end{vmatrix}} = \frac{2 \cdot (-1) - (-5)(3)}{2 \cdot 2 - (-3)(3)}$$

$$= \frac{-2+15}{4+9}$$

$$= \frac{13}{13} \text{ or } 1 \qquad \{(-1,1)\}$$

59. $\begin{cases} 5x + 4y = 12 \\ -6x + 8y = -8 \end{cases}$

$$x = \frac{\begin{vmatrix} 12 & 4 \\ -8 & 8 \end{vmatrix}}{\begin{vmatrix} 5 & 4 \\ -6 & 8 \end{vmatrix}} = \frac{12 \cdot 8 - 4 \cdot (-8)}{5 \cdot 8 - 4(-6)}$$

$$= \frac{96+32}{40+24}$$

$$= \frac{128}{64} \text{ or } 2$$

$$y = \frac{\begin{vmatrix} 5 & 12 \\ -6 & -8 \end{vmatrix}}{\begin{vmatrix} 5 & 4 \\ -6 & 8 \end{vmatrix}} = \frac{5 \cdot (-8) - 12(-6)}{64}$$

$$= \frac{-40+72}{64}$$

$$= \frac{32}{64} \text{ or } \frac{1}{2} \qquad \{(2, \tfrac{1}{2})\}$$

61. $\begin{cases} -x + 3y = 4 \\ 2x - 6y = -8 \end{cases}$

Since $\begin{vmatrix} -1 & 3 \\ 2 & -6 \end{vmatrix} = (-1)(-6) - (3)(2)$

$$= 6 - 6$$

$$= 0$$

Cramer's Rule does not apply.

63. $\begin{cases} x + y - z = -3 \\ x - y + z = -1 \\ x + y + z = -1 \end{cases}$

$$x = \frac{\begin{vmatrix} -3 & 1 & -1 \\ -1 & -1 & 1 \\ -1 & 1 & 1 \end{vmatrix}}{\begin{vmatrix} 1 & 1 & -1 \\ 1 & -1 & 1 \\ 1 & 1 & 1 \end{vmatrix}}$$

$$= \frac{-3\begin{vmatrix} -1 & 1 \\ 1 & 1 \end{vmatrix} - 1\begin{vmatrix} -1 & 1 \\ -1 & 1 \end{vmatrix} + (-1)\begin{vmatrix} -1 & 1 \\ -1 & 1 \end{vmatrix}}{1\begin{vmatrix} -1 & 1 \\ 1 & 1 \end{vmatrix} - 1\begin{vmatrix} 1 & 1 \\ 1 & 1 \end{vmatrix} + (-1)\begin{vmatrix} 1 & -1 \\ 1 & 1 \end{vmatrix}}$$

$$= \frac{-3[(-1)(1)-1 \cdot 1] - [(-1)(1)-(1)(-1)]}{[(-1)(1)-1 \cdot 1] - [(1)(1)-(1)(1)]}$$

$$\frac{-[(-1)(1)-(-1)(-1)]}{-1[(1)(1)-(-1)(1)]}$$

$$= \frac{-3(-1-1)-(-1+1)-(-1-1)}{(-1-1)-(0)-(1+1)}$$

$$= \frac{-3(-2)-0-(-2)}{(-2)-2}$$

$$= \frac{6+2}{-4}$$

$$= \frac{8}{-4} \text{ or } -2$$

$$y = \frac{\begin{vmatrix} 1 & -3 & -1 \\ 1 & -1 & 1 \\ 1 & -1 & 1 \end{vmatrix}}{\begin{vmatrix} 1 & 1 & -1 \\ 1 & -1 & 1 \\ 1 & 1 & 1 \end{vmatrix}}$$

$$= \frac{1\begin{vmatrix} -1 & 1 \\ -1 & 1 \end{vmatrix} - (-3)\begin{vmatrix} 1 & 1 \\ 1 & 1 \end{vmatrix} + (-1)\begin{vmatrix} 1 & -1 \\ 1 & -1 \end{vmatrix}}{-4}$$

$$= \frac{[(-1)(1)-(1)(-1)]+3(0)-[(1)(-1)- \quad -(-1)(1)]}{-4}$$

$$= \frac{(-1+1)+0-(-1+1)}{-4}$$

$$= \frac{0}{-4} \text{ or } 0$$

$$z = \frac{\begin{vmatrix} 1 & 1 & -3 \\ 1 & -1 & -1 \\ 1 & 1 & -1 \end{vmatrix}}{\begin{vmatrix} 1 & 1 & -1 \\ 1 & -1 & 1 \\ 1 & 1 & 1 \end{vmatrix}}$$

$$= \frac{1\begin{vmatrix} -1 & -1 \\ 1 & -1 \end{vmatrix} -1\begin{vmatrix} 1 & -1 \\ 1 & -1 \end{vmatrix} + (-3)\begin{vmatrix} 1 & -1 \\ 1 & 1 \end{vmatrix}}{-4}$$

$$= \frac{[(-1)(-1)-(-1)(1)]-[(1)(-1)-(-1)(1)] \quad -3[(1)(1)-(-1)(1)]}{-4}$$

$$= \frac{(1+1)-(-1+1)-3(1+1)}{-4}$$

$$= \frac{2-6}{-4}$$

$$= \frac{-4}{-4} \text{ or } 1 \qquad \{(-2,0,1)\}$$

65. $\quad$ x - y - z = 0

$\quad\quad$ x + 2y - z = 3

$\quad\quad$ x + y + 2z = 5

$$x = \frac{\begin{vmatrix} 0 & -1 & -1 \\ 3 & 2 & -1 \\ 5 & 1 & 2 \end{vmatrix}}{\begin{vmatrix} 1 & -1 & -1 \\ 1 & 2 & -1 \\ 1 & 1 & 2 \end{vmatrix}}$$

$$= \frac{0-(-1)\begin{vmatrix} 3 & -1 \\ 5 & 2 \end{vmatrix}+(-1)\begin{vmatrix} 3 & 2 \\ 5 & 1 \end{vmatrix}}{1\begin{vmatrix} 2 & -1 \\ 1 & 2 \end{vmatrix}-(-1)\begin{vmatrix} 1 & -1 \\ 1 & 2 \end{vmatrix}+(-1)\begin{vmatrix} 1 & 2 \\ 1 & 1 \end{vmatrix}}$$

$$= \frac{[3\cdot2-(-1)(5)]-(3\cdot1-2\cdot5)}{[2\cdot2-(-1)(1)]+[(1)(2)-(-1)(1)] \quad -[1\cdot1-2\cdot1]}$$

$$= \frac{(6+5)-(3-10)}{(4+1)+(2+1)-(1-2)}$$

$$= \frac{11+7}{5+3-(-1)}$$

$$= \frac{18}{8+1}$$

$$= \frac{18}{9} \text{ or } 2$$

$$y = \frac{\begin{vmatrix} 1 & 0 & -1 \\ 1 & 3 & -1 \\ 1 & 5 & 2 \end{vmatrix}}{\begin{vmatrix} 1 & -1 & -1 \\ 1 & 2 & -1 \\ 1 & 1 & 2 \end{vmatrix}}$$

$$= \frac{1\begin{vmatrix} 3 & -1 \\ 5 & 2 \end{vmatrix} -0+(-1)\begin{vmatrix} 1 & 3 \\ 1 & 5 \end{vmatrix}}{9}$$

$$= \frac{[3\cdot2-(-1)(5)]-[1\cdot5-3\cdot1]}{9}$$

$$= \frac{(6+5)-(5-3)}{9}$$

$$= \frac{11-2}{9}$$

$$= \frac{9}{9} \text{ or } 1$$

$$z = \frac{\begin{vmatrix} 1 & -1 & 0 \\ 1 & 2 & 3 \\ 1 & 1 & 5 \end{vmatrix}}{\begin{vmatrix} 1 & -1 & -1 \\ 1 & 2 & -1 \\ 1 & 1 & 2 \end{vmatrix}}$$

$$= \frac{1\begin{vmatrix} 2 & 3 \\ 1 & 5 \end{vmatrix} -(-1)\begin{vmatrix} 1 & 3 \\ 1 & 5 \end{vmatrix} +0}{9}$$

$$= \frac{(2\cdot5-3\cdot1)+(1\cdot5-3\cdot1)}{9}$$

$$= \frac{(10-3)+(5-3)}{9}$$

$$= \frac{7+2}{9}$$

$$= \frac{9}{9} \text{ or } 1 \qquad \{(2,1,1)\}$$

67. $\begin{cases} x - 2y + z = 17 \\ 2x + 3y + 2z = 13 \\ 3x + y - z = 14 \end{cases}$

$$x = \frac{\begin{vmatrix} 17 & -2 & 1 \\ 13 & 3 & 2 \\ 14 & 1 & -1 \end{vmatrix}}{\begin{vmatrix} 1 & -2 & 1 \\ 2 & 3 & 2 \\ 3 & 1 & -1 \end{vmatrix}}$$

$$= \frac{17\begin{vmatrix} 3 & 2 \\ 1 & -1 \end{vmatrix} - (-2)\begin{vmatrix} 13 & 2 \\ 14 & -1 \end{vmatrix} + 1\begin{vmatrix} 13 & 3 \\ 14 & 1 \end{vmatrix}}{1\begin{vmatrix} 3 & 2 \\ 1 & -1 \end{vmatrix} - (-2)\begin{vmatrix} 2 & 2 \\ 3 & -1 \end{vmatrix} + 1\begin{vmatrix} 2 & 3 \\ 3 & 1 \end{vmatrix}}$$

$$= \frac{17[(3)(-1)-2\cdot 1]+2[(13)(-1)-2\cdot 14]}{[3(-1)-2\cdot 1]+2[(2)(-1)-2\cdot 3]}$$

$$\frac{+(13\cdot 1-3\cdot 14)}{+(2\cdot 1-3\cdot 3)}$$

$$= \frac{17(-3-2)+2(-13-28)+(13-42)}{(-3-2)+2(-2-6)+(2-9)}$$

$$= \frac{17(-5)+2(-41)+(-29)}{-5+2(-8)+(-7)}$$

$$= \frac{-85-82-29}{-5-16-7}$$

$$= \frac{-196}{-28} \text{ or } 7$$

$$y = \frac{\begin{vmatrix} 1 & 17 & 1 \\ 2 & 13 & 2 \\ 3 & 14 & -1 \end{vmatrix}}{\begin{vmatrix} 1 & & 1 \\ 2 & 3 & 2 \\ 3 & 1 & -1 \end{vmatrix}}$$

$$= \frac{1\begin{vmatrix} 13 & 2 \\ 14 & -1 \end{vmatrix} - 17\begin{vmatrix} 2 & 2 \\ 3 & -1 \end{vmatrix} + 1\begin{vmatrix} 2 & 13 \\ 3 & 14 \end{vmatrix}}{-28}$$

$$= \frac{[13(-1)-2\cdot 14]-17[2(-1)-2\cdot 3]}{-28}$$

$$\frac{+[2\cdot 14-13\cdot 3]}{}$$

$$= \frac{(-13-28)-17(-2-6)+(28-39)}{-28}$$

$$= \frac{-41+136-11}{-28}$$

$$= \frac{84}{-28} \text{ or } -3$$

$$z = \frac{\begin{vmatrix} 1 & -2 & 17 \\ 2 & 3 & 13 \\ 3 & 1 & 14 \end{vmatrix}}{\begin{vmatrix} 1 & -2 & 1 \\ 2 & 3 & 2 \\ 3 & 1 & -1 \end{vmatrix}}$$

$$= \frac{1\begin{vmatrix} 3 & 13 \\ 1 & 14 \end{vmatrix} - (-2)\begin{vmatrix} 2 & 13 \\ 3 & 14 \end{vmatrix} + 17\begin{vmatrix} 2 & 3 \\ 3 & 1 \end{vmatrix}}{-28}$$

$$= \frac{(3\cdot 14-13\cdot 1)+2(2\cdot 14-13\cdot 3)+17(2\cdot 1-3\cdot 3)}{-28}$$

$$= \frac{(42-13)+2(28-39)+17(2-9)}{-28}$$

$$= \frac{29+2(-11)+17(-7)}{-28}$$

$$= \frac{29-22-119}{-28}$$

$$= \frac{-112}{-28} \text{ or } 4 \qquad \{(7,-3,4)\}$$

69. $\begin{cases} 3x - y + 4z = 9 \\ x - 2y + 3z = -2 \\ 2x - y + z = 3 \end{cases}$

$$x = \frac{\begin{vmatrix} 9 & -1 & 4 \\ -2 & -2 & 3 \\ 3 & -1 & 1 \end{vmatrix}}{\begin{vmatrix} 3 & -1 & 4 \\ 1 & -2 & 3 \\ 2 & -1 & 1 \end{vmatrix}}$$

$$= \frac{9\begin{vmatrix} -2 & 3 \\ -1 & 1 \end{vmatrix} - (-1)\begin{vmatrix} -2 & 3 \\ 3 & 1 \end{vmatrix} + 4\begin{vmatrix} -2 & -2 \\ 3 & -1 \end{vmatrix}}{3\begin{vmatrix} -2 & 3 \\ -1 & 1 \end{vmatrix} - (-1)\begin{vmatrix} 1 & 3 \\ 2 & 1 \end{vmatrix} + 4\begin{vmatrix} 1 & -2 \\ 2 & -1 \end{vmatrix}}$$

$$= \frac{9[(-2)(1)-3(-1)]+[(-2)(1)-3\cdot 3]}{3[(-2)(1)-3(-1)]+(1\cdot 1-3\cdot 2)}$$

$$\frac{+4[(-2)(-1)-(-2)(3)]}{+4[(1)(-1)-(-2)(2)]}$$

$$= \frac{9(-2+3)+(-2-9)+4(2+6)}{3(-2+3)+(1-6)+4(-1+4)}$$

$$= \frac{9(1)-11+4(8)}{3(1)+(-5)+4(3)}$$

$$= \frac{9-11+32}{3-5+12}$$

$$= \frac{30}{10} \text{ or } 3$$

$$y = \frac{\begin{vmatrix} 3 & 9 & 4 \\ 1 & -2 & 3 \\ 2 & 3 & 1 \end{vmatrix}}{\begin{vmatrix} 3 & -1 & 4 \\ 1 & -2 & 3 \\ 2 & -1 & 1 \end{vmatrix}}$$

$$= \frac{3\begin{vmatrix} -2 & 3 \\ 3 & 1 \end{vmatrix} - 9\begin{vmatrix} 1 & 3 \\ 2 & 1 \end{vmatrix} + 4\begin{vmatrix} 1 & -2 \\ 2 & 3 \end{vmatrix}}{10}$$

$$= \frac{3[(-2)(1)-3\cdot3]-9(1\cdot1-3\cdot2)}{10}$$
$$ \frac{+4[1\cdot3-(-2)(2)]}{10}$$

$$= \frac{3(-2-9)-9(1-6)+4(3+4)}{10}$$

$$= \frac{3(-11)+9(5)+4(7)}{10}$$

$$= \frac{-33+45+28}{10}$$

$$= \frac{40}{10} \text{ or } 4$$

$$z = \frac{\begin{vmatrix} 3 & -1 & 9 \\ 1 & -2 & -2 \\ 2 & -1 & 3 \end{vmatrix}}{\begin{vmatrix} 3 & -1 & 4 \\ 1 & -2 & 3 \\ 2 & -1 & 1 \end{vmatrix}}$$

$$= \frac{3\begin{vmatrix} -2 & -2 \\ -1 & 3 \end{vmatrix} - (-1)\begin{vmatrix} 1 & -2 \\ 2 & 3 \end{vmatrix} + 9\begin{vmatrix} 1 & -2 \\ 2 & -1 \end{vmatrix}}{10}$$

$$= \frac{3[(-2)3-(-2)(-1)]+[1\cdot3-(-2)(2)]}{10}$$
$$ \frac{+9[1(-1)-(-2)(2)]}{10}$$

$$= \frac{3(-6-2)+(3+4)+9(-1+4)}{10}$$

$$= \frac{3(-8)+7+9(3)}{10}$$

$$= \frac{-24+7+27}{10}$$

$$= \frac{10}{10} \text{ or } 1 \qquad \{(3,4,1)\}$$

71. $\begin{cases} 2x - 3y + 4z = 4 \\ 3x - y + z = -2 \\ x + 2y - 3z = -6 \end{cases}$

Since $\begin{vmatrix} 2 & -3 & 4 \\ 3 & -1 & 1 \\ 1 & 2 & -3 \end{vmatrix}$

$$= 2\begin{vmatrix} -1 & 1 \\ 2 & -3 \end{vmatrix} - (-3)\begin{vmatrix} 3 & 1 \\ 1 & -3 \end{vmatrix} + 4\begin{vmatrix} 3 & -1 \\ 1 & 2 \end{vmatrix}$$

$$= 2[(-1)(-3)-1\cdot2] + 3[(3)(-3)-(1)(1)]$$
$$+ 4[3\cdot2-(-1)(1)]$$

$$= 2[3-2] + 3(-9-1) + 4(6+1)$$

$$= 2(1) + 3(-10) + 4(7)$$

$$= 2 - 30 + 28$$

$$= 0$$

Cramer's Rule does not apply.

73. $\begin{cases} x + 2y = 2 \\ x - 2y = 6 \end{cases} \qquad \begin{bmatrix} 1 & 2 & | & 2 \\ 1 & -2 & | & 6 \end{bmatrix}$

$\begin{bmatrix} 1 & 2 & | & 2 \\ 1 & -2 & | & 6 \end{bmatrix} \xrightarrow[\substack{-1 \text{ and add to row} \\ 2}]{\text{Multiply row 1 by}} \begin{bmatrix} 1 & 2 & | & 2 \\ 0 & -4 & | & 4 \end{bmatrix}$

$$-4y = 4$$
$$y = -1$$

$$x + 2(-1) = 2$$
$$x - 2 = 2$$
$$x = 4 \qquad \{(4,-1)\}$$

75. $\begin{cases} 2x + 3y = 15 \\ 2x - 7y = 5 \end{cases} \qquad \begin{bmatrix} 2 & 3 & | & 15 \\ 2 & -7 & | & 5 \end{bmatrix}$

$\begin{bmatrix} 2 & 3 & | & 15 \\ 2 & -7 & | & 5 \end{bmatrix} \xrightarrow[\text{by } \frac{1}{2}]{\text{multiply row 1}} \begin{bmatrix} 1 & \frac{3}{2} & | & \frac{15}{2} \\ 2 & -7 & | & 5 \end{bmatrix}$

$\xrightarrow[\substack{-2 \text{ and add to row} \\ 2}]{\text{multiply row 1 by}} \begin{bmatrix} 1 & \frac{3}{2} & | & \frac{15}{2} \\ 0 & -10 & | & -10 \end{bmatrix}$

$$-10y = -10$$
$$y = 1$$
$$2x + 3(1) = 15$$
$$2x + 3 = 15$$
$$2x = 12$$
$$x = 6 \qquad \{(6,1)\}$$

77. $\begin{cases} 5x + 6y = -3 \\ -4x + 9y = 7 \end{cases} \qquad \begin{bmatrix} 5 & 6 & | & -3 \\ -4 & 9 & | & 7 \end{bmatrix}$

$$\begin{bmatrix} 5 & 6 & | & -3 \\ -4 & 9 & | & 7 \end{bmatrix} \xrightarrow[\text{by } \frac{1}{5}]{\text{Multiply row 1}} \begin{bmatrix} 1 & \frac{6}{5} & | & -\frac{3}{5} \\ -4 & 9 & | & 7 \end{bmatrix}$$

$$\xrightarrow[\substack{\text{4 and add to row} \\ 3}]{\text{multiply row 1 by}} \begin{bmatrix} 1 & \frac{6}{5} & | & -\frac{3}{5} \\ 0 & \frac{69}{5} & | & \frac{23}{5} \end{bmatrix}$$

$$\frac{24}{5} + 9 = \frac{24+45}{5} = \frac{69}{5}$$

$$\frac{-12}{5} + 7 = \frac{-12+35}{5} = \frac{23}{5}$$

$$\frac{69}{5}y = \frac{23}{5}$$

$$5\left(\frac{69}{5}y\right) = 5\left(\frac{23}{5}\right)$$

$$69y = 23$$

$$y = \frac{23}{69} \text{ or } \frac{1}{3}$$

$$5x + 6\left(\frac{1}{3}\right) = -3$$

$$5x + 2 = -3$$

$$5x = -5$$

$$x = -1 \qquad \{(-1, \tfrac{1}{3})\}$$

79. $\begin{cases} 24x - 18y = -1 \\ 6x - 10y = -3 \end{cases}$ $\begin{bmatrix} 24 & -18 & | & -1 \\ 6 & -10 & | & -3 \end{bmatrix}$

$$\begin{bmatrix} 24 & -18 & | & -1 \\ 6 & -10 & | & -3 \end{bmatrix} \xrightarrow[\text{by } \frac{1}{24}]{\text{Multiply row 1}} \begin{bmatrix} 1 & -\frac{3}{4} & | & -\frac{1}{24} \\ 6 & -10 & | & -3 \end{bmatrix}$$

$$-\frac{18}{24} = -\frac{3}{4}$$

$$\xrightarrow[\substack{\text{-6 and add to row} \\ 2}]{\text{Multiply row 1 by}} \begin{bmatrix} 1 & -\frac{3}{4} & | & -\frac{1}{24} \\ 0 & -\frac{11}{2} & | & -\frac{11}{4} \end{bmatrix}$$

$$-\frac{3}{4} \cdot -6 = \frac{9}{2}$$

$$\frac{9}{2} + -10 = \frac{9-20}{2} = \frac{-11}{2}$$

$$\frac{1}{4} - 3 = \frac{-11}{4}$$

$$-\frac{11}{2}y = -\frac{11}{4}$$

$$4\left(-\frac{11}{2}y\right) = 4\left(-\frac{11}{4}\right)$$

$$-22y = -11$$

$$y = \frac{-11}{-22} \text{ or } \frac{1}{2}$$

$$24x - 18\left(\frac{1}{2}\right) = -1$$

$$24x - 9 = -1$$

$$24x = 8$$

$$x = \frac{8}{24} \text{ or } \frac{1}{3} \qquad \{(\tfrac{1}{3}, \tfrac{1}{2})\}$$

81. $\begin{cases} 5x + 4y = 2 \\ 10x + 12y = 5 \end{cases}$ $\begin{bmatrix} 5 & 4 & | & 2 \\ 10 & 12 & | & 5 \end{bmatrix}$

$$\begin{bmatrix} 5 & 4 & | & 2 \\ 10 & 12 & | & 5 \end{bmatrix} \xrightarrow[\substack{\text{-2 and add to row} \\ 2}]{\text{Multiply row 1 by}} \begin{bmatrix} 5 & 4 & | & 2 \\ 0 & 4 & | & 1 \end{bmatrix}$$

$$\xrightarrow[\text{by } \frac{1}{5}]{\text{Multiply row 1}} \begin{bmatrix} 1 & \frac{4}{5} & | & \frac{2}{5} \\ 0 & 4 & | & 1 \end{bmatrix}$$

$$4y = 1$$

$$y = \frac{1}{4}$$

$$x + \frac{4}{5}\left(\frac{1}{4}\right) = \frac{2}{5}$$

$$x + \frac{1}{5} = \frac{2}{5}$$

$$x = \frac{1}{5} \qquad \{(\tfrac{1}{5}, \tfrac{1}{4})\}$$

83. $\begin{cases} x - 2y + z = 2 \\ x + y + z = 8 \\ x - y - z = 2 \end{cases}$ $\begin{bmatrix} 1 & -2 & 1 & | & 2 \\ 1 & 1 & 1 & | & 8 \\ 1 & -1 & -1 & | & 2 \end{bmatrix}$

$$\begin{bmatrix} 1 & -2 & 1 & | & 2 \\ 1 & 1 & 1 & | & 8 \\ 1 & -1 & -1 & | & 2 \end{bmatrix} \xrightarrow[\substack{\text{Also,} \\ \text{multiply} \\ \text{row 1 by} \\ \text{-1 and add} \\ \text{to row 3}}]{\substack{\text{Multiply} \\ \text{row 1 by} \\ \text{-1 and add} \\ \text{to row 2}}} \begin{bmatrix} 1 & -2 & 1 & | & 2 \\ 0 & 3 & 0 & | & 6 \\ 0 & 1 & -2 & | & 0 \end{bmatrix}$$

$$\xrightarrow[\text{by } \frac{1}{3}]{\text{multiply row 2}} \begin{bmatrix} 1 & -2 & 1 & | & 2 \\ 0 & 1 & 0 & | & 2 \\ 0 & 1 & -2 & | & 0 \end{bmatrix}$$

multiply row 2 by
2 and add to row
1
$\xrightarrow{\hspace{2cm}}$
$\begin{bmatrix} 1 & 0 & 1 & | & 6 \\ 0 & 1 & 0 & | & 2 \\ 0 & 0 & -2 & | & -2 \end{bmatrix}$
Also, multiply row
2 by -1 and add to
row 3

multiply row 3
$\xrightarrow{\hspace{2cm}}$
by $-\frac{1}{2}$
$\begin{bmatrix} 1 & 0 & 1 & | & 6 \\ 0 & 1 & 0 & | & 2 \\ 0 & 0 & 1 & | & 1 \end{bmatrix}$

$z = 1$

$y = 2$

$x + z = 6$

$x + 1 = 6$

$\quad x = 5$ $\qquad \{(5,2,1)\}$

85. $\begin{cases} 2x + 3y + 5z = 0 \\ x - 2y - z = 0 \\ 3x + 2y - 2z = 0 \end{cases}$ $\begin{bmatrix} 2 & 3 & 5 & | & 0 \\ 1 & -2 & -1 & | & 0 \\ 3 & 2 & -2 & | & 0 \end{bmatrix}$

$\begin{bmatrix} 2 & 3 & 5 & | & 0 \\ 1 & -2 & -1 & | & 0 \\ 3 & 2 & -2 & | & 0 \end{bmatrix}$ $\xrightarrow[\text{and row 2}]{\text{Exchange row 1}}$ $\begin{bmatrix} 1 & -2 & -1 & | & 0 \\ 2 & 3 & 5 & | & 0 \\ 3 & 2 & -2 & | & 0 \end{bmatrix}$

multiply row 1 by
-2 and add to row
2
$\xrightarrow{\hspace{2cm}}$
$\begin{bmatrix} 1 & -2 & -1 & | & 0 \\ 0 & 7 & 7 & | & 0 \\ 0 & 8 & 1 & | & 0 \end{bmatrix}$
Also, multiply row
1 by -3 and add to
row 3

Multiply row 2
$\xrightarrow{\hspace{2cm}}$
by $\frac{1}{7}$
$\begin{bmatrix} 1 & -2 & -1 & | & 0 \\ 0 & 1 & 1 & | & 0 \\ 0 & 8 & 1 & | & 0 \end{bmatrix}$

multiply row 2 by
$\xrightarrow{\hspace{2cm}}$
-8 and add to row
3
$\begin{bmatrix} 1 & -2 & -1 & | & 0 \\ 0 & 1 & 1 & | & 0 \\ 0 & 0 & -7 & | & 0 \end{bmatrix}$

$-7z = 0$

$\quad z = 0$

$y + 0 = 0$

$\quad y = 0$

$x - 2(0) - 0 = 0$

$\qquad x = 0$ $\qquad \{(0,0,0)\}$

87. $\begin{cases} 2x + 5y - z = -6 \\ x - y + 3z = 18 \\ 2x + 3y - 2z = -12 \end{cases}$ $\begin{bmatrix} 2 & 5 & -1 & | & -6 \\ 1 & -1 & 3 & | & 18 \\ 2 & 3 & -2 & | & -12 \end{bmatrix}$

$\begin{bmatrix} 2 & 5 & -1 & | & -6 \\ 1 & -1 & 3 & | & 18 \\ 2 & 3 & -2 & | & -12 \end{bmatrix}$ $\xrightarrow[\text{1 and row 2}]{\text{Exchange row}}$ $\begin{bmatrix} 1 & -1 & 3 & | & 18 \\ 2 & 5 & -1 & | & -6 \\ 2 & 3 & -2 & | & -12 \end{bmatrix}$

Multiply row 1 by -2
$\xrightarrow{\hspace{2cm}}$
and add to row 2;
Also, add to row 3
$\begin{bmatrix} 1 & -1 & 3 & | & 18 \\ 0 & 7 & -7 & | & -42 \\ 0 & 5 & -8 & | & -48 \end{bmatrix}$

Multiply row 2
$\xrightarrow{\hspace{2cm}}$
by $\frac{1}{7}$
$\begin{bmatrix} 1 & -1 & 3 & | & 18 \\ 0 & 1 & -1 & | & -6 \\ 0 & 5 & -8 & | & -48 \end{bmatrix}$

Multiply row 2 by
$\xrightarrow{\hspace{2cm}}$
-5 and add to row
3
$\begin{bmatrix} 1 & -1 & 3 & | & 18 \\ 0 & 1 & -1 & | & -6 \\ 0 & 0 & -3 & | & -18 \end{bmatrix}$

Multiply row 3
$\xrightarrow{\hspace{2cm}}$
by $-\frac{1}{3}$
$\begin{bmatrix} 1 & -1 & 3 & | & 18 \\ 0 & 1 & -1 & | & -6 \\ 0 & 0 & 1 & | & 6 \end{bmatrix}$

$z = 6$

$y - 6 = -6$

$\quad y = 0$

$x - 0 + 3(6) = 18$

$\quad x + 18 = 18$

$\qquad x = 0$ $\qquad \{(0,0,6)\}$

89. $\begin{cases} x + 3y + z = 1 \\ 2x + y + 2z = 2 \\ 3x - y + 2z = 0 \end{cases}$ $\begin{bmatrix} 1 & 3 & 1 & | & 1 \\ 2 & 1 & 2 & | & 2 \\ 3 & -1 & 2 & | & 0 \end{bmatrix}$

Multiply row 1 by
-2 and add to row
2
$\xrightarrow{\hspace{2cm}}$
Also, multiply row
1 by -3 and add to
row 3
$\begin{bmatrix} 1 & 3 & 1 & | & 1 \\ 0 & -5 & 0 & | & 0 \\ 0 & -10 & -1 & | & -3 \end{bmatrix}$

Multiply row 2
$\xrightarrow{\hspace{2cm}}$
by $-\frac{1}{5}$
$\begin{bmatrix} 1 & 3 & 1 & | & 1 \\ 0 & 1 & 0 & | & 0 \\ 0 & -10 & -1 & | & -3 \end{bmatrix}$

Multiply row 2 by
$\xrightarrow{\text{10 and add to row}}$ $\begin{bmatrix} 1 & 3 & 1 & | & 1 \\ 0 & 1 & 0 & | & 0 \\ 0 & 0 & -1 & | & -3 \end{bmatrix}$
3

Multiply row 3
$\xrightarrow{\text{by } -1}$ $\begin{bmatrix} 1 & 3 & 1 & | & 1 \\ 0 & 1 & 0 & | & 0 \\ 0 & 0 & 1 & | & 3 \end{bmatrix}$

$z = 3$

$y = 0$

$x + 3(0) + 3 = 1$

$\qquad x + 3 = 1$

$\qquad\qquad x = -2 \qquad \{(-2,0,3)\}$

91. $\begin{cases} x - y + 3z = 6 \\ 2x + y - z = -3 \\ 3x - 2y + z = -4 \end{cases}$ $\begin{bmatrix} 1 & -1 & 3 & | & 6 \\ 2 & 1 & -1 & | & -3 \\ 3 & -2 & 1 & | & -4 \end{bmatrix}$

Multiply row 1 by
-2 and add to row 2
$\xrightarrow{\text{Also, multiply row}}$ $\begin{bmatrix} 1 & -1 & 3 & | & 6 \\ 0 & 3 & -7 & | & -15 \\ 0 & 1 & -8 & | & -22 \end{bmatrix}$
1 by -3 and add to
row 3

Multiply row 2
$\xrightarrow{\text{by } \frac{1}{3}}$ $\begin{bmatrix} 1 & -1 & 3 & | & 6 \\ 0 & 1 & -\frac{7}{3} & | & -5 \\ 0 & 1 & -8 & | & -22 \end{bmatrix}$

$-8 + \frac{7}{3} = -\frac{17}{3}$

Multiply row 2
$\xrightarrow{\text{by } -1 \text{ and add to}}$ $\begin{bmatrix} 1 & -1 & 3 & | & 6 \\ 0 & 1 & -\frac{7}{3} & | & -5 \\ 0 & 0 & -\frac{17}{3} & | & -17 \end{bmatrix}$
row 3

$\qquad -\frac{17}{3}z = -17$

$3(-\frac{17}{3}z) = 3 \cdot -17$

$\qquad -17z = -51$

$\qquad\quad z = 3$

$y - \frac{7}{3}(3) = -5$

$\quad y - 7 = -5$

$\qquad\quad y = 2$

$x - 2 + 3(3) = 6$

$\quad x + 7 = 6$

$\qquad x = -1 \qquad \{(-1,2,3)\}$

93. $(4-d)^3$ -factored

95. $x^3 + 8 = (x+2)(x^2-2x+4)$

97. $1 + (x+2)^3$ has two terms;
$(x+2)$ is not a factor.

99. $ax - bx + 2a - 2b$ has four terms;
$ax - bx + 2a - 2b = x(a-b)$
$\qquad\qquad\qquad\qquad + 2(a-b)$
$\qquad\qquad\qquad = (a-b)(x+2)$
$(x+2)$ is a factor.

101. $-2^{-4} = -\frac{1}{2^4}$ or $-\frac{1}{16}$

103. $(-2)^{-3} = \frac{1}{(-2)^3}$

$\qquad\qquad = \frac{-1}{8}$

105. $(\frac{8x^{-6}y^9}{27y^3})^{-1/3}$

$= \frac{8^{-1/3}x^{(-6)(-1/3)}y^{9(-1/3)}}{27^{-1/3}y^{(3)(-1/3)}}$

$= \frac{(2^3)^{-1/3}x^2y^{-3}}{(3^3)^{-1/3}y^{-1}}$

$= \frac{2^{-1}x^2y}{3^{-1}y^3}$

$= \frac{3x^2}{2y^2}$

107. $\frac{a-(x+b)^2}{a^2+(x+b)^2}$ will not reduce.

109. $\qquad\qquad \frac{1}{1-x} + \frac{2}{x^2-1} = 1$

$\qquad\quad \frac{1}{-(x-1)} + \frac{2}{(x-1)(x+1)} = 1$

$\qquad\quad \frac{-1}{x-1} \quad \frac{2}{(x-1)(x+1)} = 1$

$(x+1)(x-1)(\frac{-1}{x-1} + \frac{2}{(x-1)(x+1)})$

$\qquad\qquad = 1 \cdot (x+1)(x-1)$

$\quad -(x+1) + 2 = x^2 - 1$

$$-x - 1 + 2 = x^2 - 1$$
$$-x + 1 = x^2 - 1$$
$$0 = x^2 + x - 2$$
$$0 = (x+2)(x-1)$$

$x + 2 = 0$ or $x - 1 = 0$

$\quad x = -2 \qquad\qquad x = 1 \qquad \{-2\}$

1 is not a solution since $\dfrac{1}{1-x}$

and $\dfrac{2}{x^2-1}$ are undefined when

$x = 1$.

111. $|5-x| < 3$ -- Inequality

$\quad -3 < 5 - x < 3$
$\quad -8 < -x < -2$
$\quad 8 > x > 2$

$\{x \mid 2<x<8\}$

113. $\sqrt[3]{8x^3+64x^6}$ -- Expression

$\quad \sqrt[3]{8x^3(1+8x^3)} = 2x\sqrt[3]{1+8x^3}$

Chapter Test.

1. $\begin{cases} 3x + y = 1 \\ y = x - 1 \end{cases}$

$\quad 3x + (x-1) = 1$
$\qquad 4x - 1 = 1$
$\qquad\quad 4x = 2$
$\qquad\qquad x = \dfrac{2}{4}$ or $\dfrac{1}{2}$

$y = \dfrac{1}{2} - 1$

$y = -\dfrac{1}{2}$ $\qquad\qquad \{(\dfrac{1}{2}, -\dfrac{1}{2})\}$

D.

3. $\begin{cases} 3x + 2y = -1 \\ 3x - 4y = 11 \end{cases}$

$\quad -1(3x+2y) = (-1)(-1)$

$\quad -3x - 2y = 1$
$\quad \underline{3x - 4y = 11}$
$\qquad\quad -6y = 12$

$$y = -2$$
$$3x + 2(-2) = -1$$
$$3x - 4 = -1$$
$$3x = 3$$
$$x = 1 \qquad \{(1,-2)\}$$

B.

3. $\begin{cases} x + y \quad\;\; = -1 \\ \quad\; y + z = 1 \\ x + \quad\;\; z = 4 \end{cases}$

$\quad -(x+y) = (-1)(-1)$

$\quad -x - y \qquad = 1$
$\quad \underline{x \qquad + z = 4}$
$\qquad\quad -y + z = 5$
$\qquad\quad \underline{y + z = 1}$
$\qquad\qquad\quad 2z = 6$
$\qquad\qquad\quad z = 3$

$x + 3 = 4$
$\quad x = 1$

$y + 3 = 1$
$\quad y = -2 \qquad\qquad \{(1,-2,3)\}$

D.

4. $\begin{cases} x + y \qquad\;\; = -1 \\ 2x + 4y + z = 1 \\ \quad\; 2y + z = 1 \end{cases}$

$\quad -2(x+y) = (-1(-2)$

$\quad -2x - 2y \qquad = 2$
$\quad \underline{2x + 4y + z = 1}$
$\qquad\quad 2y + z = 3$

$\quad -2y - z = -3$
$\quad \underline{2y + z = 1}$
$\qquad\quad 0 = -2$

System is inconsistent.

B.

5. $\begin{cases} 2x + 3y = 1 \\ 4x + 6y = 0 \end{cases}$

310

$-2(2x+3y) = 1 \cdot (-2)$

$-4x - 6y = -2$
$\underline{4x + 6y = 0}$
$0 + 0 = -2$
$0 = -2 \qquad \emptyset$

C.

6. $x + 2y \leq 2$

Boundary line: $x + 2y = 2$
   (included).

x	y
0	1
2	0

Test $(0,0)$
   $0 + 2(0) \leq 2$ is true.

Shade region.

7. $2x - y > 0$

Boundary line: $2x - y = 0$ (not included).

x	y
0	0
1	2

Test $(1,0)$
   $2(1) - 0 > 0$ is true.

Shade region.

8. $\begin{cases} x - 2y \geq -2 \\ 2x - y \geq 0 \end{cases}$

Boundary line 1: $x - 2y = -2$
   (included)

x	y
0	1
-2	0

Test $(0,0)$
   $0 - 2(0) \geq -2$ is true.

Region in soln. set

Boundary line 2: $2x - y \geq 0$
   (included).

x	y
0	0
1	2

Test $(1,0)$
   $2(1) - 0 \geq 0$ is true.

Region in soln. set.

9. $\begin{cases} x + y \geq 1 \\ x < 1 \end{cases}$

Boundary line 1: $x + y = 1$
   (included).

x	y
0	1
1	0

Test $(1,1)$
   $1 + 1 \geq 1$ is true.
Region in soln. set.

Boundary line 2: $x = 1$ (not included).

x	y
1	0
1	1

Test $(0,2)$
   $0 < 1$ is true.
Region in soln. set.

10. $\begin{cases} x + y = 3 \\ x^2 + y^2 = 17 \end{cases}$

$x = 3 - y$
$(3-y)^2 + y^2 = 17$
$9 - 6y + y^2 + y^2 = 17$
$2y^2 - 6y - 8 = 0$
$\frac{1}{2}(2y^2 - 6y - 8) = \frac{1}{2} \cdot 0$
$(y-4)(y+1) = 0$

$y - 4 = 0$ or $y + 1 = 0$
$ y = 4 \qquad\qquad y = -1$
$x + 4 = 3 \qquad\qquad x + (-1) = 3$
$ x = -1 \qquad\qquad\quad x = 4$

$\{(-1,4),(4,-1)\}$

311

11. $\begin{cases} 3x - 5y = 6 \\ 6x + y = 1 \end{cases}$

$y = -6x + 1$

$3x - 5(-6x+1) = 6$

$3x + 30x - 5 = 6$

$\qquad 33x = 11$

$\qquad x = \dfrac{11}{33} \quad \text{or} \quad \dfrac{1}{3}$

$3(\dfrac{1}{3}) - 5y = 6$

$\quad 1 - 5y = 6$

$\qquad -5y = 5$

$\qquad y = -1 \qquad \{(\dfrac{1}{3}, -1)\}$

12. $\begin{cases} 7x + 2y = 3 \\ 9x + 3y = 3 \end{cases}$

$-3(7x+2y) = -3(3)$

$-21x - 6y = -9$

$2(9x+3y) = 2(3)$

$18x + 6y = 6$

$\underline{-21x - 6y = -9}$

$\qquad -3x = -3$

$\qquad x = 1$

$7(1) + 2y = 3$

$\qquad 2y = -4$

$\qquad y = -2 \qquad \{(1,-2)\}$

13. $\begin{cases} y = 3x - 6 \\ 9x - 3y = 18 \end{cases}$

$9x - 3(3x-6) = 18$

$9x - 9x + 18 = 18$

$\qquad 18 = 18$

$\{(x,y) \mid y=3x-6\}$

14. $\begin{cases} 3x + 2y = 1 \\ \quad y - 3z = -10 \\ x + y + z = 3 \end{cases}$

$-3(x+y+z) = -3(3)$

$\begin{array}{r} -3x - 3y - 3z = -9 \\ \underline{3x + 2y \qquad = 1} \end{array}$

$\begin{array}{r} -y - 3z = -8 \\ \underline{y - 3z = -10} \end{array}$

$\qquad -6z = -18$

$\qquad z = 3$

$y - 3(3) = -10$

$\quad y - 9 = -10$

$\qquad y = -1$

$x - 1 + 3 = 3$

$\quad x + 2 = 3$

$\qquad x = 1 \qquad \{(1,-1,3)\}$

15. b: price of one pound of bananas.

a: price of one pound of apples.

$3b + 2a = 297$

$5b + a = 264$

$-2(5b+a) = -2(264)$

$-10b - 2a = -528$

$\underline{3b + 2a = 297}$

$\qquad -7b = -231$

$\qquad b = 33$

A pound of bananas costs 33 ¢.

16. Expand about row 3:

$\begin{vmatrix} 1 & 2 & 1 \\ 2 & 0 & -1 \\ 3 & 1 & 0 \end{vmatrix}$

$= 3\begin{vmatrix} 2 & 1 \\ 0 & -1 \end{vmatrix} - 1\begin{vmatrix} 1 & 1 \\ 2 & -1 \end{vmatrix} + 0$

$= 3[2(-1)-1\cdot 0] - [1(-1)-1\cdot 2]$

$= 3(-2) - (-1-2)$

$= -6 - (-3)$

$= -3$

17. $2x + 3y = 1$

$\quad 3x + 2y = 2$

$x = \dfrac{\begin{vmatrix} 1 & 3 \\ 2 & 2 \end{vmatrix}}{\begin{vmatrix} 2 & 3 \\ 3 & 2 \end{vmatrix}}$

$$= \frac{(1 \cdot 2 - 3 \cdot 2)}{(2 \cdot 2 - 3 \cdot 3)}$$

$$= \frac{-4}{-5} \text{ or } \frac{4}{5}$$

$$y = \frac{\begin{vmatrix} 2 & 1 \\ 3 & 2 \end{vmatrix}}{-5}$$

$$= \frac{(2 \cdot 2 - 1 \cdot 3)}{-5}$$

$$= \frac{1}{-5} \text{ or } -\frac{1}{5} \qquad \{(\frac{4}{5}, -\frac{1}{5})\}$$

18. $\begin{cases} x + 2y + z = 0 \\ \quad -y + z = 1 \\ 2x + 3y \quad = 2 \end{cases}$

$$x = \frac{\begin{vmatrix} 0 & 2 & 1 \\ 1 & -1 & 1 \\ 2 & 3 & 0 \end{vmatrix}}{\begin{vmatrix} 1 & 2 & 1 \\ 0 & -1 & 1 \\ 2 & 3 & 0 \end{vmatrix}}$$

$$= \frac{0 - 2 \begin{vmatrix} 1 & 1 \\ 2 & 0 \end{vmatrix} + 1 \begin{vmatrix} 1 & -1 \\ 2 & 3 \end{vmatrix}}{1 \begin{vmatrix} -1 & 1 \\ 3 & 0 \end{vmatrix} - 0 + 2 \begin{vmatrix} 2 & 1 \\ -1 & 1 \end{vmatrix}}$$

$$= \frac{-2(1 \cdot 0 - 1 \cdot 2) + [1 \cdot 3 - (-1)2]}{[(-1) \cdot 0 - 1 \cdot 3] + 2[2 \cdot 1 - 1(-1)]}$$

$$= \frac{-2(-2 + (3 + 2)}{-3 + 2(2 + 1)}$$

$$= \frac{4 + 5}{-3 + 6}$$

$$= \frac{9}{3} \text{ or } 3$$

$$y = \frac{\begin{vmatrix} 1 & 0 & 1 \\ 0 & 1 & 1 \\ 2 & 2 & 0 \end{vmatrix}}{\begin{vmatrix} 1 & 2 & 1 \\ 0 & -1 & 1 \\ 2 & 3 & 0 \end{vmatrix}}$$

$$= \frac{1 \begin{vmatrix} 1 & 1 \\ 2 & 0 \end{vmatrix} - 0 + 1 \begin{vmatrix} 0 & 1 \\ 2 & 2 \end{vmatrix}}{3}$$

$$= \frac{(1 \cdot 0 - 1 \cdot 2) + (0 \cdot 2 - 1 \cdot 2)}{3}$$

$$= \frac{(0 - 2) + (0 - 2)}{3}$$

$$= \frac{-4}{3}$$

$$z = \frac{\begin{vmatrix} 1 & 2 & 0 \\ 0 & -1 & 1 \\ 2 & 3 & 2 \end{vmatrix}}{\begin{vmatrix} 1 & 2 & 1 \\ 0 & -1 & 1 \\ 2 & 3 & 0 \end{vmatrix}}$$

$$= \frac{1 \begin{vmatrix} -1 & 1 \\ 3 & 2 \end{vmatrix} - 2 \begin{vmatrix} 0 & 1 \\ 2 & 2 \end{vmatrix} + 0}{3}$$

$$= \frac{[(-1)(2) - 1 \cdot 3] - 2(0 \cdot 2 - 1 \cdot 2)}{3}$$

$$= \frac{(-2 - 3) - 2(-2)}{3}$$

$$= \frac{-5 + 4}{3}$$

$$= \frac{-1}{3} \qquad \{(3, -\frac{4}{3}, -\frac{1}{3})\}$$

19. $\begin{cases} 2x + y = 1 \\ x + 7y = -2 \end{cases} \quad \begin{bmatrix} 2 & 1 & | & 1 \\ 1 & -7 & | & -2 \end{bmatrix}$

$\xrightarrow[\text{and row 2}]{\text{Exchange row 1}} \begin{bmatrix} 1 & -7 & | & -2 \\ 2 & 1 & | & 1 \end{bmatrix}$

$\xrightarrow[\substack{\text{by } -2 \text{ and add} \\ \text{to row 2}}]{\text{Multiply row 1}} \begin{bmatrix} 1 & -7 & | & 2 \\ 0 & 15 & | & 5 \end{bmatrix}$

$\xrightarrow[\text{by } \frac{1}{15}]{\text{Multiply row 2}} \begin{bmatrix} 1 & -1 & | & 2 \\ 0 & 1 & | & \frac{1}{3} \end{bmatrix}$

$$y = \frac{1}{3}$$

$$x - (\frac{7}{3}) = -2$$

$$x = -2 + \frac{7}{3} = \frac{-6}{3} + \frac{7}{3} = \frac{1}{3}$$

$$\{(\frac{1}{3}, \frac{1}{3})\}$$

20. $\begin{cases} 2x + y - z = 1 \\ x + y \quad = 2 \\ x + 3y - 4z = -2 \end{cases}$

$$\begin{bmatrix} 2 & 0 & -1 & | & 1 \\ 1 & 1 & 0 & | & 2 \\ 1 & 3 & -4 & | & -2 \end{bmatrix}$$

Exchange row 1 and row 2

$\xrightarrow{\text{Exchange row 1}}$ $\begin{bmatrix} 1 & 1 & 0 & | & 2 \\ 2 & 0 & -1 & | & 1 \\ 1 & 3 & -4 & | & -2 \end{bmatrix}$

Multiply row 1 by -2 and add to row 2

Multiply row 1 by -1 and add to row 3

$\xrightarrow{}$ $\begin{bmatrix} 1 & 1 & 0 & | & 2 \\ 0 & -2 & -1 & | & -3 \\ 0 & 2 & -4 & | & -4 \end{bmatrix}$

Multiply row 2 by $-\frac{1}{2}$

$\xrightarrow{}$ $\begin{bmatrix} 1 & 1 & 0 & | & 2 \\ 0 & 1 & \frac{1}{2} & | & \frac{3}{2} \\ 0 & 2 & -4 & | & -4 \end{bmatrix}$

Multiply row 2 by -2 and add to row 3

$\xrightarrow{}$ $\begin{bmatrix} 1 & 1 & 0 & | & 2 \\ 0 & 1 & \frac{1}{2} & | & \frac{3}{2} \\ 0 & 0 & -5 & | & -7 \end{bmatrix}$

$-5z = -7$

$z = \frac{7}{5}$

$y + \frac{1}{2}(\frac{7}{5}) = \frac{3}{2}$

$10(y + \frac{7}{10}) = 10 \cdot \frac{3}{2}$

$10y + 7 = 15$

$10y = 8$

$y = \frac{8}{10} \text{ or } \frac{4}{5}$

$x + \frac{4}{5} + 0(\frac{7}{5}) = 2$

$x = 2 - \frac{4}{5}$

$x = \frac{10-4}{5} = \frac{6}{5}$

$\{(\frac{6}{5}, \frac{4}{5}, \frac{7}{5})\}$

CHAPTER 10

Problem Set 10.1.

1. $x^2 + y^2 = 4$

   Center: (0,0)   Radius: 2

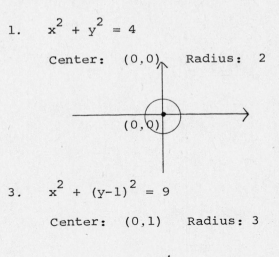

3. $x^2 + (y-1)^2 = 9$

   Center: (0,1)   Radius: 3

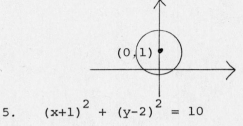

5. $(x+1)^2 + (y-2)^2 = 10$

   Center: (-1,2)   Radius: $\sqrt{10}$

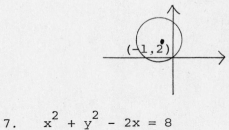

7. $x^2 + y^2 - 2x = 8$

   $x^2 - 2x + 1 + y^2 = 8 + 1$

   $(x-1)^2 + y^2 = 9$

   Center: (1,0)   Radius: 3

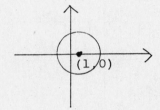

9.
$$x^2 + y^2 + 8y = 4$$
$$x^2 + y^2 + 8y + 16 = 4 + 16$$
$$x^2 + (y+4)^2 = 20$$

Center: $(0,-4)$ Radius: $\sqrt{20}$ or $2\sqrt{5}$

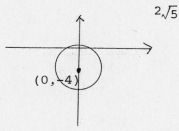

15.
$$x^2 + y^2 - x - 2 = 0$$
$$x^2 - x + \frac{1}{4} + y^2 = 2 + \frac{1}{4}$$
$$(x-\frac{1}{2})^2 + y^2 = \frac{9}{4}$$

Center: $(\frac{1}{2},0)$ Radius: $\frac{3}{2}$

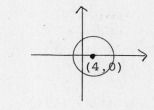

11.
$$x^2 + y^2 - 10x + 16 = 0$$
$$x^2 - 10x + 25 + y^2 = -16 + 25$$
$$(x-5)^2 + y^2 = 9$$

Center: $(5,0)$ Radius: 3

17.
$$x^2 + y^2 = 9$$

Center: $(0,0)$ Radius: 3

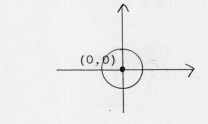

19.
$$x^2 + (y-2)^2 = 16$$

Center: $(0,2)$ Radius: 4

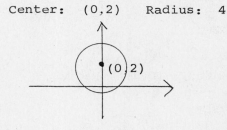

13.
$$x^2 + y^2 - 2x - 4y = 4$$
$$x^2 - 2x + 1 + y^2 - 4y + 4 = 4 + 5$$
$$(x-1)^2 + (y-2)^2 = 9$$

Center: $(1,2)$ Radius: 3

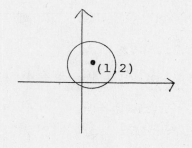

21.
$$(x+3)^2 + (y+2)^2 = 49$$

Center: $(-3,-2)$ Radius: 7

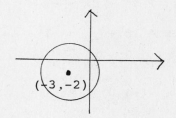

23. $x^2 + y^2 - 4x = 5$

    $x^2 - 4x + 4 + y^2 = 5 + 4$

      $(x-2)^2 + y^2 = 9$

Center: (2,0)   Radius: 3

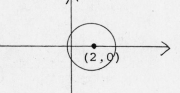

25. $x^2 + y^2 - 8y = 0$

    $x^2 + y^2 - 8y + 16 = 16 + 0$

      $x^2 + (y-4)^2 = 16$

Center: (0,4)   Radius: 4

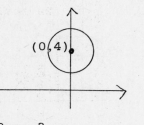

27. $x^2 + y^2 - 6y = 0$

    $x^2 + y^2 - 6y + 9 = 9 + 0$

      $x^2 + (y-3)^2 = 9$

Center: (0,3)   Radius: 3

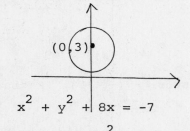

29. $x^2 + y^2 + 8x = -7$

    $x^2 + 8x + 16 + y^2 = -7 + 16$

      $(x+4)^2 + y^2 = 9$

Center: (-4,0)   Radius: 3

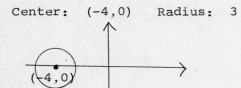

31. $x^2 + y^2 + 2y = 7$

    $x^2 + y^2 + 2y + 1 = 7 + 1$

      $x^2 + (y+1)^2 = 8$

Center: (0,-1)   Radius: $\sqrt{8}$ or

                          $2\sqrt{2}$

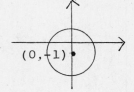

33. $x^2 + y^2 - 12x - 13 = 0$

    $x^2 - 12x + 36 + y^2 = 13 + 36$

      $(x-6)^2 + y^2 = 49$

Center: (6,0)   Radius: 7

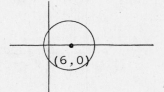

35. $x^2 + y^2 - 4x - 2y = 11$

    $x^2 - 4x + 4 + y^2 - 2y + 1 = 11 + 5$

      $(x-2)^2 + (y-1)^2 = 16$

Center: (2,1)   Radius: 4

37. $x^2 + y^2 - 4x + 4y - 1 = 0$

    $x^2 - 4x + 4 + y^2 + 4y + 4 = 1 + 8$

      $(x-2)^2 + (y+2)^2 = 9$

Center: (2,-2)   Radius: 3

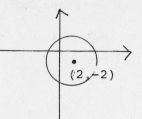
(2,-2)

39.
$$x^2 + y^2 + 6x - 6y + 9 = 0$$
$$x^2 + 6x + 9 + y^2 - 6y + 9 = 0 + 9$$
$$(x+3)^2 + (y-3)^2 = 9$$

Center (-3,3)   Radius: 3

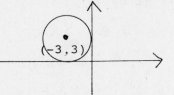
(-3,3)

41. $(x+2)^2 + (y+3)^2 = 25$

Center: (-2,-3)   Radius: 5

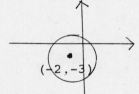
(-2,-3)

43.
$$x^2 + y^2 + 4x = -3$$
$$x^2 + 4x + 4 + y^2 = -3 + 4$$
$$(x+2)^2 + y^2 = 1$$

Center: (-2,0)   Radius: 1

(-2,0)

45.
$$x^2 + y^2 + 12x + 4y = 0$$
$$x^2 + 12x + 36 + y^2 + 4y + 4 = 0+40$$
$$(x+6)^2 + (y+2)^2 = 40$$

Center: (-6,-2)   Radius: $\sqrt{40}$
   or $2\sqrt{10}$

(-6,-2)

47.
$$x^2 + y^2 - 5x - y + 4 = 0$$
$$x^2 - 5x + \frac{25}{4} + y^2 - y + \frac{1}{4} = -4+\frac{26}{4}$$
$$(x-\frac{5}{2})^2 + (y-\frac{1}{2})^2 = \frac{10}{4}$$

Center: $(\frac{5}{2},\frac{1}{2})$ Radius: $\frac{\sqrt{10}}{2}$

$(\frac{5}{2},\frac{1}{2})$

49.
$$x^2 + y^2 + 7x + y = 0$$
$$x^2 + 7x + \frac{49}{4} + y^2 + y + \frac{1}{4} = 0 +\frac{50}{4}$$
$$(x+\frac{7}{2})^2 + (y+\frac{1}{2})^2 = \frac{50}{4}$$

Center: $(-\frac{7}{2},-\frac{1}{2})$ Radius: $\sqrt{\frac{50}{5}}$ or
$$\frac{5\sqrt{2}}{2}$$

$(-\frac{7}{2},-\frac{1}{2})$

51.
$$x^2 + y^2 + 6x + 8y + 5 = 0$$
$$x^2 + 6x + 9 + y^2 + 8y + 16$$
$$+ -5 + 25$$
$$(x+3)^2 + (y+4)^2 = 20$$

Center: (-3,-4)   Radius: $\sqrt{20}$ or

$2\sqrt{5}$

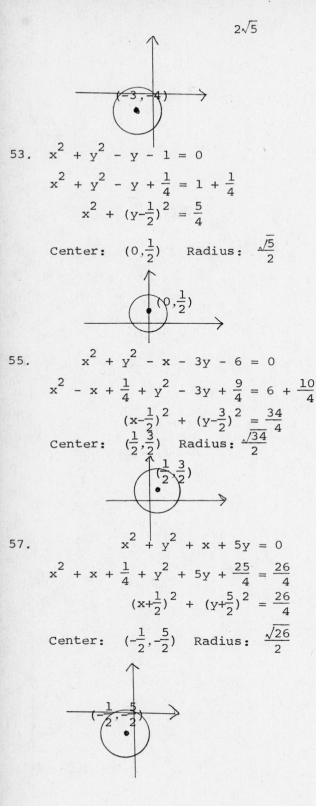

$(-3,-4)$

53. $x^2 + y^2 - y - 1 = 0$

$x^2 + y^2 - y + \dfrac{1}{4} = 1 + \dfrac{1}{4}$

$x^2 + (y-\dfrac{1}{2})^2 = \dfrac{5}{4}$

Center: $(0,\dfrac{1}{2})$ Radius: $\dfrac{\sqrt{5}}{2}$

$(0,\dfrac{1}{2})$

55. $x^2 + y^2 - x - 3y - 6 = 0$

$x^2 - x + \dfrac{1}{4} + y^2 - 3y + \dfrac{9}{4} = 6 + \dfrac{10}{4}$

$(x-\dfrac{1}{2})^2 + (y-\dfrac{3}{2})^2 = \dfrac{34}{4}$

Center: $(\dfrac{1}{2},\dfrac{3}{2})$ Radius: $\dfrac{\sqrt{34}}{2}$

$(\dfrac{1}{2},\dfrac{3}{2})$

57. $x^2 + y^2 + x + 5y = 0$

$x^2 + x + \dfrac{1}{4} + y^2 + 5y + \dfrac{25}{4} = \dfrac{26}{4}$

$(x+\dfrac{1}{2})^2 + (y+\dfrac{5}{2})^2 = \dfrac{26}{4}$

Center: $(-\dfrac{1}{2},-\dfrac{5}{2})$ Radius: $\dfrac{\sqrt{26}}{2}$

$(-\dfrac{1}{2},-\dfrac{5}{2})$

59.   Consider a circle with center at (h,k) and radius r and the point (x,y) on the circle.

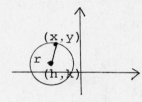

(x,y)

r

(h,k)

Using the distance formula:

$r = \sqrt{(x-h)^2+(y-k)^2}$ or

$r^2 = (x-h)^2 + (y-k)^2$

61. $2x^2 + 2y^2 - 4x - 2y + 1 = 0$

$\dfrac{1}{2}(2x^2+2y^2-4x-2y+1) = \dfrac{1}{2} \cdot 0$

$x^2 + y^2 - 2x - y + \dfrac{1}{2} = 0$

$x^2 - 2x + 1 + y^2 - y + \dfrac{1}{4} = -\dfrac{1}{2} + \dfrac{5}{4}$

$(x-1)^2 + (y-\dfrac{1}{2})^2 = \dfrac{3}{4}$

Center: $(1,\dfrac{1}{2})$ Radius: $\dfrac{\sqrt{3}}{2}$

$(1,\dfrac{1}{2})$

63. $4 + 2x + 4y - x^2 - y^2 = 0$

$-1(4+2x+4y-x^2-y^2) = 0$

$x^2 - 2x + 1 + y^2 - 4y + 4 = 4 + 5$

$(x-1)^2 + (y-2)^2 = 9$

Center: $(1,2)$ Radius: 3

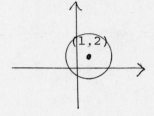

$(1,2)$

$y = x^2 + 3$

$y = (x-0)^2 + 3$

Vertex: (0,3) Axis of symmetry:

x = 0, opens up

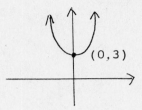

3. $y = 3x^2$

$y = 3(x-0)^2 + 0$

Vertex: (0,0) Axis of Symmetry:

x = 0, opens up

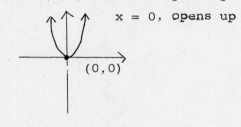

5. $y = (x-3)^2$

$y = (x-3)^2 + 0$

Vertex: (3,0) Axis of Symmetry:

x = 3, opens up

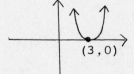

7. $y = (x+2)^2 + 1$

Vertex: (-2,1) Axis of Symmetry:

x = -2 opens up

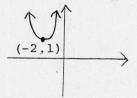

9. $y = (x-2)^2 + 3$

Vertex: (2,3)

11. $y = -(x-4)^2 - 6$

Vertex: (4,-6)

13. $y = -2x^2 + 4x$

$y = -2(x^2-2x)$

$y = -2(x^2-2x+1-1)$

$y = -2(x-1)^2 + 2$

Vertex: (1,2), opens down

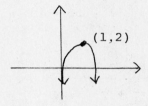

15. $y = x^2 - 4x + 2$

$y = (x^2-4x+4-4) + 2$

$y = (x-2)^2 - 2$

Vertex: (2,-2), opens up

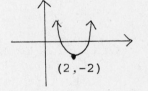

17. $x = y^2 - 3y + 2$

$x = (y^2-3y+\frac{9}{4}-\frac{9}{4}) + 2$

$x = (y-\frac{3}{2})^2 - \frac{1}{4}$

Vertex: $(-\frac{1}{4},\frac{3}{2})$, opens right

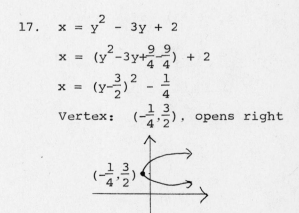

19. $x = -2y^2 + 4y$

$x = -2(y^2 - 2y)$

$x = -2(y^2 - 2y + 1 - 1)$

$x = -2(y-1)^2 + 2$

Vertex: $(2,1)$, opens left

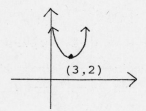

21. $x = (y-1)^2$

Vertex: $(0,1)$, opens right

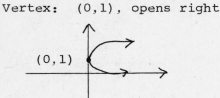

23. $y = (x-3)^2 + 2$

Vertex: $(3,2)$ opens up

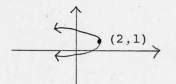

25. $x = (y+3)^2 + 3$

Vertex: $(3,-3)$ opens right

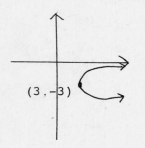

27. $y = \frac{1}{2}(x + \frac{2}{3})^2 + \frac{1}{3}$

Vertex: $(-\frac{2}{3}, \frac{1}{3})$, opens up

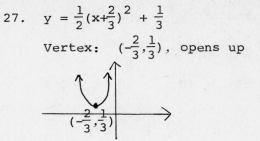

29. $y = -(x+3)^2 + 3$

Vertex: $(-3,3)$, opens down

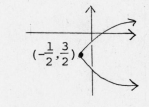

31. $x = \frac{1}{3}(y + \frac{3}{2})^2 - \frac{1}{2}$

Vertex: $(-\frac{1}{2}, -\frac{3}{2})$, opens right

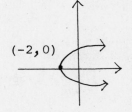

33. $y^2 - 2x - 4 = 0$

$-2x = -y^2 + 4$

$x = \frac{1}{2}y^2 - 2$

$x = \frac{1}{2}(y-0)^2 - 2$

Vertex: $(-2,0)$, opens right

35. $x = -2y^2 - 8y - 8$

$x = -2(y^2+4y+4)$

$x = -2(y+2)^2 + 0$

Vertex: $(0,-2)$, opens left

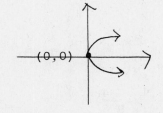
$(0,-2)$

37. $3x^2 - 9x - y + 6 = 0$

$y = 3x^2 - 9x + 6$

$y = 3(x^2-3x) + 6$

$y = 3(x^2-3x+\frac{9}{4}-\frac{9}{4}) + 6$

$y = 3(x-\frac{3}{2})^2 + 6 - \frac{27}{4}$

$y = 3(x-\frac{3}{2})^2 - \frac{3}{4}$

Vertex: $(\frac{3}{2},-\frac{3}{4})$, opens up

$(\frac{3}{2},-\frac{3}{4})$

39. $y^2 - x = 0$

$x = y^2$

$x = (y-0)^2 + 0$

Vertex: $(0,0)$, opens right

$(0,0)$

41. $x^2 - 2 = y$

$y = (x-0)^2 - 2$

Vertex: $(0,-2)$, opens up

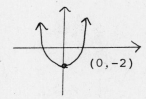
$(0,-2)$

43. $3y^2 + 3 = x$

$x = 3(y-0)^2 + 3$

Vertex: $(3,0)$, opens right

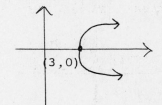
$(3,0)$

45. $x^2 + 2y + 4 = 0$

$2y = -x^2 - 4$

$y = -\frac{1}{2}x^2 - 2$

$y = -\frac{1}{2}(x-0)^2 - 2$

Vertex: $(0,-2)$, opens down

$(0,-2)$

47. $y^2 - 8y = x - 10$

$x = y^2 - 8y + 10$

$x = (y^2-8y+16-16) + 10$

$x = (y-4)^2 - 6$

Vertex: $(-6,4)$, opens right

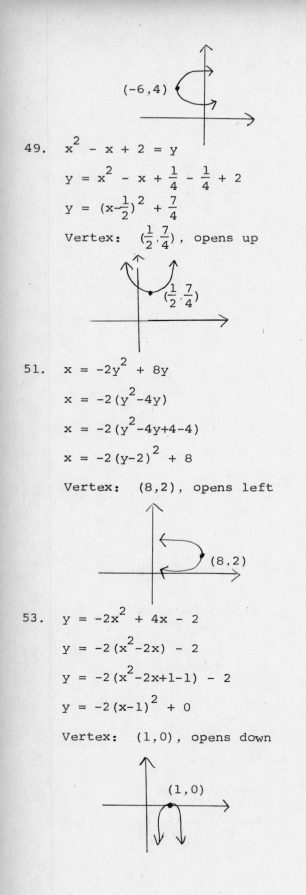

(-6,4)

49. $x^2 - x + 2 = y$

$y = x^2 - x + \frac{1}{4} - \frac{1}{4} + 2$

$y = (x-\frac{1}{2})^2 + \frac{7}{4}$

Vertex: $(\frac{1}{2},\frac{7}{4})$, opens up

51. $x = -2y^2 + 8y$

$x = -2(y^2-4y)$

$x = -2(y^2-4y+4-4)$

$x = -2(y-2)^2 + 8$

Vertex: $(8,2)$, opens left

53. $y = -2x^2 + 4x - 2$

$y = -2(x^2-2x) - 2$

$y = -2(x^2-2x+1-1) - 2$

$y = -2(x-1)^2 + 0$

Vertex: $(1,0)$, opens down

55. $3y^2 + 9y - x + 6 = 0$

$x = 3(y^2+3y) + 6$

$x = 3(y^2+3y+\frac{9}{4}-\frac{9}{4}) + 6$

$x = 3(y+\frac{3}{2})^2 - \frac{27}{4} + 6$

$x = 3(y+\frac{3}{2})^2 - \frac{3}{4}$

Vertex: $(-\frac{3}{4},-\frac{3}{2})$, opens right

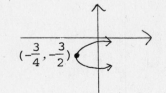

$(-\frac{3}{4},-\frac{3}{2})$

57. $2y^2 - x - 3y + 1 = 0$

$2y^2 - 3y + 1 = x$

$x = 2(y^2-\frac{3}{2}y) + 1$

$x = 2(y^2-\frac{3}{2}y+\frac{9}{16}-\frac{9}{16}) + 1$

$x = 2(y-\frac{3}{4})^2 - \frac{18}{16} + 1$

$x = 2(y-\frac{3}{4})^2 - \frac{9}{8} + \frac{8}{8}$

$x = 2(y-\frac{3}{4})^2 - \frac{1}{8}$

Vertex: $(-\frac{1}{8},\frac{3}{4})$, opens right

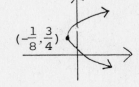

$(-\frac{1}{8},\frac{3}{4})$

59. $3x^2 - 4x - 2y = 0$

$3x^2 - 4x = 2y$

$y = \frac{3}{2}x^2 - 2x$

$y = \frac{3}{2}(x^2-\frac{4}{3}x)$

$y = \frac{3}{2}(x^2-\frac{4}{3}x+\frac{4}{9}-\frac{4}{9})$

$y = \frac{3}{2}(x-\frac{2}{3})^2 - \frac{2}{3}$

Vertex: $(\frac{2}{3},-\frac{2}{3})$, opens up

322

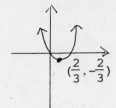

$(\frac{2}{3}, -\frac{2}{3})$

61. $2x^2 + y + 3x + 2 = 0$

$y = -2x^2 - 3x - 2$

$y = -2(x^2 + \frac{3}{2}x) - 2$

$y = -2(x^2 + \frac{3}{2}x + \frac{9}{16} - \frac{9}{16}) - 2$

$y = -2(x + \frac{3}{4})^2 + \frac{9}{8} - 2$

$y = -2(x + \frac{3}{4})^2 - \frac{7}{8}$

Vertex: $(-\frac{3}{4}, -\frac{7}{8})$, opens down

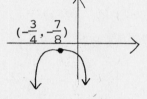

$(-\frac{3}{4}, -\frac{7}{8})$

63. $4y^2 - 5y - 2x = 0$

$-2x = -4y^2 + 5y$

$x = 2y^2 - \frac{5}{2}y$

$x = 2(y^2 - \frac{5}{4}y)$

$x = 2(y^2 - \frac{5}{4}y + \frac{25}{64} - \frac{25}{64})$

$x = 2(y - \frac{5}{8})^2 - \frac{25}{32}$, opens right

Vertex: $(\frac{-25}{32}, \frac{5}{8})$

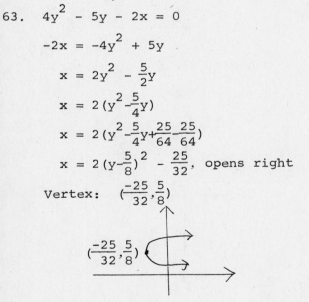

$(\frac{-25}{32}, \frac{5}{8})$

<u>Problem Set 10.3.</u>

1. $\frac{x^2}{36} + \frac{y^2}{16} = 1$

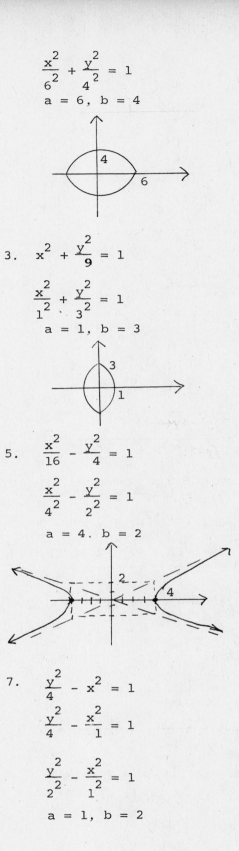

$\frac{x^2}{6^2} + \frac{y^2}{4^2} = 1$

a = 6, b = 4

4

6

3. $x^2 + \frac{y^2}{9} = 1$

$\frac{x^2}{1^2} + \frac{y^2}{3^2} = 1$

a = 1, b = 3

3

1

5. $\frac{x^2}{16} - \frac{y^2}{4} = 1$

$\frac{x^2}{4^2} - \frac{y^2}{2^2} = 1$

a = 4, b = 2

2

4

7. $\frac{y^2}{4} - x^2 = 1$

$\frac{y^2}{4} - \frac{x^2}{1} = 1$

$\frac{y^2}{2^2} - \frac{x^2}{1^2} = 1$

a = 1, b = 2

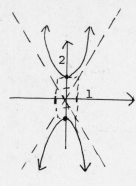

9. $\dfrac{(x-1)^2}{36} + \dfrac{(y-2)^2}{49} = 1$

$\dfrac{(x-1)^2}{6^2} + \dfrac{(y-2)^2}{7^2} = 1$

Center: $(1,2)$, $a = 6$, $b = 7$

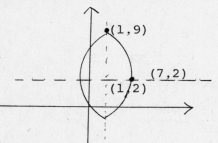

11. $9x^2 + 4y^2 - 18x - 8y - 23 = 0$

$9(x^2-2x) + 4(y^2-2y) - 23 = 0$

$9(x^2-2x+1-1) + 4(y^2-2y+1-1) - 23$
$$= 0$$

$9(x-1)^2 - 9 + 4(y-1)^2 - 4 - 23$
$$= 0$$

$9(x-1)^2 + 4(y-1)^2 - 36 = 0$

$\dfrac{(x-1)^2}{4} + \dfrac{(y-1)^2}{9} = 1$

$\dfrac{(x-1)^2}{2^2} + \dfrac{(y-1)^2}{3^2} = 1$

Center: $(1,1)$, $a = 2$ $b = 3$

13. $\dfrac{(y-1)^2}{9} - \dfrac{(x+1)^2}{4} = 1$

$\dfrac{(y-1)^2}{3^2} - \dfrac{(x+1)^2}{2^2} = 1$

Center: $(-1,1)$, $a = 2$ $b = 3$

15. $4x^2 - y^2 - 16x + 2y + 11 = 0$

$4x^2 - 16x - y^2 + 2y = -11$

$4(x^2-4x) - (y^2-2y) = -11$

$4(x^2-4x+4-4) - (y^2-2y+1-1) = -11$

$4(x-2)^2 - 16 - (y-1)^2 + 1 = -11$

$4(x-2)^2 - (y-1)^2 = 4$

$\dfrac{(x-2)^2}{1} - \dfrac{(y-1)^2}{4} = 1$

$\dfrac{(x-2)^2}{1^2} - \dfrac{(y-1)^2}{2^2} = 1$

Center: $(2,1)$

$a = 1$, $b = 2$

17. $\dfrac{x^2}{36} - \dfrac{y^2}{16} = 1$

$\dfrac{x^2}{6^2} - \dfrac{y^2}{4^2} = 1$

center: $(0,0)$

$a = 6$, $b = 4$

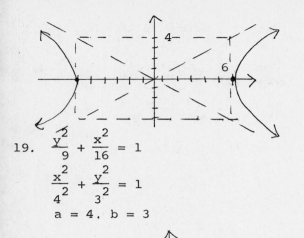

19. $\dfrac{y^2}{9} + \dfrac{x^2}{16} = 1$

$\dfrac{x^2}{4^2} + \dfrac{y^2}{3^2} = 1$

$a = 4, \ b = 3$

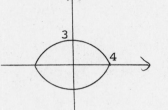

21. $\dfrac{x^2}{4} + y^2 = 1$

$\dfrac{x^2}{2^2} + \dfrac{y^2}{1^2} = 1$

$a = 2, \ b = 1$

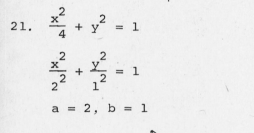

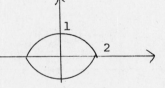

23. $\dfrac{(x+1)^2}{9} + \dfrac{(y-1)^2}{4} = 1$

$\dfrac{(x+1)^2}{3^2} + \dfrac{(y-1)^2}{2^2} = 1$

Center: $(-1,1)$

$a = 3, \ b = 2$

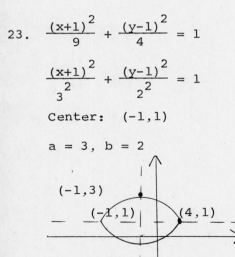

25. $\dfrac{16(x-1)^2}{25} - \dfrac{9(y-1)^2}{4} = 1$

$\dfrac{(x-1)^2}{\frac{25}{16}} - \dfrac{(y-1)^2}{\frac{4}{9}} = 1$

Center: $(1,1)$

$a = \dfrac{5}{4}, \ b = \dfrac{2}{3}$

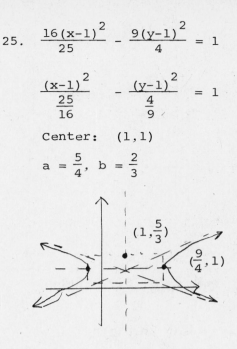

27. $2x^2 + y^2 = 8$

$\dfrac{2x^2}{8} + \dfrac{y^2}{8} = 1$

$\dfrac{x^2}{(2)^2} + \dfrac{y^2}{(\sqrt{8})^2} = 1$

$a = 2, \ b = 2\sqrt{2}$

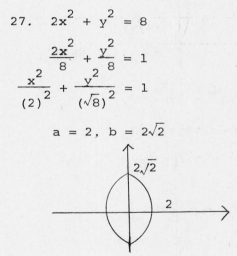

29. $x^2 - 4y^2 + 16y = 0$

$x^2 - 4(y^2 - 4y) = 0$

$x^2 - 4(y^2 - 4y + 4 - 4) = 0$

$x^2 - 4(y-2)^2 + 16 = 0$

$16 = 4(y-2)^2 - x^2$

$\dfrac{4(y-2)^2}{16} - \dfrac{x^2}{16} = 1$

$\dfrac{(y-2)^2}{(2)^2} - \dfrac{x^2}{(4)^2} = 1$

Center: (0,2)

a = 4, b = 2

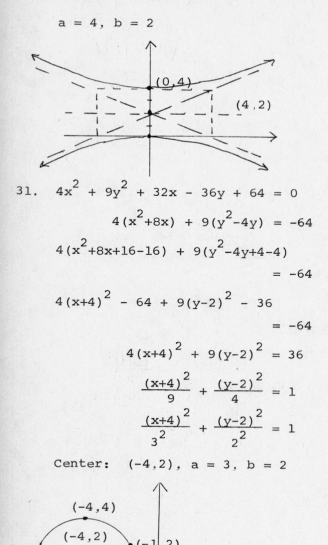

(0,4)

(4,2)

31. $4x^2 + 9y^2 + 32x - 36y + 64 = 0$

$$4(x^2+8x) + 9(y^2-4y) = -64$$

$$4(x^2+8x+16-16) + 9(y^2-4y+4-4)$$
$$= -64$$

$$4(x+4)^2 - 64 + 9(y-2)^2 - 36$$
$$= -64$$

$$4(x+4)^2 + 9(y-2)^2 = 36$$

$$\frac{(x+4)^2}{9} + \frac{(y-2)^2}{4} = 1$$

$$\frac{(x+4)^2}{3^2} + \frac{(y-2)^2}{2^2} = 1$$

Center: (-4,2), a = 3, b = 2

(-4,4)

(-4,2)   (-1,2)

33. $16x^2 + y^2 + 64x - 8y + 64 = 0$

$$16(x^2+4x) + y^2 - 8y = -64$$

$$16(x^2+4x+4-4) + y^2 - 8y + 16 - 16$$
$$= -64$$

$$16(x+2)^2 - 64 + (y-4)^2 - 16$$
$$= -64$$

$$16(x+2)^2 + (y-4)^2 = 16$$

$$\frac{(x+2)^2}{1^2} + \frac{(y-4)^2}{4^2} = 1$$

Center: (2-,4),   a = 1, b = 4

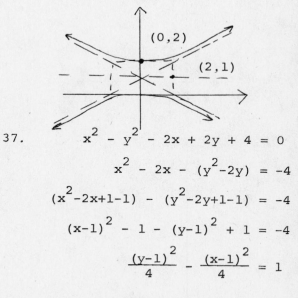

(-2,8)

(-2,4)   (-1,4)

35. $9x^2 - 36y^2 + 72y = 0$

$$9x^2 - 36(y^2-2y) = 0$$

$$9x^2 - 36(y^2-2y+1-1) = 0$$

$$9x^2 - 36(y-1)^2 + 36 = 0$$

$$36 = 36(y-1)^2 - 9x^2$$

$$\frac{(y-1)^2}{1^2} - \frac{x^2}{2^2} = 1$$

Center: (0,1), a = 2, b = 1

(0,2)

(2,1)

37. $x^2 - y^2 - 2x + 2y + 4 = 0$

$$x^2 - 2x - (y^2-2y) = -4$$

$$(x^2-2x+1-1) - (y^2-2y+1-1) = -4$$

$$(x-1)^2 - 1 - (y-1)^2 + 1 = -4$$

$$\frac{(y-1)^2}{4} - \frac{(x-1)^2}{4} = 1$$

Center: (1,1), a = 2, b = 2

326

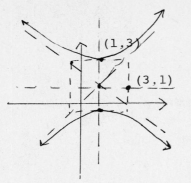

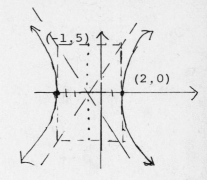

39. $x^2 - 4y^2 + 16y - 32 = 0$

$$x^2 - 4(y^2 - 4y) = 32$$

$$x^2 - 4(y^2 - 4y + 4 - 4) = 32$$

$$x^2 - 4(y-2)^2 + 16 = 32$$

$$x^2 - 4(y-2)^2 = 16$$

$$\frac{x^2}{16} - \frac{(y-2)^2}{4} = 1$$

$$\frac{x^2}{4^2} - \frac{(y-2)^2}{2^2} = 1$$

Center: $(0,2)$, $a = 4$, $b = 2$

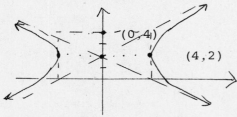

41. $25x^2 - 9y^2 + 50x - 200 = 0$

$$25(x^2 + 2x) - 9y^2 = 200$$

$$25(x^2 + 2x + 1 - 1) - 9y^2 = 200$$

$$25(x+1)^2 - 25 - 9y^2 = 200$$

$$25(x+1)^2 - 9y^2 = 225$$

$$\frac{(x+1)^2}{9} - \frac{y^2}{25} = 1$$

$$\frac{(x+1)^2}{3^2} - \frac{y^2}{5^2} = 1$$

Center: $(-1,0)$

$a = 3$, $b = 5$

43. $x^2 - y^2 + 6x + 4y + 14 = 0$

$$x^2 + 6x - (y^2 - 4y) = -14$$

$$(x^2 + 6x + 9) - 9 - (y^2 - 4y + 4 - 4)$$
$$= -14$$

$$(x+3)^2 - (y-2)^2 - 5 = -14$$

$$(x+3)^2 - (y-2)^2 = -9$$

$$\frac{(y-2)^2}{9} - \frac{(x+3)^2}{9} = 1$$

$$\frac{(y-2)^2}{3^2} - \frac{(x+3)^2}{3^2} = 1$$

Center: $(-3,2)$, $a = 3$, $b = 3$

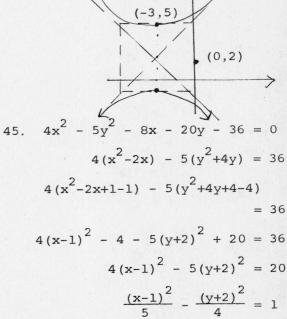

45. $4x^2 - 5y^2 - 8x - 20y - 36 = 0$

$$4(x^2 - 2x) - 5(y^2 + 4y) = 36$$

$$4(x^2 - 2x + 1 - 1) - 5(y^2 + 4y + 4 - 4)$$
$$= 36$$

$$4(x-1)^2 - 4 - 5(y+2)^2 + 20 = 36$$

$$4(x-1)^2 - 5(y+2)^2 = 20$$

$$\frac{(x-1)^2}{5} - \frac{(y+2)^2}{4} = 1$$

$$\frac{(x-1)^2}{(\sqrt{5})^2} - \frac{(y+2)^2}{2^2} = 1$$

Center: $(1,-2)$, $\quad a = \sqrt{5}$, $\quad b = 2$

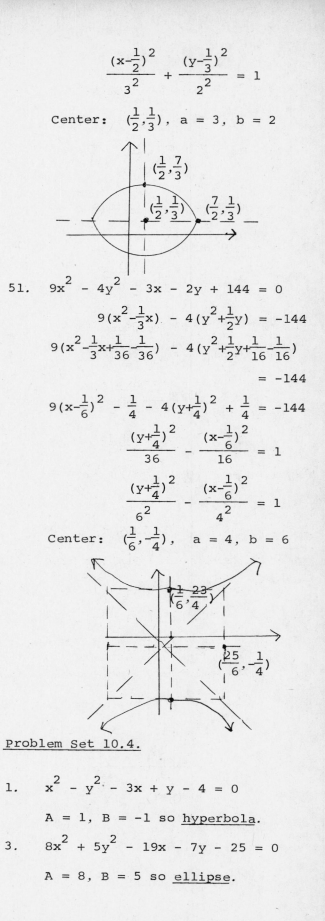

47. $9x^2 + 36y^2 + 72y + 32 = 0$

$$9x^2 + 36(y^2+2y) = -32$$

$$9x^2 + 36(y^2+2y+1-1) = -32$$

$$9x^2 + 36(y+1)^2 - 36 = -32$$

$$9x^2 + 36(y+1)^2 = 4$$

$$\frac{9x^2}{4} + 9(y+1)^2 = 1$$

$$\frac{x^2}{\frac{4}{9}} + \frac{(y+1)^2}{\frac{1}{9}} = 1$$

Center: $(0,-1)$, $a = \frac{2}{3}$, $b = \frac{1}{3}$

49. $4x^2 + 9y^2 - 4x - 6y - 34 = 0$

$$4(x^2-x) + 9(y^2-\tfrac{2}{3}y) = 34$$

$$4(x^2-x+\tfrac{1}{4}-\tfrac{1}{4}) + 9(y^2-\tfrac{2}{3}y+\tfrac{1}{9}-\tfrac{1}{9}) = 34$$

$$4(x-\tfrac{1}{2})^2 - 1 + 9(y-\tfrac{1}{3})^2 - 1 = 34$$

$$4(x-\tfrac{1}{2})^2 + 9(y-\tfrac{1}{3})^2 = 36$$

$$\frac{(x-\frac{1}{2})^2}{9} + \frac{(y-\frac{1}{3})^2}{4} = 1$$

$$\frac{(x-\frac{1}{2})^2}{3^2} + \frac{(y-\frac{1}{3})^2}{2^2} = 1$$

Center: $(\frac{1}{2},\frac{1}{3})$, $a = 3$, $b = 2$

51. $9x^2 - 4y^2 - 3x - 2y + 144 = 0$

$$9(x^2-\tfrac{1}{3}x) - 4(y^2+\tfrac{1}{2}y) = -144$$

$$9(x^2-\tfrac{1}{3}x+\tfrac{1}{36}-\tfrac{1}{36}) - 4(y^2+\tfrac{1}{2}y+\tfrac{1}{16}-\tfrac{1}{16}) = -144$$

$$9(x-\tfrac{1}{6})^2 - \tfrac{1}{4} - 4(y+\tfrac{1}{4})^2 + \tfrac{1}{4} = -144$$

$$\frac{(y+\frac{1}{4})^2}{36} - \frac{(x-\frac{1}{6})^2}{16} = 1$$

$$\frac{(y+\frac{1}{4})^2}{6^2} - \frac{(x-\frac{1}{6})^2}{4^2} = 1$$

Center: $(\frac{1}{6},-\frac{1}{4})$, $\quad a = 4$, $b = 6$

Problem Set 10.4.

1. $x^2 - y^2 - 3x + y - 4 = 0$

   $A = 1$, $B = -1$ so __hyperbola__.

3. $8x^2 + 5y^2 - 19x - 7y - 25 = 0$

   $A = 8$, $B = 5$ so __ellipse__.

328

5. $3x^2 + 3y^2 + 13y = 0$

   A = 3, B = 3 so <u>circle</u>.

7. $x^2 - 4x + 36y + 31 = 0$

   A = 1, B = 0 so <u>parabola</u>.

9. $13 - 2y^2 + 3x - 7y = 0$

   A = 0, B = -2 so <u>parabola.</u>

11. $3x^2 + 2y^2 - 2x - 2y - 14 = 0$

   A = 3, B = 2 so <u>ellipse</u>.

13. $11x^2 + 11y - 13x - 5 = 0$

   A = 11, B = 0 so <u>parabola.</u>

15. $5x^2 + 6x - 6y^2 - 5y = 0$

   A = 5, B = -6 so <u>hyperbola.</u>

17. $2x - 3y + 4x^2 + 5y^2 - 6 = 0$

   A = 4, B = 5 so <u>ellipse.</u>

19. $7x - 8y - 4x^2 - 4y^2 = 13$

   A = -4, B = -4 so <u>circle</u>.

21. $\quad 4x^2 + 3y^2 - 8x + 6y + 7 = 0$

   $4(x^2-2x+1-1) + 3(y^2+2y+1-1) = -7$

   $4(x-1)^2 - 4 + 3(y+1)^2 - 3 = -7$

   $\qquad 4(x-1)^2 + 3(y+1)^2 = 0$

   Degenerate ellipse.

   The point (1,-1) satisfies the
   equation.

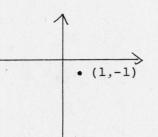

Review.

1. $\quad x^2 - y^2 - 2x - 6y = 0$

   A = 1, B = -1 so <u>hyperbola</u>.

3. $\quad x^2 + 5y^2 - 10x - 13 = 0$

   A = 1, B = 5 so <u>ellipse</u>.

5. $\quad 2x^2 + 3y^2 - 4x + 6y = 21$

   A = 2, B = 3 so <u>ellipse</u>.

7. $\quad 3x^2 - 5y^2 - 18x - 20y - 100 = 0$

   A = 3, B = -5 so <u>hyperbola</u>.

9. $\quad 2x^2 + x - y + 8 = 0$

   A = 2, B = 0 so <u>parabola</u>.

11. $\dfrac{x^2}{4} + \dfrac{y^2}{25} = 1$

   Center: (0,0), a = 2, b = 5

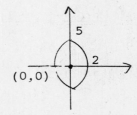

13. $x + 2 = 2(y-1)^2$

   $x = 2(y-1)^2 - 2$

   Vertex: (-2,1), opens right

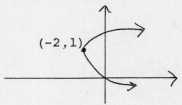

15. $\quad x^2 - y^2 - 4x - 4y - 16 = 0$

   $(x^2-4x+4-4) - (y^2+4y+4-4) = 16$

   $(x-2)^2 - (y+2)^2 = 16$

   $\dfrac{(x-2)^2}{} - \dfrac{(y+2)^2}{} = 1$

   Center: (2,-2) a = 4, b = 4

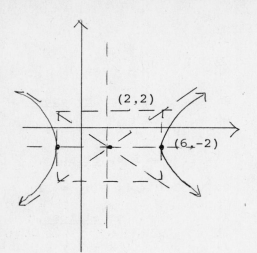

(2,2)

(6,-2)

17. $16x^2 + 9y^2 - 32x + 18y - 119 = 0$

$$16(x^2-2x) + 9(y^2+2y) = 119$$

$$16(x^2-2x+1-1) + 9(y^2+2y+1-1) = 119$$

$$16(x-1)^2 - 16 + 9(y+1)^2 - 9 = 119$$

$$16(x-1)^2 + 9(y+1)^2 = 144$$

$$\frac{(x-1)^2}{9} + \frac{(y+1)^2}{16} = 1$$

Center: $(1,-1)$, $a = 3$, $b = 4$

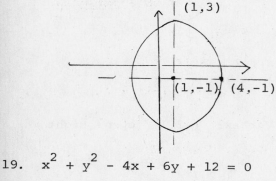

(1,3)

(1,-1) (4,-1)

19. $x^2 + y^2 - 4x + 6y + 12 = 0$

$$(x^2-4x) + (y^2+6y) = -12$$

$$(x^2-4x+4-4) + (y^2+6y+9-9) = -12$$

$$(x-2)^2 - 4 + (y+3)^2 - 9 = -12$$

$$(x-2)^2 + (y+3)^2 = 1$$

Center: $(2,-3)$ $r = 1$

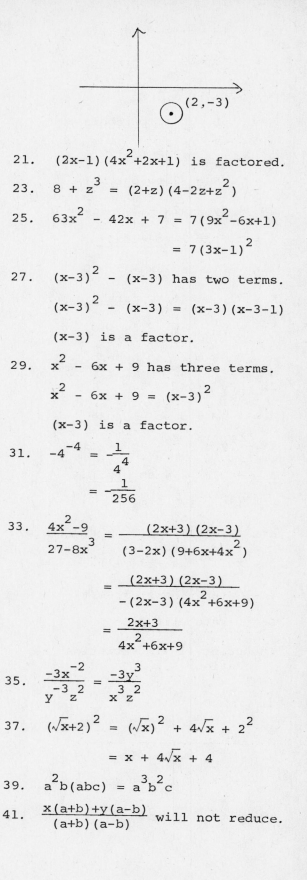

(2,-3)

21. $(2x-1)(4x^2+2x+1)$ is factored.

23. $8 + z^3 = (2+z)(4-2z+z^2)$

25. $63x^2 - 42x + 7 = 7(9x^2-6x+1)$

$$= 7(3x-1)^2$$

27. $(x-3)^2 - (x-3)$ has two terms.

$(x-3)^2 - (x-3) = (x-3)(x-3-1)$

$(x-3)$ is a factor.

29. $x^2 - 6x + 9$ has three terms.

$x^2 - 6x + 9 = (x-3)^2$

$(x-3)$ is a factor.

31. $-4^{-4} = -\dfrac{1}{4^4}$

$$= -\dfrac{1}{256}$$

33. $\dfrac{4x^2-9}{27-8x^3} = \dfrac{(2x+3)(2x-3)}{(3-2x)(9+6x+4x^2)}$

$$= \dfrac{(2x+3)(2x-3)}{-(2x-3)(4x^2+6x+9)}$$

$$= \dfrac{2x+3}{4x^2+6x+9}$$

35. $\dfrac{-3x^{-2}}{y^{-3}z^2} = \dfrac{-3y^3}{x^3z^2}$

37. $(\sqrt{x}+2)^2 = (\sqrt{x})^2 + 4\sqrt{x} + 2^2$

$$= x + 4\sqrt{x} + 4$$

39. $a^2b(abc) = a^3b^2c$

41. $\dfrac{x(a+b)+y(a-b)}{(a+b)(a-b)}$ will not reduce.

330

43.
$$\frac{x^2}{x^2-25} + \frac{1}{5-x} = \frac{x}{5+x}$$

$$\frac{x^2}{(x+5)(x-5)} - \frac{1}{x-5} = \frac{x}{x+5}$$

$$(x+5)(x-5)\left[\frac{x^2}{(x+5)(x-5)} - \frac{1}{x-5}\right]$$

$$= (x+5)(x-5)\frac{x}{x+5}$$

$$x^2 - (x+5) = x(x-5)$$

$$x^2 - x - 5 = x^2 - 5x$$

$$4x = 5$$

$$x = \frac{5}{4} \qquad \{\frac{5}{4}\}$$

45. $(x-7)^2$ is an expression.

$$(x-7)^2 = x^2 - 14x + 49$$

47. $\left|\frac{7-5x}{11}\right| = 3$ is an equation.

$$\frac{7-5x}{11} = 3 \quad \text{or} \quad \frac{7-5x}{11} = -3$$

$$7 - 5x = 33 \qquad 7 - 5x = -33$$

$$-5x = 26 \qquad\qquad -5x = -40$$

$$x = \frac{26}{-5} \text{ or} \qquad x = 8$$

$$-\frac{26}{5} \qquad\qquad (-\frac{26}{5}, 8\}$$

49. $\frac{3-2i}{1+i}$ is an expression

$$\frac{3-2i}{1+i} \cdot \frac{1-i}{1-i} = \frac{3-5i+2i^2}{1-i^2}$$

$$= \frac{1-5i}{2} \text{ or } \frac{1}{2} - \frac{5}{2}i$$

Chapter Test.

1.
$$x^2 + y^2 + 2x + 4y = 4$$

$$x^2 + 2x + 1 - 1 + y^2 + 4y + 4 - 4 = 4$$

$$(x+1)^2 + (y+2)^2 = 9 \quad r = 3$$

B.

2. $x = y^2 - 4y + 3$

$x = y^2 - 4y + 4 - 4 + 3$

$x = (y-2)^2 - 1$

Vertex: $(-1, 2)$

A.

3. $5x^2 + 6y^2 + 50x - 24y + 119 = 0$

$5(x^2+10x) + 6(y^2-4y) = -119$

$5(x^2+10x+25-25) + 6(y^2-4y+4-4)$
$$= -119$$

$5(x+5)^2 - 125 + 6(y-2)^2 - 24$
$$= -119$$

$$5(x+5)^2 + 6(y-2)^2 = 30$$

Center at $(-5, 2)$

B.

4. $x^2 + y + 2x - 3 = 0$

$A = 1$, $B = 0$ so a __parabola__.

$y = -x^2 - 2x + 3$

$y = -(x^2+2x) + 3$

$y = -(x^2+2x+1-1) + 3$

$y = -(x+1)^2 + 4$

Opens downward

D.

5. $2x^2 + 2y^2 + 2x - 3 = 0$

$A = 2$, $B = 2$ so a __circle.__

B.

6. $4x^2 + 8x - 4y^2 + 8y - 4 = 0$

$A = 4$, $B = -4$ so a __hyperbola.__

D.

331

7. $2x^2 + 2y + y^2 = 0$

A = 2, B = 1 so an <u>ellipse</u>.

A.

8. $2x^2 + 3y^2 - 8x + 18y + 29 = 0$

$2(x^2-4x) + 3(y^2+6y) = -29$

$2(x^2-4x+4-4) + 3(y^2+6y+9-9)$
$$= -29$$

$2(x-2)^2 - 8 + 3(y+3)^2 - 27 = -29$

$2(x-2)^2 + 3(y+3)^2 = 6$

$$\frac{(x-2)^2}{3} + \frac{(y+3)^2}{2} = 1$$

$a = \sqrt{3}$, $b = \sqrt{2}$ Center at (2,-3)

A.

9. $y^2 - x - 4y + 5 = 0$

$x = y^2 - 4y + 5$

$x = y^2 - 4y + 4 - 4 + 5$

$x = (y-2)^2 + 1$

Vertex: (1,2), opens right.

C.

10. $x^2 + y^2 - 4y = 1$

$x^2 + y^2 - 4y + 4 - 4 = 1$

$x^2 + (y-2)^2 = 5$

Center: (0,2) radius: $\sqrt{5}$

11. $y = -2x^2 - 4x - 3$

$y = -2(x^2+2x) - 3$

$y = -2(x^2+2x+1-1) - 3$

$y = -2(x+1)^2 + 2 - 3$

$y = -2(x+1)^2 - 1$

Vertex: (-1,-1), opens down

12. $x^2 - y^2 + 4x + 2y + 4 = 0$

$x^2 + 4x - (y^2-2y) = -4$

$(x^2+4x+4-4) - (y^2-2y+1-1) = -4$

$(x+2)^2 - (y-1)^2 - 4 + 1 = -4$

$(x+2)^2 - (y-1)^2 = -1$

$$\frac{(y-1)^2}{1^2} - \frac{(x+2)^2}{1^2} = 1$$

Center: (-2,1), a = 1, b = 1

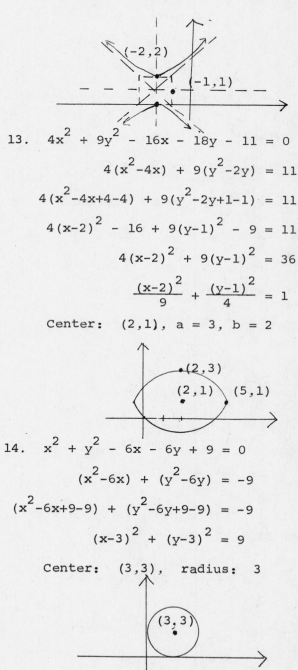

13. $4x^2 + 9y^2 - 16x - 18y - 11 = 0$

$4(x^2-4x) + 9(y^2-2y) = 11$

$4(x^2-4x+4-4) + 9(y^2-2y+1-1) = 11$

$4(x-2)^2 - 16 + 9(y-1)^2 - 9 = 11$

$4(x-2)^2 + 9(y-1)^2 = 36$

$$\frac{(x-2)^2}{9} + \frac{(y-1)^2}{4} = 1$$

Center: (2,1), a = 3, b = 2

14. $x^2 + y^2 - 6x - 6y + 9 = 0$

$(x^2-6x) + (y^2-6y) = -9$

$(x^2-6x+9-9) + (y^2-6y+9-9) = -9$

$(x-3)^2 + (y-3)^2 = 9$

Center: (3,3), radius: 3

15. $x = y^2 - 6y + 9$

$x = (y-3)^2$

Vertex at $(0,3)$, opens right.

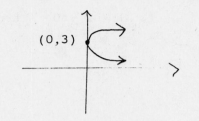

CHAPTER 11

Problem Set 11.1.

1. Yes

   $(10,100)$, $(20,400)$

3. Yes

   $(\sqrt{5},1)$, $(\frac{1}{2},1)$, $(10,\sqrt{7})$, $(12,\sqrt{7})$

5. $f(x) = 2x - 5$

   $f(2) = 2(2) - 5$

   $\qquad = 4 - 5$

   $\qquad = -1$

7. $f(x) = 2x - 5$

   $f(0) = 2(0) - 5$

   $\qquad = 0 - 5$

   $\qquad = -5$

9. $g(x) = \sqrt{x+1}$

   $g(3) = \sqrt{3+1}$

   $\qquad = \sqrt{4}$

   $\qquad = 2$

11. $g(x) = \sqrt{x+1}$

   $g(-1) = \sqrt{-1+1}$

   $\qquad = \sqrt{0}$

   $\qquad = 0$

13. $f(x) = x^2 \qquad g(x) = 2x - 3$

   $f(3) - g(3) = 3^2 - [2(3)-3]$

   $\qquad\qquad = 9 - (6 - 3)$

   $\qquad\qquad = 9 - 3$

   $\qquad\qquad = 6$

15. $f(x) = x^2 \qquad g(x) = 2x - 3$

   $\dfrac{f(3)}{g(3)} = \dfrac{3^2}{2(3)-3}$

   $\qquad = \dfrac{9}{3}$

   $\qquad = 3$

17. $f(x) = 2x^2 + x - 1$

$f(t) = 2t^2 + t - 1$

19. $f(x) = 2x^2 + x - 1$

$f(a) + f(b) = 2a^2 + a - 1 + 2b^2$
$\qquad\qquad\qquad + b - 1$

$\qquad\qquad = 2a^2 + a + 2b^2 + b$
$\qquad\qquad\qquad -2$

21. $f(x) = 2x^2 + x - 1$

$f(\sqrt{a}) = 2(\sqrt{a})^2 + \sqrt{a} - 1$

$\qquad = 2a + \sqrt{a} - 1$

23. $h(x) = x^2 - 4$

Natural domain: $\{x \mid x$ is a real number$\}$.

25. $f(x) = (x)$

Natural domain: $\{x \mid x$ is a real number$\}$.

27. $f(x) = \dfrac{3}{x} + 2$

Natural domain: $\{x \mid x \neq 0\}$

29. $g(x) = \dfrac{6}{(x+2)(x-7)}$

Natural domain: $\{x \mid x \neq -2, x \neq 7\}$

31. $g(x) = \sqrt{x-1}$

$x - 1 \geq 0$ so $x \geq 1$

Natural domain: $\{x \mid x \geq 1\}$

33. $p(x) = \sqrt{x^2+x-2}$

$p(x)$ will be real if $x^2 + x - 2 \geq 0$.

Solve: $x^2 + x - 2 \geq 0$

$(x+2)(x-1) \geq 0$

Find boundary numbers:

$(x+2)(x-1) = 0$

$x + 2 = 0$ or $x - 1 = 0$

$\quad x = -2 \qquad\qquad x = 1$

A   B   C

$$\underset{\;-2 \qquad\quad 1}{\rule{3cm}{0.4pt}}$$

Test region: A, $x = -3$

$(-3)^2 + (-3) - 2 \geq 0$ is true.

B, $x = 0$

$0^2 + 0 - 2 \geq 0$ is false.

C, $x = 2$

$2^2 + 2 - 2 \geq 0$ is true

$$\longleftarrow\!\!\underset{-2 \qquad\quad 1}{\rule{3cm}{0.4pt}}\!\!\longrightarrow$$

Natural domain: $\{x \mid x \leq -2$ or $x \geq 1\}$

35. $f(x) = x - 7$

$D = \{1, 4, 7, 11, 14\}$

$f(1) = 1 - 7$
$\quad\;\; = -6$

$f(4) = 4 - 7$
$\quad\;\; = -3$

$f(7) = 7 - 7$
$\quad\;\; = 0$

$f(11) = 11 - 7$
$\quad\;\;\; = 4$

$f(14) = 14 - 7$
$\quad\;\;\; = 7$

$R = \{-6, -3, 0, 4, 7\}$

37. $f(x) = 2x - 1$

$D = \{x \mid x$ is an even natural number$\}$

$R = \{y \mid y$ is an odd natural number$\}$

39. $f(x) = 11$

$D = \{x \mid x$ is a real number$\}$

$R = \{11\}$

334

41. $g(x) = x - 1$

Natural domain: $\{x \mid x \text{ is a real number}\}$

43. $h(x) = \dfrac{x}{3} - \dfrac{1}{4}$

Natural domain: $\{x \mid x \text{ is a real number}\}$

45. $r(x) = \dfrac{3}{x-1}$

Natural domain: $\{x \mid x \neq 1\}$

47. $h(x) = \dfrac{x}{x-3}$

Natural domain: $\{x \mid x \neq 3\}$

49. $h(x) = \dfrac{x}{x+3}$

Natural domain: $\{x \mid x \neq -3\}$

51. $f(x) = \sqrt{x-2}$

$x - 2 \geq 0$ so $x \geq 2$

Natural domain: $\{x \mid x \geq 2\}$

53. $h(x) = x^2 - 3$

Natural domain: $\{x \mid x \text{ is a real number}\}$

55. $d(x) = \sqrt[3]{x} + 1$

Natural domain: $\{x \mid x \text{ is a real number}\}$

57. $g(x) = \sqrt{x^2+1}$

$x^2 + 1 \geq 0$ for all values x, so

Natural domain: $\{x \mid x \text{ is a real number}\}$

59. $f(x) = |x-5|$

Natural domain: $\{x \mid x \text{ is a real number}\}$

61. $f(x) = 3x + 1$

$f(2) = 3(2) + 1$

$\quad = 7$

63. $f(x) = 3x + 1$

$f(0) = 3(0) + 1$

$\quad = 0 + 1$

$\quad = 1$

65. $f(x) = 3x + 1$

$f(\sqrt{3}) = 3(\sqrt{3}) + 1$

$\quad = 3\sqrt{3} + 1$

67. $f(x) = 3x + 1$

$f(a-b) = 3(a-b) + 1$

69. $f(x) = 3x + 1$

$f(2t) = 3(2t) + 1$

$\quad = 6t + 1$

71. $f(x) = 3x + 1$

$\sqrt{f(a)} = \sqrt{3a+1}$

73. $g(x) = \sqrt{x-1}$

$g(6) = \sqrt{6-1}$

$\quad = \sqrt{5}$

75. $g(2) = \sqrt{2-1}$

$\quad = \sqrt{1}$

$\quad = 1$

77. $g(x) = \sqrt{x-1}$

$2g(5) - 1 = 2\sqrt{5-1} - 1$

$\quad = 2\sqrt{4} - 1$

$\quad = 2 \cdot 2 - 1$

$\quad = 4 - 1$

$\quad = 3$

79. $g(x) = \sqrt{x-1}$

$g(2K+3) = \sqrt{(2K+3)-1}$

$\quad = \sqrt{2K+2}$

81. $g(x) = \sqrt{x-1}$

$[g(a)]^2 = [\sqrt{a-1}]^2$

$\quad = a - 1$

83. $f(x) = 1 - 2x^2$

$f(t+h) = 1 - 2(t+h)^2$

$$= 1 - 2(t^2 + 2ht + h^2)$$

$$= 1 - 2t^2 - 4ht - 2h^2$$

85. $f(x) = 1 - 2x^2$

$$f(t+h) - f(t) = 1 - 2t^2 - 4ht$$
$$- 2h^2 - (1-2t^2)$$

$$= 1 - 2t^2 - 4ht$$
$$- 2h^2 - 1 + 2t^2$$

$$= -4ht - 2h^2$$

87. $f(x) = 1 - 2x^2$

$$2f(t) = 2(1-2t^2)$$

$$= 2 - 4t^2$$

89. $f(x) = 1 - 2x^2$

$$Kf(t) = K(1-2t^2)$$

$$= K - 2Kt^2$$

91. $f(x) = 1 - 2x^2$

$$f(3t) - f(2t) = [1-2(3t)^2]$$
$$- [1-2(2t)^2]$$

$$= 1 - 18t^2 - 1 + 8t^2$$

$$= -10t^2$$

93. $g(x) = \dfrac{1}{x-1}$

$$g(0) = \dfrac{1}{-1}$$

$$= -1$$

95. $g(x) = \dfrac{1}{x-1}$

$$g(1) = \dfrac{1}{0}$$

$g(1)$ is undefined.

97. $g(x) = \dfrac{1}{x-1}$

$$\dfrac{3}{g(7)} = \dfrac{3}{\dfrac{1}{7-1}}$$

$$= \dfrac{3}{\dfrac{1}{6}}$$

$$= 3 \cdot 6 \text{ or } 18$$

99. $g(x) = \dfrac{1}{x-1}$

$\dfrac{g(1)}{g(2)}$ is undefined since $g(1)$ is undefined.

101. $f(x) = 2x^2 \quad g(x) = x + 5$

$$f(3) + g(3) = 2(3)^2 + (3+5)$$

$$= 2 \cdot 9 + 8$$

$$= 18 + 8$$

$$= 26$$

103. $f(x) = 2x^2 \quad g(x) = x + 5$

$$f(3)g(3) = 2(3)^2(3+5)$$

$$= 18(8)$$

$$= 144$$

105. $f(x) = 2x^2 \quad g(x) = x + 5$

$$f(g(3)) = 2(3+5)^2$$

$$= 2 \cdot 8^2$$

$$= 2 \cdot 64$$

$$= 128$$

107. $F(x) = 0.25x + 1.5$

a) $F(10) = 0.25(10) + 1.5$

$$= 2.5 + 1.5$$

$$= 4.0$$

The fare is $4.00.

b) $F(3) = 0.25(3) + 1.5$

$$= 0.75 + 1.5$$

$$= 2.25$$

$2.25 is the fare for a 3-mile ride.

c) $3 = 0.25x + 1.5$

$$0.25x = 1.5$$

$$x = \dfrac{1.5}{0.25}$$

$$x = 6$$

$3.00 will take you 6 miles.

109. $N(t) = t^3 - 2t^2 + t$

    a) $N(1) = 1^3 - 2(1) + 1$

           $= 0$

    There are no ants after 1
    minute.

    b) $N(2) = 2^3 - 2(2)^2 + 2$

           $= 8 - 8 + 2$

           $= 2$

    There are two ants after 2
    minutes.

    c) $N(10) = 10^3 - 2(10)^2 + 10$

            $= 1000 - 200 + 10$

            $= 810$

    There are 810 ants after 10
    minutes.

111. $f(x) = \dfrac{\sqrt{x+1}}{\sqrt{x-2}}$

    $x + 1 \geq 0$ and $x - 2 > 0$

    $x \geq -1$ and $x > 2$

    So, $x > 2$

    Natural domain: $\{x \mid x > 2\}$

Problem Set 11.2.

1. $f(x) = 2x + 1$

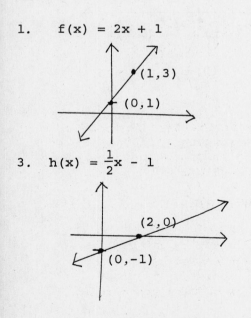

3. $h(x) = \frac{1}{2}x - 1$

5. $f(x) = 3x^2$

    Vertex: $(0,0)$

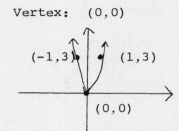

7. $h(x) = \frac{1}{2}x^2 - 2$

    Vertex: $(0,-2)$

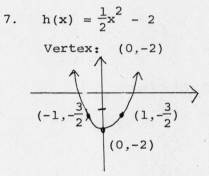

9. $g(x) = (x+4)^2$

    Vertex: $(-4,0)$

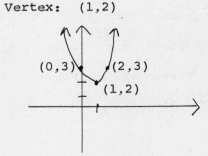

11. $g(x) = x^2 - 2x + 3$

           $= x^2 - 2x + 1 - 1 + 3$

           $= (x-1)^2 + 2$

    Vertex: $(1,2)$

13. $g(x) = |x-4|$

Vertex: $(4,0)$

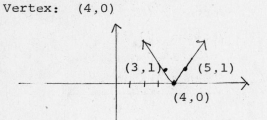

15. $f(x) = 2|x-1| - 2$

Vertex: $(1,-2)$

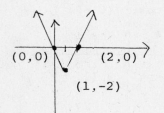

17. $h(x) = |x| + 2$

Vertex: $(0,2)$

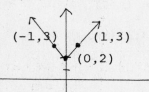

19. D: $\{x \mid x \text{ is a real number}\}$

R: $\{y \mid y \geq -1\}$

21. D: $\{x \mid x \text{ is a real number}\}$

R: $\{y \mid y \geq -2\}$

23. D: $\{x \mid x \geq 0\}$

R: $\{y \mid \geq 0\}$

25. Yes, passes vertical line test.

27. No, fails vertical line test.

29. Yes, passes vertical line test.

31. $f(x) = 3x + 2$

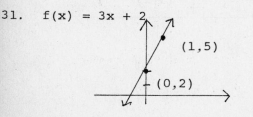

D: $\{x \mid x \text{ is a real number}\}$

R: $\{y \mid y \text{ is a real number}\}$

33. $h(x) = \frac{1}{4}x + 2$

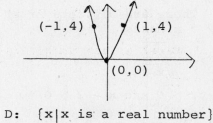

D: $\{x \mid x \text{ is a real number}\}$

R: $\{y \mid y \text{ is a real number}\}$

35. $f(x) = 4x^2$

Vertex: $(0,0)$

D: $\{x \mid x \text{ is a real number}\}$

R: $\{y \mid y \geq 0\}$

37. $h(x) = \frac{1}{3}x^2 - 1$

Vertex: $(0,-1)$

D: $\{x \mid x \text{ is a real number}\}$

R: $\{y \mid y \geq -1\}$

39. $f(x) = x^2 - 4$

Vertex: $(0,-4)$

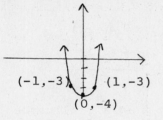

(-1,-3)   (1,-3)

(0,-4)

D: {x|x is any real number}

R: {y|y≥-4}

41. $g(x) = (x-3)^2$

Vertex: (3,0)

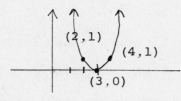

(2,1)   (4,1)

(3,0)

D: {x|x is a real number}

R: {y|y≥0}

43. $h(x) = \frac{1}{2}(x-2)^2 + 1$

Vertex: (2,1)

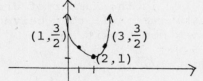

$(1,\frac{3}{2})$ $(3,\frac{3}{2})$

(2,1)

D: {x|x is a real number}

R: {y|y≥1}

45. $f(x) = -(x-1)^2 + 4$

Vertex: (1,4)

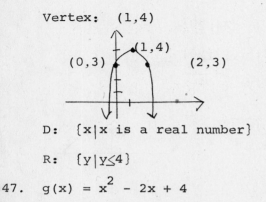

(1,4)

(0,3)   (2,3)

D: {x|x is a real number}

R: {y|y≤4}

47. $g(x) = x^2 - 2x + 4$

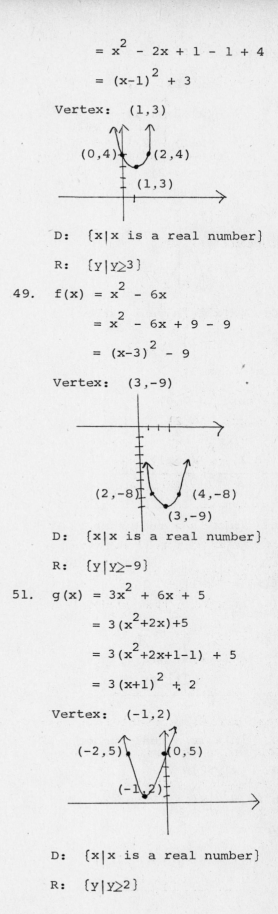

$= x^2 - 2x + 1 - 1 + 4$

$= (x-1)^2 + 3$

Vertex: (1,3)

(0,4)   (2,4)

(1,3)

D: {x|x is a real number}

R: {y|y≥3}

49. $f(x) = x^2 - 6x$

$= x^2 - 6x + 9 - 9$

$= (x-3)^2 - 9$

Vertex: (3,-9)

(2,-8)   (4,-8)

(3,-9)

D: {x|x is a real number}

R: {y|y≥-9}

51. $g(x) = 3x^2 + 6x + 5$

$= 3(x^2+2x)+5$

$= 3(x^2+2x+1-1) + 5$

$= 3(x+1)^2 + 2$

Vertex: (-1,2)

(-2,5)   (0,5)

(-1,2)

D: {x|x is a real number}

R: {y|y≥2}

53. $f(x) = -x^2 - 2x - 3$

$\quad = -(x^2+2x) - 3$

$\quad = -(x^2+2x+1-1) - 3$

$\quad = -(x+1) - 2$

Vertex: $(-1,-2)$

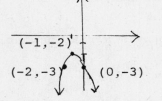

D: $\{x \mid x \text{ is a real number}\}$

R: $\{y \mid y \le -2\}$

55. $g(x) = |x+7|$

Vertex: $(-7,0)$

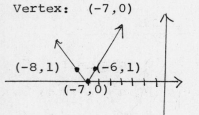

D: $\{x \mid x \text{ is a real number}\}$

R: $\{y \mid y \ge 0\}$

57. $f(x) = |x-1| + 2$

Vertex: $(1,2)$

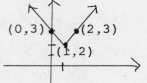

D: $\{x \mid x \text{ is a real number}\}$

R: $\{y \mid y \ge 2\}$

59. $h(x) = 2|x| + 1$

Vertex: $(0,1)$

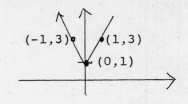

D: $\{x \mid x \text{ is a real number}\}$

R: $\{y \mid y \ge 1\}$

61. $f(x) = x^2 + 1$

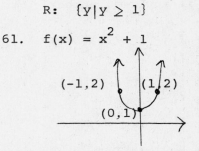

Minimum y value is 1.

63. $P(x) = -(x-250)^2 + 20,000$

Largest profit is the y coordinate of the vertex since the vertex is the highest point on the parabola.

Vertex: $(250, 20,000)$, turns down.

20,000 is the number of dresses she must sell to receive a maximum profit.

65. $f(x) = \sqrt{x}$

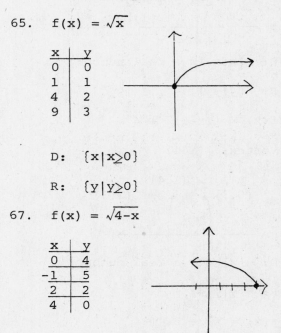

x	y
0	0
1	1
4	2
9	3

D: $\{x \mid x \ge 0\}$

R: $\{y \mid y \ge 0\}$

67. $f(x) = \sqrt{4-x}$

x	y
0	4
-1	5
2	2
4	0

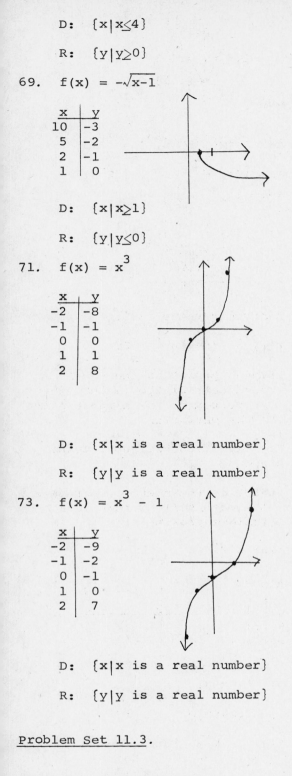

D: $\{x|x\leq 4\}$

R: $\{y|y\geq 0\}$

69. $f(x) = -\sqrt{x-1}$

x	y
10	-3
5	-2
2	-1
1	0

D: $\{x|x\geq 1\}$

R: $\{y|y\leq 0\}$

71. $f(x) = x^3$

x	y
-2	-8
-1	-1
0	0
1	1
2	8

D: $\{x|x$ is a real number$\}$

R: $\{y|y$ is a real number$\}$

73. $f(x) = x^3 - 1$

x	y
-2	-9
-1	-2
0	-1
1	0
2	7

D: $\{x|x$ is a real number$\}$

R: $\{y|y$ is a real number$\}$

Problem Set 11.3.

1. $f(x) = 2x \quad g(x) = x - 5$

$(f+g)(x) = 2x + x - 5$
$= 3x - 5$

$(f-g)(x) = 2x - (x-5)$
$= x + 5$

$(fg)(x) = 2x(x-5)$
$= 2x^2 - 10x$

$(\frac{f}{g})x = \frac{2x}{x-5}$

3. $f(x) = 3 - x^2 \quad g(x) = x + 1$

$(f+g)(x) = 3 - x^2 + x + 1$
$= -x^2 + x + 4$

$(f-g)(x) = 3 - x^2 - (x+1)$
$= -x^2 - x + 2$

$(fg)(x) = (3-x^2)(x+1)$
$= 3x + 3 - x^3 - x^2$
$= -x^3 - x^2 + 3x + 3$

$(\frac{f}{g})(x) = \frac{3-x^2}{x+1}$

5. $f(x) = x - 1 \quad g(x) = 1 - x^2$

$(g-f)(0) = (1-0^2) - (0-1)$
$= 1 + 1$
$= 2$

7. $f(x) = x - 1 \quad g(x) = 1 - x^2$

$(\frac{f}{g})(2) = \frac{2-1}{1-4}$
$= \frac{1}{-3} \quad or \quad -\frac{1}{3}$

9. $f(x) = 5x + 8 \quad g(x) = 7x - 4$

$(f \circ g)(x) = 5(7x-4) + 8$
$= 35x - 20 + 8$
$= 35x - 12$

$(g \circ f)(x) = 7(5x+8) - 4$
$= 35x + 56 - 4$
$= 35x + 52$

11. $f(x) = x^2 + 2 \quad g(x) = x - 3$

$(f \circ g)x = (x-3)^2 + 2$

$$= x^2 - 6x + 9 + 2$$

$$= x^2 - 6x + 11$$

$$(g \circ f)x = (x^2 + 2) - 3$$

$$= x^2 + 2 - 3$$

$$= x^2 - 1$$

13. $f(x) = x - 1 \quad g(x) = 1 - x^2$

$$(f \circ g)(-1) = f(g(-1))$$

$$= [1 - (-1)^2] - 1$$

$$= 1 - 1 - 1$$

$$= -1$$

15. $f(x) = x - 1 \quad g(x) = 1 - x^2$

$$(f \circ f)(1) = f(f(1))$$

$$= (1 - 1) - 1$$

$$= -1$$

17. $f(x) = 3x \quad g(x) = x + 8$

$$(f+g)(x) = 3x + (x+8)$$

$$= 4x + 8$$

$$(f-g)(x) = 3x - (x+8)$$

$$= 2x - 8$$

$$(fg)(x) = 3x(x+8)$$

$$= 3x^2 + 24$$

$$\left(\frac{f}{g}\right)(x) = \frac{3x}{x+8}$$

$$(f \circ g)(x) = 3(x+8)$$

$$= 3x + 24$$

19. $f(x) = 4x + 2 \quad g(x) = 3x - 9$

$$(f+g)(x) = (4x+2) + (3x-9)$$

$$= 7x - 7$$

$$(f-g)(x) = (4x+2) - (3x-9)$$

$$= x + 11$$

$$(fg)(x) = (4x+2)(3x-9)$$

$$= 12x^2 - 30x - 18$$

$$\left(\frac{f}{g}\right)(x) = \frac{4x+2}{3x-9}$$

$$(f \circ g)(x) = 4(3x-9) + 2$$

$$= 12x - 34$$

21. $f(x) = x - 3 \quad g(x) = \frac{1}{3}x+3$

$$(f+g)(x) = (x-3) + (\frac{1}{3}x+3)$$

$$= \frac{4}{3}x$$

$$(f-g)(x) = (x-3) - (\frac{1}{3}x+3)$$

$$= \frac{2}{3}x - 6$$

$$(fg)(x) = (x-3)(\frac{1}{3}x+3)$$

$$= \frac{1}{3}x^2 + 2x - 9$$

$$\left(\frac{f}{g}\right)(x) = \frac{x-3}{\frac{1}{3}x+3} \cdot \frac{3}{3}$$

$$= \frac{3(x-3)}{x+9}$$

$$(f \circ g)(x) = (\frac{1}{3}x+3) - 3$$

$$= \frac{1}{3}x$$

23. $f(x) = 2x^2 + x + 3 \quad g(x) = 2x - 5$

$$(f+g)(x) = (2x^2+x+3) + (2x-5)$$

$$= 2x^2 + 3x - 2$$

$$(f-g)(x) = (2x^2+x+3) - (2x-5)$$

$$= 2x^2 - x + 8$$

$$(fg)(x) = (2x^2+x+3)(2x-5)$$

$$= 2x^2(2x^2-5) + x(2x-5)$$

$$+ 3(2x-5)$$

$$= 4x^3 - 10x^2 + 2x^2 - 5x$$

$$+ 6x - 15$$

$$= 4x^3 - 8x^2 + x - 15$$

$$\left(\frac{f}{g}\right)(x) = \frac{2x^2+x+3}{2x-5}$$

$$(f \circ g)(x) = 2(2x-5)^2 + (2x-5) + 3$$

$$= 2(4x^2-20x+25) + 2x$$

$$-5 + 3$$

$$= 8x^2 - 40 + 50 + 2x - 2$$

$$= 8x^2 - 38x + 48$$

25. $f(x) = 1 - x^2 \quad g(x) = x + 3$

$$(f+g)(x) = (1-x^2) + (x+3)$$

$$= -x^2 + x + 4$$

$$(f-g)(x) = 1 - x^2 - (x+3)$$

$$= -x^2 - x - 2$$

$$(fg)(x) = (1-x^2)(x+3)$$

$$= 1(x+3) - x^2(x+3)$$

$$= x + 3 - x^3 - 3x^2$$

$$= -x^3 - 3x^2 + x + 3$$

$$\left(\frac{f}{g}\right)(x) = \frac{1-x^2}{x+3}$$

$$(f \circ g)(x) = 1 - (x+3)^2$$

$$= 1 - (x^2+6x+9)$$

$$= -x^2 - 6x - 8$$

27. $f(x) = x^2 - x - 2 \quad g(x) = x^2 - 2x$

$$(f+g)(x) = (x^2-x-2) + (x^2-2x)$$

$$= 2x^2 - 3x - 2$$

$$(f-g)(x) = (x^2-x-2) - (x^2-2x)$$

$$= x^2 - x - 2 - x^2 + 2x$$

$$= x - 2$$

$$(fg)(x) = (x^2-x-2)(x^2-2x)$$

$$= (x^2(x^2-2x) - x(x^2-2x)$$

$$\qquad - 2(x^2-2)$$

$$= x^4 - 2x^3 - x^3 + 2x^2$$

$$\qquad - 2x^2 + 4x$$

$$= x^4 - 3x^3 + 4x$$

$$\left(\frac{f}{g}\right)(x) = \frac{x^2-x-2}{x^2-2x}$$

$$= \frac{(x-2)(x+1)}{x(x-2)}$$

$$= \frac{x+1}{x}, \quad x \neq 2$$

$$(f \circ g)(x) = (x^2-2x)^2 - (x^2-2x) - 2$$

$$= x^4 - 4x^3 + 4x^2 - x^2$$

$$\qquad + 2x - 2$$

$$= x^4 - 4x^3 + 3x^2 + 2x$$

$$\qquad -2$$

29. $f(x) = 2x - 5 \quad g(x) = 4 - x^2$

$$(g-f)(0) = (4-0^2) - (2 \cdot 0-5)$$

$$= 4 + 5$$
$$= 9$$

31. $f(x) = 2x - 5 \quad g(x) = 4 - x^2$

$$\left(\frac{f}{g}\right)(1) = \frac{2(1)-5}{4-1^2}$$

$$= \frac{2-5}{4-1}$$

$$= \frac{-3}{3}$$

$$= -1$$

33. $f(x) = 2x - 5 \quad g(x) = 4 - x^2$

$$(f \circ g)(-1) = f(g(-1))$$

$$= 2[4-(-1)^2] - 5$$

$$= 2(4-1) - 5$$

$$= 2(3) - 5$$

$$= 6 - 5$$

$$= 1$$

35. $f(x) = 2x - 5$

$$(f \circ f)(1) = f(f(1))$$

$$= 2[2(1)-5] - 5$$

$$= 2(2-5) - 5$$

$$= 2(-3) - 5$$

$$= -6 - 5$$

$$= -11$$

37. $f(x) = x + 3 \quad g(x) = x - 3$

$$(f \circ g)(x) = (x-3) + 3$$

$$= x$$

$(g \circ f)(x) = (x+3) - 3$

$\qquad\qquad = x$

39. $f(x) = x - 1 \quad g(x) = 1 - x^2$

$\left(\dfrac{f}{g}\right)(x) = \dfrac{x-1}{1-x^2}$

1 is not in the domain of $\dfrac{f}{g}$.

Problem Set 11.4.

1. Passes horizontal line test so
   is one-to-one.

3. Passes horizontal line test so
   is one-to-one.

5. Fails horizontal line test so
   is not one-to-one.

7. Passes horizontal line test so
   is one-to-one.

9. $f(x) = 3x - 1$

$\qquad y = 3x - 1$

$\qquad x = 3y - 1$

$\quad x + 1 = 3y$

$\quad \dfrac{x+1}{3} = y$

$\quad f^{-1}(x) = \dfrac{x+1}{3} \text{ or } \dfrac{1}{3}(x+1)$

11. $f(x) = \dfrac{1}{2}x + 3$

$\qquad y = \dfrac{1}{2}x + 3$

$\qquad x = \dfrac{1}{2}y + 3$

$\quad x - 3 = \dfrac{1}{2}y$

$\quad 2(x-3) = y$

$\quad f^{-1}(x) = 2(x-3)$

13. $f(x) = x^3$

$\qquad y = x^3$

$\qquad x = y^3$

$\quad \sqrt[3]{x} = y$

$\quad f^{-1}(x) = \sqrt[3]{x}$

15. $f(x) = 3x + 1$

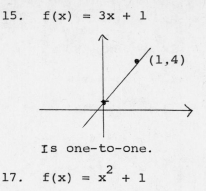

(1,4)

Is one-to-one.

17. $f(x) = x^2 + 1$

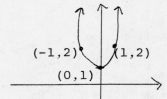

$(-1,2) \qquad (1,2)$

$\qquad (0,1)$

Is not one-to-one.

19. $g(x) = (x+1)^2 - 1$

Vertex: $(-1,-1)$

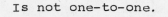

$(-2,0) \qquad (0,0)$

$\qquad (-1,-1)$

Is not one-to-one.

21. $h(x) = |x+1|$

Vertex: $(-1,0)$

$(-3,1) \qquad (0,1)$

$\qquad (-1,0)$

Is not one-to-one.

23. $f(x) = 5x - 1$

$\qquad y = 5x - 1$

$\qquad x = 5y - 1$

$\quad x + 1 = 5y$

$\quad \dfrac{x+1}{5} = y$

$\quad f^{-1}(x) = \dfrac{x+1}{5} \text{ or } \dfrac{1}{5}(x+1)$

25. $f(x) = \frac{1}{3}x - 1$

$\qquad y = \frac{1}{3}x - 1$

$\qquad x = \frac{1}{3}y - 1$

$\qquad x + 1 = \frac{1}{3}y$

$\qquad 3(x+1) = y$

$\qquad f^{-1}(x) = 3(x+1)$

27. $f(x) = x^3 + 2$

$\qquad y = x^3 + 2$

$\qquad x = y^3 + 2$

$\qquad x - 2 = y^3$

$\qquad \sqrt[3]{x-2} = y$

$\qquad f^{-1}(x) = \sqrt[3]{x-2}$

29. $f(x) = 2x + 1 \quad f^{-1}(x) = \frac{x-1}{2}$

$\qquad f(f^{-1}(x)) = 2(\frac{x-1}{2}) + 1$

$\qquad\qquad\qquad = x - 1 + 1$

$\qquad\qquad\qquad = x$

$\qquad f^{-1}(f(x)) = \frac{(2x+1)-1}{2}$

$\qquad\qquad\qquad = \frac{2x}{2}$

$\qquad\qquad\qquad = x$

31. $f(x) = x + 1 \quad f^{-1}(x) = x - 1$

$\qquad f(f^{-1}(x)) = (x-1) + 1$

$\qquad\qquad\qquad = x$

$\qquad f^{-1}(f(x)) = (x+1) - 1$

$\qquad\qquad\qquad = x$

33. $f(x) = x + 2 \quad f^{-1}(x) = x - 2$

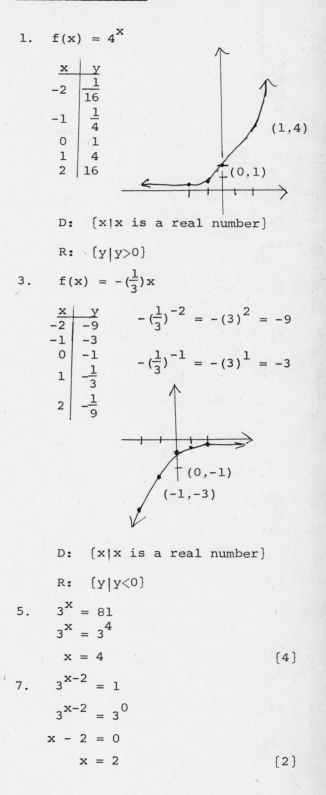

The graph of f^{-1} is the graph of
f reflected about the line
$y = x$.

Problem Set 11.5.

1. $f(x) = 4^x$

x	y
-2	$\frac{1}{16}$
-1	$\frac{1}{4}$
0	1
1	4
2	16

(1,4)

(0,1)

D: $\{x \mid x \text{ is a real number}\}$

R: $\{y \mid y > 0\}$

3. $f(x) = -(\frac{1}{3})x$

x	y
-2	-9
-1	-3
0	-1
1	$-\frac{1}{3}$
2	$-\frac{1}{9}$

$-(\frac{1}{3})^{-2} = -(3)^2 = -9$

$-(\frac{1}{3})^{-1} = -(3)^1 = -3$

(0,-1)

(-1,-3)

D: $\{x \mid x \text{ is a real number}\}$

R: $\{y \mid y < 0\}$

5. $3^x = 81$

$\quad 3^x = 3^4$

$\quad x = 4$ $\qquad\qquad \{4\}$

7. $3^{x-2} = 1$

$\quad 3^{x-2} = 3^0$

$\quad x - 2 = 0$

$\quad x = 2$ $\qquad\qquad \{2\}$

9. $f(x) = \log_6 x$

    $y = \log_6 x$ is equivalent to $x = 6^y$

x	y
$\frac{1}{36}$	-2
$\frac{1}{6}$	-1
1	0
6	1
36	2

    (0,1)

    D: $\{x \mid x > 0\}$

    R: $\{y \mid y$ is a real number$\}$

11. $\log_2 8 = 3 \qquad 2^3 = 8$

13. $\log_8 64 = 2 \qquad 8^2 = 64$

15. $\log_5 1 = 0 \qquad 5^0 = 1$

17. $\log_9 27 = \frac{3}{2} \qquad 9^{3/2} = 27$

19. $2^3 = 8 \qquad \log_2 8 = 3$

21. $(\frac{1}{3})^2 = \frac{1}{9} \qquad \log_{\frac{1}{3}} \frac{1}{9} = 2$

23. $3^{-1} = \frac{1}{3} \qquad \log_3 \frac{1}{3} = -1$

25. $4^3 = 64 \qquad \log_4 64 = 3$

27. $\log_4 x = 2$

    $x = 4^2$

    $x = 16 \qquad\qquad \{16\}$

29. $\log_5 x = 3$

    $x = 5^3$

    $x = 125 \qquad\qquad \{125\}$

31. $\log_2 x = 1$

    $x = 2^1$

    $= 2 \qquad\qquad \{2\}$

33. $\log_{\frac{1}{3}} x = -1$

    $x = (\frac{1}{3})^{-1}$

    $x = 3^1 \qquad\qquad \{3\}$

35. $\log_7 7 = x$

    $7^x = 7$

    $x = 1 \qquad\qquad \{1\}$

37. $\log_{10}(x+2) = 2$

    $x + 2 = 10^2$

    $x + 2 = 100$

    $x = 98 \qquad\qquad \{98\}$

39. $\log_5 125 = x$

    $5^x = 125$

    $5^x = 5^3$

    $x = 3$

    So, $\log_5 125 = 3$

41. $\log_3 -9$ is undefined since $\log_3 x$
     is not defined when $x < 0$.

43. $\log_3 3^2 = x$

    $3^x = 3^2$

    $x = 2$

    So, $\log_3 3^2 = 2$

45. $\log_{100} 10,000 = x$

    $100^x = 10,000$

    $100^x = 100^2$

    $x = 2$

    So, $\log_{100} 10,000 = 2$

47. $P = 14.7\, e^{-0.00004x}, \quad x = 5280$

    $P = 14.7\, e^{-0.00004(5280)}$

    $= 14.7\, e^{-0.2112}$

    $\approx 14.7\,(0.8096)$ or 11.9

    The atmospheric pressure is
    approximately 11.9 lb/sq. in.

49. $A = P(1+i)^t, \quad P = 3000, \quad i = 0.12,$
     $t = 5,$

    $A = 3000(1+0.12)^5$

346

$$= 3000(1.12)^5$$

$$\approx 3000(1.7623) \text{ or } 5287.03$$

The return on the investment is approximately $5287.03.

51. $f(x) = (\frac{1}{3})^x$

x	y
-2	9
-1	3
0	1
1	$\frac{1}{3}$
2	$\frac{1}{9}$

$(\frac{1}{3})^{-2} = 3^2 = 9$

$(\frac{1}{3})^{-1} = 3^1 = 3$

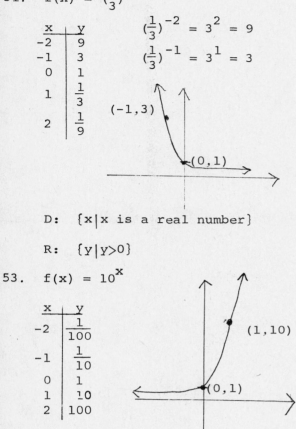

D: $\{x \mid x \text{ is a real number}\}$

R: $\{y \mid y > 0\}$

53. $f(x) = 10^x$

x	y
-2	$\frac{1}{100}$
-1	$\frac{1}{10}$
0	1
1	10
2	100

D: $\{x \mid x \text{ is a real number}\}$

R: $\{y \mid y > 0\}$

55. $f(x) = \log_2 x$

$y = \log_2 x$ is equivalent to $x = 2^4$.

x	y
$\frac{1}{4}$	-2
$\frac{1}{2}$	-1
1	0
2	1
4	2

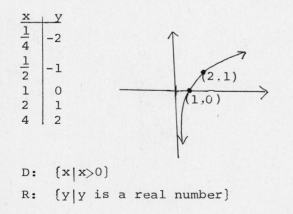

D: $\{x \mid x > 0\}$

R: $\{y \mid y \text{ is a real number}\}$

57. $f(x) = \log_{10} x$

$y = \log_{10} x$ is equivalent to $x = 10^y$.

x	y
$\frac{1}{100}$	-2
$\frac{1}{10}$	-1
1	0
10	1
100	2

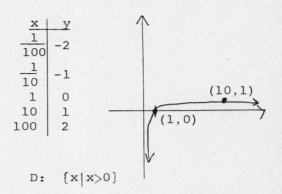

D: $\{x \mid x > 0\}$

R: $\{y \mid y \text{ is a real number}\}$

59. $f(x) = -\log_4 x$

Since $y = -\log_4 x$ is the same as $-y = \log_4 x$ which is equivalent to $x = 4^{-4}$.

x	y
16	-2
4	-1
1	0
$\frac{1}{4}$	1
$\frac{1}{16}$	2

D: $\{x \mid x > 0\}$

R: $\{y \mid y \text{ is a real number}\}$.

61. $\log_3 9 = x$

$$3^x = 9$$

$$3^x = 3^2$$

$$x = 2 \qquad \{2\}$$

63. $\log_x 1 = 0$

$$x^0 = 1 \qquad \{x \mid x > 0, x \neq 1\}$$

65. $\log_4 x = \frac{3}{2}$

$$x = 4^{3/2}$$

$$= (4^{1/2})^3$$

$$= 2^3$$
$$= 8 \quad \{8\}$$

$$-x = 2$$
$$x = -2 \quad \{-2\}$$

67. $\log_2 x = 5$

$$x = 2^5$$
$$x = 72 \quad \{32\}$$

81. $\log_{10} 10 = x$

$$10^x = 10^1$$
$$x = 1 \quad \{1\}$$

69. $\log_{27} 3 = x$

$$27^x = 3$$
$$(3^3)^x = 3$$
$$3^{3x} = 3^1$$
$$3x = 1$$
$$x = \frac{1}{3} \quad \left\{\frac{1}{3}\right\}$$

83. $\log_{25} 5 = x$

$$25^x = 5$$
$$(5^2)^x = 5$$
$$5^{2x} = 5^1$$
$$2x = 1$$
$$x = \frac{1}{2} \quad \left\{\frac{1}{2}\right\}$$

71. $2^{2x} = 16$

$$2^{2x} = 2^4$$
$$2x = 4$$
$$x = 2 \quad \{2\}$$

85. $N = N_0 e^{0.3t}$, $t = 3$, $N_0 = 50$

$$N = 50 e^{0.3(3)}$$
$$= 50 e^{0.9}$$
$$\approx 50(2.4596) \text{ or } 122.98$$

There will be approximately 123 rabbits.

73. $3^{x-7} = 27$

$$3^{x-7} = 3^3$$
$$x - 7 = 3$$
$$x = 10 \quad \{10\}$$

87. $P = P_0 e^{0.05t}$, $t = 30$, $P_0 = 50{,}000$

$$P = 50{,}000 \, e^{0.05(30)}$$
$$\approx 50{,}000(4.4817) \text{ or}$$
$$224{,}084.45$$

The population will be approximately 224,084.

75. $\log_3 (2x-1) = 2$

$$2x - 1 = 3^2$$
$$2x - 1 = 9$$
$$2x = 10$$
$$x = 5 \quad \{5\}$$

89. $N = N_0 e^{0.3t}$, $N = 100$, $N_0 = 20$

$$100 = 20 \, e^{0.3t}$$
$$e^{0.3t} = 5$$
$$e^{0.3t} = e^{\ln 5}$$
$$0.3t = \ln 5$$
$$t = \frac{\ln 5}{0.3}$$
$$\approx 5.3648$$

It will take approximately 5 months.

77. $\log_5 25 = x$

$$5^x = 25$$
$$5^x = 5^2$$
$$x = 2 \quad \{2\}$$

79. $\log_{\frac{1}{3}} 9 = x$

$$\frac{1}{3}^x = 9$$
$$(3^{-1})^x = 9$$
$$3^{-x} = 3^2$$

91. a)

1. $f(x) = 2^x$

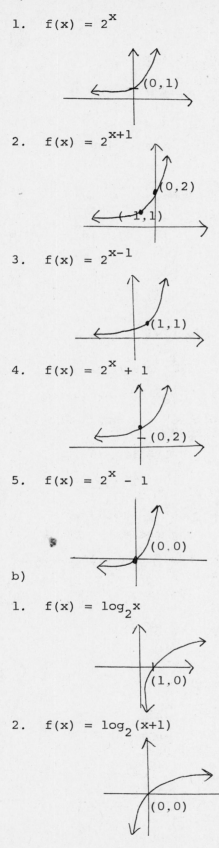

2. $f(x) = 2^{x+1}$

3. $f(x) = 2^{x-1}$

4. $f(x) = 2^x + 1$

5. $f(x) = 2^x - 1$

b)

1. $f(x) = \log_2 x$

2. $f(x) = \log_2(x+1)$

3. $f(x) = \log_2(x-1)$

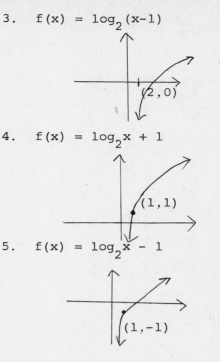

4. $f(x) = \log_2 x + 1$

5. $f(x) = \log_2 x - 1$

Rules: The graph of $f(x) = 2^{x-h}$ is the graph of $f(x) = 2^x$ shifted h units horizontally; the graph of $f(x) = \log_2(x-h)$ is the graph of $f(x) = \log_2 x$ shifted h units horizontally.

The graph of $f(x) = 2^x - K$ is the graph of $f(x) = 2^x$ shifted K units vertically; the graph of $f(x) = \log_2 x - K$ is the graph of $y = \log_2 x$ shifted K units vertically.

93. $(-2)^{1/2}$ is not real.

Problem Set 11.6.

1. $\log_b 6 = \log_b 3 + \log_b 2$
$\approx 1.62 + 1.32$
≈ 2.94

3. $\log_b 2^2 = 2 \log_b 2$
$\approx 2(1.32)$
≈ 2.64

5. $\log_b \frac{1}{2} = \log_b 2^{-1}$

$= -1 \log_b 2$

$\approx -(1.32)$ or -1.32

7. $\log_b \frac{4}{3} = \log_b 4 - \log_b 3$

$= \log_b 2^2 - \log_b 3$

$= 2 \log_b 2 - \log_b 3$

$= 2(1.32) - 1.62$

$= 2.64 - 1.62$

$= 1.02$

9. $\log_3 x + \log_3 2 = 2$

$\log_3 x(2) = 2$

$2x = 3^2$

$2x = 9$

$x = \frac{9}{2}$

Checking,

LS: $\log_3 \frac{9}{2} + \log_3 2 = \log_3 9 - \log$

$- \log_3 2 + \log_3 2$

$= \log_3 9$

$= 2$

RS: 2

$\frac{9}{2}$ checks. $\{\frac{9}{2}\}$

11. $\log x + \log 2 = 0$

$\log x(2) = 0$

$2x = 10^0$

$2x = 1$

$x = \frac{1}{2}$

Checking,

LS: $\log \frac{1}{2} + \log 2 = \log \frac{1}{2}(2)$

$= \log 1$

$= 0$

RS: 0

$\frac{1}{2}$ checks. $\{\frac{1}{2}\}$

13. $\log_{16} x + \log_4 = 1$

$\log_{16} x(4) = 1$

$\log_{16} 4x = 1$

$4x = 16^1$

$x = 4$

Checking,

LS: $\log_{16} 4 + \log_{16} 4 = \log_{16} 16$

$= 1$

RS: 1

4 checks. $\{4\}$

15. $\log_7 (x+1) - \log_7 49 = 1$

$\log_7 (\frac{x+1}{49}) = 1$

$\frac{x+1}{49} = 7$

$49(\frac{x+1}{49}) = 49 \cdot 7$

$x + 1 = 343$

$x = 342$

Checking,

LS: $\log_7 (342+1) - \log_7 49$

$= \log_7 343 - \log_7 49$

$= \log_7 \frac{343}{49}$

$= \log_7 7$

$= 1$

RS: 1

342 checks. $\{342\}$

17. $\log_8 (2x+2) = \log_8 8$

$2x + 2 = 8$

$2x = 6$

$x = 3$

Checking,

LS: $\log_8(2(3)+2) = \log_8 8$

RS: $\log_8 8$

3 checks. {3}

19. $\log x + \log (x-3) = 1$

$\log x(x-3) = 1$

$x(x-3) = 10^1$

$x^2 - 3x - 10 = 0$

$(x-5)(x+2) = 0$

$x - 5 = 0$ or $x + 2 = 0$

$x = 5$ $\qquad x = -2$

Checking 5,

LS: $\log 5 + \log(5-3) = \log 5(2)$

$= \log 10$

$= 1$

RS: 1

5 checks.

Checking −2,

LS: $\log(-2) + \log(-2-3)$ is undefined.

{5}

21. $\log_2 x^2 = 2$

$x^2 = 2^2$

$x^2 = 4$

$x = \pm 2$

Checking 2,

LS: $\log_2 2^2 = \log_2 4$

$= 2$

RS: 2

2 checks.

Checking −2,

LS: $\log_2(-2)^2 = \log_2 4$

$= 2$

RS: 2

−2 checks. {± 2}

23. $\log_b 15 = \log_b 3(5)$

$= \log_b 3 + \log_b 5$

$\approx 1.62 + 2.52$

≈ 4.14

25. $\log_b 5^2 = 2 \log_b 5$

$\approx 2(2.52)$

≈ 5.04

27. $\log_b \frac{1}{3} = \log_b 3^{-1}$

$= -\log_b 3$

$\approx -(1.62)$ or -1.62

29. $\log_b \frac{9}{5} = \log_b 9 - \log_b 5$

$= \log_b 3^2 - \log_b 5$

$= 2 \log_b 3 - \log_b 5$

$\approx 2(1.62) - 2.52$

$\approx 3.24 - 3.52$

≈ 0.72

31. $\log_b 14 = \log_b 7 + \log_b 2$

True, since $\log_b 7 + \log_b 2$

$= \log_b 2(7)$

$= \log_b 14$

33. $\log_b 13 = \dfrac{\log_b 26}{\log_b 2}$ is false.

35. $\log_b(17^2) = (\log_b 17)^2$ is false.

37. $\sqrt{\log_b 5} = \log_b \sqrt{5}$ is false.

39. $\log_2 5x = \log_2 (x+1)$

$5x = x + 1$

$4x = 1$

$x = \frac{1}{4}$

Checking,

LS: $\log_2 5(\frac{1}{4}) = \log_2 \frac{5}{4}$

RS: $\log_2 (\frac{1}{4}+1) = \log_2 \frac{5}{4}$

$\frac{1}{4}$ checks. $\{\frac{1}{4}\}$

41. $\log_2 x - \log_2 3 = 4$

$\log_2 \frac{x}{3} = 4$

$\frac{x}{3} = 2^4$

$\frac{x}{3} = 16$

$x = 48$

Checking,

LS: $\log_2 48 - \log_2 3 = \log_2 \frac{48}{3}$

$= \log_2 16$

$= \log_2 2^4$

$= 4$

RS: 4

48 checks. $\{48\}$

43. $\log_{16} 2x + \log_{16} 2 = 2$

$\log_{16} 2x(2) = 2$

$4x = 16^2$

$4x = 256$

$x = 64$

Checking,

LS: $\log_{16} 2(64) + \log_{16} 2$

$= \log_{16} 128 + \log_{16} 2$

$= \log_{16} 256$

$= \log_{16} 16^2$

$= 2$

RS: 2

64 checks. $\{64\}$

45. $\log_2 (x-1) - \log_2 16 = 1$

$\log_2 \frac{x-1}{16} = 1$

$\frac{x-1}{16} = 2^1$

$x - 1 = 32$

$x = 33$

Checking.

LS: $\log_2 (33-1) - \log_2 16$

$= \log_2 32 - \log_2 16$

$= \log_2 \frac{32}{16}$

$= \log_2 2$

$= 1$

RS: 1

33 checks. $\{33\}$

47. $\ln(2x+1) = \ln e$

$2x + 1 = e$

$2x = e - 1$

$x = \frac{e-1}{2}$

Checking,

LS: $\ln[2(\frac{e-1}{2})+1] = \ln(e-1+1)$

$= \ln e$

RS: $\ln e$

$\frac{e-1}{2}$ checks $\{\frac{e-1}{2}\}$

49. $\log_3 |x| = 1$

$|x| = 3^1$

$x = 3$ or $x = -3$

Checking 3,

LS: $\log_3 |3| = \log_3 3$

$= 1$

RS: 1

3 checks.

Checking -3,

LS: $\log_3 |-3| = \log_3 3$

$= 1$

RS: 1

-3 checks.   {±3}

51. $\log_2 x(x-3) = 2$

$x(x-3) = 2^2$

$x^2 - 3x = 4$

$x^2 - 3x - 4 = 0$

$(x-4)(x+1) = 0$

$x - 4 = 0$ or $x + 1 = 0$

$x = 4$ $x = -1$

Checking 4,

LS: $\log_2 4(4-3) = \log_2 4(1)$

$= \log_2 2^2$

$= 2$

RS: 2

4 checks.

Checking -1,

LS: $\log_2 (-1)(-1-3) = \log_2 4$

$= \log_2 2^2$

$= 2$

RS: 2

Checks.   {$-1,4$}

53. $\log_5 x + \log_5 (x-4) = 1$

$\log_5 x(x-4) = 1$

$x(x-4) = 5$

$x^2 - 4x - 5 = 0$

$(x-5)(x+1) = 0$

$x - 5 = 0$ or $x + 1 = 0$

$x = 5$ $x = -1$

Checking 5,

LS: $\log_5 5 + \log_5 (5-4)$

$= 1 + \log_5 1$

$= 1 + 0$

$= 1$

RS: 1

5 checks.

Checking -1,

LS: $\log_5 (-1) + \log_5 (-1-4)$ is undefined.

{5}

Review

1. Range: {$y \mid y$ is a negative integer}

3. $f(x) = |x-7|$

Natural domain: {$x \mid x$ is a real number}

5. $f(x) = \sqrt{x^2 - x}$

$x^2 - x \geq 0$

$x(x-1) \geq 0$

Find boundary number:

$x(x-1) = 0$

$x = 0$ or $x - 1 = 0$

$x = 1$

A	B	C
0	1	

Test regions: A, $x = -1$

$(-1)^2 - (-1) \geq 0$ is true.

B, $x = \frac{1}{2}$

$(\frac{1}{2})^2 - (\frac{1}{2}) \geq 0$ is false.

C, $x = 2$

$2^2 - 2 \geq 0$ is true.

Soln.set:

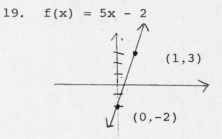

$\{x|x \leq 0 \text{ or } x \geq 1\}$

Natural domain: $\{x|x \leq 0 \text{ or } x \geq 1\}$

7. $f(x) = \dfrac{x+3}{(x+1)(x-2)}$

Natural domain: $\{x|x \neq -1, 2\}$

9. $f(x) = \dfrac{3}{x+5}$

$f(-5) = \dfrac{3}{-5+5}$

$= \dfrac{3}{0}$

$f(-5)$ is undefined.

11. $f(x) = \dfrac{3}{x+5}$

$f(f(x)) = f(\dfrac{3}{1+5})$

$= f(\dfrac{3}{6})$

$= f(\dfrac{1}{2})$

$= \dfrac{3}{\dfrac{1}{2}+5}$

$= \dfrac{3}{\dfrac{11}{2}}$

$= 3 \cdot \dfrac{2}{11}$

$= \dfrac{6}{11}$

13. $f(x) = \dfrac{3}{x+5}$

$f(-3) = \dfrac{3}{-3+5}$

$= \dfrac{3}{2}$

15. $f(x) = \dfrac{3}{x+5}$

$f(a^2) = \dfrac{3}{a^2+5}$

17. $f(x) = \dfrac{1}{4}x^2 + 3$

Vertex: $(0,3)$

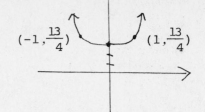

D: $\{x|x \text{ is a real number}\}$

R: $\{y|y \geq 3\}$

Not one-to-one.

19. $f(x) = 5x - 2$

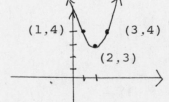

D: $\{x|x \text{ is a real number}\}$

R: $\{y|y \text{ is a real number}\}$

Is one-to-one.

21. $f(x) = (x-2)^2 + 3$

Vertex: $(2,3)$

D: $\{x|x \text{ is a real number}\}$

R: $\{y|y \geq 3\}$

Not one-to-one.

23. $f(x) = -8$

D: $\{x|x \text{ is a real number}\}$

R: {-8}

Not one-to-one.

25. $f(x) = |x+7|$

Vertex: $(-7,0)$

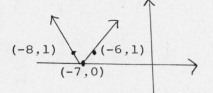

(-8,1)   (-6,1)

(-7,0)

D: {x|x is a real number}

R: {y|y ≥ 0

Not one-to-one.

27. $f(x) = -\frac{1}{2}x^2$

Vertex: $(0,0)$, opens down

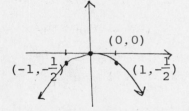

(0,0)

$(-1,-\frac{1}{2})$ $(1,-\frac{1}{2})$

D: {x|x is a real number}

R: {y|y ≤ 0}

Not one-to-one.

29. $f(x) = x^2 - 4x + 3$

$= x^2 - 4x + 4 - 4 + 3$

$= (x-2)^2 - 1$

Vertex: $(2,-1)$

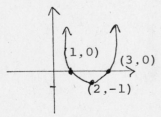

(1,0)   (3,0)

(2,-1)

D: {x|x is a real number}

R: {y|y ≥ -1}

Not one-to-one.

31. $f(x) = -2x^2 + 12x + 4$

$= -2(x^2-6x) + 4$

$= -2(x^2-6x+9-9) + 4$

$= -2(x-3)^2 + 22$

Vertex: $(3,22)$

(3,22)

(2,20)   (4,20)

D: {x|x is a real number}

R: {y|y ≤ 22}

Not one-to-one.

33. $f(x) = 3x - 5$ $g(x) = x^2$

$(\frac{f}{g})(x) = \frac{3x-5}{x^2}$

35. $(f \circ g)x = 3(x^2) - 5$

$= 3x^2 - 5$

37. $f(x) = 3x - 5$ $g(x) = x^2$

$(g \circ f)(x) = (3x-5)^2$ or

$9x^2 - 20x + 25$

39. $2^x = 128$

$2^x = 2^7$

$x = 7$ {7}

41. $\log_{10} 10^x = 1$

$10^x = 10^1$

$x = 1$

Checking,

LS: $\log_{10} 10^1 = 1$

355

RS: 1

1 checks.   {1}

43. $\ell n(x+e) - \ell n\ e = 1$

$\ell n\ \dfrac{x+e}{e} = 1$

$\dfrac{x+e}{e} = e$

$x + e = e^2$

$x = e^2 - e$

Checking,

LS: $\ell n[(e^2-e)+e] - \ell n\ e$

$= \ell n\ e^2 - \ell n\ e$

$= \ell n\ \dfrac{e^2}{e}$

$= \ell n\ e$

$= 1$

RS: 1

$e^2 - e$ checks. $\{e^2-e\}$

45. $3^{x+1} = 9$

$3^{x+1} = 3^2$

$x + 1 = 2$

$x = 1$ {1}

47. $25^x = 625$

$25^x = 25^2$

$x = 2$ {2}

49. $\log x + \log(x+3) = 1$

$\log x(x+3) = 1$

$x(x+3) = 10^1$

$x^2 + 3x - 10 = 0$

$(x+5)(x-2) = 0$

$x + 5 = 0$ or $x - 2 = 0$

$x = -5$ $x = 2$

Checking -5,

LS: $\log -5 + \log(-5+3)$ is

undefined.

-5 does not check.

Checking 2,

LS: $\log 2 + \log(2+3)$

$= \log_2 + \log_5$

$= \log 2(5)$

$= \log 10$

$= 1$

RS: 1

2 checks   {2}

51. $(a+2)^2$ is factored.

53. $4 - (a+b)^2 = [2+(a+b)][2-(a+b)]$

$= (2+a+b)(2-a-b)$

55. $a^3b + c^2b = b(a^3+c^2)$

57. $a^3 - b^3$ has two terms.

$a^3 - b^3 = (a-b)(a^2+ab+b^2)$

$(a-b)$ is a factor.

59. $w(a-b) + y(b-a)$ has two terms.

$w(a-b) + y(b-a) = w(a-b) - y(a-b)$

$= (a-b)(w-y)$

$(a-b)$ is a factor.

61. $\sqrt[5]{64x^5-128y^5} = \sqrt[5]{32(2x^5-4y^5)}$

$= \sqrt[5]{2^5(2x^5-4y^5)}$

$= 2\sqrt[5]{2x^5-4y^5}$

63. $\sqrt[3]{(x-3)^3} = x - 3$

65. $(2^{-1}+4^{-1})^{-1} = (\dfrac{1}{2}+\dfrac{1}{4})^{-1}$

$= (\dfrac{4}{8}+\dfrac{2}{8})^{-1}$

$= (\dfrac{6}{8})^{-1}$

$= (\dfrac{3}{4})^{-1}$

$= \dfrac{4}{3}$

67. $\dfrac{-5x^{-3}}{y} = \dfrac{-5}{x^3 y}$

69. $(3x-1)^3 = (3x)^3 - 3(3x)^2(1)$

$\qquad + 3(3x)(1)^2 - (1)^3$

$\qquad = 27x^3 - 27x^2 + 9x - 1$

71. $\dfrac{2(x-1)+a(x+1)}{4(x-1)+a(x+1)}$ will not reduce.

73. $\dfrac{3x}{x^2+6x+9} + \dfrac{1}{x+3} = \dfrac{3x}{(x+3)^2} + \dfrac{1}{x+3}$

$\qquad\qquad = \dfrac{3x}{(x+3)^2} + \dfrac{x+3}{(x+3)^2}$

$\qquad\qquad = \dfrac{4x+3}{(x+3)^2}$

75. $\dfrac{\dfrac{1}{x+3}-1}{\dfrac{x+2}{x^2+6x+9}} = \dfrac{\dfrac{1}{x+3}-1}{\dfrac{x+2}{(x+3)^2}}$

$\qquad = \dfrac{\left(\dfrac{1}{x+3}-1\right)(x+3)^2}{\left[\dfrac{x+2}{(x+3)^2}\right](x+3)^2}$

$\qquad = \dfrac{x+3-(x+3)^2}{x+2}$

$\qquad = \dfrac{x+3-(x^2+6x+9)}{x+2}$

$\qquad = \dfrac{-x^2-5x-6}{x+2}$

$\qquad = \dfrac{-(x^2+5x+6)}{x+2}$

$\qquad = \dfrac{-(x+3)(x+2)}{x+2}$

$\qquad = -(x+3)$ or $-x - 3$

77. $\dfrac{1}{x-2} = \dfrac{4}{2-x}$ Equation

$\dfrac{1}{x-2} = \dfrac{4}{-(x-2)}$

$\dfrac{1}{x-2} = \dfrac{-4}{x-2}$

$(x-2)\left(\dfrac{1}{x-2}\right) = (x-2)\left(\dfrac{-4}{x-2}\right)$

$\qquad 1 = -4 \qquad\qquad\qquad \emptyset$

79. -2^2 Expression

$-[(2)^2] = -4$

81. $2x + 3(x-7) \le 5$ Inequality

$2x + 3x - 21 \le 5$

$5x - 21 \le 5$

$5x \le 26$

$x \le \dfrac{26}{5} \qquad\qquad \left\{x \,\middle|\, x \le \dfrac{26}{5}\right\}$

83. $|x+11| = 0$ Equation

$x + 11 = 0$ or $-(x+11) = 0$

$\quad x = -11 \qquad -x - 11 = 0$

$\qquad\qquad\qquad\qquad -x = 11$

$\qquad\qquad\qquad\qquad\quad x = -11$

$\qquad\qquad\qquad\qquad\qquad \{-11\}$

85. $\sqrt{48} - \sqrt{12}$ Expression

$\sqrt{48} - \sqrt{12} = \sqrt{16\cdot 3} - \sqrt{4\cdot 3}$

$\qquad\qquad\quad = 4\sqrt{3} - 2\sqrt{3}$

$\qquad\qquad\quad = 2\sqrt{3}$

87. $a^2(a^{-3}b)^3$ Expression

$a^2(a^{-3}b)^3 = a^2 a^{-9} b^3$

$\qquad\qquad = a^{-7}b^3$

$\qquad\qquad = \dfrac{b^3}{a^7}$

89. $ab^{-3}(ab^4-b^5)$ Expression

$ab^{-3}(ab^9-b^5) = a^2 b - ab^2$

91. $|x+7| \ge 11$

$x + 7 \ge 11$ or $x + 7 \le -1$

$\quad x \ge 4 \qquad\qquad\qquad x \le -18$

$\qquad\qquad \{x \,|\, x \le -18 \text{ or } x \ge 4\}$

Chapter Test.

1. $\log_b x = y$

D.

357

2. $g(x) = x^2$ D: $\{-2,-1,0,1,2\}$

$g(-2) = (-2)^2 = 4$

$g(-1) = (-1)^2 = 1$

$g(0) = 0^2 = 0$

$g(1) = 1^2 = 1$

$g(2) = 2^2 = 4$

Range: $\{0,1,4\}$

C.

3. $f(x) = 1 - 2x + x^2$

$f(-3) = 1 - 2(-3) + (-3)^2$

$= 1 + 6 + 9$

$= 16$

4. $f(x) = x^2 + 2x + 2$

$= x^2 + 2x + 1 - 1 + 2$

$= (x+1)^2 + 1$

Vertex: $(-1,1)$

A.

5. The graph in A passes the vertical line test.

A.

6. a. $\log_3 x = 3$

$x = 3^3$

$= 27$

Checking,

LS: $\log_3 27 = \log_3 3^3$

$= 3$

RS: 3

27 checks. $\{27\}$

b. $5^x = 12r$

$5^x = 5^3$

$x = 3$ $\{3\}$

c. $\log_2 2 + \log_2 4 = x$

$\log_2 2(4) = x$

$\log_2 8 = x$

$2^x = 8$

$2^x = 2^3$

$x = 3$ $\{3\}$

d. $\log 10 = x$

$10^x = 10^1$

$x = 1$ $\{1\}$

e. $\log_5 1 = x$

$5^x = 1$

$5^x = 5^0$

$x = 0$ $\{0\}$

7. a. $\log 4.73 = x$

$x \approx 0.67$

b. $\log x = -0.8174$

$x \approx 0.15$

c. $\ln 10.1 = x$

$x \approx 2.31$

8. $f(x) = x - 3$ $g(x) = x^2$

a. $(f+g)(x) = (x-3) + x^2$

or $x^2 + x - 3$

b. $(g \circ f)(x) = (x-3)^2$

or $x^2 - 6x + 9$

9. $f(x) = 2x + 3$

$y = 2x + 3$

$x = 2y + 3$

$x - 3 = 2y$

$y = \frac{x-3}{2}$

$f^{-1}(x) = \frac{x-3}{2}$

10. a. $f(x) = \sqrt{(x+1)(x-2)}$

Solve: $(x+1)(x-2) \geq 0$

Find boundary numbers:

$(x+1)(x-2) = 0$

$x + 1 = 0$ or $x - 2 = 0$

   $x = -1$ $x = 2$

```
     A      B      C
   ─────┼──────┼────────
       -1      2
```

Test regions: <u>A</u>, $x = -2$

$(-2+1)(-2-2) \geq 0$ is true.

<u>B</u>, $x = 0$
$(1)(-2) \geq$ is false.

<u>C</u>, $x = 3$
$(3+1)(3-2) \geq 0$ is true.

Shade regions in soln. set.:

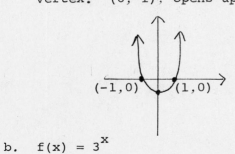

$\{x \mid x \leq -1 \text{ or } x \geq 2\}$

Natural domain: $\{x \mid x \leq -1 \text{ or } x \geq 2\}$

b. $g(x) = \dfrac{1}{x-7}$

Natural domain: $\{x \mid x \neq 7\}$

11. a. $f(x) = x^2 - 1$

Vertex: $(0,-1)$, opens up

b. $f(x) = 3^x$

c) $f(x) = |x-3|$

Vertex: $(3,0)$

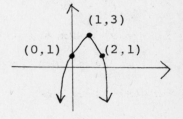

d) $f(x) = -2(x-1)^2 + 3$

Vertex: $(1,3)$, opens down

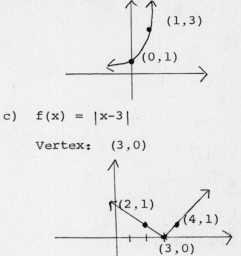

CHAPTER 12

Problem Set 12.1.

1. $a_n = n$

    $1, 2, 3, 4, 5$

3. $a_n = 2(n+1)$

    $n = 1$ $2(2) = 4$

    $n = 2$ $2(3) = 6$

    $n = 3$ $2(4) = 8$

    $n = 4$ $2(5) = 10$

    $n = 5$ $2(6) = 12$

    $4,6,8,10,12$

5. $c_n = n^2$

    $n = 1$ $1^2 = 1$

    $n = 2$ $2^2 = 4$

    $n = 3$ $3^2 = 9$

    $n = 4$ $4^2 = 16$

    $n = 5$ $5^2 = 25$

    $1,4,9,16,25$

7. $a_n = 3$

    $3,3,3,3,3$

9. $K_n = (-1)^n(1-n)$

    $n = 1$ $(-1)^1(1-1) = 0$

    $n = 2$ $(-1)^2(1-2) = 1(-1) = -1$

    $n = 3$ $(-1)^3(1-3) = (-1)(-2) = 2$

    $n = 4$ $(-1)^4(1-4) = 1(-3) = -3$

    $n = 5$ $(-1)^5(1-5) = (-1)(-4) = 4$

    $0,-1,2,-3,4$

11. $1,4,9,16,\ldots\ n^2$

13. $-1,2,-3,4,\ldots (-1)^n n$

15. $2,-4,8,-16,\ldots (-1)^{n+1}2^n$

17. $a_n = 3 - 2n$

$n = 1$ $3 - 2(1) = 1$

$n = 2$ $3 - 2(2) = -1$

$n = 3$ $3 - 2(3) = -3$

$n = 4$ $3 - 2(4) = -5$

The sequence is decreasing.

19. $a_n = (-n)^{-1}$

    $n = 1$ $(-1)^{-1} = -1$

    $n = 2$ $(-2)^{-1} = -\frac{1}{2}$

    $n = 3$ $(-3)^{-1} = -\frac{1}{3}$

    $n = 4$ $(-4)^{-1} = -\frac{1}{4}$

The sequence is increasing.

21. $K_n = 1 - n^{-1}$

    $n = 1$ $1 - 1^{-1} = 1 - 1 = 0$

    $n = 2$ $1 - 2^{-1} = 1 - \frac{1}{2} = \frac{1}{2}$

    $n = 3$ $1 - 3^{-1} = 1 - \frac{1}{3} = \frac{2}{3}$

    $n = 4$ $1 - 4^{-1} = 1 - \frac{1}{4} = \frac{3}{4}$

The sequence is increasing.

23. $2,3,4,\ldots$

    $d = 3 - 2 = 1$

    So, $a_n = 2 + (n-1)1$

25. $5,15,25,\ldots$

    $d = 15 - 5 = 10$

    So, $a_n = 5 + (n-1)10$

27. $\frac{1}{2},0,-\frac{1}{2},\ldots$

    $d = 0 - \frac{1}{2} = \frac{1}{2}$

    $a_n = \frac{1}{2} + (n-1)(-\frac{1}{2})$

29. $1,5,25,\ldots$

    $r = \frac{5}{1} = 5$

    $a_n = 1 \cdot 5^{n-1}$

31. $2,-4,8,\ldots$

$r = \dfrac{-4}{2} = -2$

$a_n = 2(-2)^{n-1}$

33. $1,-\dfrac{1}{4},\dfrac{1}{16},\ldots$

$r = \dfrac{-1/4}{1} = -\dfrac{1}{4}$

$a_n = 1(-\dfrac{1}{4})^{n-1}$

35. $a_n = 3_n - 1$

$n = 1 \quad 3(1) - 1 = 2$

$n = 2 \quad 3(2) - 1 = 5$

$n = 3 \quad 3(3) - 1 = 8$

$n = 4 \quad 3(4) - 1 = 11$

$n = 5 \quad 3(5) - 1 = 14$

$2,5,8,11,14$

37. $A_n = 8 - 2n$

$n = 1 \quad 8 - 2(1) = 6$

$n = 2 \quad 8 - 2(2) = 4$

$n = 3 \quad 8 - 2(3) = 2$

$n = 4 \quad 8 - 2(4) = 0$

$n = 5 \quad 8 - 2(5) = -2$

$6,4,2,0,-2$

39. $h_n = n^2 - n + 1$

$n = 1 \quad 1^2 - 1 + 1 = 1$

$n = 2 \quad 2^2 - 2 + 1 = 3$

$n = 3 \quad 3^2 - 3 + 1 = 7$

$n = 4 \quad 4^2 - 4 + 1 = 13$

$n = 5 \quad 5^2 - 5 + 1 = 21$

$1,3,7,13,21$

41. $j_n = (-1)^{n-1}n^2$

$n = 1 \quad (-1)^{1-1}(1)^2 = 1$

$n = 2 \quad (-1)^{2-1}(2)^2 = (-1)4 = -4$

$n = 3 \quad (-1)^{3-1}(3)^2 = (1)(9) = 9$

$n = 4 \quad (-1)^{4-1}(4)^2 = (-1)(16)$

$\qquad\qquad = -16$

$n = 5 \quad (-1)^{5-1}(5)^2 = (1)(25)$

$\qquad\qquad = 25$

$1,-4,9,-16,25$

43. $4,6,8,10,\ldots,2n + 2$

45. $-1,3,7,11,\ldots,4n - 5$

47. $0,1,8,27,\ldots,(n-1)^3$

49. $a_n = -4 + n$

$n = 1 \quad -4 + 1 = -3$

$n = 2 \quad -4 + 2 = -2$

$n = 3 \quad -4 + 3 = -1$

$n = 4 \quad -4 + 4 = 0$

$n = 5 \quad -4 + 5 = 1$

The sequence is increasing.

51. $b_n = n^{-2} - 2$

$n = 1 \quad 1^{-2} - 2 = 1 - 2 = -1$

$n = 2 \quad 2^{-2} - 2 = \dfrac{1}{4} - 2 = -1\dfrac{3}{4}$

$n = 3 \quad 3^{-2} - 2 = \dfrac{1}{9} - 2 = -1\dfrac{8}{9}$

$n = 4 \quad 4^{-2} - 2 = \dfrac{1}{16} - 2 = -1\dfrac{15}{16}$

The sequence is decreasing.

53. $d_n = (-2)^{-2n}$

$n = 1 \quad (-2)^{-2} = \dfrac{1}{4}$

$n = 2 \quad (-2)^{-4} = \dfrac{1}{16}$

$n = 3 \quad (-2)^{-6} = \dfrac{1}{64}$

$n = 4 \quad (-2)^{-8} = \dfrac{1}{256}$

The sequence is decreasing.

55. $1,4,7,\ldots$

$d = 4 - 1 = 3$

$a_n = 1 + (n-1)(3)$

57. $10,8,6,\ldots$

361

$$d = 8 - 10 = -2$$

$$a_n = 10 + (n-1)(-2)$$

59. $-\frac{1}{2}, 0, \frac{1}{2}, \ldots$

$$d = 0 - (-\frac{1}{2}) = \frac{1}{2}$$

$$a_n = -\frac{1}{2} + (n-1)(\frac{1}{2})$$

61. $1, 3, 9, \ldots$

$$r = \frac{3}{1} = 3$$

$$a_n = 1 \cdot 3^{n-1}$$

63. $2, -6, 18, \ldots$

$$r = \frac{-6}{2} = -3$$

$$a_n = 2 \cdot (-2)^{n-1}$$

65. $27, 9, 3, \ldots$

$$r = \frac{9}{27} = \frac{1}{3}$$

$$a_n = 27 \cdot (\frac{1}{3})^{n-1}$$

Problem Set 12.2.

1. $\displaystyle\sum_{j=1}^{5} 2j = 2(1) + 2(2) + 2(3)$
$$+ 2(4) + 2(5)$$
$$= 2 + 4 + 6 + 8 + 10$$

3. $\displaystyle\sum_{j=1}^{7} j^2 = 0^2 + 1^2 + 2^2 + 3^2 + 4^2$
$$+ 5^2 + 6^2 + 7^2$$
$$= 0 + 1 + 4 + 9 + 16 + 25$$
$$+ 36 + 49$$

5. $\displaystyle\sum_{j=0}^{4} (3-j)^2 = (3-0)^2 + (3-1)^2$
$$+ (3-2)^2 + (3-3)^2$$
$$+ (3-4)^2$$
$$= 3^2 + 2^2 + 1^2 + 0^2$$

$$+ (-1)^2$$
$$= 9 + 4 + 1 + 0 + 1$$

7. $\displaystyle\sum_{j=1}^{6} (-1)^{j-1}_{j} = (-1)^{1-1}(1)$
$$+ (-1)^{2-1}(2) + (-1)^{3-1}(3)$$
$$+ (-1)^{4-1}(4) + (-1)^{5-1}(5)$$
$$+ (-1)^{6-1}(6)$$
$$= (1)(1) + (-1)(2) + (1)(3)$$
$$+ (-1)(4) + (1)(5) + (-1)(6)$$
$$= 1 - 2 + 3 - 4 + 5 - 6$$

9. $\displaystyle\sum_{j=1}^{5} \frac{j-1}{j+1}(-1)^{j+1}$

$$= \frac{1-1}{1+1}(-1)^2 + \frac{2-1}{2+1}(-1)^3 + \frac{3-1}{3+1}(-1)^4$$

$$+ \frac{4-1}{4+1}(-1)^5 + \frac{5-1}{5+1}(-1)^6$$

$$= 0 + \frac{1}{3}(-1) + \frac{2}{4}(1) + \frac{3}{5}(-1)$$

$$+ \frac{4}{6}(1)$$

$$= 0 - \frac{1}{3} + \frac{1}{2} - \frac{3}{5} + \frac{2}{3}$$

11. $1 - 3 + 5 - 7 + 9 - 11$

$$= \sum_{j=1}^{6} (-1)^{j+1}(2j-1)$$

13. $1 + \frac{x}{2} + \frac{x^2}{3} + \frac{x^3}{4} + \frac{x^4}{5} + \frac{x^5}{6} + \frac{x^6}{7}$

$$= \sum_{j=1}^{7} \frac{x^{j-1}}{j}$$

15. $1 - \sqrt{2}x^2 + \sqrt{3}x^4 - 2x^6 + \sqrt{5}x^8$
$$- \sqrt{6}x^{10} + \sqrt{7}x^{12}$$

$$= \sum_{K=1}^{7} (-1)^{K+1}\sqrt{K}x^{2K-2}$$

17. $\displaystyle\sum_{j=0}^{4} 2(j-5) = 2(0-5) + 2(1-5)$

$\qquad\qquad + 2(2-5) + 2(3-5) + 2(4-5)$

$\qquad = 2(-5) + 2(-4) + 2(-3) + 2(-2)$
$\qquad\qquad + 2(-1)$

$\qquad = -10 - 8 - 6 - 4 - 2$

19. $\displaystyle\sum_{j=1}^{7} 2^{j-1} = 2^0 + 2^1 + 2^2 + 2^3 + 2^4$

$\qquad\qquad\qquad + 2^5 + 2^6$

$\qquad\qquad = 1 + 2 + 4 + 8 + 16$

$\qquad\qquad\qquad + 32 + 64$

21. $\displaystyle\sum_{j=0}^{5} (j-1)^3 = (0-1)^3 + (1-1)^3$

$\qquad\qquad + (2-1)^3 + (3-1)^3 + (4-1)^3$

$\qquad\qquad + (5-1)^3$

$\qquad = (-1)^3 + 0^3 + 1^3 + 2^3 + 3^3 + 4^3$

$\qquad = -1 + 0 + 1 + 8 + 27 + 64$

23. $\displaystyle\sum_{j=1}^{5} (-1)^j 2^{j-1} = (-1)^1 2^0 + (-1)^2 2^1$

$\qquad\qquad + (-1)^3 2^2 + (-1)^4 2^3 + (-1)^5 2^4$

$\qquad = -1 + 2 - 4 + 8 - 16$

25. $3 + 4 + 5 + 6 + 7 + 8 + 9 + 10$

$\qquad\qquad + 11 + 12 + 13 + 14$

$\qquad = \displaystyle\sum_{K=3}^{14} K$

27. $1 + \dfrac{x^2}{3} + \dfrac{x^4}{5} + \dfrac{x^6}{7} + \dfrac{x^8}{9}$

$\qquad = \displaystyle\sum_{K=0}^{4} \dfrac{x^{2K}}{2K+1}$

29. $-\pi + \dfrac{1-\pi}{10} + \dfrac{2-\pi}{100} + \dfrac{3-\pi}{1000} + \dfrac{4-\pi}{10,000}$

$\qquad + \dfrac{5-\pi}{100,000} + \dfrac{6-\pi}{1,000,000}$

$= \displaystyle\sum_{k=0}^{6} \dfrac{K-\pi}{10^K}$

31. $\displaystyle\sum_{i=1}^{5} i = \sum_{j=1}^{5} j = \sum_{K=1}^{5} K = 1 + 2 + 3$

$\qquad\qquad\qquad\qquad\qquad + 4 + 5$

33. $\displaystyle\sum_{j=1}^{4} 5A_j = 5A_1 + 5A_2 + 5A_3 + 5A_4$

$5 \displaystyle\sum_{j=1}^{4} A_j = 5(A_1+A_2+A_3+A_4)$

Property: $\displaystyle\sum_{j=1}^{n} KA_j = K\sum_{j=1}^{n} A_j$

Problem Set 12.3.

1. $6! = 1\cdot2\cdot3\cdot4\cdot5\cdot6$
   $\qquad = 720$

3. $12! = 1\cdot2\cdot3\cdot4\cdot5\cdot6\cdot7\cdot8\cdot9\cdot10\cdot11\cdot12$
   $\qquad = 479,001,600$

5. $\dfrac{14!}{13!} = \dfrac{13!\,14}{13!} = 14$

7. $\dfrac{8!}{4!\,4!} = \dfrac{4!\,5\cdot6\cdot7\cdot8}{4!\,1\cdot2\cdot3\cdot4}$
   $\qquad = 5\cdot7\cdot2$
   $\qquad = 70$

9. $\dfrac{8!}{2!\,6!} = \dfrac{6!\,7\cdot8}{1\cdot2\cdot6!}$
   $\qquad = 4\cdot7$
   $\qquad = 28$

11. $\dfrac{20!}{1!\,19!} = \dfrac{19!\,20}{1\cdot19!}$
   $\qquad = 20$

13. $\dbinom{8}{5} = \dfrac{8!}{5!\,3!}$
   $\qquad = \dfrac{5!\,6\cdot7\cdot8}{5!\,1\cdot2\cdot3}$
   $\qquad = 7\cdot8$
   $\qquad = 56$

15. $\dbinom{5}{3} = \dfrac{5!}{3!\,2!}$

$$= \frac{3! \cdot 4 \cdot 5}{3! \cdot 1 \cdot 2}$$

$$= 2 \cdot 5$$

$$= 10$$

17. $\binom{6}{1} = \frac{6!}{1! \cdot 5!}$

$$= \frac{5! \cdot 6}{1 \cdot 5!}$$

$$= 6$$

19. $\binom{6}{3} = \frac{6!}{3! \cdot 3!}$

$$= \frac{3! \cdot 4 \cdot 5 \cdot 6}{3! \cdot 1 \cdot 2 \cdot 3}$$

$$= 4 \cdot 5$$

$$= 20$$

21. $\binom{6}{5} = \frac{6!}{5! \cdot 1!}$

$$= \frac{5! \cdot 6}{5! \cdot 1}$$

$$= 6$$

23. $\binom{500}{0} = \frac{500!}{0! \cdot 500!}$

$$= 1$$

25. $7! = 1 \cdot 2 \cdot 3 \cdot 4 \cdot 5 \cdot 6 \cdot 7$

$$= 5040$$

27. $11! = 1 \cdot 2 \cdot 3 \cdot 4 \cdot 5 \cdot 6 \cdot 7 \cdot 8 \cdot 9 \cdot 10 \cdot 11$

$$= 39,916,800$$

29. $\frac{17!}{18!} = \frac{17!}{17! \cdot 18}$

$$= \frac{1}{18}$$

31. $\frac{9!}{4! \cdot 5!} = \frac{5! \cdot 6 \cdot 7 \cdot 8 \cdot 9}{5! \cdot 1 \cdot 2 \cdot 3 \cdot 4}$

$$= 2 \cdot 7 \cdot 9$$

$$= 126$$

33. $\frac{9!}{2! \cdot 7!} = \frac{7! \cdot 8 \cdot 9}{7! \cdot 1 \cdot 2}$

$$= 4 \cdot 9$$

$$= 36$$

35. $\frac{30!}{1! \cdot 29!} = \frac{29! \cdot 30}{29! \cdot 1}$

$$= 30$$

37. $\binom{9}{6} = \frac{9!}{6! \cdot 3!}$

$$= \frac{6! \cdot 7 \cdot 8 \cdot 9}{6! \cdot 1 \cdot 2 \cdot 3}$$

$$= 7 \cdot 4 \cdot 3$$

$$= 84$$

39. $\binom{4}{1} = \frac{4!}{1! \cdot 3!}$

$$= \frac{3! \cdot 4}{3! \cdot 1}$$

$$= 4$$

41. $\binom{7}{1} = \frac{7!}{1! \cdot 6!}$

$$= \frac{6! \cdot 7}{6! \cdot 1}$$

$$= 7$$

43. $\binom{7}{3} = \frac{7!}{3! \cdot 4!}$

$$= \frac{4! \cdot 5 \cdot 6 \cdot 7}{4! \cdot 1 \cdot 2 \cdot 3}$$

$$= 5 \cdot 7$$

$$= 35$$

45. $\binom{7}{5} = \frac{7!}{5! \cdot 2!}$

$$= \frac{5! \cdot 6 \cdot 7}{5! \cdot 1 \cdot 2}$$

$$= 3 \cdot 7$$

$$= 21$$

47. $\binom{7}{7} = \frac{7!}{7! \cdot 1!}$

$$= 1$$

49. Show: $\binom{n}{r} = \binom{n}{n-r}$

$$\binom{n}{r} = \frac{r!}{r! \cdot (n-r)!}$$

and

$$\binom{n}{n-r} = \frac{n!}{(n-r)! \cdot (n-(n-r))!}$$

$$= \frac{n!}{(n-r)! \cdot r!}$$

$$= \frac{n!}{r!(n-r)!}$$

So, $\binom{n}{r} = \binom{n}{n-r}$

<u>Problem Set 12.4.</u>

1. $(a+b)^{12}$

First three times: $\binom{12}{0}a^{12}b^0$

    $+ \binom{12}{1}a^{11}b^1 + \binom{12}{2}a^{10}b^2$

$\binom{12}{0} = \frac{12!}{0!12!} = 1$

$\binom{12}{1} = \frac{12!}{1!11!}$

    $= \frac{11!\,12}{11!\,1}$

    $= 12$

$\binom{12}{2} = \frac{12!}{2!10!}$

    $= \frac{10!\,11\cdot12}{10!\cdot1\cdot2}$

    $= 11\cdot6$

    $= 66$

So the first three terms are:

    $a^{12} + 12a^{11}b + 66a^{10}b^2.$

3. $(s+2)^{15}$

First three terms: $\binom{15}{0}s^{15}\cdot2^0$

    $+ \binom{15}{1}s^{14}\cdot2^1 + \binom{15}{2}s^{13}\cdot2^2$

$\binom{15}{0} = \frac{15!}{0!15!} = 1$

$\binom{15}{1} = \frac{15!}{1!14!}$

    $= \frac{14!\,15}{14!\cdot1}$

    $= 15$

$\binom{15}{2} = \frac{15!}{2!13!}$

    $= \frac{13!\,14\cdot15}{13!\,1\cdot2}$

    $= 7\cdot15$

    $= 105$

So the first three terms are:

    $s^{15} + 15(s^{14})(2) + 105(s^{13})(4)$

    $= s^{15} + 30s^{14} + 420\,s^{13}$

5. $(2a+3b)^6$

First three terms: $\binom{6}{0}(2a)^6(3b)^6$

    $+ \binom{6}{1}(2a)^5(3b)^1 + \binom{6}{2}(2a)^4(3b)^2$

$\binom{6}{0} = \frac{6!}{0!6!}$

$\binom{6}{1} = \frac{6!}{1!5!}$

    $= \frac{5!\,6}{5!\,1}$

    $= 6$

$\binom{6}{2} = \frac{6!}{2!4!}$

    $= \frac{4!\cdot5\cdot6}{4!\cdot1\cdot2}$

    $= 5\cdot3$

    $= 15$

So the first three terms are:

    $1(64a^6) + 5(32a^5)(3b)$

    $+ 15(16a^4)(9b^2)$

    $= 64a^6 + 576a^5b + 2160a^4b^2$

7. $(a+b)^{13}$

Fifth term: $\binom{13}{4}a^9b^4 = 715a^9b^4$

$\binom{13}{4} = \frac{13!}{4!9!}$

    $= \frac{9!\,10\cdot11\cdot12\cdot13}{9!\,1\cdot2\cdot3\cdot4}$

    $= 5\cdot11\cdot13$

    $= 715$

9. $(3x + \frac{1}{2})^{11}$

Fourth term: $\binom{11}{3}(3x)^8(\frac{1}{2})^3$

$= 165(6561x^8)(\frac{1}{8})$

$= \frac{1,082,565}{8}x^8$

$\binom{11}{3} = \frac{11!}{3!8!}$

$= \frac{8!9\cdot10\cdot11}{8!1\cdot2\cdot3}$

$= 3\cdot5\cdot11$

$= 165$

11. $(a+b)^6 = \binom{6}{0}a^6b^0 + \binom{6}{1}a^5b^1$

$\quad + \binom{6}{2}a^4b^2 + \binom{6}{3}a^3b^3 + \binom{6}{4}a^2b^4$

$\quad + \binom{6}{5}ab^5 + \binom{6}{6}a^0b^6$

$\binom{6}{0} = \frac{6!}{0!6!} = 1$

$\binom{6}{1} = \frac{6!}{1!5!} = \frac{5!\cdot6}{5!\cdot1} = 6$

$\binom{6}{2} = \frac{6!}{2!4!} = \frac{4!5\cdot6}{4!1\cdot2} = 15$

$\binom{6}{3} = \frac{6!}{3!3!} = \frac{3!4\cdot5\cdot6}{3!1\cdot2\cdot3} = 20$

$\binom{6}{4} = \binom{6}{2} = 15$

$\binom{6}{5} = \binom{6}{1} = 6$

$\binom{6}{6} = \binom{6}{0} = 1$

So, $(a+b)^6 = a^6 + 6a^5b + 15a^4b^2$

$\quad + 20a^3b^3 + 15a^2b^4 + 6ab^5 + b^6$

13. $(x+1)^9 = \binom{9}{0}x^9(1)^0 + \binom{9}{1}x^8(1)^1$

$\quad + \binom{9}{2}x^7(1)^2 + \binom{9}{3}x^6(1)^3$

$\quad + \binom{9}{4}x^5(1)^4 + \binom{9}{5}x^4(1)^5$

$\quad + \binom{9}{6}x^3(1)^6 + \binom{9}{7}x^2(1)^7$

$\quad + \binom{9}{8}x^1(1)^8 + \binom{9}{9}x^0(1)^9$

$\binom{9}{0} = \frac{9!}{0!9!} = 1$

$\binom{9}{1} = \frac{9!}{1!8!} = \frac{8!9}{8!1} = 9$

$\binom{9}{2} = \frac{9!}{2!7!} = \frac{7!8\cdot9}{7!1\cdot2} = 36$

$\binom{9}{3} = \frac{9!}{3!6!} = \frac{6!7\cdot8\cdot9}{6!1\cdot2\cdot3} = 7\cdot4\cdot3 = 84$

$\binom{9}{4} = \frac{9!}{4!5!} = \frac{5!6\cdot7\cdot8\cdot9}{5!1\cdot2\cdot3\cdot4} = 7\cdot2\cdot9$

$= 126$

$\binom{9}{5} = \binom{9}{4} = 126$

$\binom{9}{6} = \binom{9}{3} = 84$

$\binom{9}{7} = \binom{9}{2} = 36$

$\binom{9}{8} = \binom{9}{1} = 9$

$\binom{9}{9} = \binom{9}{0} = 1$

So, $(x+1)^9 = x^9 + 9x^8 + 36x^7$

$\quad + 84x^6 + 126x^5 + 126x^4 + 84x^3$

$\quad + 36x^2 + 9x + 1$

15. $(2x+y)^6 = \binom{6}{0}(2x)^6(y)^0$

$\quad + \binom{6}{1}(2x)^5(y)^1 + \binom{6}{2}(2x)^4(y)^2$

$\quad + \binom{6}{3}(2x)^3(y)^3 + \binom{6}{4}(2x)^2(y)^4$

$\quad + \binom{6}{5}(2x)^1(y)^5 + \binom{6}{6}(2x)^0(y)^6$

$\binom{6}{0} = \frac{6!}{0!6!} = 1$

$\binom{6}{1} = \frac{6!}{1!5!} = \frac{5!6}{5!\cdot1} = 6$

$\binom{6}{2} = \frac{6!}{2!4!} = \frac{4!5\cdot6}{4!1\cdot2} = 5\cdot3 = 15$

$\binom{6}{3} = \frac{6!}{3!3!} = \frac{3!4\cdot5\cdot6}{3!1\cdot2\cdot3} = 4\cdot5 = 20$

$\binom{6}{4} = \binom{6}{2} = 15$

$\binom{6}{5} = \binom{6}{1} = 6$

$\binom{6}{6} = \binom{6}{0} = 1$

So, $(2x+y)^6 = 64x^6 + 6(32x^5)y$

$\quad + 15(16x^4)(y) + 20(8x^3)y^3$

$+ 15(4x)y^4 + 6(2x)y^5$

$+ (1)(1)y^6$

$= 64x^6 + 192x^5y + 240x^4y^2$

$+ 160x^3y^3 + 60x^2y^4 + 12xy^5$

$+ y^6$

17. $(a+b)^9 = \binom{9}{0}a^9b^0 + \binom{9}{1}$

$+ \binom{9}{2}a^7b^2 + \binom{9}{3}a^6b^3 + \binom{9}{4}a^5b^4$

$+ \binom{9}{5}a^4b^5 + \binom{9}{6}a^3b^6 + \binom{9}{7}a^3b^6$

$+ \binom{9}{8}a^1b^8 + \binom{9}{9}a^0b^9$

$\binom{9}{0} = \frac{9!}{0!\,9!} = 1$

$\binom{9}{1} = \frac{9!}{1!\,8!} = \frac{8!\,9}{8!\,1} = 9$

$\binom{9}{2} = \frac{9!}{2!\,7!} = \frac{7!\cdot 8\cdot 9}{7!\cdot 1\cdot 2} = 36$

$\binom{9}{3} = \frac{9!}{3!\,6!} = \frac{6!\cdot 7\cdot 8\cdot 9}{6!\cdot 1\cdot 2\cdot 3} = 7\cdot 4\cdot 3 = 84$

$\binom{9}{4} = \frac{9!}{4!\,5!} = \frac{5!\cdot 6\cdot 7\cdot 8\cdot 9}{5!\cdot 1\cdot 2\cdot 3\cdot 4} = 7.2.9$

$= 126$

$\binom{9}{5} = \binom{9}{4} = 126$

$\binom{9}{6} = \binom{9}{3} = 84$

$\binom{9}{7} = \binom{9}{2} = 36$

$\binom{9}{8} = \binom{9}{1} = 9$

$\binom{9}{9} = \binom{9}{0} = 1$

So, $(a+b)^9 = a^9 + 9a^8b + 36a^7b^2$

$+ 84a^6b^3 + 126a^5b^4 + 126a^4b^5$

$+ 84a^3b^6 + 36a^2b^7 + 9ab^8 + b^9$

19. $(x+y)^9 = \binom{9}{0}x^9y^0 + \binom{9}{1}x^8y^1$

$+ \binom{9}{2}x^7y^2 + \binom{9}{3}x^6y^3 + \binom{9}{4}x^5y^4$

$+ \binom{9}{5}x^4y^5 + \binom{9}{6}x^3y^6 + \binom{9}{7}x^2y^7$

$+ \binom{9}{8}x^1y^8 + \binom{9}{9}x^0y^9$

$\binom{9}{0} = \frac{9!}{0!\,9!} = 1$

$\binom{9}{1} = \frac{9!}{1!\,8!} = \frac{8!\,9}{8!\,1} = 9$

$\binom{9}{2} = \frac{9!}{2!\,7!} = \frac{7!\cdot 8\cdot 9}{7!\cdot 1\cdot 2} = 36$

$\binom{9}{3} = \frac{9!}{3!\,6!} = \frac{6!\cdot 7\cdot 8\cdot 9}{6!\cdot 1\cdot 2\cdot 3} = 7\cdot 4\cdot 3 = 84$

$\binom{9}{4} = \frac{9!}{4!\,5!} = \frac{5!\cdot 6\cdot 7\cdot 8\cdot 9}{5!\cdot 2\cdot 3\cdot 4\cdot 5} = 7\cdot 2\cdot 9$

$= 126$

$\binom{9}{5} = \binom{9}{4} = 126$

$\binom{9}{6} = \binom{9}{3} = 84$

$\binom{9}{7} = \binom{9}{2} = 36$

$\binom{9}{8} = \binom{9}{1} = 9$

$\binom{9}{9} = \binom{9}{0} = 1$

So, $(x+y)^9 = x^9 + 9x^8y + 36x^7y^2$

$+ 84x^6y^3 + 126x^5y^4 + 126x^4y^5$

$+ 84x^3y^6 + 36x^2y^7 + 9xy^8$

$+ 1y^9$

21. $(2x+y)^7 = \binom{7}{0}(2x)^7(y)^0$

$+ \binom{7}{1}(2x)^6(y)^1 + \binom{7}{2}(2x)^5(y)^2$

$+ \binom{7}{3}(2x)^4(y)^3 + \binom{7}{4}(2x)^3(y)^4$

$+ \binom{7}{5}(2x)^2(y)^5 + \binom{7}{6}(2x)^1(y)^6$

$+ \binom{7}{7}(2x)^0y^7$

$\binom{7}{0} = \frac{7!}{0!\,7!} = 1$

$\binom{7}{1} = \frac{7!}{1!\,6!} = \frac{6!\,7}{6!\,1} = 7$

$\binom{7}{2} = \frac{7!}{2!5!} = \frac{5!6\cdot7}{5!1\cdot2} = 3\cdot7 = 21$

$\binom{7}{3} = \frac{7!}{3!4!} = \frac{4!5\cdot6\cdot7}{4!1\cdot2\cdot3} = 5\cdot7 = 35$

$\binom{7}{4} = \binom{7}{3} = 35$

$\binom{7}{5} = \binom{7}{2} = 21$

$\binom{7}{6} = \binom{7}{1} = 7$

$\binom{7}{7} = \binom{7}{0} = 1$

So, $(2x+y)^7 = 128x^7 + 7(64x^6)y$

$\qquad + 21(32x^5)y^2 = 35(16x^4)y^3$

$\qquad + 35(8x^3)y^4 + 21(4x^2)y^5$

$\qquad + 7(2x)y^6 + y^7$

$\quad = 128x^7 + 448x^6y + 672x^5y^2$

$\qquad + 560x^4y^3 + 280x^3y^4 + 84x^2y^5$

$\qquad + 14xy^6 + y^7$

23. $(a+b)^{13}$

Last three terms: $\binom{13}{11}a^2b^{11}$

$\qquad + \binom{13}{12}a^1b^{12} + \binom{13}{13}a^0b^{13}$

$\binom{13}{11} = \frac{13!}{11!2!} = \frac{11!12\cdot13}{11!1\cdot2} = 6\cdot13$

$\qquad = 78$

$\binom{13}{12} = \frac{13!}{12!1!} = \frac{12!13}{12!1!} = 13$

$\binom{13}{13} = \frac{13!}{13!0!} = 1$

So the last three terms are:

$78a^2b^{11} + 13ab^{12} + b^{13}$

25. $(s+3)^5$

Last three terms: $\binom{5}{3}s^2(3)^3$

$\qquad + \binom{5}{4}s^1(3)^4 + \binom{5}{5}s^0(3)^5$

$\binom{5}{3} = \frac{5!}{3!2!} = \frac{3!4\cdot5}{3!1\cdot2} = 2\cdot5 = 10$

$\binom{5}{4} = \frac{5!}{4!1!} = \frac{4!5}{4!\cdot1} = 5$

$\binom{5}{5} = \frac{5!}{5!0!} = 1$

So the last three terms are:

$10s^2(27) + 5s(81) + 243$

$\qquad = 270s^2 + 405s + 243$

27. $(3x+2y)^7$

Last three terms: $\binom{7}{5}(3x)^2(2y)^5$

$\qquad + \binom{7}{6}(3x)^1(2y)^6 + \binom{7}{7}(3x)^0(2y)^7$

$\binom{7}{5} = \frac{7!}{5!2!} = \frac{5!6\cdot7}{5!1\cdot2} = 3\cdot7 = 21$

$\binom{7}{6} = \frac{7!}{6!1!} = \frac{6!7}{6!\cdot1} = 7$

$\binom{7}{7} = \frac{7!}{7!0!} = 1$

So, the last three terms are:

$21(9x^2)(32y^5) + 7(3x)(64y^6)$

$\qquad + 128y^7$

$\qquad = 6048x^2y^5 + 1344xy^6 + 128y^7$

29. $(a+b)^{12}$

Last three terms: $\binom{12}{10}a^2b^{10}$

$\qquad + \binom{12}{11}a^1b^{11} + \binom{12}{12}a^0b^{12}$

$\binom{12}{10} = \frac{12!}{10!a!} = \frac{10!10\cdot12}{10!1\cdot2} = 11\cdot6$

$\qquad = 66$

$\binom{12}{11} = \frac{12!}{11!1!} = \frac{11!12}{11!\cdot1} = 12$

$\binom{12}{12} = \frac{12!}{12!0!} = 1$

So, the last three terms are:

$66a^2b^{10} + 12ab^{11} + b^{12}$

31. $(s+3)^6$

Last three terms: $\binom{6}{4}s^2(3)^4$

$\qquad + \binom{6}{5}s^1(3)^5 + \binom{6}{6}s^0(3)^6$

$\binom{6}{4} = \frac{6!}{4!2!} = \frac{4!5\cdot 6}{4!1\cdot 2} = 15$

$\binom{6}{5} = \frac{6!}{5!1!} = \frac{5!\cdot 6}{5!\cdot 1} = 6$

$\binom{6}{6} = \frac{6!}{6!0!} = 1$

So, the last three terms are:

$(15)s^2(81) + (6)5(243) + 729$

$= 1215s^2 + 1458s + 729$

33. $(2x+3y)^7$

Last three terms: $\binom{7}{5}(2x)^2(3y)^5$

$\qquad + \binom{7}{6}(2x)^1(3y)^6$

$\qquad + \binom{7}{7}(2x)^0(3y)^7$

$\binom{7}{5} = \frac{7!}{5!2!} = \frac{5!6\cdot 7}{5!1\cdot 2} = 3\cdot 7 = 21$

$\binom{7}{6} = \frac{7!}{6!1!} = \frac{6!7}{6!\cdot 1} = 7$

$\binom{7}{7} = \frac{7!}{7!0!} = 1$

So, the last three terms are:

$21(4x^2)(243y^5) + 7(2x)(729y^6)$

$\qquad + 2187y^7$

$\quad = 20,412x^2y^5 + 10,206xy^6$

$\qquad + 2,187y^7$

35. $(a+b)^{50}$

First two terms: $\binom{50}{0}a^{50}b^0$

$\qquad + \binom{50}{1}a^{49}b^1$

$\binom{50}{0} = \frac{50!}{0!50!} = 1$

$\binom{50}{1} = \frac{50!}{1!49!} = \frac{49!\cdot 50}{49!\cdot 1} = 50$

So, the first two terms are:

$a^{50} + 50a^{49}b$

37. $(s+3)^{500}$

First two terms: $\binom{500}{0}s^{500}(3)^0$

$\qquad + \binom{500}{1}s^{499}\cdot 3^1$

$\binom{500}{0} = \frac{500!}{0!500!} = 1$

$\binom{500}{1} = \frac{500!}{1!499!} = \frac{499!500}{499!\cdot 1} = 500$

So the first two terms are:

$s^{500} + 500(s^{499})(3)$

$\quad = s^{500} + 1500s^{499}$

39. $(1+x)^{100}$

First two terms: $\binom{100}{0}1^{100}(x)^0$

$\qquad + \binom{100}{1}1^{99}(x)^1$

$\binom{100}{0} = \frac{100!}{0!100!} = 1$

$\binom{100}{1} = \frac{100!}{1!99!} = \frac{99!100}{99!\cdot 1} = 100$

So, the first two terms are:

$(1)(1)(1) + 100(1)x = 1 + 100x$

41. $(\frac{x}{2}+\frac{1}{3})^{12}$

Fourth term: $\binom{12}{3}(\frac{x}{2})^9(\frac{1}{3})^3$

$\binom{12}{3} = \frac{12!}{3!9!} = \frac{9!10\cdot 11\cdot 12}{9!1\cdot 2\cdot 3}$

$\qquad = 5\cdot 11\cdot 4 = 220$

So, the fourth term is

$(220)(\frac{x^9}{512})(\frac{1}{27}) = 4\cdot 55(\frac{x^9}{4\cdot 128})(\frac{1}{27})$

$\qquad = \frac{55x^9}{.3456}$

43. $(\frac{1}{2}+\frac{1}{2})^6 = \binom{6}{0}(\frac{1}{2})^6(\frac{1}{2})^0$

$\qquad + \binom{6}{1}(\frac{1}{2})^5(\frac{1}{2})^1 + \binom{6}{2}(\frac{1}{2})^4(\frac{1}{2})^2$

$\qquad + \binom{6}{3}(\frac{1}{2})^3(\frac{1}{2})^3 + \binom{6}{4}(\frac{1}{2})^2(\frac{1}{2})^4$

$\qquad + \binom{6}{5}(\frac{1}{2})^1(\frac{1}{2})^5 + \binom{6}{6}(\frac{1}{2})^0(\frac{1}{2})^6$

$\binom{6}{0} = \frac{6!}{0! \, 6!} = 1$

$\binom{6}{1} = \frac{6!}{1! \, 5!} = \frac{5 \cdot 6}{5! \cdot 1} = 6$

$\binom{6}{2} = \frac{6!}{2! \, 4!} = \frac{4! \, 5 \cdot 6}{4! \cdot 1 \cdot 2} = 5 \cdot 3 = 15$

$\binom{6}{3} = \frac{6!}{3! \, 3!} = \frac{4 \cdot 5 \cdot 6}{3! \cdot 1 \cdot 2 \cdot 3} = 2 \cdot 5 \cdot 2 = 20$

$\binom{6}{4} = \binom{6}{2} = 15$

$\binom{6}{5} = \binom{6}{1} = 6$

$\binom{6}{6} = \binom{6}{0} = 1$

So, $\left(\frac{1}{2} + \frac{1}{2}\right)^6 = 1\left(\frac{1}{2}\right)^6 + 6\left(\frac{1}{2}\right)^6$

$+ \, 15\left(\frac{1}{2}\right)^6 + 20\left(\frac{1}{2}\right)^6 + 15\left(\frac{1}{2}\right)^6$

$+ \, 6\left(\frac{1}{2}\right)^6 + \left(\frac{1}{2}\right)^6$

$= \frac{1}{64} + \frac{6}{64} + \frac{15}{64} + \frac{20}{64} + \frac{15}{64} + \frac{6}{64} + \frac{1}{64}$

$= \frac{64}{64}$

$= 1$

45. $\displaystyle\sum_{j=0}^{n} (-1)^j \binom{n}{j} a^{n-j} b^j$

47. $(x-y)^6 = (-1)^0 \binom{6}{0} (x)^6 y^0$

$+ \, (-1)^1 \binom{6}{1} x^5 y^1$

$+ \, (-1)^2 \binom{6}{2} x^4 y^2$

$+ \, (-1)^3 \binom{6}{3} x^3 y^3$

$+ \, (-1)^4 \binom{6}{4} x^2 y^4$

$+ \, (-1)^5 \binom{6}{5} x^1 y^5$

$+ \, (-1)^6 \binom{6}{6} x^0 y^6$

$\binom{6}{0} = \frac{6!}{6! \, 0!} = 1$

$\binom{6}{1} = \frac{6!}{1! \, 5!} = \frac{5! \cdot 6}{5! \cdot 1} = 6$

$\binom{6}{2} = \frac{6!}{2! \, 4!} = \frac{4! \cdot 5 \cdot 6}{4! \cdot 1 \cdot 2} = 5 \cdot 3 = 15$

$\binom{6}{3} = \frac{6!}{3! \, 3!} = \frac{3! \, 4 \cdot 5 \cdot 6}{3! \cdot 1 \cdot 2 \cdot 3} = 2 \cdot 5 \cdot 2 = 20$

$\binom{6}{4} = \binom{6}{2} = 15$

$\binom{6}{5} = \binom{6}{1} = 6$

$\binom{6}{6} = \binom{6}{0} = 1$

So, $(x-y)^6 = x^6 - 6x^5 y + 15x^4 y^2$

$- \, 20x^3 y^3 + 15x^2 y^4 - 6x^5 y + y^6$

49. $(q-2)^8 = (-1)^0 \binom{8}{0} q^8 (2)^0$

$+ \, (-1)^1 \binom{8}{1} q^7 (2)^1$

$+ \, (-1)^2 \binom{8}{2} q^6 (2)^2$

$+ \, (-1)^3 \binom{8}{3} q^5 (2)^3$

$+ \, (-1)^4 \binom{8}{4} q^4 (2)^4$

$+ \, (-1)^5 \binom{8}{5} q^3 (2)^5$

$+ \, (-1)^6 \binom{8}{6} q^2 (2)^6$

$+ \, (-1)^7 \binom{8}{7} q^1 (2)^7$

$+ \, (-1)^8 \binom{8}{8} q^0 (2)^8$

$\binom{8}{0} = \frac{8!}{0! \, 8!} = 1$

$\binom{8}{1} = \frac{8!}{1! \, 7!} = \frac{7! \, 8}{7! \cdot 1} = 8$

$\binom{8}{2} = \frac{8!}{2! \, 6!} = \frac{6! \, 7 \cdot 8}{6! \cdot 1 \cdot 2} = 7 \cdot 4 = 28$

$\binom{8}{3} = \frac{8!}{3! \, 5!} = \frac{5! \, 6 \cdot 7 \cdot 8}{5! \cdot 1 \cdot 2 \cdot 3} = 7 \cdot 8 = 56$

$\binom{8}{4} = \frac{8!}{4! \, 4!} = \frac{4! \, 5 \cdot 6 \cdot 7 \cdot 8}{4! \cdot 1 \cdot 2 \cdot 3 \cdot 4} = 5 \cdot 2 \cdot 7$

$= 70$

$\binom{8}{5} = \binom{8}{3} = 56$

$$\binom{8}{6} = \binom{8}{2} = 28$$

$$\binom{8}{7} = \binom{8}{1} = 8$$

$$\binom{8}{8} = \binom{8}{0} = 1$$

So, $(q-2)^8 = q^8 - 8(q^7)(2)$

$\qquad + 28(q^6)(4) - 56(q^5)(8)$

$\qquad + 70(q^4)(16) - 56(q^3)(32)$

$\qquad + 28(q^2)(64) - 8(q)(128)$

$\qquad + 256$

$\quad = q^8 - 16q^7 + 112q^6 - 448q^5$

$\qquad + 1120q^4 - 1792q^3 + 1792q^2$

$\qquad - 1024q + 256$

51. $(3x^2 - 2y^2)^4$

$\quad = (-1)^0 \binom{4}{0}(3x^2)^4(2y^2)^0$

$\qquad + (-1)^1 \binom{4}{1}(3x^2)^3(2y^2)^1$

$\qquad + (-1)^2 \binom{4}{2}(3x^2)^2(2y^2)^2$

$\qquad + (-1)^3 \binom{4}{3}(3x^2)^1(2y^2)^2$

$\qquad + (-1)^4 \binom{4}{4}(3x^2)^0(2y^2)^4$

$$\binom{4}{0} = \frac{4!}{0! \, 4!} = 1$$

$$\binom{4}{1} = \frac{4!}{1! \, 3!} = \frac{3! \cdot 4}{3! \cdot 1} = 4$$

$$\binom{4}{2} = \frac{4!}{2! \, 2!} = \frac{2! \cdot 3 \cdot 4}{2! \cdot 1 \cdot 2} = 3 \cdot 2 = 6$$

$$\binom{4}{3} = \binom{4}{1} = 4$$

$$\binom{4}{4} = \binom{4}{0} = 1$$

So, $(3x^2-2y^2)^4 = 81x^8$

$\qquad - 4(27x^6)(2y^2)$

$\qquad + 6(9x^4)(2y^2)^2$

$\qquad - 4(3x^2)(8y^6) + 16y^8$

$= 81x^8 - 216x^6y^2 + 216x^4y^4$

$\qquad - 96x^2y^6 + 16y^8$

Problem Set 12.5.

1. $P(4,2) = \dfrac{4!}{2!}$

$\qquad = \dfrac{4 \cdot 3 \cdot 2!}{2!}$

$\qquad = 4 \cdot 3$

$\qquad = 12$

3. $P(5,1) = \dfrac{5!}{4!}$

$\qquad = \dfrac{5! \, 4!}{4!}$

$\qquad = 5$

5. $P(5,3) = \dfrac{5!}{2!}$

$\qquad = \dfrac{5 \cdot 4 \cdot 3 \cdot 2!}{2!}$

$\qquad = 5 \cdot 4 \cdot 3$

$\qquad = 60$

7. $P(5,5) = \dfrac{5!}{0!}$

$\qquad = \dfrac{5 \cdot 4 \cdot 3 \cdot 2 \cdot 1}{1}$

$\qquad = 120$

9. $C(9,0) = \dfrac{9!}{0! \, 9!}$

$\qquad = 1$

11. $C(9,2) = \dfrac{9!}{2! \, 7!}$

$\qquad = \dfrac{9 \cdot 8 \cdot 7!}{2 \cdot 1 \cdot 7!}$

$\qquad = 9 \cdot 4$

$\qquad = 36$

13. $C(9,9) = \dfrac{9!}{9! \, 0!}$

$\qquad = 1$

15. $P(6,3) = \dfrac{6!}{3!}$

$\qquad = \dfrac{6 \cdot 5 \cdot 4 \cdot 3!}{3!}$

$\qquad = 6 \cdot 5 \cdot 4$

= 120

There are 120 three-letter "words" that can be made with the letters of TIMERS.

17. $C(13,7) = \dfrac{13!}{7!6!}$

$= \dfrac{13 \cdot 12 \cdot 11 \cdot 10 \cdot 9 \cdot 8 \cdot 7!}{6 \cdot 5 \cdot 4 \cdot 3 \cdot 2 \cdot 1 \cdot 7!}$

$= 13 \cdot 11 \cdot 2 \cdot 3 \cdot 2$

$= 1716$

There are 1716 ways to choose seven players from a roster of 13.

19. $P(8,4) = \dfrac{8!}{4!}$

$= \dfrac{8 \cdot 7 \cdot 6 \cdot 5 \cdot 4!}{4!}$

$= 1680$

21. $P(6,0) = \dfrac{6!}{6!}$

$= 1$

23. $P(6,2) = \dfrac{6!}{4!}$

$= \dfrac{6 \cdot 5 \cdot 4!}{4!}$

$= 30$

25. $P(6,4) = \dfrac{6!}{2!}$

$= \dfrac{6 \cdot 5 \cdot 4 \cdot 3 \cdot 2!}{2!}$

$= 360$

27. $P(6,6) = \dfrac{6!}{0!}$

$= 6 \cdot 5 \cdot 4 \cdot 3 \cdot 2 \cdot 1$

$= 720$

29. $C(7,5) = \dfrac{7!}{5!2!}$

$= \dfrac{7 \cdot 6 \cdot 5!}{1 \cdot 2 \cdot 5!}$

$= 7 \cdot 3$

$= 21$

31. $C(8,0) = \dfrac{8!}{0!8!}$

$= 1$

33. $C(8,2) = \dfrac{8!}{2!6!}$

$= \dfrac{8 \cdot 7 \cdot 6!}{2 \cdot 1 \cdot 6!}$

$= 4 \cdot 7$

$= 28$

35. $C(8,8) = \dfrac{8!}{8!0!}$

$= 1$

37. $C(8,6) = \dfrac{8!}{6!2!}$

$= \dfrac{8 \cdot 7 \cdot 6!}{1 \cdot 2 \cdot 6!}$

$= 4 \cdot 7$

$= 28$

39. $P(14,4) = \dfrac{14!}{10!}$

$= \dfrac{14 \cdot 13 \cdot 12 \cdot 11 \cdot 10!}{10!}$

$= 14 \cdot 13 \cdot 12 \cdot 11$

$= 24{,}024$

41. $C(14,4) = \dfrac{14!}{4!10!}$

$= \dfrac{14 \cdot 13 \cdot 12 \cdot 11 \cdot 10!}{4 \cdot 3 \cdot 2 \cdot 1 \cdot 10!}$

$= 7 \cdot 13 \cdot 11$

$= 1001$

43. $P(8,4) = \dfrac{8!}{4!}$

$= \dfrac{8 \cdot 7 \cdot 6 \cdot 5 \cdot 4!}{4!}$

$= 8 \cdot 7 \cdot 6 \cdot 5$

$= 1680$

There are 1680 four-letter "words" that can be made with the letters of OUTFIELD.

45. $C(16,9) = \dfrac{16!}{9!7!}$

$= \dfrac{16 \cdot 15 \cdot 14 \cdot 13 \cdot 12 \cdot 11 \cdot 10 \cdot 9!}{7 \cdot 6 \cdot 5 \cdot 4 \cdot 3 \cdot 2 \cdot 1 \cdot 9!}$

$$= 2 \cdot 2 \cdot 13 \cdot 2 \cdot 11 \cdot 10$$
$$= 11{,}440$$

47. $P(N,N) = \dfrac{N!}{0!}$

$$= N!$$

49. $P(N,N-2) = \dfrac{N!}{[N-(N-2)]!}$

$$= \dfrac{N!}{2!}$$

$$= \dfrac{N!}{2 \cdot 1}$$

$$= \dfrac{1}{2}N!$$

51. $C(N,0) = \dfrac{N!}{0!N!}$

$$= 1$$

53. $C(N+2,N) = \dfrac{(N+2)!}{N![(N+2)-N]!}$

$$= \dfrac{(N+2)(N+1)\cdot N!}{2 \cdot 1 \cdot N!}$$

$$= \dfrac{(N+2)(N+1)}{2}$$

55. $C(N+1,N-1) = \dfrac{(N+1)!}{(N-1)![(N+1)-(N-1)]!}$

$$= \dfrac{(N+1)!}{(N-1)!2!}$$

$$= \dfrac{(N+1)N \cdot (N-1)!}{2 \cdot 1 \cdot (N-1)!}$$

$$= \dfrac{(N+1)N}{2} \text{ or } \dfrac{N(N+1)}{2}$$

Review.

1. $a_n = 3n + 1$

$n = 1 \quad 3(1) + 1 = 4$

$n = 2 \quad 3(2) + 1 = 7$

$n = 3 \quad 3(3) + 1 = 10$

$n = 4 \quad 3(4) + 1 = 13$

$n = 5 \quad 3(5) + 1 = 16$

$4,7,10,13,16$

3. $a_n = 3 \cdot 5^{n-1}$

$n = 1 \quad 3 \cdot 5^{1-1} = 3 \cdot 1 = 3$

$n = 2 \quad 3 \cdot 5^{2-1} = 3 \cdot 5 = 15$

$n = 3 \quad 3 \cdot 5^{3-1} = 3 \cdot 5^2 = 75$

$n = 4 \quad 3 \cdot 5^{4-1} = 3 \cdot 5^3 = 375$

$n = 5 \quad 3 \cdot 5^{5-1} = 3 \cdot 5^4 = 1875$

$3,15,75,275,1875$

5. $c_n = (-1)^n \cdot 3n$

$n = 1 \quad (-1)^1(3) = -3$

$n = 2 \quad (-1)^2(3)(2) = 6$

$n = 3 \quad (-1)^3(3)(3) = -9$

$n = 4 \quad (-1)^4(3)(4) = 12$

$n = 5 \quad (-1)^5(3)(5) = -15$

$-3,6,-9,12,-15$

7. $a_n = 10 + 3n$

$n = 1 \quad 10 + 3 = 13$

$n = 2 \quad 10 + 6 = 16$

$n = 3 \quad 10 + 9 = 19$

The sequence is increasing.

9. $c_n = 3 - n^{-1}$

$n = 1 \quad 3 - 1^{-1} = 3 - 1 = 2$

$n = 2 \quad 3 - 2^{-1} = 3 - \dfrac{1}{2} = 2\dfrac{1}{2}$

$n = 3 \quad 3 - 3^{-1} = 3 - \dfrac{1}{3} = 2\dfrac{2}{3}$

$n = 4 \quad 3 - 4^{-1} = 3 - \dfrac{1}{4} = 2\dfrac{3}{4}$

The sequence is increasing.

11. $-2,0,2,\ldots$

$d = 0 - (-2) = 2$

Next term: $2 + 2 = 4$

13. $1,4,16,\ldots$

$r = \dfrac{4}{1} = 4$

Next term: $16(4) = 64$

15. $40,60,90,\ldots$

$r = \dfrac{60}{40} = \dfrac{3}{2}$

Next term: $90 \cdot \dfrac{2}{3} = 135$

17. $\displaystyle\sum_{j=1}^{6} (1-j)^2 = (1-1)^2 + (1-2)^2$

$+ (1-3)^2 + (1-4)^2 + (1-5)^2$

$+ (1-6)^2$

$= 0^2 + (-1)^2 + (-2)^2 + (-7)^2$

$+ (-4)^2 + (-5)^2$

$= 0 + 1 + 4 + 9 + 16 + 25$

19. $\displaystyle\sum_{j=0}^{5} (2j)^2 = (2\cdot 0)^2 + (2\cdot 1)^2$

$+ (2\cdot 2)^2 + (2\cdot 3)^2 + (2\cdot 4)^2$

$+ (2\cdot 5)^2$

$= 0^2 + 2^2 + 4^2 + 6^2 + 8^2 + 10^2$

$= 0 + 4 + 16 + 36 + 64 + 100$

21. $\displaystyle\sum_{j=1}^{4} (-1)^{j+1} j^j = (-1)^2 \cdot 1^1 + (-1)^3 \cdot 2^2$

$+ (-1)^4 \cdot 3^3 + (-1)^5 \cdot 4^4$

$= 1 - 4 + 27 - 256$

23. $1 + 2K + 3K^2 + 4K^3 + 5K^4 + 6K^5$

$+ 7K^6$

$= \displaystyle\sum_{j=0}^{6} (j+1)K^j$

25. $9! = 9\cdot 8\cdot 7\cdot 6\cdot 5\cdot 4\cdot 3\cdot 2\cdot 1$

$= 362,880$

27. $0!\cdot 1!\cdot 2!\cdot 3! = 1\cdot 1\cdot 1\cdot 2\cdot 1\cdot 2\cdot 3$

$= 12$

29. $\dfrac{41!}{39!} = \dfrac{41\cdot 40\cdot 39!}{39!}$

$= 41\cdot 40$

$= 1,640$

31. $\dbinom{9}{3} = \dfrac{9!}{3!\,6!}$

$= \dfrac{9\cdot 8\cdot 7\cdot 6!}{3\cdot 2\cdot 1\cdot 6!}$

$= 3\cdot 4\cdot 7$

$= 84$

33. $\dbinom{10}{5} = \dfrac{10!}{5!\,5!}$

$= \dfrac{10\cdot 9\cdot 8\cdot 7\cdot 6\cdot 5!}{5\cdot 4\cdot 3\cdot 2\cdot 1\cdot 5!}$

$= 2\cdot 9\cdot 7\cdot 2$

$= 252$

35. $(x+1)^7 = \dbinom{7}{0}x^7 \cdot 1^0 + \dbinom{7}{1}x^6 \cdot 1^1$

$+ \dbinom{7}{2}x^5 \cdot 1^2 + \dbinom{7}{3}x^4 \cdot 1^3$

$+ \dbinom{7}{4}x^3 \cdot 1^4 + \dbinom{7}{5}x^2 \cdot 1^5$

$+ \dbinom{7}{6}x^1 \cdot 1^6 + \dbinom{7}{7}x^0 \cdot 1^7$

$\dbinom{7}{0} = \dfrac{7!}{0!\,7!} = 1$

$\dbinom{7}{1} = \dfrac{7!}{1!\,6!} = \dfrac{7}{6!} = 7$

$\dbinom{7}{2} = \dfrac{7!}{2!\,5!} = \dfrac{7\cdot 6\cdot 5!}{2\cdot 1\cdot 5!} = 7\cdot 3 = 21$

$\dbinom{7}{3} = \dfrac{7!}{3!\,4!} = \dfrac{7\cdot 6\cdot 5\cdot 4!}{3\cdot 2\cdot 1\cdot 4!} = 7\cdot 5 = 35$

$\dbinom{7}{4} = \dbinom{7}{3} = 35$

$\dbinom{7}{5} = \dbinom{7}{2} = 21$

$\dbinom{7}{6} = \dbinom{7}{1} = 7$

$\dbinom{7}{7} = \dbinom{7}{0} = 1$

So, $(x+1)^7 = x^7 + 7x^6 + 21x^5$

$+ 35x^4 + 35x^3 + 21x^2 + 7x + 1$

37. $(2+3y)^6 = \dbinom{6}{0}(2)^6(3y)^0$

$+ \dbinom{6}{1}(2)^5(3y)^1 + \dbinom{6}{2}(2)^4(3y)^2$

$+ \dbinom{6}{3}(2)^3(3y)^3 + \dbinom{6}{4}(2)^2(3y)^4$

$+ \dbinom{6}{5}(2)^1(3y)^5 + \dbinom{6}{6}2^0(3y)^6$

$\dbinom{6}{0} = \dfrac{6!}{0!\,6!} = 1$

$\binom{6}{1} = \frac{6!}{1!5!} = \frac{6 \cdot 5!}{5!} = 6$

$\binom{6}{2} = \frac{6!}{2!4!} = \frac{6 \cdot 5 \cdot 4!}{2 \cdot 1 \cdot 4!} = 3 \cdot 5 = 15$

$\binom{6}{3} = \frac{6!}{3!3!} = \frac{6 \cdot 5 \cdot 4 \cdot 3!}{3 \cdot 2 \cdot 1 \cdot 3!} = 5 \cdot 4 = 20$

$\binom{6}{4} = \binom{6}{2} = 15$

$\binom{6}{5} = \binom{6}{1} = 6$

$\binom{6}{6} = \binom{6}{0} = 1$

So, $(2+3y)^6 = 64 = 6(32)(3y)$

$+ 15(16)(9y^2) + 20(8)(27y^3)$

$+ 15(4)(81y^4) + 6(2)(243y^5)$

$+ 729y^6$

$= 64 + 576y + 2160y^2 + 4320y^3$

$+ 4860y^4 + 2916y^5 + 729y^6$

39. $(1+s)^{10} = \binom{10}{0}1^{10} \cdot s^{10} + \binom{10}{1}1^9 \cdot s^1$

$+ \binom{10}{2}1^8 \cdot s^2 + \binom{10}{3}1^7 \cdot s^3$

$+ \binom{10}{4}1^6 \cdot s^4 + \binom{10}{5}1^5 \cdot s^5$

$+ \binom{10}{6}1^4 \cdot s^6 + \binom{10}{7}1^3 \cdot s^7$

$+ \binom{10}{8} 1^2 \cdot s^8 + \binom{10}{9}1^1 \cdot s^9$

$+ \binom{10}{10}1^0 \cdot s^{10}$

$\binom{10}{0} = \frac{10!}{0!10!} = 1$

$\binom{10}{1} = \frac{10!}{1!9!} = 10$

$\binom{10}{2} = \frac{10!}{2!8!} = \frac{10 \cdot 9 \cdot 8!}{2 \cdot 1 \cdot 8!} = 5 \cdot 9 = 45$

$\binom{10}{3} = \frac{10!}{3!7!} = \frac{10 \cdot 9 \cdot 8 \cdot 7!}{3 \cdot 2 \cdot 1 \cdot 7!} = 5 \cdot 3 \cdot 8$

$= 120$

$\binom{10}{4} = \frac{10!}{4!6!} = \frac{10 \cdot 9 \cdot 8 \cdot 7 \cdot 6!}{4 \cdot 3 \cdot 2 \cdot 1 \cdot 6!}$

$= 10 \cdot 3 \cdot 7 = 210$

$\binom{10}{5} = \frac{10!}{5!5!} = \frac{10 \cdot 9 \cdot 8 \cdot 7 \cdot 6 \cdot 5!}{5 \cdot 4 \cdot 3 \cdot 2 \cdot 1 \cdot 5!}$

$= 2 \cdot 3 \cdot 7 \cdot 6 = 252$

$\binom{10}{6} = \binom{10}{4} = 210$

$\binom{10}{7} = \binom{10}{3} = 120$

$\binom{10}{8} = \binom{10}{2} = 45$

$\binom{10}{9} = \binom{10}{1} = 10$

$\binom{10}{10} = \binom{10}{0} = 1$

So, $(1+s)^{10} = 1 + 10s + 45s^2$

$+ 120s^3 + 210s^4 + 252s^5$

$+ 210s^6 + 120s^7 + 45s^8$

$+ 10s^9 + s^{10}$

41. $(2+5t)^8$

First three terms: $\binom{8}{0}2^8(5t)^0$

$+ \binom{8}{1}2^7(5t)^1 + \binom{8}{2}2^6(5t)^2$

$\binom{8}{0} = \frac{8!}{0!8!} = 1$

$\binom{8}{1} = \frac{8!}{1!7!} = 8$

$\binom{8}{2} = \frac{8!}{2!6!} = \frac{8 \cdot 7 \cdot 6!}{2 \cdot 1 \cdot 6!} = 4 \cdot 7 = 28$

So, the first three terms are:

$256 + 8(128)(5t) + 28(64)(25t^2)$

$= 256 + 7040t + 44,800t^2$

43. $(a+b)^{14}$

Middle term (8th term): $\binom{14}{7}a^7b^7$

$\binom{14}{7} = \frac{14!}{7!7!}$

$= \frac{14 \cdot 13 \cdot 12 \cdot 11 \cdot 10 \cdot 9 \cdot 8 \cdot 7!}{7 \cdot 6 \cdot 5 \cdot 4 \cdot 3 \cdot 2 \cdot 1 \cdot 7!}$

$= 13 \cdot 11 \cdot 3 \cdot 8$

$= 3432$

So, the middle term is $3432\ a^7b^7$.

45. $C(10,4) = \dfrac{10!}{4!6!}$

$= \dfrac{10 \cdot 9 \cdot 8 \cdot 7 \cdot 6!}{4 \cdot 3 \cdot 2 \cdot 1 \cdot 6!}$

$= 10 \cdot 3 \cdot 7$

$= 210$

47. $P(11,6) = \dfrac{11!}{5!}$

$= \dfrac{11 \cdot 10 \cdot 9 \cdot 8 \cdot 7 \cdot 6 \cdot 5!}{5!}$

$= 11 \cdot 10 \cdot 9 \cdot 8 \cdot 7 \cdot 6$

$= 332,640$

There are 332,640 ways to draw 6 balls from an urn containing 11 balls if order is important.

49. $8x^3 - 27 = (2x-3)(4x^2+6x+9)$

51. $(2x-3)^3$ is factored.

53. $x^3 - 3x^2 + 3x - 1 = (x-1)^3$

55. $t(7-y) + y - 7 = 5(7-y) - (7-y)$

$= (7-y)(t-1)$

$7 - y$ is a factor of $t(7-y) + y - 7$.

57. $-2^{-4} = -\dfrac{1}{2^4} = -\dfrac{1}{16}$

59. $\dfrac{16x^2-25}{125-64x^3} = \dfrac{(4x+5)(4x-5)}{(5-4x)(25+20x+16x^2)}$

$= \dfrac{(4x+5)(4x-5)}{-(4x-5)(25+20x+16x^2)}$

$= -\dfrac{4x+5}{25+20x+16x^2}$ or

$= -\dfrac{4x+5}{16x^2+20x+25}$

61. $\dfrac{2^{-3}+8}{x^{-3}+2^{-2}} = \dfrac{\frac{1}{8}+8}{\frac{1}{3}+\frac{1}{4}}$

$= \dfrac{\frac{65}{8} \cdot 8x^3}{(\frac{1}{3}+\frac{1}{4}) \cdot 8x^3}$

$= \dfrac{65x^3}{8+2x^3}$

63. $(3x+2y)^3 = (3x)^3 + 3(3x)^2(2y)$

$+ 3(3x)(2y)^2 + (2y)^3$

$= 27x^3 + 54x^2y + 36xy^2$

$+ 8y^3$

65. $\dfrac{-14+\sqrt{-28}}{14} = \dfrac{-14+2i\sqrt{7}}{14}$

$= -1 + \dfrac{\sqrt{7}}{7}i$

67. $\dfrac{1}{x} + \dfrac{1}{x^2} = \dfrac{x}{x^2} + \dfrac{1}{x^2}$

$= \dfrac{x+1}{x^2}$

69. $\dfrac{\frac{1}{x}-1}{\frac{1}{x^2}-1} = \dfrac{(\frac{1}{x}-1)\ x^2}{(\frac{1}{x^2}-1)\ x^2}$

$= \dfrac{x-x^2}{1-x^2}$

$= \dfrac{x(1-x)}{(1-x)(1+x)}$

$= \dfrac{x}{1+x}$ or $\dfrac{x}{x+1}$

71. $\dfrac{1-\frac{x}{x+1}}{1+\frac{1}{x+1}}$ Expression

$\dfrac{(1-\frac{x}{x+1})x+1}{(1+\frac{1}{x+1})x+1} = \dfrac{x+1-x}{x+1+1}$

$= \dfrac{1}{x+2}$

73. $\left|\dfrac{2-3x}{4}\right| = -3$ Equation

Solution Set: $\emptyset$

75. $\dfrac{i}{2-3i}$ Expression

$\dfrac{i}{2-3i} \cdot \dfrac{2+3i}{2+3i} = \dfrac{2i+3i^2}{4-9i^2}$

$= \dfrac{2i-3}{4+9}$

$= \dfrac{-3+2i}{13}$

$= \dfrac{-3}{13} + \dfrac{2}{13}i$

376

Chapter Test.

1. $a_n = (-1)^n \cdot n^2$

   $n = 1 \quad (-1)^1(1)^2 = -1$

   $n = 2 \quad (-1)^2(2)^2 = 4$

   $n = 3 \quad (-1)^3(3)^2 = -9$

   D.

3. $a_n = 3 \cdot 2^{n-1}$

   $n = 1 \quad 3 \cdot 2^{1-1} = 3 \cdot 1 = 3$

   $n = 2 \quad 3 \cdot 2^{2-1} = 3 \cdot 2 = 6$

   $n = 3 \quad 3 \cdot 2^{3-1} = 3 \cdot 4 = 12$

   $n = 4 \quad 3 \cdot 2^{4-1} = 3 \cdot 8 = 24$

   $r = \dfrac{6}{3} = 2$

   B.

5. $\displaystyle\sum_{j=0}^{4} j(j+1) = 0 \cdot 1 + 1 \cdot 2 + 2 \cdot 3$

   $\qquad\qquad\qquad + 3 \cdot 4 + 4 \cdot 5$

   D.

4. $\displaystyle\sum_{j=1}^{6} (-1)^{j+1} j = (-1)^2(1) + (-1)^3(2)$

   $\qquad + (-1)^4(3) + (-1)^5(4)$

   $\qquad + (-1)^6(5) + (-1)^7(6)$

   $= 1 - 2 + 3 - 4 + 5 - 6$

   $= -3$

   B.

5. $6! = 6 \cdot 5 \cdot 4 \cdot 3 \cdot 2 \cdot 1$

   $\qquad = 720$

   D.

6. $\dfrac{12!}{10!} = \dfrac{12 \cdot 11 \cdot 10!}{10!}$

   $\qquad = 12 \cdot 11$

   $\qquad = 132$

   B.

7. $\dbinom{9}{3} = \dfrac{9!}{3! \, 6!}$

   $\qquad = \dfrac{9 \cdot 8 \cdot 7 \cdot 6!}{3 \cdot 2 \cdot 1 \cdot 6!}$

   $\qquad = 3 \cdot 4 \cdot 7$

   $\qquad = 84$

   A.

8. $(x+2)^5 = \dbinom{5}{0}x^5(2)^0 + \dbinom{5}{1}x^4(2)^1$

   $\qquad + \dbinom{5}{2}x^3(2)^2 + \dbinom{5}{3}x^2(2)^3$

   $\qquad + \dbinom{5}{4}x^1(2)^4 + \dbinom{5}{5}x^0(2)^5$

   $\dbinom{5}{0} = \dfrac{5!}{0! \, 5!} = 1$

   $\dbinom{5}{1} = \dfrac{5!}{1! \, 4!} = 5$

   $\dbinom{5}{2} = \dfrac{5!}{2! \, 3!} = \dfrac{5 \cdot 4 \cdot 3!}{2 \cdot 1 \cdot 3!}$

   $\qquad = 10$

   $\dbinom{5}{3} = \dbinom{5}{2} = 10$

   $\dbinom{5}{4} = \dbinom{5}{1} = 5$

   $\dbinom{5}{5} = \dbinom{5}{0} = 1$

   So, $(x+2)^5 = x^5 + 5x^4(2)$

   $\qquad + 10x^3(4) + 10x^2(8) + 5x(16)$

   $\qquad + 32$

   $= x^5 + 10x^4 + 40x^3 + 80x^2 + 80x$

   $\qquad + 32$

   C.

9. $(a+b)^{12}$

   Middle term (7th term): $\dbinom{12}{6}a^6 b^6$

   $\dbinom{12}{6} = \dfrac{12!}{6! \, 6!}$

   $\qquad = \dfrac{12 \cdot 11 \cdot 10 \cdot 9 \cdot 8 \cdot 7 \cdot 6!}{6 \cdot 5 \cdot 4 \cdot 3 \cdot 2 \cdot 1 \cdot 6!}$

   $\qquad = 11 \cdot 2 \cdot 3 \cdot 2 \cdot 7$

$= 924$

Middle term: $924a^6b^6$

D.

10. $4,7,10,13,\ldots,n+3$

11. $a_n = (-1)^{n+1} \cdot 2^n$

$n = 1 \quad (-1)^2 \cdot 2^1$

$n = 2 \quad (-1)^3 \cdot 2^2$

$n = 3 \quad (-1)^4 \cdot 2^3$

$n = 4 \quad (-1)^5 \cdot 2^4$

$n = 5 \quad (-1)^6 \cdot 2^5$

$2,-2^2,2^3,-2^4,2^5$

12. $\sum_{j=1}^{5} (2j-1) = [2(1)-1] + [2(2)-1]$

$+ [2(3)-1] + [2(4)-1]$

$+ [2(5)-1]$

$= (2-1) + (4-1) + (6-1) + (8-1)$

$+ (10-1)$

$= 1 + 3 + 5 + 7 + 9$

$= 25$

13. $P(8,5) = \dfrac{8!}{3!} = \dfrac{8 \cdot 7 \cdot 6 \cdot 5 \cdot 4 \cdot 3!}{3!}$

$= 8 \cdot 7 \cdot 6 \cdot 5 \cdot 4$

$= 6720$

There are 6720 five-letter "words" that can be read from the letters of COMPUTER.

14. $(3+t)^4 = \binom{4}{0}(3)^4 t^0 + \binom{4}{1}(3)^3 t^1$

$+ \binom{4}{2}(3)^2 t^2 + \binom{4}{3}(3)^1 t^3$

$+ \binom{4}{4}(3)^0 t^4$

$\binom{4}{0} = \dfrac{4!}{0! 4!} = 1$

$\binom{4}{1} = \dfrac{4!}{1! 3!} = 4$

$\binom{4}{2} = \dfrac{4!}{2! 2!} = \dfrac{4 \cdot 3 \cdot 2!}{2 \cdot 1 \cdot 2!} = 2 \cdot 3 = 6$

$\binom{4}{3} = \binom{4}{1} = 4$

$\binom{4}{4} = \binom{4}{0} = 1$

So, $(3+t)^4 = 81 + 4(27)t$

$+ 6(9)t^2 + 4(3)t^3 + t^4$

$= 81 + 108t + 54t^2 + 12t^3 + t^4$

15. $(a+b)^{18}$

Last three terms: $\binom{18}{16}a^2 b^{16}$

$+ \binom{18}{17}a^1 b^{17} + \binom{18}{18}a^0 b^{18}$

$\binom{18}{16} = \dfrac{18!}{16! 2!} = \dfrac{18 \cdot 17 \cdot 16!}{2 \cdot 1 \cdot 16}$

$= 9 \cdot 17 = 153$

$\binom{18}{17} = \dfrac{18!}{17! 1!} = 18$

$\binom{18}{18} = \dfrac{18!}{18! 0!} = 1$

So, the last three terms are:

$153a^2 b^{16} + 18ab^{17} + b^{18}.$